Little Lulu®

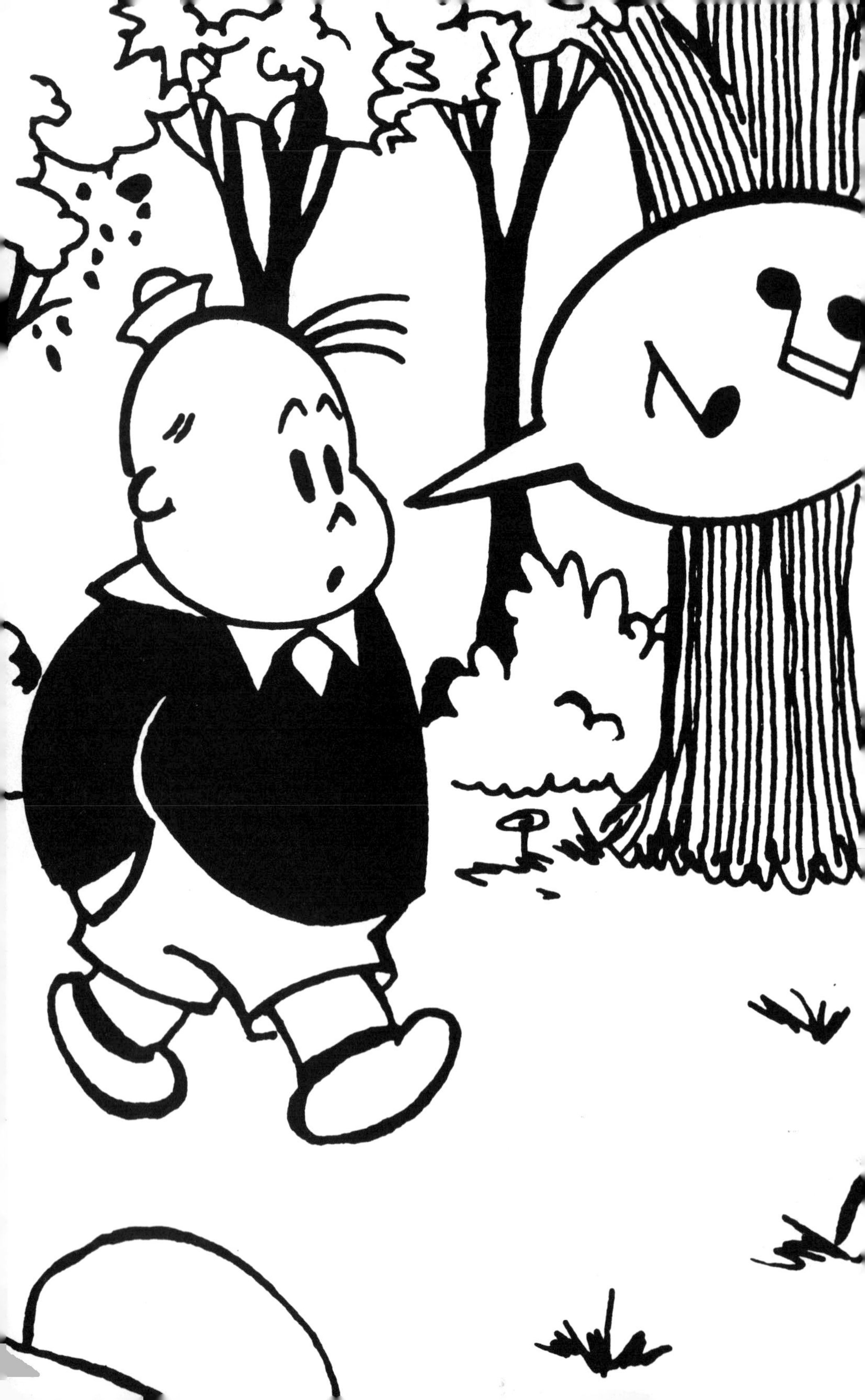

Little Lulu®

Lulu Takes A Trip

Story and Art

John Stanley
and
Irving Tripp

Based on the character

created by

Marge Buell

DARK HORSE BOOKS™

Publisher
Mike Richardson

Editor
Shawna Gore

Collection Designer
Debra Bailey

Art Director
Lia Ribacchi

Published by
Dark Horse Books
A division of Dark Horse Comics, Inc.
10956 SE Main Street
Milwaukie, OR 97222

darkhorse.com

First edition: February 2005
ISBN-10: 1-59307-317-8
ISBN-13: 978-1-59307-317-6

3 5 7 9 10 8 6 4 2
Printed in U.S.A.

A note about Lulu

Little Lulu came into the world through the pen of cartoonist Marjorie "Marge" Henderson Buell in 1935. Originally commissioned as a series of single-panel cartoons by *The Saturday Evening Post*, Lulu took the world by storm with her charm, smarts, and sass. Within ten years, she not only was the star of her own cartoon series, but a celebrity spokesgirl for a variety of high-profile commercial products.

Little Lulu truly hit her stride as America's sweetheart in the comic books published by Dell Comics starting in 1945. While Buell was solely responsible for Lulu's original single-panel shenanigans, the comic book stories were put into the able hands of comics legend John Stanley. Stanley wrote and laid out the comics while artist Irving Tripp provided the finished drawings. After a number of trial appearances in Dell comics, Lulu's appeal was undeniable, and she was granted her very own comic book series, called *Marge's Little Lulu*, which was published regularly through 1984.

This volume contains every comic story from issues thirteen through seventeen of *Marge's Little Lulu*.

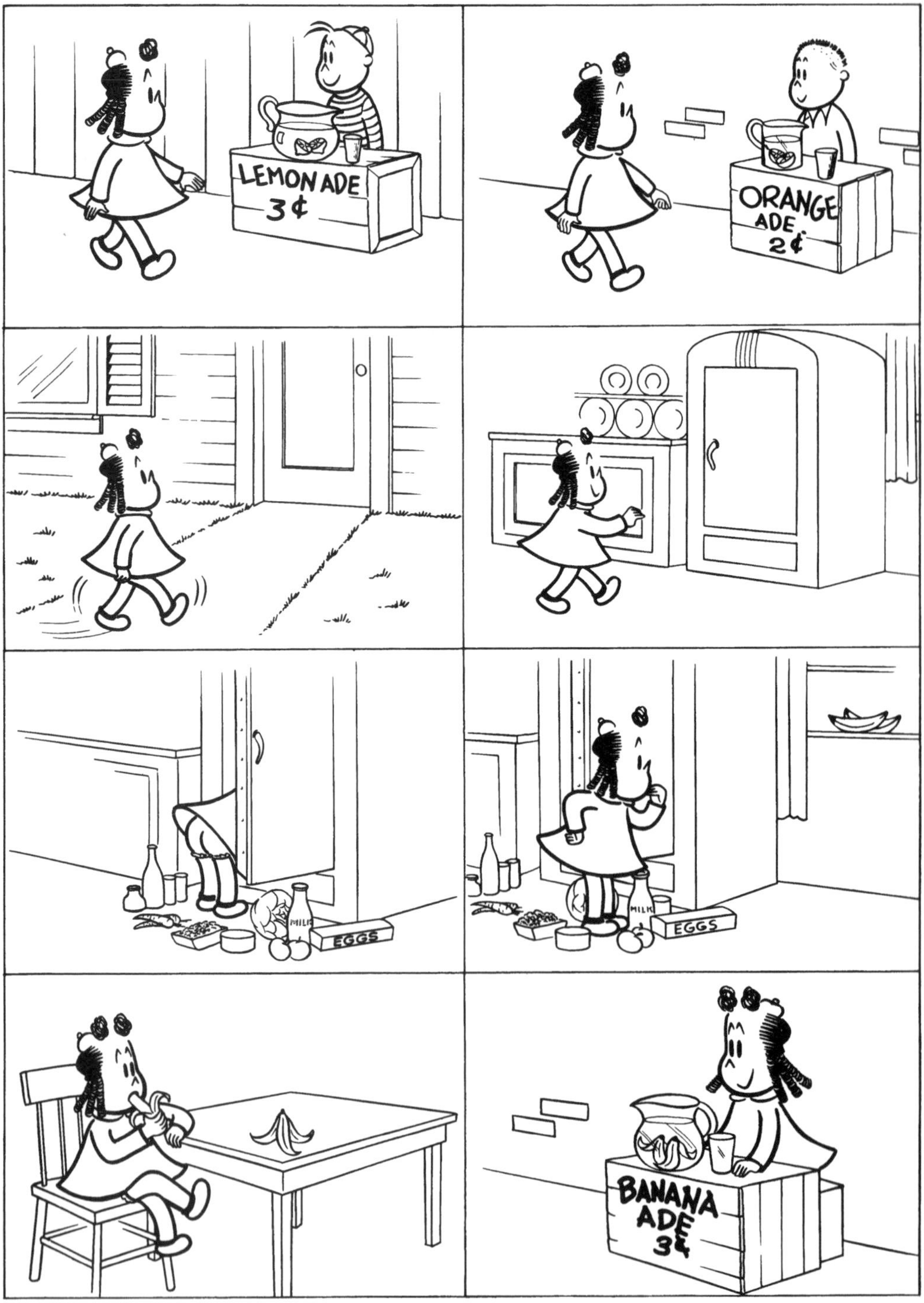
LEMONADE
3¢
ORANGE
ADE
2¢
MILK
EGGS
MILK
EGGS
BANANA
ADE
3¢

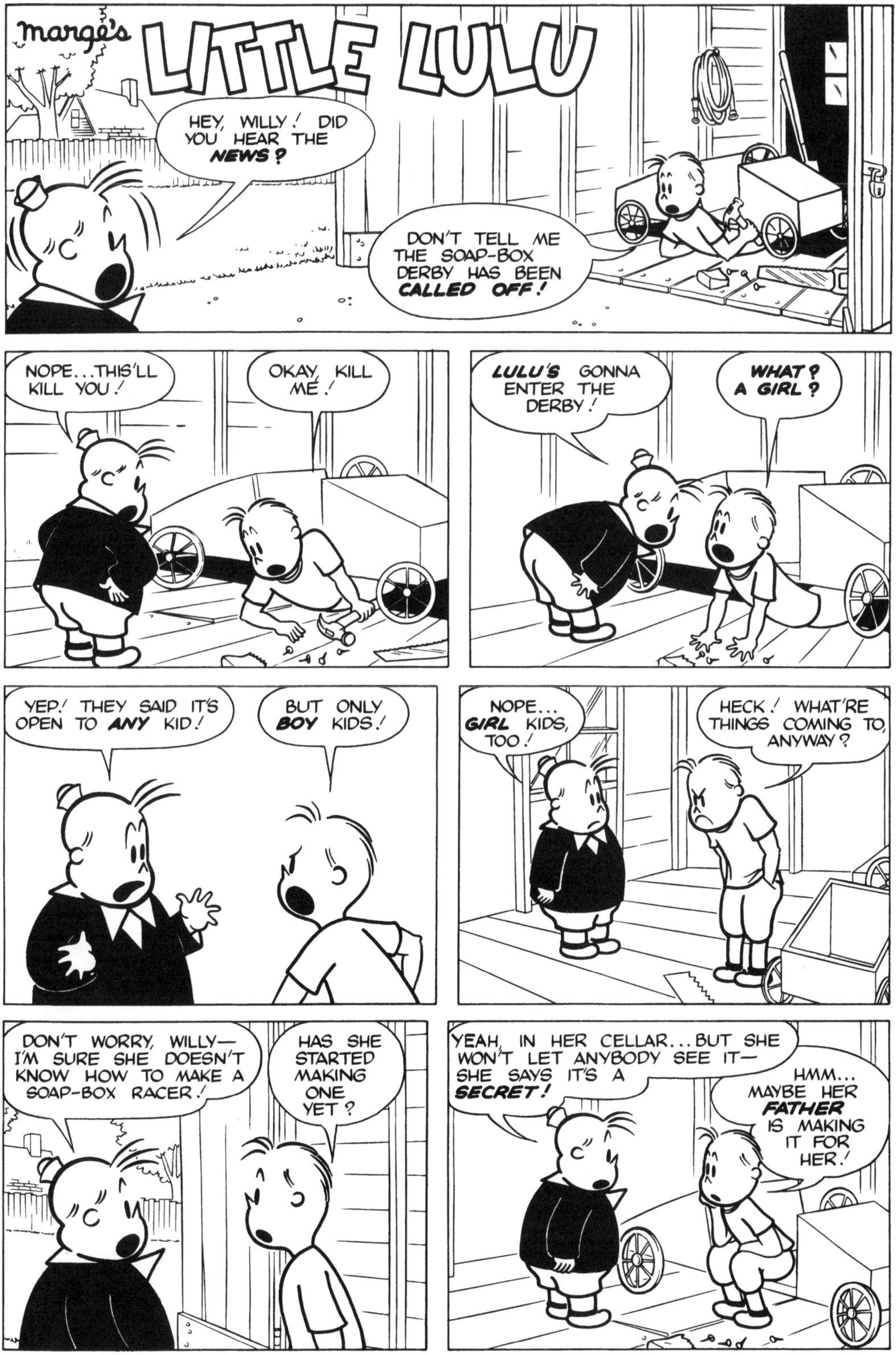

marge's LITTLE LULU
HEY, WILLY! DID YOU HEAR THE NEWS?
DON'T TELL ME THE SOAP-BOX DERBY HAS BEEN CALLED OFF!
NOPE...THIS'LL KILL YOU!
OKAY, KILL ME!
LULU'S GONNA ENTER THE DERBY!
WHAT? A GIRL?
YEP! THEY SAID IT'S OPEN TO ANY KID!
BUT ONLY BOY KIDS!
NOPE... GIRL KIDS, TOO!
HECK! WHAT'RE THINGS COMING TO, ANYWAY?
DON'T WORRY, WILLY— I'M SURE SHE DOESN'T KNOW HOW TO MAKE A SOAP-BOX RACER!
HAS SHE STARTED MAKING ONE YET?
YEAH, IN HER CELLAR...BUT SHE WON'T LET ANYBODY SEE IT— SHE SAYS IT'S A SECRET!
HMM... MAYBE HER FATHER IS MAKING IT FOR HER!

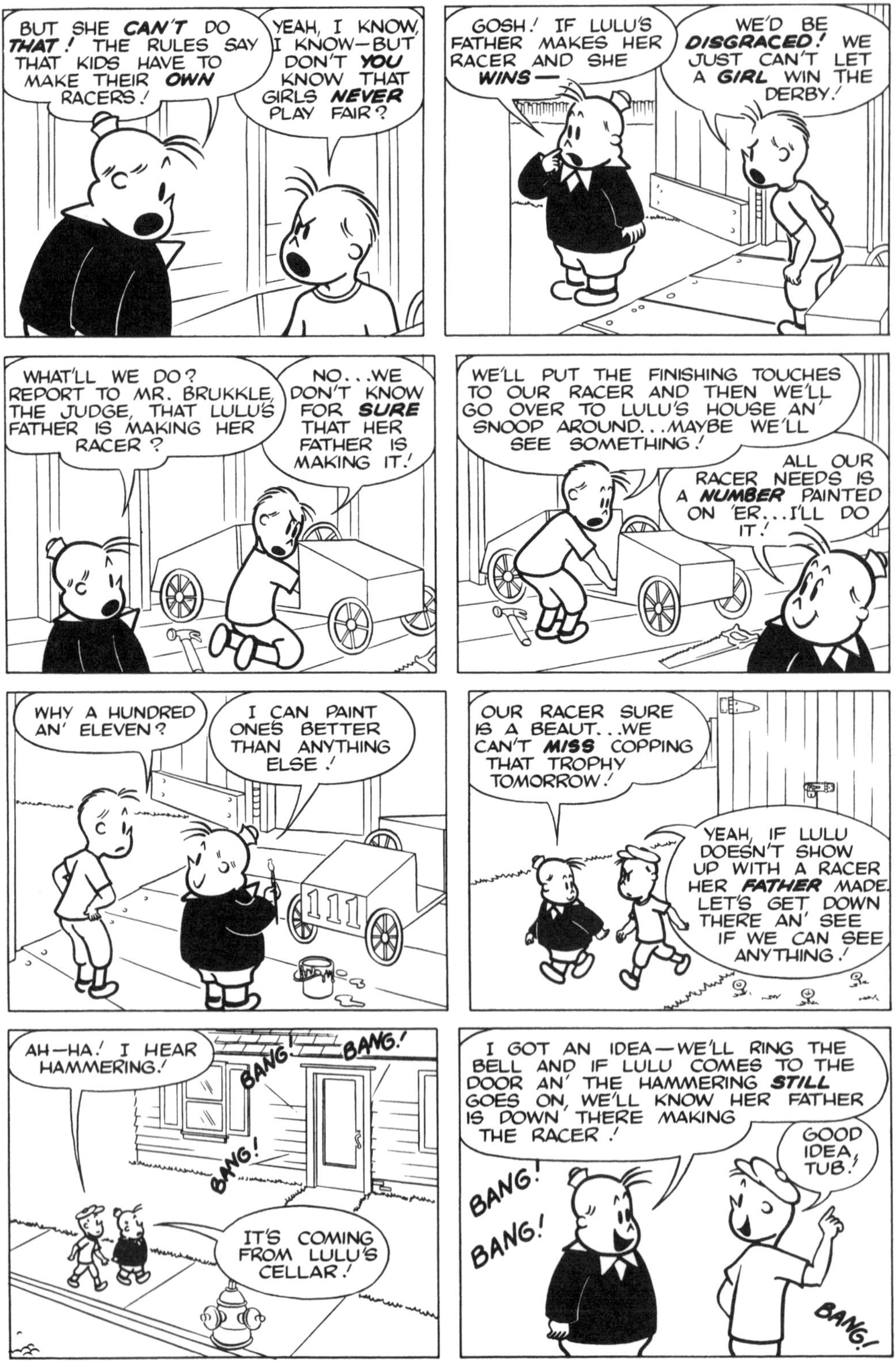

BUT SHE CAN'T DO THAT! THE RULES SAY THAT KIDS HAVE TO MAKE THEIR OWN RACERS!
YEAH, I KNOW, I KNOW—BUT DON'T YOU KNOW THAT GIRLS NEVER PLAY FAIR?
GOSH! IF LULU'S FATHER MAKES HER RACER AND SHE WINS—
WE'D BE DISGRACED! WE JUST CAN'T LET A GIRL WIN THE DERBY!
WHAT'LL WE DO? REPORT TO MR. BRUKKLE, THE JUDGE, THAT LULU'S FATHER IS MAKING HER RACER?
NO...WE DON'T KNOW FOR SURE THAT HER FATHER IS MAKING IT!
WE'LL PUT THE FINISHING TOUCHES TO OUR RACER AND THEN WE'LL GO OVER TO LULU'S HOUSE AN' SNOOP AROUND...MAYBE WE'LL SEE SOMETHING!
ALL OUR RACER NEEDS IS A NUMBER PAINTED ON 'ER...I'LL DO IT!
WHY A HUNDRED AN' ELEVEN?
I CAN PAINT ONE'S BETTER THAN ANYTHING ELSE!
111
OUR RACER SURE IS A BEAUT...WE CAN'T MISS COPPING THAT TROPHY TOMORROW!
YEAH, IF LULU DOESN'T SHOW UP WITH A RACER HER FATHER MADE. LET'S GET DOWN THERE AN' SEE IF WE CAN SEE ANYTHING!
AH-HA! I HEAR HAMMERING!
BANG! BANG!
BANG!
BANG!
IT'S COMING FROM LULU'S CELLAR!
I GOT AN IDEA—WE'LL RING THE BELL AND IF LULU COMES TO THE DOOR AN' THE HAMMERING STILL GOES ON, WE'LL KNOW HER FATHER IS DOWN THERE MAKING THE RACER!
GOOD IDEA, TUB!
BANG!
BANG!
BANG!

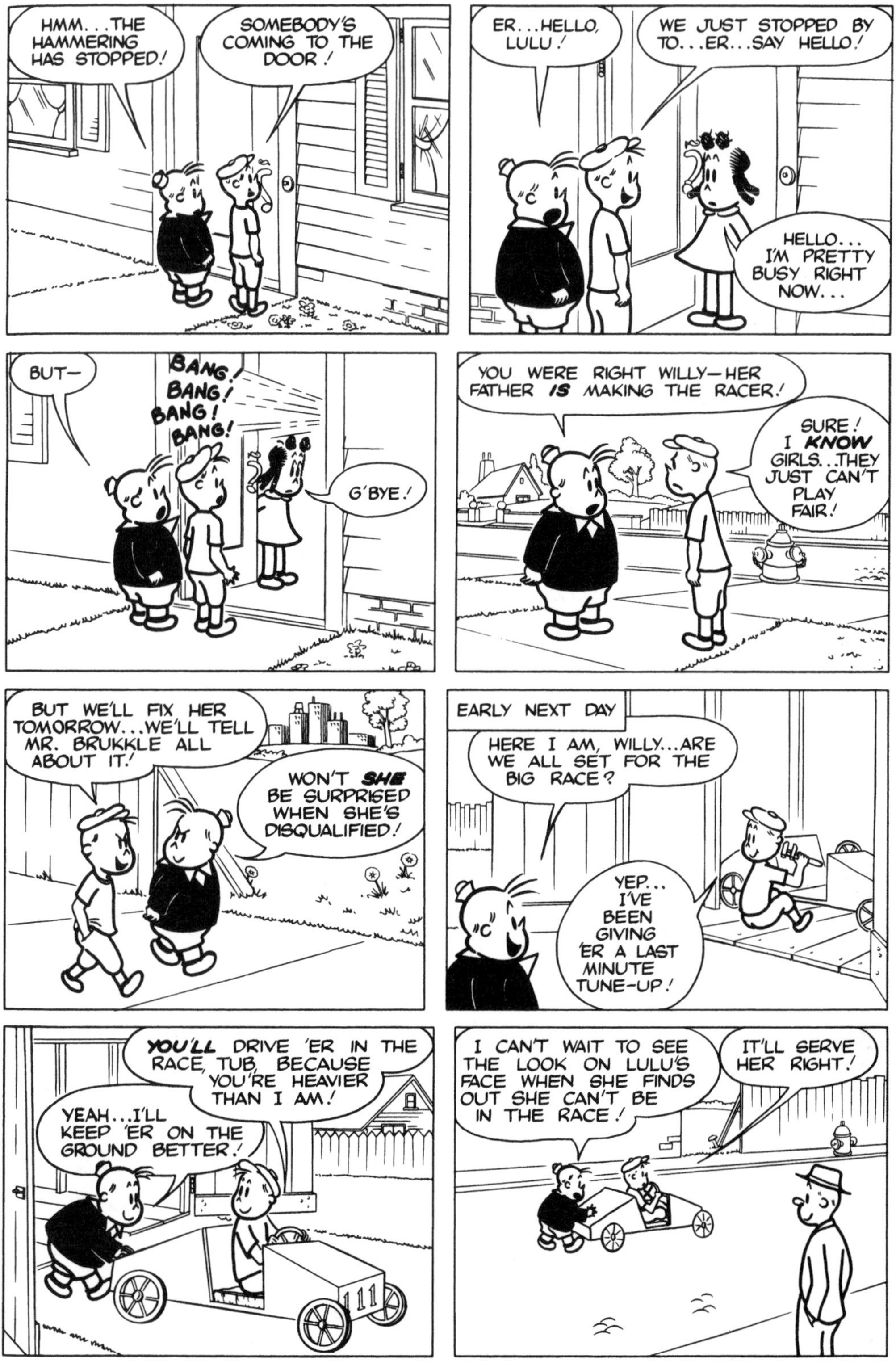
HMM...THE HAMMERING HAS STOPPED!
SOMEBODY'S COMING TO THE DOOR!
ER...HELLO, LULU!
WE JUST STOPPED BY TO...ER...SAY HELLO!
HELLO... I'M PRETTY BUSY RIGHT NOW...
BUT—
BANG! BANG! BANG! BANG!
G'BYE!
YOU WERE RIGHT WILLY—HER FATHER IS MAKING THE RACER!
SURE! I KNOW GIRLS...THEY JUST CAN'T PLAY FAIR!
BUT WE'LL FIX HER TOMORROW...WE'LL TELL MR. BRUKKLE ALL ABOUT IT!
WON'T SHE BE SURPRISED WHEN SHE'S DISQUALIFIED!
EARLY NEXT DAY
HERE I AM, WILLY...ARE WE ALL SET FOR THE BIG RACE?
YEP... I'VE BEEN GIVING 'ER A LAST MINUTE TUNE-UP!
YOU'LL DRIVE 'ER IN THE RACE, TUB, BECAUSE YOU'RE HEAVIER THAN I AM!
YEAH...I'LL KEEP 'ER ON THE GROUND BETTER!
111
I CAN'T WAIT TO SEE THE LOOK ON LULU'S FACE WHEN SHE FINDS OUT SHE CAN'T BE IN THE RACE!
IT'LL SERVE HER RIGHT!

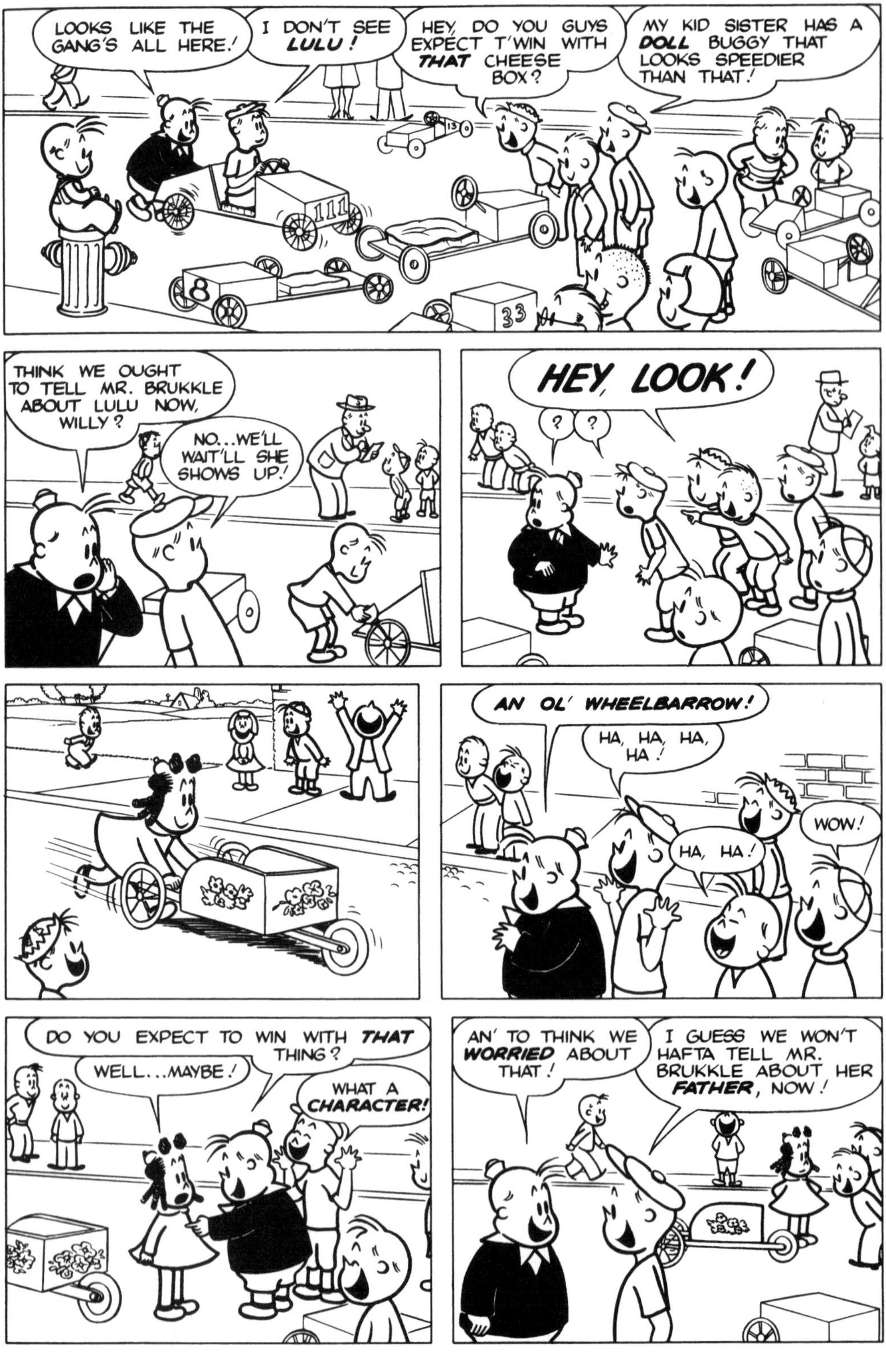
LOOKS LIKE THE GANG'S ALL HERE!
I DON'T SEE **LULU**!
HEY, DO YOU GUYS EXPECT T'WIN WITH **THAT** CHEESE BOX?
MY KID SISTER HAS A **DOLL** BUGGY THAT LOOKS SPEEDIER THAN THAT!
111
8
33
13
THINK WE OUGHT TO TELL MR. BRUKKLE ABOUT LULU NOW, WILLY?
NO...WE'LL WAIT'LL SHE SHOWS UP!
HEY, LOOK!
?
?
AN OL' WHEELBARROW!
HA, HA, HA, HA!
HA, HA!
WOW!
DO YOU EXPECT TO WIN WITH **THAT** THING?
WELL...MAYBE!
WHAT A **CHARACTER**!
AN' TO THINK WE **WORRIED** ABOUT THAT!
I GUESS WE WON'T HAFTA TELL MR. BRUKKLE ABOUT HER **FATHER**, NOW!

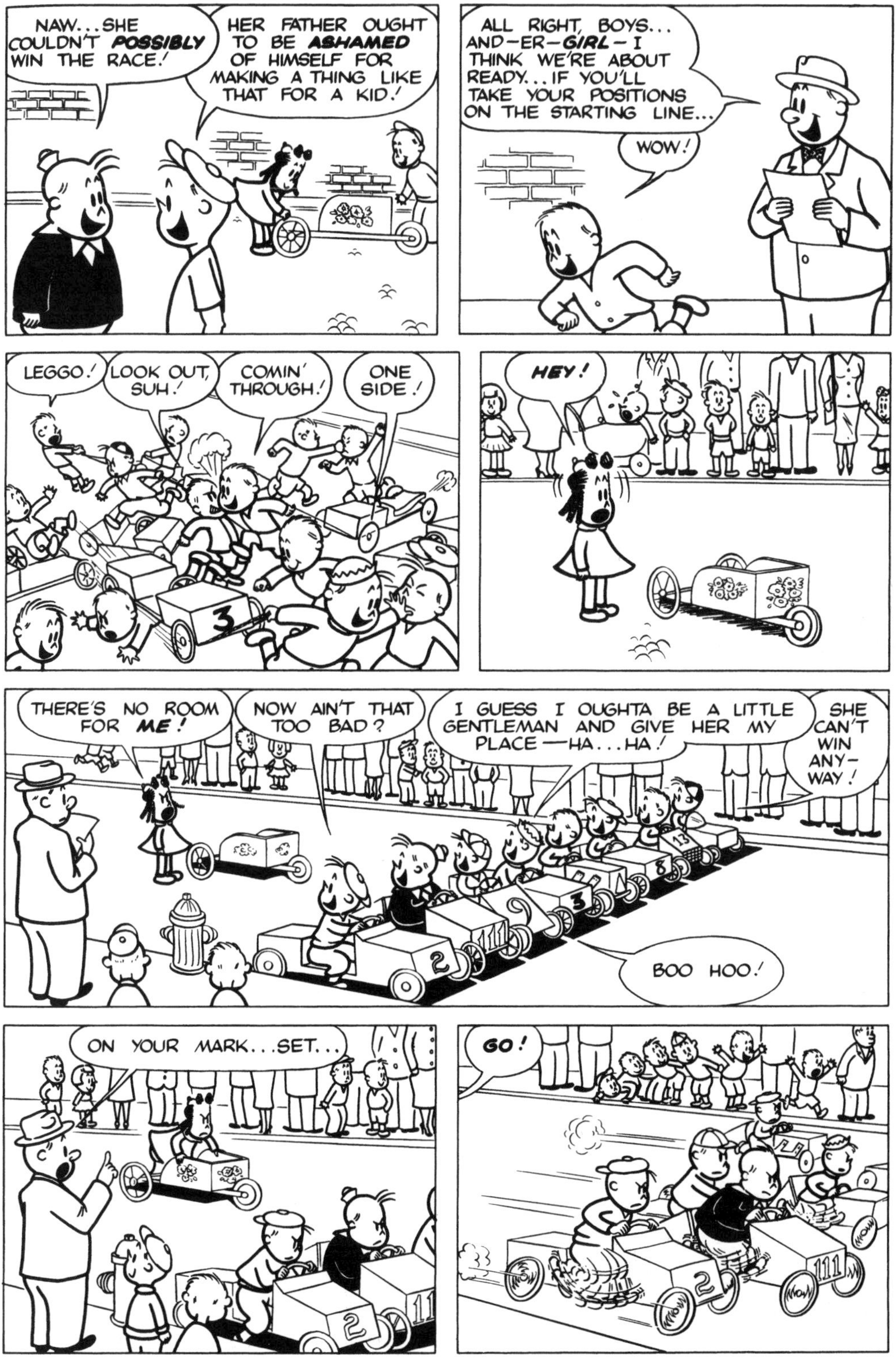
NAW...SHE COULDN'T POSSIBLY WIN THE RACE!
HER FATHER OUGHT TO BE ASHAMED OF HIMSELF FOR MAKING A THING LIKE THAT FOR A KID!
ALL RIGHT, BOYS... AND—ER—GIRL—I THINK WE'RE ABOUT READY...IF YOU'LL TAKE YOUR POSITIONS ON THE STARTING LINE...
WOW!
LEGGO!
LOOK OUT, SUH!
COMIN' THROUGH!
ONE SIDE!
HEY!
THERE'S NO ROOM FOR ME!
NOW AIN'T THAT TOO BAD?
I GUESS I OUGHTA BE A LITTLE GENTLEMAN AND GIVE HER MY PLACE—HA...HA!
SHE CAN'T WIN ANY-WAY!
BOO HOO!
ON YOUR MARK...SET...
GO!

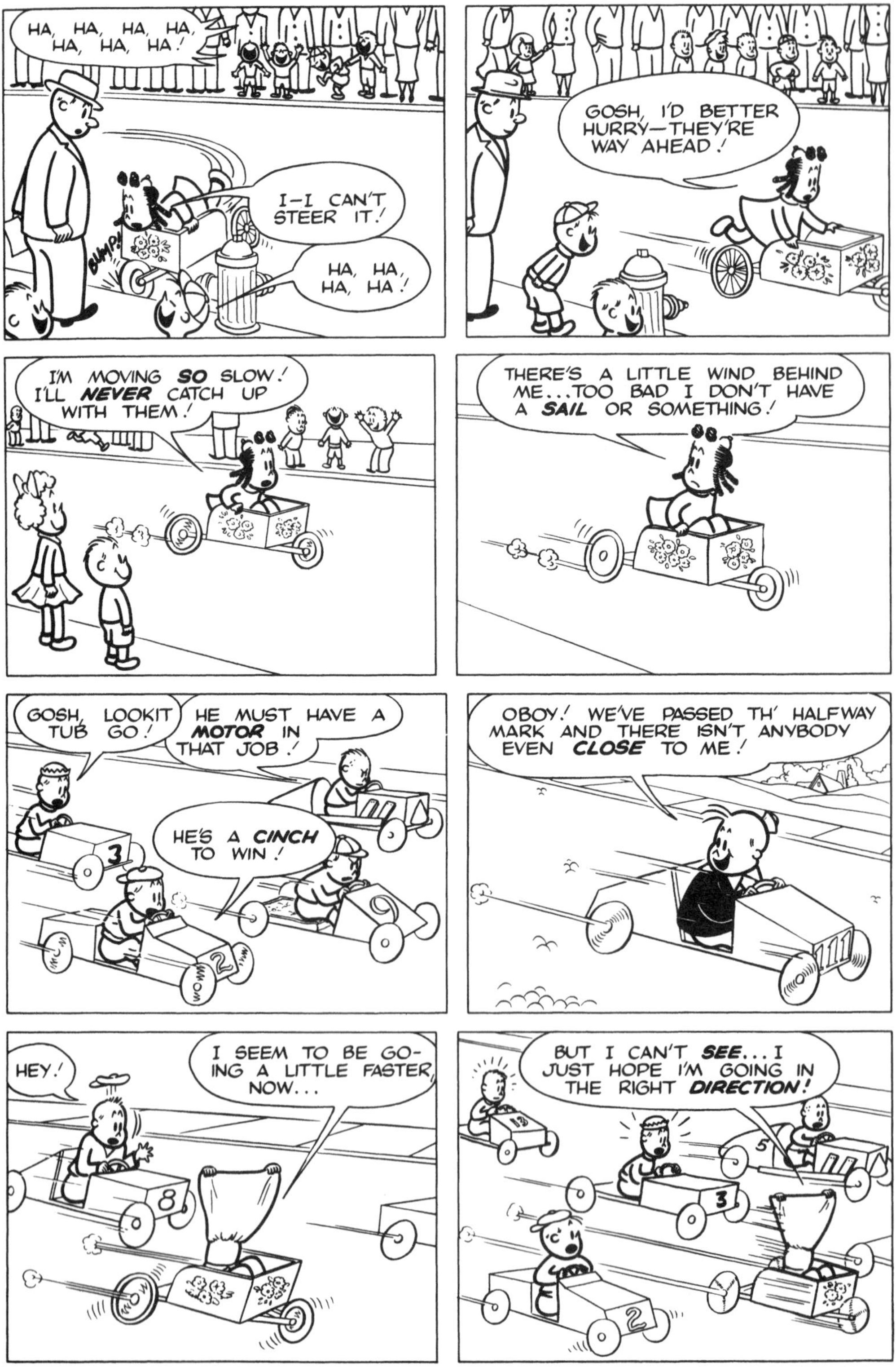
HA, HA, HA, HA, HA, HA, HA!
I-I CAN'T STEER IT!
BUMP!
HA, HA, HA, HA!
GOSH, I'D BETTER HURRY—THEY'RE WAY AHEAD!
I'M MOVING SO SLOW! I'LL NEVER CATCH UP WITH THEM!
THERE'S A LITTLE WIND BEHIND ME...TOO BAD I DON'T HAVE A SAIL OR SOMETHING!
GOSH, LOOKIT TUB GO!
HE MUST HAVE A MOTOR IN THAT JOB!
HE'S A CINCH TO WIN!
OBOY! WE'VE PASSED TH' HALFWAY MARK AND THERE ISN'T ANYBODY EVEN CLOSE TO ME!
HEY!
I SEEM TO BE GO-ING A LITTLE FASTER NOW...
BUT I CAN'T SEE... I JUST HOPE I'M GOING IN THE RIGHT DIRECTION!

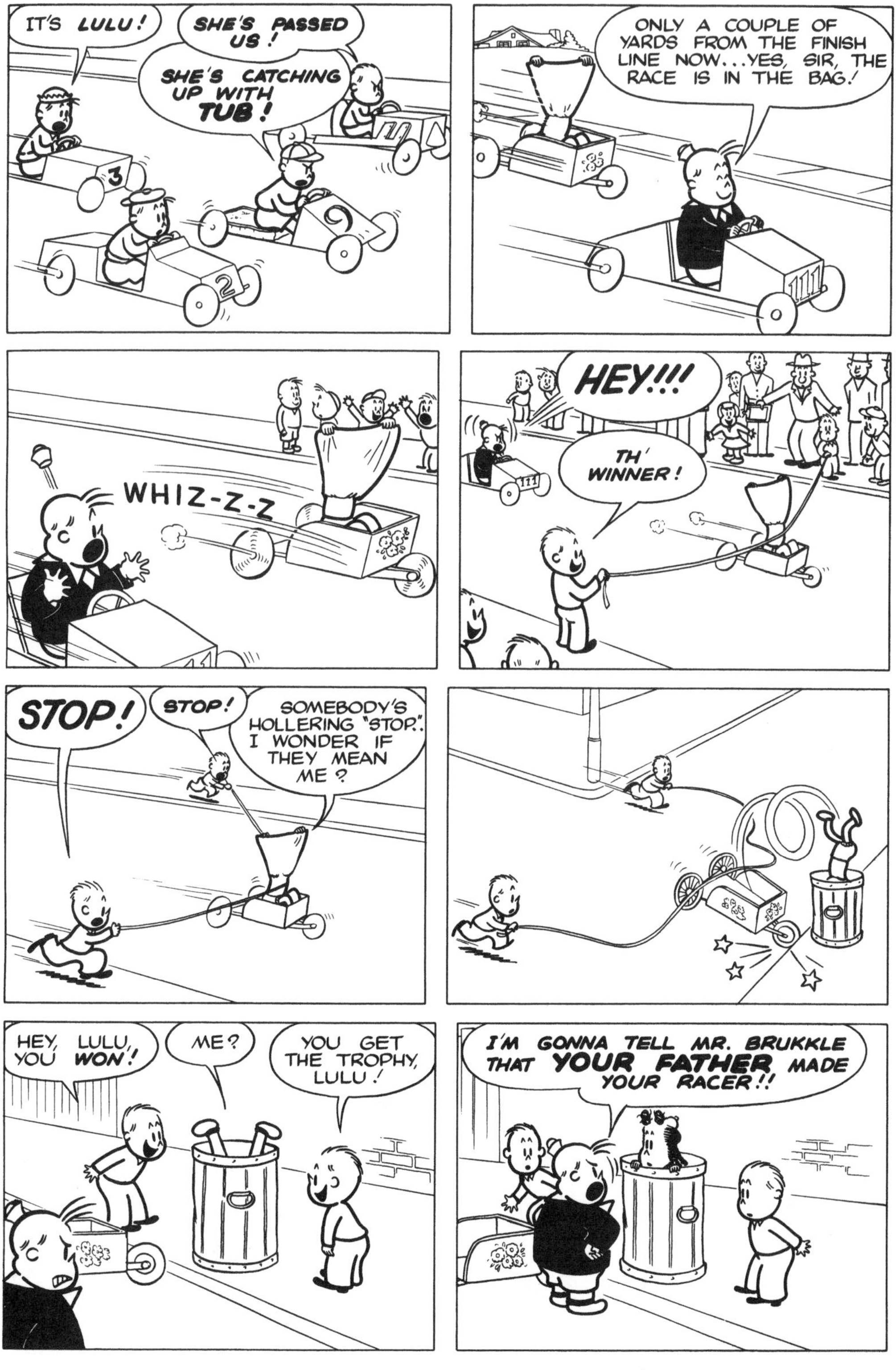
IT'S LULU!
SHE'S PASSED US!
SHE'S CATCHING UP WITH TUB!
ONLY A COUPLE OF YARDS FROM THE FINISH LINE NOW...YES, SIR, THE RACE IS IN THE BAG!
WHIZ-Z-Z
HEY!!!
TH' WINNER!
STOP!
STOP!
SOMEBODY'S HOLLERING "STOP". I WONDER IF THEY MEAN ME?
HEY, LULU, YOU WON!
ME?
YOU GET THE TROPHY, LULU!
I'M GONNA TELL MR. BRUKKLE THAT YOUR FATHER MADE YOUR RACER!!

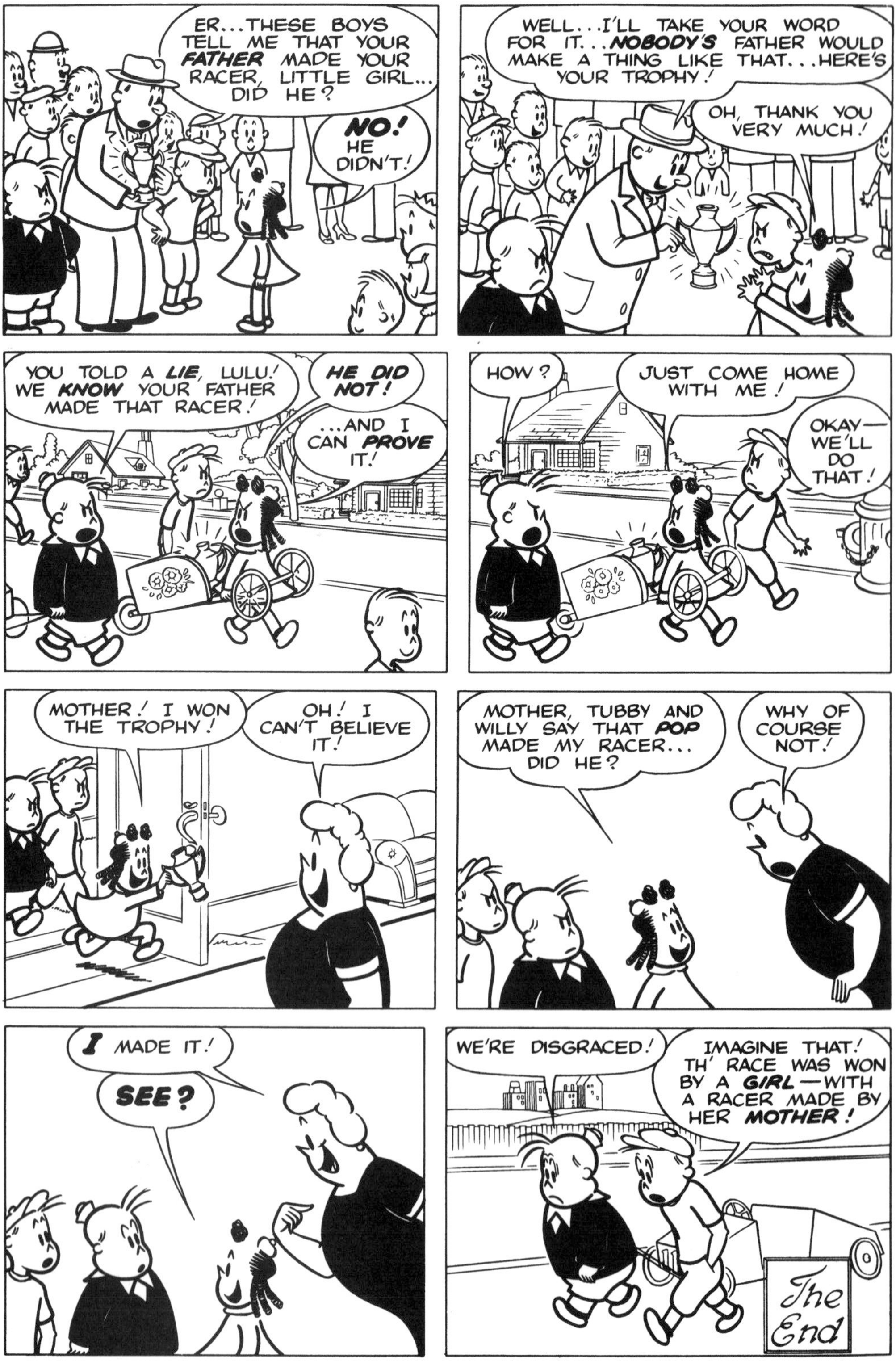
ER...THESE BOYS TELL ME THAT YOUR **FATHER** MADE YOUR RACER, LITTLE GIRL... DID HE?
NO! HE DIDN'T!
WELL...I'LL TAKE YOUR WORD FOR IT...**NOBODY'S** FATHER WOULD MAKE A THING LIKE THAT...HERE'S YOUR TROPHY!
OH, THANK YOU VERY MUCH!
YOU TOLD A **LIE**, LULU! WE **KNOW** YOUR FATHER MADE THAT RACER!
HE DID NOT!
...AND I CAN **PROVE** IT!
HOW?
JUST COME HOME WITH ME!
OKAY—WE'LL DO THAT!
MOTHER! I WON THE TROPHY!
OH! I CAN'T BELIEVE IT!
MOTHER, TUBBY AND WILLY SAY THAT **POP** MADE MY RACER... DID HE?
WHY OF COURSE NOT!
I MADE IT!
SEE?
WE'RE DISGRACED!
IMAGINE THAT! TH' RACE WAS WON BY A **GIRL**—WITH A RACER MADE BY HER **MOTHER**!
The End

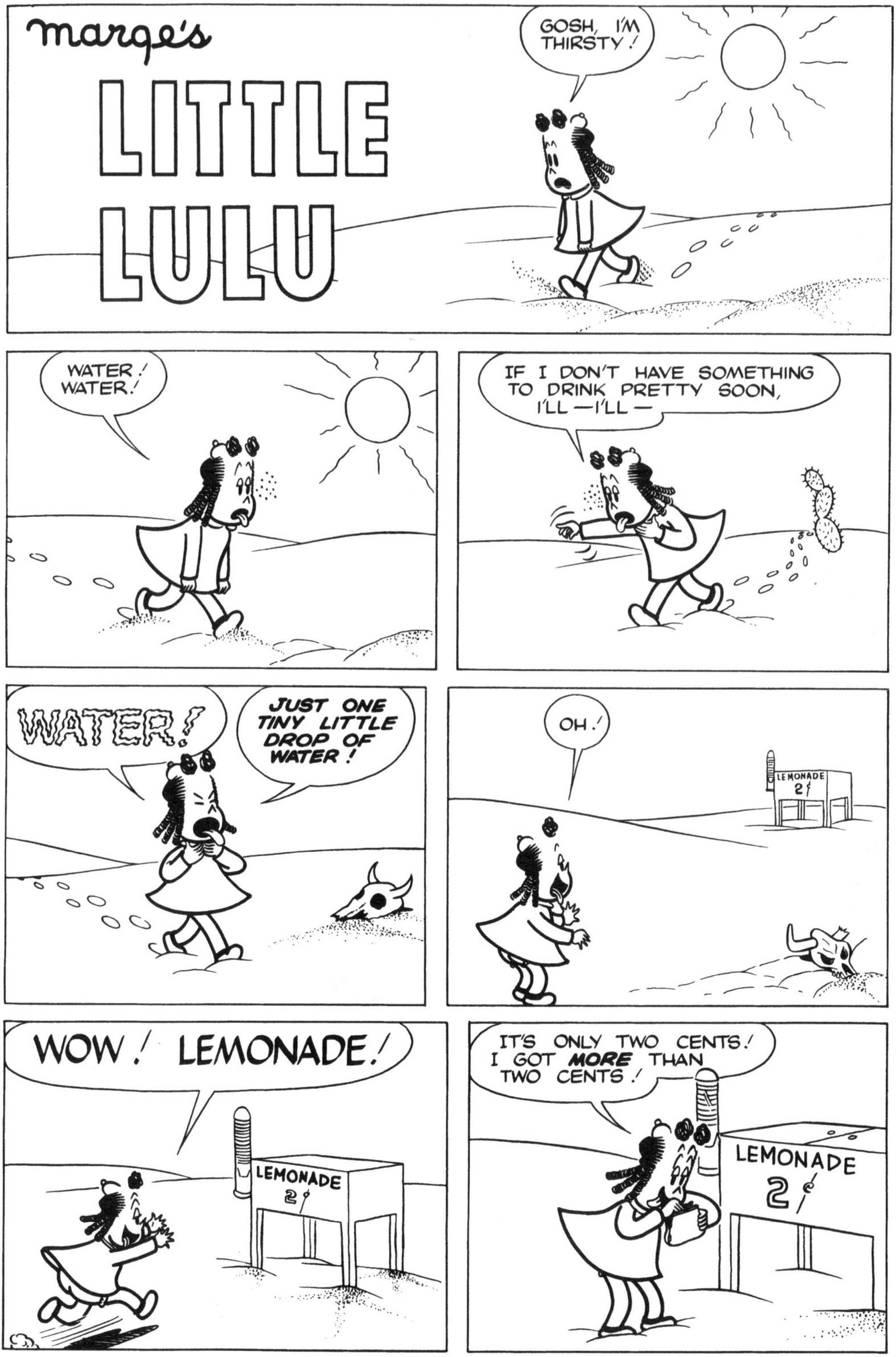
marge's
LITTLE LULU
GOSH, I'M THIRSTY!
WATER! WATER!
IF I DON'T HAVE SOMETHING TO DRINK PRETTY SOON, I'LL—I'LL—
WATER!
JUST ONE TINY LITTLE DROP OF WATER!
OH!
LEMONADE 2¢
WOW! LEMONADE!
LEMONADE 2¢
IT'S ONLY TWO CENTS! I GOT MORE THAN TWO CENTS!
LEMONADE 2¢

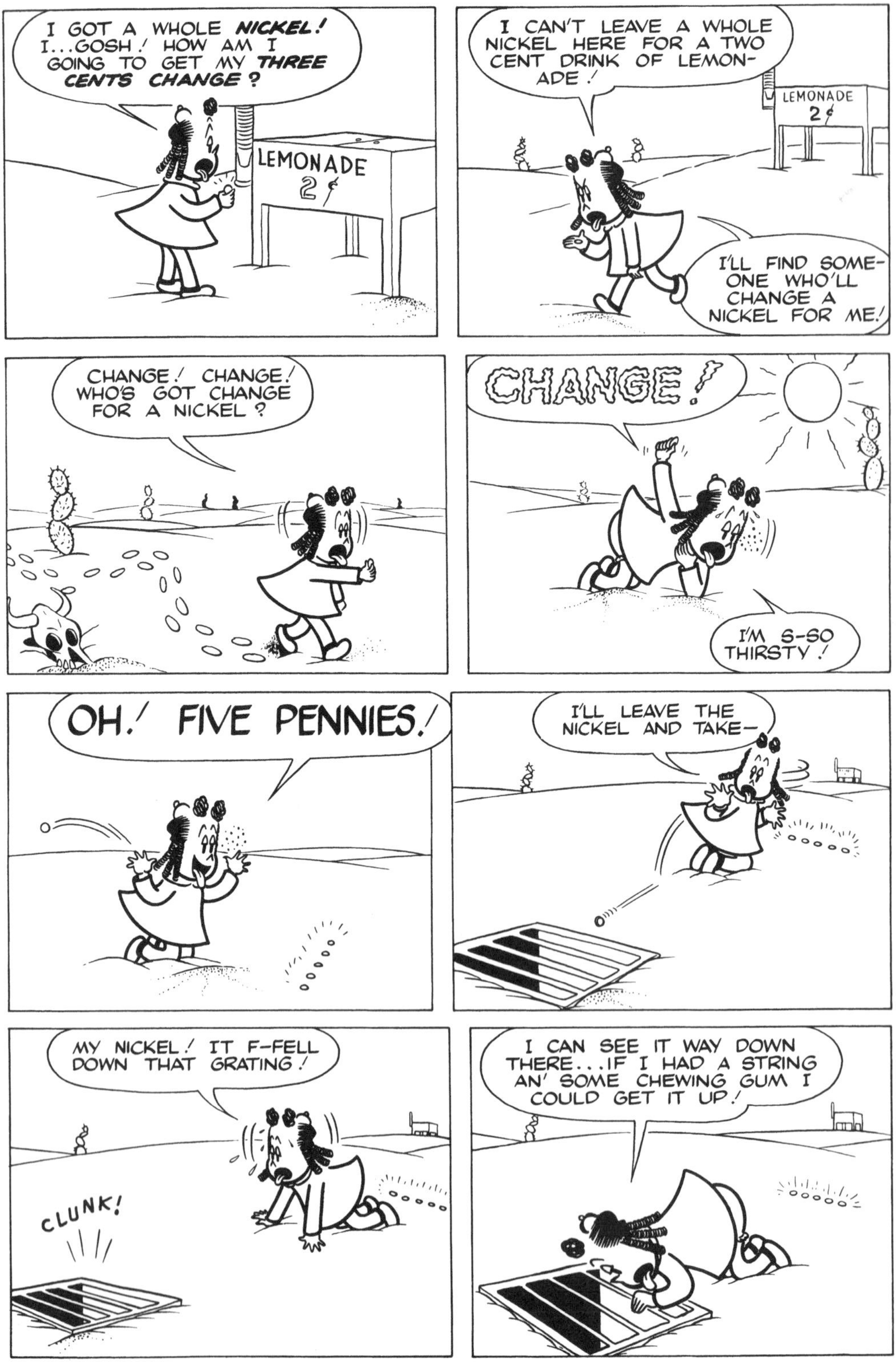

I GOT A WHOLE NICKEL! I...GOSH! HOW AM I GOING TO GET MY THREE CENTS CHANGE?
LEMONADE 2¢
I CAN'T LEAVE A WHOLE NICKEL HERE FOR A TWO CENT DRINK OF LEMONADE!
LEMONADE 2¢
I'LL FIND SOMEONE WHO'LL CHANGE A NICKEL FOR ME!
CHANGE! CHANGE! WHO'S GOT CHANGE FOR A NICKEL?
CHANGE!
I'M S-SO THIRSTY!
OH! FIVE PENNIES!
I'LL LEAVE THE NICKEL AND TAKE—
MY NICKEL! IT F-FELL DOWN THAT GRATING!
CLUNK!
I CAN SEE IT WAY DOWN THERE...IF I HAD A STRING AN' SOME CHEWING GUM I COULD GET IT UP!

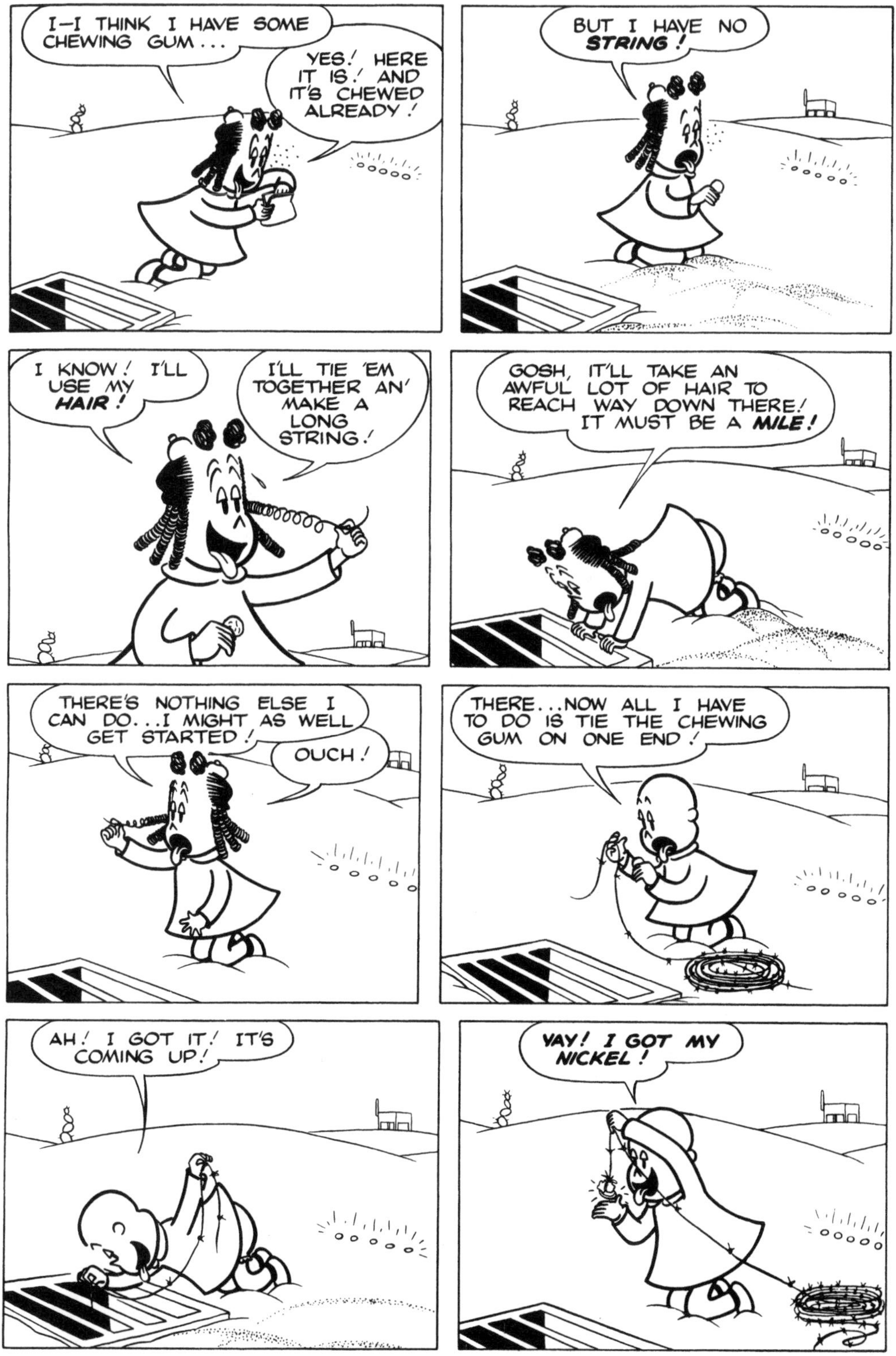
I—I THINK I HAVE SOME CHEWING GUM...
YES! HERE IT IS! AND IT'S CHEWED ALREADY!
BUT I HAVE NO STRING!
I KNOW! I'LL USE MY HAIR!
I'LL TIE 'EM TOGETHER AN' MAKE A LONG STRING!
GOSH, IT'LL TAKE AN AWFUL LOT OF HAIR TO REACH WAY DOWN THERE! IT MUST BE A MILE!
THERE'S NOTHING ELSE I CAN DO...I MIGHT AS WELL GET STARTED!
OUCH!
THERE...NOW ALL I HAVE TO DO IS TIE THE CHEWING GUM ON ONE END!
AH! I GOT IT! IT'S COMING UP!
YAY! I GOT MY NICKEL!

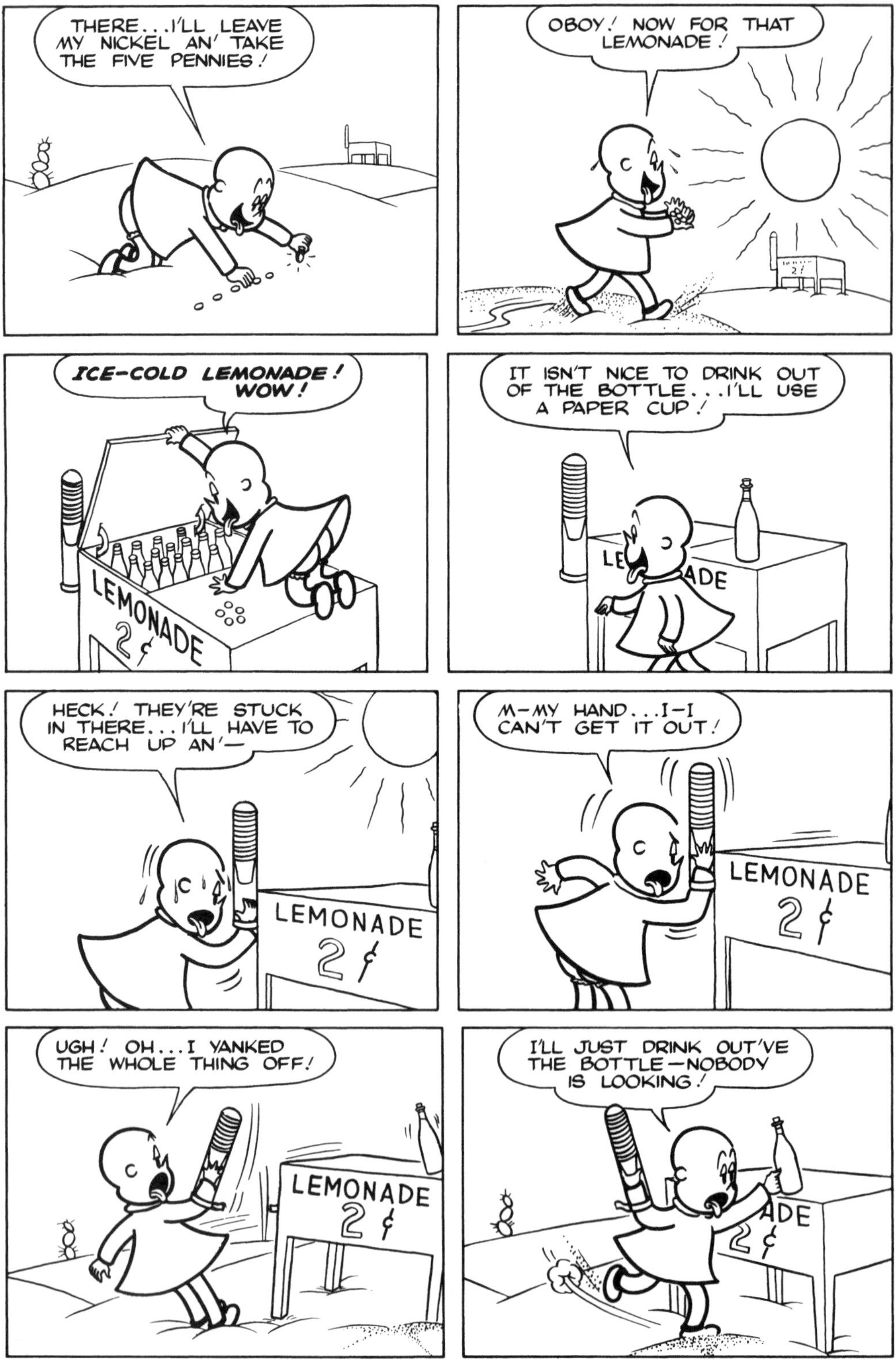
THERE...I'LL LEAVE MY NICKEL AN' TAKE THE FIVE PENNIES!
OBOY! NOW FOR THAT LEMONADE!
2¢
ICE-COLD LEMONADE! WOW!
LEMONADE 2¢
IT ISN'T NICE TO DRINK OUT OF THE BOTTLE...I'LL USE A PAPER CUP!
HECK! THEY'RE STUCK IN THERE...I'LL HAVE TO REACH UP AN'—
LEMONADE 2¢
M-MY HAND...I-I CAN'T GET IT OUT!
LEMONADE 2¢
UGH! OH...I YANKED THE WHOLE THING OFF!
LEMONADE 2¢
I'LL JUST DRINK OUT'VE THE BOTTLE—NOBODY IS LOOKING!
ADE 2¢

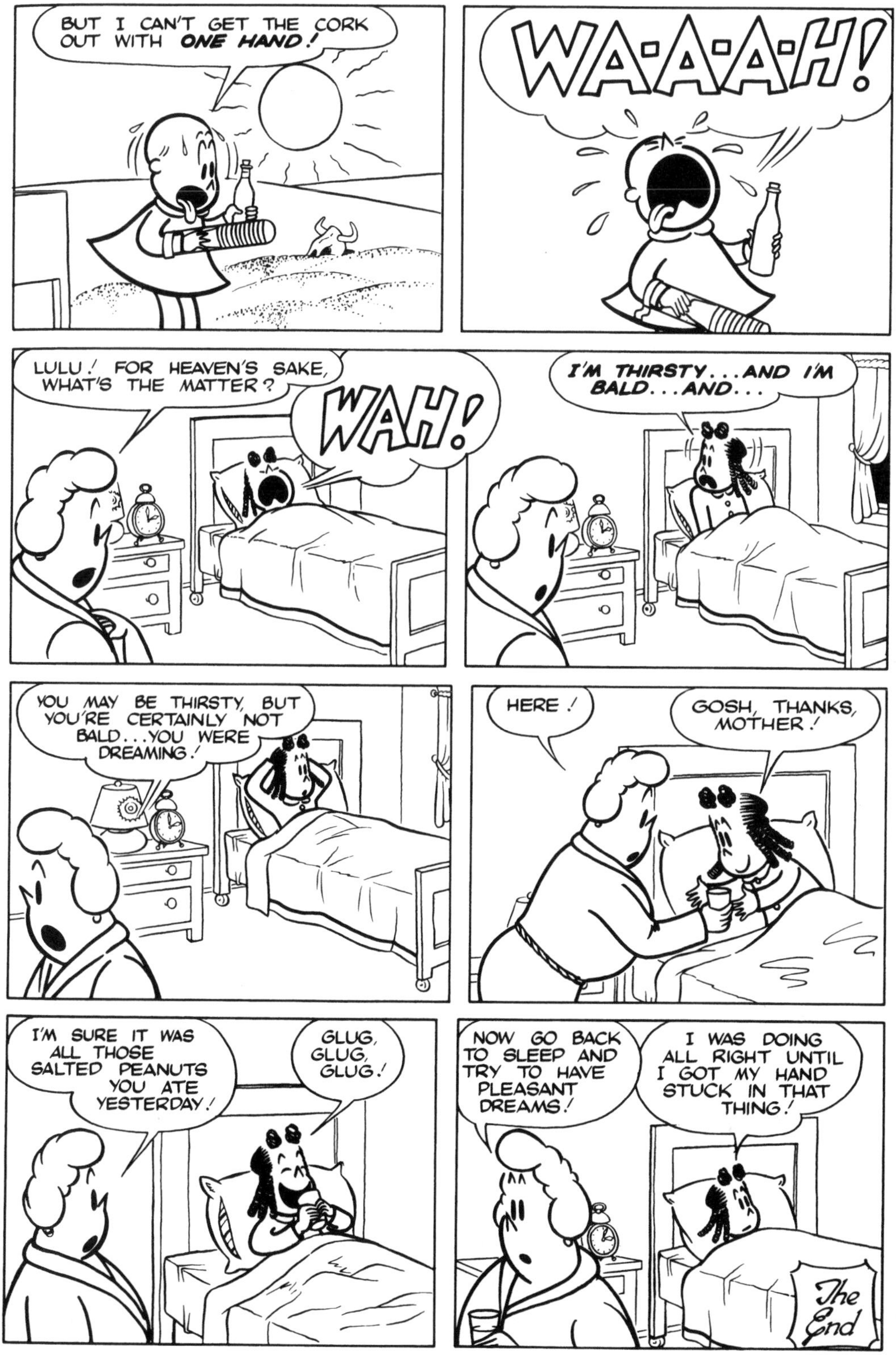

BUT I CAN'T GET THE CORK OUT WITH ONE HAND!
WA-A-A-H!
LULU! FOR HEAVEN'S SAKE, WHAT'S THE MATTER?
WAH!
I'M THIRSTY... AND I'M BALD... AND...
YOU MAY BE THIRSTY, BUT YOU'RE CERTAINLY NOT BALD... YOU WERE DREAMING!
HERE!
GOSH, THANKS, MOTHER!
I'M SURE IT WAS ALL THOSE SALTED PEANUTS YOU ATE YESTERDAY!
GLUG, GLUG, GLUG!
NOW GO BACK TO SLEEP AND TRY TO HAVE PLEASANT DREAMS!
I WAS DOING ALL RIGHT UNTIL I GOT MY HAND STUCK IN THAT THING!
The End

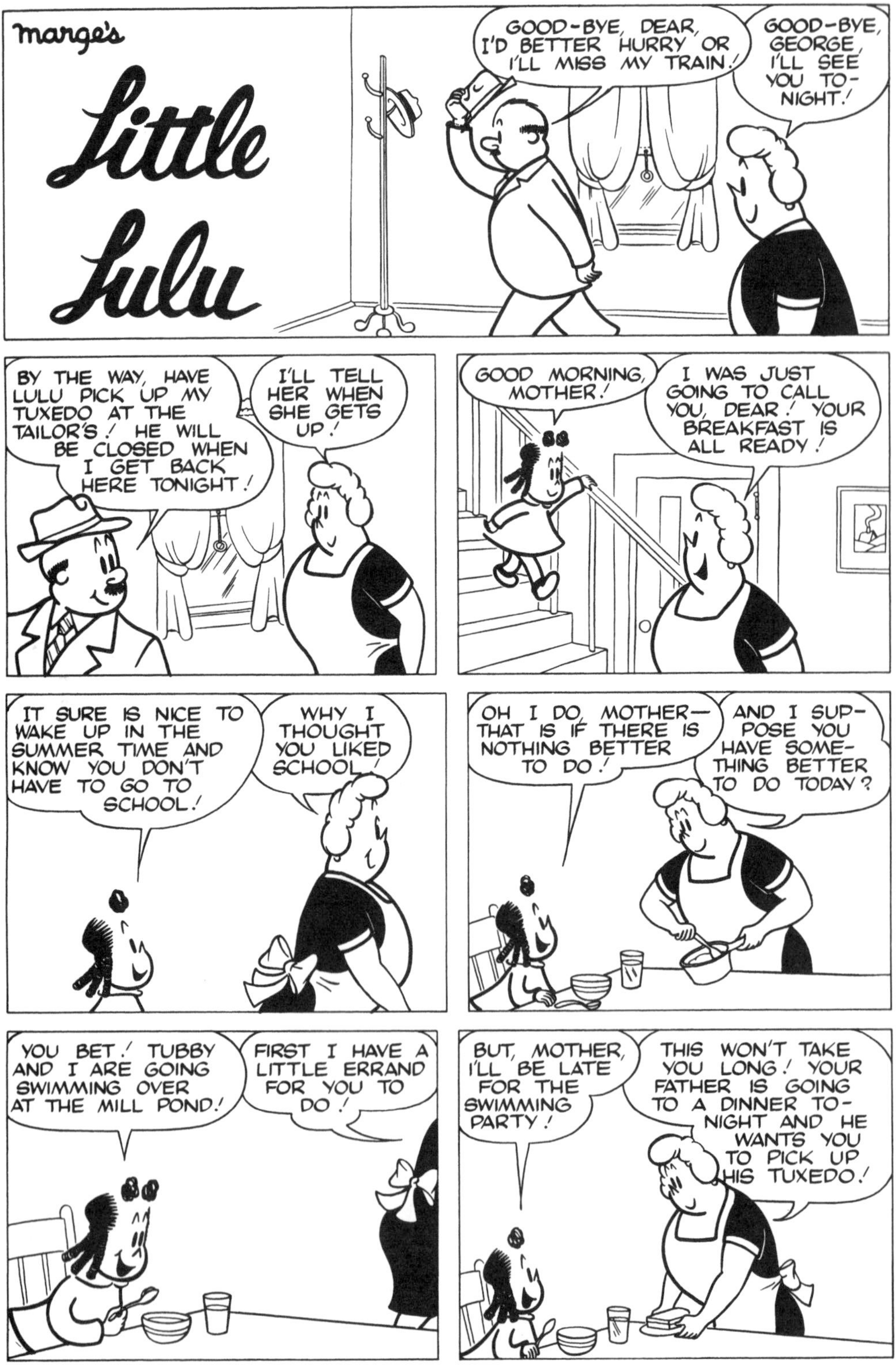
marge's
Little Lulu
GOOD-BYE, DEAR, I'D BETTER HURRY OR I'LL MISS MY TRAIN!
GOOD-BYE, GEORGE, I'LL SEE YOU TO-NIGHT!
BY THE WAY, HAVE LULU PICK UP MY TUXEDO AT THE TAILOR'S! HE WILL BE CLOSED WHEN I GET BACK HERE TONIGHT!
I'LL TELL HER WHEN SHE GETS UP!
GOOD MORNING, MOTHER!
I WAS JUST GOING TO CALL YOU, DEAR! YOUR BREAKFAST IS ALL READY!
IT SURE IS NICE TO WAKE UP IN THE SUMMER TIME AND KNOW YOU DON'T HAVE TO GO TO SCHOOL!
WHY I THOUGHT YOU LIKED SCHOOL!
OH I DO, MOTHER— THAT IS IF THERE IS NOTHING BETTER TO DO!
AND I SUPPOSE YOU HAVE SOMETHING BETTER TO DO TODAY?
YOU BET! TUBBY AND I ARE GOING SWIMMING OVER AT THE MILL POND!
FIRST I HAVE A LITTLE ERRAND FOR YOU TO DO!
BUT, MOTHER, I'LL BE LATE FOR THE SWIMMING PARTY!
THIS WON'T TAKE YOU LONG! YOUR FATHER IS GOING TO A DINNER TO-NIGHT AND HE WANTS YOU TO PICK UP HIS TUXEDO!

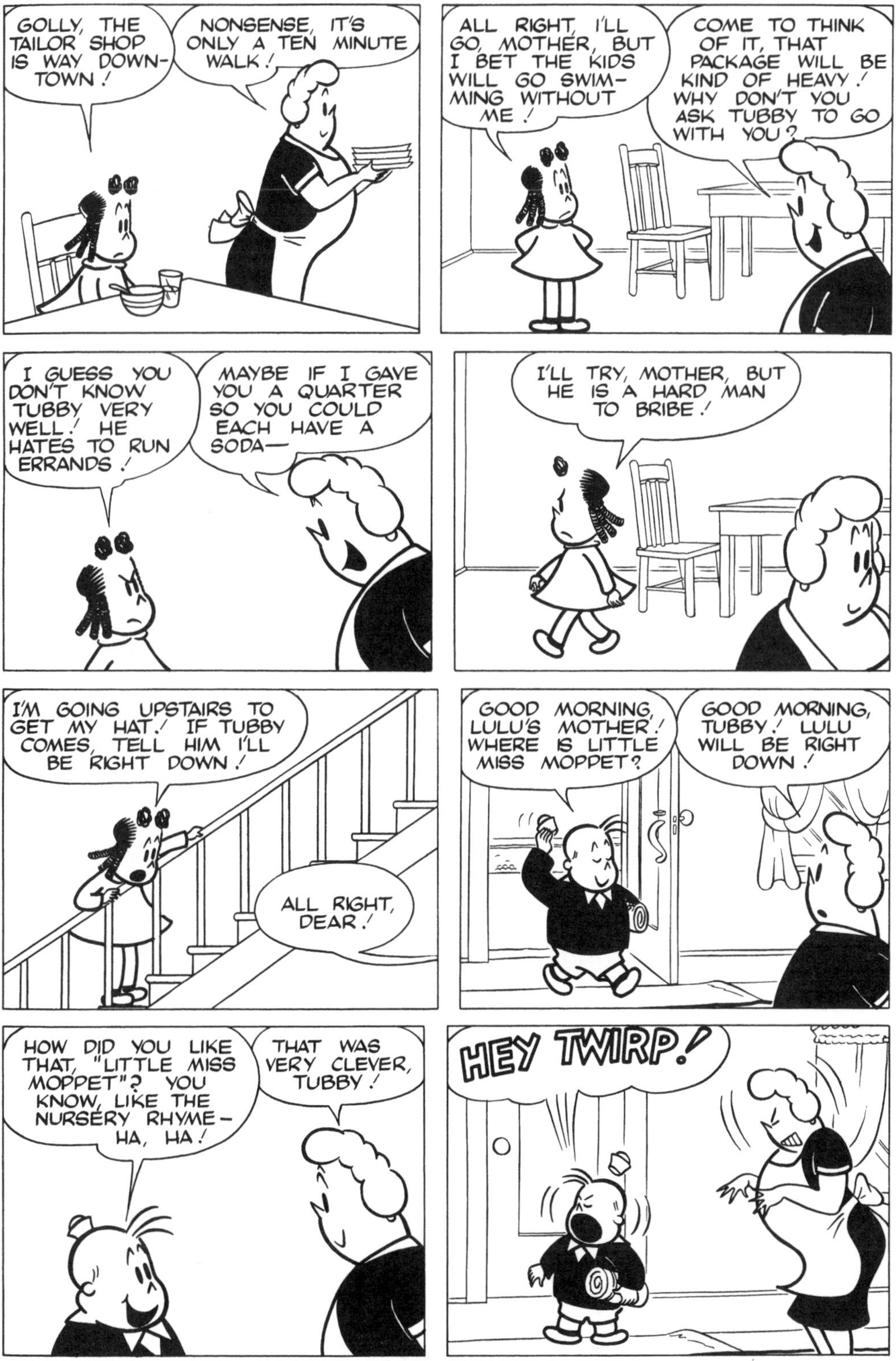
GOLLY, THE TAILOR SHOP IS WAY DOWN-TOWN!
NONSENSE, IT'S ONLY A TEN MINUTE WALK!
ALL RIGHT, I'LL GO, MOTHER, BUT I BET THE KIDS WILL GO SWIM-MING WITHOUT ME!
COME TO THINK OF IT, THAT PACKAGE WILL BE KIND OF HEAVY! WHY DON'T YOU ASK TUBBY TO GO WITH YOU?
I GUESS YOU DON'T KNOW TUBBY VERY WELL! HE HATES TO RUN ERRANDS!
MAYBE IF I GAVE YOU A QUARTER SO YOU COULD EACH HAVE A SODA—
I'LL TRY, MOTHER, BUT HE IS A HARD MAN TO BRIBE!
I'M GOING UPSTAIRS TO GET MY HAT! IF TUBBY COMES, TELL HIM I'LL BE RIGHT DOWN!
ALL RIGHT, DEAR!
GOOD MORNING, LULU'S MOTHER! WHERE IS LITTLE MISS MOPPET?
GOOD MORNING, TUBBY! LULU WILL BE RIGHT DOWN!
HOW DID YOU LIKE THAT, "LITTLE MISS MOPPET"? YOU KNOW, LIKE THE NURSERY RHYME— HA, HA!
THAT WAS VERY CLEVER, TUBBY!
HEY TWIRP!

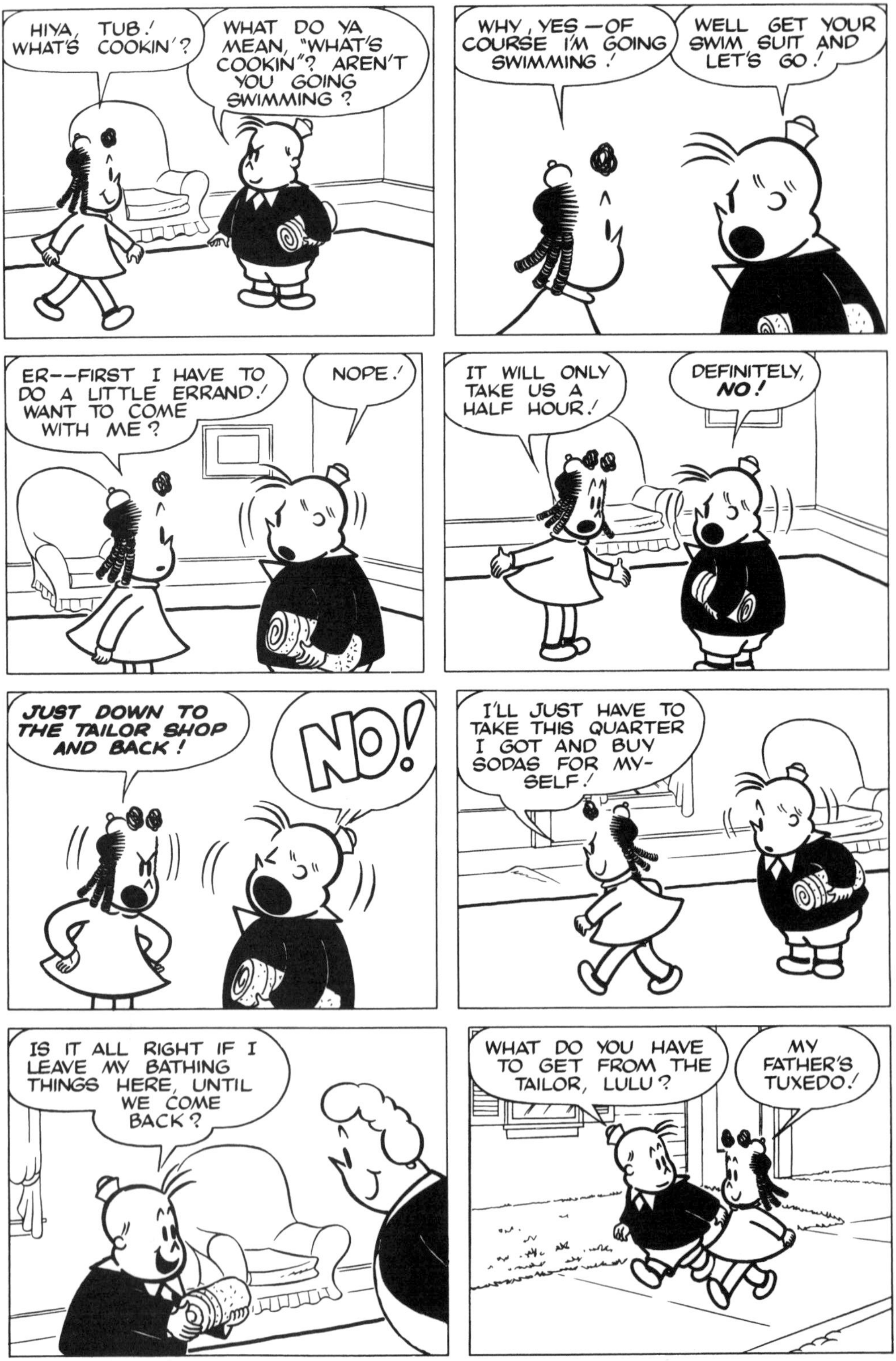
HIYA, TUB! WHAT'S COOKIN'?
WHAT DO YA MEAN, "WHAT'S COOKIN'"? AREN'T YOU GOING SWIMMING?
WHY, YES—OF COURSE I'M GOING SWIMMING!
WELL GET YOUR SWIM SUIT AND LET'S GO!
ER--FIRST I HAVE TO DO A LITTLE ERRAND! WANT TO COME WITH ME?
NOPE!
IT WILL ONLY TAKE US A HALF HOUR!
DEFINITELY, NO!
JUST DOWN TO THE TAILOR SHOP AND BACK!
NO!
I'LL JUST HAVE TO TAKE THIS QUARTER I GOT AND BUY SODAS FOR MY-SELF!
IS IT ALL RIGHT IF I LEAVE MY BATHING THINGS HERE, UNTIL WE COME BACK?
WHAT DO YOU HAVE TO GET FROM THE TAILOR, LULU?
MY FATHER'S TUXEDO!

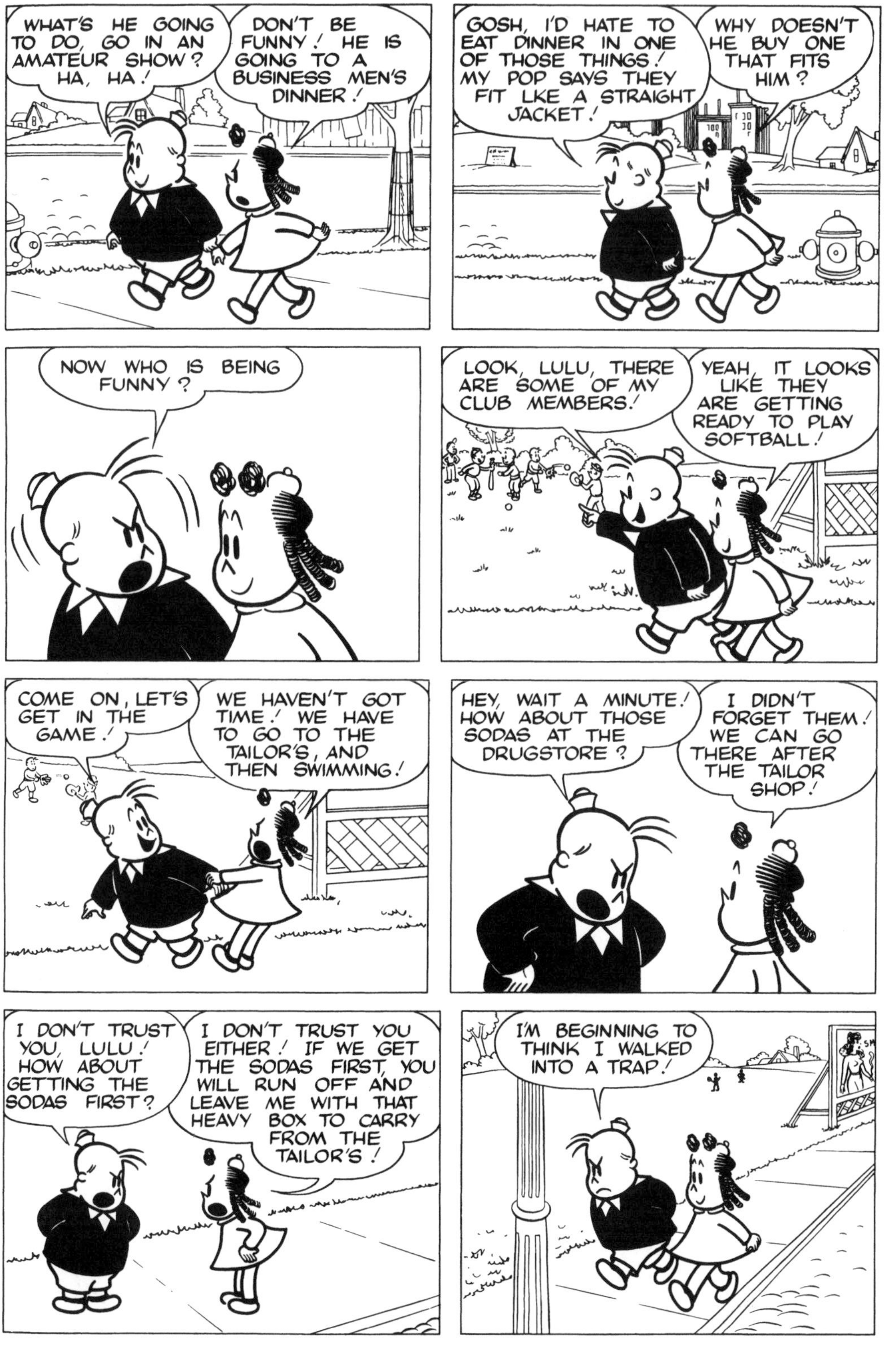
WHAT'S HE GOING TO DO, GO IN AN AMATEUR SHOW? HA, HA!
DON'T BE FUNNY! HE IS GOING TO A BUSINESS MEN'S DINNER!
GOSH, I'D HATE TO EAT DINNER IN ONE OF THOSE THINGS! MY POP SAYS THEY FIT LKE A STRAIGHT JACKET!
WHY DOESN'T HE BUY ONE THAT FITS HIM?
NOW WHO IS BEING FUNNY?
LOOK, LULU, THERE ARE SOME OF MY CLUB MEMBERS!
YEAH, IT LOOKS LIKE THEY ARE GETTING READY TO PLAY SOFTBALL!
COME ON, LET'S GET IN THE GAME!
WE HAVEN'T GOT TIME! WE HAVE TO GO TO THE TAILOR'S, AND THEN SWIMMING!
HEY, WAIT A MINUTE! HOW ABOUT THOSE SODAS AT THE DRUGSTORE?
I DIDN'T FORGET THEM! WE CAN GO THERE AFTER THE TAILOR SHOP!
I DON'T TRUST YOU, LULU! HOW ABOUT GETTING THE SODAS FIRST?
I DON'T TRUST YOU EITHER! IF WE GET THE SODAS FIRST, YOU WILL RUN OFF AND LEAVE ME WITH THAT HEAVY BOX TO CARRY FROM THE TAILOR'S!
I'M BEGINNING TO THINK I WALKED INTO A TRAP!

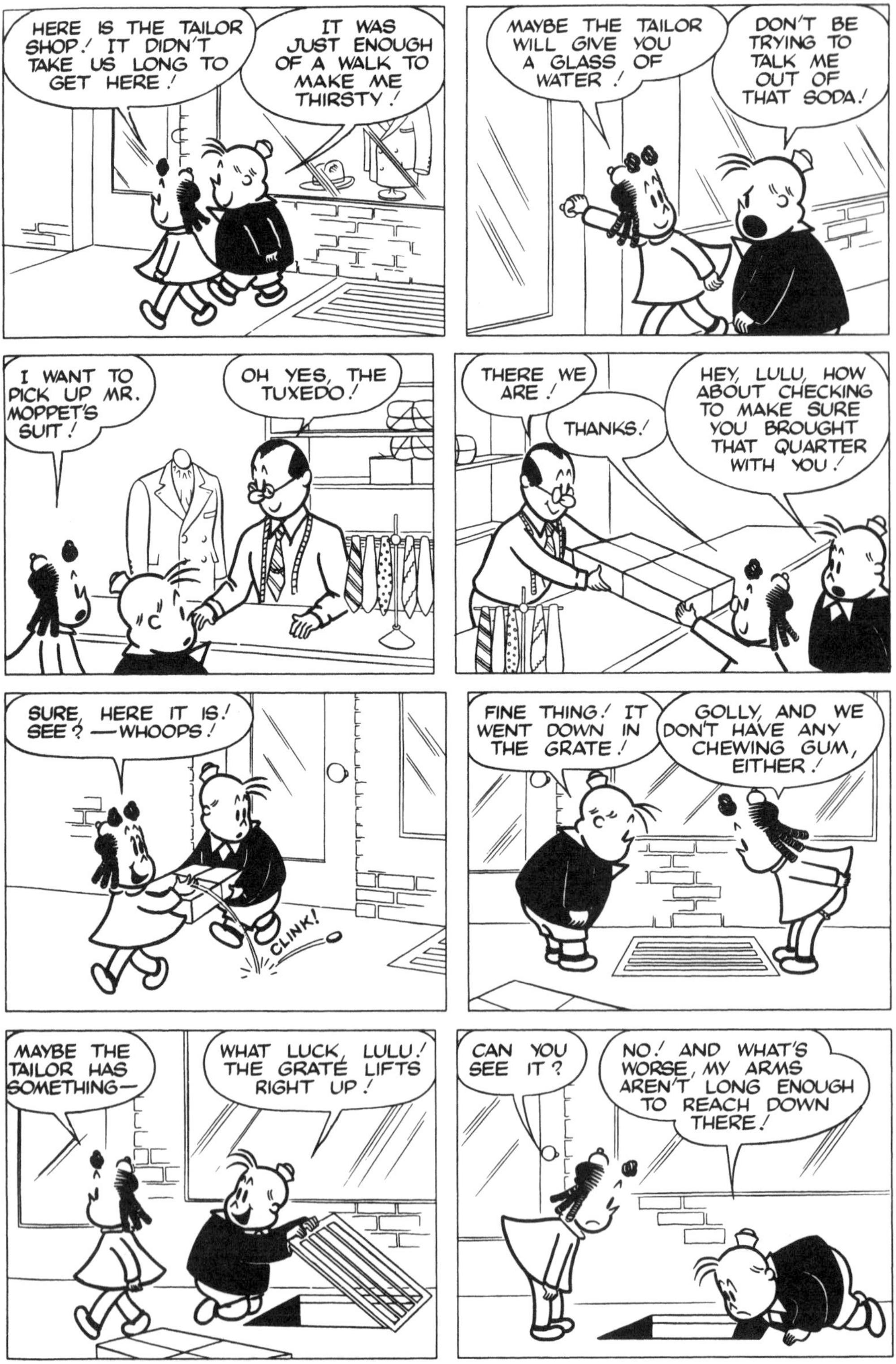
HERE IS THE TAILOR SHOP! IT DIDN'T TAKE US LONG TO GET HERE!
IT WAS JUST ENOUGH OF A WALK TO MAKE ME THIRSTY!
MAYBE THE TAILOR WILL GIVE YOU A GLASS OF WATER!
DON'T BE TRYING TO TALK ME OUT OF THAT SODA!
I WANT TO PICK UP MR. MOPPET'S SUIT!
OH YES, THE TUXEDO!
THERE WE ARE!
THANKS!
HEY, LULU, HOW ABOUT CHECKING TO MAKE SURE YOU BROUGHT THAT QUARTER WITH YOU!
SURE, HERE IT IS! SEE? —WHOOPS!
CLINK!
FINE THING! IT WENT DOWN IN THE GRATE!
GOLLY, AND WE DON'T HAVE ANY CHEWING GUM, EITHER!
MAYBE THE TAILOR HAS SOMETHING—
WHAT LUCK, LULU! THE GRATE LIFTS RIGHT UP!
CAN YOU SEE IT?
NO! AND WHAT'S WORSE, MY ARMS AREN'T LONG ENOUGH TO REACH DOWN THERE!

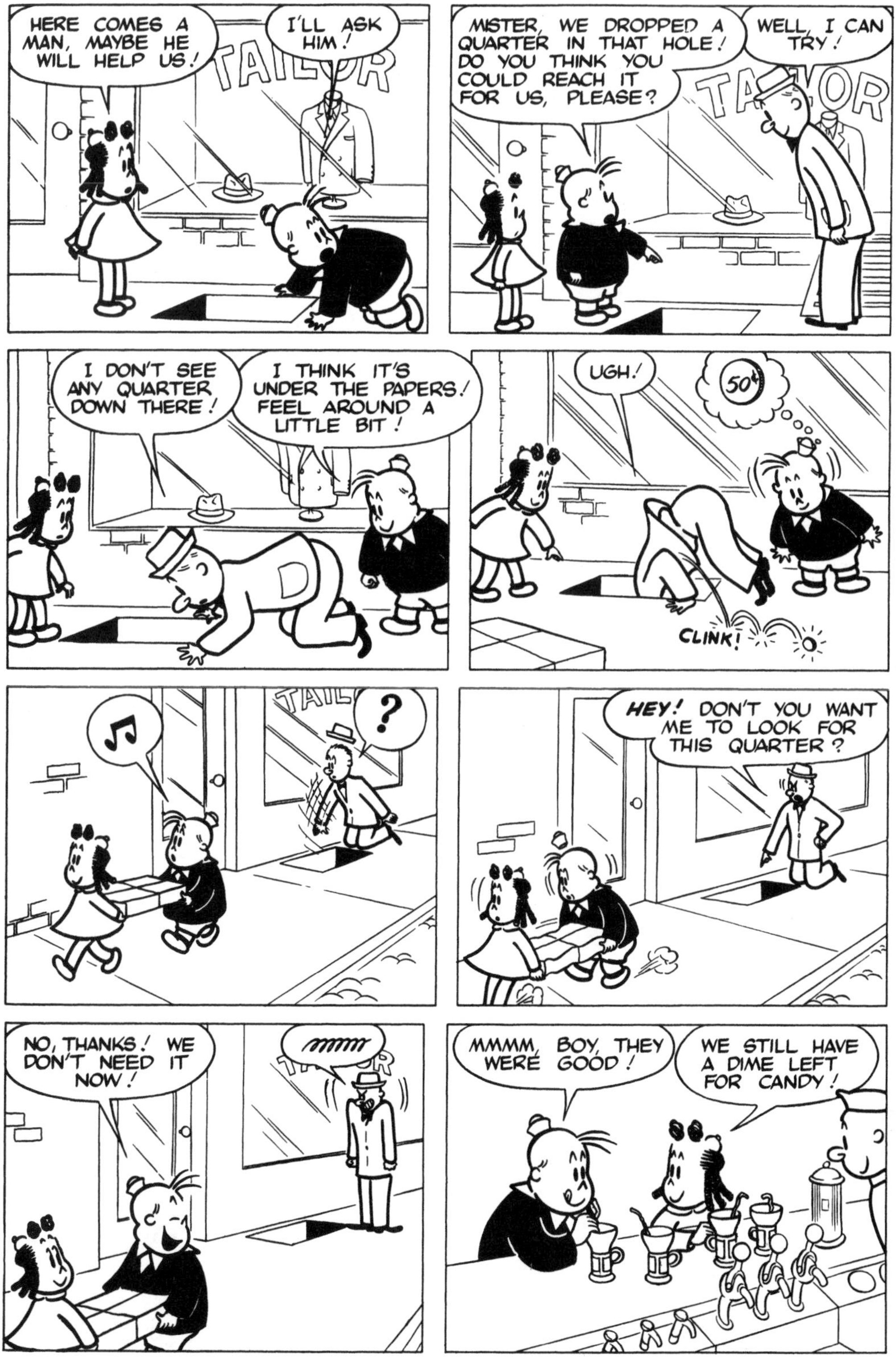
HERE COMES A MAN, MAYBE HE WILL HELP US!
I'LL ASK HIM!
MISTER, WE DROPPED A QUARTER IN THAT HOLE! DO YOU THINK YOU COULD REACH IT FOR US, PLEASE?
WELL, I CAN TRY!
I DON'T SEE ANY QUARTER DOWN THERE!
I THINK IT'S UNDER THE PAPERS! FEEL AROUND A LITTLE BIT!
UGH!
50¢
CLINK!
?
HEY! DON'T YOU WANT ME TO LOOK FOR THIS QUARTER?
NO, THANKS! WE DON'T NEED IT NOW!
MMMM, BOY, THEY WERE GOOD!
WE STILL HAVE A DIME LEFT FOR CANDY!

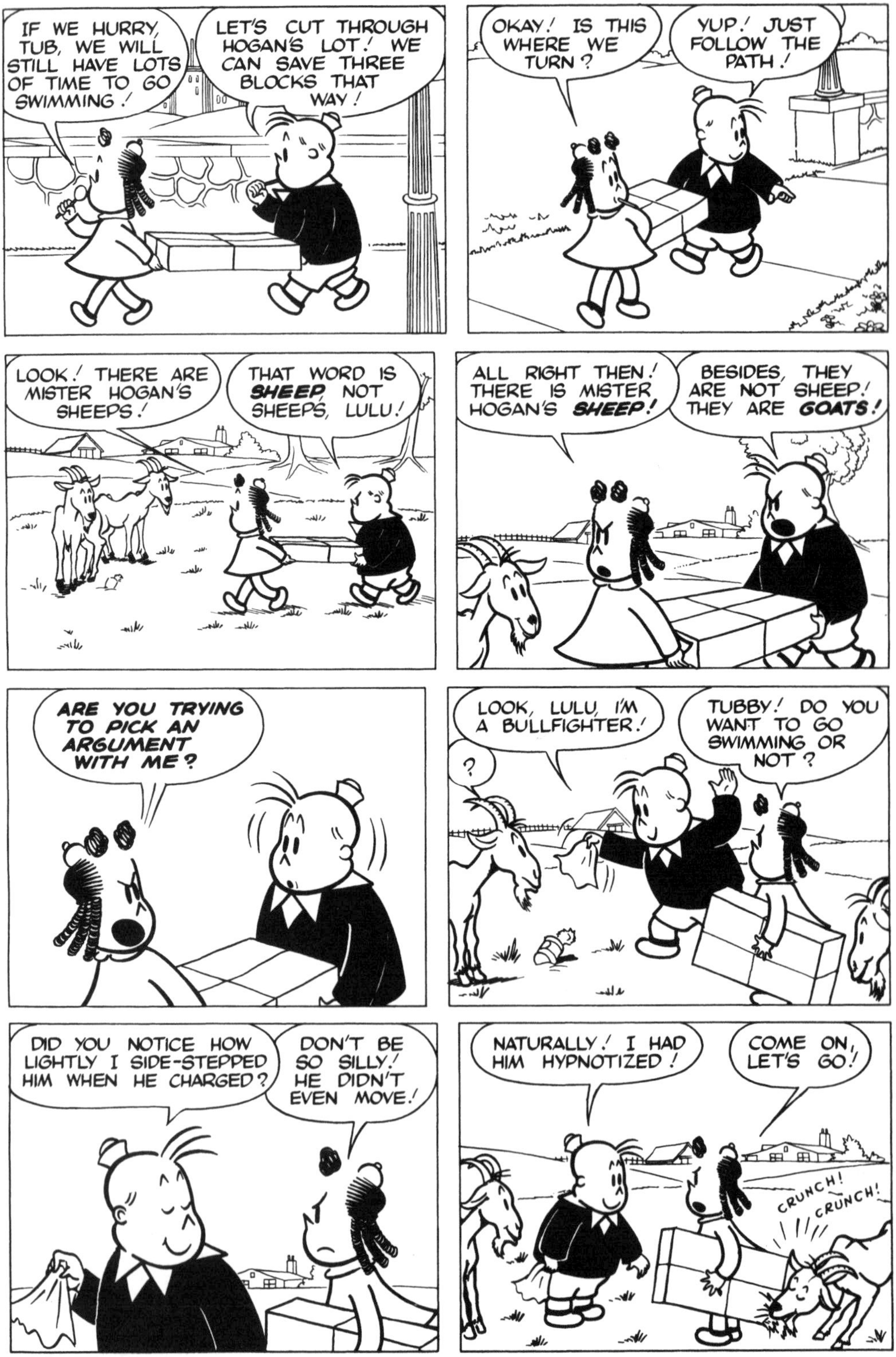
IF WE HURRY, TUB, WE WILL STILL HAVE LOTS OF TIME TO GO SWIMMING!
LET'S CUT THROUGH HOGAN'S LOT! WE CAN SAVE THREE BLOCKS THAT WAY!
OKAY! IS THIS WHERE WE TURN?
YUP! JUST FOLLOW THE PATH!
LOOK! THERE ARE MISTER HOGAN'S SHEEPS!
THAT WORD IS SHEEP, NOT SHEEPS, LULU!
ALL RIGHT THEN! THERE IS MISTER HOGAN'S SHEEP!
BESIDES, THEY ARE NOT SHEEP! THEY ARE GOATS!
ARE YOU TRYING TO PICK AN ARGUMENT WITH ME?
LOOK, LULU, I'M A BULLFIGHTER!
?
TUBBY! DO YOU WANT TO GO SWIMMING OR NOT?
DID YOU NOTICE HOW LIGHTLY I SIDE-STEPPED HIM WHEN HE CHARGED?
DON'T BE SO SILLY! HE DIDN'T EVEN MOVE!
NATURALLY! I HAD HIM HYPNOTIZED!
COME ON, LET'S GO!
CRUNCH! CRUNCH!

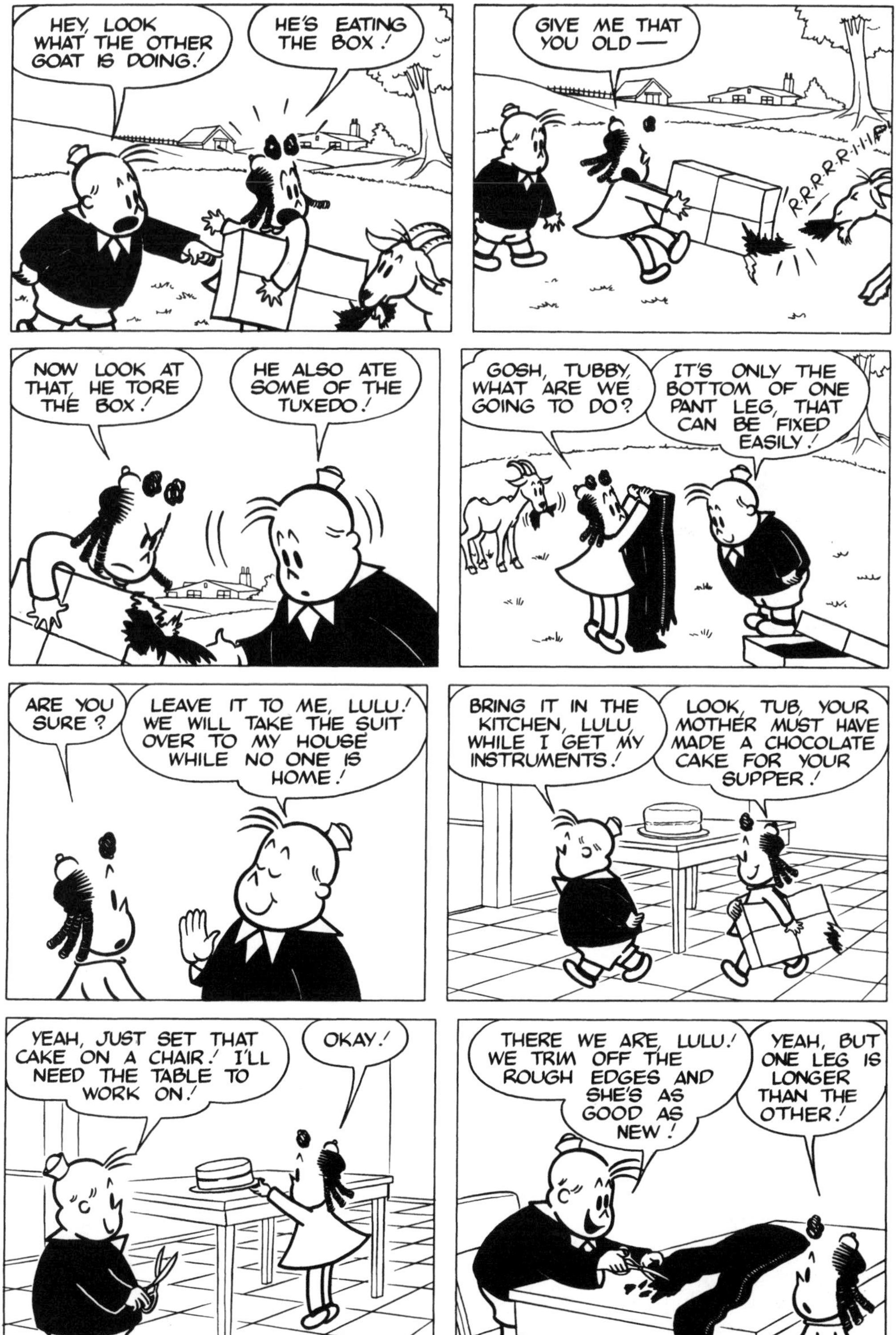
HEY, LOOK WHAT THE OTHER GOAT IS DOING!
HE'S EATING THE BOX!
GIVE ME THAT YOU OLD—
R-R-R-R-R-I-I-I-P
NOW LOOK AT THAT, HE TORE THE BOX!
HE ALSO ATE SOME OF THE TUXEDO!
GOSH, TUBBY, WHAT ARE WE GOING TO DO?
IT'S ONLY THE BOTTOM OF ONE PANT LEG, THAT CAN BE FIXED EASILY!
ARE YOU SURE?
LEAVE IT TO ME, LULU! WE WILL TAKE THE SUIT OVER TO MY HOUSE WHILE NO ONE IS HOME!
BRING IT IN THE KITCHEN, LULU, WHILE I GET MY INSTRUMENTS!
LOOK, TUB, YOUR MOTHER MUST HAVE MADE A CHOCOLATE CAKE FOR YOUR SUPPER!
YEAH, JUST SET THAT CAKE ON A CHAIR! I'LL NEED THE TABLE TO WORK ON!
OKAY!
THERE WE ARE, LULU! WE TRIM OFF THE ROUGH EDGES AND SHE'S AS GOOD AS NEW!
YEAH, BUT ONE LEG IS LONGER THAN THE OTHER!

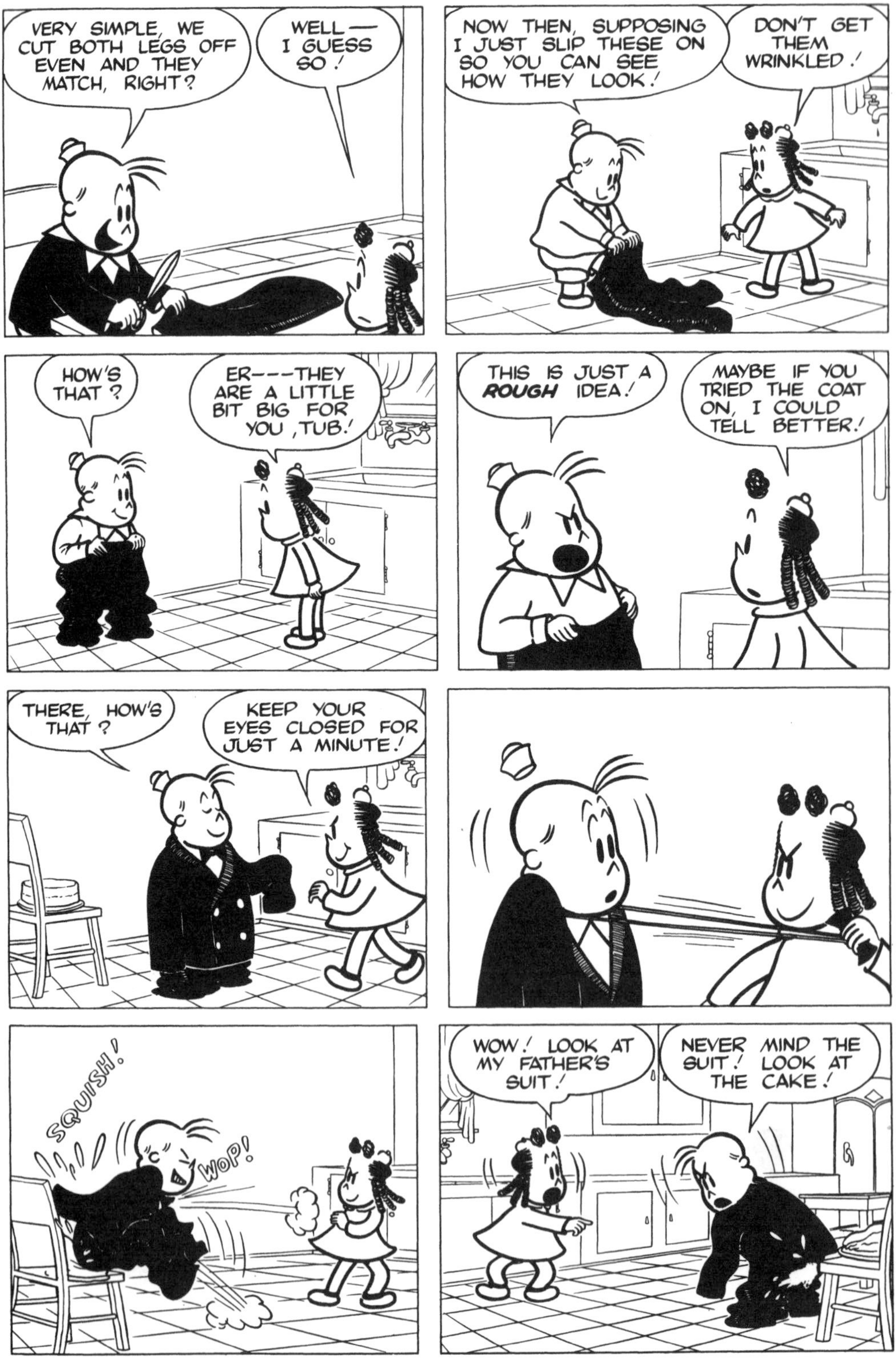
VERY SIMPLE, WE CUT BOTH LEGS OFF EVEN AND THEY MATCH, RIGHT?
WELL— I GUESS SO!
NOW THEN, SUPPOSING I JUST SLIP THESE ON SO YOU CAN SEE HOW THEY LOOK!
DON'T GET THEM WRINKLED!
HOW'S THAT?
ER---THEY ARE A LITTLE BIT BIG FOR YOU, TUB!
THIS IS JUST A ROUGH IDEA!
MAYBE IF YOU TRIED THE COAT ON, I COULD TELL BETTER!
THERE, HOW'S THAT?
KEEP YOUR EYES CLOSED FOR JUST A MINUTE!
SQUISH!
WOP!
WOW! LOOK AT MY FATHER'S SUIT!
NEVER MIND THE SUIT! LOOK AT THE CAKE!

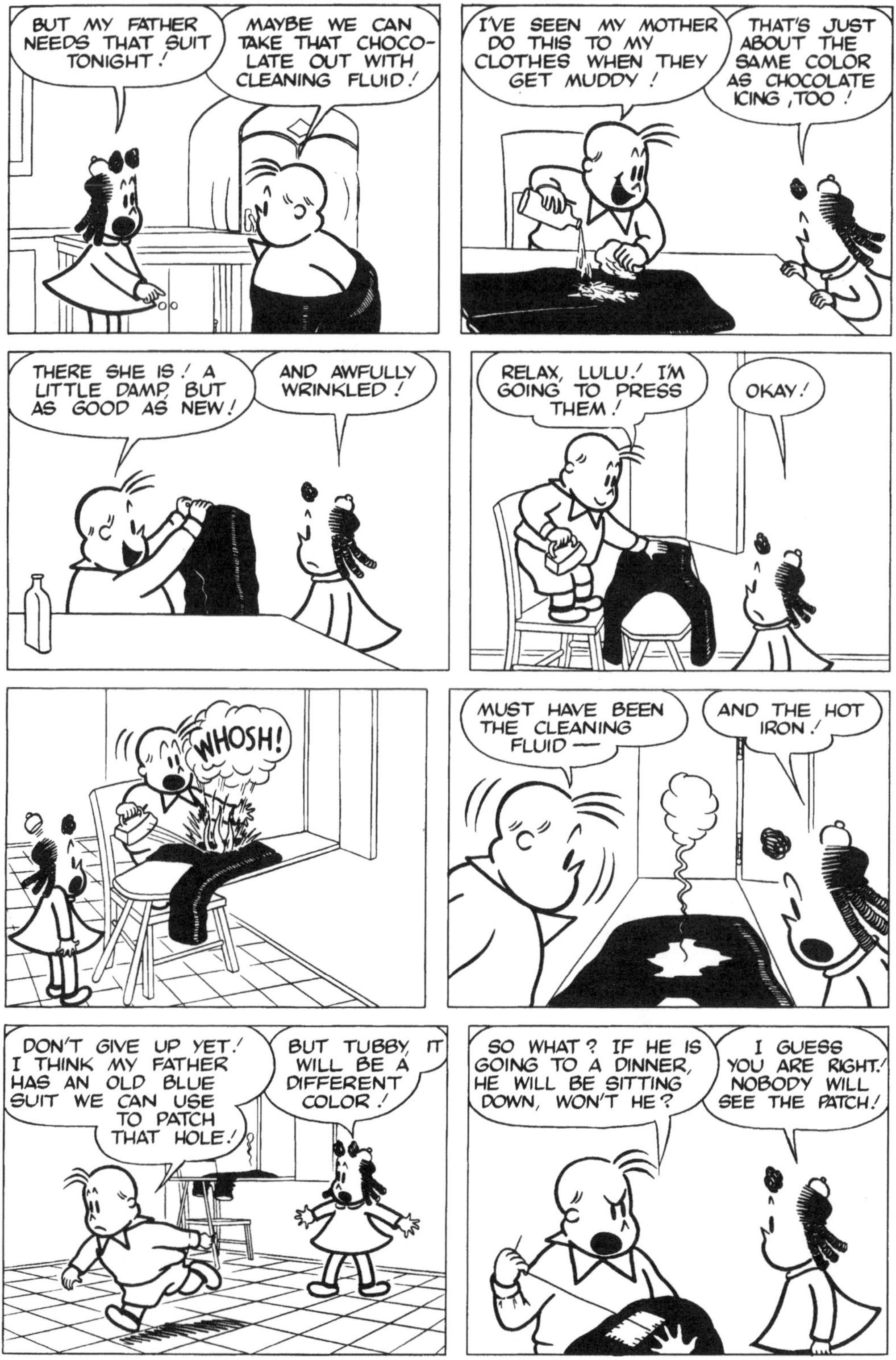
BUT MY FATHER NEEDS THAT SUIT TONIGHT!
MAYBE WE CAN TAKE THAT CHOCO-LATE OUT WITH CLEANING FLUID!
I'VE SEEN MY MOTHER DO THIS TO MY CLOTHES WHEN THEY GET MUDDY!
THAT'S JUST ABOUT THE SAME COLOR AS CHOCOLATE ICING, TOO!
THERE SHE IS! A LITTLE DAMP, BUT AS GOOD AS NEW!
AND AWFULLY WRINKLED!
RELAX, LULU! I'M GOING TO PRESS THEM!
OKAY!
WHOSH!
MUST HAVE BEEN THE CLEANING FLUID —
AND THE HOT IRON!
DON'T GIVE UP YET! I THINK MY FATHER HAS AN OLD BLUE SUIT WE CAN USE TO PATCH THAT HOLE!
BUT TUBBY, IT WILL BE A DIFFERENT COLOR!
SO WHAT? IF HE IS GOING TO A DINNER, HE WILL BE SITTING DOWN, WON'T HE?
I GUESS YOU ARE RIGHT! NOBODY WILL SEE THE PATCH!

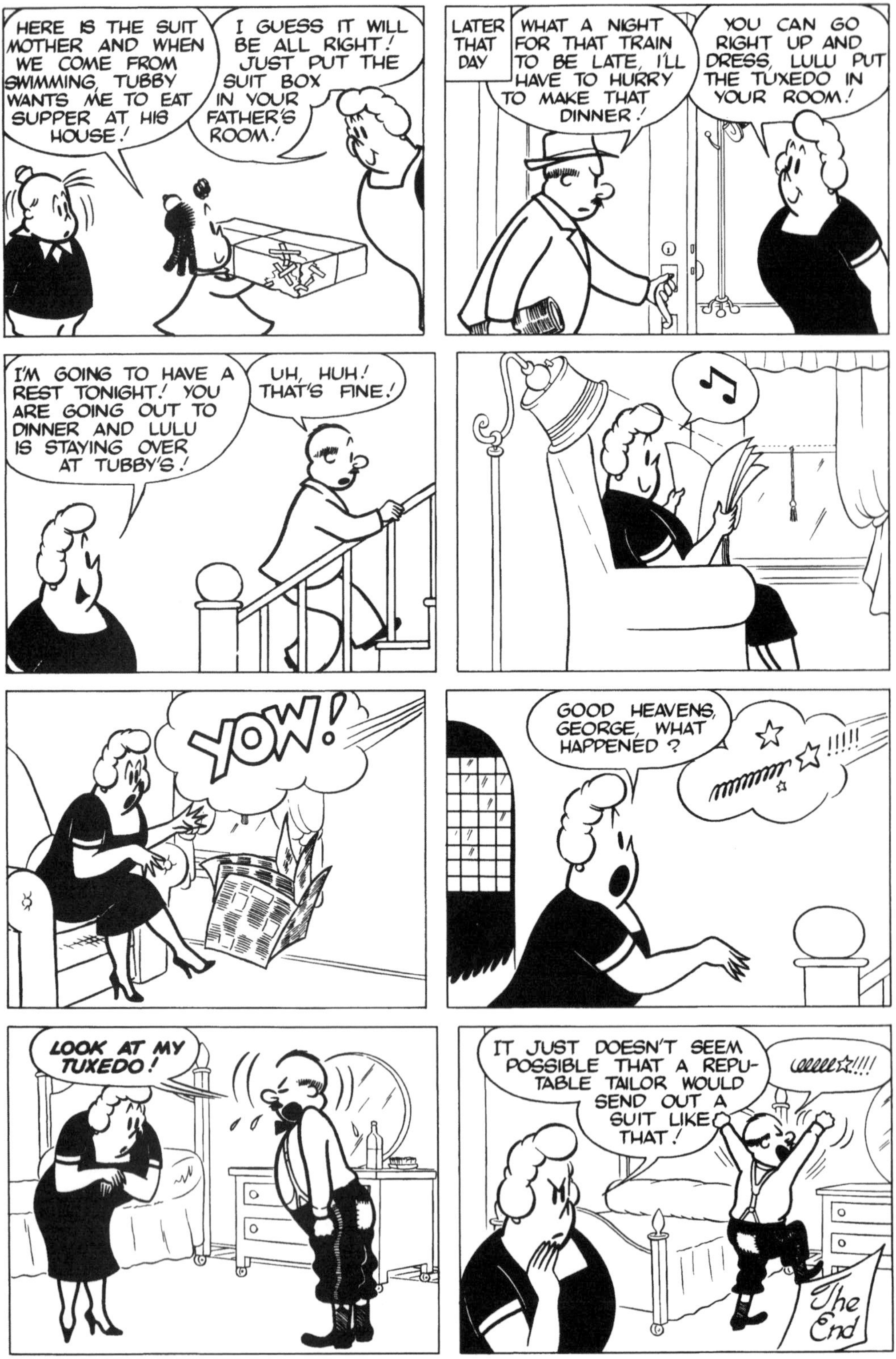
HERE IS THE SUIT MOTHER AND WHEN WE COME FROM SWIMMING, TUBBY WANTS ME TO EAT SUPPER AT HIS HOUSE!
I GUESS IT WILL BE ALL RIGHT! JUST PUT THE SUIT BOX IN YOUR FATHER'S ROOM!
LATER THAT DAY
WHAT A NIGHT FOR THAT TRAIN TO BE LATE, I'LL HAVE TO HURRY TO MAKE THAT DINNER!
YOU CAN GO RIGHT UP AND DRESS, LULU PUT THE TUXEDO IN YOUR ROOM!
I'M GOING TO HAVE A REST TONIGHT! YOU ARE GOING OUT TO DINNER AND LULU IS STAYING OVER AT TUBBY'S!
UH, HUH! THAT'S FINE!
YOW!
GOOD HEAVENS, GEORGE, WHAT HAPPENED?
!!!!!
LOOK AT MY TUXEDO!
IT JUST DOESN'T SEEM POSSIBLE THAT A REPUTABLE TAILOR WOULD SEND OUT A SUIT LIKE THAT!
!!!!
The End

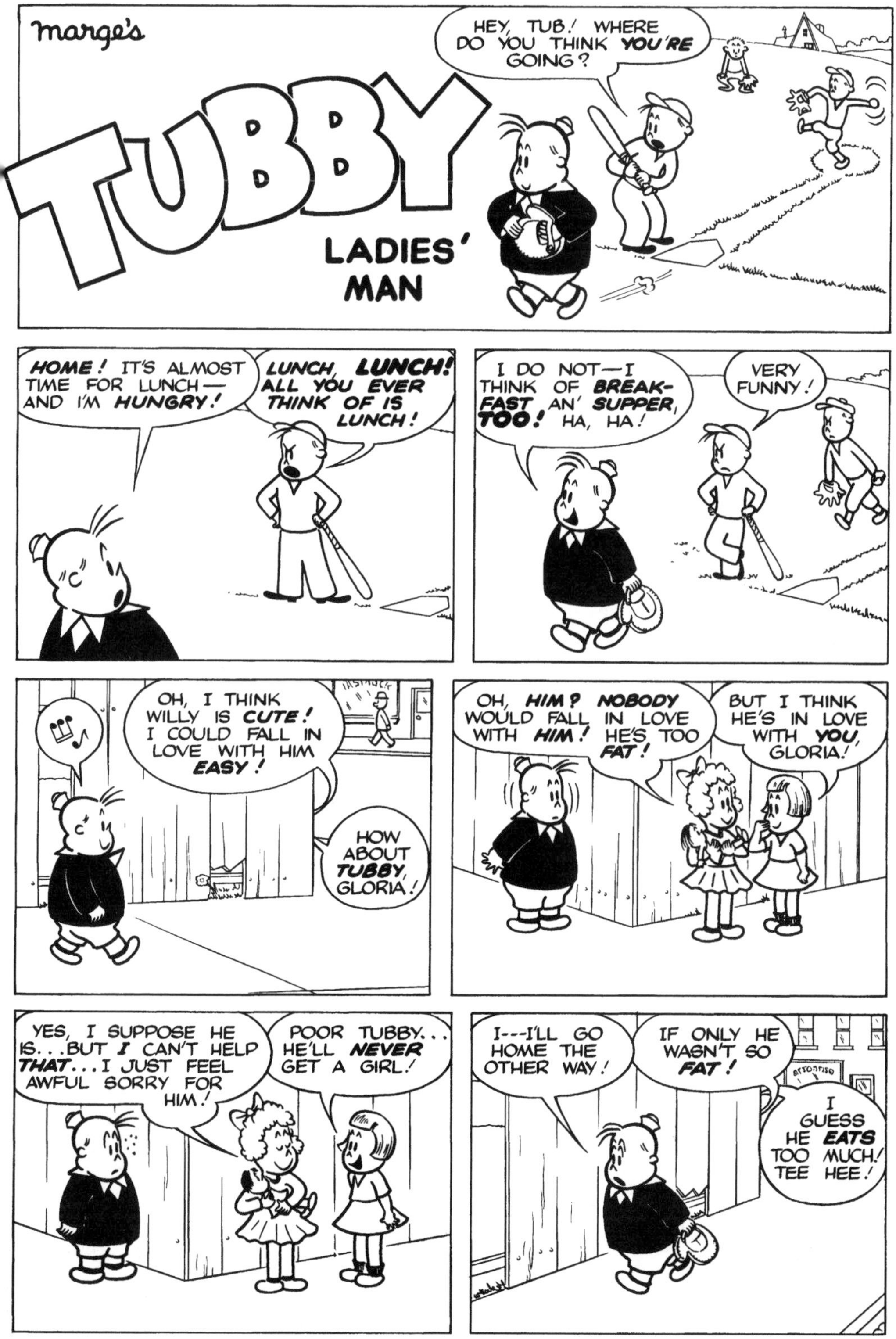
marge's
TUBBY
LADIES' MAN
HEY, TUB! WHERE DO YOU THINK YOU'RE GOING?
HOME! IT'S ALMOST TIME FOR LUNCH— AND I'M HUNGRY!
LUNCH, LUNCH! ALL YOU EVER THINK OF IS LUNCH!
I DO NOT—I THINK OF BREAKFAST AN' SUPPER, TOO! HA, HA!
VERY FUNNY!
OH, I THINK WILLY IS CUTE! I COULD FALL IN LOVE WITH HIM EASY!
HOW ABOUT TUBBY, GLORIA!
OH, HIM? NOBODY WOULD FALL IN LOVE WITH HIM! HE'S TOO FAT!
BUT I THINK HE'S IN LOVE WITH YOU, GLORIA!
YES, I SUPPOSE HE IS...BUT I CAN'T HELP THAT...I JUST FEEL AWFUL SORRY FOR HIM!
POOR TUBBY... HE'LL NEVER GET A GIRL!
I---I'LL GO HOME THE OTHER WAY!
IF ONLY HE WASN'T SO FAT!
I GUESS HE EATS TOO MUCH! TEE HEE!

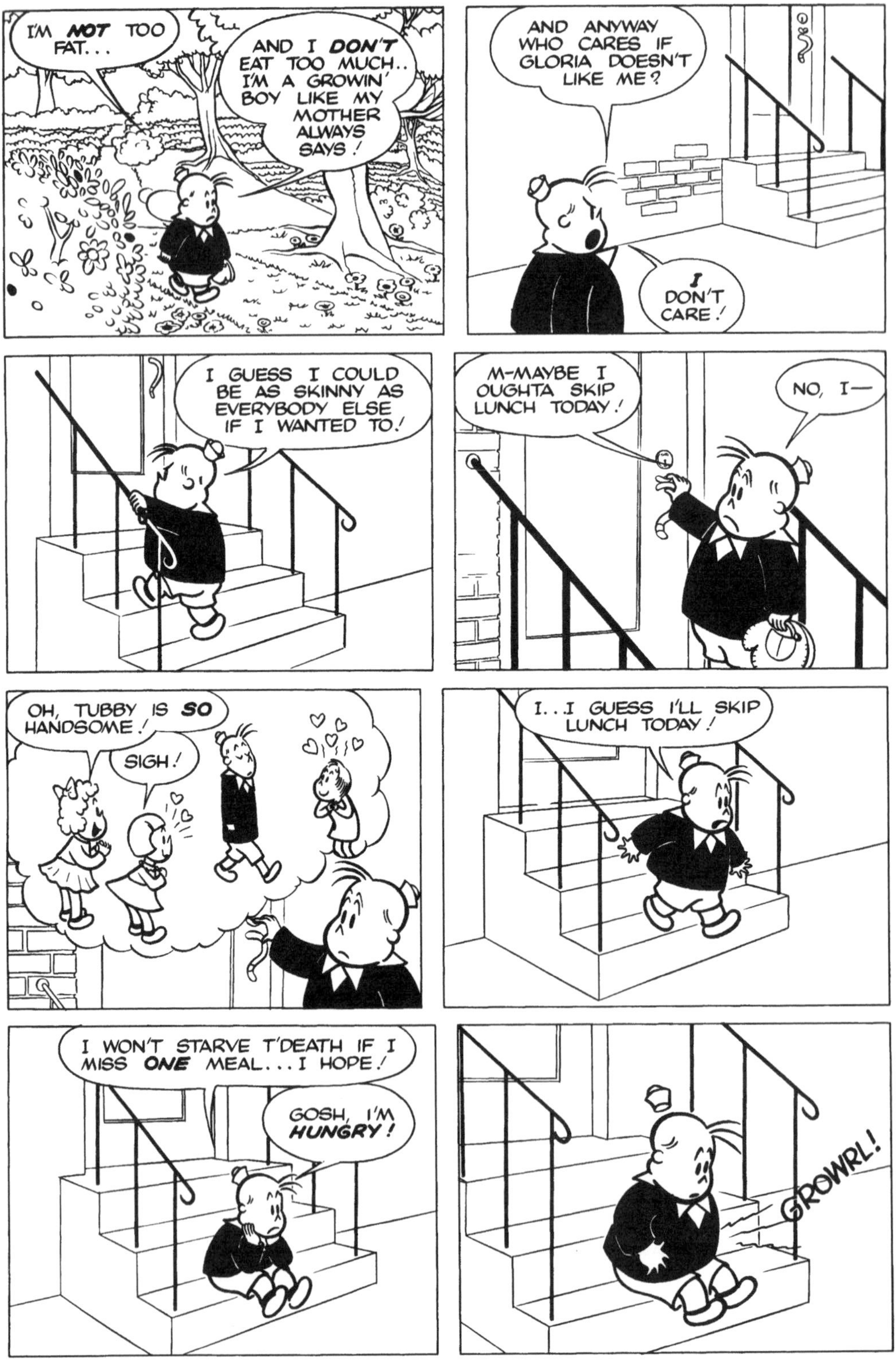

I'M **NOT** TOO FAT...
AND I **DON'T** EAT TOO MUCH.. I'M A GROWIN' BOY LIKE MY MOTHER ALWAYS SAYS!
AND ANYWAY WHO CARES IF GLORIA DOESN'T LIKE ME?
I DON'T CARE!
I GUESS I COULD BE AS SKINNY AS EVERYBODY ELSE IF I WANTED TO!
M-MAYBE I OUGHTA SKIP LUNCH TODAY!
NO, I—
OH, TUBBY IS **SO** HANDSOME!
SIGH!
I...I GUESS I'LL SKIP LUNCH TODAY!
I WON'T STARVE T'DEATH IF I MISS **ONE** MEAL...I HOPE!
GOSH, I'M **HUNGRY**!
GROWRL!

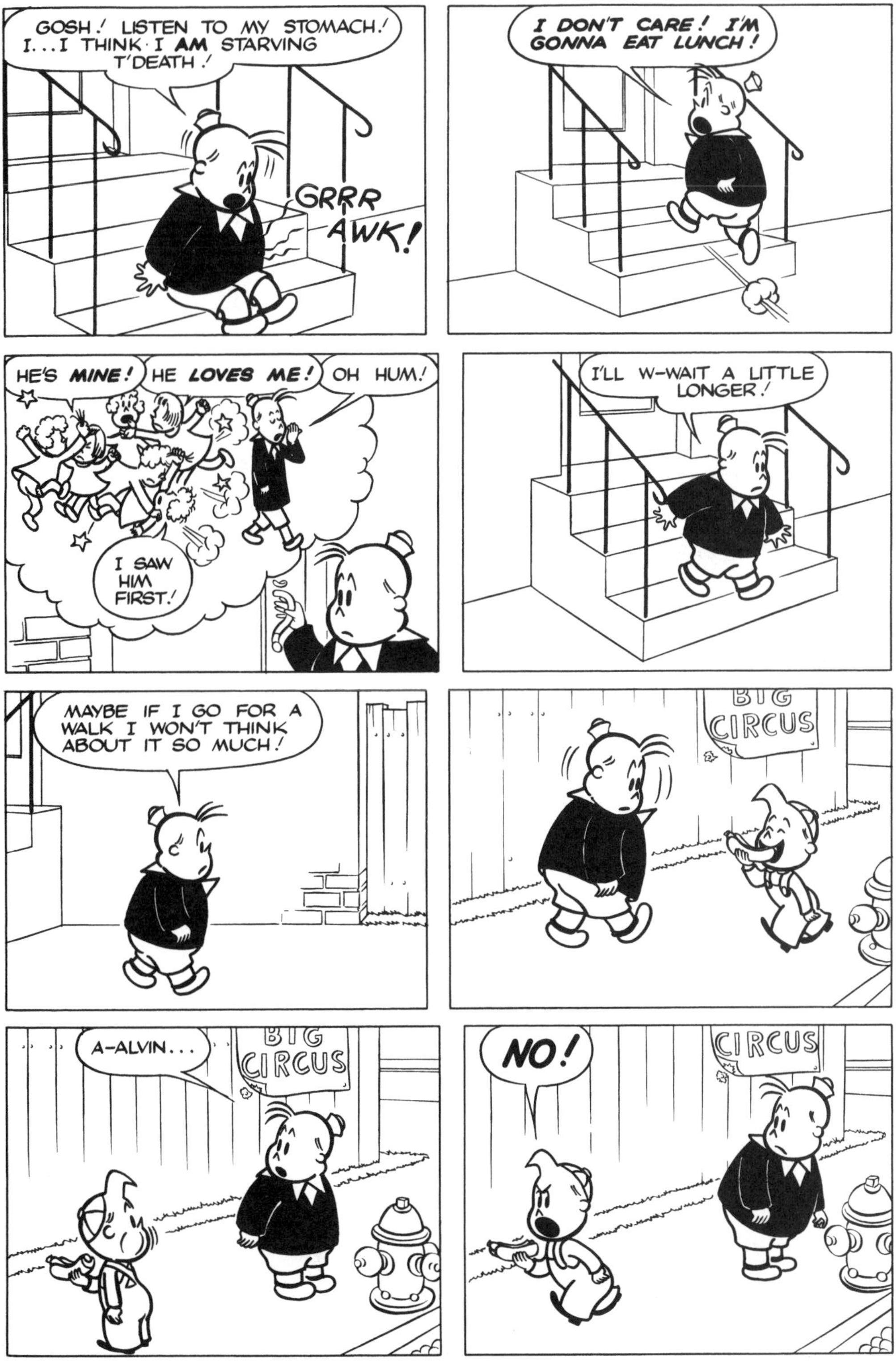
GOSH! LISTEN TO MY STOMACH! I...I THINK I AM STARVING T'DEATH!
GRRR AWK!
I DON'T CARE! I'M GONNA EAT LUNCH!
HE'S MINE!
HE LOVES ME!
OH HUM!
I SAW HIM FIRST!
I'LL W-WAIT A LITTLE LONGER!
MAYBE IF I GO FOR A WALK I WON'T THINK ABOUT IT SO MUCH!
BIG CIRCUS
A-ALVIN...
BIG CIRCUS
NO!
CIRCUS

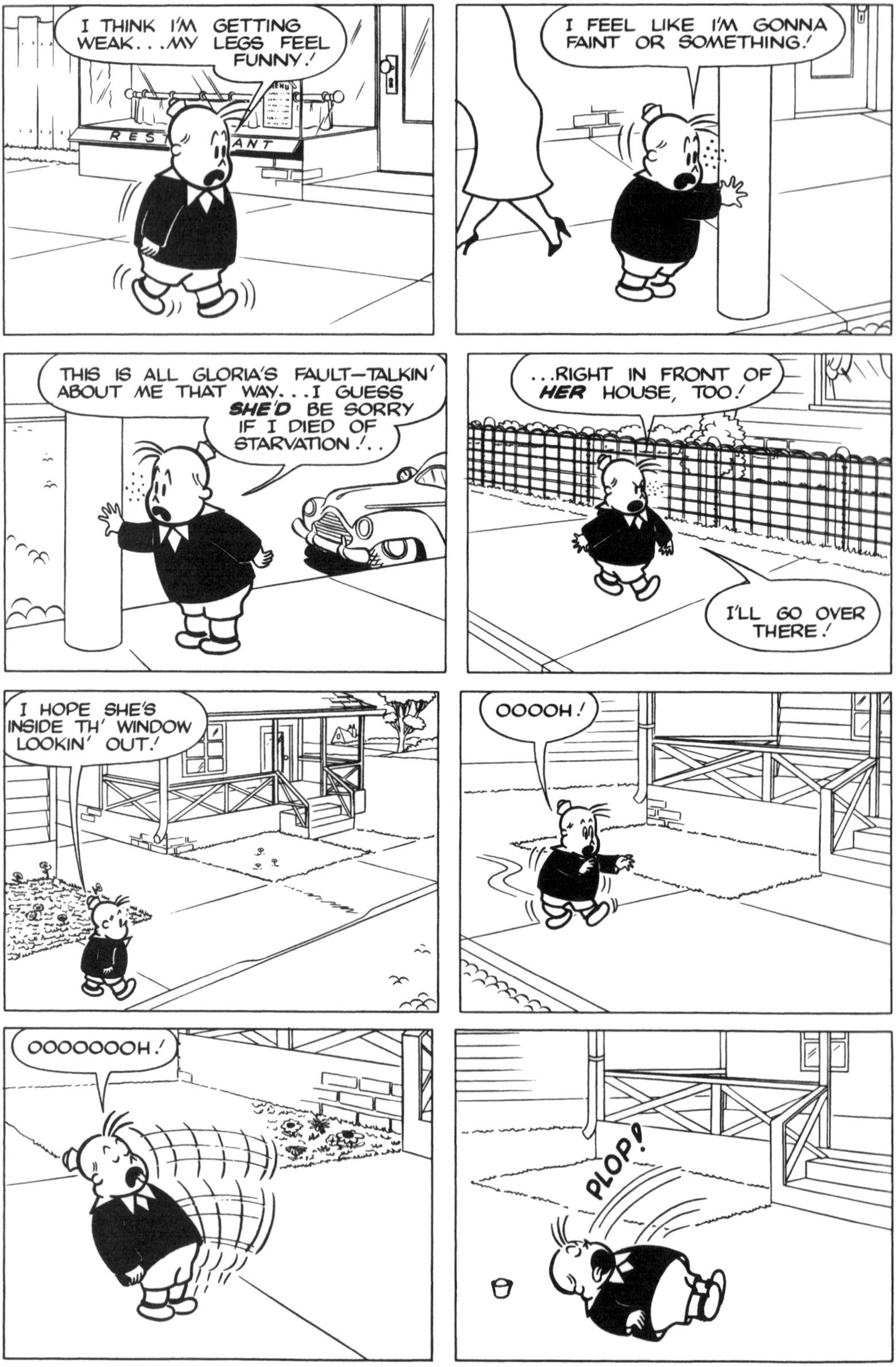
I THINK I'M GETTING WEAK...MY LEGS FEEL FUNNY!
I FEEL LIKE I'M GONNA FAINT OR SOMETHING!
THIS IS ALL GLORIA'S FAULT—TALKIN' ABOUT ME THAT WAY...I GUESS SHE'D BE SORRY IF I DIED OF STARVATION!..
...RIGHT IN FRONT OF HER HOUSE, TOO!
I'LL GO OVER THERE!
I HOPE SHE'S INSIDE TH' WINDOW LOOKIN' OUT!
OOOOH!
OOOOOOOH!
PLOP!

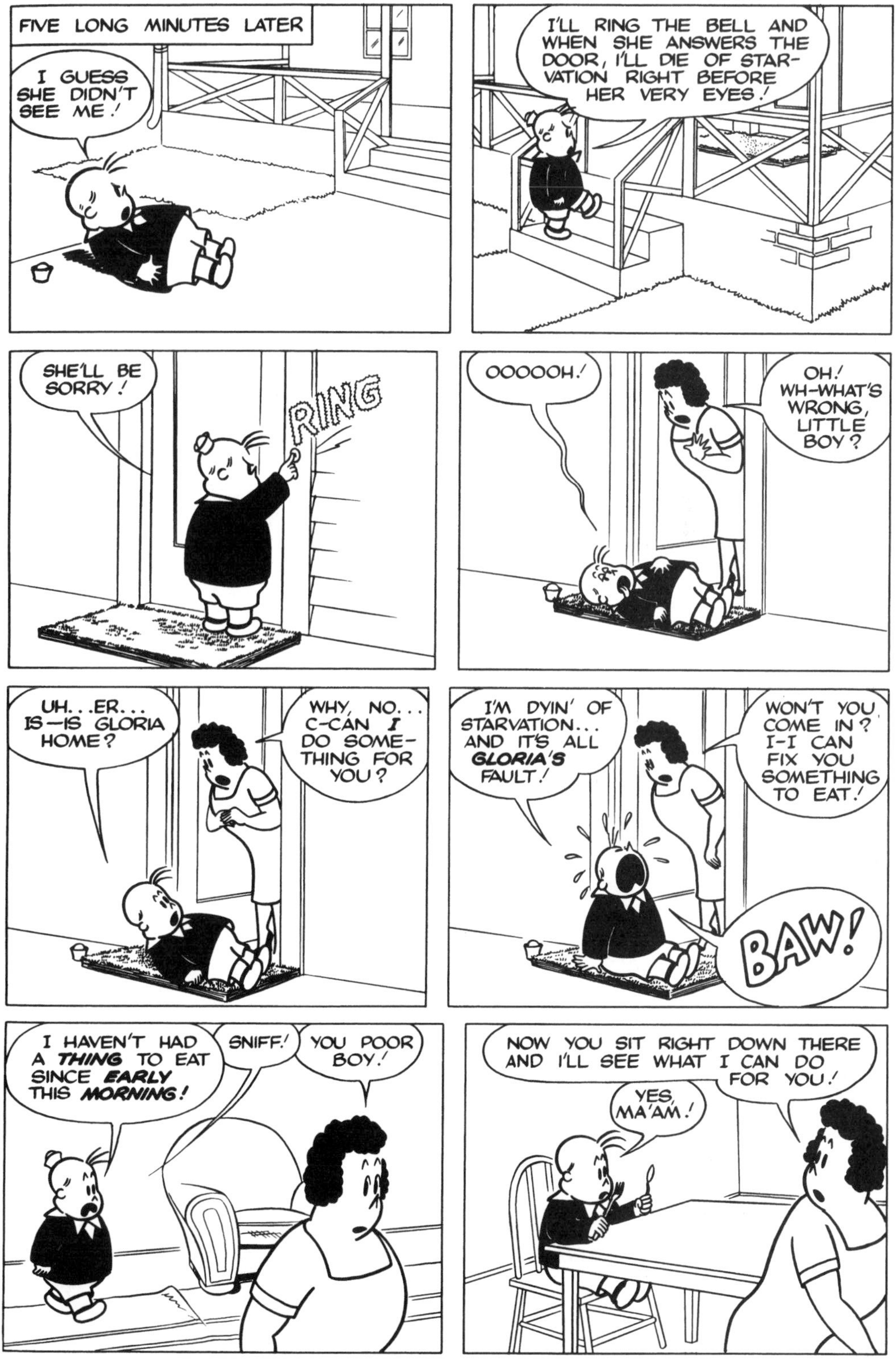
FIVE LONG MINUTES LATER
I GUESS SHE DIDN'T SEE ME!
I'LL RING THE BELL AND WHEN SHE ANSWERS THE DOOR, I'LL DIE OF STARVATION RIGHT BEFORE HER VERY EYES!
SHE'LL BE SORRY!
RING
OOOOOH!
OH! WH-WHAT'S WRONG, LITTLE BOY?
UH...ER... IS—IS GLORIA HOME?
WHY, NO... C-CAN I DO SOMETHING FOR YOU?
I'M DYIN' OF STARVATION... AND IT'S ALL GLORIA'S FAULT!
WON'T YOU COME IN? I-I CAN FIX YOU SOMETHING TO EAT!
BAW!
I HAVEN'T HAD A THING TO EAT SINCE EARLY THIS MORNING!
SNIFF!
YOU POOR BOY!
NOW YOU SIT RIGHT DOWN THERE AND I'LL SEE WHAT I CAN DO FOR YOU!
YES, MA'AM!

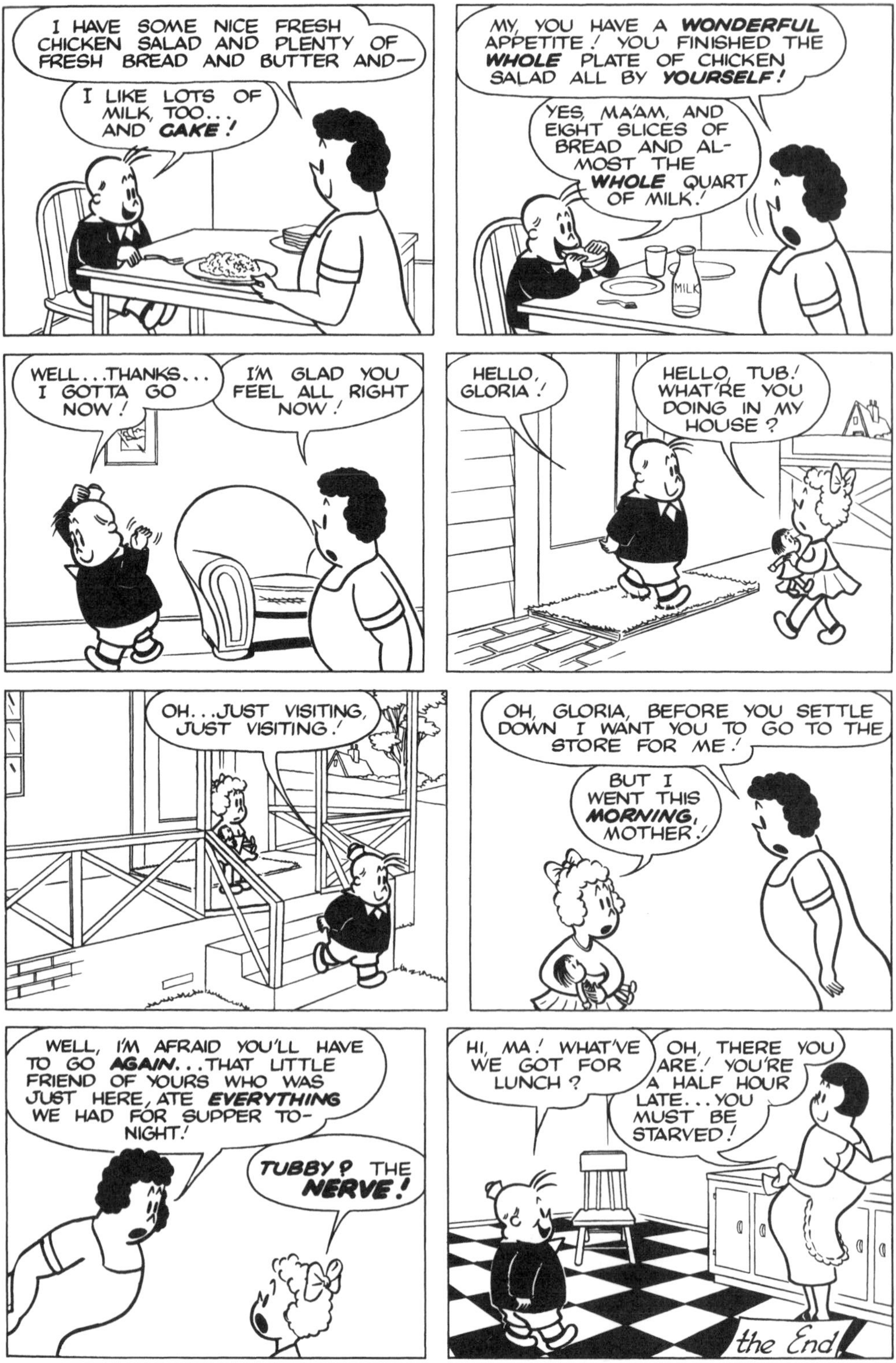
I HAVE SOME NICE FRESH CHICKEN SALAD AND PLENTY OF FRESH BREAD AND BUTTER AND—
I LIKE LOTS OF MILK, TOO..., AND CAKE!
MY, YOU HAVE A WONDERFUL APPETITE! YOU FINISHED THE WHOLE PLATE OF CHICKEN SALAD ALL BY YOURSELF!
YES, MA'AM, AND EIGHT SLICES OF BREAD AND ALMOST THE WHOLE QUART OF MILK!
MILK
WELL...THANKS... I GOTTA GO NOW!
I'M GLAD YOU FEEL ALL RIGHT NOW!
HELLO, GLORIA!
HELLO, TUB! WHAT'RE YOU DOING IN MY HOUSE?
OH...JUST VISITING, JUST VISITING!
OH, GLORIA, BEFORE YOU SETTLE DOWN I WANT YOU TO GO TO THE STORE FOR ME!
BUT I WENT THIS MORNING, MOTHER!
WELL, I'M AFRAID YOU'LL HAVE TO GO AGAIN...THAT LITTLE FRIEND OF YOURS WHO WAS JUST HERE, ATE EVERYTHING WE HAD FOR SUPPER TONIGHT!
TUBBY? THE NERVE!
HI, MA! WHAT'VE WE GOT FOR LUNCH?
OH, THERE YOU ARE! YOU'RE A HALF HOUR LATE...YOU MUST BE STARVED!
the End

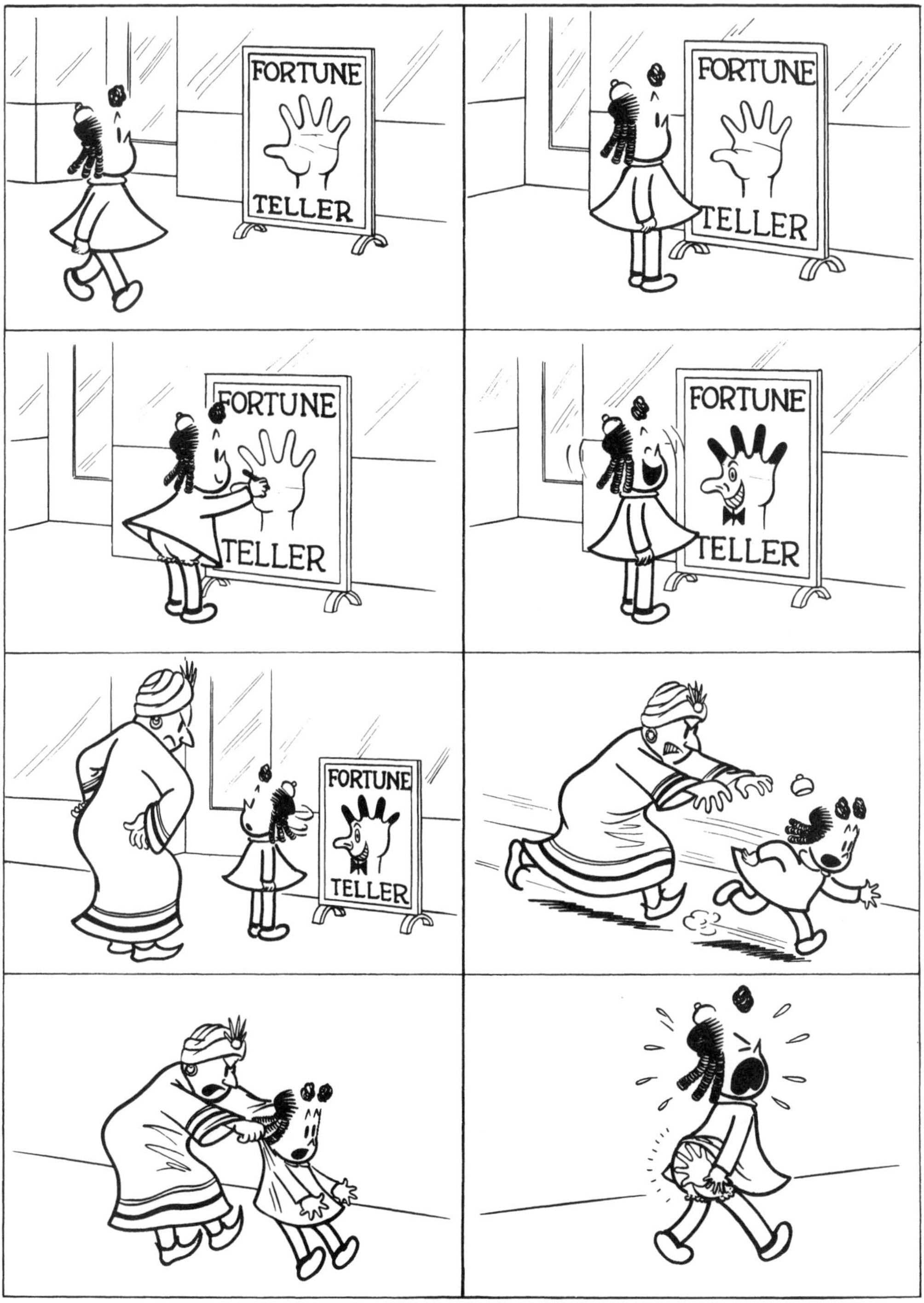
FORTUNE
TELLER
FORTUNE
TELLER
FORTUNE
TELLER
FORTUNE
TELLER
FORTUNE
TELLER

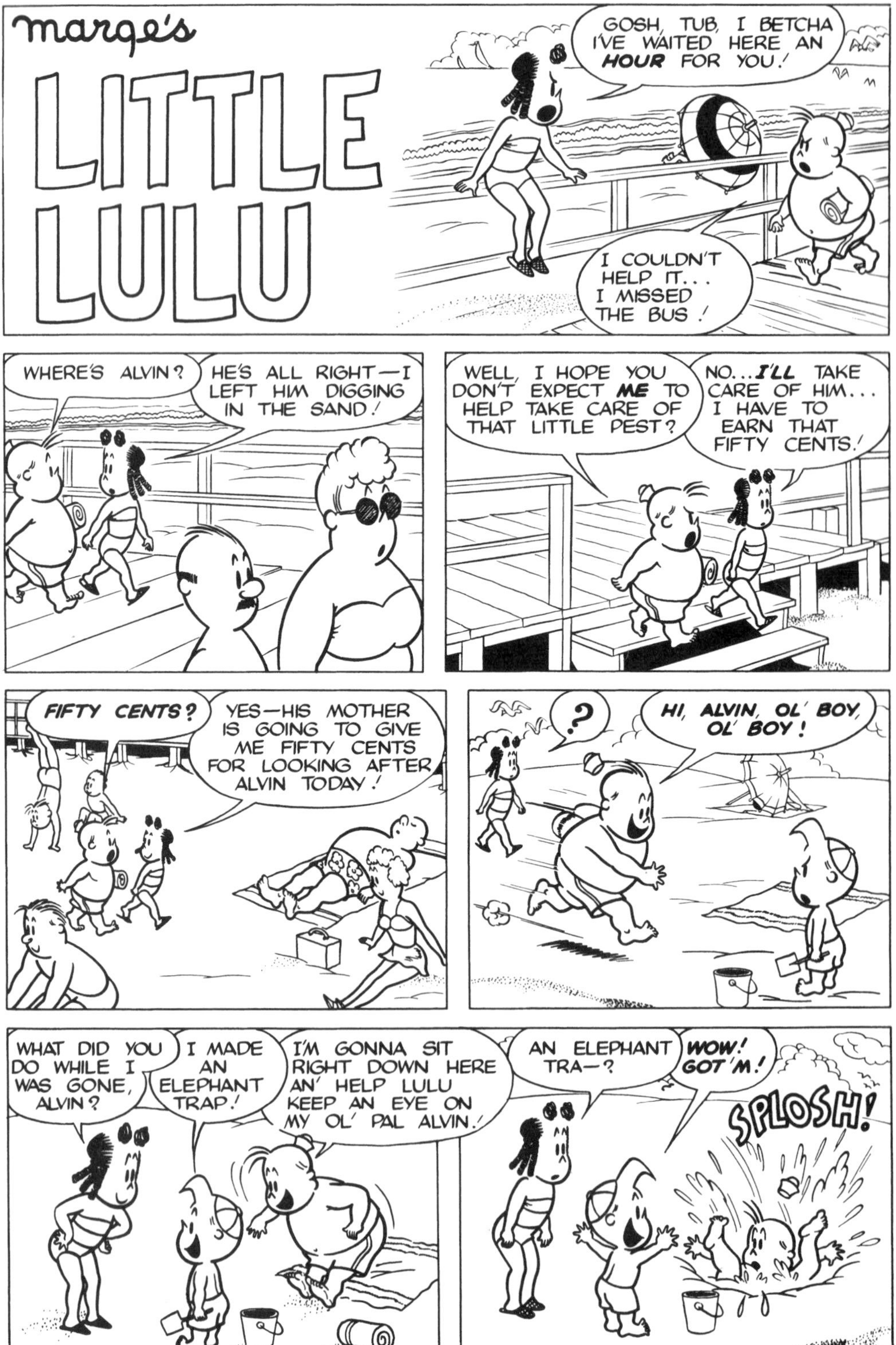
marge's
LITTLE LULU
GOSH, TUB, I BETCHA I'VE WAITED HERE AN HOUR FOR YOU!
I COULDN'T HELP IT... I MISSED THE BUS!
WHERE'S ALVIN?
HE'S ALL RIGHT—I LEFT HIM DIGGING IN THE SAND!
WELL, I HOPE YOU DON'T EXPECT ME TO HELP TAKE CARE OF THAT LITTLE PEST?
NO...I'LL TAKE CARE OF HIM... I HAVE TO EARN THAT FIFTY CENTS!
FIFTY CENTS?
YES—HIS MOTHER IS GOING TO GIVE ME FIFTY CENTS FOR LOOKING AFTER ALVIN TODAY!
?
HI, ALVIN, OL' BOY, OL' BOY!
WHAT DID YOU DO WHILE I WAS GONE, ALVIN?
I MADE AN ELEPHANT TRAP!
I'M GONNA SIT RIGHT DOWN HERE AN' HELP LULU KEEP AN EYE ON MY OL' PAL ALVIN!
AN ELEPHANT TRA—?
WOW! GOT 'M!
SPLOSH!

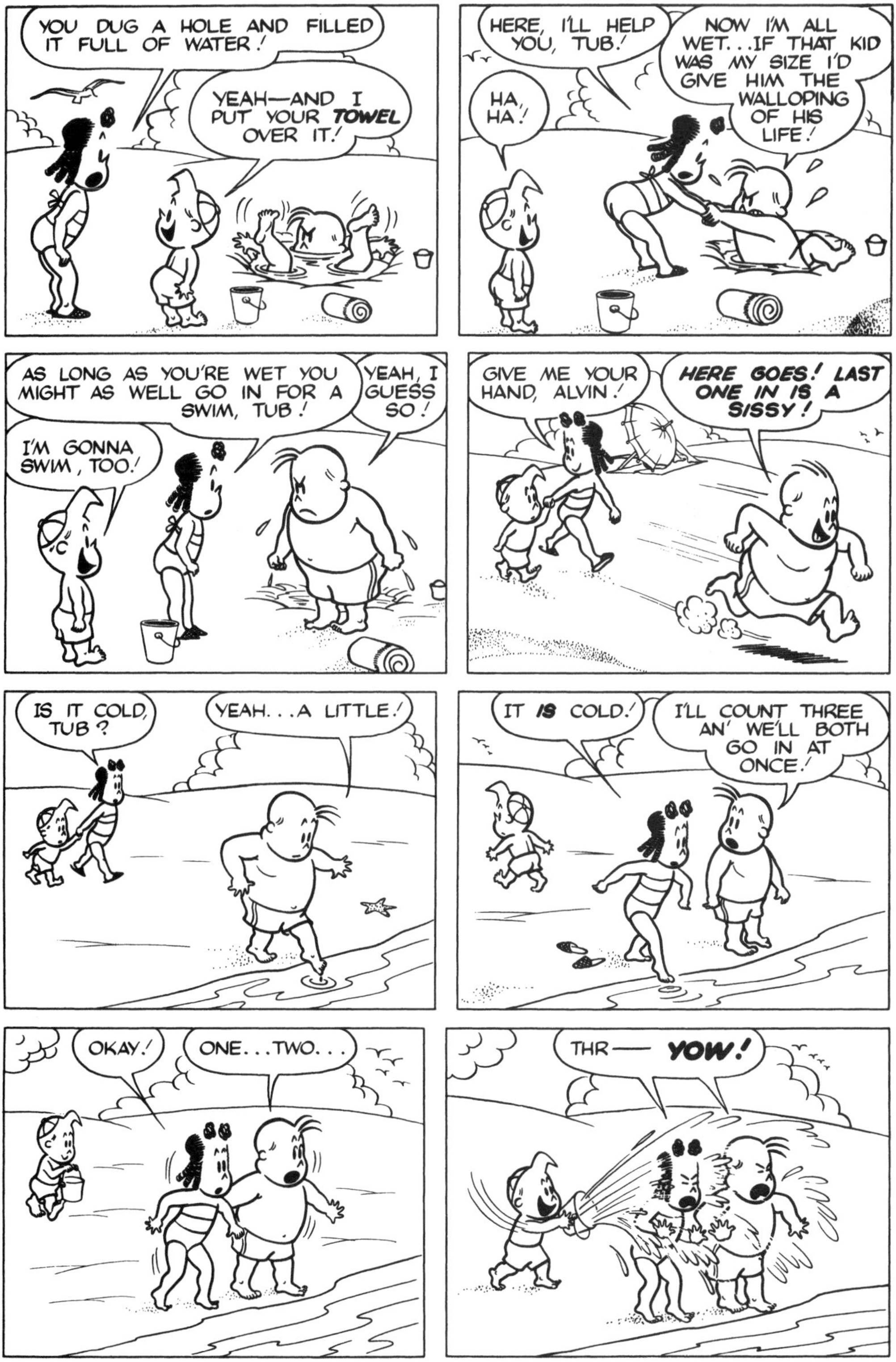
YOU DUG A HOLE AND FILLED IT FULL OF WATER!
YEAH—AND I PUT YOUR TOWEL OVER IT!
HERE, I'LL HELP YOU, TUB!
HA, HA!
NOW I'M ALL WET...IF THAT KID WAS MY SIZE I'D GIVE HIM THE WALLOPING OF HIS LIFE!
AS LONG AS YOU'RE WET YOU MIGHT AS WELL GO IN FOR A SWIM, TUB!
YEAH, I GUESS SO!
I'M GONNA SWIM, TOO!
GIVE ME YOUR HAND, ALVIN!
HERE GOES! LAST ONE IN IS A SISSY!
IS IT COLD, TUB?
YEAH...A LITTLE!
IT IS COLD!
I'LL COUNT THREE AN' WE'LL BOTH GO IN AT ONCE!
OKAY!
ONE...TWO...
THR— YOW!

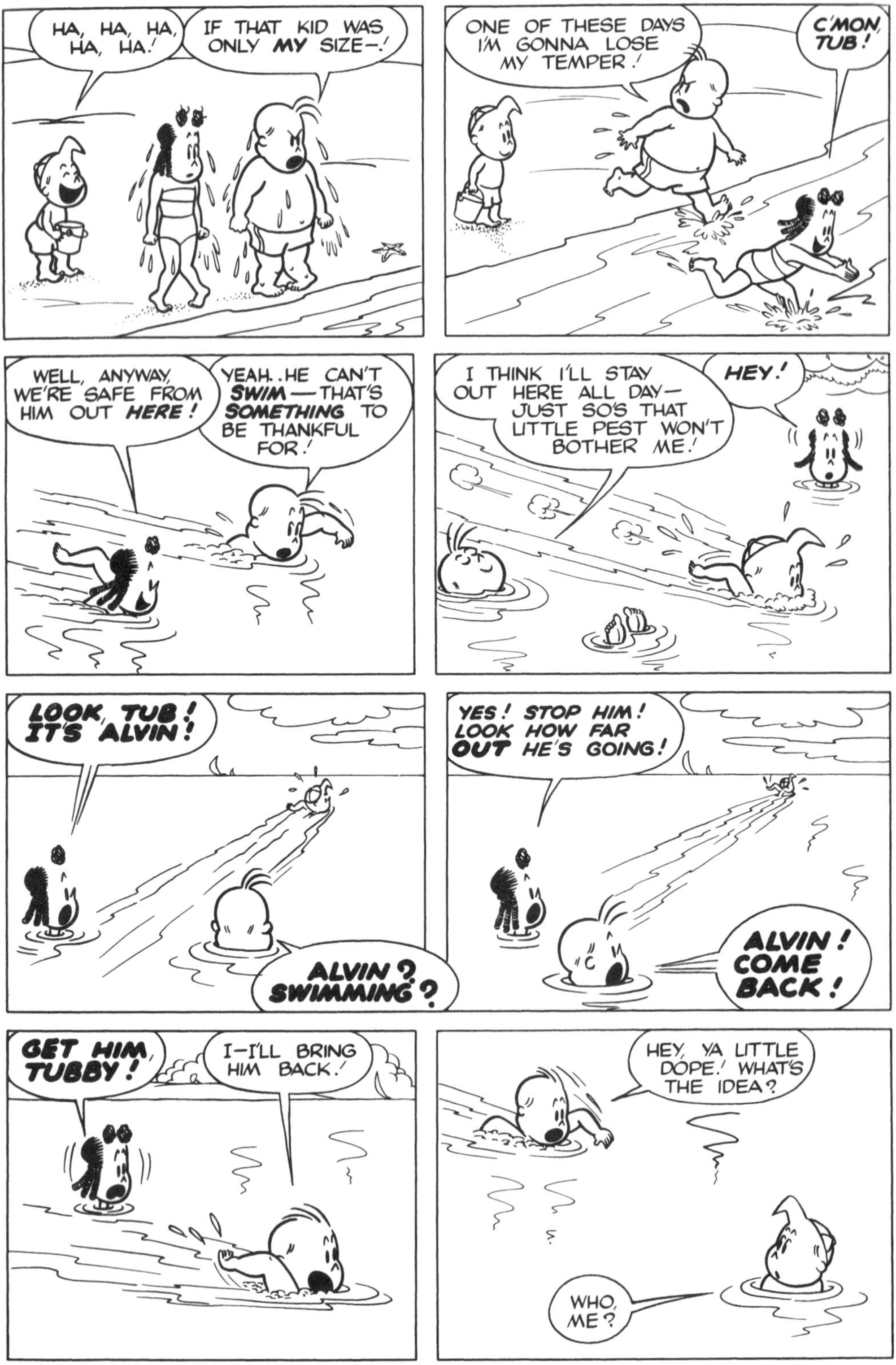
HA, HA, HA, HA, HA!
IF THAT KID WAS ONLY MY SIZE—!
ONE OF THESE DAYS I'M GONNA LOSE MY TEMPER!
C'MON, TUB!
WELL, ANYWAY, WE'RE SAFE FROM HIM OUT HERE!
YEAH..HE CAN'T SWIM—THAT'S SOMETHING TO BE THANKFUL FOR!
I THINK I'LL STAY OUT HERE ALL DAY— JUST SO'S THAT LITTLE PEST WON'T BOTHER ME!
HEY!
LOOK, TUB! IT'S ALVIN!
ALVIN? SWIMMING?
YES! STOP HIM! LOOK HOW FAR OUT HE'S GOING!
ALVIN! COME BACK!
GET HIM, TUBBY!
I-I'LL BRING HIM BACK!
HEY, YA LITTLE DOPE! WHAT'S THE IDEA?
WHO, ME?

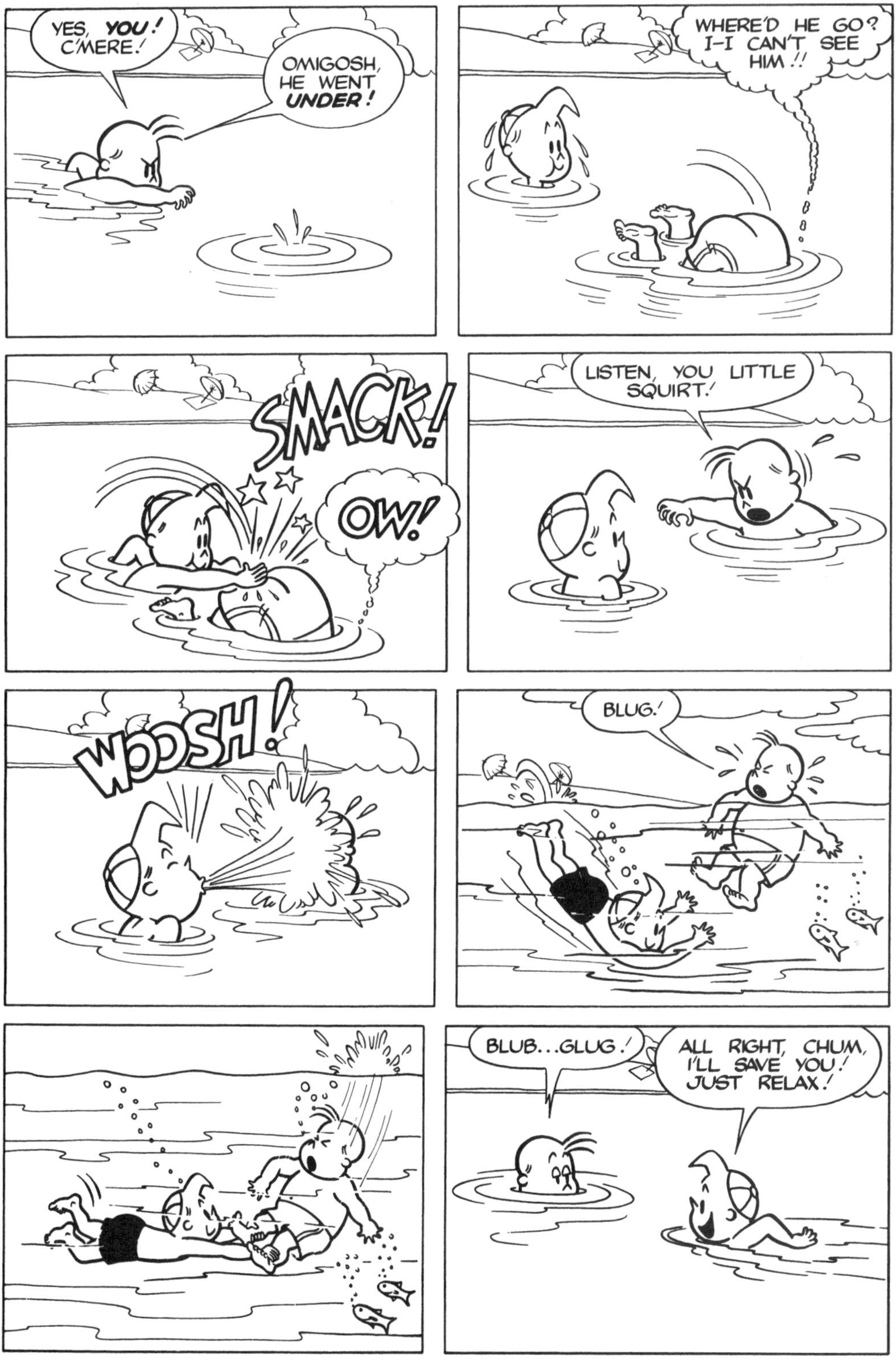
YES, YOU! C'MERE!
OMIGOSH, HE WENT UNDER!
WHERE'D HE GO? I-I CAN'T SEE HIM!!
SMACK!
OW!
LISTEN, YOU LITTLE SQUIRT!
WOOSH!
BLUG!
BLUB...GLUG!
ALL RIGHT, CHUM, I'LL SAVE YOU! JUST RELAX!

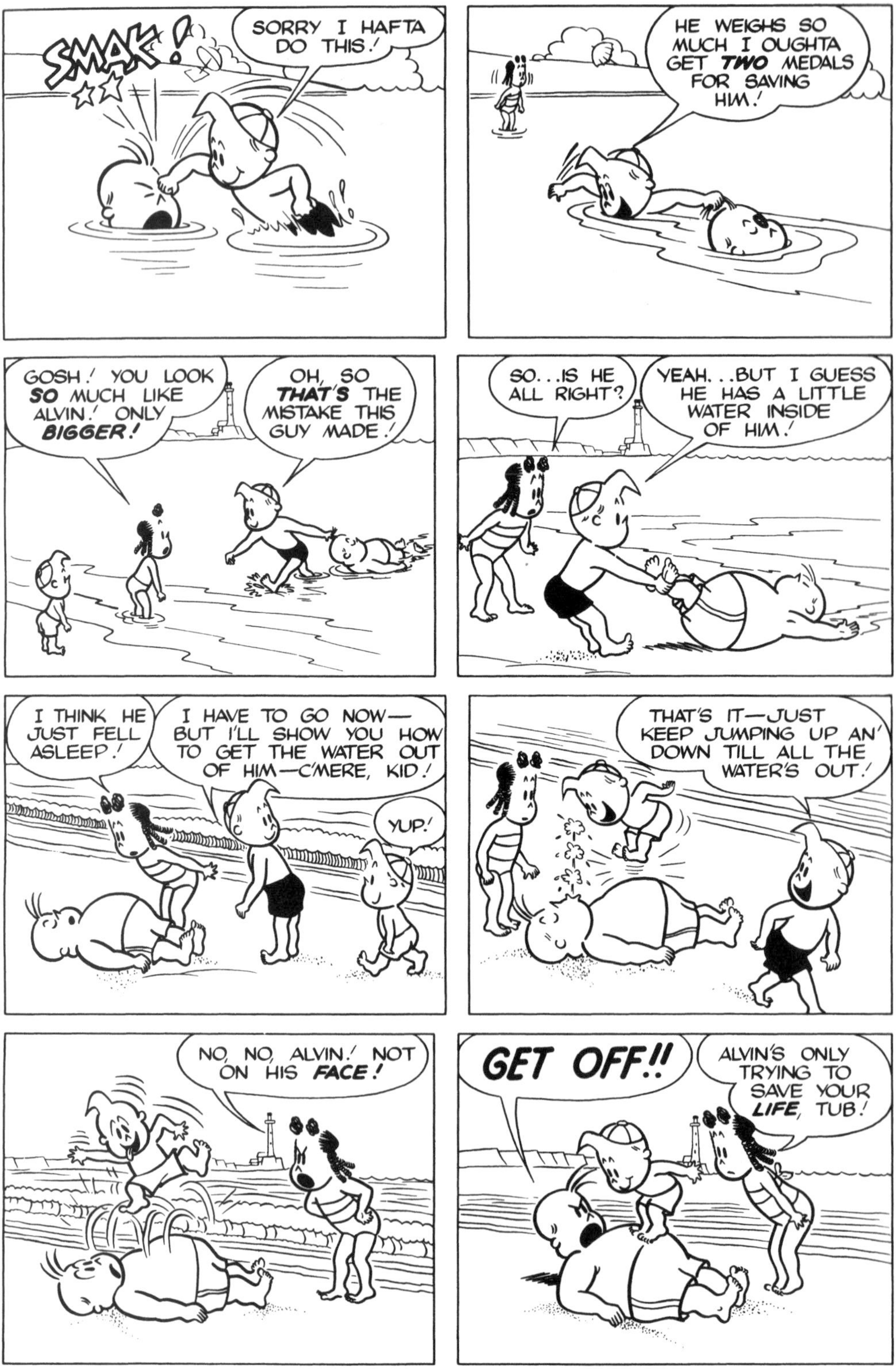
SMAK!
SORRY I HAFTA DO THIS!
HE WEIGHS SO MUCH I OUGHTA GET **TWO** MEDALS FOR SAVING HIM!
GOSH! YOU LOOK **SO** MUCH LIKE ALVIN! ONLY **BIGGER!**
OH, SO **THAT'S** THE MISTAKE THIS GUY MADE!
SO...IS HE ALL RIGHT?
YEAH...BUT I GUESS HE HAS A LITTLE WATER INSIDE OF HIM!
I THINK HE JUST FELL ASLEEP!
I HAVE TO GO NOW— BUT I'LL SHOW YOU HOW TO GET THE WATER OUT OF HIM—C'MERE, KID!
YUP!
THAT'S IT—JUST KEEP JUMPING UP AN' DOWN TILL ALL THE WATER'S OUT!
NO, NO, ALVIN! NOT ON HIS **FACE!**
GET OFF!!
ALVIN'S ONLY TRYING TO SAVE YOUR **LIFE**, TUB!

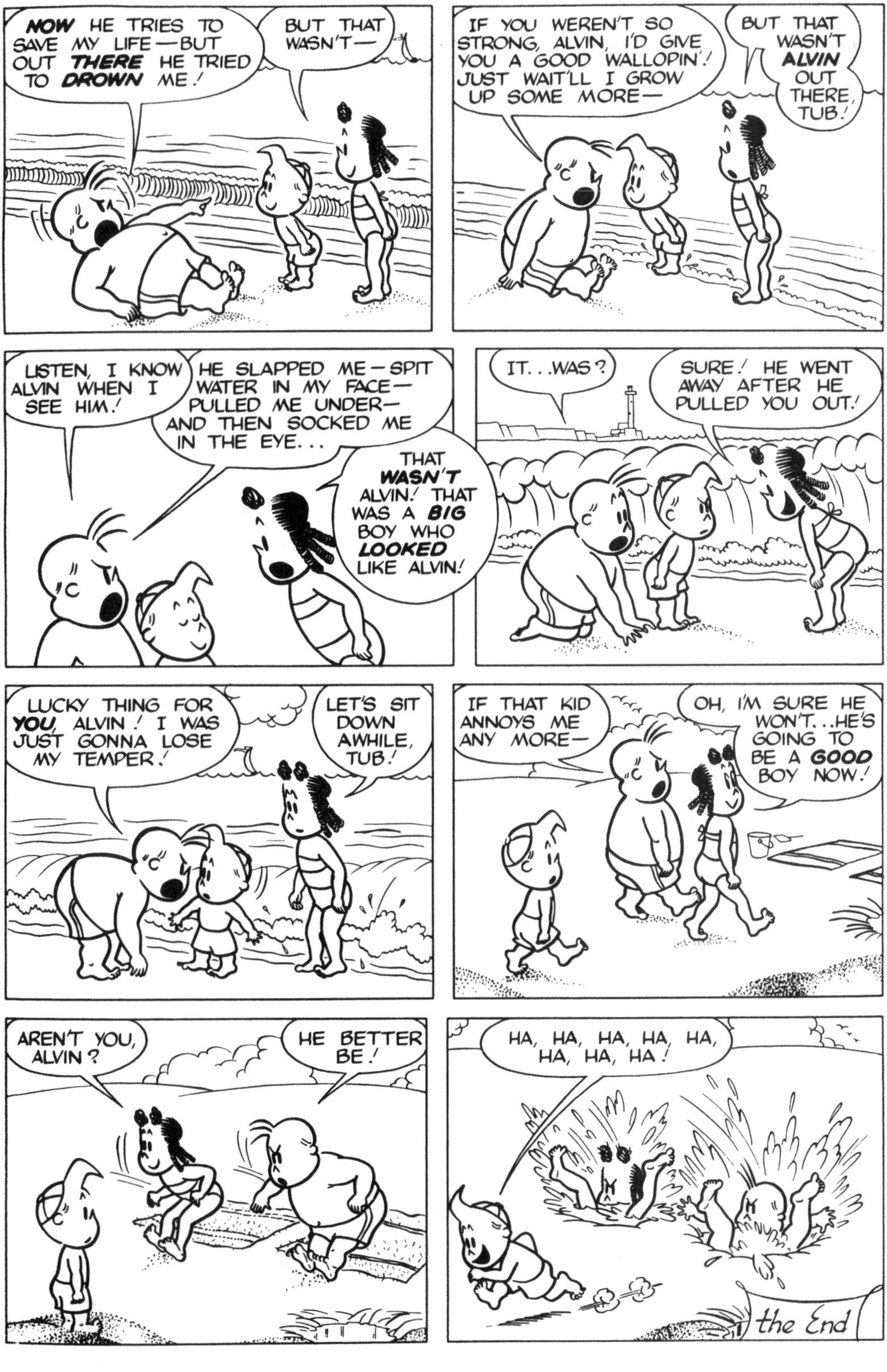
NOW HE TRIES TO SAVE MY LIFE—BUT OUT THERE HE TRIED TO DROWN ME!
BUT THAT WASN'T—
IF YOU WEREN'T SO STRONG, ALVIN, I'D GIVE YOU A GOOD WALLOPIN'! JUST WAIT'LL I GROW UP SOME MORE—
BUT THAT WASN'T ALVIN OUT THERE, TUB!
LISTEN, I KNOW ALVIN WHEN I SEE HIM!
HE SLAPPED ME—SPIT WATER IN MY FACE—PULLED ME UNDER—AND THEN SOCKED ME IN THE EYE...
THAT WASN'T ALVIN! THAT WAS A BIG BOY WHO LOOKED LIKE ALVIN!
IT...WAS?
SURE! HE WENT AWAY AFTER HE PULLED YOU OUT!
LUCKY THING FOR YOU, ALVIN! I WAS JUST GONNA LOSE MY TEMPER!
LET'S SIT DOWN AWHILE, TUB!
IF THAT KID ANNOYS ME ANY MORE—
OH, I'M SURE HE WON'T...HE'S GOING TO BE A GOOD BOY NOW!
AREN'T YOU, ALVIN?
HE BETTER BE!
HA, HA, HA, HA, HA, HA, HA, HA!
the End

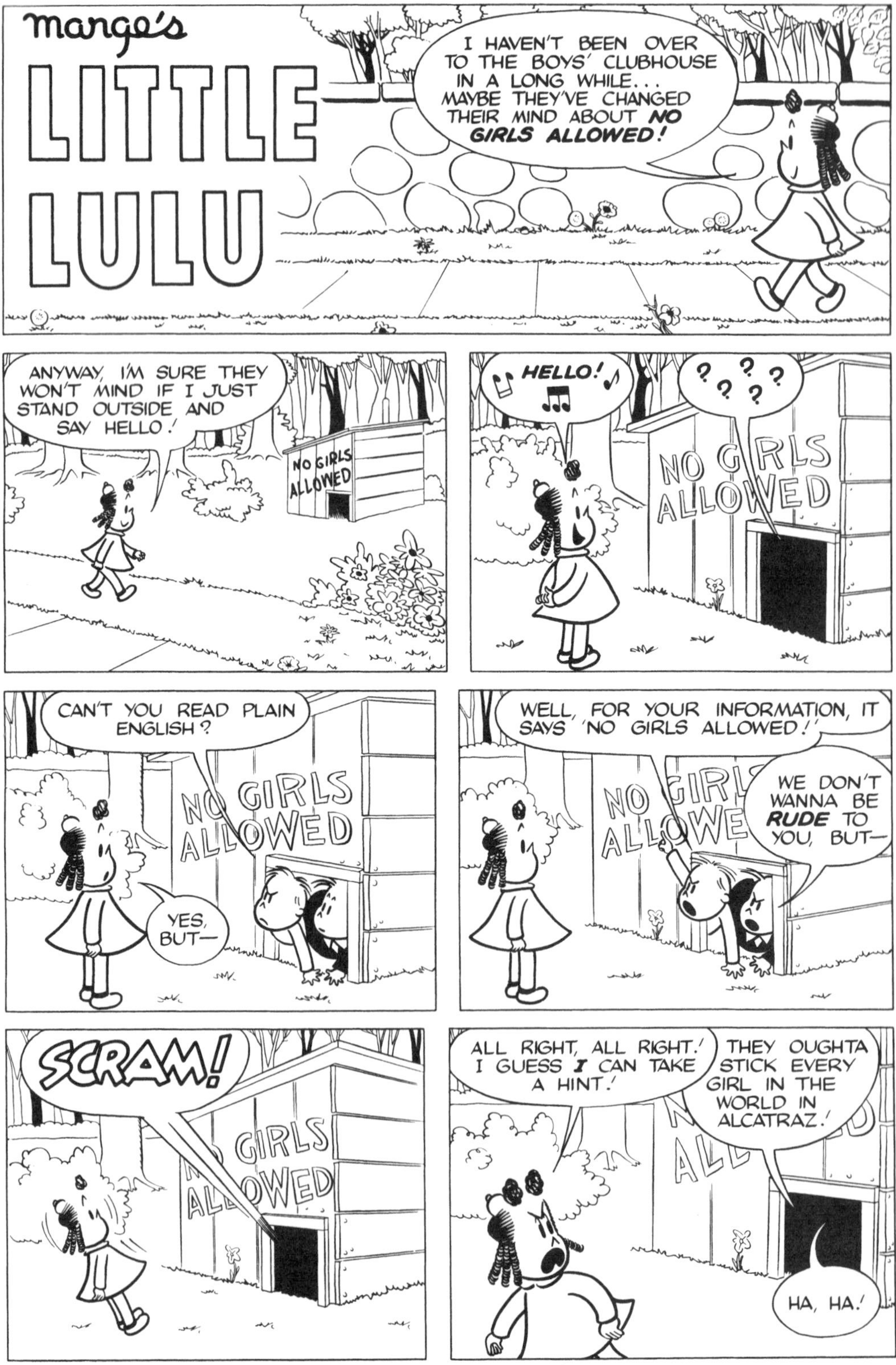
marge's
LITTLE LULU
I HAVEN'T BEEN OVER TO THE BOYS' CLUBHOUSE IN A LONG WHILE... MAYBE THEY'VE CHANGED THEIR MIND ABOUT **NO GIRLS ALLOWED**!
ANYWAY, I'M SURE THEY WON'T MIND IF I JUST STAND OUTSIDE AND SAY HELLO!
NO GIRLS ALLOWED
HELLO!
? ? ? ? ?
NO GIRLS ALLOWED
CAN'T YOU READ PLAIN ENGLISH?
NO GIRLS ALLOWED
YES, BUT—
WELL, FOR YOUR INFORMATION, IT SAYS 'NO GIRLS ALLOWED!'
WE DON'T WANNA BE ***RUDE*** TO YOU, BUT—
SCRAM!
ALL RIGHT, ALL RIGHT! I GUESS ***I*** CAN TAKE A HINT!
THEY OUGHTA STICK EVERY GIRL IN THE WORLD IN ALCATRAZ!
HA, HA!

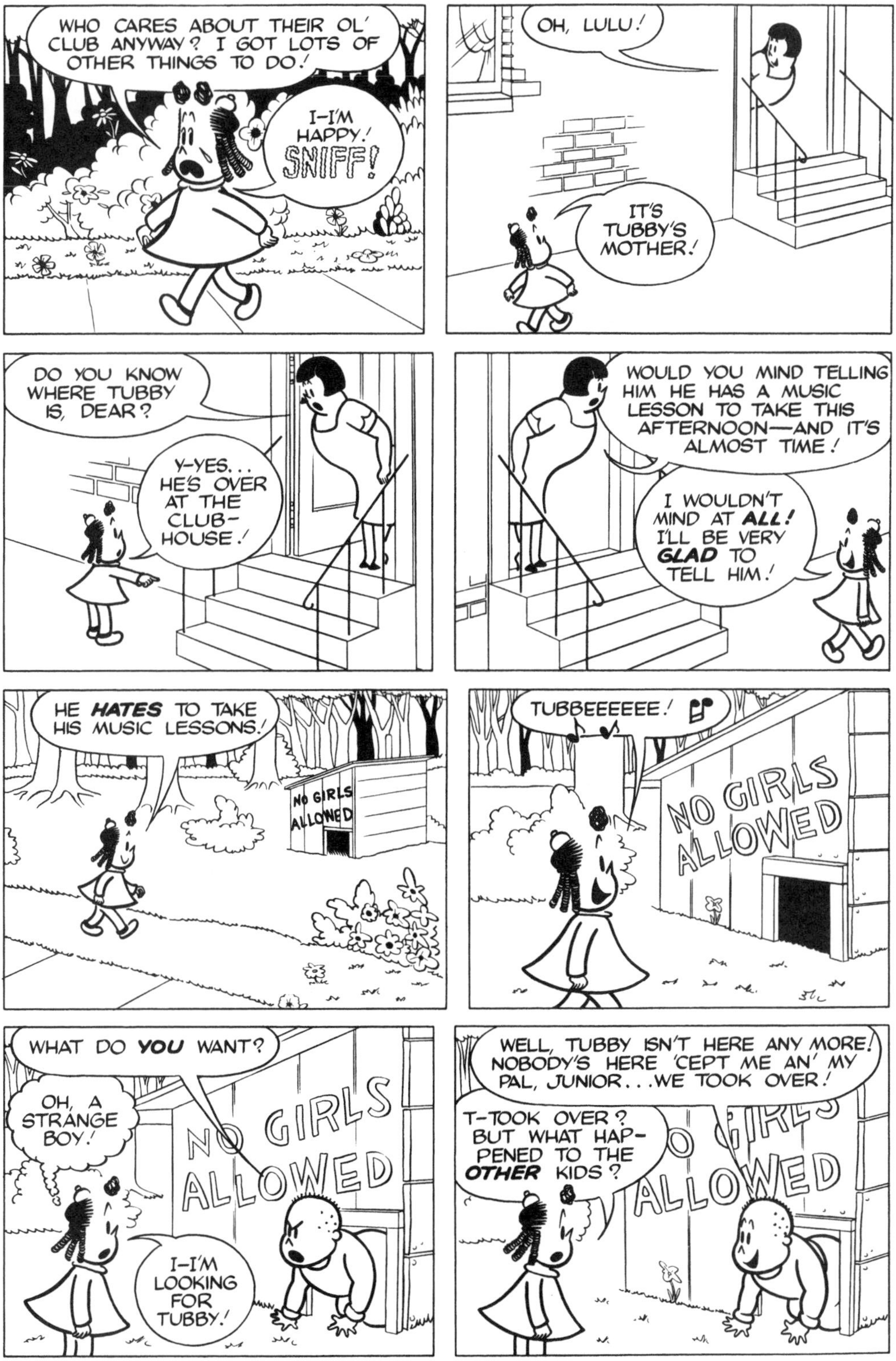
WHO CARES ABOUT THEIR OL' CLUB ANYWAY? I GOT LOTS OF OTHER THINGS TO DO!
I-I'M HAPPY! SNIFF!
OH, LULU!
IT'S TUBBY'S MOTHER!
DO YOU KNOW WHERE TUBBY IS, DEAR?
Y-YES... HE'S OVER AT THE CLUB-HOUSE!
WOULD YOU MIND TELLING HIM HE HAS A MUSIC LESSON TO TAKE THIS AFTERNOON—AND IT'S ALMOST TIME!
I WOULDN'T MIND AT ALL! I'LL BE VERY GLAD TO TELL HIM!
HE HATES TO TAKE HIS MUSIC LESSONS!
NO GIRLS ALLOWED
TUBBEEEEEE!
NO GIRLS ALLOWED
WHAT DO YOU WANT?
OH, A STRANGE BOY!
NO GIRLS ALLOWED
I-I'M LOOKING FOR TUBBY!
WELL, TUBBY ISN'T HERE ANY MORE! NOBODY'S HERE 'CEPT ME AN' MY PAL, JUNIOR... WE TOOK OVER!
T-TOOK OVER? BUT WHAT HAP-PENED TO THE OTHER KIDS?

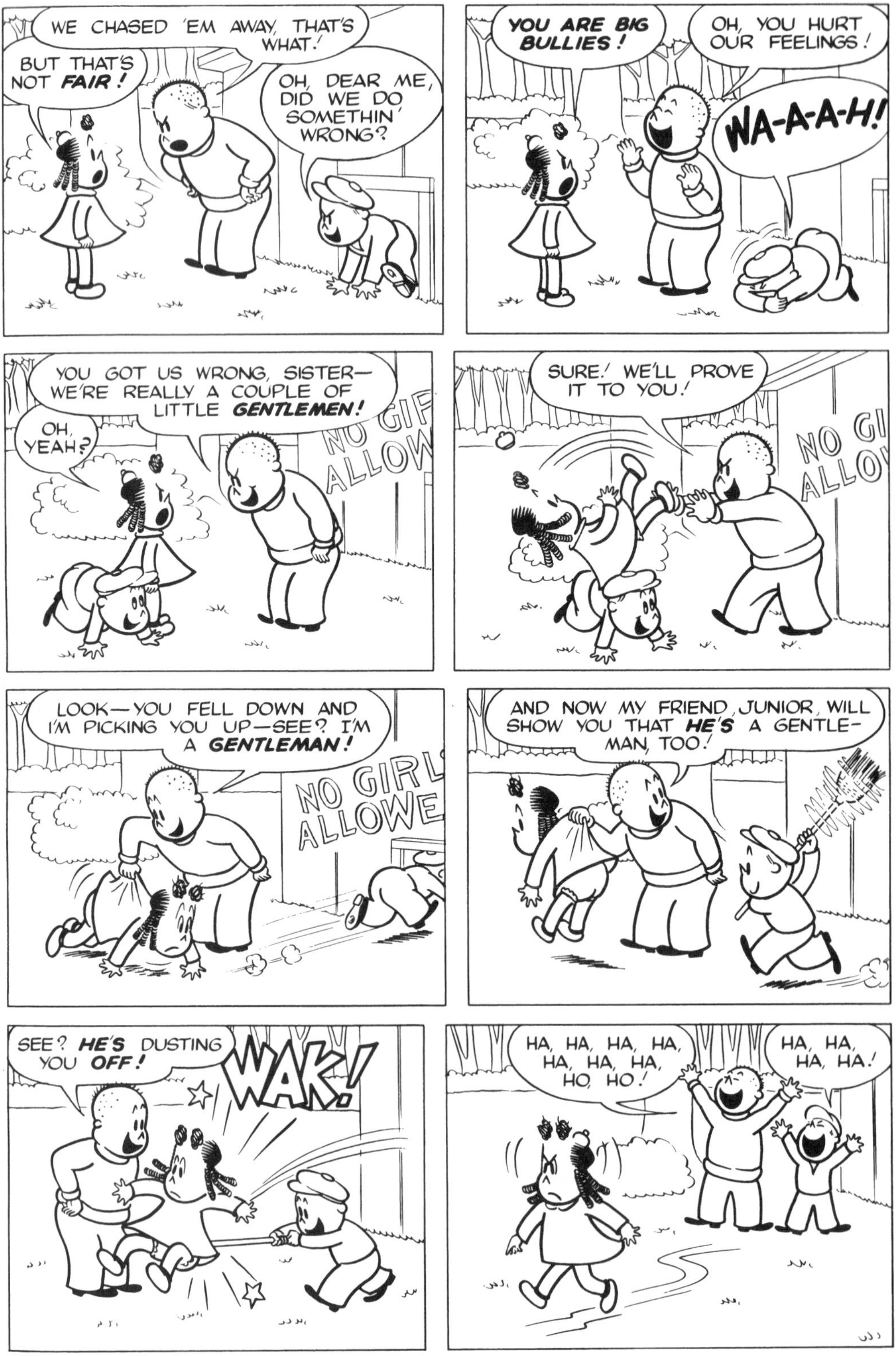
WE CHASED 'EM AWAY, THAT'S WHAT!
BUT THAT'S NOT FAIR!
OH, DEAR ME, DID WE DO SOMETHIN' WRONG?
YOU ARE BIG BULLIES!
OH, YOU HURT OUR FEELINGS!
WA-A-A-H!
YOU GOT US WRONG, SISTER— WE'RE REALLY A COUPLE OF LITTLE GENTLEMEN!
OH, YEAH?
NO GIRLS ALLOWED
SURE! WE'LL PROVE IT TO YOU!
LOOK—YOU FELL DOWN AND I'M PICKING YOU UP—SEE? I'M A GENTLEMAN!
AND NOW MY FRIEND, JUNIOR, WILL SHOW YOU THAT HE'S A GENTLEMAN, TOO!
SEE? HE'S DUSTING YOU OFF!
WAK!
HA, HA, HA, HA, HA, HA, HA, HO, HO!
HA, HA, HA, HA!

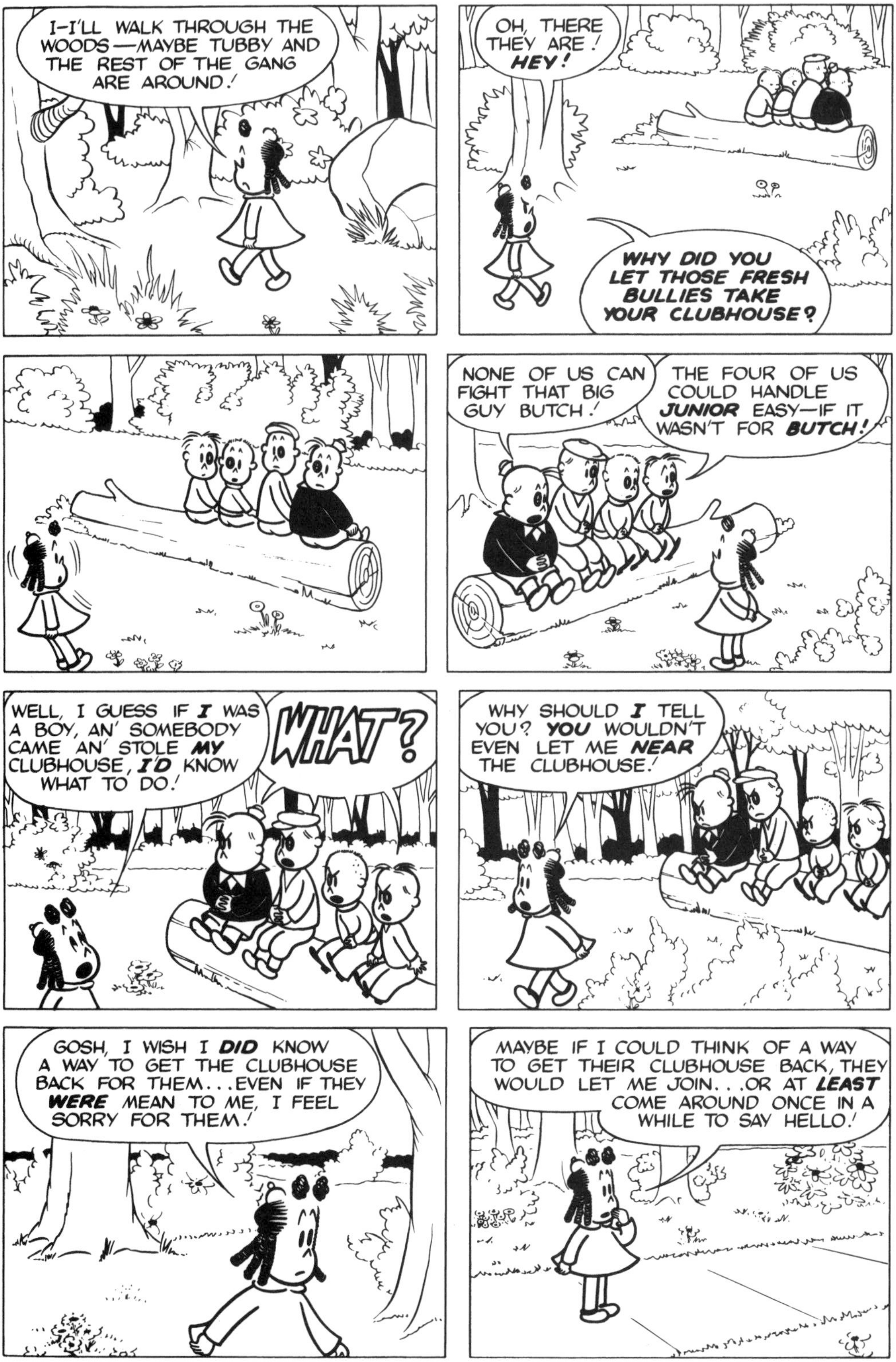
I-I'LL WALK THROUGH THE WOODS—MAYBE TUBBY AND THE REST OF THE GANG ARE AROUND!
OH, THERE THEY ARE! HEY!
WHY DID YOU LET THOSE FRESH BULLIES TAKE YOUR CLUBHOUSE?
NONE OF US CAN FIGHT THAT BIG GUY BUTCH!
THE FOUR OF US COULD HANDLE JUNIOR EASY—IF IT WASN'T FOR BUTCH!
WELL, I GUESS IF I WAS A BOY, AN' SOMEBODY CAME AN' STOLE MY CLUBHOUSE, I'D KNOW WHAT TO DO!
WHAT?
WHY SHOULD I TELL YOU? YOU WOULDN'T EVEN LET ME NEAR THE CLUBHOUSE!
GOSH, I WISH I DID KNOW A WAY TO GET THE CLUBHOUSE BACK FOR THEM...EVEN IF THEY WERE MEAN TO ME, I FEEL SORRY FOR THEM!
MAYBE IF I COULD THINK OF A WAY TO GET THEIR CLUBHOUSE BACK, THEY WOULD LET ME JOIN...OR AT LEAST COME AROUND ONCE IN A WHILE TO SAY HELLO!

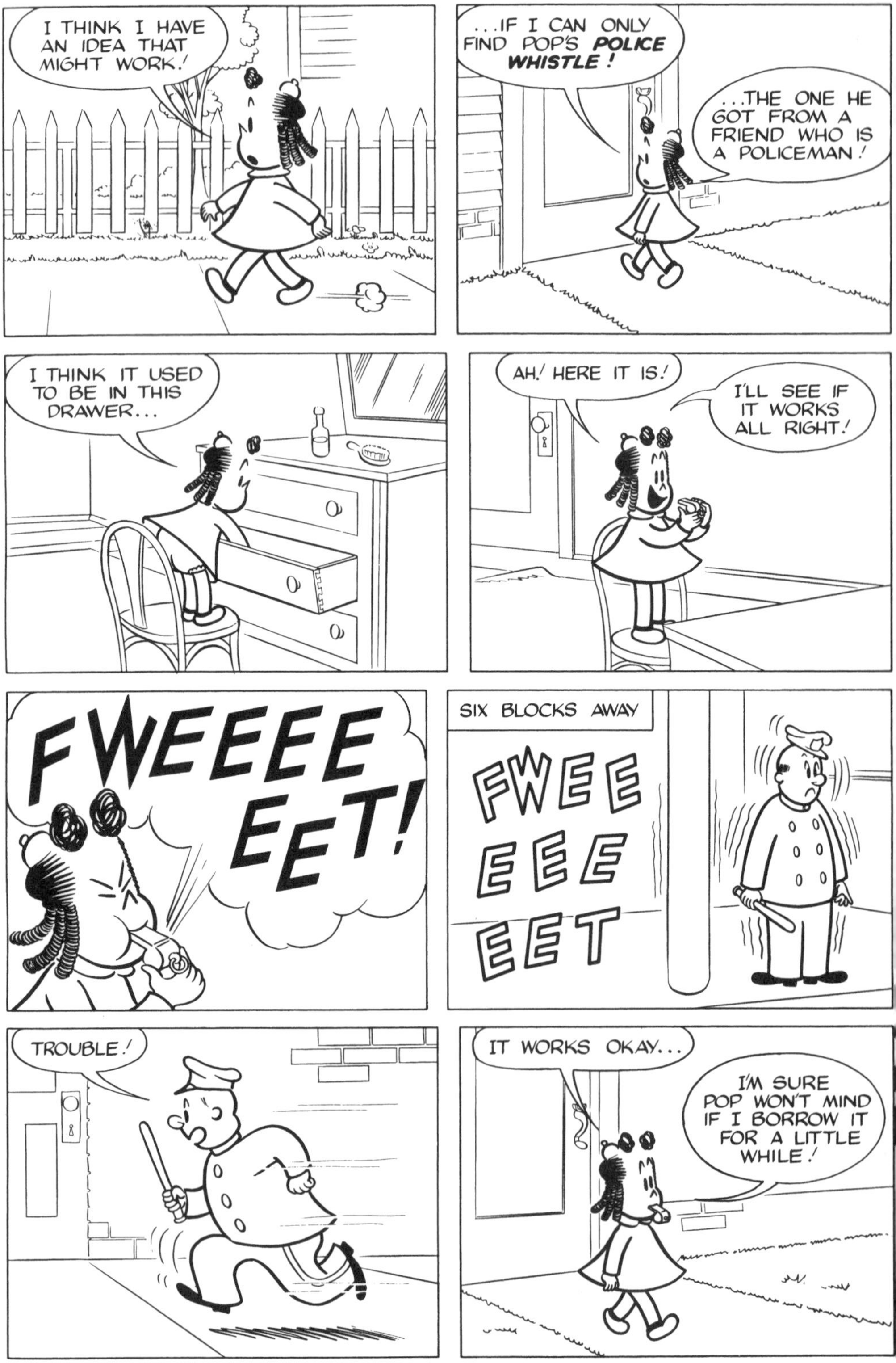
I THINK I HAVE AN IDEA THAT MIGHT WORK!
...IF I CAN ONLY FIND POP'S **POLICE WHISTLE**!
...THE ONE HE GOT FROM A FRIEND WHO IS A POLICEMAN!
I THINK IT USED TO BE IN THIS DRAWER...
AH! HERE IT IS!
I'LL SEE IF IT WORKS ALL RIGHT!
FWEEEE EET!
SIX BLOCKS AWAY
FWEE EEE EET
TROUBLE!
IT WORKS OKAY...
I'M SURE POP WON'T MIND IF I BORROW IT FOR A LITTLE WHILE!

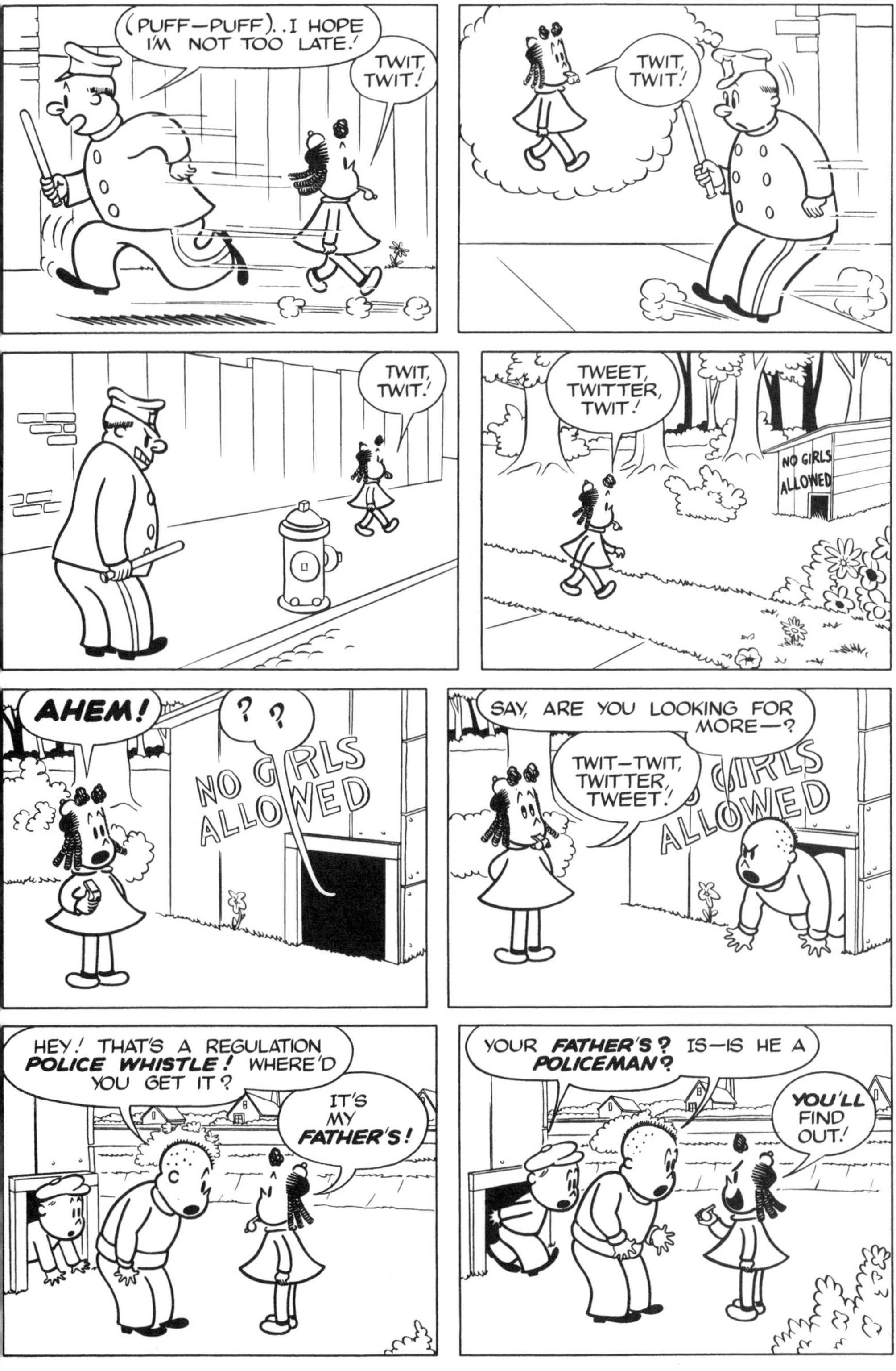

(PUFF—PUFF)..I HOPE I'M NOT TOO LATE!
TWIT, TWIT!
TWIT, TWIT!
TWIT, TWIT!
TWEET, TWITTER, TWIT!
NO GIRLS ALLOWED
AHEM!
? ?
NO GIRLS ALLOWED
SAY, ARE YOU LOOKING FOR MORE—?
TWIT—TWIT, TWITTER, TWEET!
HEY! THAT'S A REGULATION POLICE WHISTLE! WHERE'D YOU GET IT?
IT'S MY FATHER'S!
YOUR FATHER'S? IS—IS HE A POLICEMAN?
YOU'LL FIND OUT!

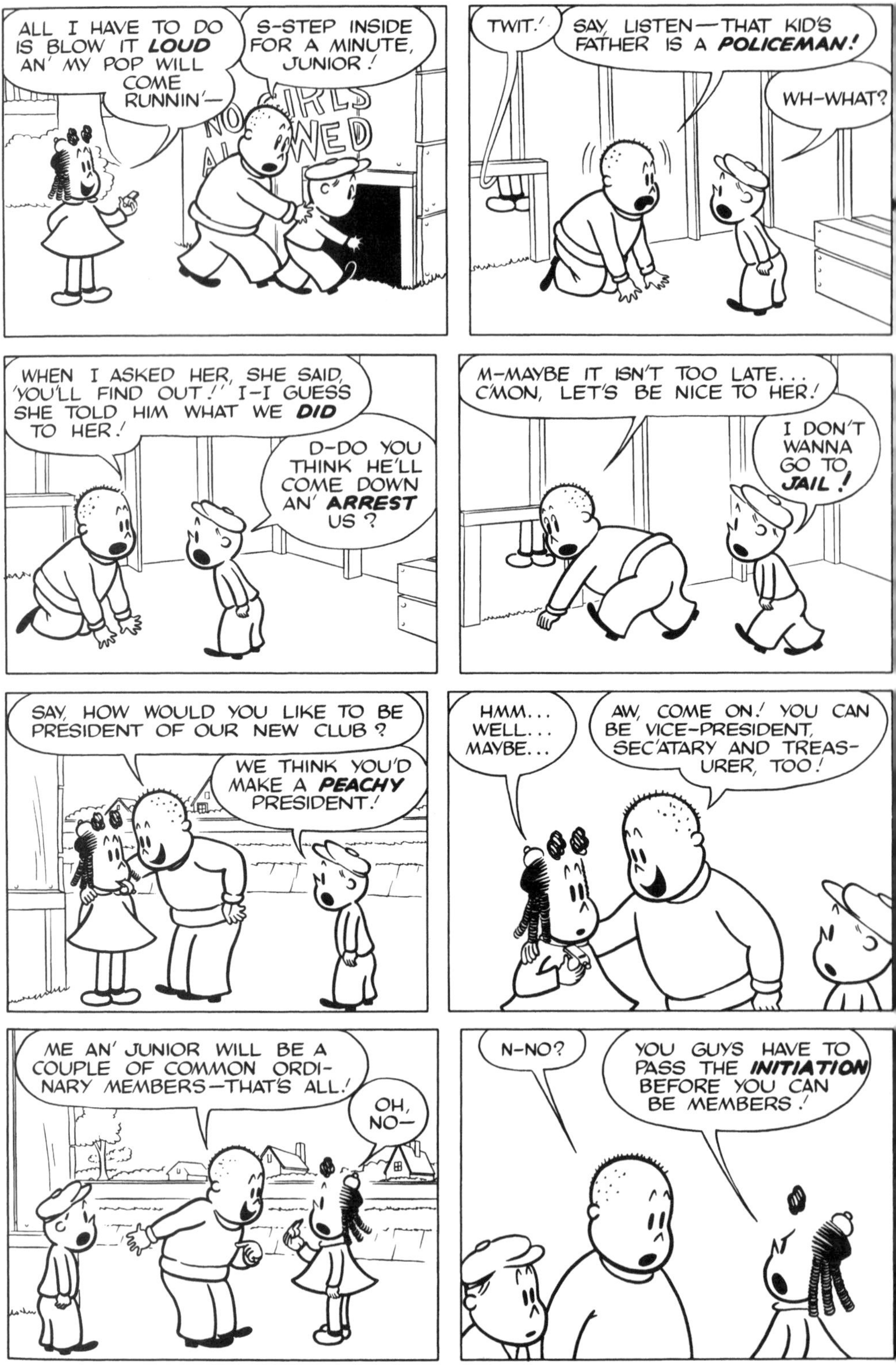
ALL I HAVE TO DO IS BLOW IT LOUD AN' MY POP WILL COME RUNNIN'—
S-STEP INSIDE FOR A MINUTE, JUNIOR!
NO GIRLS ALLOWED
TWIT!
SAY, LISTEN—THAT KID'S FATHER IS A POLICEMAN!
WH-WHAT?
WHEN I ASKED HER, SHE SAID, 'YOU'LL FIND OUT!' I-I GUESS SHE TOLD HIM WHAT WE DID TO HER!
D-DO YOU THINK HE'LL COME DOWN AN' ARREST US?
M-MAYBE IT ISN'T TOO LATE... C'MON, LET'S BE NICE TO HER!
I DON'T WANNA GO TO JAIL!
SAY, HOW WOULD YOU LIKE TO BE PRESIDENT OF OUR NEW CLUB?
WE THINK YOU'D MAKE A PEACHY PRESIDENT!
HMM... WELL... MAYBE...
AW, COME ON! YOU CAN BE VICE-PRESIDENT, SEC'ATARY AND TREAS-URER, TOO!
ME AN' JUNIOR WILL BE A COUPLE OF COMMON ORDI-NARY MEMBERS—THAT'S ALL!
OH, NO—
N-NO?
YOU GUYS HAVE TO PASS THE INITIATION BEFORE YOU CAN BE MEMBERS!

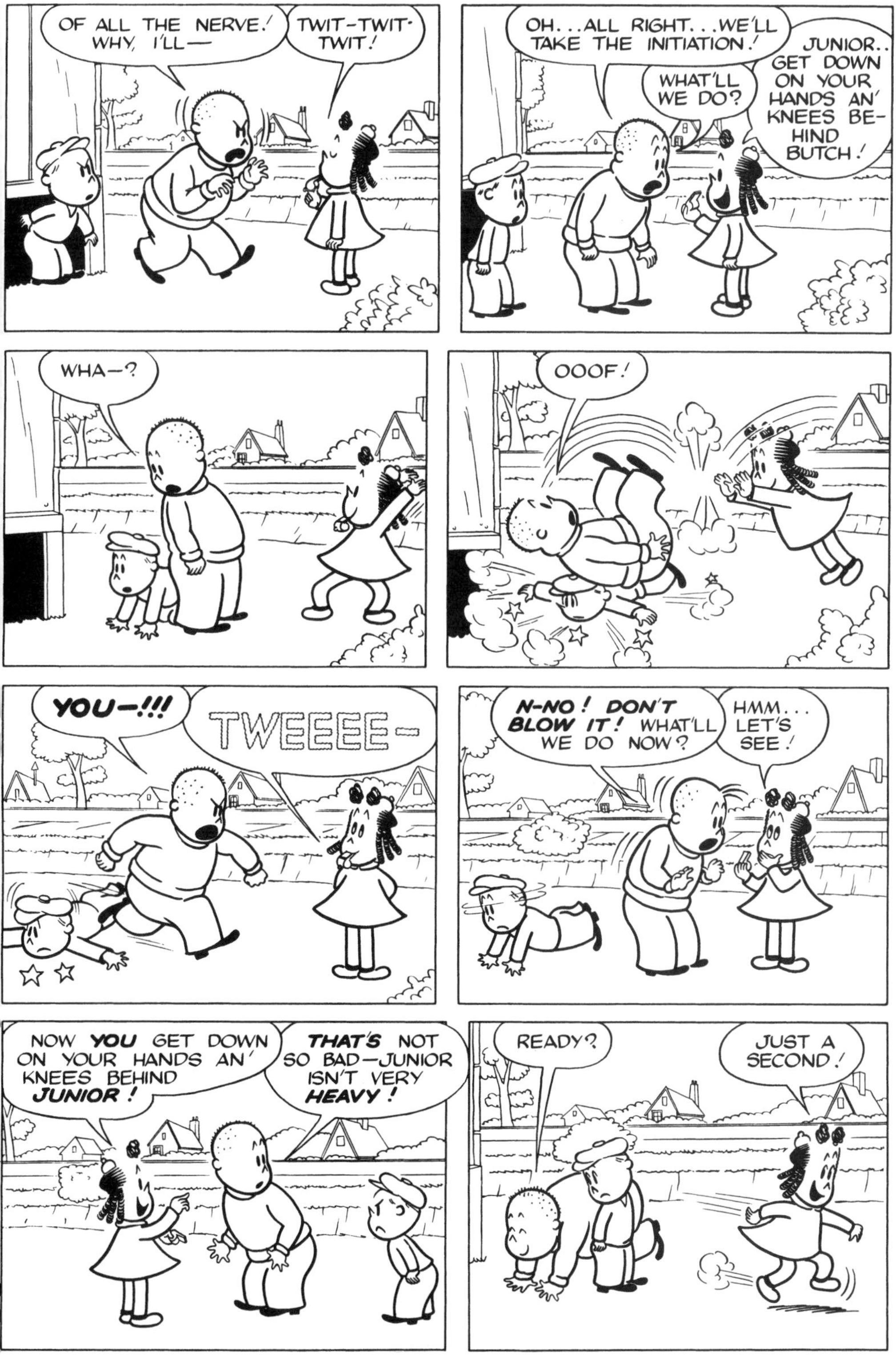
OF ALL THE NERVE! WHY, I'LL—
TWIT-TWIT-TWIT!
OH...ALL RIGHT...WE'LL TAKE THE INITIATION!
WHAT'LL WE DO?
JUNIOR.. GET DOWN ON YOUR HANDS AN' KNEES BEHIND BUTCH!
WHA—?
OOOF!
YOU—!!!
TWEEEE-
N-NO! DON'T BLOW IT! WHAT'LL WE DO NOW?
HMM... LET'S SEE!
NOW YOU GET DOWN ON YOUR HANDS AN' KNEES BEHIND JUNIOR!
THAT'S NOT SO BAD—JUNIOR ISN'T VERY HEAVY!
READY?
JUST A SECOND!

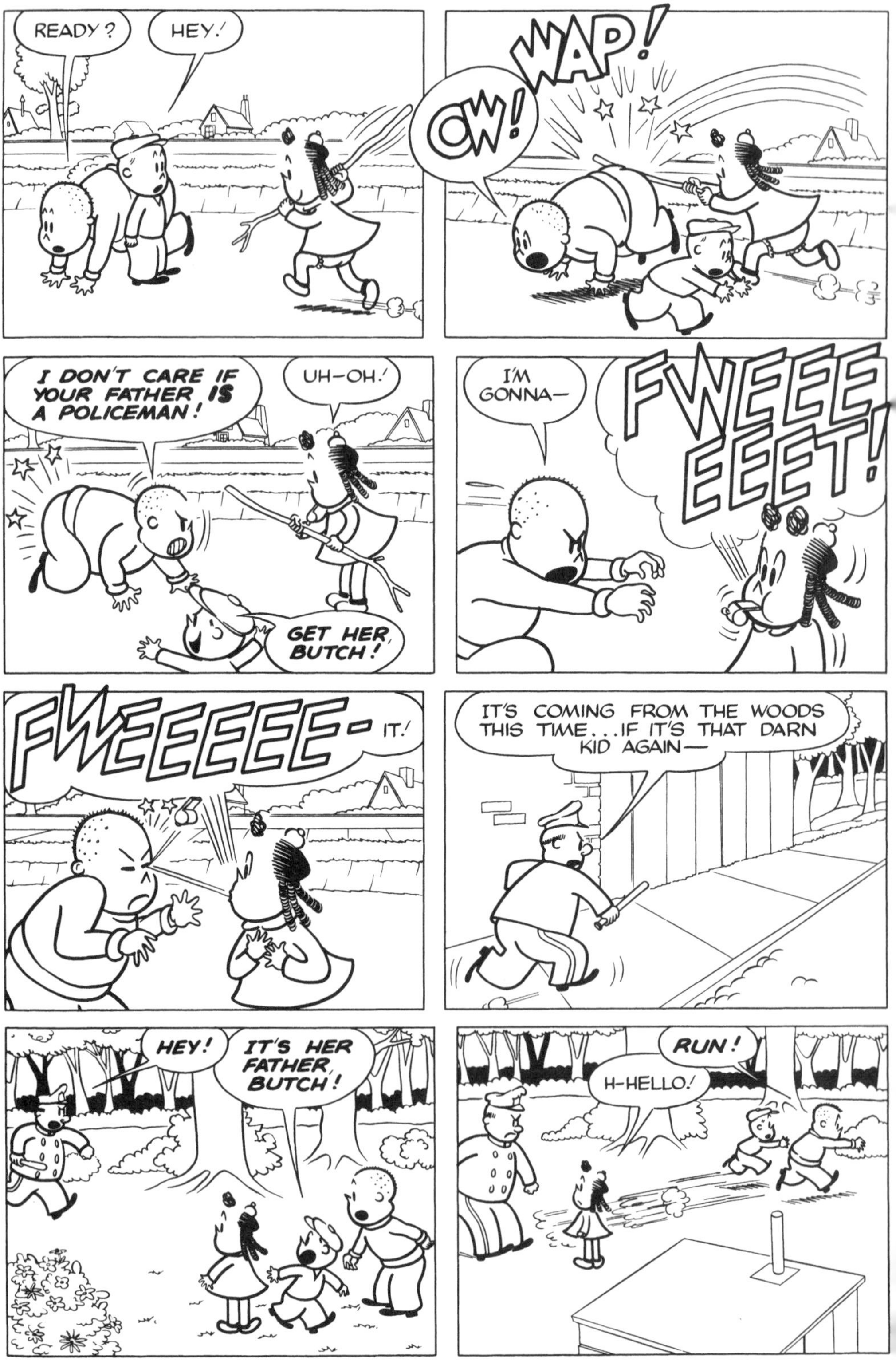
READY?
HEY!
WAP!
OW!
I DON'T CARE IF YOUR FATHER IS A POLICEMAN!
UH-OH!
GET HER, BUTCH!
I'M GONNA—
FWEEE EEET!
FWEEEEEE-IT!
IT'S COMING FROM THE WOODS THIS TIME...IF IT'S THAT DARN KID AGAIN—
HEY!
IT'S HER FATHER, BUTCH!
RUN!
H-HELLO!

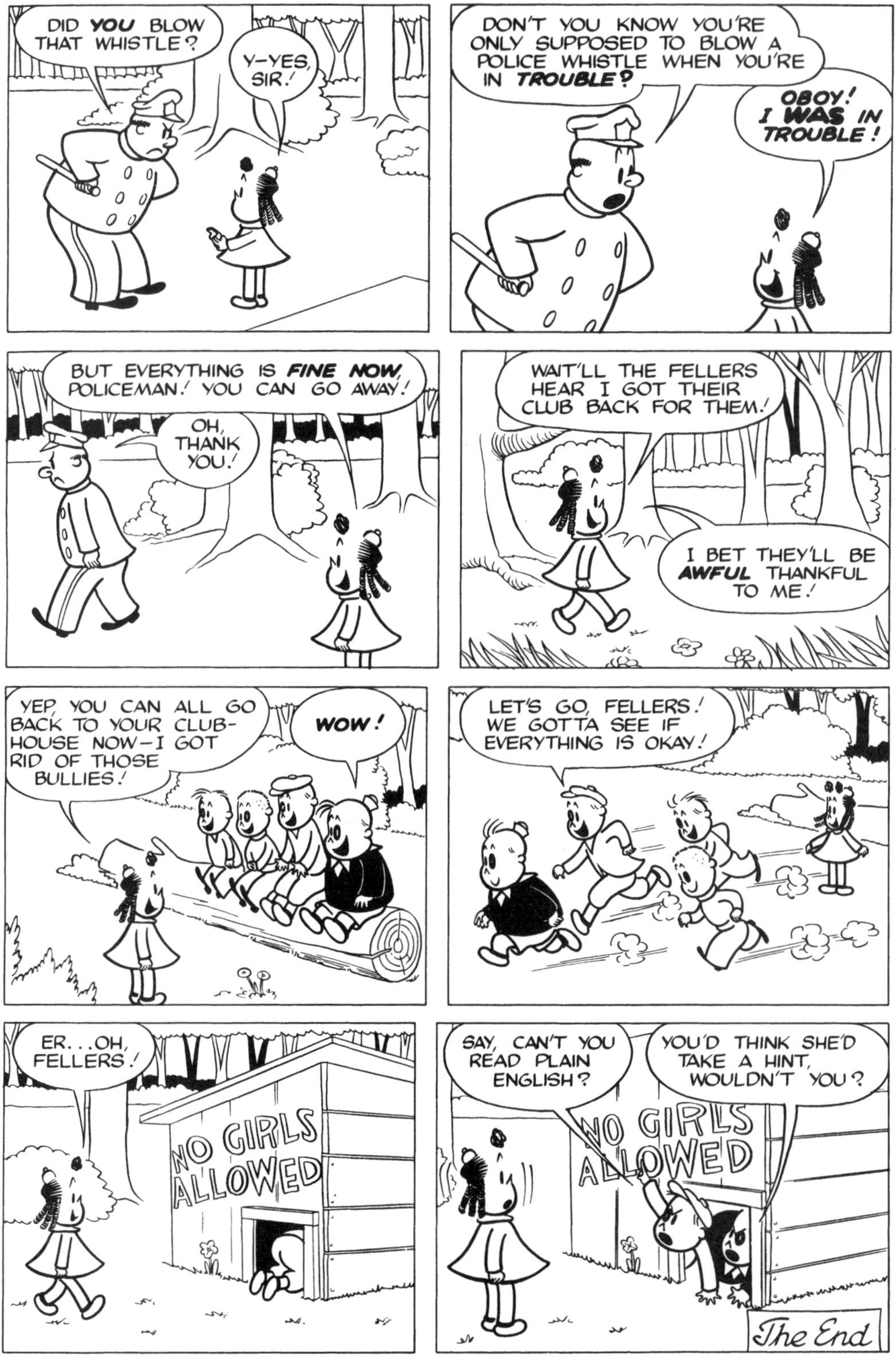
DID **YOU** BLOW THAT WHISTLE?
Y-YES, SIR.!
DON'T YOU KNOW YOU'RE ONLY SUPPOSED TO BLOW A POLICE WHISTLE WHEN YOU'RE IN ***TROUBLE?***
OBOY! I **WAS** IN TROUBLE!
BUT EVERYTHING IS ***FINE NOW,*** POLICEMAN! YOU CAN GO AWAY!
OH, THANK YOU!
WAIT'LL THE FELLERS HEAR I GOT THEIR CLUB BACK FOR THEM!
I BET THEY'LL BE ***AWFUL*** THANKFUL TO ME!
YEP, YOU CAN ALL GO BACK TO YOUR CLUB-HOUSE NOW—I GOT RID OF THOSE BULLIES!
WOW!
LET'S GO, FELLERS! WE GOTTA SEE IF EVERYTHING IS OKAY!
ER...OH, FELLERS!
NO GIRLS ALLOWED
SAY, CAN'T YOU READ PLAIN ENGLISH?
YOU'D THINK SHE'D TAKE A HINT, WOULDN'T YOU?
NO GIRLS ALLOWED
The End

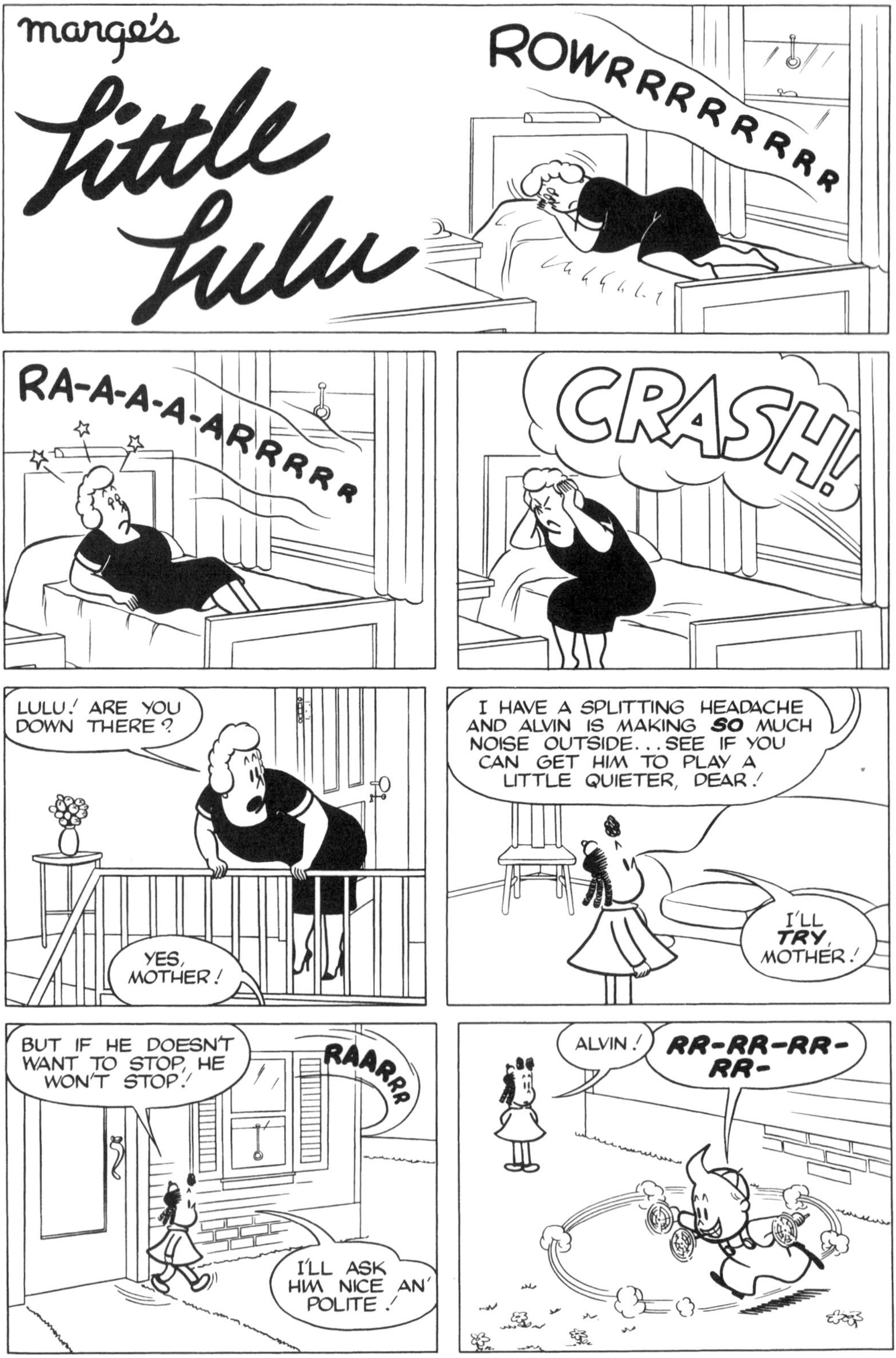
marge's
Little Lulu
ROWRRRRRRRRRR
RA-A-A-A-ARRRRRR
CRASH!
LULU! ARE YOU DOWN THERE?
YES, MOTHER!
I HAVE A SPLITTING HEADACHE AND ALVIN IS MAKING SO MUCH NOISE OUTSIDE...SEE IF YOU CAN GET HIM TO PLAY A LITTLE QUIETER, DEAR!
I'LL TRY, MOTHER!
BUT IF HE DOESN'T WANT TO STOP, HE WON'T STOP!
RAARRR
I'LL ASK HIM NICE AN' POLITE!
ALVIN!
RR-RR-RR-RR-

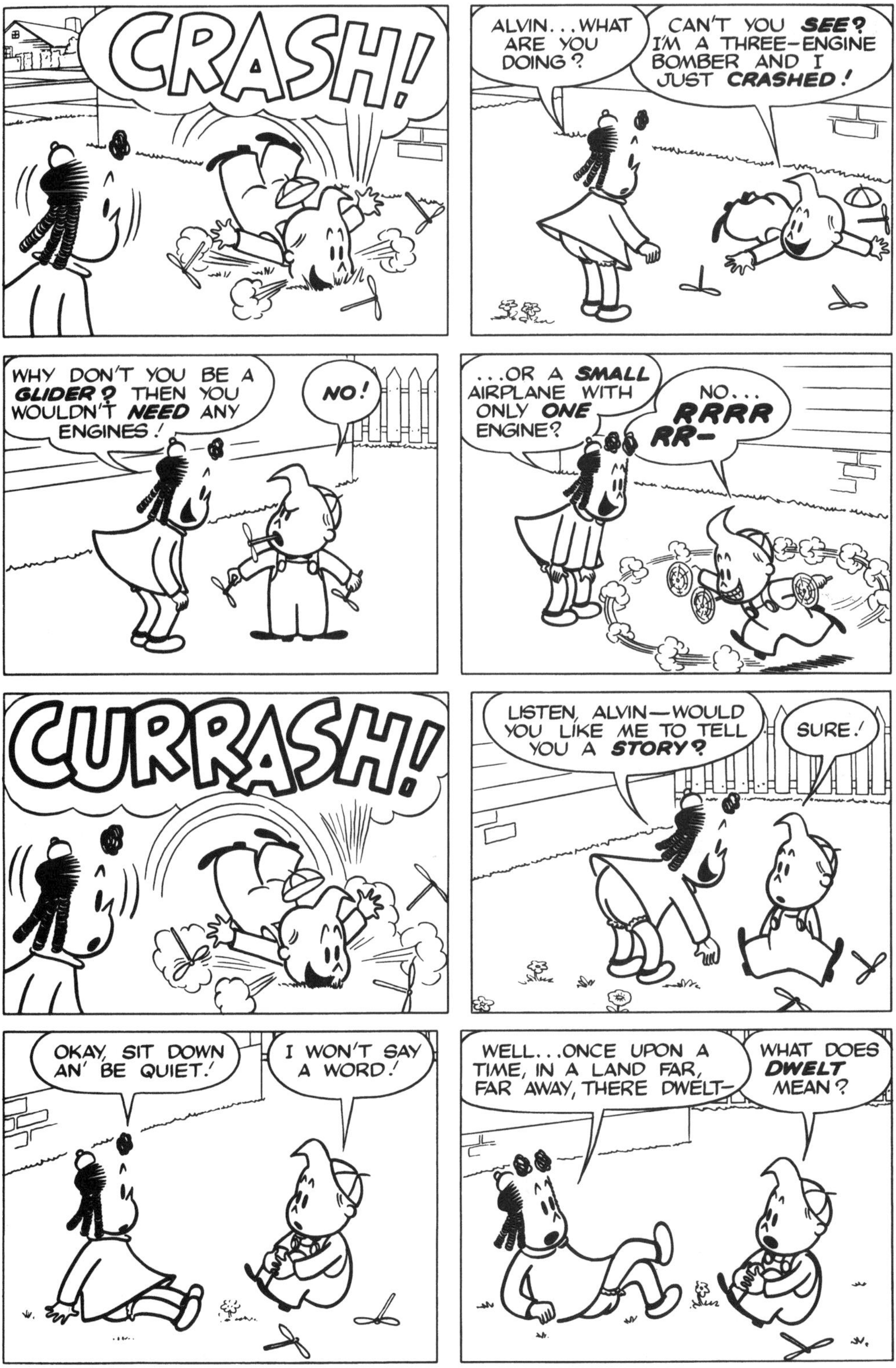
CRASH!
ALVIN...WHAT ARE YOU DOING?
CAN'T YOU SEE? I'M A THREE-ENGINE BOMBER AND I JUST CRASHED!
WHY DON'T YOU BE A GLIDER? THEN YOU WOULDN'T NEED ANY ENGINES!
NO!
...OR A SMALL AIRPLANE WITH ONLY ONE ENGINE?
NO... RRRR RR—
CURRASH!
LISTEN, ALVIN—WOULD YOU LIKE ME TO TELL YOU A STORY?
SURE!
OKAY, SIT DOWN AN' BE QUIET!
I WON'T SAY A WORD!
WELL...ONCE UPON A TIME, IN A LAND FAR, FAR AWAY, THERE DWELT—
WHAT DOES DWELT MEAN?

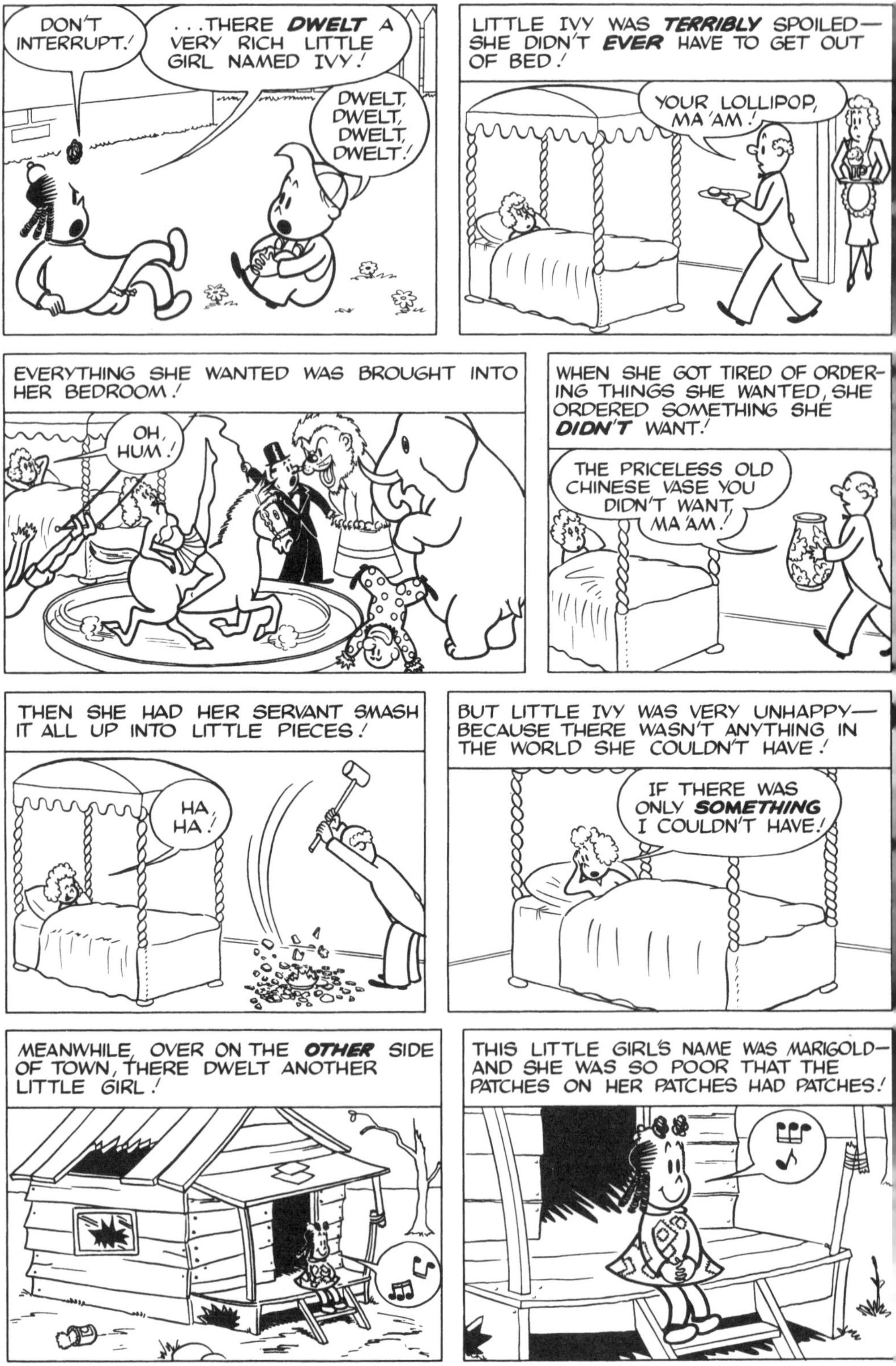
DON'T INTERRUPT!
...THERE DWELT A VERY RICH LITTLE GIRL NAMED IVY!
DWELT, DWELT, DWELT, DWELT!
LITTLE IVY WAS TERRIBLY SPOILED—SHE DIDN'T EVER HAVE TO GET OUT OF BED!
YOUR LOLLIPOP, MA'AM!
EVERYTHING SHE WANTED WAS BROUGHT INTO HER BEDROOM!
OH, HUM!
WHEN SHE GOT TIRED OF ORDERING THINGS SHE WANTED, SHE ORDERED SOMETHING SHE DIDN'T WANT!
THE PRICELESS OLD CHINESE VASE YOU DIDN'T WANT, MA'AM!
THEN SHE HAD HER SERVANT SMASH IT ALL UP INTO LITTLE PIECES!
HA, HA!
BUT LITTLE IVY WAS VERY UNHAPPY—BECAUSE THERE WASN'T ANYTHING IN THE WORLD SHE COULDN'T HAVE!
IF THERE WAS ONLY SOMETHING I COULDN'T HAVE!
MEANWHILE, OVER ON THE OTHER SIDE OF TOWN, THERE DWELT ANOTHER LITTLE GIRL!
THIS LITTLE GIRL'S NAME WAS MARIGOLD—AND SHE WAS SO POOR THAT THE PATCHES ON HER PATCHES HAD PATCHES!

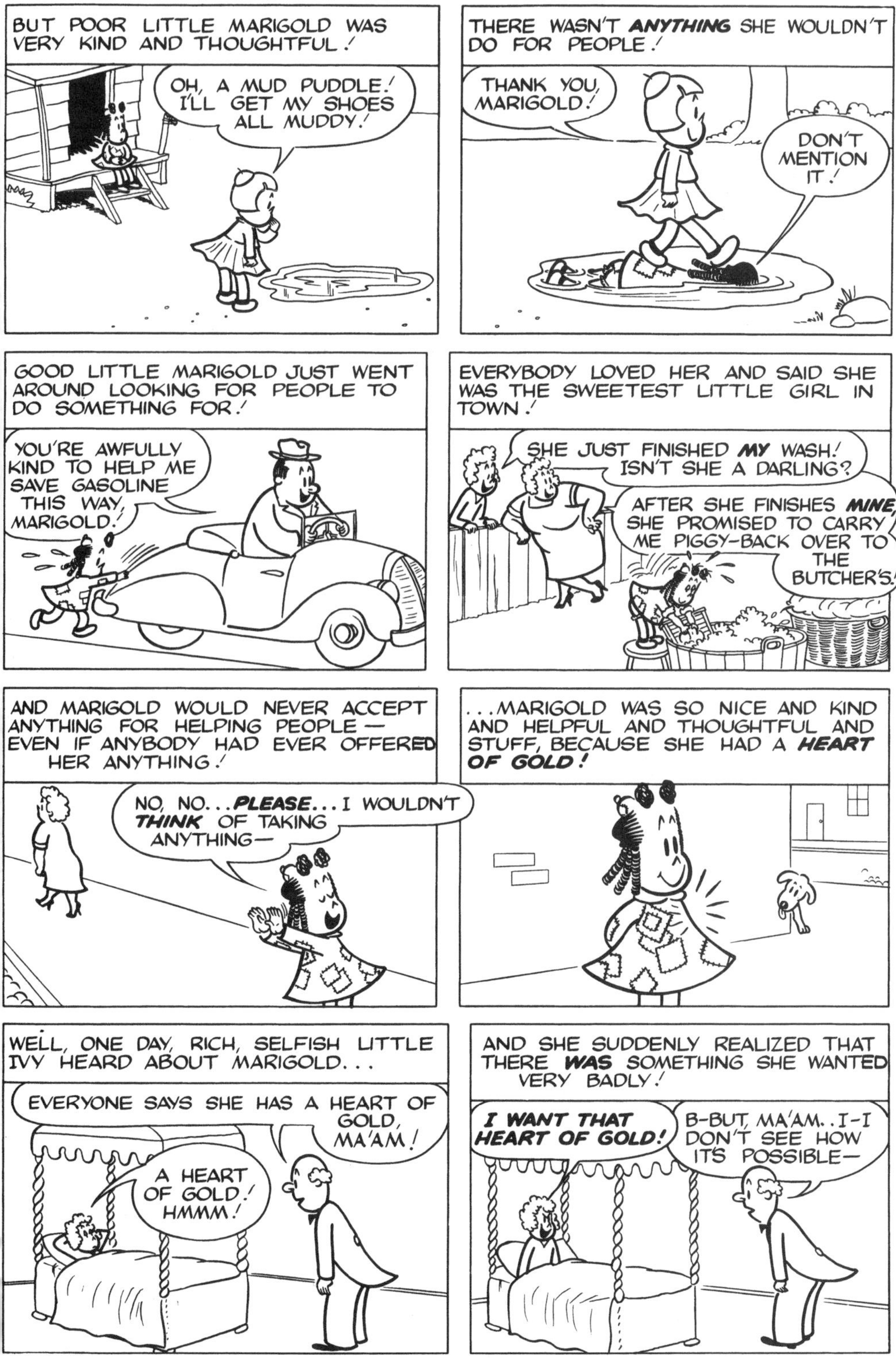

BUT POOR LITTLE MARIGOLD WAS VERY KIND AND THOUGHTFUL!
OH, A MUD PUDDLE! I'LL GET MY SHOES ALL MUDDY!
THERE WASN'T **ANYTHING** SHE WOULDN'T DO FOR PEOPLE!
THANK YOU, MARIGOLD!
DON'T MENTION IT!
GOOD LITTLE MARIGOLD JUST WENT AROUND LOOKING FOR PEOPLE TO DO SOMETHING FOR!
YOU'RE AWFULLY KIND TO HELP ME SAVE GASOLINE THIS WAY, MARIGOLD!
EVERYBODY LOVED HER AND SAID SHE WAS THE SWEETEST LITTLE GIRL IN TOWN!
SHE JUST FINISHED **MY** WASH! ISN'T SHE A DARLING?
AFTER SHE FINISHES **MINE**, SHE PROMISED TO CARRY ME PIGGY-BACK OVER TO THE BUTCHER'S!
AND MARIGOLD WOULD NEVER ACCEPT ANYTHING FOR HELPING PEOPLE— EVEN IF ANYBODY HAD EVER OFFERED HER ANYTHING!
NO, NO...**PLEASE**...I WOULDN'T **THINK** OF TAKING ANYTHING—
...MARIGOLD WAS SO NICE AND KIND AND HELPFUL AND THOUGHTFUL AND STUFF, BECAUSE SHE HAD A **HEART OF GOLD!**
WELL, ONE DAY, RICH, SELFISH LITTLE IVY HEARD ABOUT MARIGOLD...
EVERYONE SAYS SHE HAS A HEART OF GOLD, MA'AM!
A HEART OF GOLD! HMMM!
AND SHE SUDDENLY REALIZED THAT THERE **WAS** SOMETHING SHE WANTED VERY BADLY!
I WANT THAT HEART OF GOLD!
B-BUT, MA'AM..I-I DON'T SEE HOW IT'S POSSIBLE—

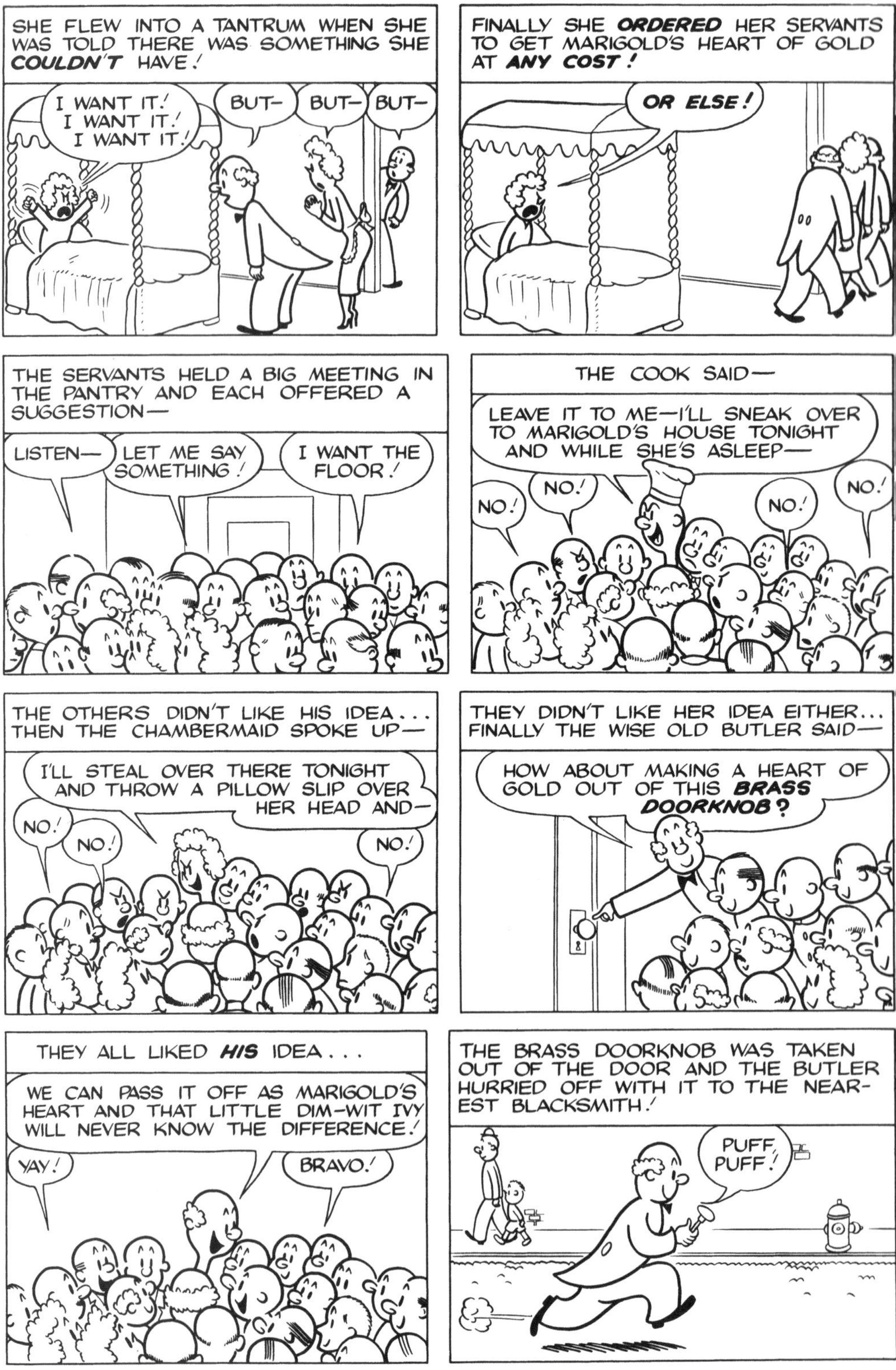
SHE FLEW INTO A TANTRUM WHEN SHE WAS TOLD THERE WAS SOMETHING SHE COULDN'T HAVE!
I WANT IT! I WANT IT! I WANT IT!
BUT–
BUT–
BUT–
FINALLY SHE ORDERED HER SERVANTS TO GET MARIGOLD'S HEART OF GOLD AT ANY COST!
OR ELSE!
THE SERVANTS HELD A BIG MEETING IN THE PANTRY AND EACH OFFERED A SUGGESTION—
LISTEN—
LET ME SAY SOMETHING!
I WANT THE FLOOR!
THE COOK SAID—
LEAVE IT TO ME—I'LL SNEAK OVER TO MARIGOLD'S HOUSE TONIGHT AND WHILE SHE'S ASLEEP—
NO!
NO!
NO!
NO!
THE OTHERS DIDN'T LIKE HIS IDEA... THEN THE CHAMBERMAID SPOKE UP—
I'LL STEAL OVER THERE TONIGHT AND THROW A PILLOW SLIP OVER HER HEAD AND—
NO!
NO!
NO!
THEY DIDN'T LIKE HER IDEA EITHER... FINALLY THE WISE OLD BUTLER SAID—
HOW ABOUT MAKING A HEART OF GOLD OUT OF THIS BRASS DOORKNOB?
THEY ALL LIKED HIS IDEA...
WE CAN PASS IT OFF AS MARIGOLD'S HEART AND THAT LITTLE DIM-WIT IVY WILL NEVER KNOW THE DIFFERENCE!
YAY!
BRAVO!
THE BRASS DOORKNOB WAS TAKEN OUT OF THE DOOR AND THE BUTLER HURRIED OFF WITH IT TO THE NEAREST BLACKSMITH!
PUFF, PUFF!

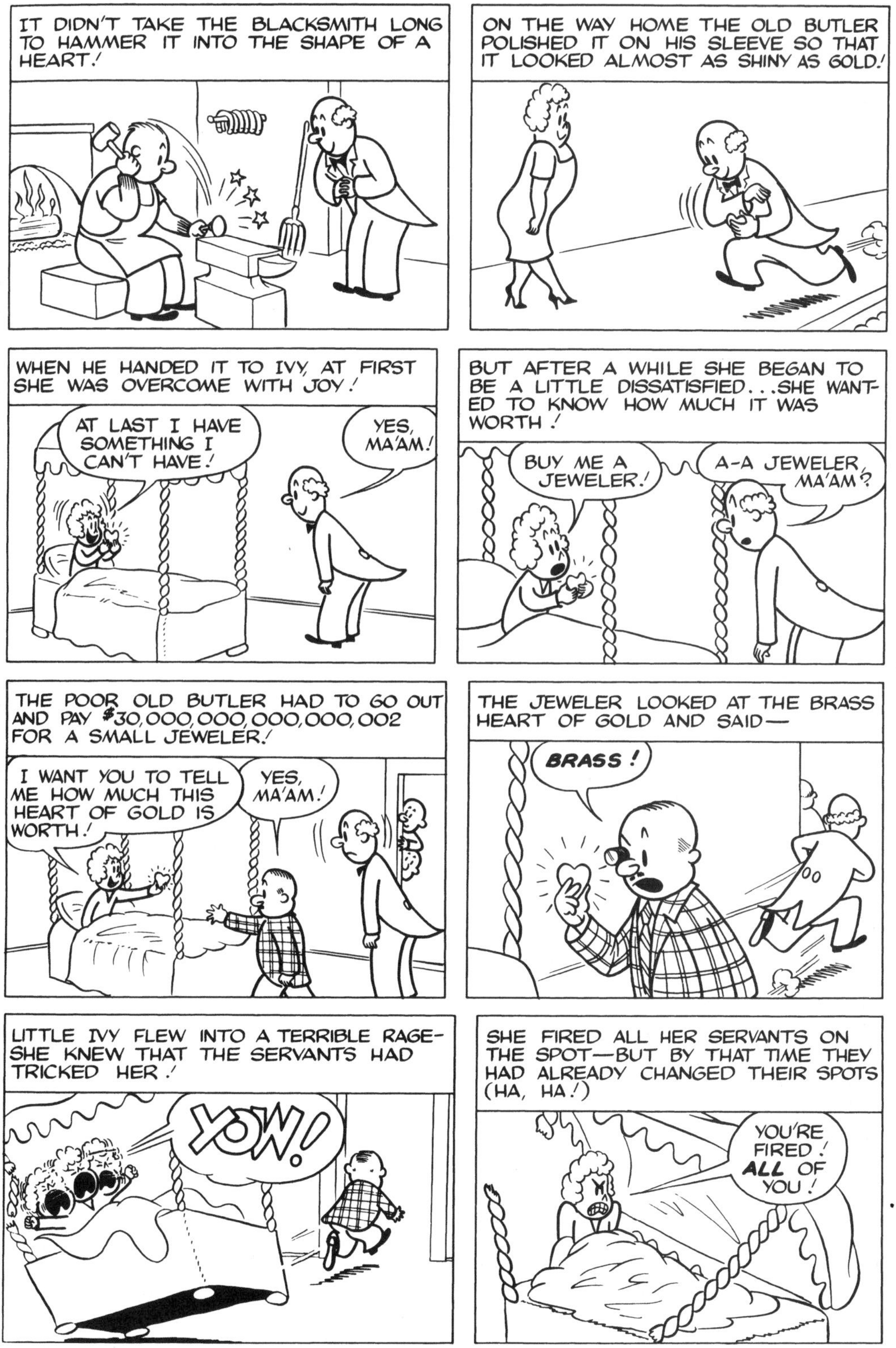
IT DIDN'T TAKE THE BLACKSMITH LONG TO HAMMER IT INTO THE SHAPE OF A HEART!
ON THE WAY HOME THE OLD BUTLER POLISHED IT ON HIS SLEEVE SO THAT IT LOOKED ALMOST AS SHINY AS GOLD!
WHEN HE HANDED IT TO IVY, AT FIRST SHE WAS OVERCOME WITH JOY!
AT LAST I HAVE SOMETHING I CAN'T HAVE!
YES, MA'AM!
BUT AFTER A WHILE SHE BEGAN TO BE A LITTLE DISSATISFIED...SHE WANTED TO KNOW HOW MUCH IT WAS WORTH!
BUY ME A JEWELER!
A-A JEWELER, MA'AM?
THE POOR OLD BUTLER HAD TO GO OUT AND PAY $30,000,000,000,000,002 FOR A SMALL JEWELER!
I WANT YOU TO TELL ME HOW MUCH THIS HEART OF GOLD IS WORTH!
YES, MA'AM!
THE JEWELER LOOKED AT THE BRASS HEART OF GOLD AND SAID—
BRASS!
LITTLE IVY FLEW INTO A TERRIBLE RAGE-SHE KNEW THAT THE SERVANTS HAD TRICKED HER!
YOW!
SHE FIRED ALL HER SERVANTS ON THE SPOT—BUT BY THAT TIME THEY HAD ALREADY CHANGED THEIR SPOTS (HA, HA!)
YOU'RE FIRED! ALL OF YOU!

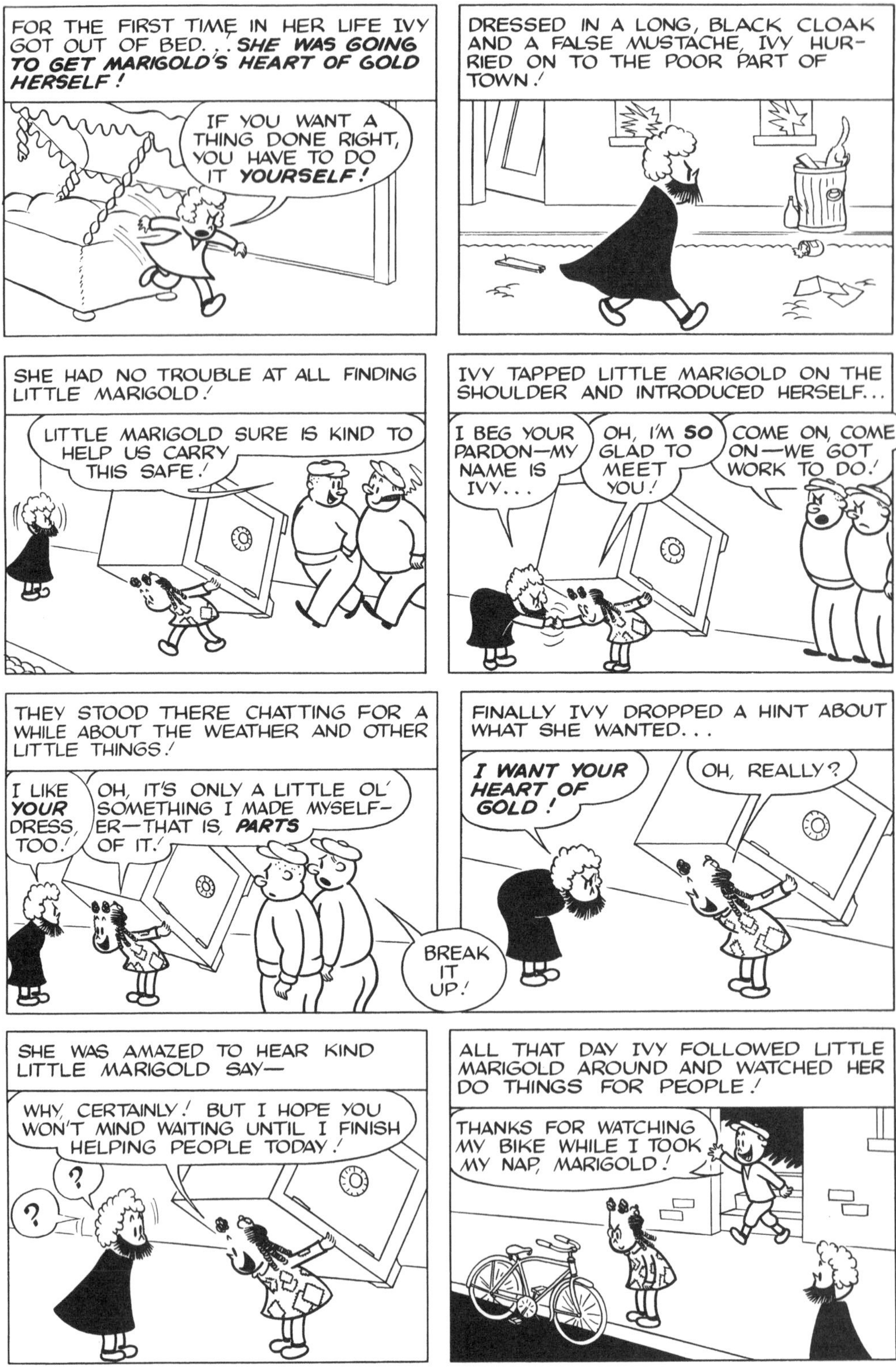
FOR THE FIRST TIME IN HER LIFE IVY GOT OUT OF BED. . . **SHE WAS GOING TO GET MARIGOLD'S HEART OF GOLD HERSELF!**
IF YOU WANT A THING DONE RIGHT, YOU HAVE TO DO IT **YOURSELF!**
DRESSED IN A LONG, BLACK CLOAK AND A FALSE MUSTACHE, IVY HURRIED ON TO THE POOR PART OF TOWN!
SHE HAD NO TROUBLE AT ALL FINDING LITTLE MARIGOLD!
LITTLE MARIGOLD SURE IS KIND TO HELP US CARRY THIS SAFE!
IVY TAPPED LITTLE MARIGOLD ON THE SHOULDER AND INTRODUCED HERSELF...
I BEG YOUR PARDON—MY NAME IS IVY...
OH, I'M **SO** GLAD TO MEET YOU!
COME ON, COME ON—WE GOT WORK TO DO!
THEY STOOD THERE CHATTING FOR A WHILE ABOUT THE WEATHER AND OTHER LITTLE THINGS!
I LIKE **YOUR** DRESS, TOO!
OH, IT'S ONLY A LITTLE OL' SOMETHING I MADE MYSELF—ER—THAT IS, **PARTS** OF IT!
BREAK IT UP!
FINALLY IVY DROPPED A HINT ABOUT WHAT SHE WANTED...
I WANT YOUR HEART OF GOLD!
OH, REALLY?
SHE WAS AMAZED TO HEAR KIND LITTLE MARIGOLD SAY—
WHY, CERTAINLY! BUT I HOPE YOU WON'T MIND WAITING UNTIL I FINISH HELPING PEOPLE TODAY!
?
?
ALL THAT DAY IVY FOLLOWED LITTLE MARIGOLD AROUND AND WATCHED HER DO THINGS FOR PEOPLE!
THANKS FOR WATCHING MY BIKE WHILE I TOOK MY NAP, MARIGOLD!

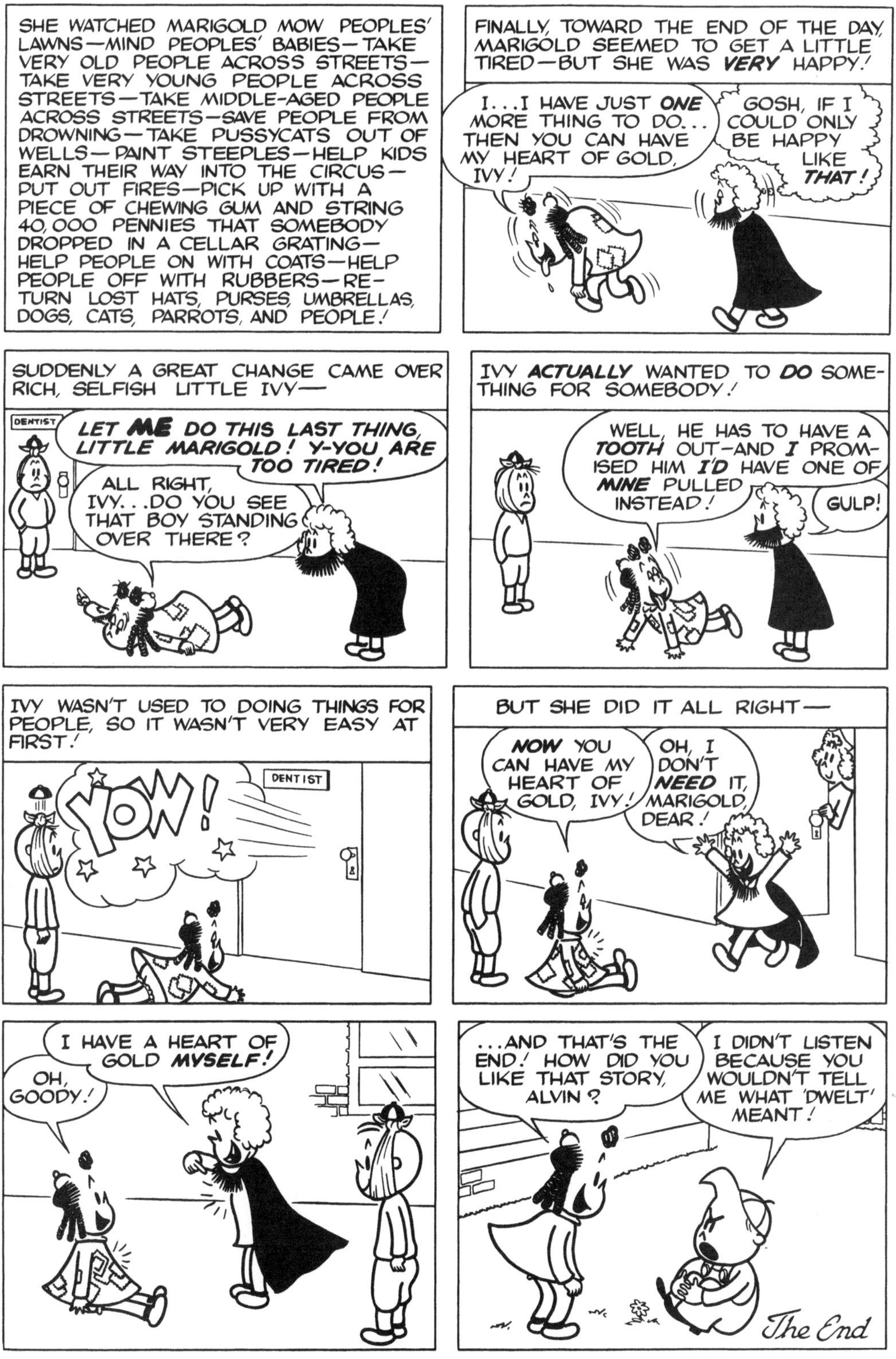

SHE WATCHED MARIGOLD MOW PEOPLES' LAWNS—MIND PEOPLES' BABIES—TAKE VERY OLD PEOPLE ACROSS STREETS—TAKE VERY YOUNG PEOPLE ACROSS STREETS—TAKE MIDDLE-AGED PEOPLE ACROSS STREETS—SAVE PEOPLE FROM DROWNING—TAKE PUSSYCATS OUT OF WELLS—PAINT STEEPLES—HELP KIDS EARN THEIR WAY INTO THE CIRCUS—PUT OUT FIRES—PICK UP WITH A PIECE OF CHEWING GUM AND STRING 40,000 PENNIES THAT SOMEBODY DROPPED IN A CELLAR GRATING—HELP PEOPLE ON WITH COATS—HELP PEOPLE OFF WITH RUBBERS—RETURN LOST HATS, PURSES, UMBRELLAS, DOGS, CATS, PARROTS, AND PEOPLE!
FINALLY, TOWARD THE END OF THE DAY, MARIGOLD SEEMED TO GET A LITTLE TIRED—BUT SHE WAS VERY HAPPY!
I...I HAVE JUST ONE MORE THING TO DO... THEN YOU CAN HAVE MY HEART OF GOLD, IVY!
GOSH, IF I COULD ONLY BE HAPPY LIKE THAT!
SUDDENLY A GREAT CHANGE CAME OVER RICH, SELFISH LITTLE IVY—
DENTIST
LET ME DO THIS LAST THING, LITTLE MARIGOLD! Y-YOU ARE TOO TIRED!
ALL RIGHT, IVY...DO YOU SEE THAT BOY STANDING OVER THERE?
IVY ACTUALLY WANTED TO DO SOMETHING FOR SOMEBODY!
WELL, HE HAS TO HAVE A TOOTH OUT—AND I PROMISED HIM I'D HAVE ONE OF MINE PULLED INSTEAD!
GULP!
IVY WASN'T USED TO DOING THINGS FOR PEOPLE, SO IT WASN'T VERY EASY AT FIRST!
YOW!
DENTIST
BUT SHE DID IT ALL RIGHT—
NOW YOU CAN HAVE MY HEART OF GOLD, IVY!
OH, I DON'T NEED IT, MARIGOLD, DEAR!
I HAVE A HEART OF GOLD MYSELF!
OH, GOODY!
...AND THAT'S THE END! HOW DID YOU LIKE THAT STORY, ALVIN?
I DIDN'T LISTEN BECAUSE YOU WOULDN'T TELL ME WHAT 'DWELT' MEANT!
The End

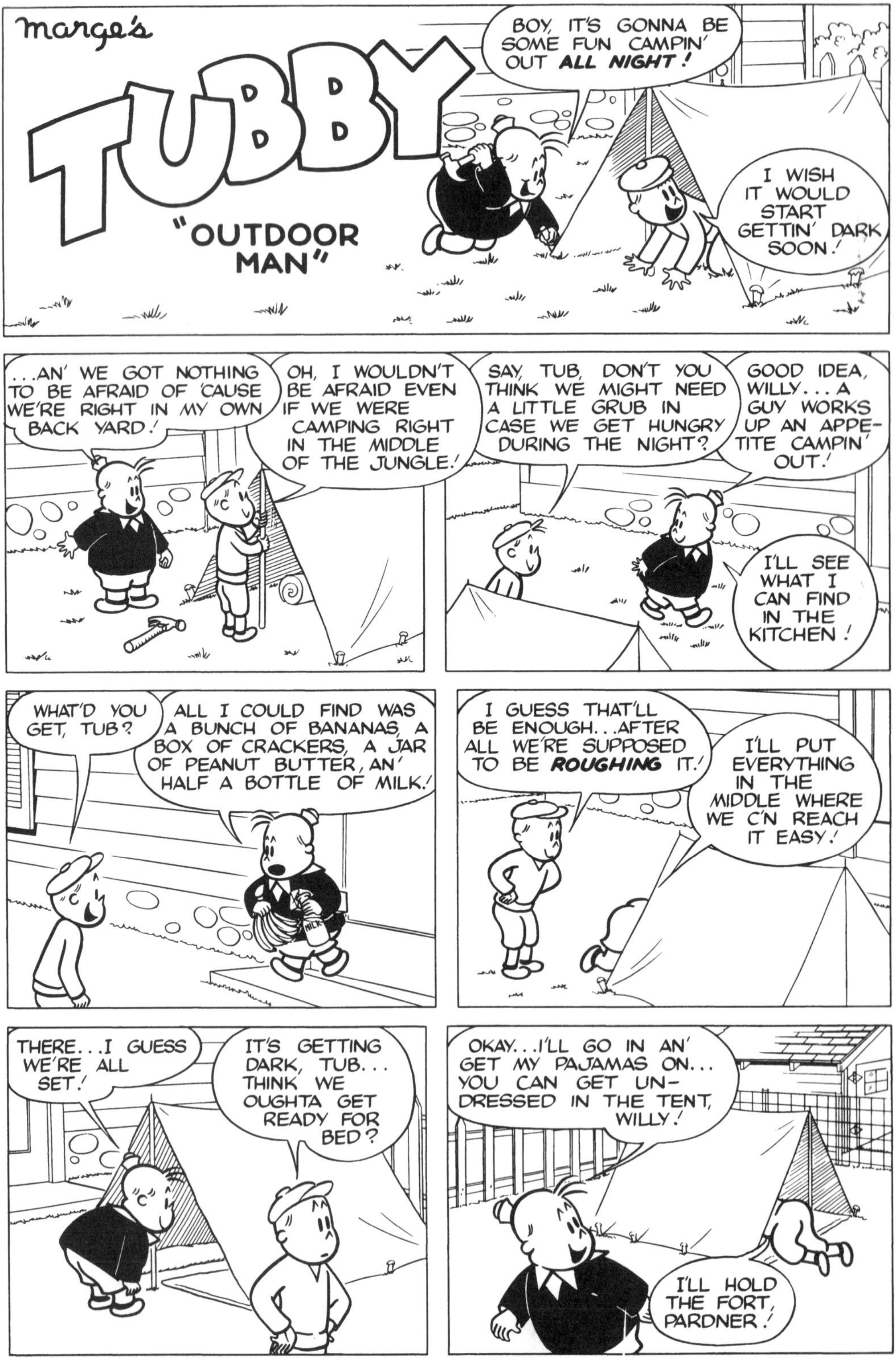
marge's
TUBBY
"OUTDOOR MAN"
BOY, IT'S GONNA BE SOME FUN CAMPIN' OUT ALL NIGHT!
I WISH IT WOULD START GETTIN' DARK SOON!
...AN' WE GOT NOTHING TO BE AFRAID OF 'CAUSE WE'RE RIGHT IN MY OWN BACK YARD!
OH, I WOULDN'T BE AFRAID EVEN IF WE WERE CAMPING RIGHT IN THE MIDDLE OF THE JUNGLE!
SAY, TUB, DON'T YOU THINK WE MIGHT NEED A LITTLE GRUB IN CASE WE GET HUNGRY DURING THE NIGHT?
GOOD IDEA, WILLY... A GUY WORKS UP AN APPE-TITE CAMPIN' OUT!
I'LL SEE WHAT I CAN FIND IN THE KITCHEN!
WHAT'D YOU GET, TUB?
ALL I COULD FIND WAS A BUNCH OF BANANAS, A BOX OF CRACKERS, A JAR OF PEANUT BUTTER, AN' HALF A BOTTLE OF MILK!
MILK
I GUESS THAT'LL BE ENOUGH...AFTER ALL WE'RE SUPPOSED TO BE ROUGHING IT!
I'LL PUT EVERYTHING IN THE MIDDLE WHERE WE C'N REACH IT EASY!
THERE...I GUESS WE'RE ALL SET!
IT'S GETTING DARK, TUB... THINK WE OUGHTA GET READY FOR BED?
OKAY...I'LL GO IN AN' GET MY PAJAMAS ON... YOU CAN GET UN-DRESSED IN THE TENT, WILLY!
I'LL HOLD THE FORT, PARDNER!

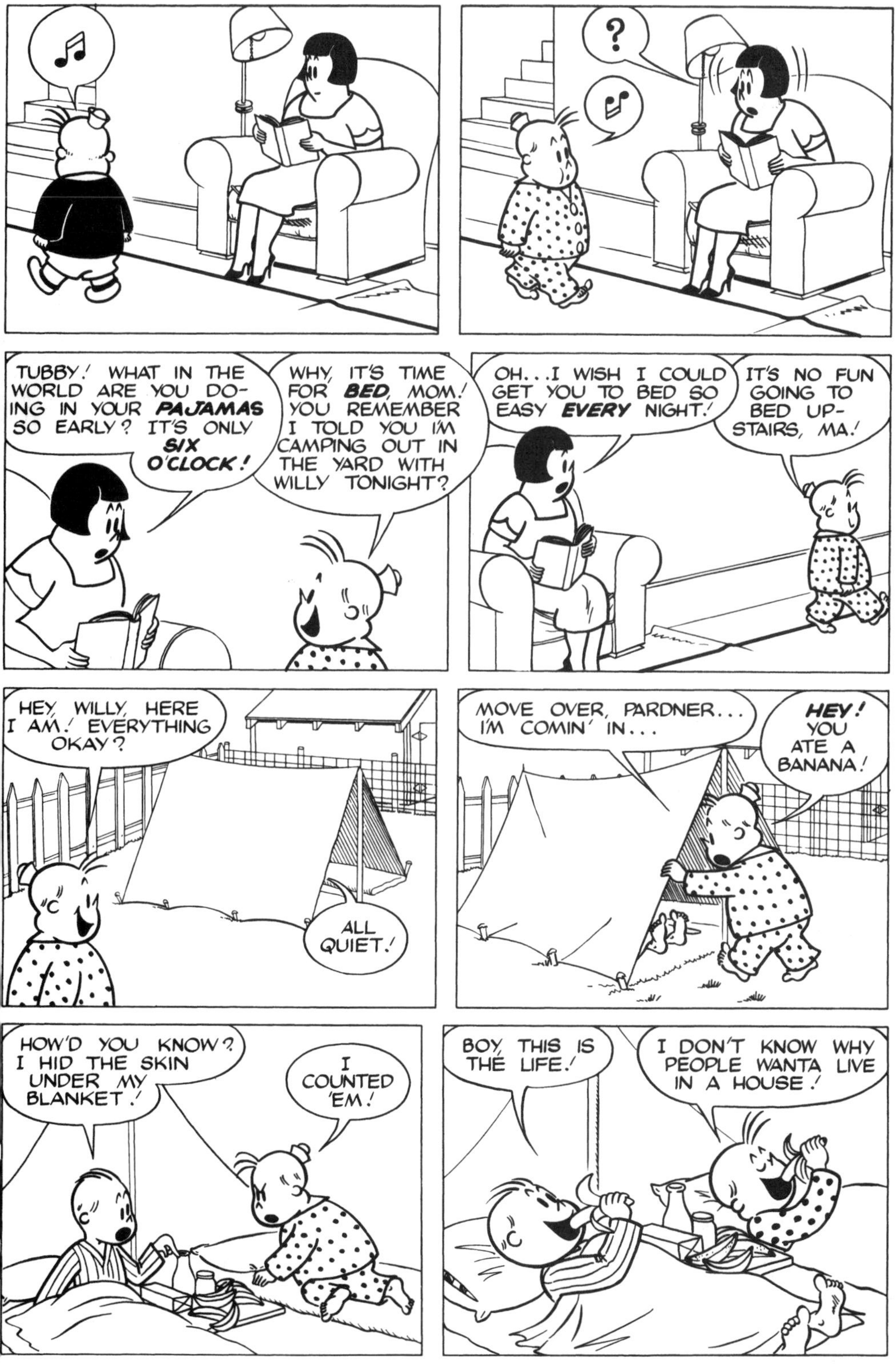
TUBBY! WHAT IN THE WORLD ARE YOU DOING IN YOUR PAJAMAS SO EARLY? IT'S ONLY SIX O'CLOCK!
WHY, IT'S TIME FOR BED, MOM! YOU REMEMBER I TOLD YOU I'M CAMPING OUT IN THE YARD WITH WILLY TONIGHT?
OH... I WISH I COULD GET YOU TO BED SO EASY EVERY NIGHT!
IT'S NO FUN GOING TO BED UPSTAIRS, MA!
HEY, WILLY, HERE I AM! EVERYTHING OKAY?
ALL QUIET!
MOVE OVER, PARDNER... I'M COMIN' IN...
HEY! YOU ATE A BANANA!
HOW'D YOU KNOW? I HID THE SKIN UNDER MY BLANKET!
I COUNTED 'EM!
BOY, THIS IS THE LIFE!
I DON'T KNOW WHY PEOPLE WANTA LIVE IN A HOUSE!

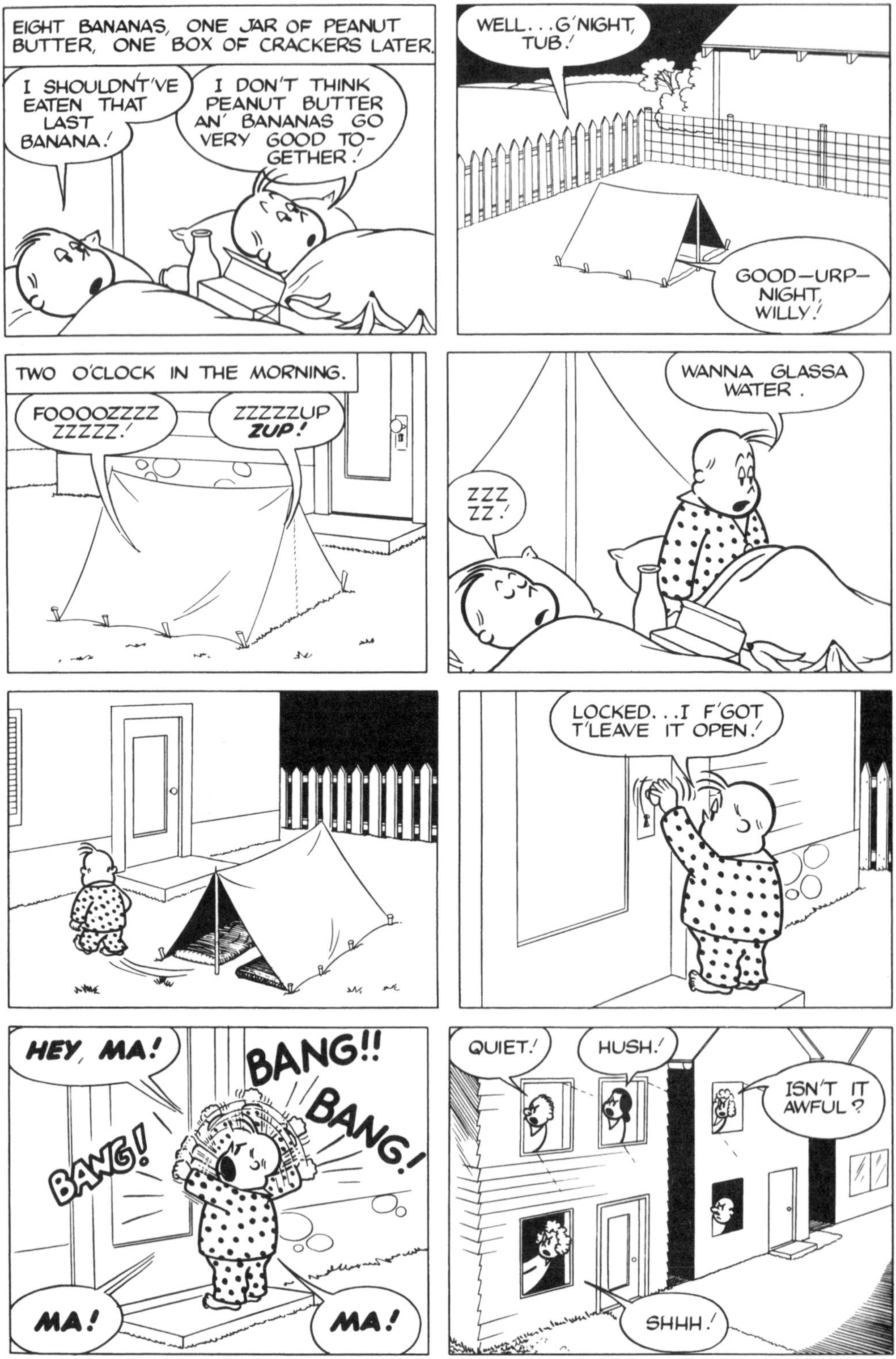

EIGHT BANANAS, ONE JAR OF PEANUT BUTTER, ONE BOX OF CRACKERS LATER.
I SHOULDN'T'VE EATEN THAT LAST BANANA!
I DON'T THINK PEANUT BUTTER AN' BANANAS GO VERY GOOD TO-GETHER!
WELL...G'NIGHT, TUB!
GOOD—URP—NIGHT, WILLY!
TWO O'CLOCK IN THE MORNING.
FOOOOZZZZ ZZZZZ!
ZZZZZUP ZUP!
WANNA GLASSA WATER.
ZZZ ZZ!
LOCKED...I F'GOT T'LEAVE IT OPEN!
HEY, MA!
BANG!!
BANG!
BANG!
MA!
MA!
QUIET!
HUSH!
ISN'T IT AWFUL?
SHHH!

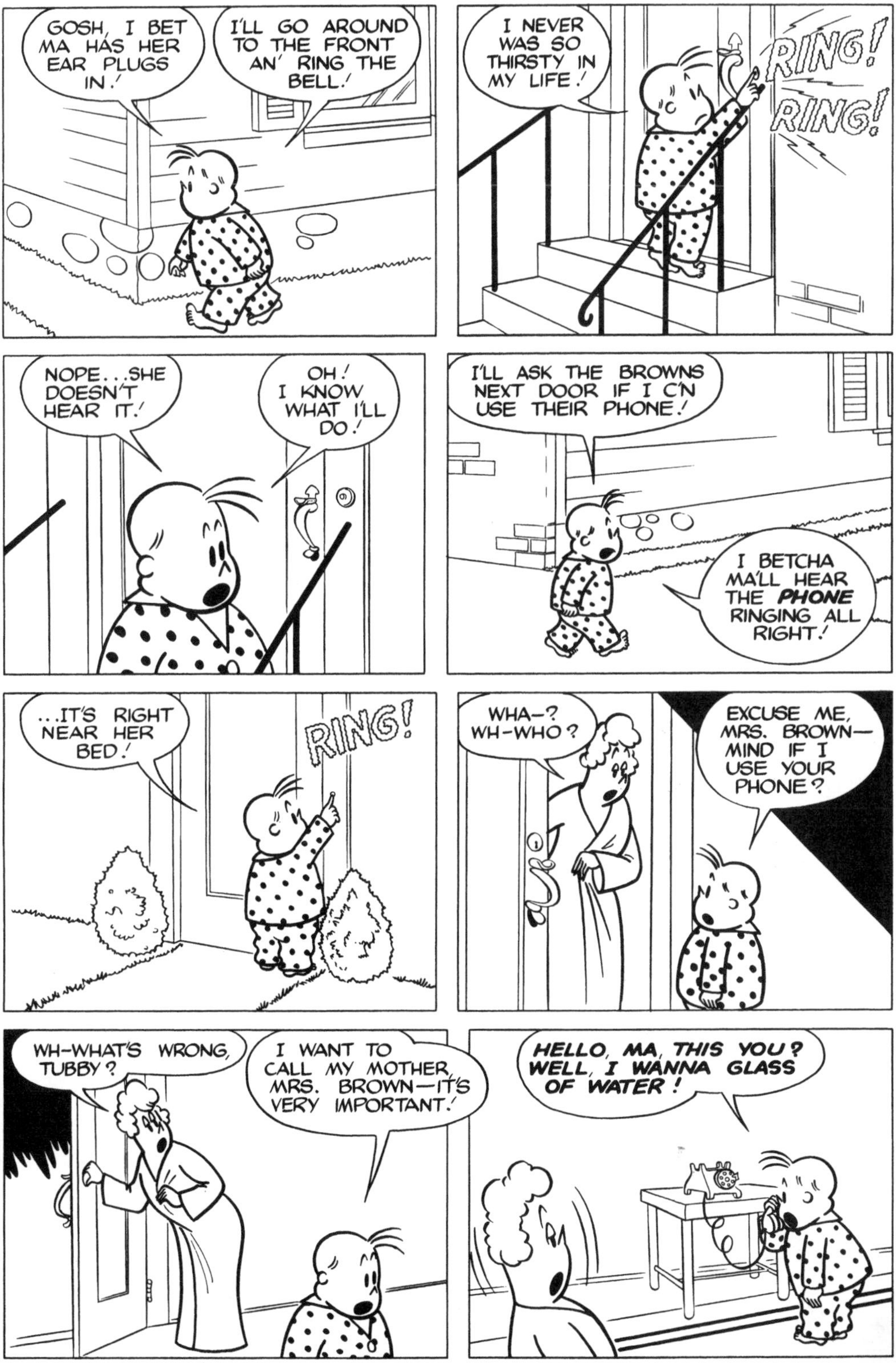
GOSH, I BET MA HAS HER EAR PLUGS IN.!
I'LL GO AROUND TO THE FRONT AN' RING THE BELL.!
I NEVER WAS SO THIRSTY IN MY LIFE.!
RING! RING!
NOPE...SHE DOESN'T HEAR IT.!
OH! I KNOW WHAT I'LL DO.!
I'LL ASK THE BROWNS NEXT DOOR IF I C'N USE THEIR PHONE.!
I BETCHA MA'LL HEAR THE PHONE RINGING ALL RIGHT.!
...IT'S RIGHT NEAR HER BED.!
RING!
WHA-? WH-WHO?
EXCUSE ME, MRS. BROWN— MIND IF I USE YOUR PHONE?
WH-WHAT'S WRONG, TUBBY?
I WANT TO CALL MY MOTHER, MRS. BROWN—IT'S VERY IMPORTANT.!
HELLO, MA, THIS YOU? WELL, I WANNA GLASS OF WATER!

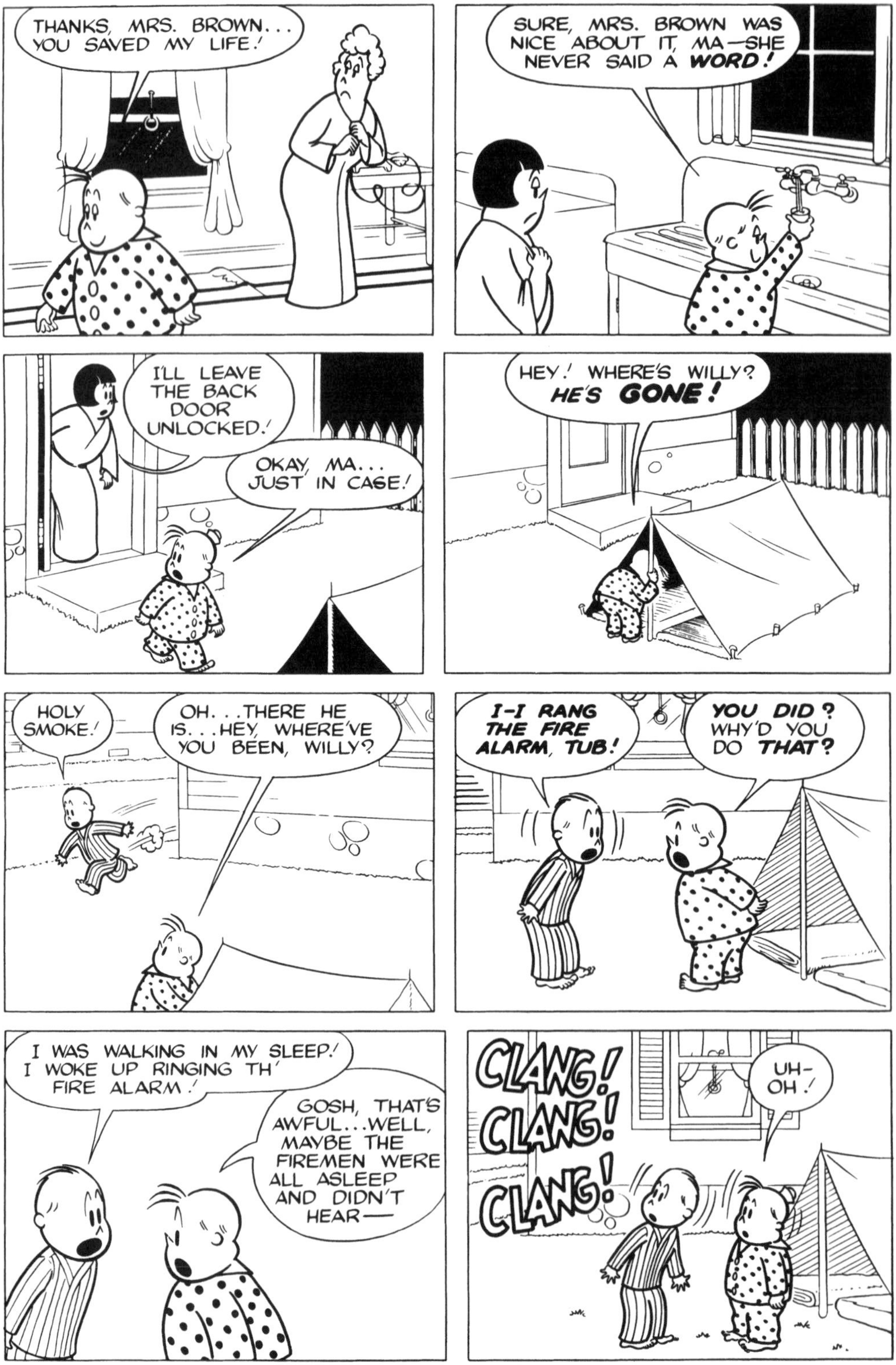
THANKS, MRS. BROWN... YOU SAVED MY LIFE!
SURE, MRS. BROWN WAS NICE ABOUT IT, MA—SHE NEVER SAID A **WORD**!
I'LL LEAVE THE BACK DOOR UNLOCKED!
OKAY, MA... JUST IN CASE!
HEY! WHERE'S WILLY? HE'S **GONE**!
HOLY SMOKE!
OH...THERE HE IS...HEY, WHERE'VE YOU BEEN, WILLY?
I-I RANG THE FIRE ALARM, TUB!
YOU DID? WHY'D YOU DO THAT?
I WAS WALKING IN MY SLEEP! I WOKE UP RINGING TH' FIRE ALARM!
GOSH, THAT'S AWFUL...WELL, MAYBE THE FIREMEN WERE ALL ASLEEP AND DIDN'T HEAR—
CLANG! CLANG! CLANG!
UH-OH!

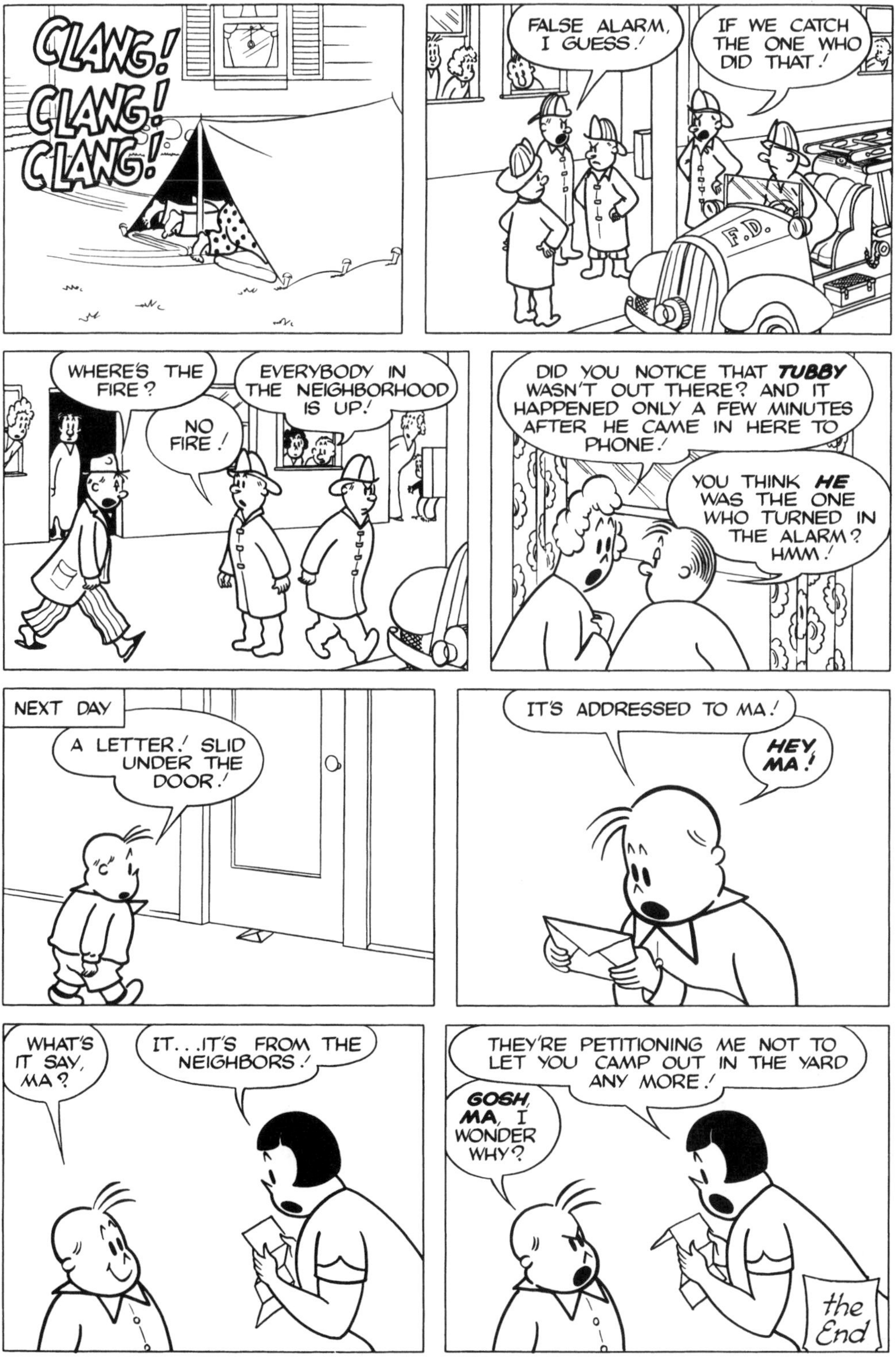
CLANG! CLANG! CLANG!
FALSE ALARM, I GUESS!
IF WE CATCH THE ONE WHO DID THAT!
WHERE'S THE FIRE?
NO FIRE!
EVERYBODY IN THE NEIGHBORHOOD IS UP!
DID YOU NOTICE THAT TUBBY WASN'T OUT THERE? AND IT HAPPENED ONLY A FEW MINUTES AFTER HE CAME IN HERE TO PHONE!
YOU THINK HE WAS THE ONE WHO TURNED IN THE ALARM? HMM!
NEXT DAY
A LETTER! SLID UNDER THE DOOR!
IT'S ADDRESSED TO MA!
HEY, MA!
WHAT'S IT SAY, MA?
IT...IT'S FROM THE NEIGHBORS!
THEY'RE PETITIONING ME NOT TO LET YOU CAMP OUT IN THE YARD ANY MORE!
GOSH, MA, I WONDER WHY?
the End

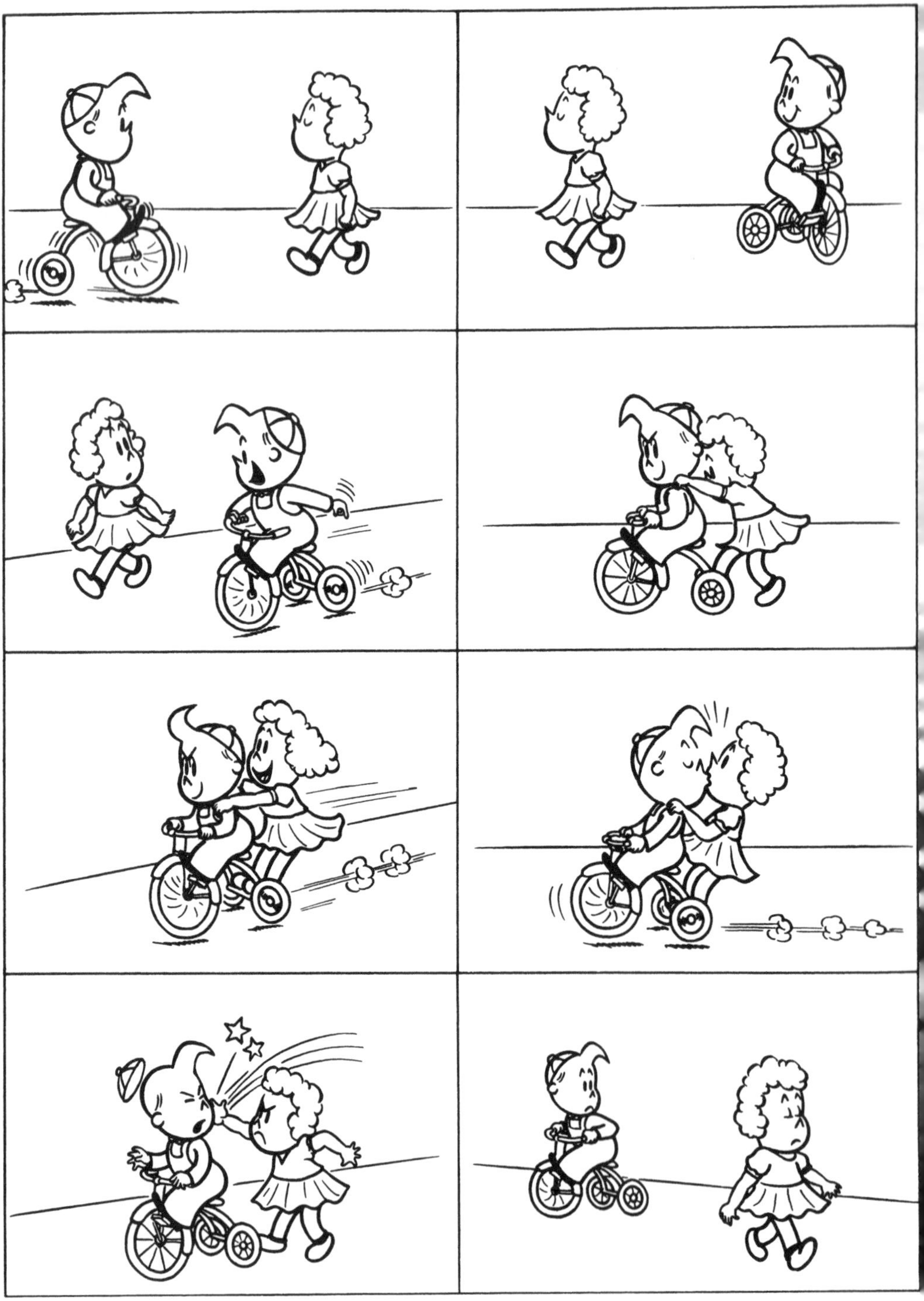

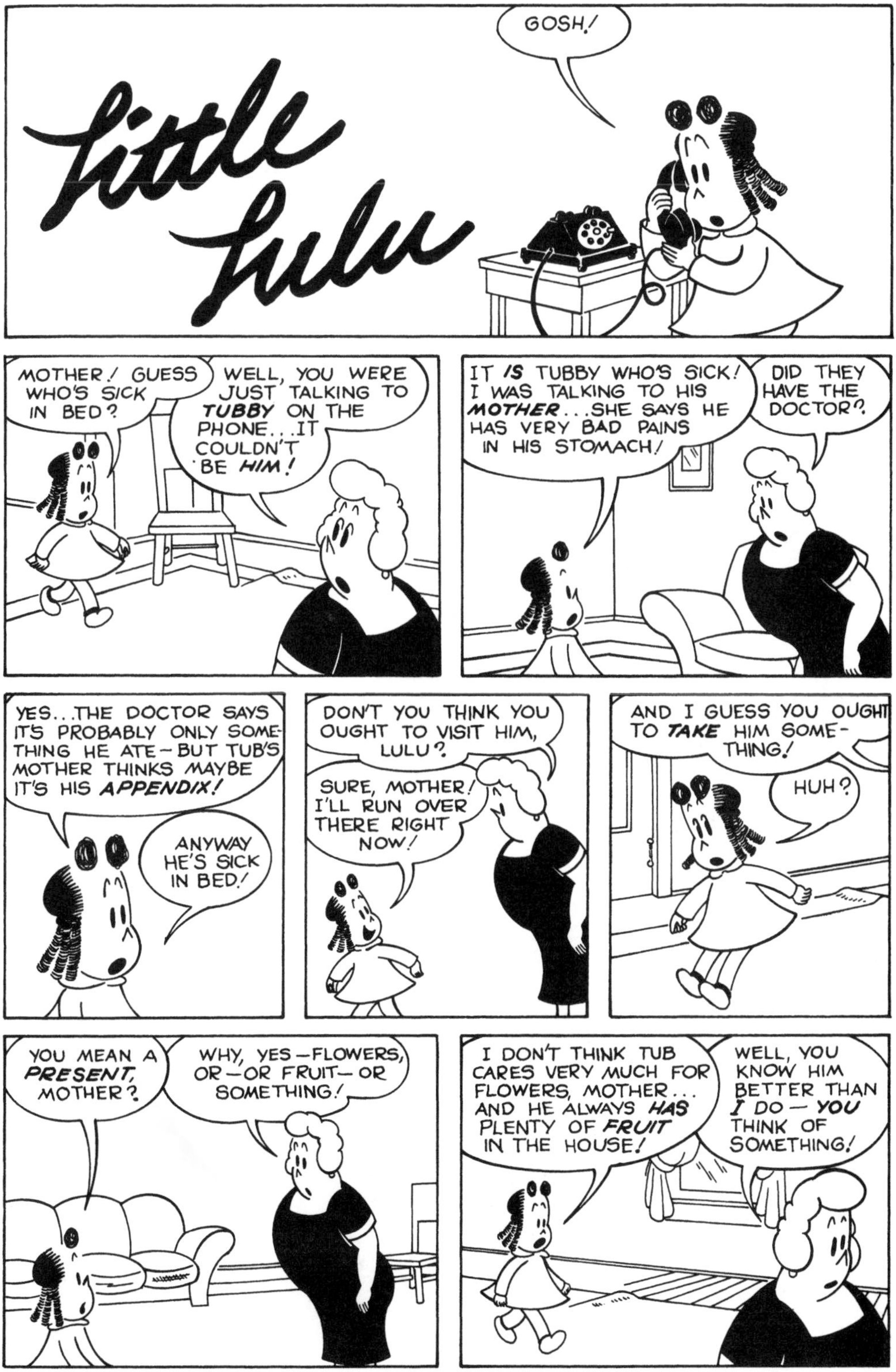
little lulu
GOSH!
MOTHER! GUESS WHO'S SICK IN BED?
WELL, YOU WERE JUST TALKING TO TUBBY ON THE PHONE...IT COULDN'T BE HIM!
IT IS TUBBY WHO'S SICK! I WAS TALKING TO HIS MOTHER...SHE SAYS HE HAS VERY BAD PAINS IN HIS STOMACH!
DID THEY HAVE THE DOCTOR?
YES...THE DOCTOR SAYS IT'S PROBABLY ONLY SOMETHING HE ATE—BUT TUB'S MOTHER THINKS MAYBE IT'S HIS APPENDIX!
ANYWAY HE'S SICK IN BED!
DON'T YOU THINK YOU OUGHT TO VISIT HIM, LULU?
SURE, MOTHER! I'LL RUN OVER THERE RIGHT NOW!
AND I GUESS YOU OUGHT TO TAKE HIM SOMETHING!
HUH?
YOU MEAN A PRESENT, MOTHER?
WHY, YES—FLOWERS, OR—OR FRUIT—OR SOMETHING!
I DON'T THINK TUB CARES VERY MUCH FOR FLOWERS, MOTHER... AND HE ALWAYS HAS PLENTY OF FRUIT IN THE HOUSE!
WELL, YOU KNOW HIM BETTER THAN I DO—YOU THINK OF SOMETHING!

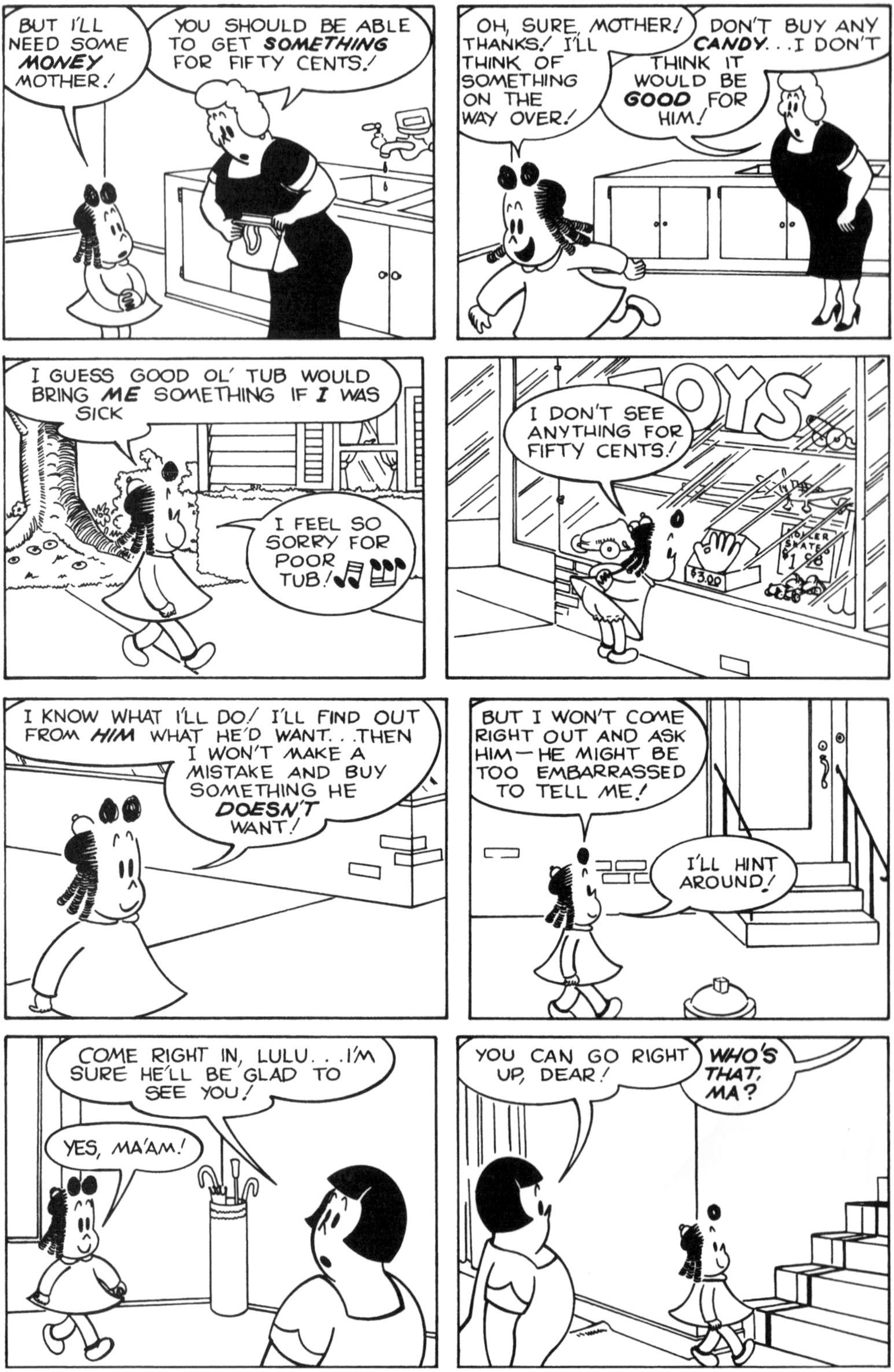
BUT I'LL NEED SOME MONEY MOTHER!
YOU SHOULD BE ABLE TO GET SOMETHING FOR FIFTY CENTS!
OH, SURE, MOTHER! THANKS! I'LL THINK OF SOMETHING ON THE WAY OVER!
DON'T BUY ANY CANDY...I DON'T THINK IT WOULD BE GOOD FOR HIM!
I GUESS GOOD OL' TUB WOULD BRING ME SOMETHING IF I WAS SICK
I FEEL SO SORRY FOR POOR TUB!
TOYS
I DON'T SEE ANYTHING FOR FIFTY CENTS!
$3.00
I KNOW WHAT I'LL DO! I'LL FIND OUT FROM HIM WHAT HE'D WANT...THEN I WON'T MAKE A MISTAKE AND BUY SOMETHING HE DOESN'T WANT!
BUT I WON'T COME RIGHT OUT AND ASK HIM—HE MIGHT BE TOO EMBARRASSED TO TELL ME!
I'LL HINT AROUND!
COME RIGHT IN, LULU...I'M SURE HE'LL BE GLAD TO SEE YOU!
YES, MA'AM!
YOU CAN GO RIGHT UP, DEAR!
WHO'S THAT, MA?

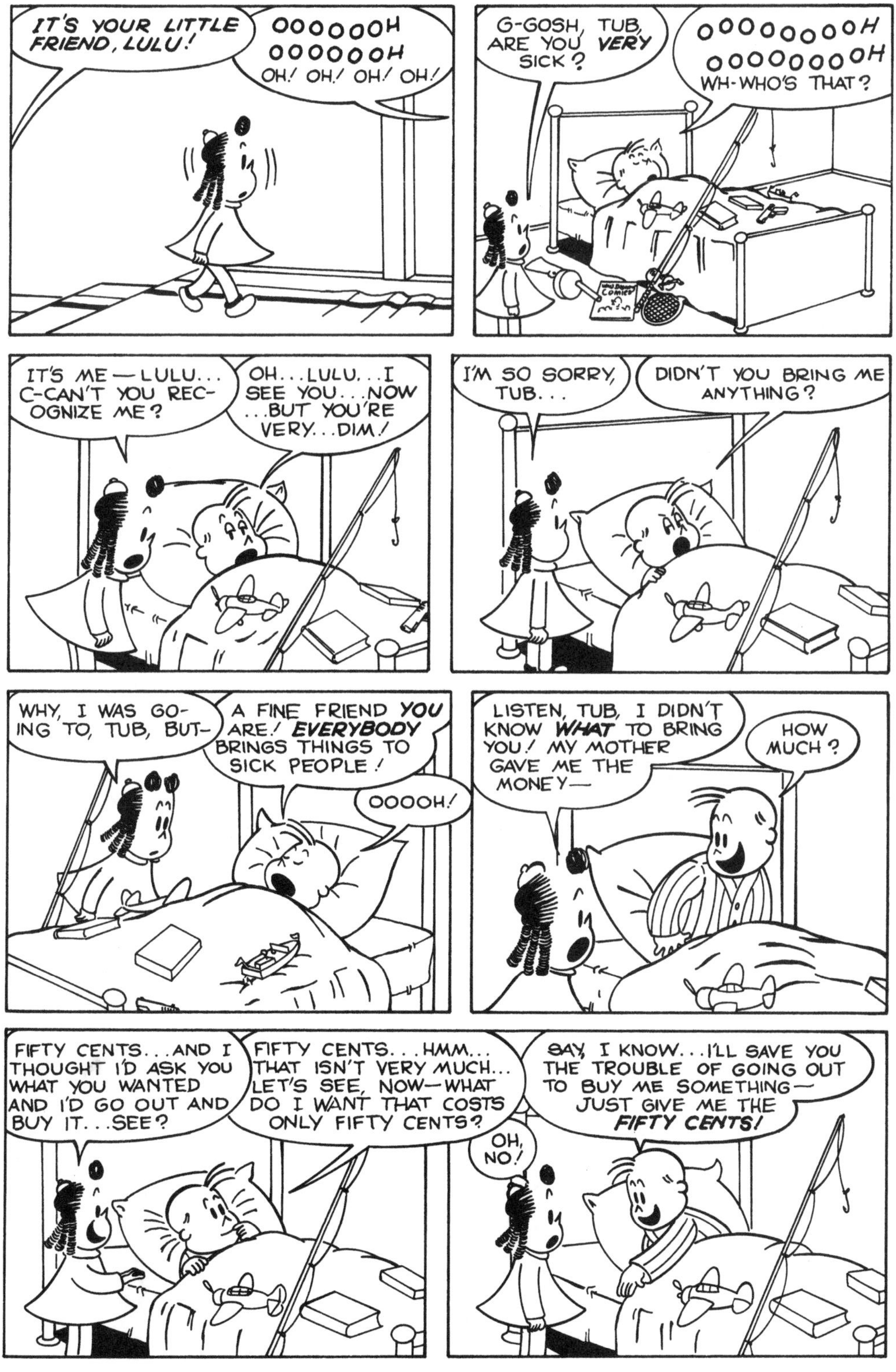
IT'S YOUR LITTLE FRIEND, LULU!
OOOOOOOH OOOOOOOH OH! OH! OH! OH!
G-GOSH, TUB, ARE YOU VERY SICK?
OOOOOOOOOH OOOOOOOOOH WH-WHO'S THAT?
IT'S ME—LULU... C-CAN'T YOU RECOGNIZE ME?
OH...LULU...I SEE YOU...NOW ...BUT YOU'RE VERY...DIM!
I'M SO SORRY, TUB...
DIDN'T YOU BRING ME ANYTHING?
WHY, I WAS GOING TO, TUB, BUT-
A FINE FRIEND YOU ARE! EVERYBODY BRINGS THINGS TO SICK PEOPLE!
OOOOH!
LISTEN, TUB, I DIDN'T KNOW WHAT TO BRING YOU! MY MOTHER GAVE ME THE MONEY—
HOW MUCH?
FIFTY CENTS...AND I THOUGHT I'D ASK YOU WHAT YOU WANTED AND I'D GO OUT AND BUY IT...SEE?
FIFTY CENTS...HMM... THAT ISN'T VERY MUCH... LET'S SEE, NOW—WHAT DO I WANT THAT COSTS ONLY FIFTY CENTS?
SAY, I KNOW...I'LL SAVE YOU THE TROUBLE OF GOING OUT TO BUY ME SOMETHING— JUST GIVE ME THE FIFTY CENTS!
OH, NO!

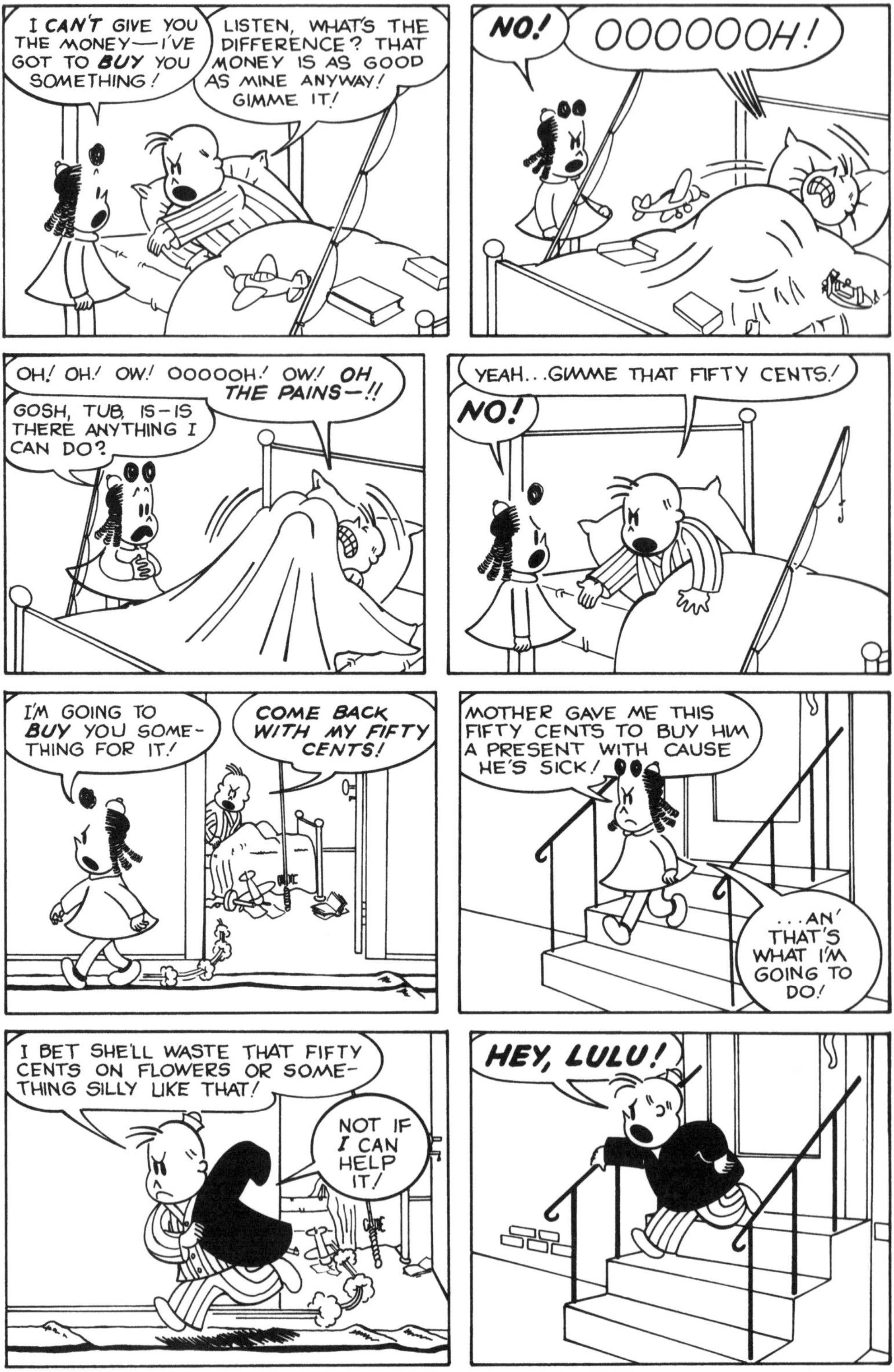
I CAN'T GIVE YOU THE MONEY—I'VE GOT TO BUY YOU SOMETHING!
LISTEN, WHAT'S THE DIFFERENCE? THAT MONEY IS AS GOOD AS MINE ANYWAY! GIMME IT!
NO!
OOOOOOH!
OH! OH! OW! OOOOOH! OW! OH THE PAINS—!!
GOSH, TUB, IS—IS THERE ANYTHING I CAN DO?
YEAH...GIMME THAT FIFTY CENTS!
NO!
I'M GOING TO BUY YOU SOMETHING FOR IT!
COME BACK WITH MY FIFTY CENTS!
MOTHER GAVE ME THIS FIFTY CENTS TO BUY HIM A PRESENT WITH CAUSE HE'S SICK!
...AN' THAT'S WHAT I'M GOING TO DO!
I BET SHE'LL WASTE THAT FIFTY CENTS ON FLOWERS OR SOMETHING SILLY LIKE THAT!
NOT IF I CAN HELP IT!
HEY, LULU!

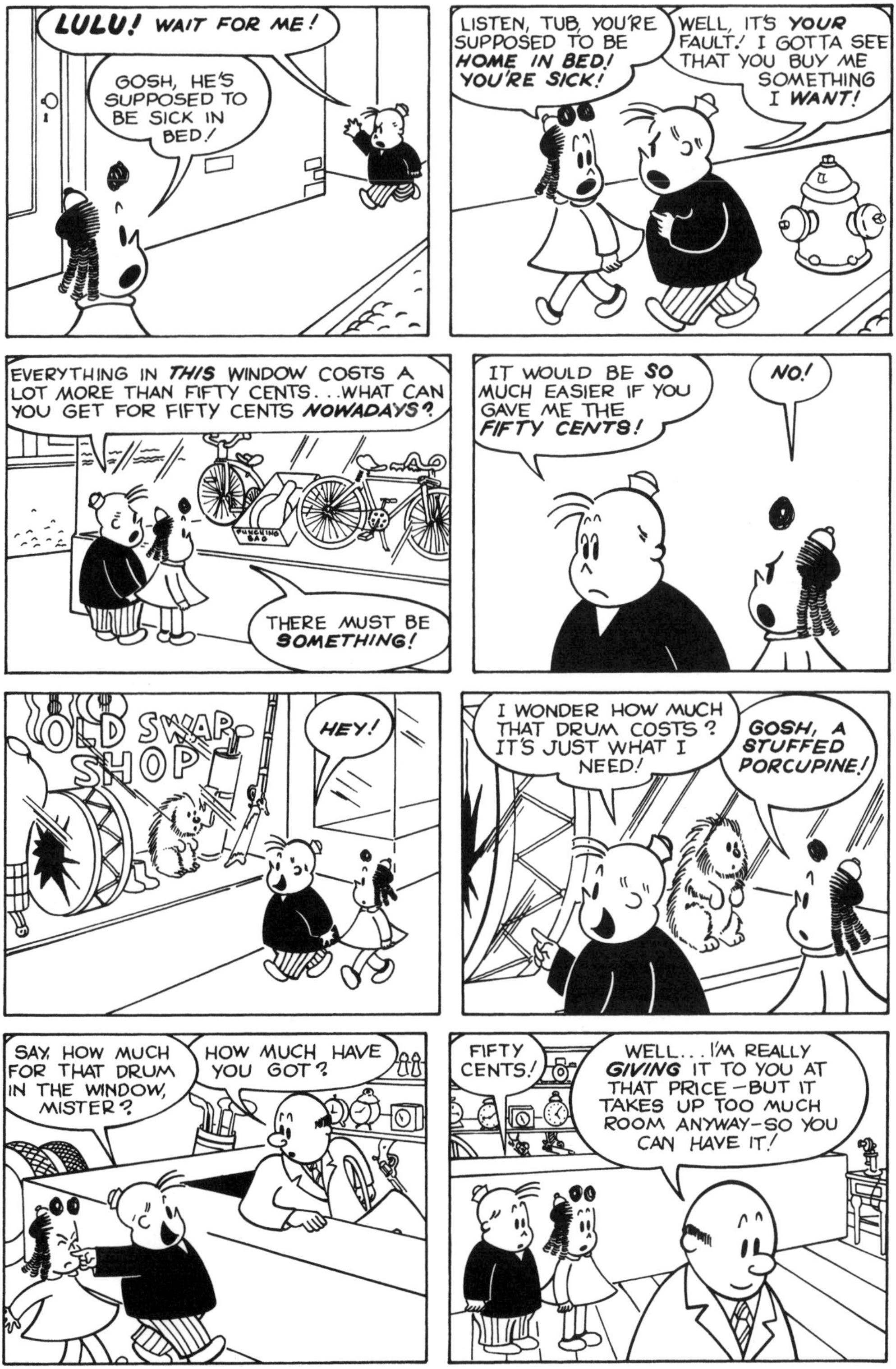
LULU! WAIT FOR ME!
GOSH, HE'S SUPPOSED TO BE SICK IN BED!
LISTEN, TUB, YOU'RE SUPPOSED TO BE HOME IN BED! YOU'RE SICK!
WELL, IT'S YOUR FAULT! I GOTTA SEE THAT YOU BUY ME SOMETHING I WANT!
EVERYTHING IN THIS WINDOW COSTS A LOT MORE THAN FIFTY CENTS...WHAT CAN YOU GET FOR FIFTY CENTS NOWADAYS?
PUNCHING BAG
THERE MUST BE SOMETHING!
IT WOULD BE SO MUCH EASIER IF YOU GAVE ME THE FIFTY CENTS!
NO!
OLD SWAP SHOP
HEY!
I WONDER HOW MUCH THAT DRUM COSTS? IT'S JUST WHAT I NEED!
GOSH, A STUFFED PORCUPINE!
SAY, HOW MUCH FOR THAT DRUM IN THE WINDOW, MISTER?
HOW MUCH HAVE YOU GOT?
FIFTY CENTS!
WELL... I'M REALLY GIVING IT TO YOU AT THAT PRICE—BUT IT TAKES UP TOO MUCH ROOM ANYWAY—SO YOU CAN HAVE IT!

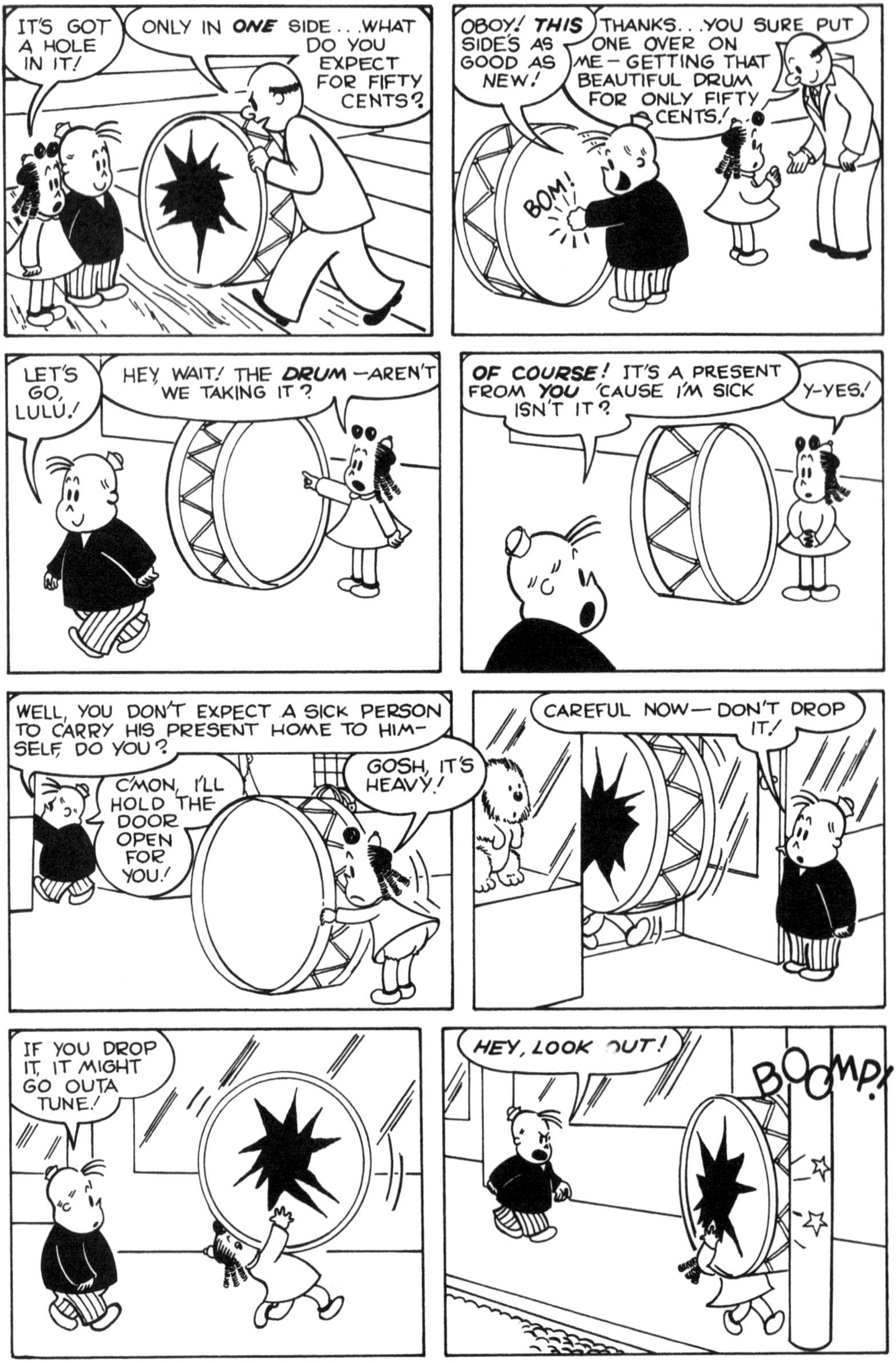
IT'S GOT A HOLE IN IT!
ONLY IN ONE SIDE...WHAT DO YOU EXPECT FOR FIFTY CENTS?
OBOY! THIS SIDE'S AS GOOD AS NEW!
THANKS...YOU SURE PUT ONE OVER ON ME—GETTING THAT BEAUTIFUL DRUM FOR ONLY FIFTY CENTS!
BOM!
LET'S GO, LULU!
HEY, WAIT! THE DRUM—AREN'T WE TAKING IT?
OF COURSE! IT'S A PRESENT FROM YOU 'CAUSE I'M SICK ISN'T IT?
Y-YES!
WELL, YOU DON'T EXPECT A SICK PERSON TO CARRY HIS PRESENT HOME TO HIMSELF, DO YOU?
C'MON, I'LL HOLD THE DOOR OPEN FOR YOU!
GOSH, IT'S HEAVY!
CAREFUL NOW—DON'T DROP IT!
IF YOU DROP IT, IT MIGHT GO OUTA TUNE!
HEY, LOOK OUT!
BOOMP!

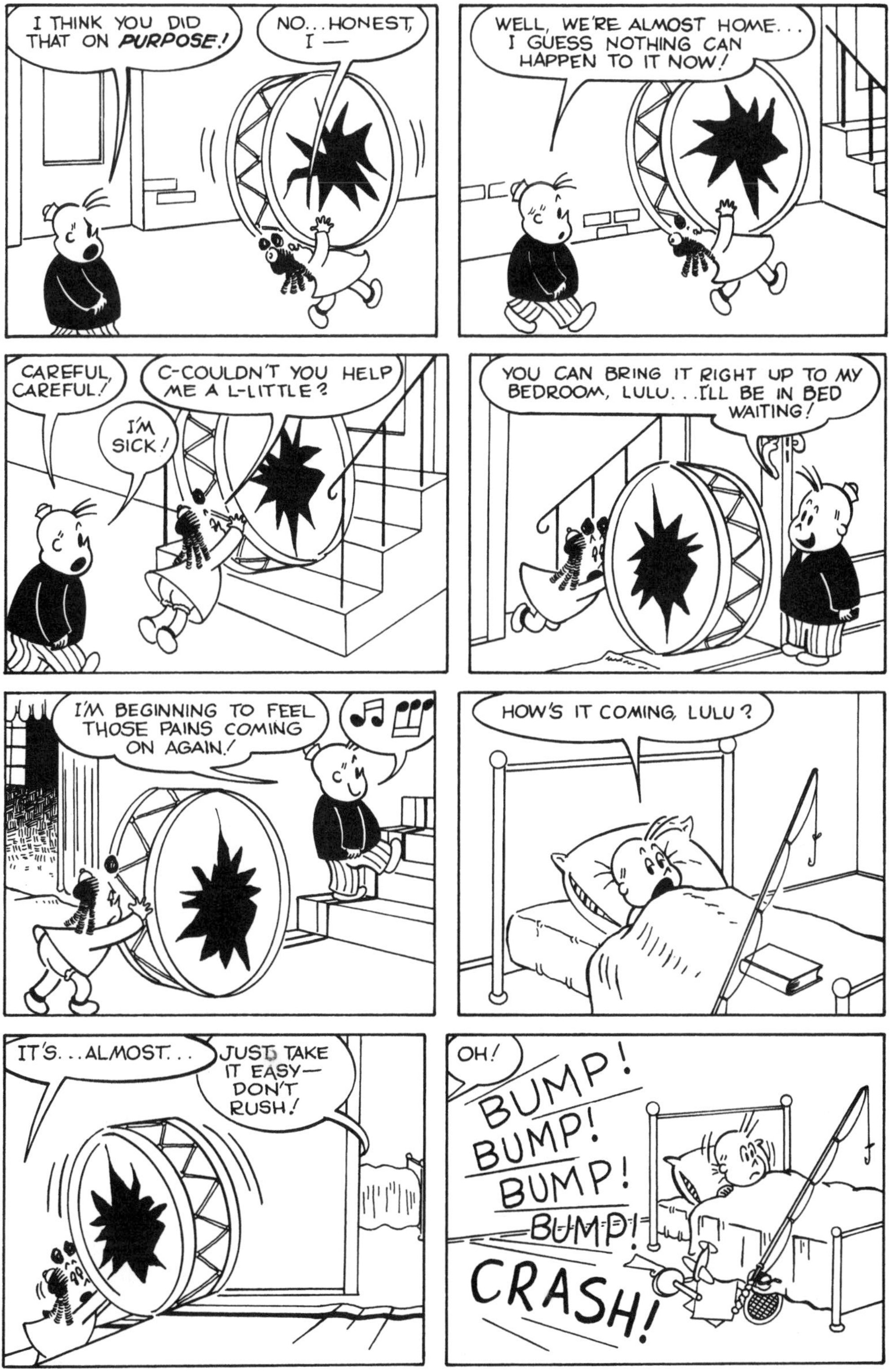
I THINK YOU DID THAT ON *PURPOSE*!
NO...HONEST, I —
WELL, WE'RE ALMOST HOME... I GUESS NOTHING CAN HAPPEN TO IT NOW!
CAREFUL, CAREFUL!
C-COULDN'T YOU HELP ME A L-LITTLE?
I'M SICK!
YOU CAN BRING IT RIGHT UP TO MY BEDROOM, LULU...I'LL BE IN BED WAITING!
I'M BEGINNING TO FEEL THOSE PAINS COMING ON AGAIN!
HOW'S IT COMING, LULU?
IT'S...ALMOST...
JUST TAKE IT EASY— DON'T RUSH!
OH!
BUMP!
BUMP!
BUMP!
BUMP!
CRASH!

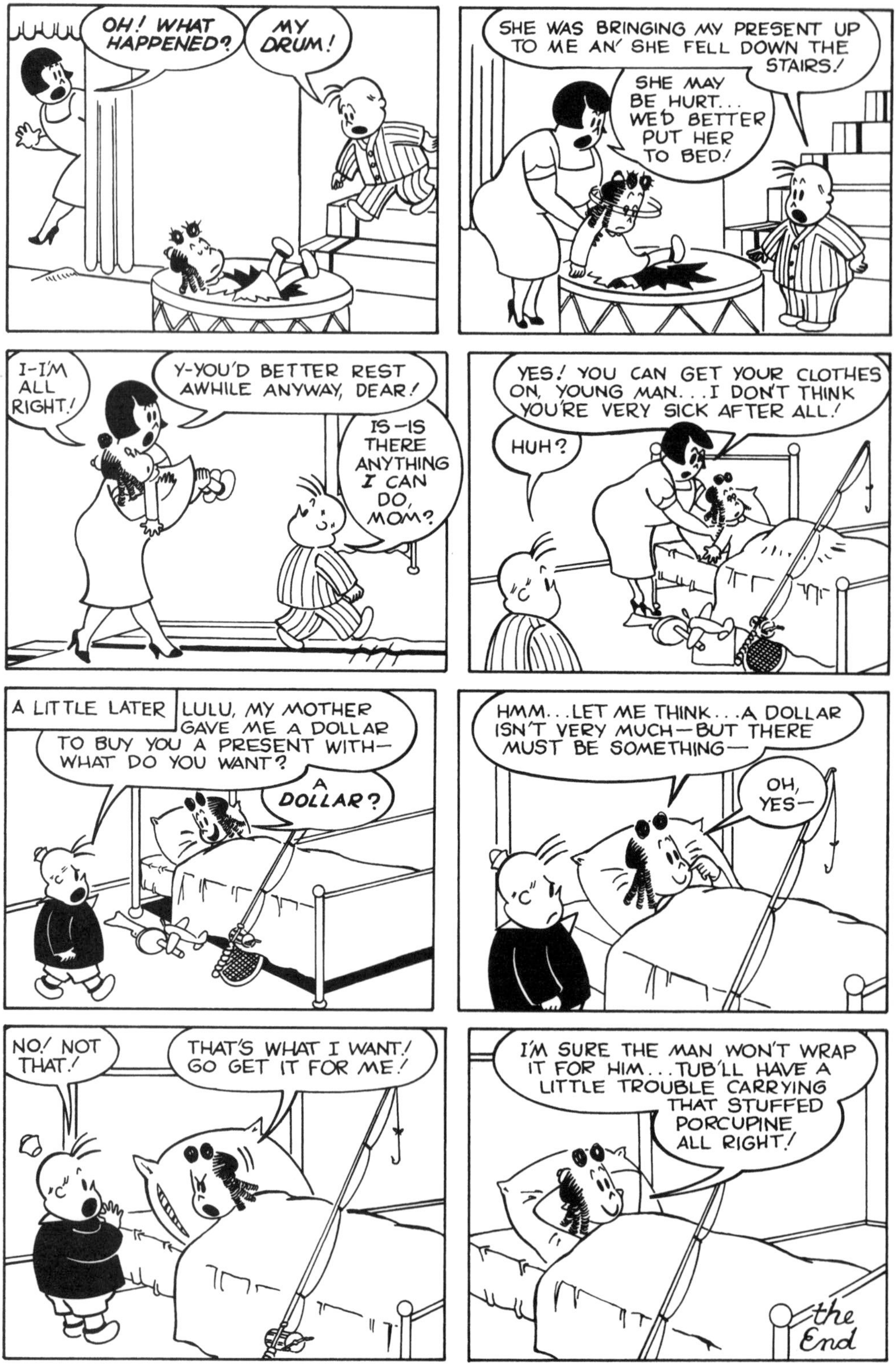
OH! WHAT HAPPENED?
MY DRUM!
SHE WAS BRINGING MY PRESENT UP TO ME AN' SHE FELL DOWN THE STAIRS!
SHE MAY BE HURT... WE'D BETTER PUT HER TO BED!
I-I'M ALL RIGHT!
Y-YOU'D BETTER REST AWHILE ANYWAY, DEAR!
IS-IS THERE ANYTHING I CAN DO, MOM?
YES! YOU CAN GET YOUR CLOTHES ON, YOUNG MAN... I DON'T THINK YOU'RE VERY SICK AFTER ALL!
HUH?
A LITTLE LATER
LULU, MY MOTHER GAVE ME A DOLLAR TO BUY YOU A PRESENT WITH— WHAT DO YOU WANT?
A DOLLAR?
HMM... LET ME THINK... A DOLLAR ISN'T VERY MUCH—BUT THERE MUST BE SOMETHING—
OH, YES—
NO! NOT THAT!
THAT'S WHAT I WANT! GO GET IT FOR ME!
I'M SURE THE MAN WON'T WRAP IT FOR HIM... TUB'LL HAVE A LITTLE TROUBLE CARRYING THAT STUFFED PORCUPINE ALL RIGHT!
the End

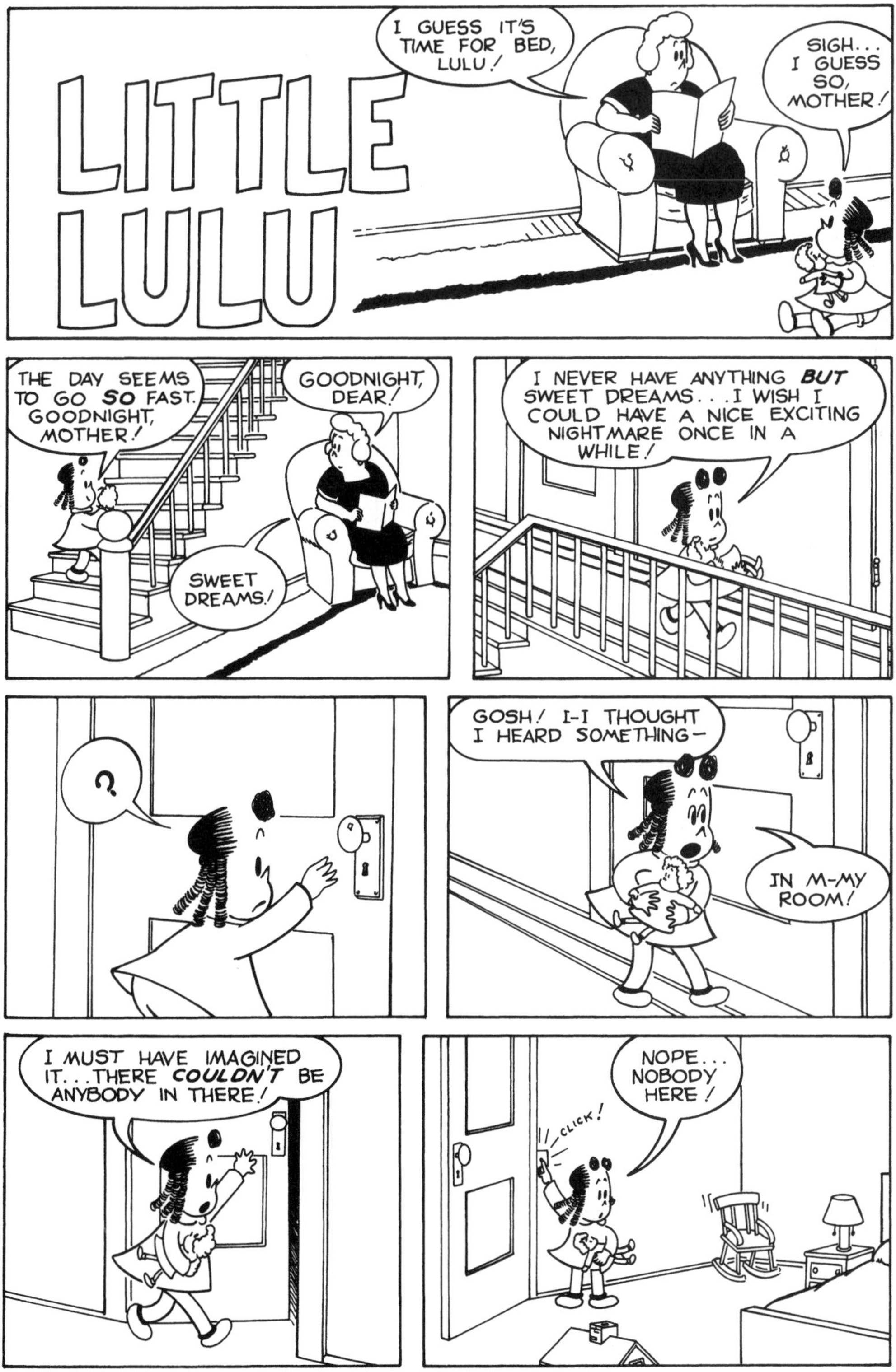
LITTLE LULU
I GUESS IT'S TIME FOR BED, LULU!
SIGH... I GUESS SO, MOTHER!
THE DAY SEEMS TO GO **SO** FAST. GOODNIGHT, MOTHER!
GOODNIGHT, DEAR!
SWEET DREAMS!
I NEVER HAVE ANYTHING **BUT** SWEET DREAMS...I WISH I COULD HAVE A NICE EXCITING NIGHTMARE ONCE IN A WHILE!
?
GOSH! I-I THOUGHT I HEARD SOMETHING—
IN M-MY ROOM!
I MUST HAVE IMAGINED IT...THERE **COULDN'T** BE ANYBODY IN THERE!
CLICK!
NOPE... NOBODY HERE!

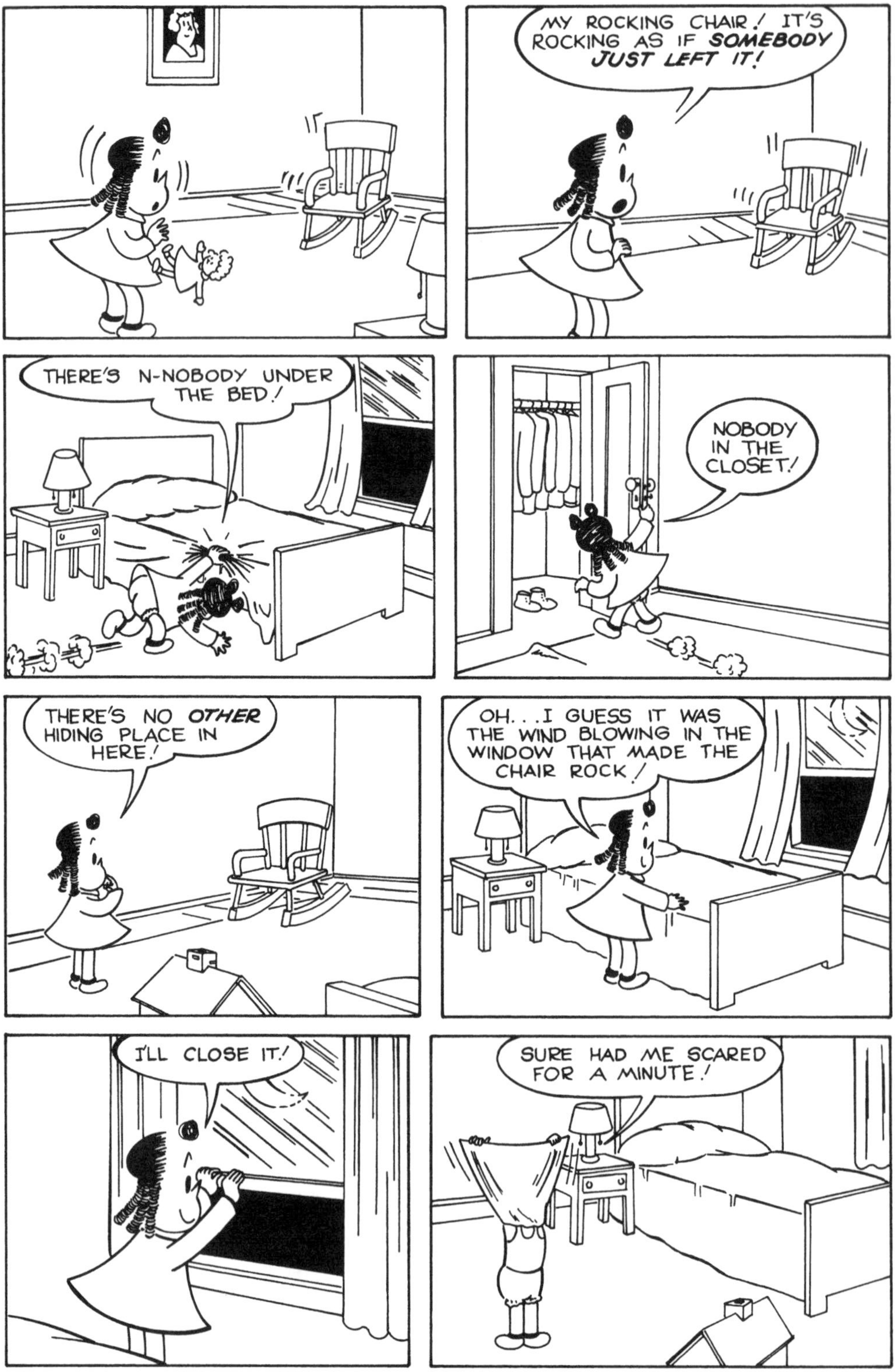
MY ROCKING CHAIR! IT'S ROCKING AS IF SOMEBODY JUST LEFT IT!
THERE'S N-NOBODY UNDER THE BED!
NOBODY IN THE CLOSET!
THERE'S NO OTHER HIDING PLACE IN HERE!
OH...I GUESS IT WAS THE WIND BLOWING IN THE WINDOW THAT MADE THE CHAIR ROCK!
I'LL CLOSE IT!
SURE HAD ME SCARED FOR A MINUTE!

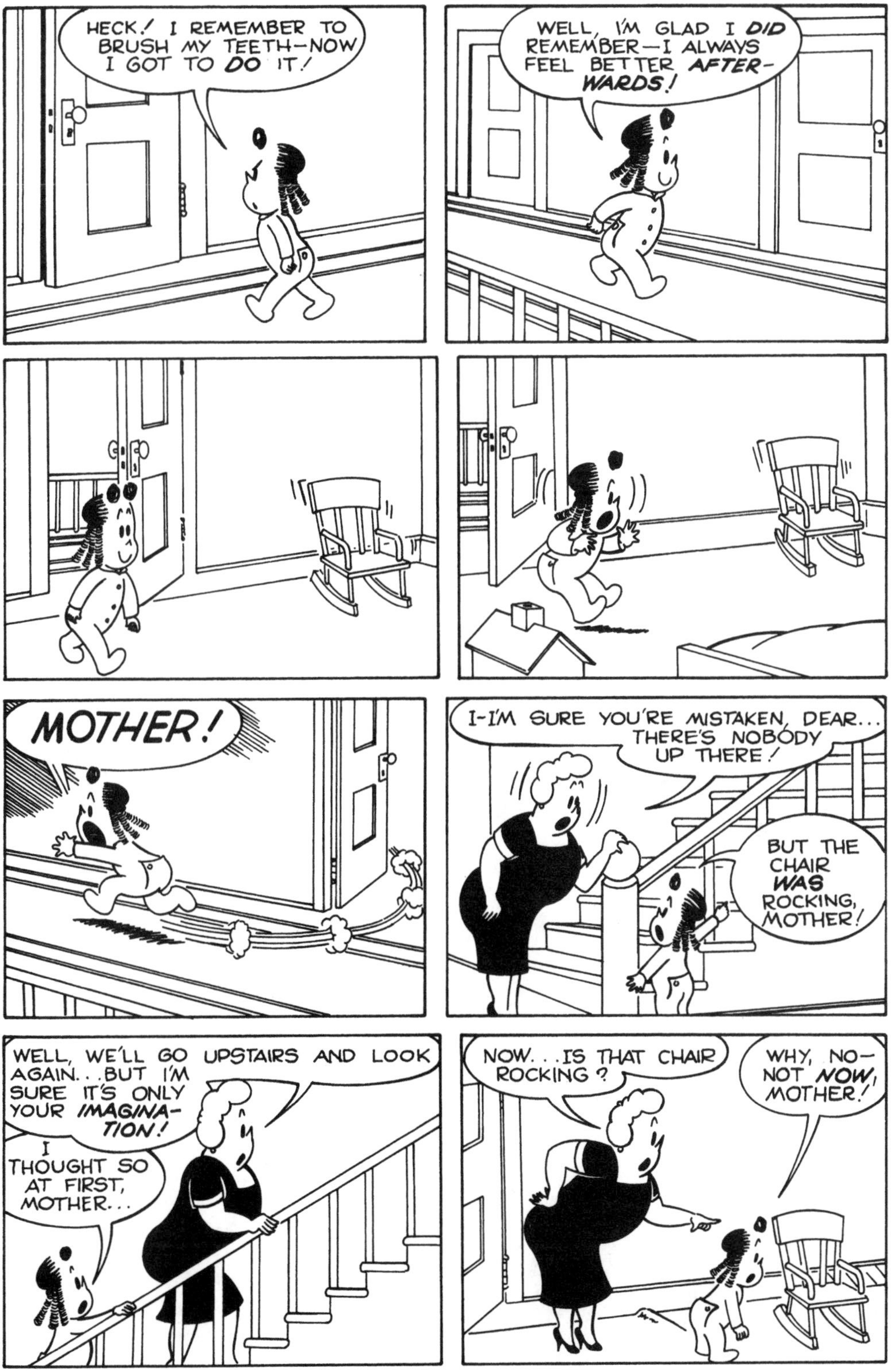
HECK! I REMEMBER TO BRUSH MY TEETH—NOW I GOT TO DO IT!
WELL, I'M GLAD I DID REMEMBER—I ALWAYS FEEL BETTER AFTER-WARDS!
MOTHER!
I-I'M SURE YOU'RE MISTAKEN, DEAR... THERE'S NOBODY UP THERE!
BUT THE CHAIR WAS ROCKING, MOTHER!
WELL, WE'LL GO UPSTAIRS AND LOOK AGAIN...BUT I'M SURE IT'S ONLY YOUR IMAGINA-TION!
I THOUGHT SO AT FIRST, MOTHER...
NOW...IS THAT CHAIR ROCKING?
WHY, NO—NOT NOW, MOTHER!

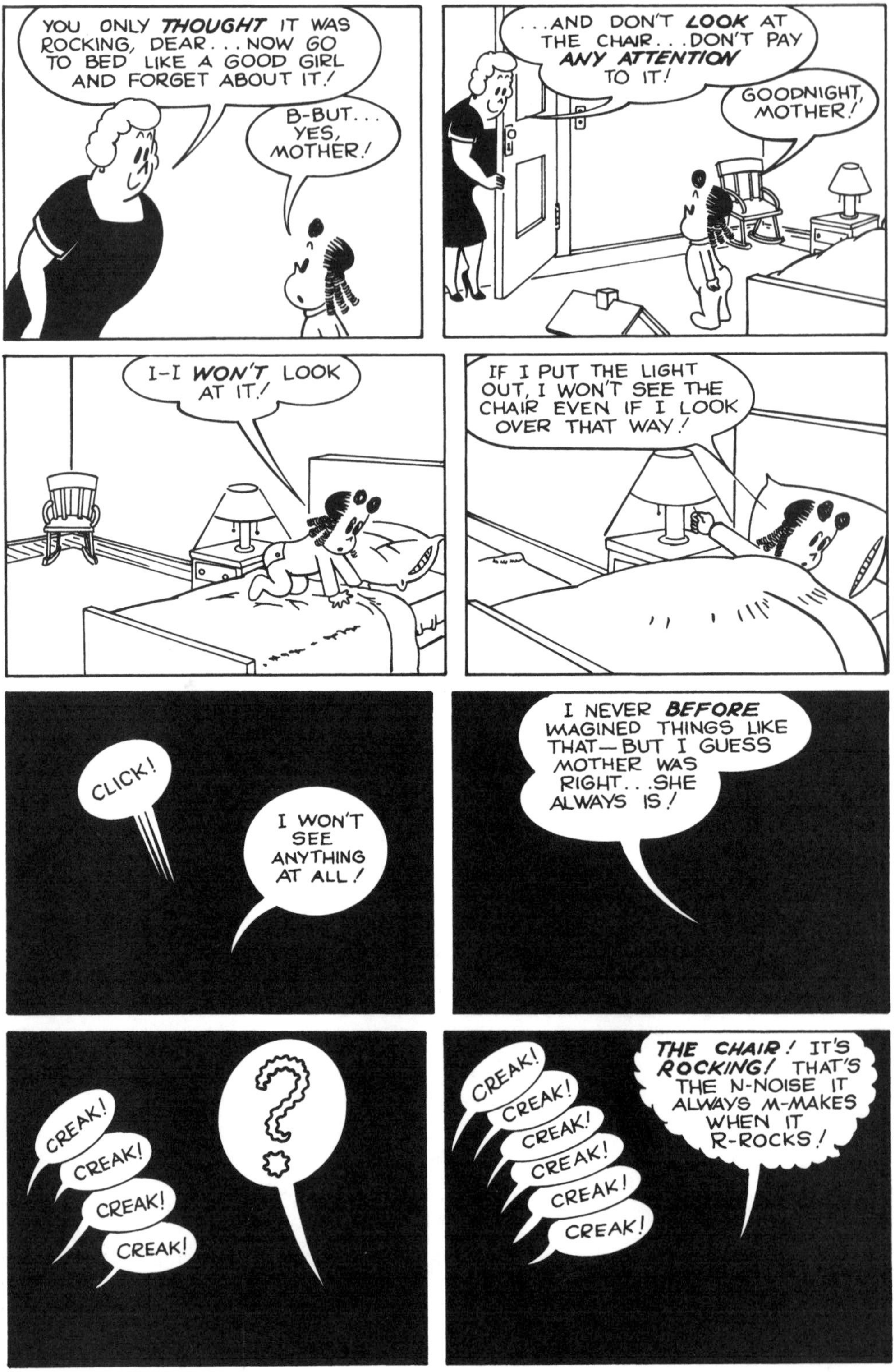

YOU ONLY THOUGHT IT WAS ROCKING, DEAR... NOW GO TO BED LIKE A GOOD GIRL AND FORGET ABOUT IT!
B-BUT... YES, MOTHER!
...AND DON'T LOOK AT THE CHAIR... DON'T PAY ANY ATTENTION TO IT!
GOODNIGHT, MOTHER!
I-I WON'T LOOK AT IT!
IF I PUT THE LIGHT OUT, I WON'T SEE THE CHAIR EVEN IF I LOOK OVER THAT WAY!
CLICK!
I WON'T SEE ANYTHING AT ALL!
I NEVER BEFORE IMAGINED THINGS LIKE THAT—BUT I GUESS MOTHER WAS RIGHT... SHE ALWAYS IS!
CREAK!
CREAK!
CREAK!
CREAK!
?
CREAK!
CREAK!
CREAK!
CREAK!
CREAK!
CREAK!
THE CHAIR! IT'S ROCKING! THAT'S THE N-NOISE IT ALWAYS M-MAKES WHEN IT R-ROCKS!

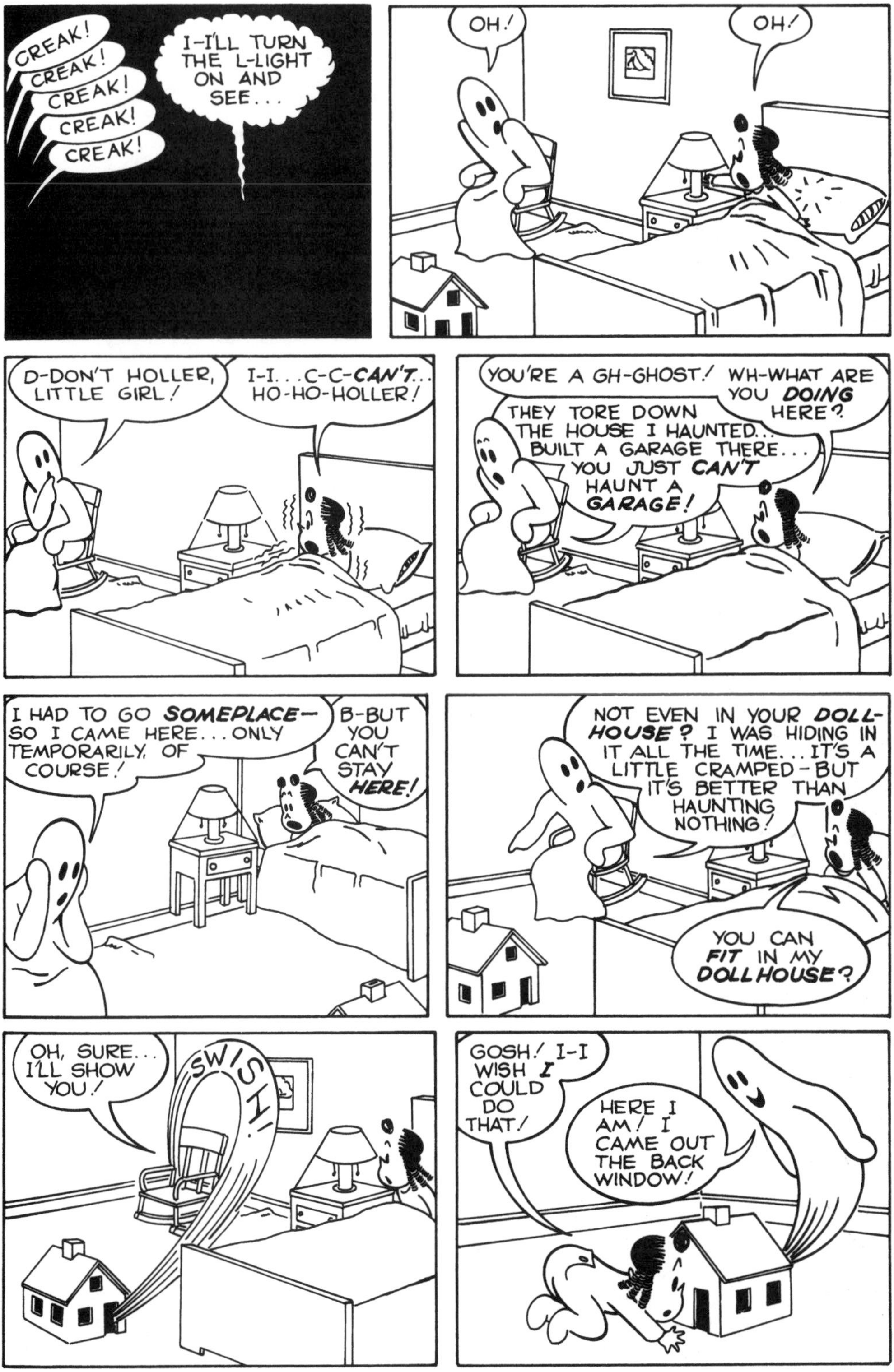
CREAK!
CREAK!
CREAK!
CREAK!
CREAK!
I-I'LL TURN THE L-LIGHT ON AND SEE...
OH!
OH!
D-DON'T HOLLER, LITTLE GIRL!
I-I...C-C-CAN'T...HO-HO-HOLLER!
YOU'RE A GH-GHOST! WH-WHAT ARE YOU DOING HERE?
THEY TORE DOWN THE HOUSE I HAUNTED... BUILT A GARAGE THERE... YOU JUST CAN'T HAUNT A GARAGE!
I HAD TO GO SOMEPLACE— SO I CAME HERE...ONLY TEMPORARILY, OF COURSE!
B-BUT YOU CAN'T STAY HERE!
NOT EVEN IN YOUR DOLL-HOUSE? I WAS HIDING IN IT ALL THE TIME...IT'S A LITTLE CRAMPED-BUT IT'S BETTER THAN HAUNTING NOTHING!
YOU CAN FIT IN MY DOLLHOUSE?
OH, SURE... I'LL SHOW YOU!
SWISH!
GOSH! I-I WISH I COULD DO THAT!
HERE I AM! I CAME OUT THE BACK WINDOW!

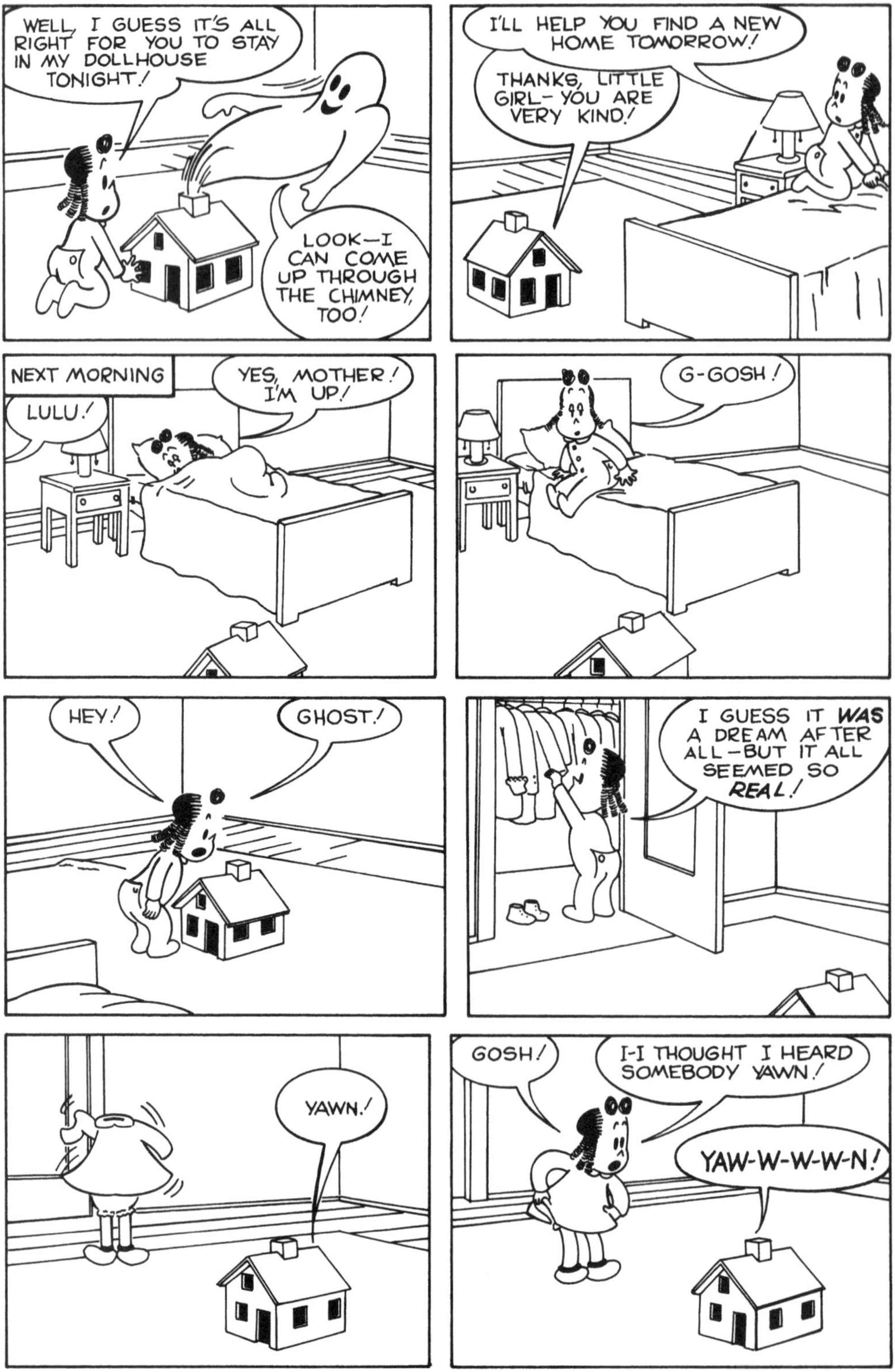
WELL, I GUESS IT'S ALL RIGHT FOR YOU TO STAY IN MY DOLLHOUSE TONIGHT!
LOOK—I CAN COME UP THROUGH THE CHIMNEY, TOO!
I'LL HELP YOU FIND A NEW HOME TOMORROW!
THANKS, LITTLE GIRL—YOU ARE VERY KIND!
NEXT MORNING
LULU!
YES, MOTHER! I'M UP!
G-GOSH!
HEY!
GHOST!
I GUESS IT WAS A DREAM AFTER ALL—BUT IT ALL SEEMED SO REAL!
YAWN!
GOSH!
I-I THOUGHT I HEARD SOMEBODY YAWN!
YAW-W-W-W-N!

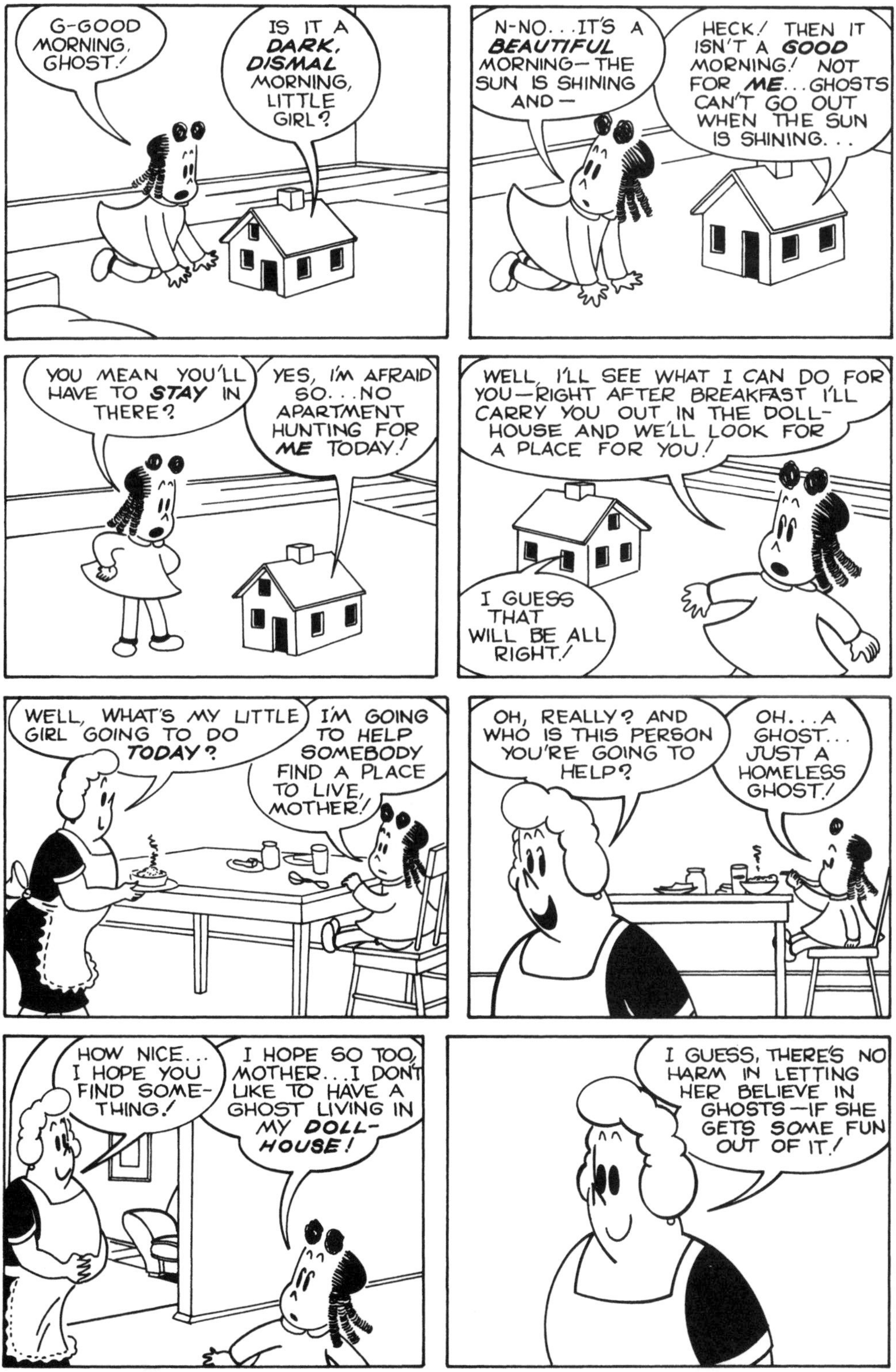
G-GOOD MORNING, GHOST!
IS IT A DARK, DISMAL MORNING, LITTLE GIRL?
N-NO...IT'S A BEAUTIFUL MORNING—THE SUN IS SHINING AND—
HECK! THEN IT ISN'T A GOOD MORNING! NOT FOR ME...GHOSTS CAN'T GO OUT WHEN THE SUN IS SHINING...
YOU MEAN YOU'LL HAVE TO STAY IN THERE?
YES, I'M AFRAID SO...NO APARTMENT HUNTING FOR ME TODAY!
WELL, I'LL SEE WHAT I CAN DO FOR YOU—RIGHT AFTER BREAKFAST I'LL CARRY YOU OUT IN THE DOLL-HOUSE AND WE'LL LOOK FOR A PLACE FOR YOU!
I GUESS THAT WILL BE ALL RIGHT!
WELL, WHAT'S MY LITTLE GIRL GOING TO DO TODAY?
I'M GOING TO HELP SOMEBODY FIND A PLACE TO LIVE, MOTHER!
OH, REALLY? AND WHO IS THIS PERSON YOU'RE GOING TO HELP?
OH...A GHOST... JUST A HOMELESS GHOST!
HOW NICE... I HOPE YOU FIND SOME-THING!
I HOPE SO TOO, MOTHER...I DON'T LIKE TO HAVE A GHOST LIVING IN MY DOLL-HOUSE!
I GUESS, THERE'S NO HARM IN LETTING HER BELIEVE IN GHOSTS—IF SHE GETS SOME FUN OUT OF IT!

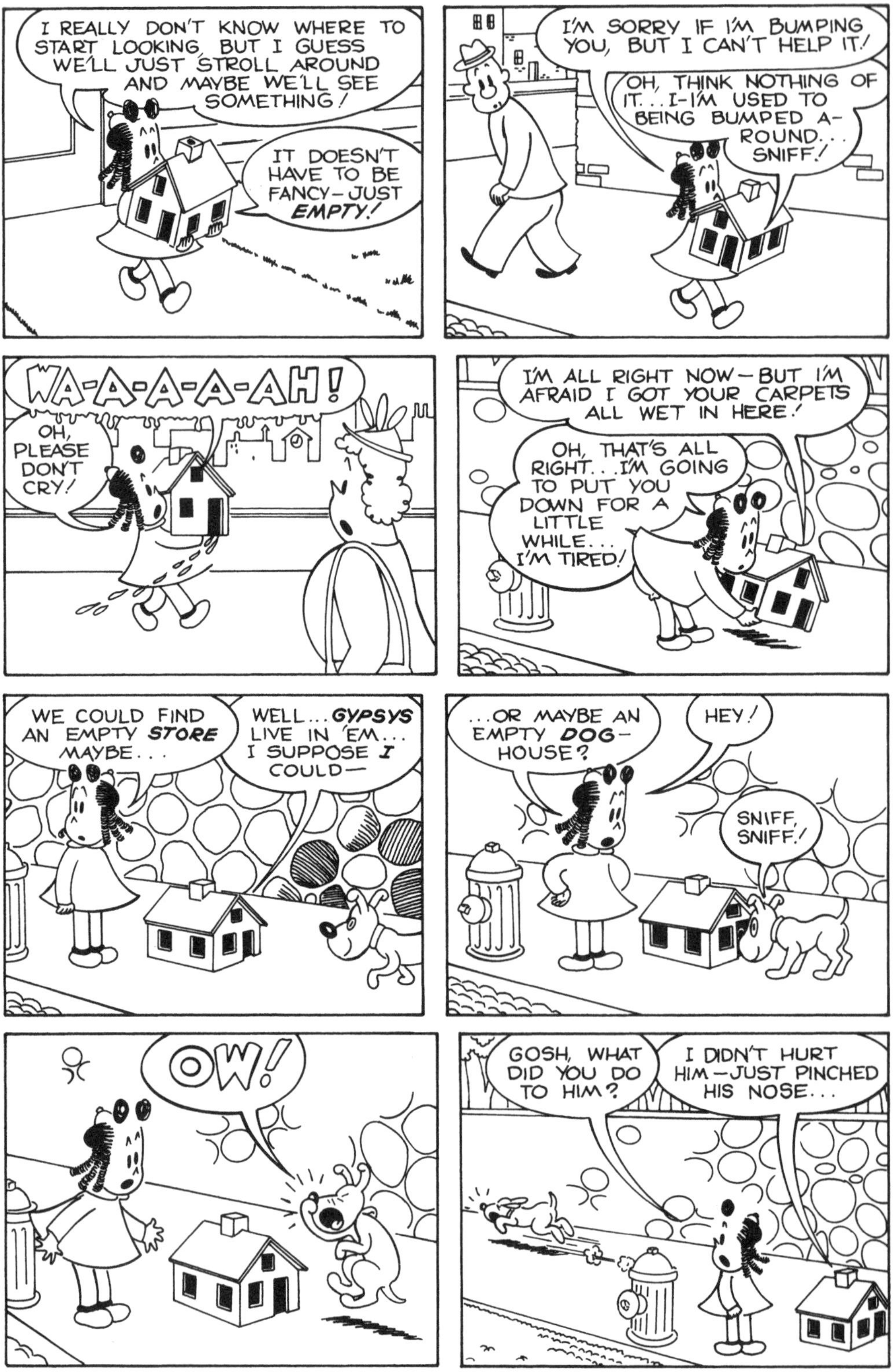

I REALLY DON'T KNOW WHERE TO START LOOKING, BUT I GUESS WE'LL JUST STROLL AROUND AND MAYBE WE'LL SEE SOMETHING!
IT DOESN'T HAVE TO BE FANCY—JUST EMPTY!
I'M SORRY IF I'M BUMPING YOU, BUT I CAN'T HELP IT!
OH, THINK NOTHING OF IT... I-I'M USED TO BEING BUMPED A-ROUND... SNIFF!
WA-A-A-A-AH!
OH, PLEASE DON'T CRY!
I'M ALL RIGHT NOW—BUT I'M AFRAID I GOT YOUR CARPETS ALL WET IN HERE!
OH, THAT'S ALL RIGHT... I'M GOING TO PUT YOU DOWN FOR A LITTLE WHILE... I'M TIRED!
WE COULD FIND AN EMPTY STORE MAYBE...
WELL... GYPSYS LIVE IN 'EM... I SUPPOSE I COULD—
...OR MAYBE AN EMPTY DOG-HOUSE?
HEY!
SNIFF, SNIFF!
OW!
GOSH, WHAT DID YOU DO TO HIM?
I DIDN'T HURT HIM—JUST PINCHED HIS NOSE...

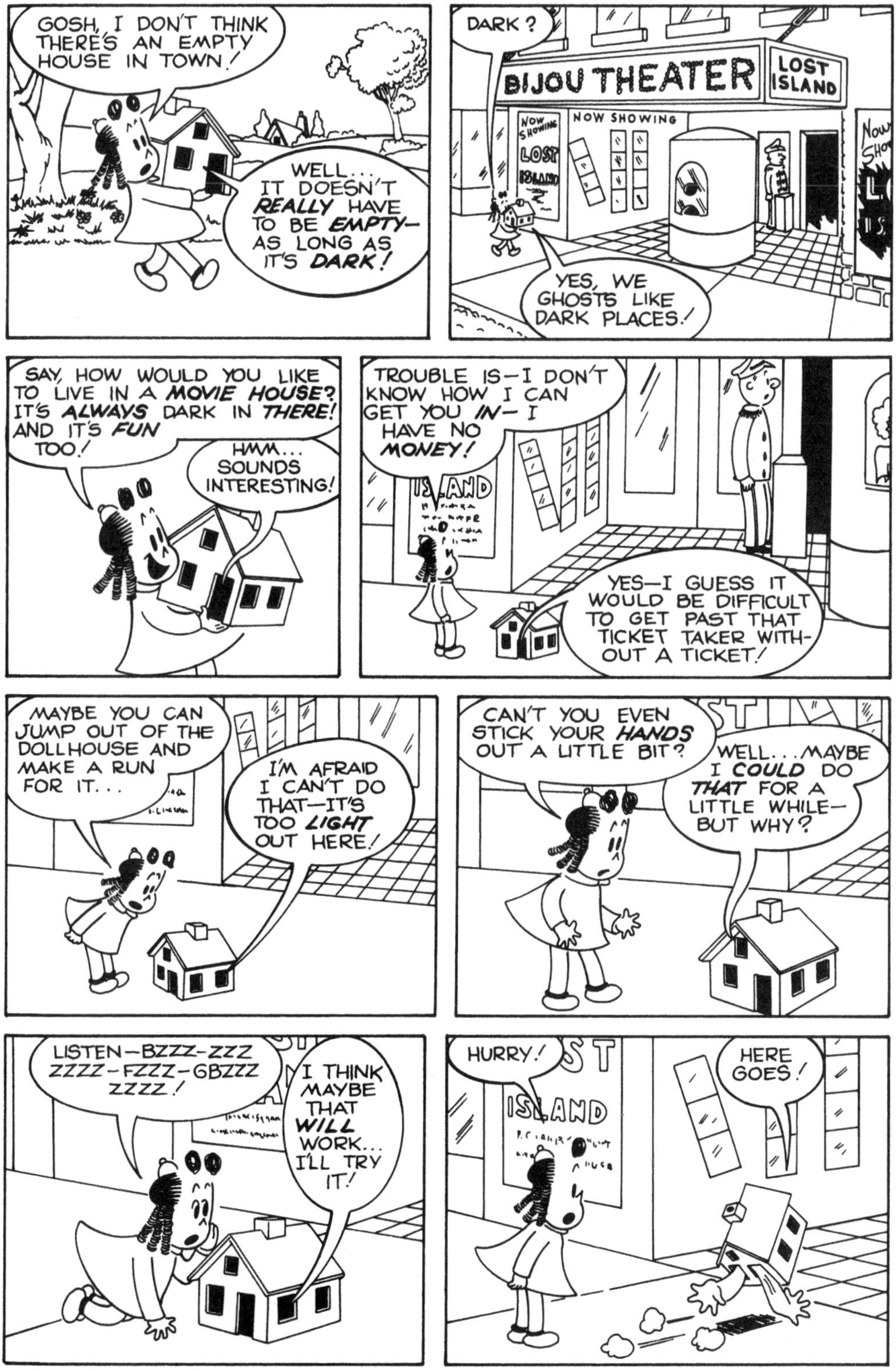
GOSH, I DON'T THINK THERE'S AN EMPTY HOUSE IN TOWN!
WELL... IT DOESN'T REALLY HAVE TO BE EMPTY— AS LONG AS IT'S DARK!
DARK?
BIJOU THEATER
LOST ISLAND
NOW SHOWING
NOW SHOWING LOST ISLAND
YES, WE GHOSTS LIKE DARK PLACES!
SAY, HOW WOULD YOU LIKE TO LIVE IN A MOVIE HOUSE? IT'S ALWAYS DARK IN THERE! AND IT'S FUN TOO!
HMM... SOUNDS INTERESTING!
TROUBLE IS—I DON'T KNOW HOW I CAN GET YOU IN— I HAVE NO MONEY!
ISLAND
YES—I GUESS IT WOULD BE DIFFICULT TO GET PAST THAT TICKET TAKER WITHOUT A TICKET!
MAYBE YOU CAN JUMP OUT OF THE DOLLHOUSE AND MAKE A RUN FOR IT...
I'M AFRAID I CAN'T DO THAT—IT'S TOO LIGHT OUT HERE!
CAN'T YOU EVEN STICK YOUR HANDS OUT A LITTLE BIT?
WELL... MAYBE I COULD DO THAT FOR A LITTLE WHILE— BUT WHY?
LISTEN—BZZZ-ZZZ ZZZZ-FZZZ-GBZZZ ZZZZ!
I THINK MAYBE THAT WILL WORK... I'LL TRY IT!
HURRY!
ISLAND
HERE GOES!

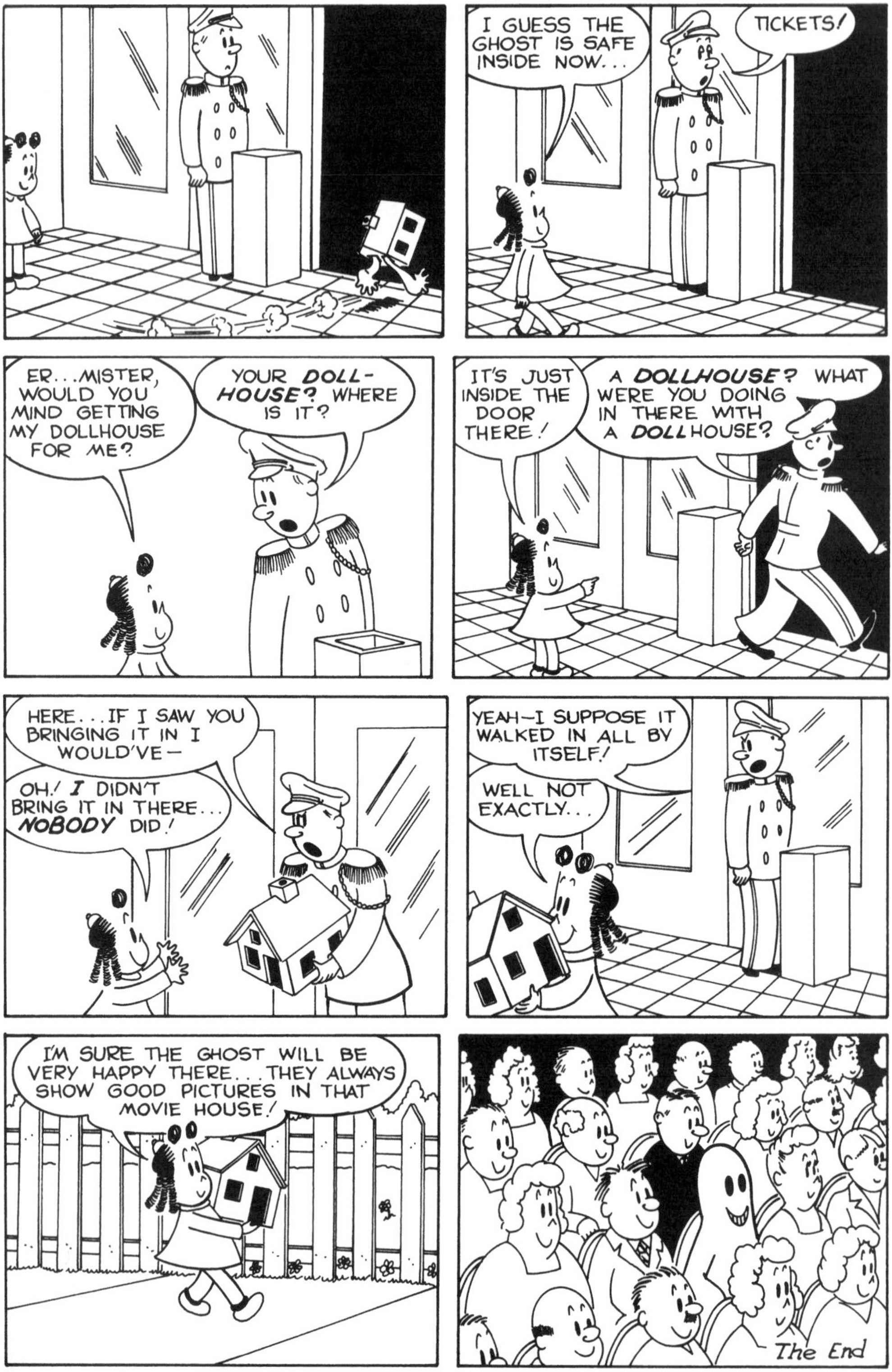
I GUESS THE GHOST IS SAFE INSIDE NOW...
TICKETS!
ER...MISTER, WOULD YOU MIND GETTING MY DOLLHOUSE FOR ME?
YOUR DOLL-HOUSE? WHERE IS IT?
IT'S JUST INSIDE THE DOOR THERE!
A DOLLHOUSE? WHAT WERE YOU DOING IN THERE WITH A DOLLHOUSE?
HERE...IF I SAW YOU BRINGING IT IN I WOULD'VE—
OH! I DIDN'T BRING IT IN THERE... NOBODY DID!
YEAH—I SUPPOSE IT WALKED IN ALL BY ITSELF!
WELL NOT EXACTLY...
I'M SURE THE GHOST WILL BE VERY HAPPY THERE...THEY ALWAYS SHOW GOOD PICTURES IN THAT MOVIE HOUSE!
The End

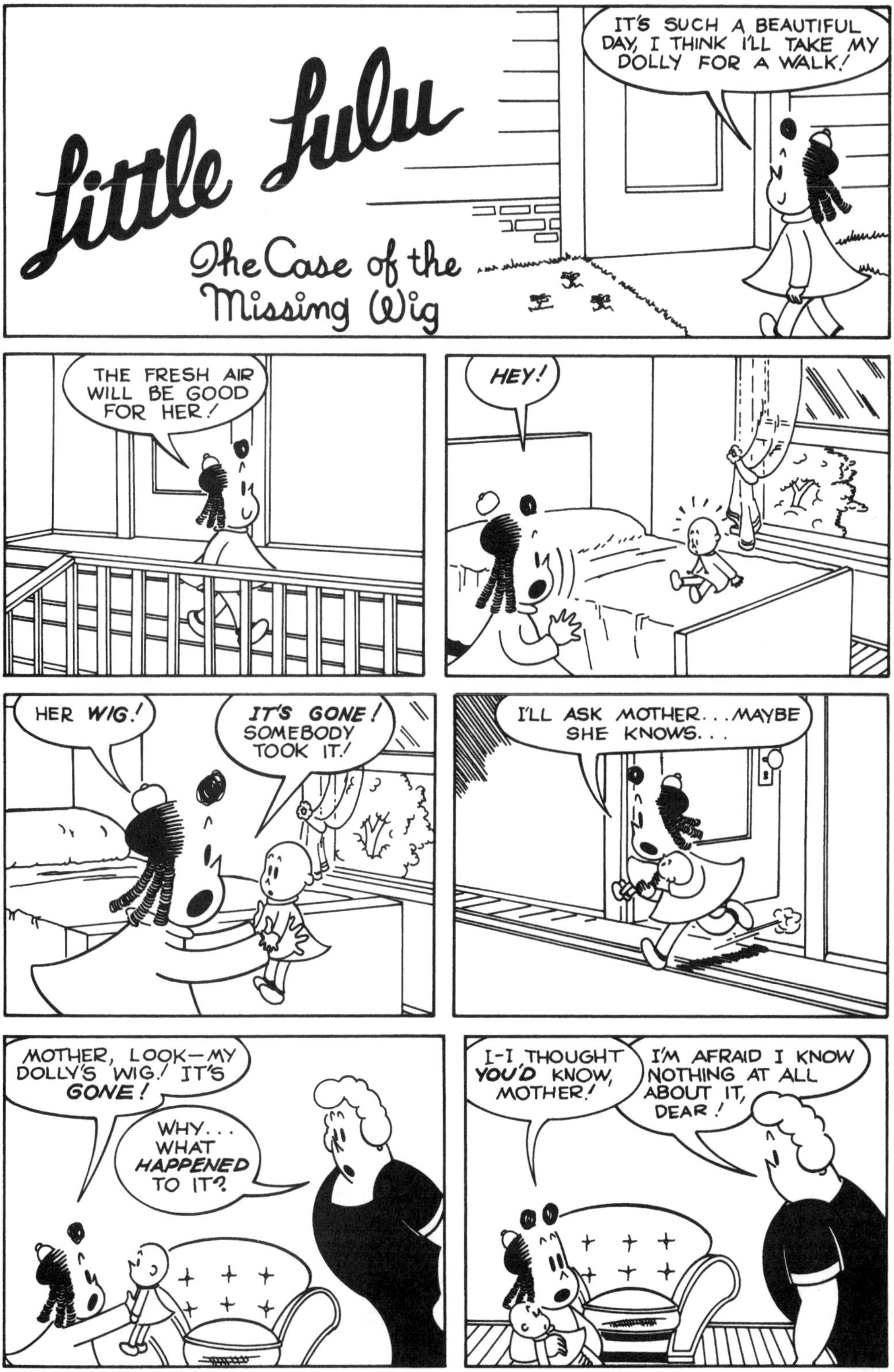
Little Lulu
The Case of the Missing Wig
IT'S SUCH A BEAUTIFUL DAY, I THINK I'LL TAKE MY DOLLY FOR A WALK!
THE FRESH AIR WILL BE GOOD FOR HER!
HEY!
HER WIG!
IT'S GONE! SOMEBODY TOOK IT!
I'LL ASK MOTHER... MAYBE SHE KNOWS...
MOTHER, LOOK—MY DOLLY'S WIG! IT'S GONE!
WHY... WHAT HAPPENED TO IT?
I-I THOUGHT YOU'D KNOW, MOTHER!
I'M AFRAID I KNOW NOTHING AT ALL ABOUT IT, DEAR!

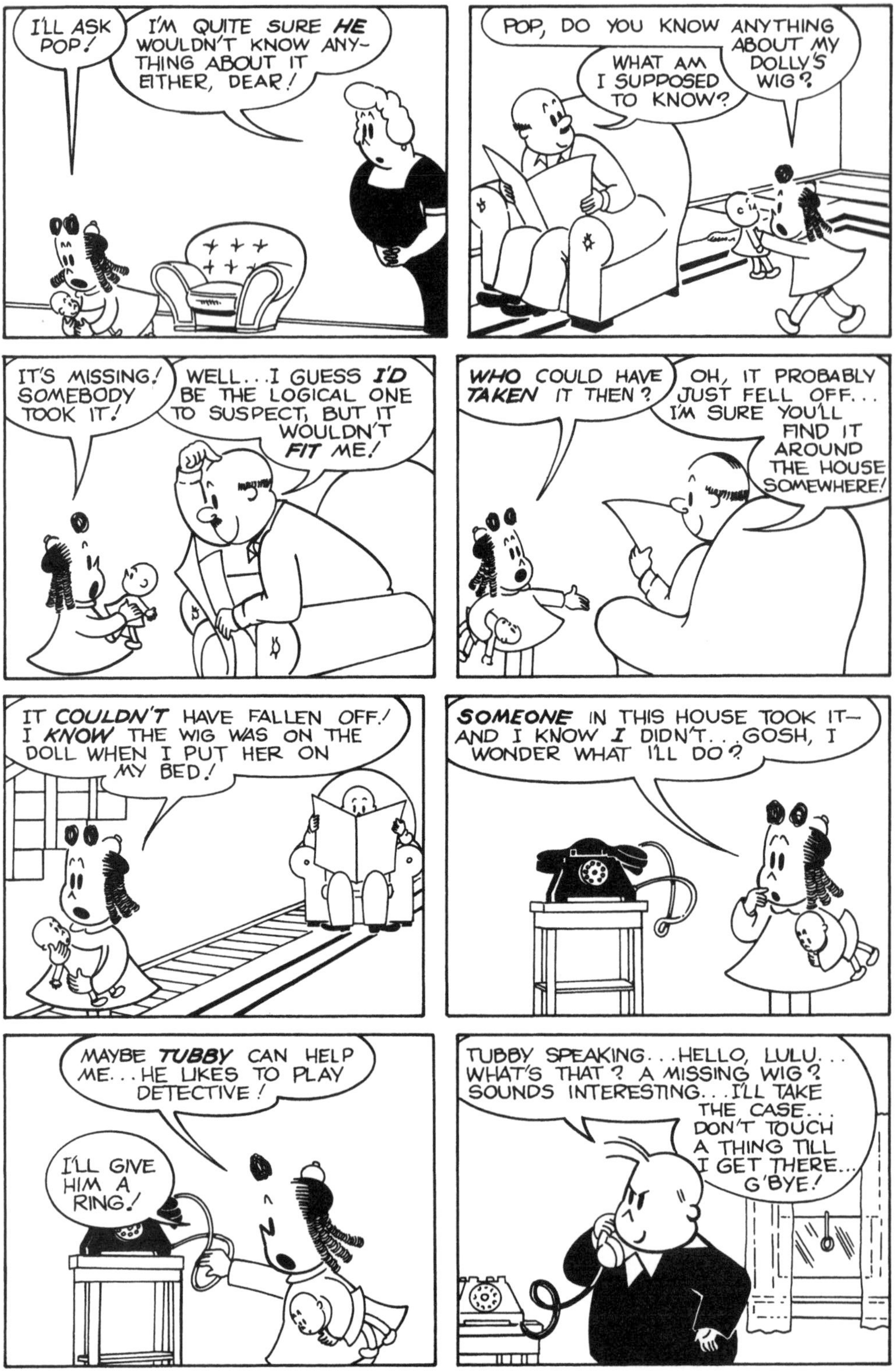
I'LL ASK POP!
I'M QUITE SURE HE WOULDN'T KNOW ANYTHING ABOUT IT EITHER, DEAR!
POP, DO YOU KNOW ANYTHING ABOUT MY DOLLY'S WIG?
WHAT AM I SUPPOSED TO KNOW?
IT'S MISSING! SOMEBODY TOOK IT!
WELL...I GUESS I'D BE THE LOGICAL ONE TO SUSPECT, BUT IT WOULDN'T FIT ME!
WHO COULD HAVE TAKEN IT THEN?
OH, IT PROBABLY JUST FELL OFF... I'M SURE YOU'LL FIND IT AROUND THE HOUSE SOMEWHERE!
IT COULDN'T HAVE FALLEN OFF! I KNOW THE WIG WAS ON THE DOLL WHEN I PUT HER ON MY BED!
SOMEONE IN THIS HOUSE TOOK IT— AND I KNOW I DIDN'T...GOSH, I WONDER WHAT I'LL DO?
MAYBE TUBBY CAN HELP ME...HE LIKES TO PLAY DETECTIVE!
I'LL GIVE HIM A RING!
TUBBY SPEAKING...HELLO, LULU... WHAT'S THAT? A MISSING WIG? SOUNDS INTERESTING...I'LL TAKE THE CASE... DON'T TOUCH A THING TILL I GET THERE... G'BYE!

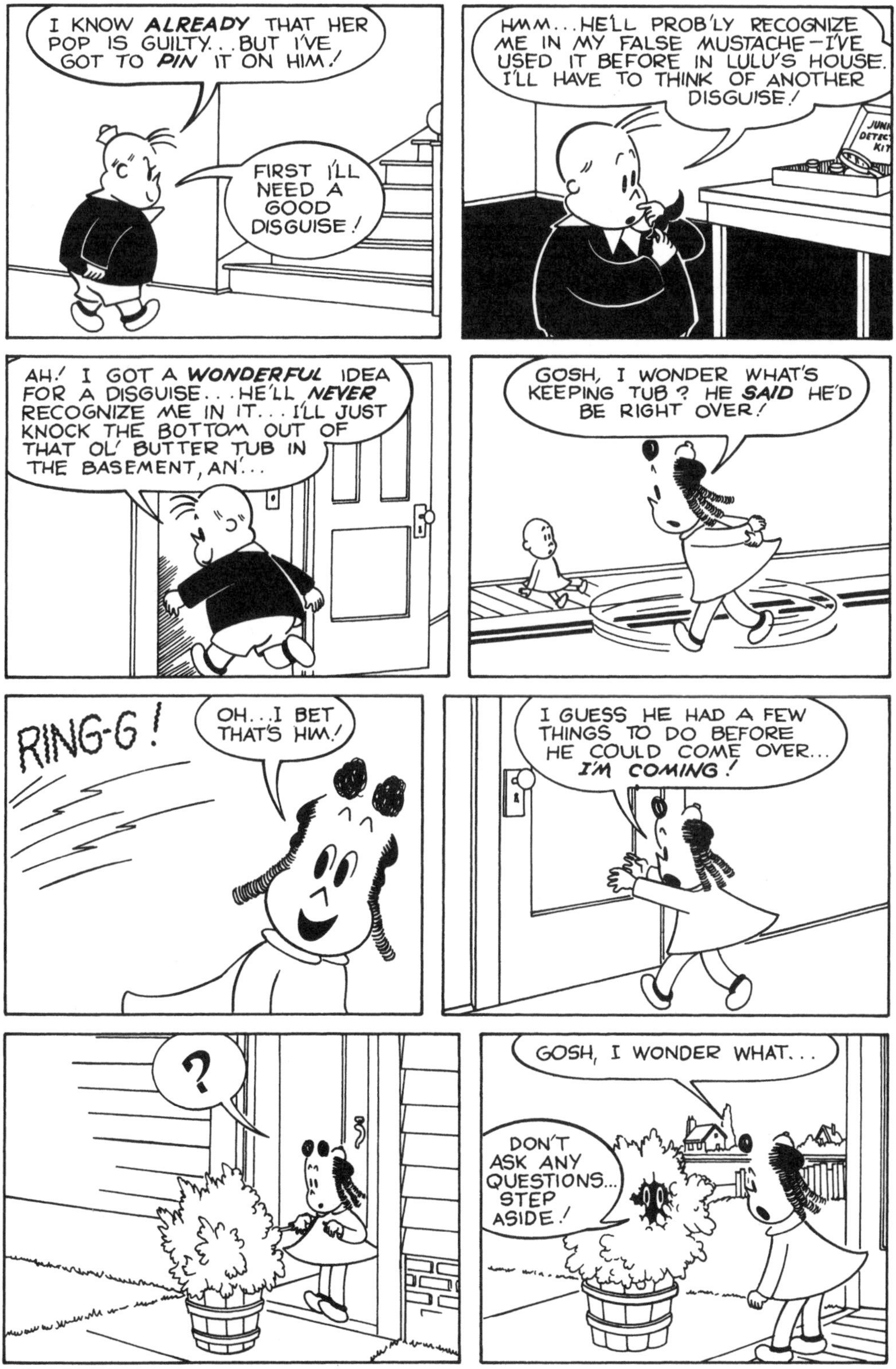
I KNOW ALREADY THAT HER POP IS GUILTY...BUT I'VE GOT TO PIN IT ON HIM!
FIRST I'LL NEED A GOOD DISGUISE!
HMM...HE'LL PROB'LY RECOGNIZE ME IN MY FALSE MUSTACHE—I'VE USED IT BEFORE IN LULU'S HOUSE. I'LL HAVE TO THINK OF ANOTHER DISGUISE!
AH! I GOT A WONDERFUL IDEA FOR A DISGUISE...HE'LL NEVER RECOGNIZE ME IN IT...I'LL JUST KNOCK THE BOTTOM OUT OF THAT OL' BUTTER TUB IN THE BASEMENT, AN'...
GOSH, I WONDER WHAT'S KEEPING TUB? HE SAID HE'D BE RIGHT OVER!
RING-G!
OH...I BET THAT'S HIM!
I GUESS HE HAD A FEW THINGS TO DO BEFORE HE COULD COME OVER... I'M COMING!
?
GOSH, I WONDER WHAT...
DON'T ASK ANY QUESTIONS... STEP ASIDE!

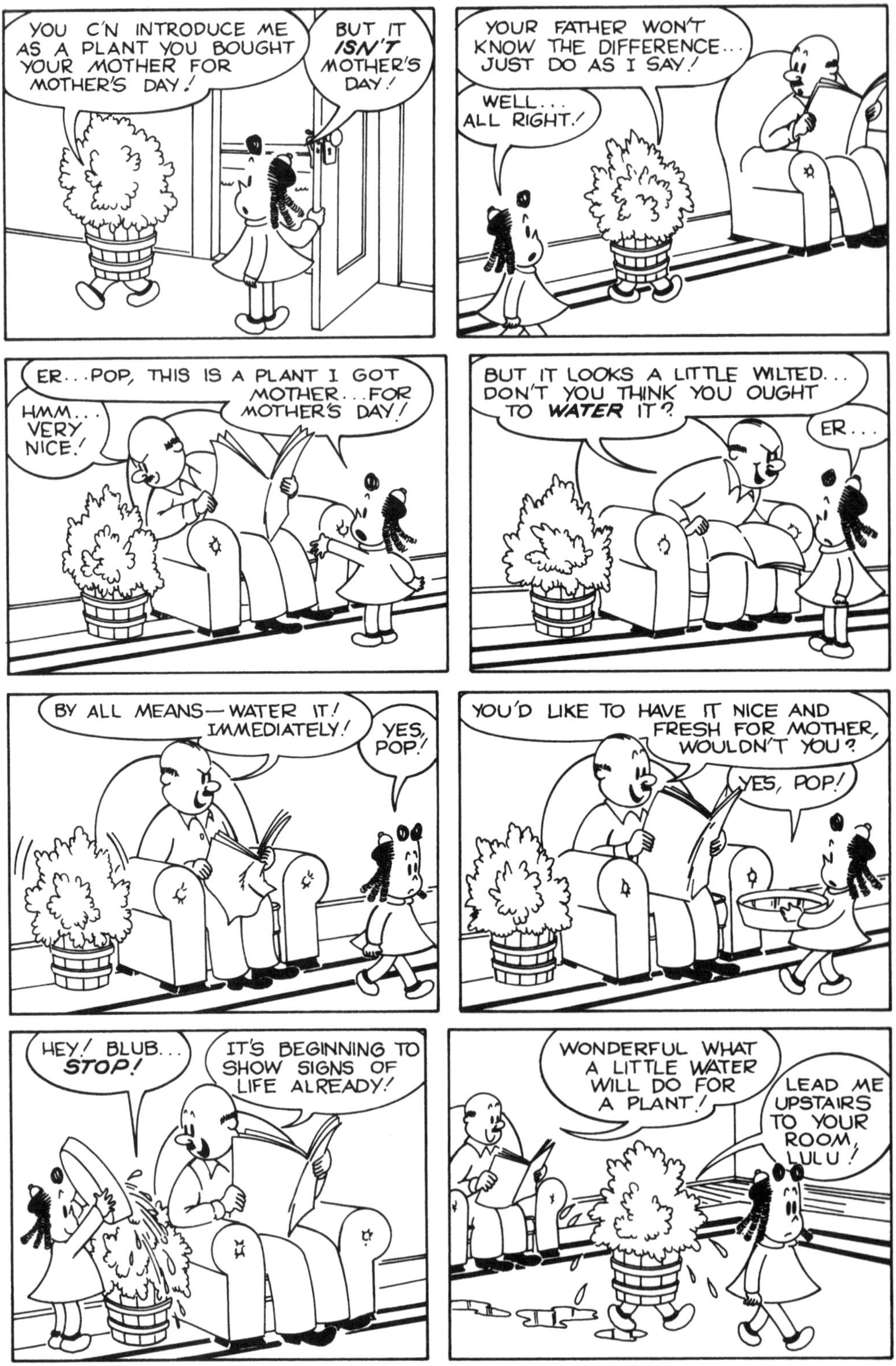
YOU C'N INTRODUCE ME AS A PLANT YOU BOUGHT YOUR MOTHER FOR MOTHER'S DAY!
BUT IT *ISN'T* MOTHER'S DAY!
YOUR FATHER WON'T KNOW THE DIFFERENCE... JUST DO AS I SAY!
WELL... ALL RIGHT!
ER...POP, THIS IS A PLANT I GOT MOTHER...FOR MOTHER'S DAY!
HMM... VERY NICE!
BUT IT LOOKS A LITTLE WILTED... DON'T YOU THINK YOU OUGHT TO *WATER* IT?
ER...
BY ALL MEANS—WATER IT! IMMEDIATELY!
YES, POP!
YOU'D LIKE TO HAVE IT NICE AND FRESH FOR MOTHER, WOULDN'T YOU?
YES, POP!
HEY! BLUB... *STOP!*
IT'S BEGINNING TO SHOW SIGNS OF LIFE ALREADY!
WONDERFUL WHAT A LITTLE WATER WILL DO FOR A PLANT!
LEAD ME UPSTAIRS TO YOUR ROOM, LULU!

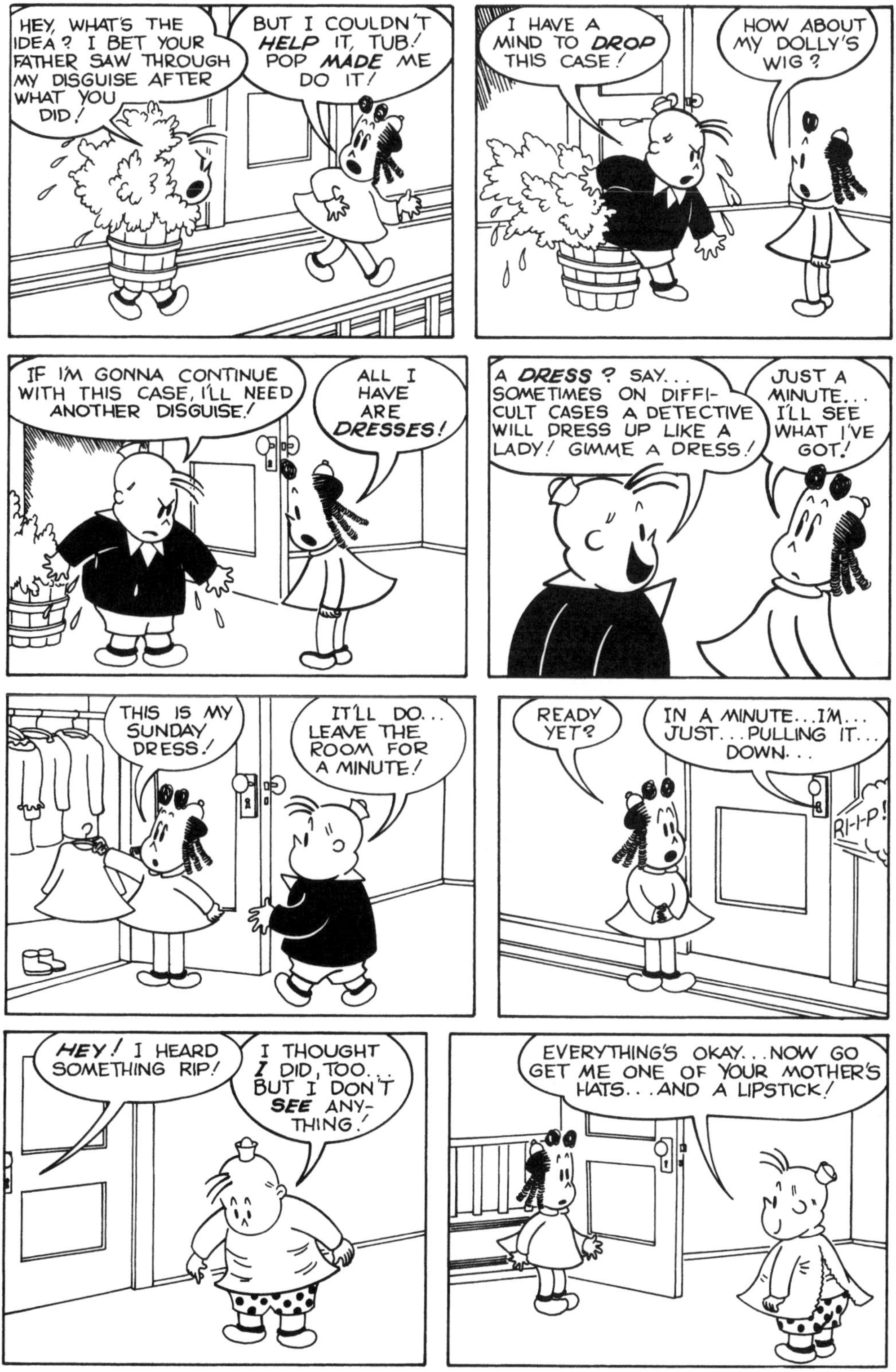
HEY, WHAT'S THE IDEA? I BET YOUR FATHER SAW THROUGH MY DISGUISE AFTER WHAT YOU DID!
BUT I COULDN'T HELP IT, TUB! POP MADE ME DO IT!
I HAVE A MIND TO DROP THIS CASE!
HOW ABOUT MY DOLLY'S WIG?
IF I'M GONNA CONTINUE WITH THIS CASE, I'LL NEED ANOTHER DISGUISE!
ALL I HAVE ARE DRESSES!
A DRESS? SAY... SOMETIMES ON DIFFI-CULT CASES A DETECTIVE WILL DRESS UP LIKE A LADY! GIMME A DRESS!
JUST A MINUTE... I'LL SEE WHAT I'VE GOT!
THIS IS MY SUNDAY DRESS!
IT'LL DO... LEAVE THE ROOM FOR A MINUTE!
READY YET?
IN A MINUTE...I'M... JUST...PULLING IT... DOWN...
RI-I-P!
HEY! I HEARD SOMETHING RIP!
I THOUGHT I DID, TOO... BUT I DON'T SEE ANY-THING!
EVERYTHING'S OKAY...NOW GO GET ME ONE OF YOUR MOTHER'S HATS...AND A LIPSTICK!

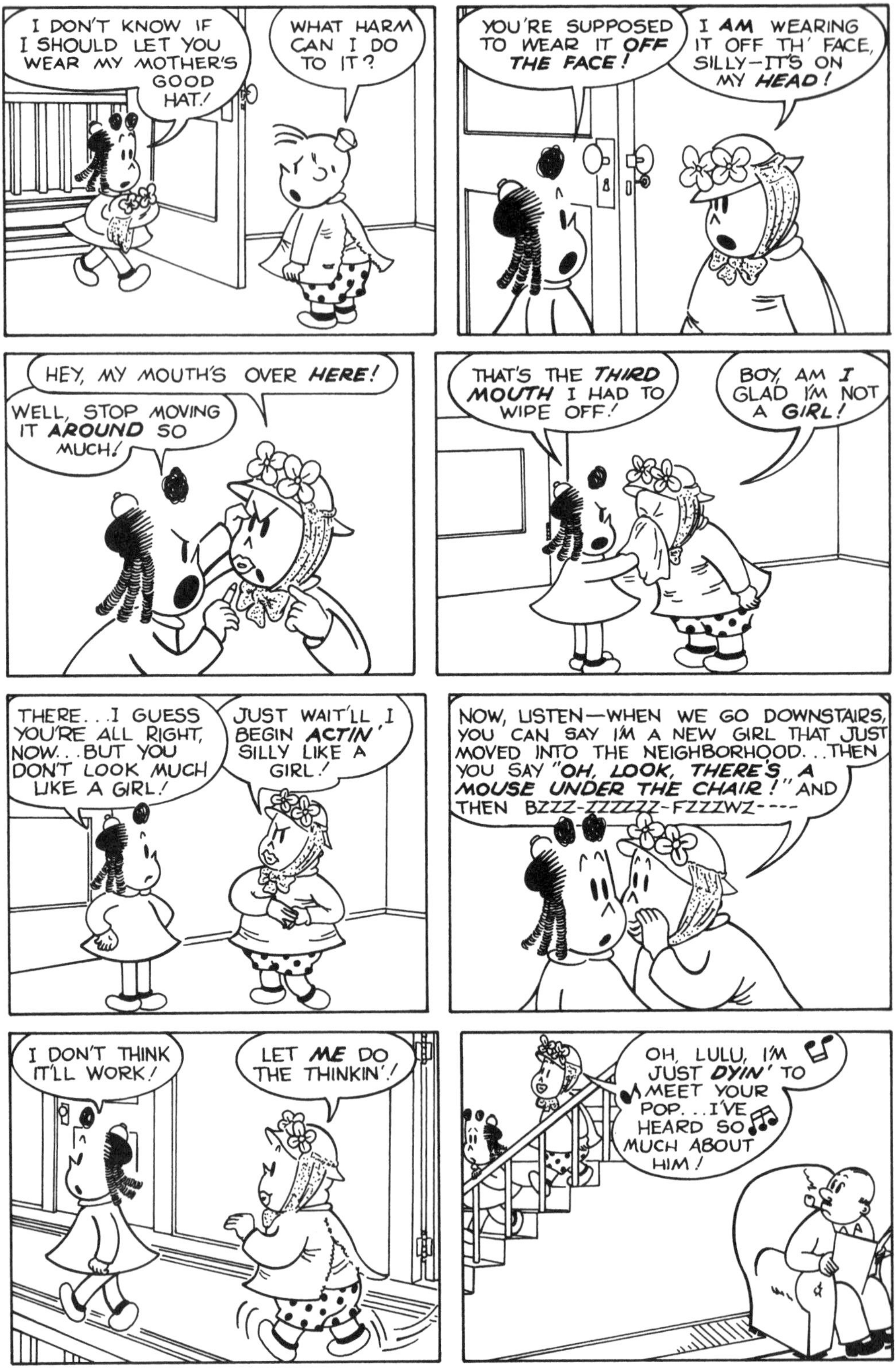

I DON'T KNOW IF I SHOULD LET YOU WEAR MY MOTHER'S GOOD HAT!
WHAT HARM CAN I DO TO IT?
YOU'RE SUPPOSED TO WEAR IT **OFF THE FACE!**
I **AM** WEARING IT OFF TH' FACE, SILLY—IT'S ON MY **HEAD!**
HEY, MY MOUTH'S OVER **HERE!**
WELL, STOP MOVING IT **AROUND** SO MUCH!
THAT'S THE **THIRD MOUTH** I HAD TO WIPE OFF!
BOY, AM **I** GLAD I'M NOT A **GIRL!**
THERE...I GUESS YOU'RE ALL RIGHT, NOW...BUT YOU DON'T LOOK MUCH LIKE A GIRL!
JUST WAIT'LL I BEGIN **ACTIN'** SILLY LIKE A GIRL!
NOW, LISTEN—WHEN WE GO DOWNSTAIRS, YOU CAN SAY I'M A NEW GIRL THAT JUST MOVED INTO THE NEIGHBORHOOD...THEN YOU SAY "**OH, LOOK, THERE'S A MOUSE UNDER THE CHAIR!**" AND THEN BZZZ-ZZZZZZ-FZZZWZ----
I DON'T THINK IT'LL WORK!
LET **ME** DO THE THINKIN'!
OH, LULU, I'M JUST **DYIN'** TO MEET YOUR POP...I'VE HEARD SO MUCH ABOUT HIM!

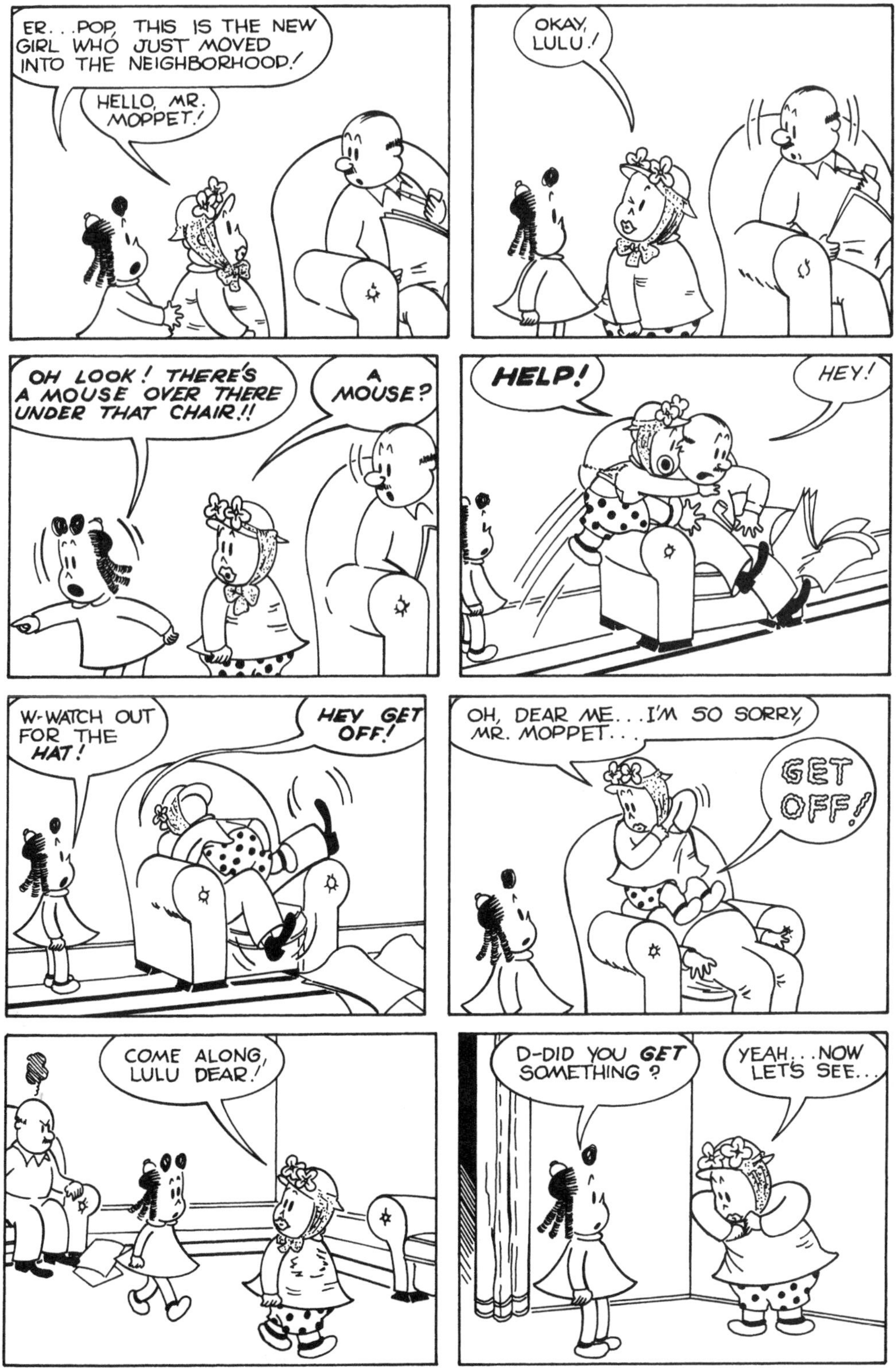
ER...POP, THIS IS THE NEW GIRL WHO JUST MOVED INTO THE NEIGHBORHOOD!
HELLO, MR. MOPPET!
OKAY, LULU!
OH LOOK! THERE'S A MOUSE OVER THERE UNDER THAT CHAIR!!
A MOUSE?
HELP!
HEY!
W-WATCH OUT FOR THE HAT!
HEY GET OFF!
OH, DEAR ME...I'M SO SORRY, MR. MOPPET...
GET OFF!
COME ALONG, LULU DEAR!
D-DID YOU GET SOMETHING?
YEAH...NOW LET'S SEE...

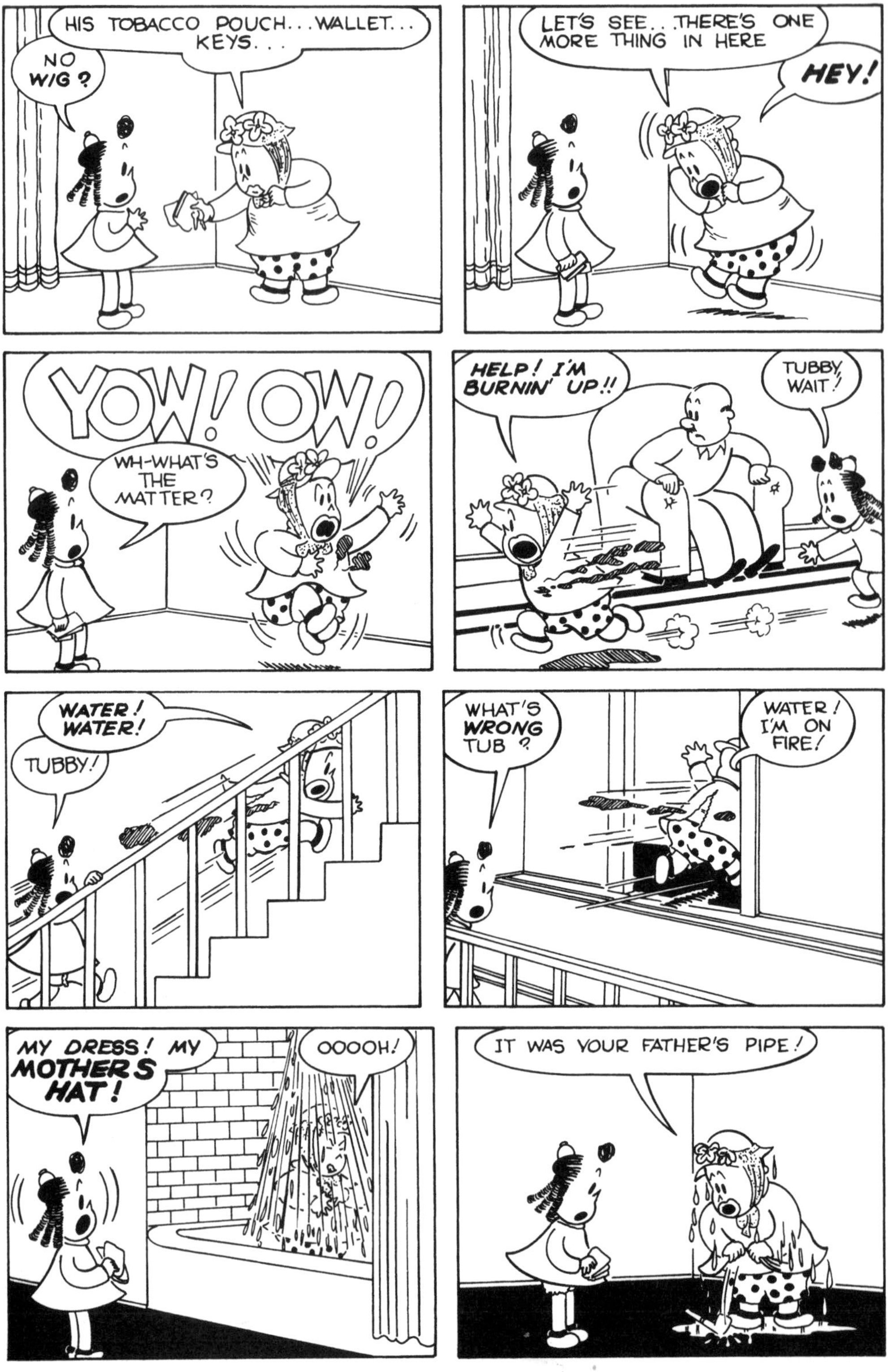
HIS TOBACCO POUCH...WALLET... KEYS...
NO WIG ?
LET'S SEE.. THERE'S ONE MORE THING IN HERE
HEY!
YOW! OW!
WH-WHAT'S THE MATTER?
HELP! I'M BURNIN' UP!!
TUBBY, WAIT!
WATER! WATER!
TUBBY!
WHAT'S WRONG TUB ?
WATER! I'M ON FIRE!
MY DRESS! MY MOTHERS HAT!
OOOOH!
IT WAS YOUR FATHER'S PIPE!

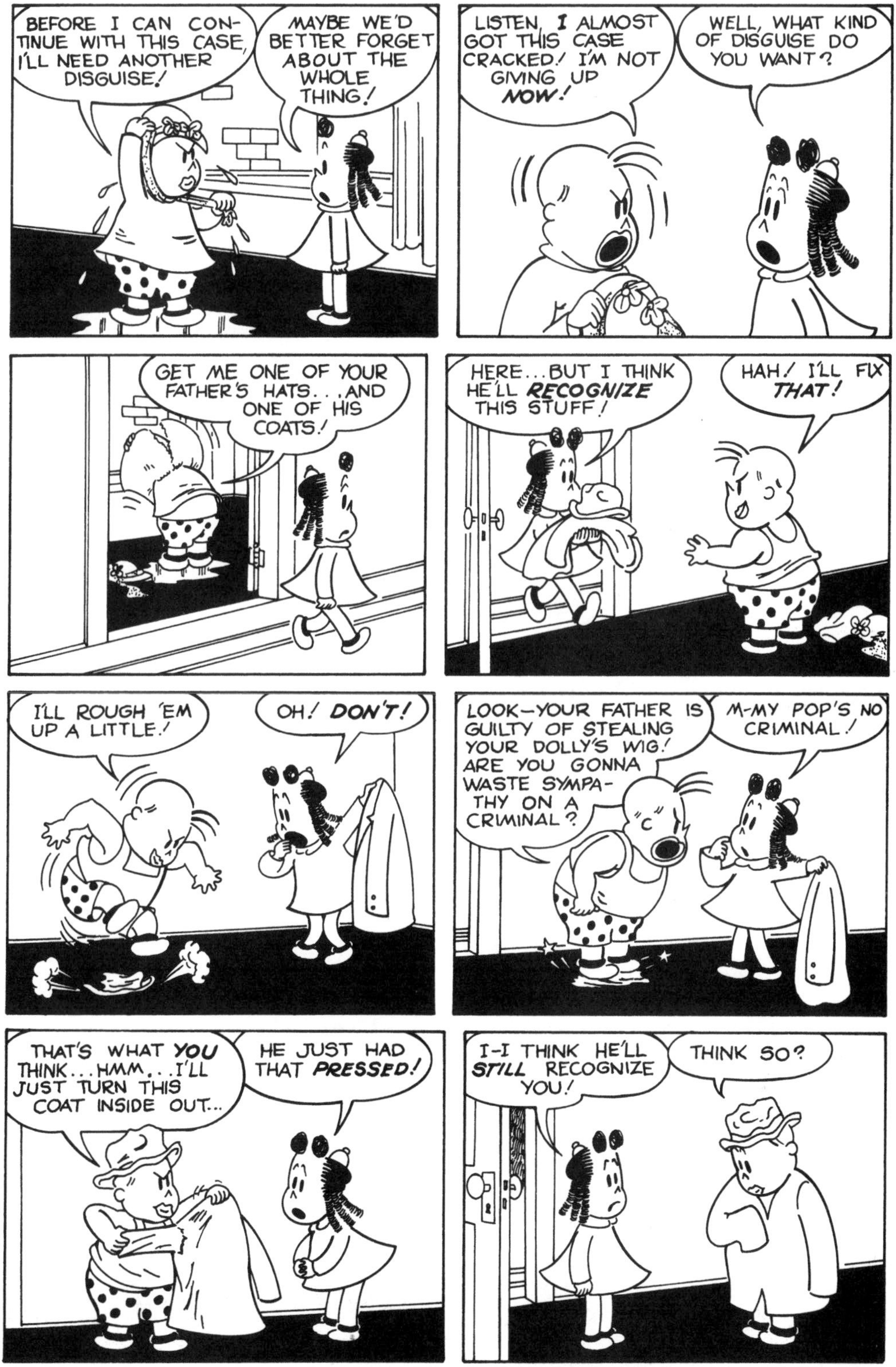
BEFORE I CAN CONTINUE WITH THIS CASE, I'LL NEED ANOTHER DISGUISE!
MAYBE WE'D BETTER FORGET ABOUT THE WHOLE THING!
LISTEN, I ALMOST GOT THIS CASE CRACKED! I'M NOT GIVING UP NOW!
WELL, WHAT KIND OF DISGUISE DO YOU WANT?
GET ME ONE OF YOUR FATHER'S HATS...AND ONE OF HIS COATS!
HERE...BUT I THINK HE'LL RECOGNIZE THIS STUFF!
HAH! I'LL FIX THAT!
I'LL ROUGH 'EM UP A LITTLE!
OH! DON'T!
LOOK—YOUR FATHER IS GUILTY OF STEALING YOUR DOLLY'S WIG! ARE YOU GONNA WASTE SYMPATHY ON A CRIMINAL?
M-MY POP'S NO CRIMINAL!
THAT'S WHAT YOU THINK...HMM...I'LL JUST TURN THIS COAT INSIDE OUT...
HE JUST HAD THAT PRESSED!
I-I THINK HE'LL STILL RECOGNIZE YOU!
THINK SO?

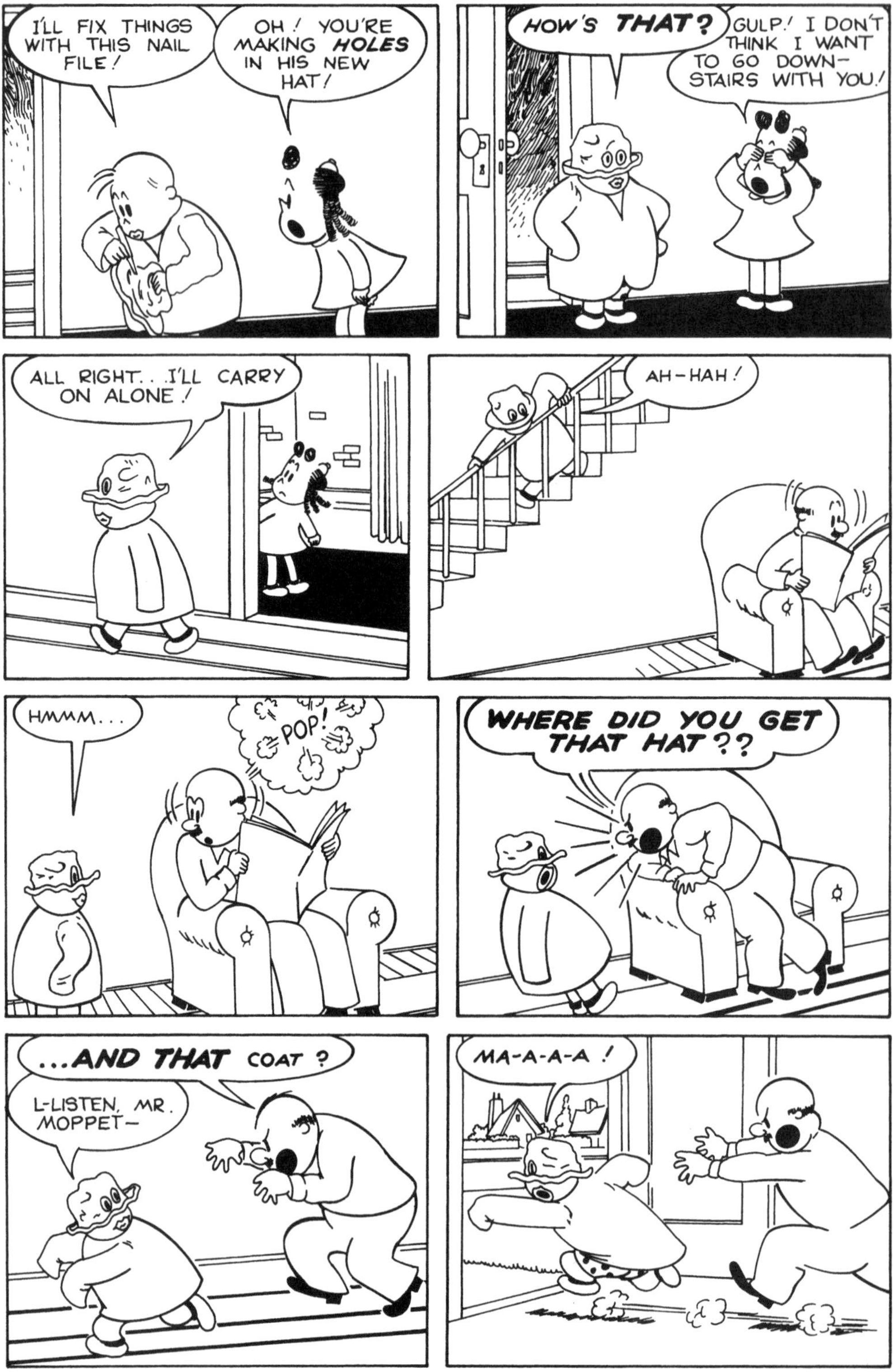
I'LL FIX THINGS WITH THIS NAIL FILE!
OH! YOU'RE MAKING **HOLES** IN HIS NEW HAT!
HOW'S **THAT?**
GULP! I DON'T THINK I WANT TO GO DOWN-STAIRS WITH YOU!
ALL RIGHT. . .I'LL CARRY ON ALONE!
AH-HAH!
HMMM...
POP!
WHERE DID YOU GET THAT HAT??
...AND THAT COAT?
L-LISTEN, MR. MOPPET—
MA-A-A-A!

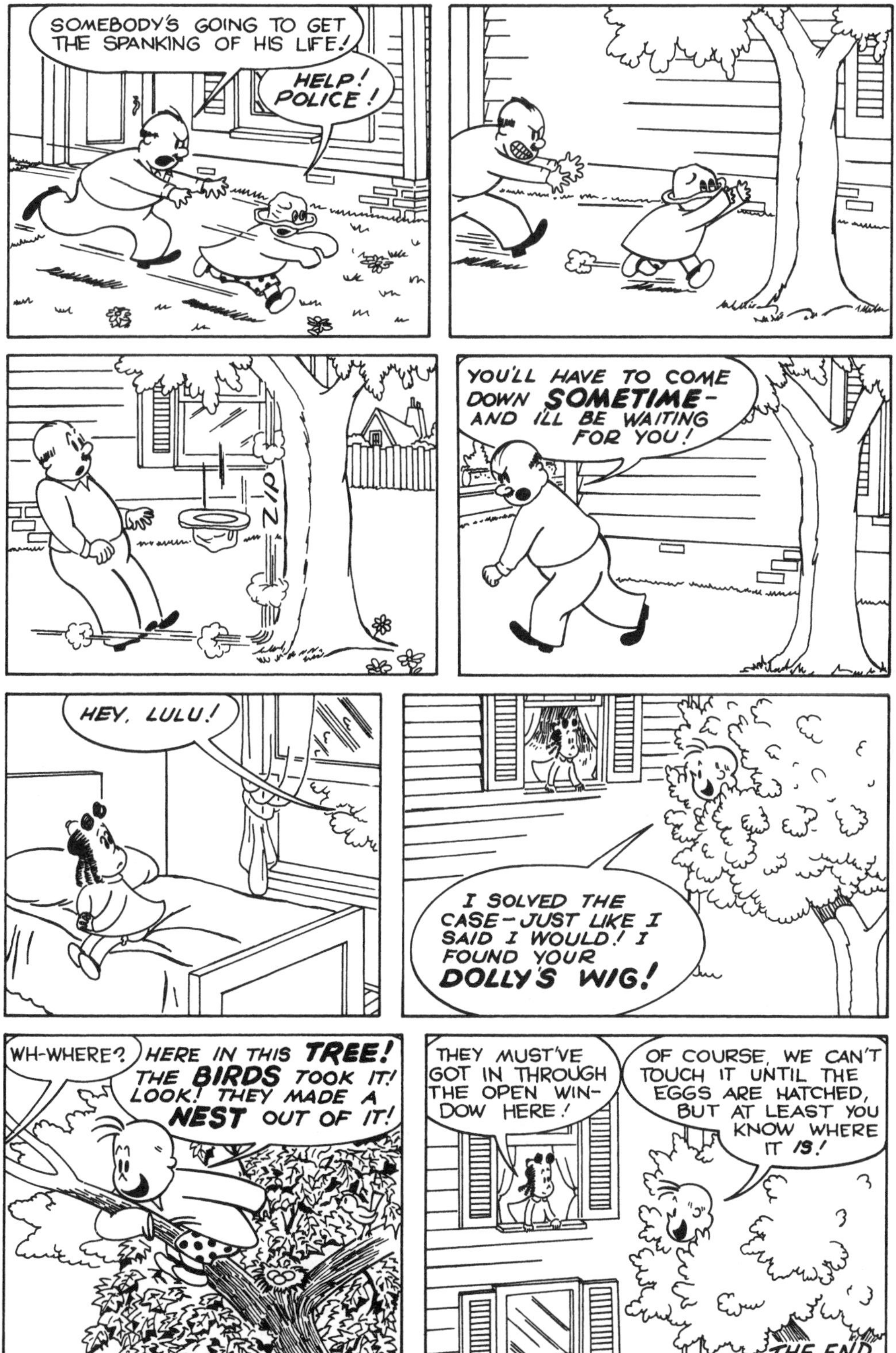
SOMEBODY'S GOING TO GET THE SPANKING OF HIS LIFE!
HELP! POLICE!
ZIP
YOU'LL HAVE TO COME DOWN SOMETIME- AND I'LL BE WAITING FOR YOU!
HEY, LULU!
I SOLVED THE CASE-JUST LIKE I SAID I WOULD! I FOUND YOUR DOLLY'S WIG!
WH-WHERE?
HERE IN THIS TREE! THE BIRDS TOOK IT! LOOK! THEY MADE A NEST OUT OF IT!
THEY MUST'VE GOT IN THROUGH THE OPEN WIN-DOW HERE!
OF COURSE, WE CAN'T TOUCH IT UNTIL THE EGGS ARE HATCHED, BUT AT LEAST YOU KNOW WHERE IT IS!
THE END

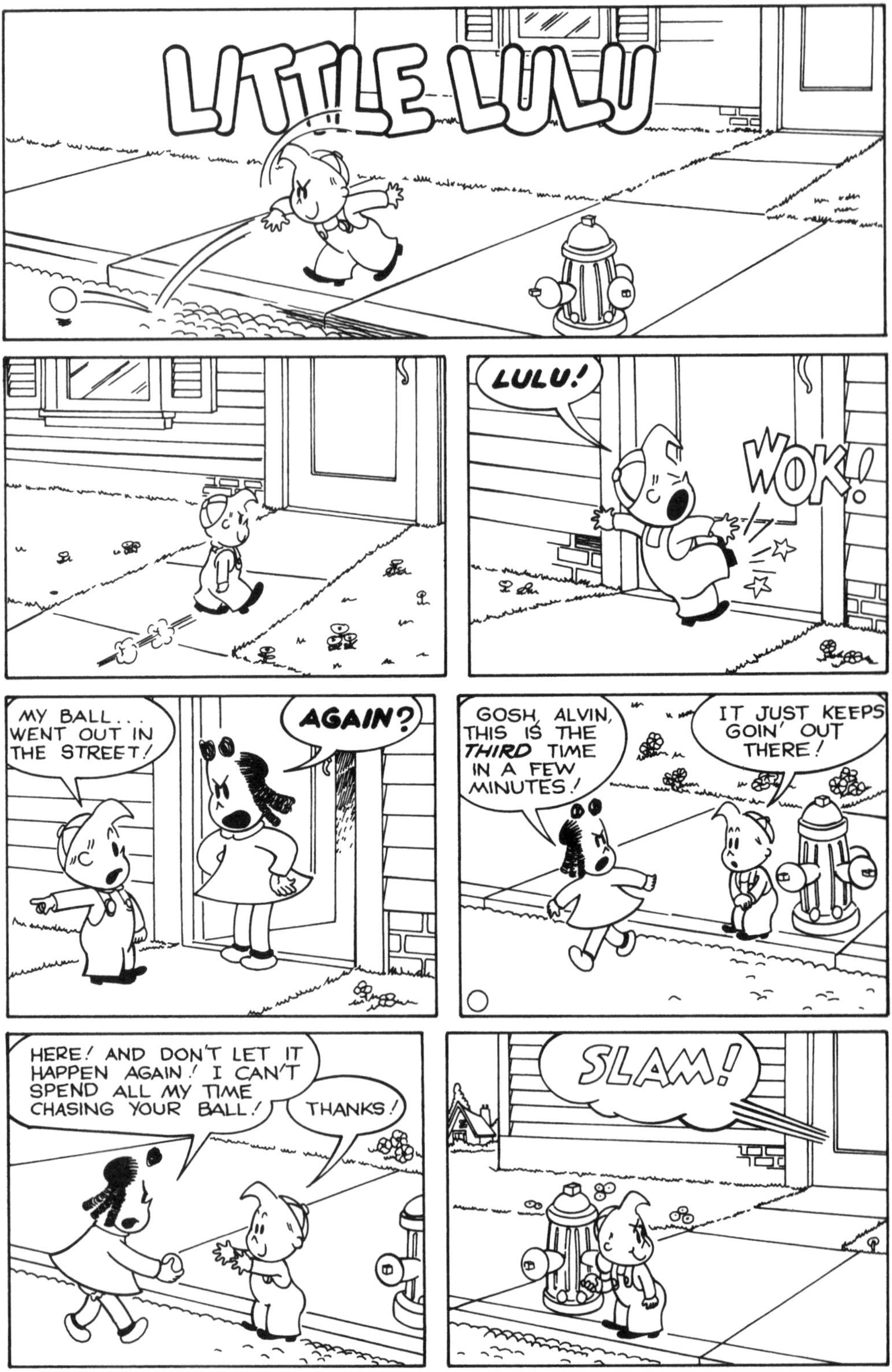
LITTLE LULU
LULU!
WOK!
MY BALL... WENT OUT IN THE STREET!
AGAIN?
GOSH, ALVIN, THIS IS THE *THIRD* TIME IN A FEW MINUTES!
IT JUST KEEPS GOIN' OUT THERE!
HERE! AND DON'T LET IT HAPPEN AGAIN! I CAN'T SPEND ALL MY TIME CHASING YOUR BALL!
THANKS!
SLAM!

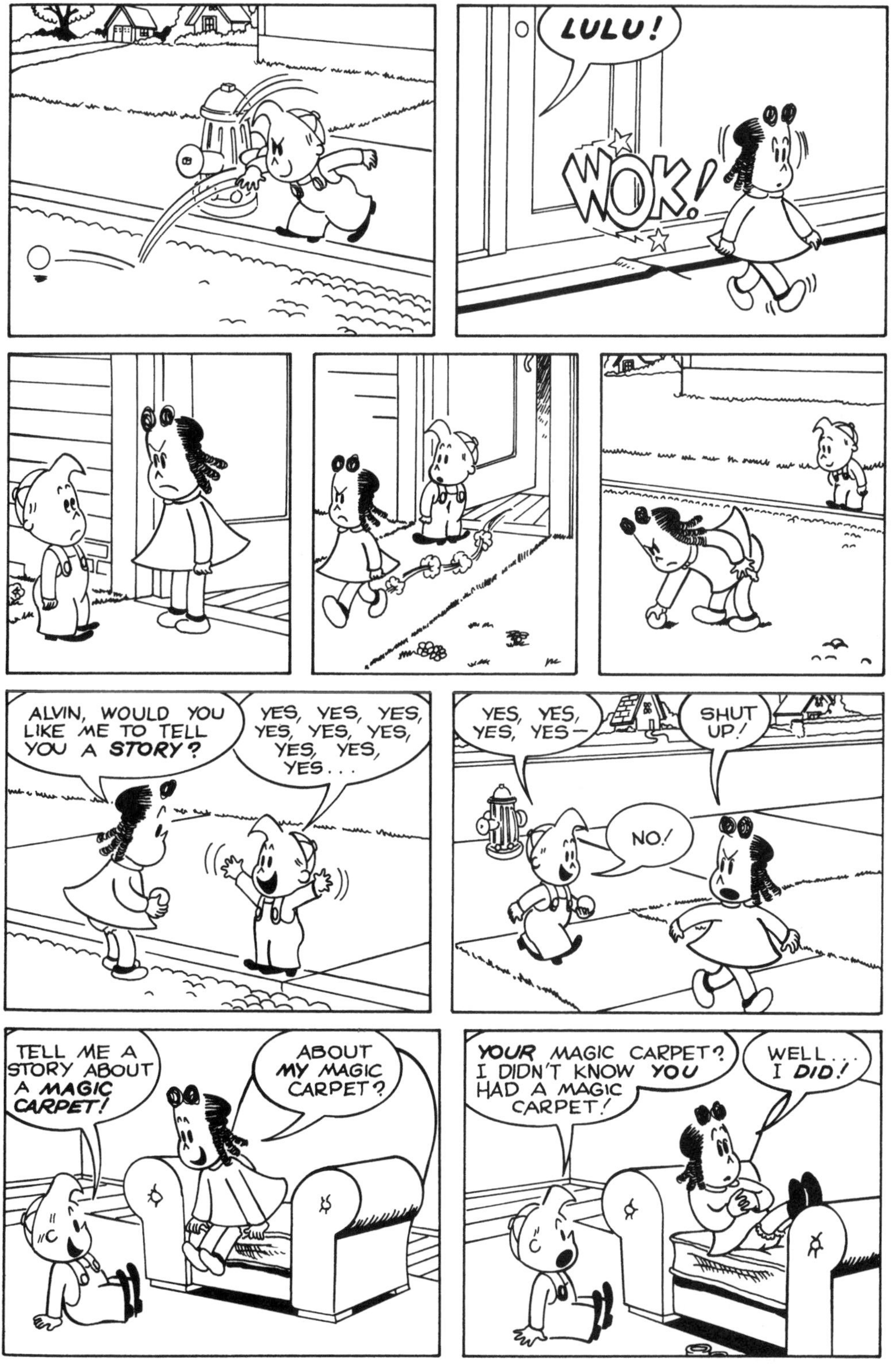
LULU!
WOK!
ALVIN, WOULD YOU LIKE ME TO TELL YOU A STORY?
YES, YES, YES, YES, YES, YES, YES, YES, YES...
YES, YES, YES, YES—
SHUT UP!
NO!
TELL ME A STORY ABOUT A MAGIC CARPET!
ABOUT MY MAGIC CARPET?
YOUR MAGIC CARPET? I DIDN'T KNOW YOU HAD A MAGIC CARPET!
WELL... I DID!

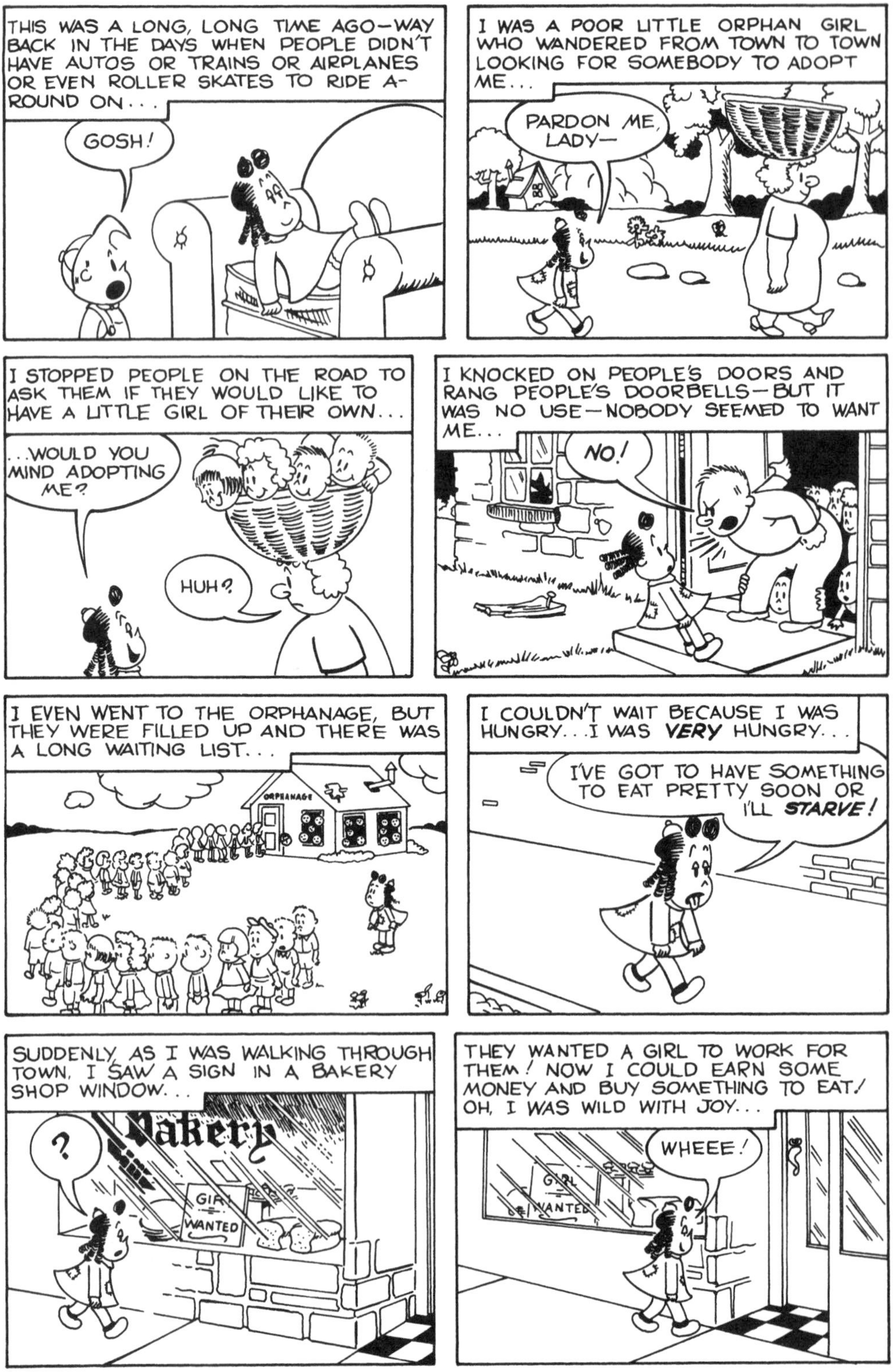
THIS WAS A LONG, LONG TIME AGO—WAY BACK IN THE DAYS WHEN PEOPLE DIDN'T HAVE AUTOS OR TRAINS OR AIRPLANES OR EVEN ROLLER SKATES TO RIDE A-ROUND ON...
GOSH!
I WAS A POOR LITTLE ORPHAN GIRL WHO WANDERED FROM TOWN TO TOWN LOOKING FOR SOMEBODY TO ADOPT ME...
PARDON ME, LADY—
I STOPPED PEOPLE ON THE ROAD TO ASK THEM IF THEY WOULD LIKE TO HAVE A LITTLE GIRL OF THEIR OWN...
...WOULD YOU MIND ADOPTING ME?
HUH?
I KNOCKED ON PEOPLE'S DOORS AND RANG PEOPLE'S DOORBELLS—BUT IT WAS NO USE—NOBODY SEEMED TO WANT ME...
NO!
I EVEN WENT TO THE ORPHANAGE, BUT THEY WERE FILLED UP AND THERE WAS A LONG WAITING LIST...
ORPHANAGE
I COULDN'T WAIT BECAUSE I WAS HUNGRY...I WAS **VERY** HUNGRY...
I'VE GOT TO HAVE SOMETHING TO EAT PRETTY SOON OR I'LL **STARVE!**
SUDDENLY, AS I WAS WALKING THROUGH TOWN, I SAW A SIGN IN A BAKERY SHOP WINDOW...
?
Bakery
GIRL WANTED
THEY WANTED A GIRL TO WORK FOR THEM! NOW I COULD EARN SOME MONEY AND BUY SOMETHING TO EAT! OH, I WAS WILD WITH JOY...
WHEEE!
GIRL WANTED

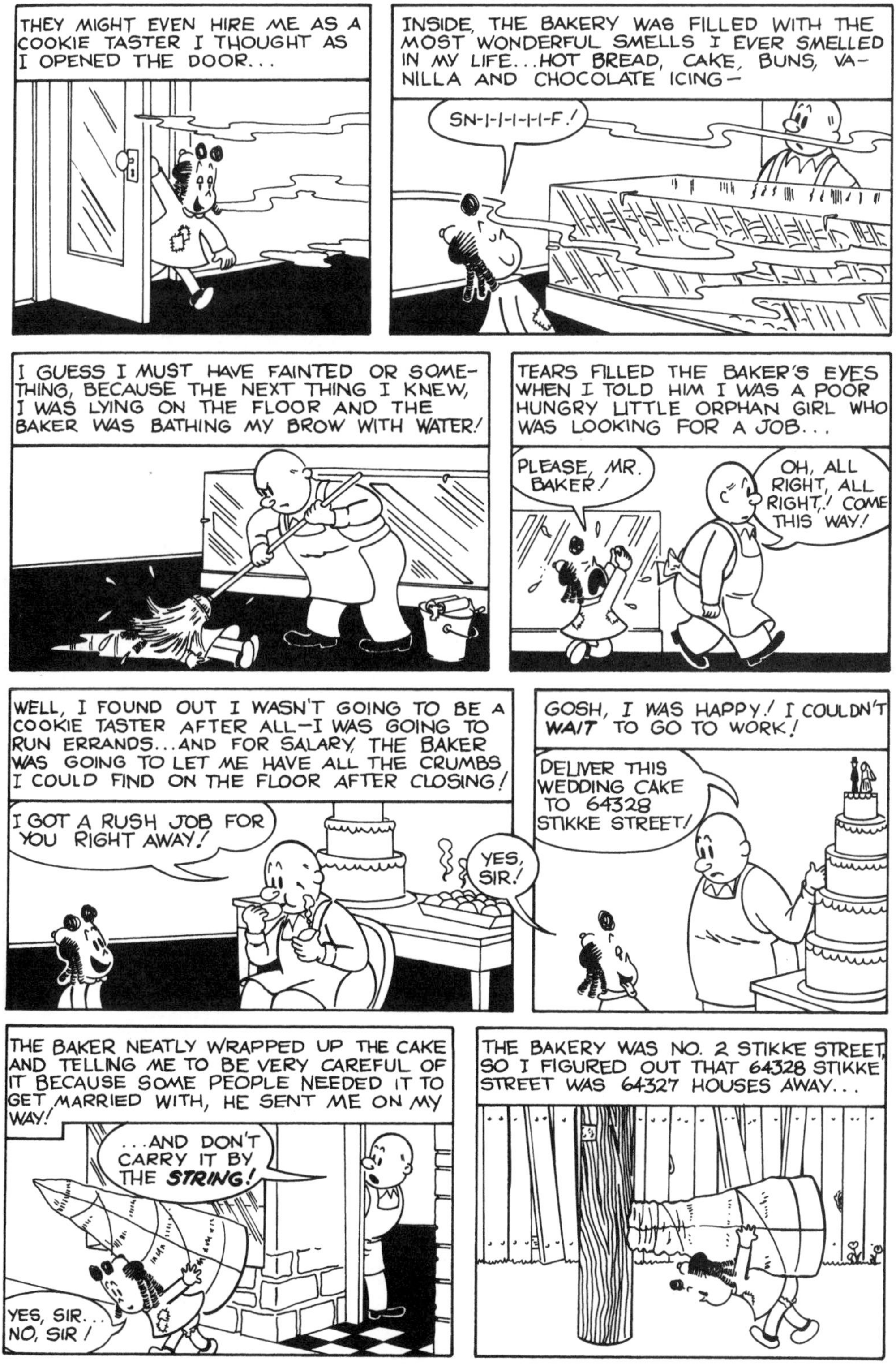
THEY MIGHT EVEN HIRE ME AS A COOKIE TASTER I THOUGHT AS I OPENED THE DOOR...
INSIDE, THE BAKERY WAS FILLED WITH THE MOST WONDERFUL SMELLS I EVER SMELLED IN MY LIFE...HOT BREAD, CAKE, BUNS, VA-NILLA AND CHOCOLATE ICING—
SN-I-I-I-I-I-F!
I GUESS I MUST HAVE FAINTED OR SOME-THING, BECAUSE THE NEXT THING I KNEW, I WAS LYING ON THE FLOOR AND THE BAKER WAS BATHING MY BROW WITH WATER!
TEARS FILLED THE BAKER'S EYES WHEN I TOLD HIM I WAS A POOR HUNGRY LITTLE ORPHAN GIRL WHO WAS LOOKING FOR A JOB...
PLEASE, MR. BAKER!
OH, ALL RIGHT, ALL RIGHT! COME THIS WAY!
WELL, I FOUND OUT I WASN'T GOING TO BE A COOKIE TASTER AFTER ALL—I WAS GOING TO RUN ERRANDS...AND FOR SALARY, THE BAKER WAS GOING TO LET ME HAVE ALL THE CRUMBS I COULD FIND ON THE FLOOR AFTER CLOSING!
I GOT A RUSH JOB FOR YOU RIGHT AWAY!
YES, SIR!
GOSH, I WAS HAPPY! I COULDN'T WAIT TO GO TO WORK!
DELIVER THIS WEDDING CAKE TO 64328 STIKKE STREET!
THE BAKER NEATLY WRAPPED UP THE CAKE AND TELLING ME TO BE VERY CAREFUL OF IT BECAUSE SOME PEOPLE NEEDED IT TO GET MARRIED WITH, HE SENT ME ON MY WAY!
...AND DON'T CARRY IT BY THE STRING!
YES, SIR... NO, SIR!
THE BAKERY WAS NO. 2 STIKKE STREET, SO I FIGURED OUT THAT 64328 STIKKE STREET WAS 64327 HOUSES AWAY...

AT FIRST THE CAKE DIDN'T SEEM VERY HEAVY, BUT I HAD ONLY GONE A FEW STEPS DOWN THE BLOCK WHEN IT SEEMED TO GET *SO* HEAVY I COULDN'T MOVE ANOTHER STEP!

I PUT THE CAKE DOWN AND RESTED FOR A LITTLE WHILE... AND I GUESS MAYBE I CRIED A LITTLE, TOO!

BAW!

I DIDN'T KNOW *WHAT* TO DO... I COULDN'T TAKE A TROLLEY CAR OR A BUS OR ANYTHING BECAUSE THERE JUST *WEREN'T* ANY IN THOSE DAYS...

WAH!

TSK, TSK, TSK... LITTLE GIRLS SHOULD NEVER CRY!

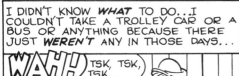

SUDDENLY I HEARD A SOFT VOICE BEHIND ME AND WHEN I TURNED TO LOOK, THERE WAS THE STRANGEST LITTLE MAN I EVER SAW...

GOSH!

YOU SEEM TO BE IN TROUBLE LITTLE GIRL?

HE WAS VERY NICE... WHEN I TOLD HIM WHY I WAS CRYING, HE SAID MAYBE HE COULD HELP ME...

NOW THIS CARPET— IF YOU WILL BUY IT FROM ME—

HE WANTED TO SELL ME A CARPET... IT WASN'T EVEN A *NEW* CARPET- IT WAS VERY OLD AND FADED AND WORN--- IMAGINE!

B-BUT I DON'T *NEED* A CARPET! AND EVEN IF I DID, I HAVEN'T ANY MONEY TO BUY IT WITH!

YOU NEED *THIS* CARPET.. AND I DON'T WANT ANY *MONEY* FOR IT!

THEN HE TOLD ME TO PUT THE CAKE ON THE CARPET WHICH HE HAD SPREAD ON THE SIDEWALK!

WELL, ALL RIGHT, BUT—

AFTER THE CAKE WAS ON THE CARPET HE TOLD ME TO SIT ON THE CARPET MYSELF...

WELL?

NOW SAY *GIDDYBAB!*

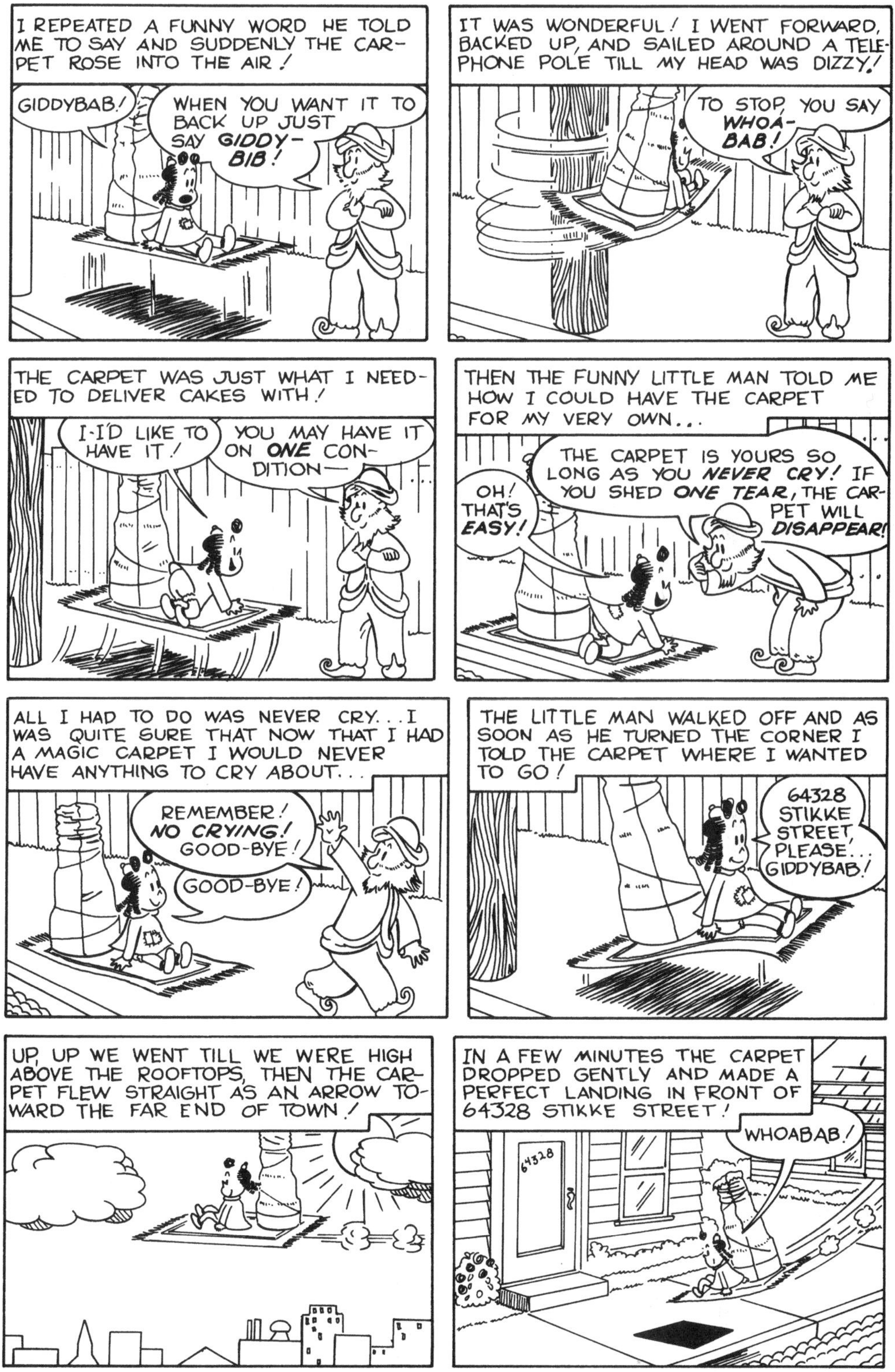

I REPEATED A FUNNY WORD HE TOLD ME TO SAY AND SUDDENLY THE CARPET ROSE INTO THE AIR!
GIDDYBAB!
WHEN YOU WANT IT TO BACK UP JUST SAY GIDDY-BIB!
IT WAS WONDERFUL! I WENT FORWARD, BACKED UP, AND SAILED AROUND A TELEPHONE POLE TILL MY HEAD WAS DIZZY!
TO STOP, YOU SAY WHOA-BAB!
THE CARPET WAS JUST WHAT I NEEDED TO DELIVER CAKES WITH!
I-I'D LIKE TO HAVE IT!
YOU MAY HAVE IT ON ONE CONDITION—
THEN THE FUNNY LITTLE MAN TOLD ME HOW I COULD HAVE THE CARPET FOR MY VERY OWN...
THE CARPET IS YOURS SO LONG AS YOU NEVER CRY! IF YOU SHED ONE TEAR, THE CARPET WILL DISAPPEAR!
OH! THAT'S EASY!
ALL I HAD TO DO WAS NEVER CRY... I WAS QUITE SURE THAT NOW THAT I HAD A MAGIC CARPET I WOULD NEVER HAVE ANYTHING TO CRY ABOUT...
REMEMBER! NO CRYING! GOOD-BYE!
GOOD-BYE!
THE LITTLE MAN WALKED OFF AND AS SOON AS HE TURNED THE CORNER I TOLD THE CARPET WHERE I WANTED TO GO!
64328 STIKKE STREET, PLEASE... GIDDYBAB!
UP, UP WE WENT TILL WE WERE HIGH ABOVE THE ROOFTOPS, THEN THE CARPET FLEW STRAIGHT AS AN ARROW TOWARD THE FAR END OF TOWN!
IN A FEW MINUTES THE CARPET DROPPED GENTLY AND MADE A PERFECT LANDING IN FRONT OF 64328 STIKKE STREET!
64328
WHOABAB!

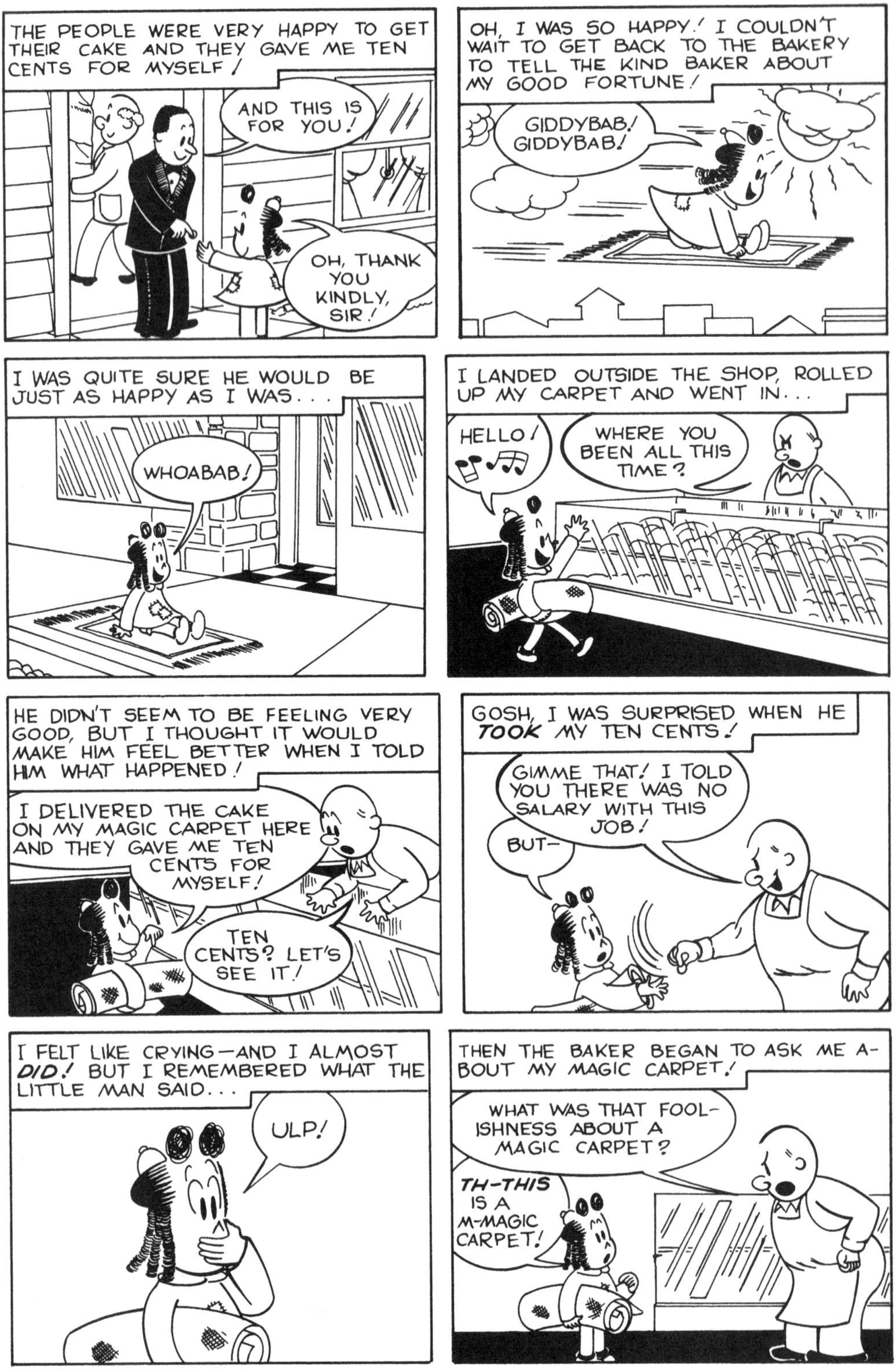
THE PEOPLE WERE VERY HAPPY TO GET THEIR CAKE AND THEY GAVE ME TEN CENTS FOR MYSELF!
AND THIS IS FOR YOU!
OH, THANK YOU KINDLY, SIR!
OH, I WAS SO HAPPY! I COULDN'T WAIT TO GET BACK TO THE BAKERY TO TELL THE KIND BAKER ABOUT MY GOOD FORTUNE!
GIDDYBAB! GIDDYBAB!
I WAS QUITE SURE HE WOULD BE JUST AS HAPPY AS I WAS...
WHOABAB!
I LANDED OUTSIDE THE SHOP, ROLLED UP MY CARPET AND WENT IN...
HELLO!
WHERE YOU BEEN ALL THIS TIME?
HE DIDN'T SEEM TO BE FEELING VERY GOOD, BUT I THOUGHT IT WOULD MAKE HIM FEEL BETTER WHEN I TOLD HIM WHAT HAPPENED!
I DELIVERED THE CAKE ON MY MAGIC CARPET HERE AND THEY GAVE ME TEN CENTS FOR MYSELF!
TEN CENTS? LET'S SEE IT!
GOSH, I WAS SURPRISED WHEN HE TOOK MY TEN CENTS!
GIMME THAT! I TOLD YOU THERE WAS NO SALARY WITH THIS JOB!
BUT—
I FELT LIKE CRYING—AND I ALMOST DID! BUT I REMEMBERED WHAT THE LITTLE MAN SAID...
ULP!
THEN THE BAKER BEGAN TO ASK ME A-BOUT MY MAGIC CARPET!
WHAT WAS THAT FOOL-ISHNESS ABOUT A MAGIC CARPET?
TH-THIS IS A M-MAGIC CARPET!

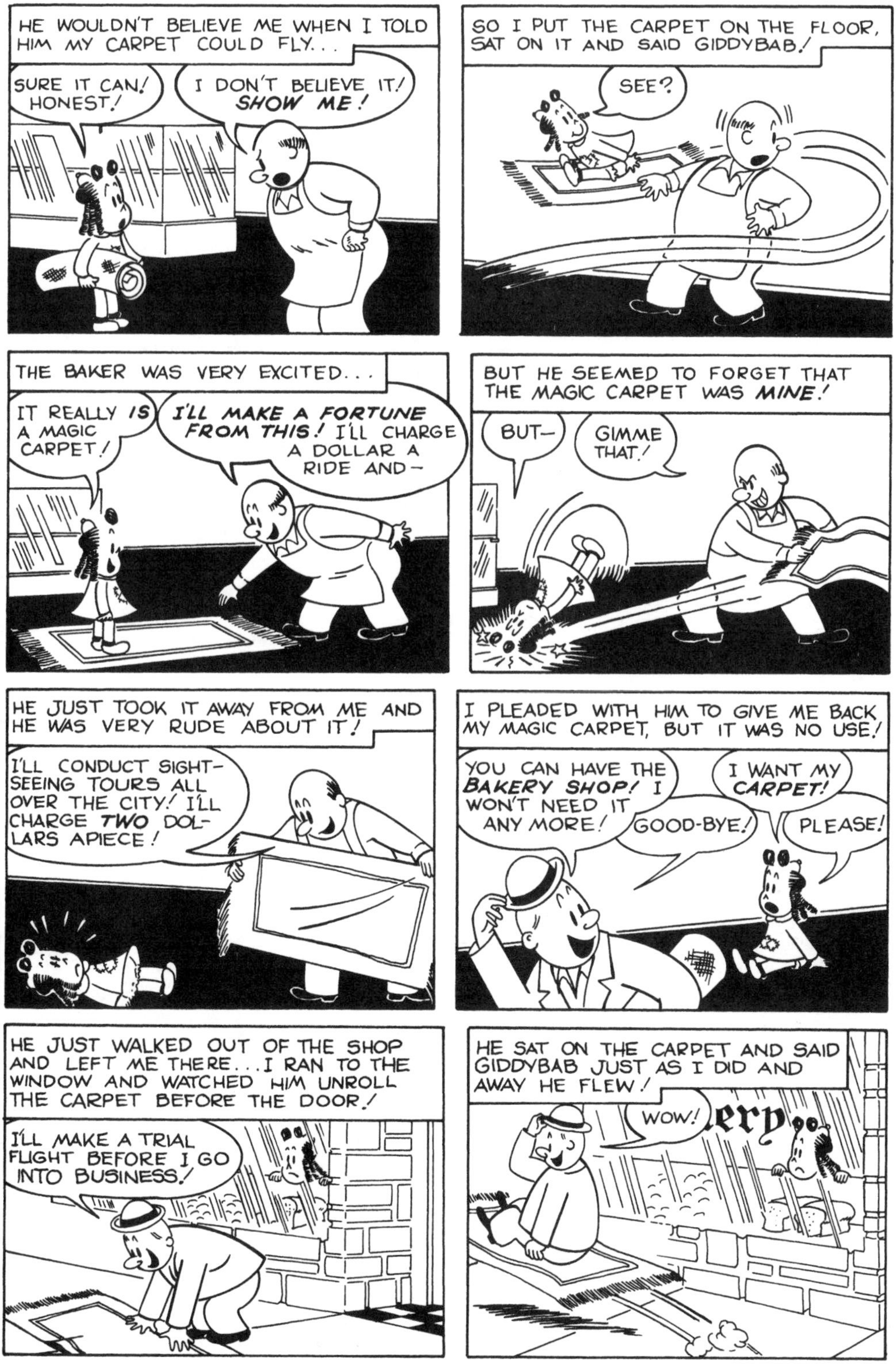
HE WOULDN'T BELIEVE ME WHEN I TOLD HIM MY CARPET COULD FLY...
SURE IT CAN! HONEST!
I DON'T BELIEVE IT! SHOW ME!
SO I PUT THE CARPET ON THE FLOOR, SAT ON IT AND SAID GIDDYBAB!
SEE?
THE BAKER WAS VERY EXCITED...
IT REALLY IS A MAGIC CARPET!
I'LL MAKE A FORTUNE FROM THIS! I'LL CHARGE A DOLLAR A RIDE AND–
BUT HE SEEMED TO FORGET THAT THE MAGIC CARPET WAS MINE!
BUT–
GIMME THAT!
HE JUST TOOK IT AWAY FROM ME AND HE WAS VERY RUDE ABOUT IT!
I'LL CONDUCT SIGHT-SEEING TOURS ALL OVER THE CITY! I'LL CHARGE TWO DOLLARS APIECE!
I PLEADED WITH HIM TO GIVE ME BACK MY MAGIC CARPET, BUT IT WAS NO USE!
YOU CAN HAVE THE BAKERY SHOP! I WON'T NEED IT ANY MORE!
I WANT MY CARPET!
GOOD-BYE!
PLEASE!
HE JUST WALKED OUT OF THE SHOP AND LEFT ME THERE... I RAN TO THE WINDOW AND WATCHED HIM UNROLL THE CARPET BEFORE THE DOOR!
I'LL MAKE A TRIAL FLIGHT BEFORE I GO INTO BUSINESS!
HE SAT ON THE CARPET AND SAID GIDDYBAB JUST AS I DID AND AWAY HE FLEW!
WOW!

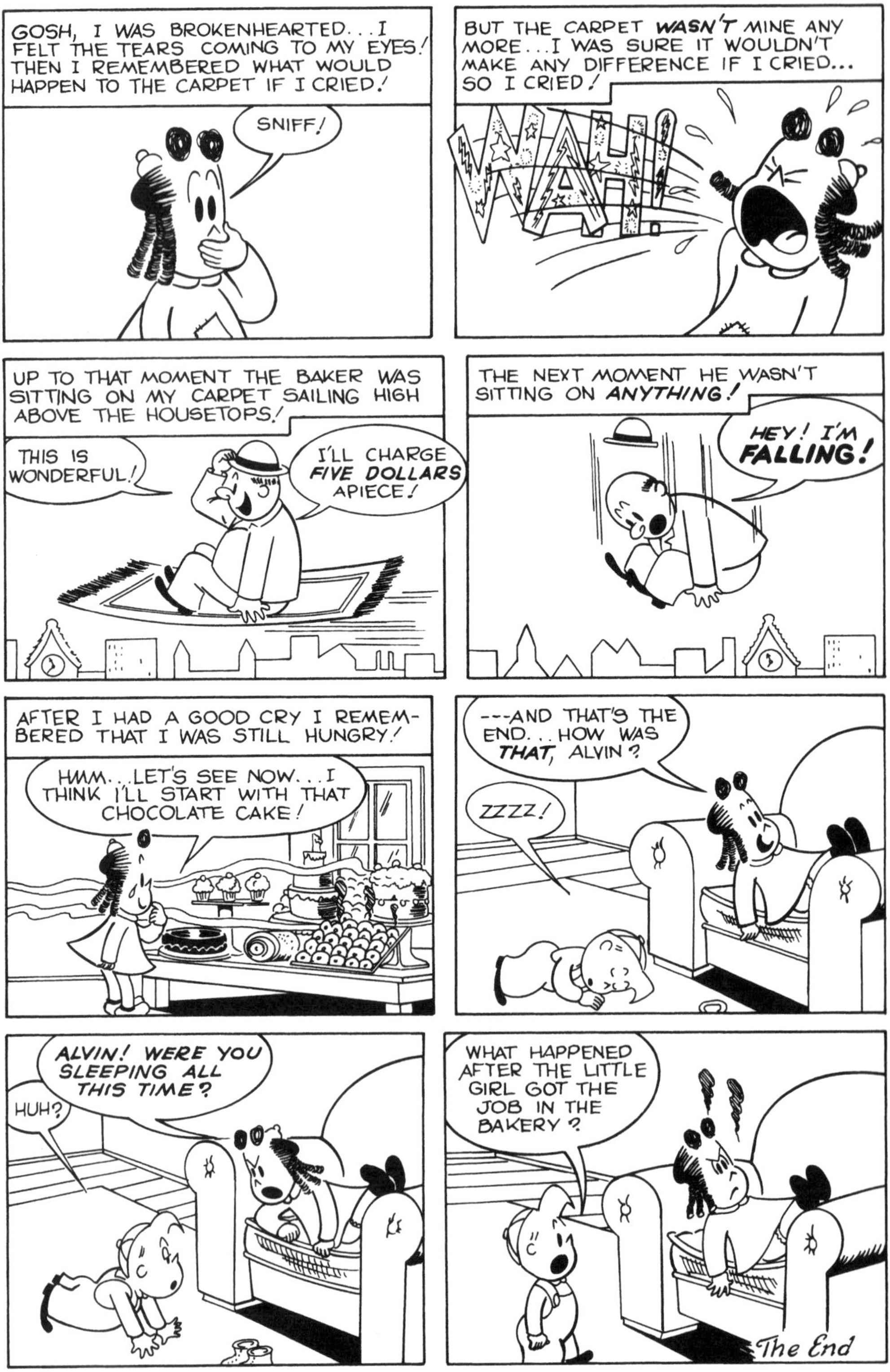
GOSH, I WAS BROKENHEARTED... I FELT THE TEARS COMING TO MY EYES! THEN I REMEMBERED WHAT WOULD HAPPEN TO THE CARPET IF I CRIED!
SNIFF!
BUT THE CARPET WASN'T MINE ANY MORE... I WAS SURE IT WOULDN'T MAKE ANY DIFFERENCE IF I CRIED... SO I CRIED!
WAH!
UP TO THAT MOMENT THE BAKER WAS SITTING ON MY CARPET SAILING HIGH ABOVE THE HOUSETOPS!
THIS IS WONDERFUL!
I'LL CHARGE FIVE DOLLARS APIECE!
THE NEXT MOMENT HE WASN'T SITTING ON ANYTHING!
HEY! I'M FALLING!
AFTER I HAD A GOOD CRY I REMEMBERED THAT I WAS STILL HUNGRY!
HMM... LET'S SEE NOW... I THINK I'LL START WITH THAT CHOCOLATE CAKE!
---AND THAT'S THE END... HOW WAS THAT, ALVIN?
ZZZZ!
ALVIN! WERE YOU SLEEPING ALL THIS TIME?
HUH?
WHAT HAPPENED AFTER THE LITTLE GIRL GOT THE JOB IN THE BAKERY?
The End

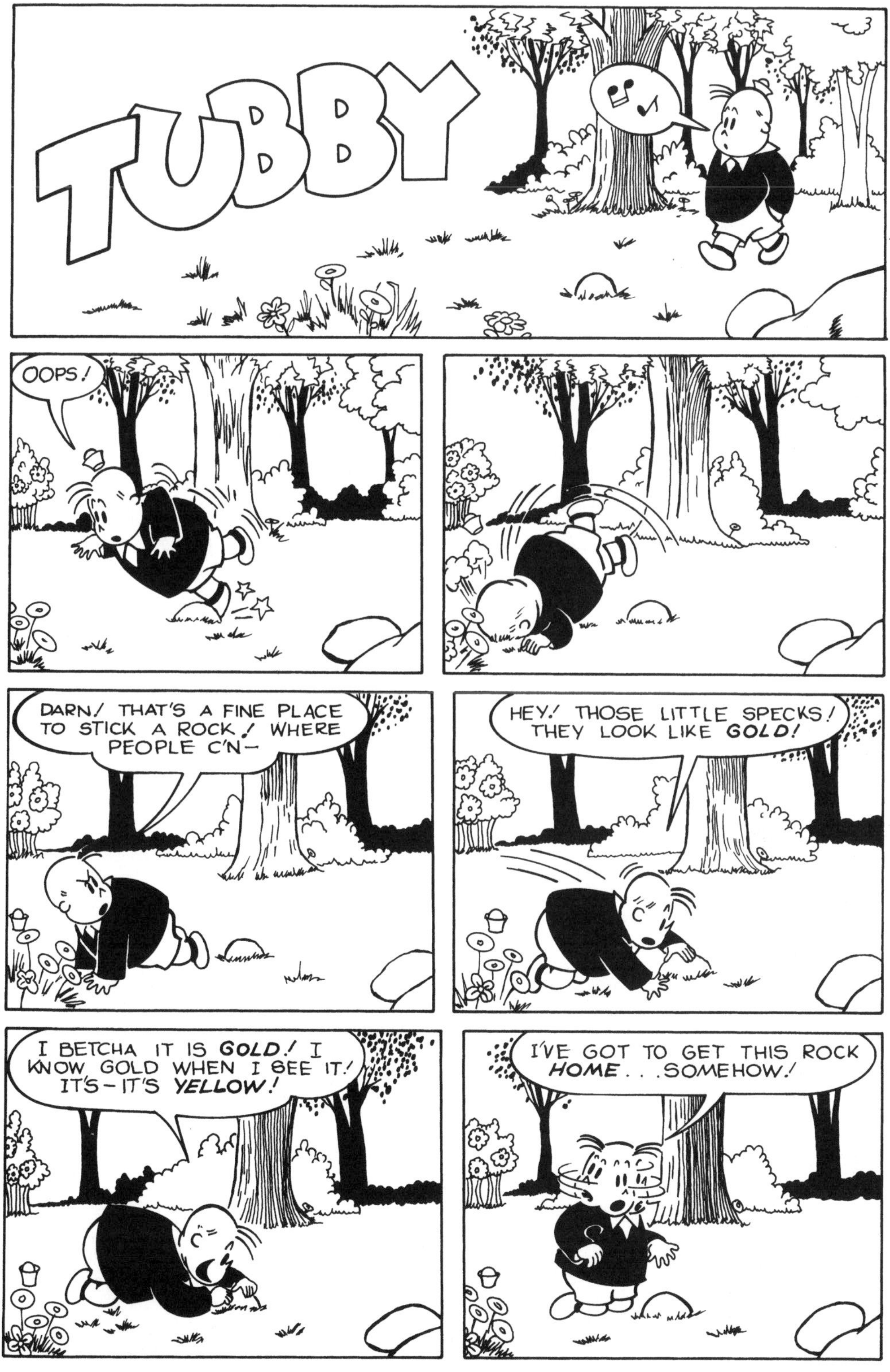
TUBBY
OOPS!
DARN! THAT'S A FINE PLACE TO STICK A ROCK! WHERE PEOPLE C'N—
HEY! THOSE LITTLE SPECKS! THEY LOOK LIKE GOLD!
I BETCHA IT IS GOLD! I KNOW GOLD WHEN I SEE IT! IT'S—IT'S YELLOW!
I'VE GOT TO GET THIS ROCK HOME...SOMEHOW!

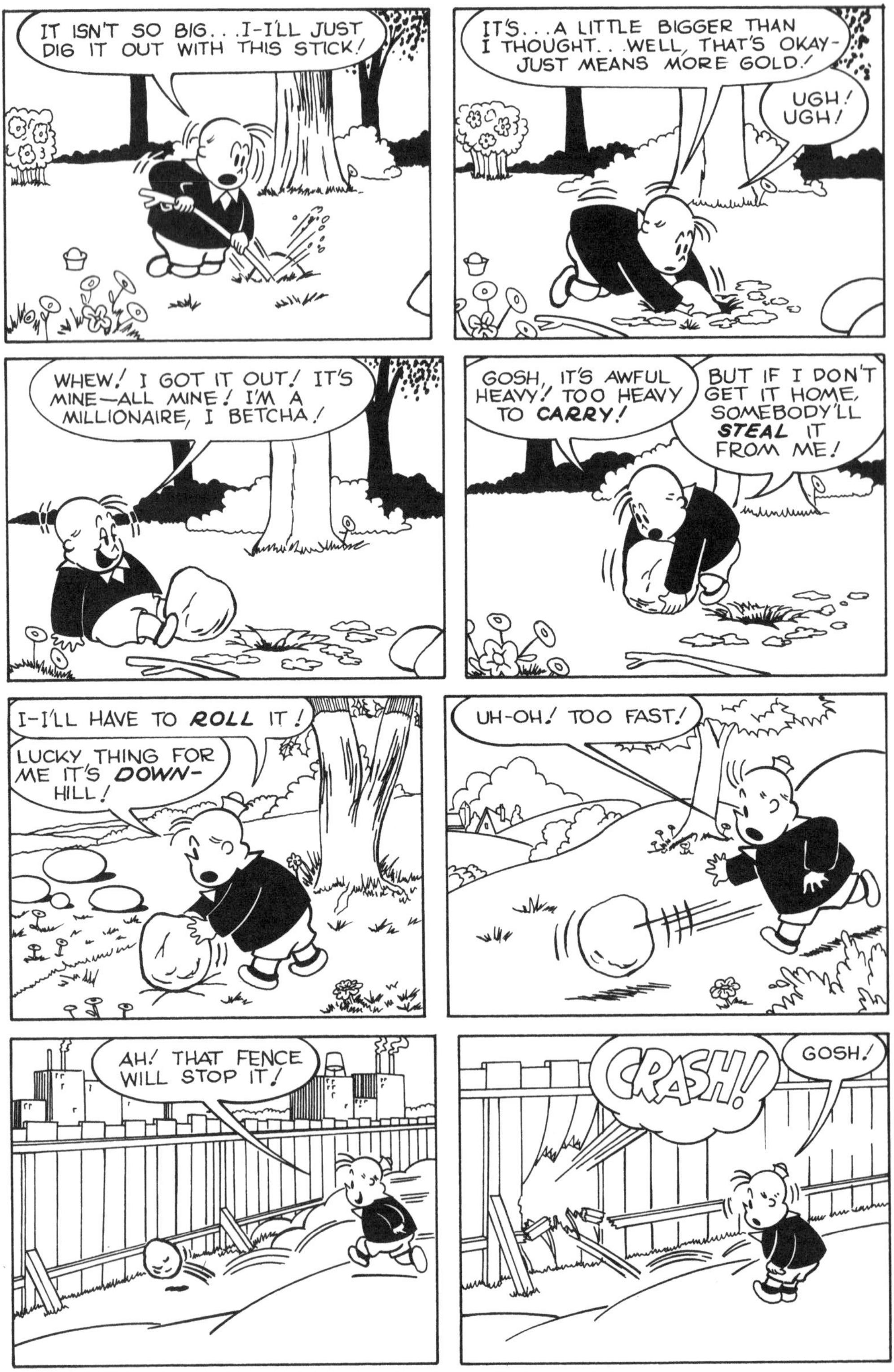
IT ISN'T SO BIG. . .I-I'LL JUST DIG IT OUT WITH THIS STICK!
IT'S. . .A LITTLE BIGGER THAN I THOUGHT. . .WELL, THAT'S OKAY-JUST MEANS MORE GOLD!
UGH! UGH!
WHEW! I GOT IT OUT! IT'S MINE—ALL MINE! I'M A MILLIONAIRE, I BETCHA!
GOSH, IT'S AWFUL HEAVY! TOO HEAVY TO CARRY!
BUT IF I DON'T GET IT HOME, SOMEBODY'LL STEAL IT FROM ME!
I-I'LL HAVE TO ROLL IT!
LUCKY THING FOR ME IT'S DOWN-HILL!
UH-OH! TOO FAST!
AH! THAT FENCE WILL STOP IT!
CRASH!
GOSH!

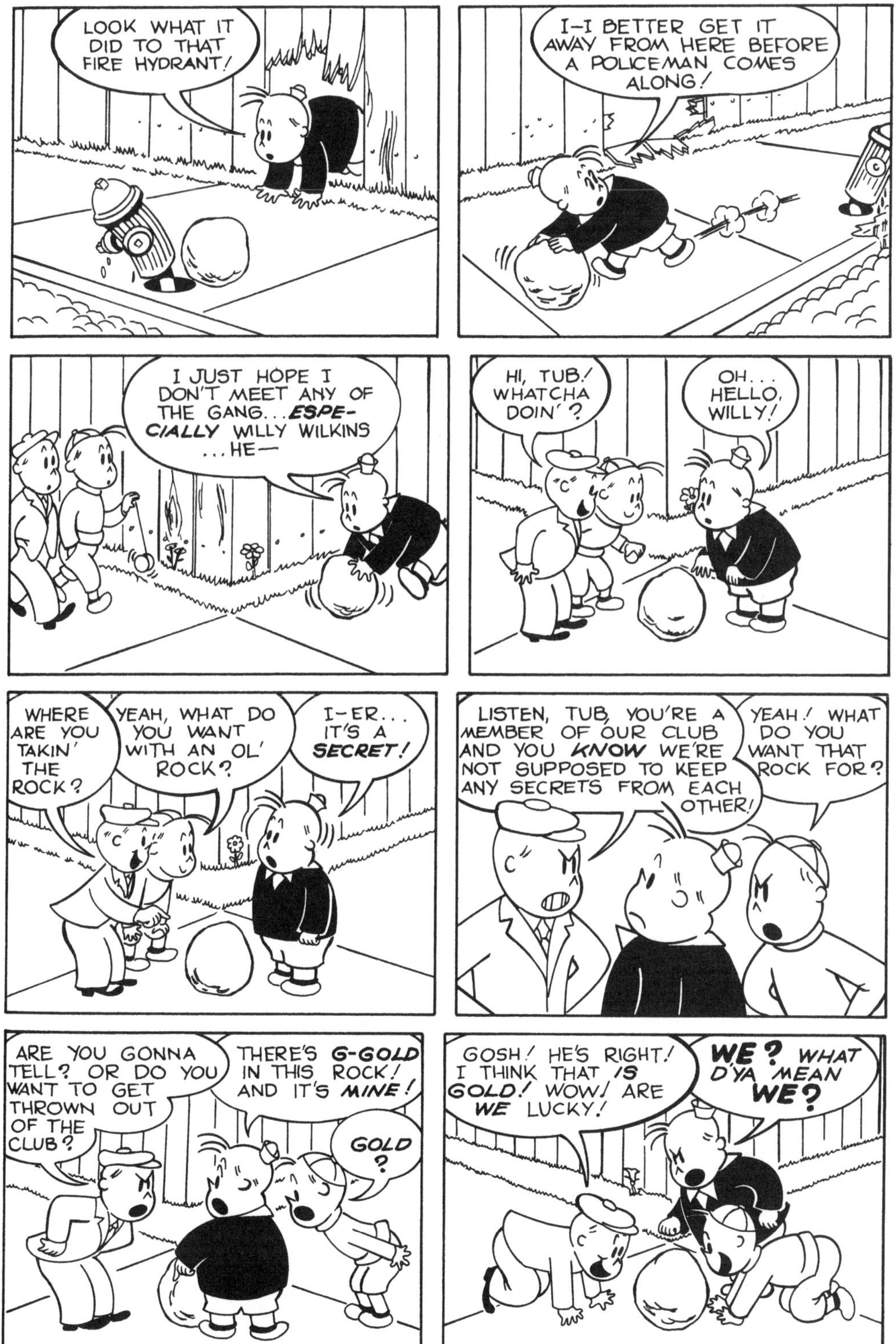
LOOK WHAT IT DID TO THAT FIRE HYDRANT!
I-I BETTER GET IT AWAY FROM HERE BEFORE A POLICEMAN COMES ALONG!
I JUST HOPE I DON'T MEET ANY OF THE GANG... ESPE-CIALLY WILLY WILKINS ...HE—
HI, TUB! WHATCHA DOIN'?
OH... HELLO, WILLY!
WHERE ARE YOU TAKIN' THE ROCK?
YEAH, WHAT DO YOU WANT WITH AN OL' ROCK?
I-ER... IT'S A SECRET!
LISTEN, TUB, YOU'RE A MEMBER OF OUR CLUB AND YOU KNOW WE'RE NOT SUPPOSED TO KEEP ANY SECRETS FROM EACH OTHER!
YEAH! WHAT DO YOU WANT THAT ROCK FOR?
ARE YOU GONNA TELL? OR DO YOU WANT TO GET THROWN OUT OF THE CLUB?
THERE'S G-GOLD IN THIS ROCK! AND IT'S MINE!
GOLD?
GOSH! HE'S RIGHT! I THINK THAT IS GOLD! WOW! ARE WE LUCKY!
WE? WHAT D'YA MEAN WE?

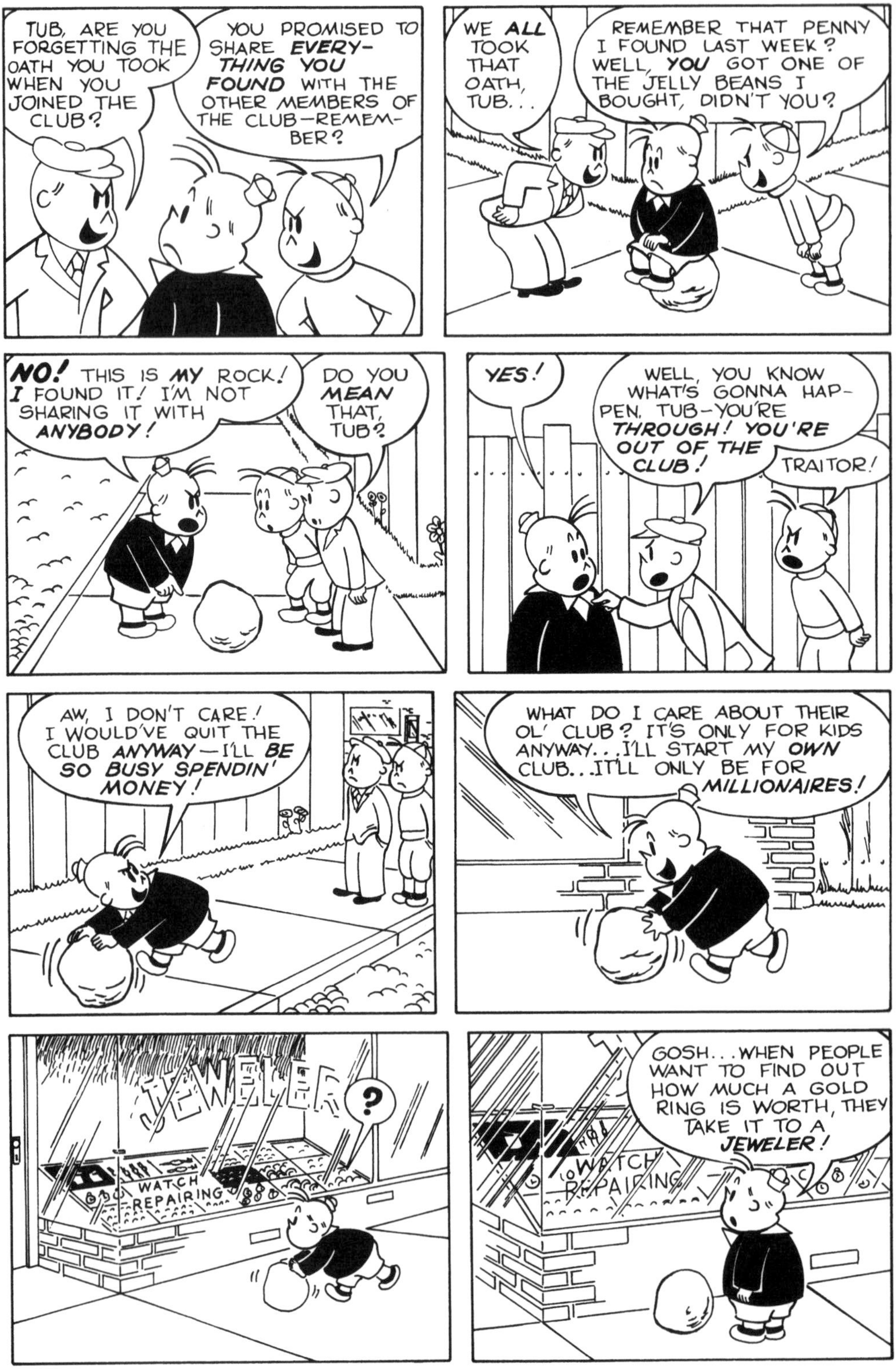
TUB, ARE YOU FORGETTING THE OATH YOU TOOK WHEN YOU JOINED THE CLUB?
YOU PROMISED TO SHARE EVERY-THING YOU FOUND WITH THE OTHER MEMBERS OF THE CLUB—REMEMBER?
WE ALL TOOK THAT OATH, TUB...
REMEMBER THAT PENNY I FOUND LAST WEEK? WELL, YOU GOT ONE OF THE JELLY BEANS I BOUGHT, DIDN'T YOU?
NO! THIS IS MY ROCK! I FOUND IT! I'M NOT SHARING IT WITH ANYBODY!
DO YOU MEAN THAT, TUB?
YES!
WELL, YOU KNOW WHAT'S GONNA HAP-PEN, TUB—YOU'RE THROUGH! YOU'RE OUT OF THE CLUB!
TRAITOR!
AW, I DON'T CARE! I WOULD'VE QUIT THE CLUB ANYWAY—I'LL BE SO BUSY SPENDIN' MONEY!
WHAT DO I CARE ABOUT THEIR OL' CLUB? IT'S ONLY FOR KIDS ANYWAY...I'LL START MY OWN CLUB...IT'LL ONLY BE FOR MILLIONAIRES!
JEWELER
WATCH REPAIRING
?
GOSH...WHEN PEOPLE WANT TO FIND OUT HOW MUCH A GOLD RING IS WORTH, THEY TAKE IT TO A JEWELER!
WATCH REPAIRING

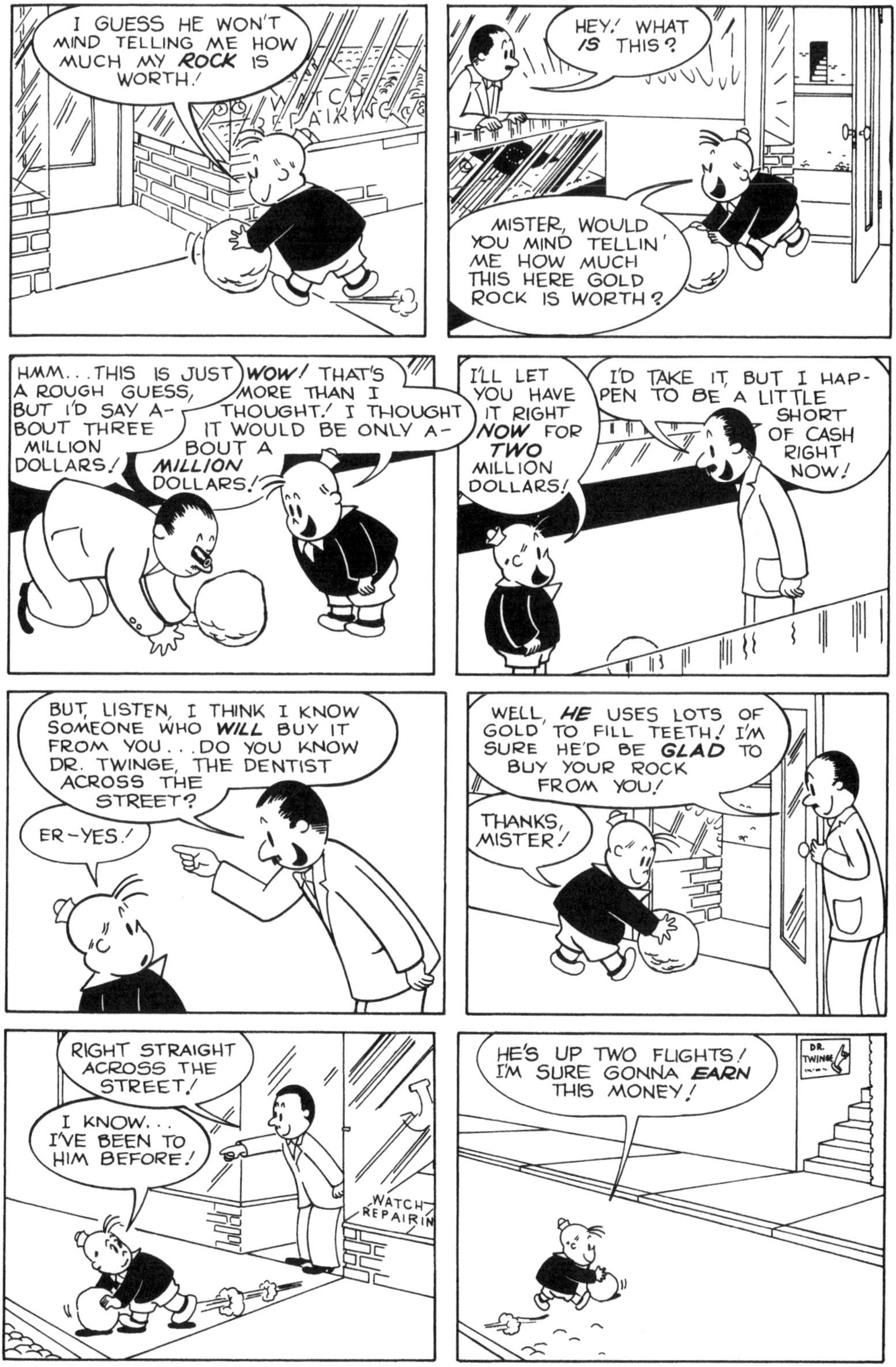
I GUESS HE WON'T MIND TELLING ME HOW MUCH MY ROCK IS WORTH!
WATCH REPAIRING
HEY! WHAT IS THIS?
MISTER, WOULD YOU MIND TELLIN' ME HOW MUCH THIS HERE GOLD ROCK IS WORTH?
HMM... THIS IS JUST A ROUGH GUESS, BUT I'D SAY A-BOUT THREE MILLION DOLLARS!
WOW! THAT'S MORE THAN I THOUGHT! I THOUGHT IT WOULD BE ONLY A-BOUT A MILLION DOLLARS!
I'LL LET YOU HAVE IT RIGHT NOW FOR TWO MILLION DOLLARS!
I'D TAKE IT, BUT I HAPPEN TO BE A LITTLE SHORT OF CASH RIGHT NOW!
BUT, LISTEN, I THINK I KNOW SOMEONE WHO WILL BUY IT FROM YOU... DO YOU KNOW DR. TWINGE, THE DENTIST ACROSS THE STREET?
ER-YES!
WELL, HE USES LOTS OF GOLD TO FILL TEETH! I'M SURE HE'D BE GLAD TO BUY YOUR ROCK FROM YOU!
THANKS, MISTER!
RIGHT STRAIGHT ACROSS THE STREET!
I KNOW... I'VE BEEN TO HIM BEFORE!
WATCH REPAIRIN
HE'S UP TWO FLIGHTS! I'M SURE GONNA EARN THIS MONEY!
DR. TWINGE

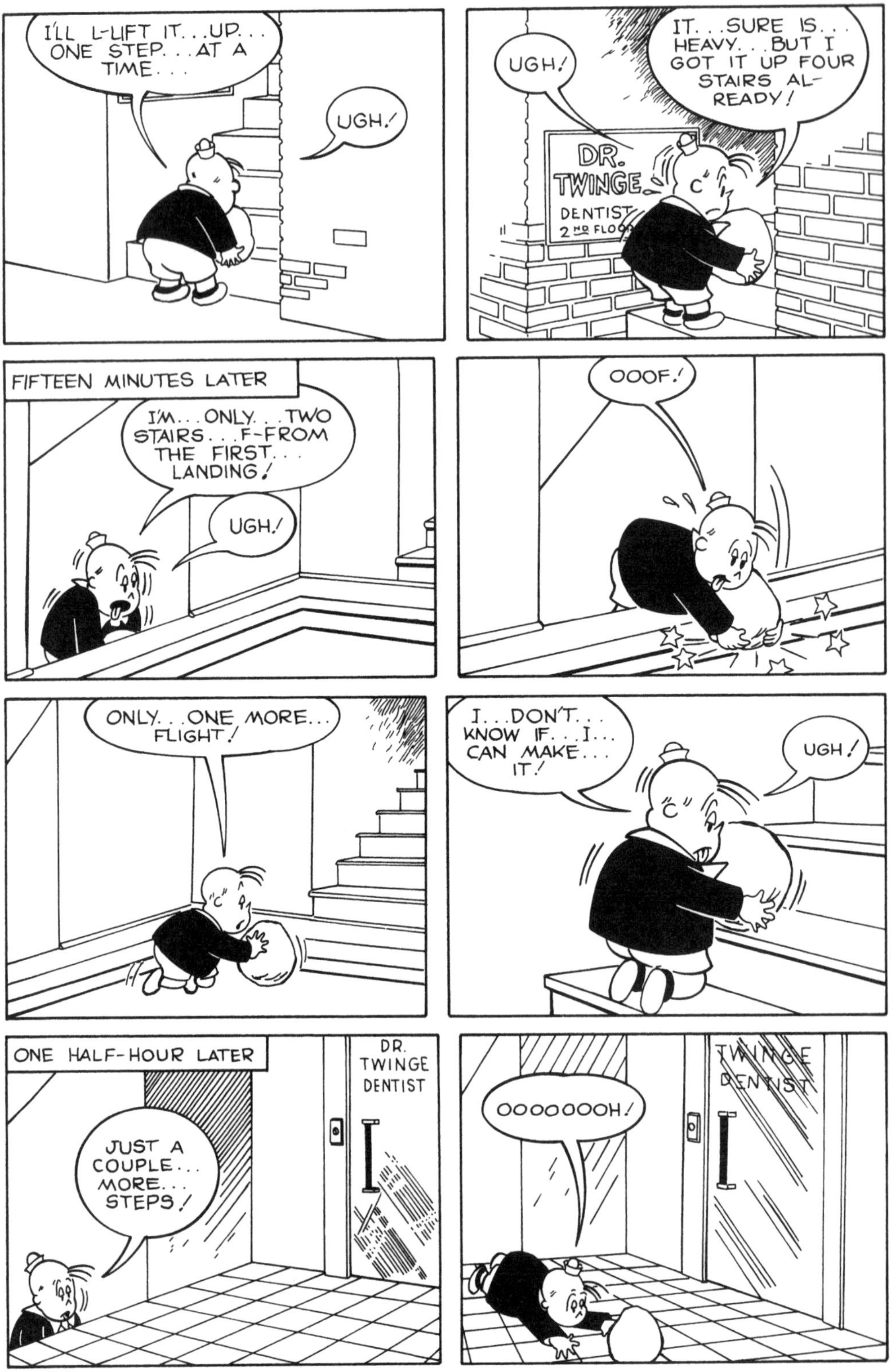
I'LL L-LIFT IT... UP... ONE STEP... AT A TIME...
UGH!
UGH!
IT... SURE IS... HEAVY... BUT I GOT IT UP FOUR STAIRS AL-READY!
DR. TWINGE DENTIST 2ND FLOOR
FIFTEEN MINUTES LATER
I'M... ONLY... TWO STAIRS... F-FROM THE FIRST... LANDING!
UGH!
OOOF!
ONLY... ONE MORE... FLIGHT!
I... DON'T... KNOW IF... I... CAN MAKE... IT!
UGH!
ONE HALF-HOUR LATER
DR. TWINGE DENTIST
JUST A COUPLE... MORE... STEPS!
OOOOOOOH!
TWINGE DENTIST

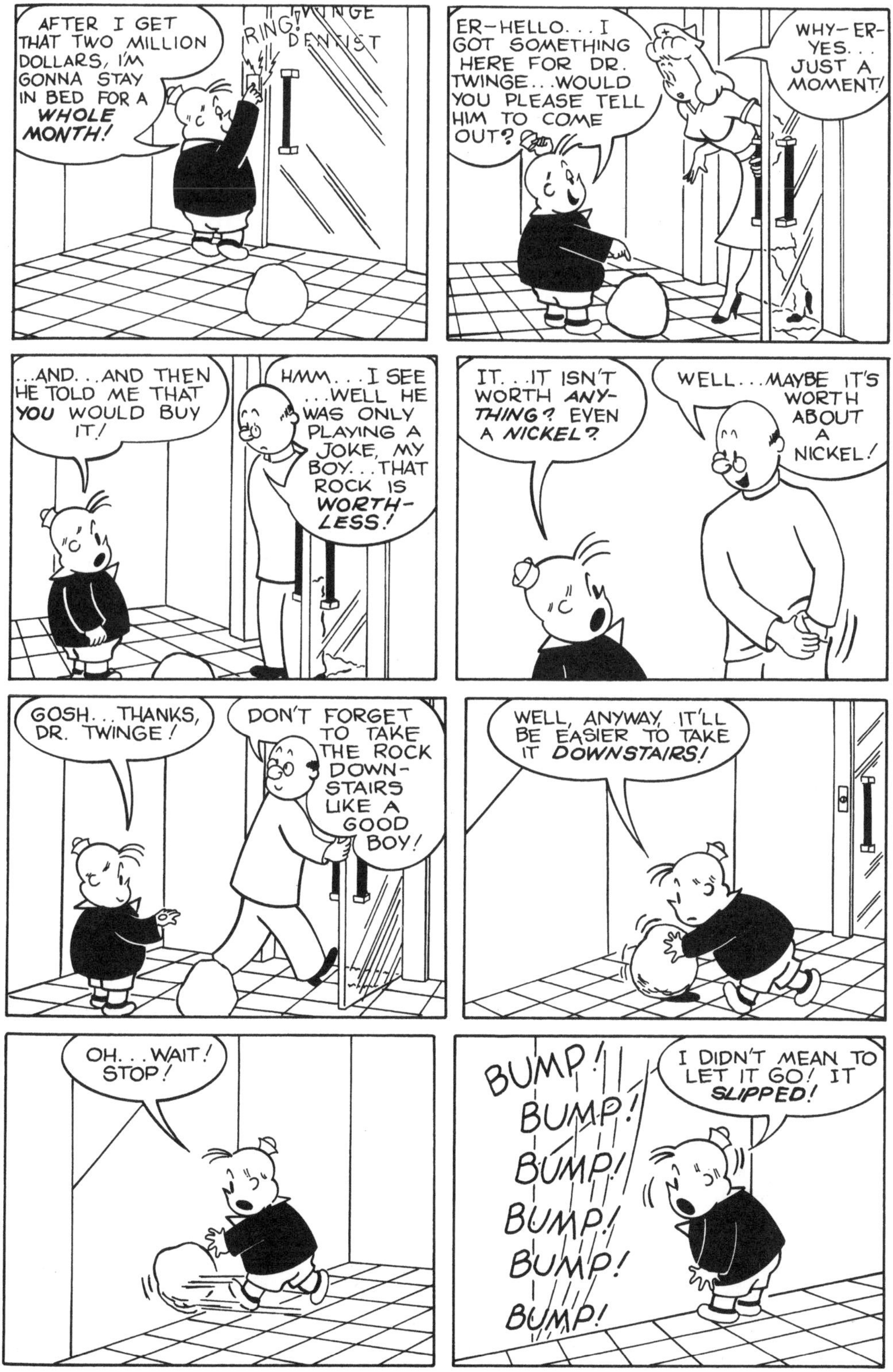
AFTER I GET THAT TWO MILLION DOLLARS, I'M GONNA STAY IN BED FOR A WHOLE MONTH!
RING!
TWINGE DENTIST
ER—HELLO... I GOT SOMETHING HERE FOR DR. TWINGE... WOULD YOU PLEASE TELL HIM TO COME OUT?
WHY—ER—YES... JUST A MOMENT!
...AND... AND THEN HE TOLD ME THAT YOU WOULD BUY IT!
HMM... I SEE ...WELL HE WAS ONLY PLAYING A JOKE, MY BOY... THAT ROCK IS WORTHLESS!
IT... IT ISN'T WORTH ANYTHING? EVEN A NICKEL?
WELL... MAYBE IT'S WORTH ABOUT A NICKEL!
GOSH... THANKS, DR. TWINGE!
DON'T FORGET TO TAKE THE ROCK DOWNSTAIRS LIKE A GOOD BOY!
WELL, ANYWAY, IT'LL BE EASIER TO TAKE IT DOWNSTAIRS!
OH... WAIT! STOP!
BUMP! BUMP! BUMP! BUMP! BUMP! BUMP!
I DIDN'T MEAN TO LET IT GO! IT SLIPPED!

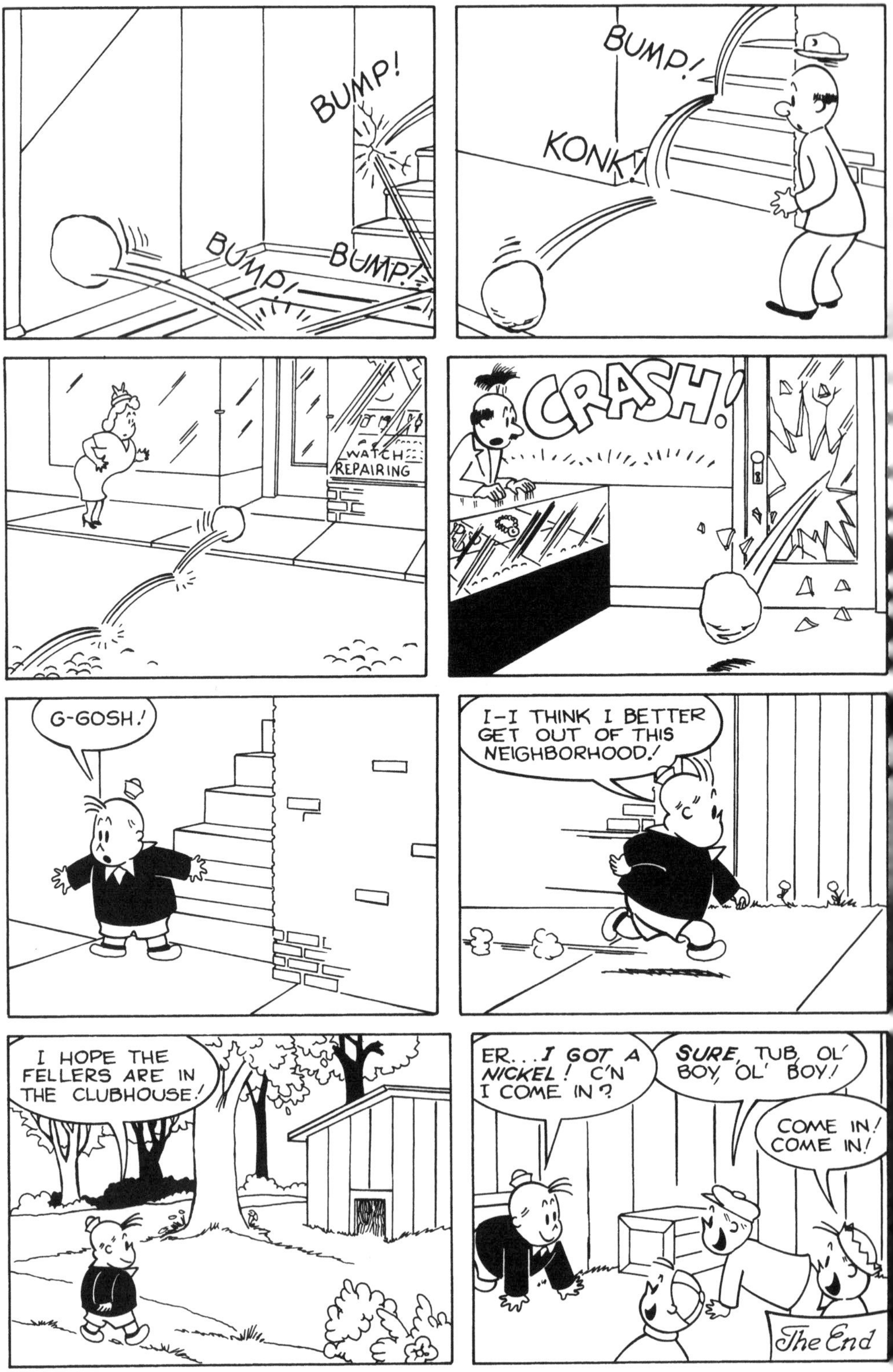
BUMP!
BUMP!
BUMP!
BUMP!
KONK!
WATCH REPAIRING
CRASH!
G-GOSH!
I-I THINK I BETTER GET OUT OF THIS NEIGHBORHOOD!
I HOPE THE FELLERS ARE IN THE CLUBHOUSE!
ER... I GOT A NICKEL! C'N I COME IN?
SURE, TUB, OL' BOY, OL' BOY!
COME IN! COME IN!
The End

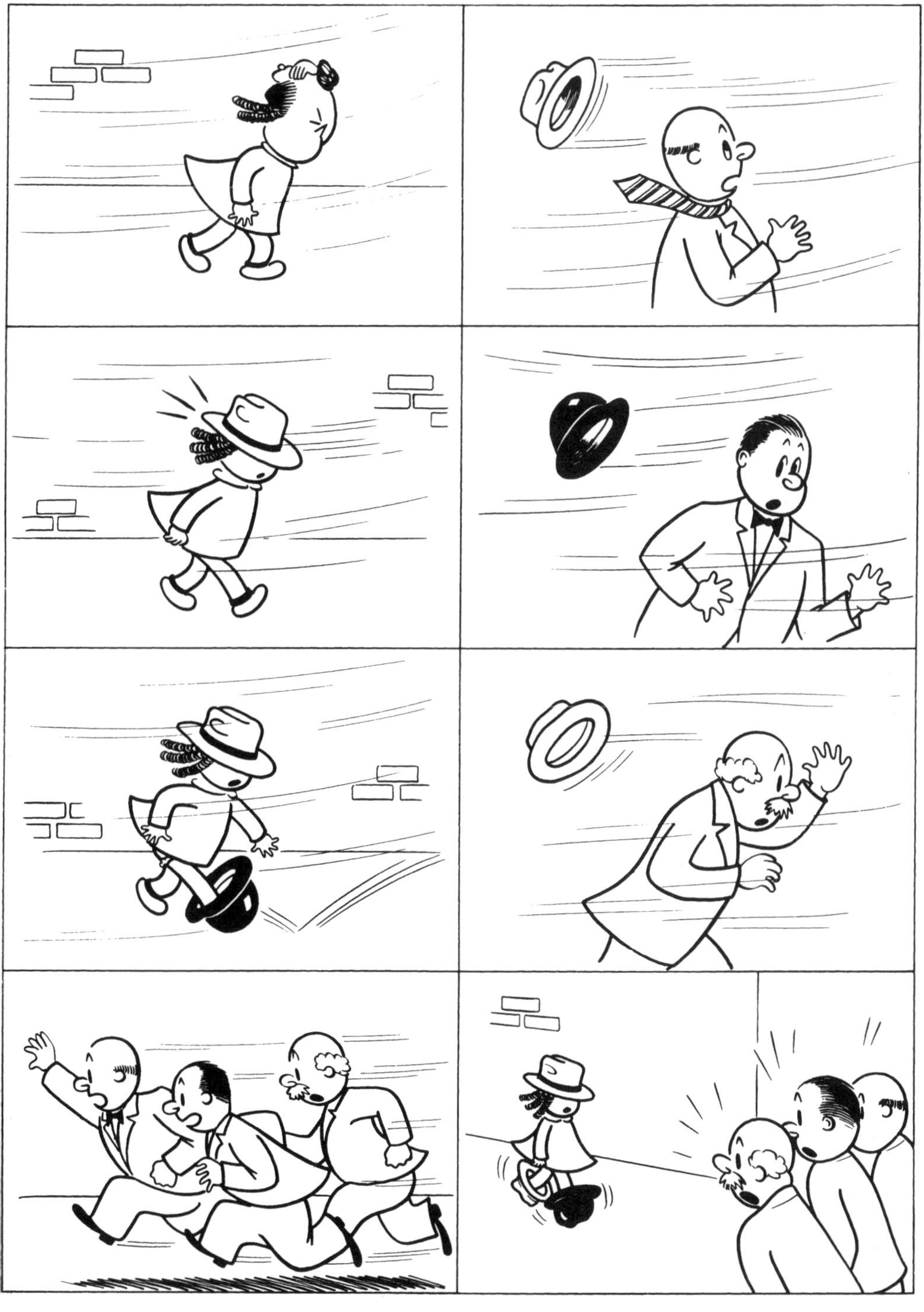

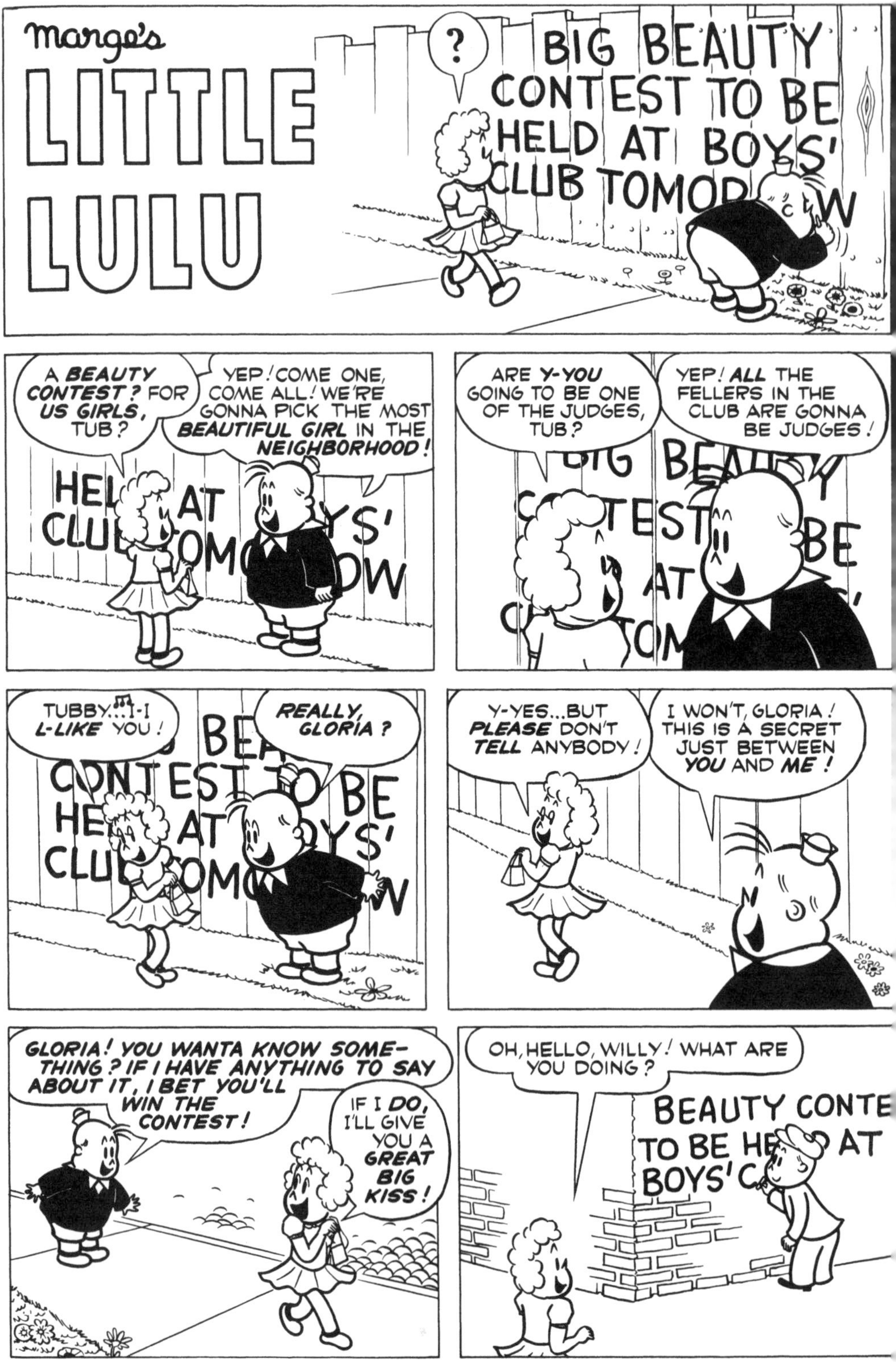
marge's
LITTLE LULU
?
BIG BEAUTY
CONTEST TO BE
HELD AT BOYS'
A BEAUTY CONTEST? FOR US GIRLS, TUB?
YEP! COME ONE, COME ALL! WE'RE GONNA PICK THE MOST BEAUTIFUL GIRL IN THE NEIGHBORHOOD!
ARE Y-YOU GOING TO BE ONE OF THE JUDGES, TUB?
YEP! ALL THE FELLERS IN THE CLUB ARE GONNA BE JUDGES!
TUBBY...I-I L-LIKE YOU!
REALLY, GLORIA?
Y-YES...BUT PLEASE DON'T TELL ANYBODY!
I WON'T, GLORIA! THIS IS A SECRET JUST BETWEEN YOU AND ME!
GLORIA! YOU WANTA KNOW SOMETHING? IF I HAVE ANYTHING TO SAY ABOUT IT, I BET YOU'LL WIN THE CONTEST!
IF I DO, I'LL GIVE YOU A GREAT BIG KISS!
OH, HELLO, WILLY! WHAT ARE YOU DOING?

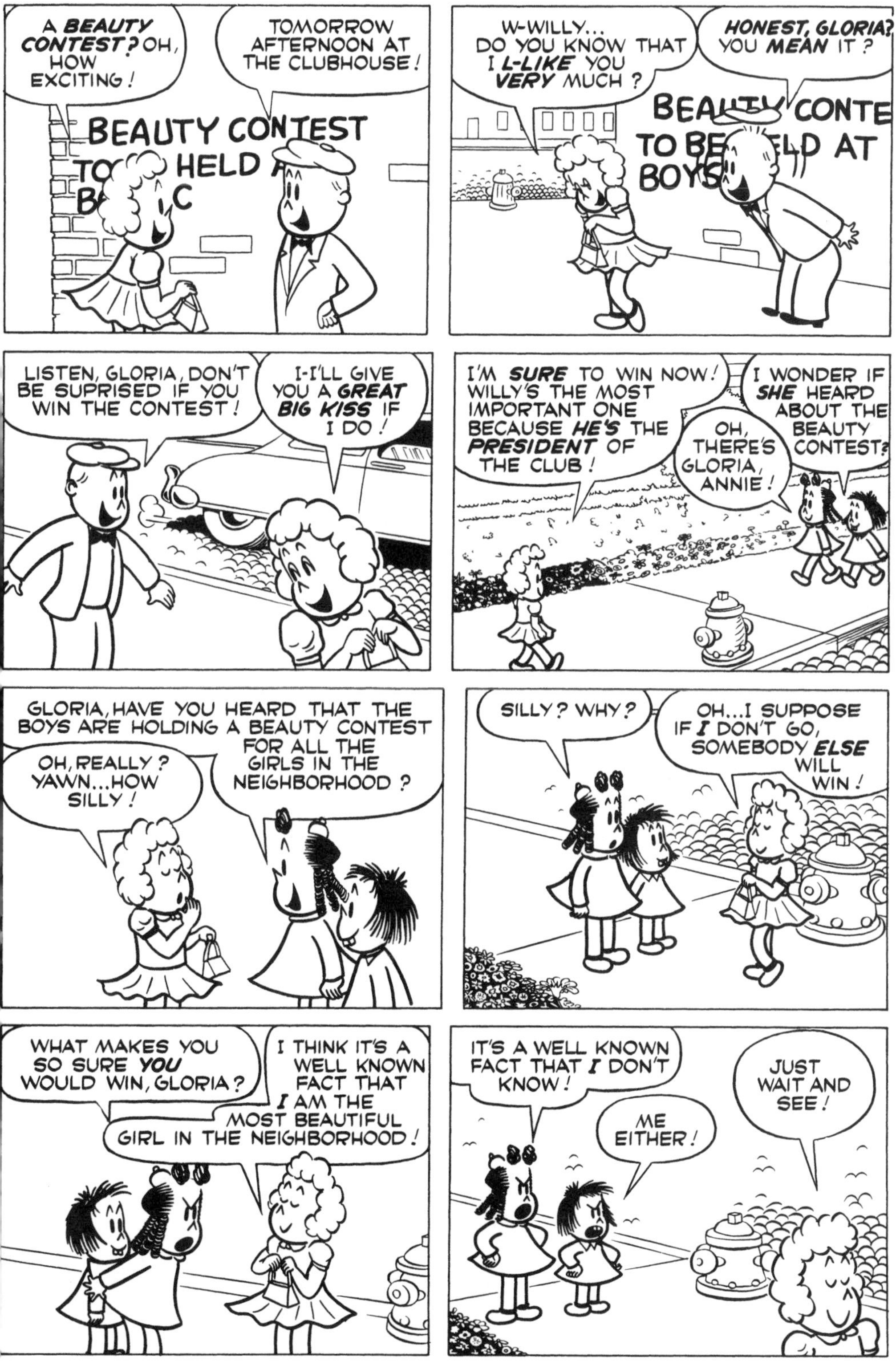

A BEAUTY CONTEST? OH, HOW EXCITING!
TOMORROW AFTERNOON AT THE CLUBHOUSE!
BEAUTY CONTEST
W-WILLY... DO YOU KNOW THAT I L-LIKE YOU VERY MUCH?
HONEST, GLORIA? YOU MEAN IT?
LISTEN, GLORIA, DON'T BE SUPRISED IF YOU WIN THE CONTEST!
I-I'LL GIVE YOU A GREAT BIG KISS IF I DO!
I'M SURE TO WIN NOW! WILLY'S THE MOST IMPORTANT ONE BECAUSE HE'S THE PRESIDENT OF THE CLUB!
OH, THERE'S GLORIA, ANNIE!
I WONDER IF SHE HEARD ABOUT THE BEAUTY CONTEST?
GLORIA, HAVE YOU HEARD THAT THE BOYS ARE HOLDING A BEAUTY CONTEST FOR ALL THE GIRLS IN THE NEIGHBORHOOD?
OH, REALLY? YAWN...HOW SILLY!
SILLY? WHY?
OH...I SUPPOSE IF I DON'T GO, SOMEBODY ELSE WILL WIN!
WHAT MAKES YOU SO SURE YOU WOULD WIN, GLORIA?
I THINK IT'S A WELL KNOWN FACT THAT I AM THE MOST BEAUTIFUL GIRL IN THE NEIGHBORHOOD!
IT'S A WELL KNOWN FACT THAT I DON'T KNOW!
ME EITHER!
JUST WAIT AND SEE!

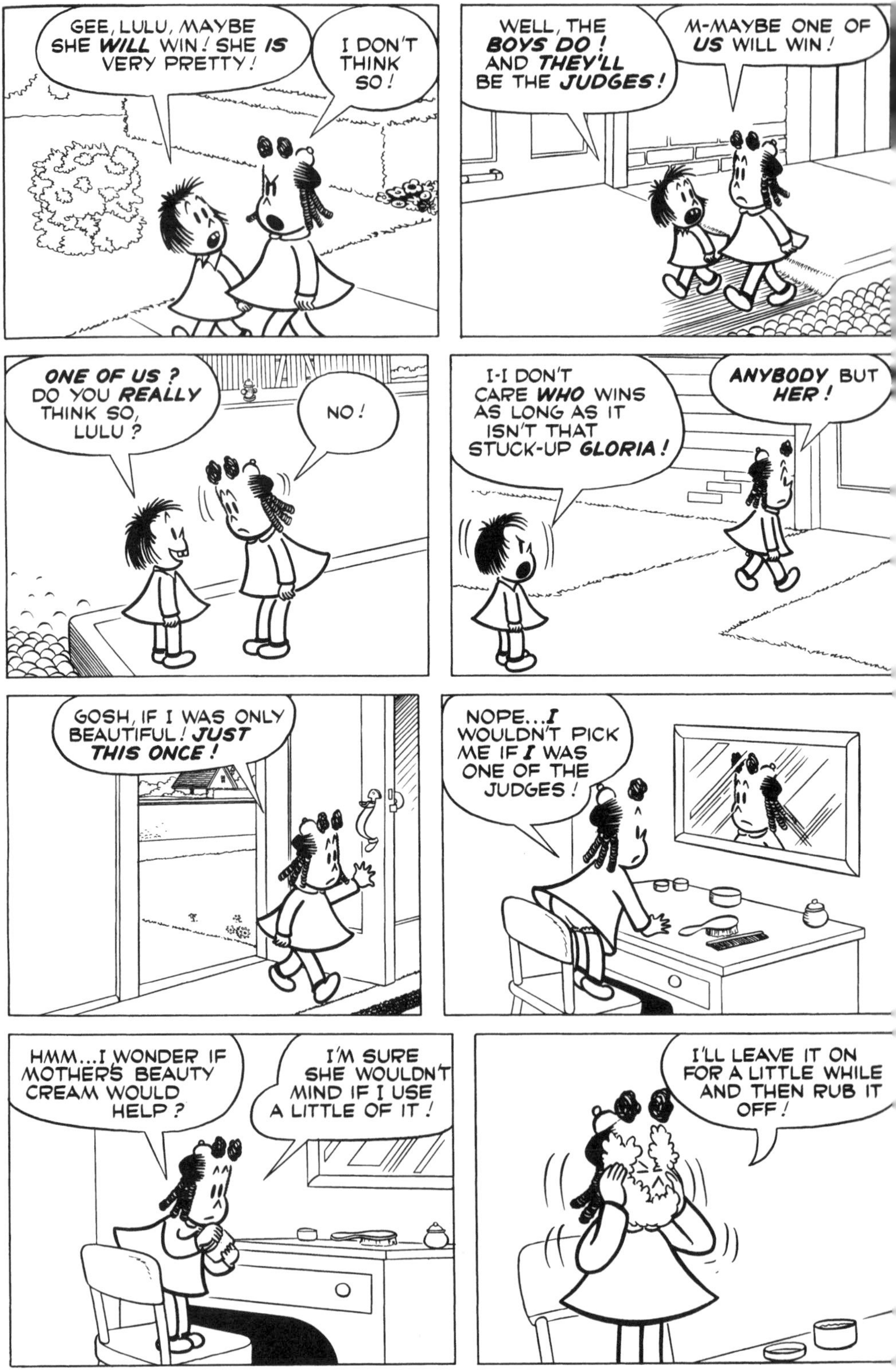
GEE, LULU, MAYBE SHE WILL WIN! SHE IS VERY PRETTY!
I DON'T THINK SO!
WELL, THE BOYS DO! AND THEY'LL BE THE JUDGES!
M-MAYBE ONE OF US WILL WIN!
ONE OF US? DO YOU REALLY THINK SO, LULU?
NO!
I-I DON'T CARE WHO WINS AS LONG AS IT ISN'T THAT STUCK-UP GLORIA!
ANYBODY BUT HER!
GOSH, IF I WAS ONLY BEAUTIFUL! JUST THIS ONCE!
NOPE...I WOULDN'T PICK ME IF I WAS ONE OF THE JUDGES!
HMM...I WONDER IF MOTHER'S BEAUTY CREAM WOULD HELP?
I'M SURE SHE WOULDN'T MIND IF I USE A LITTLE OF IT!
I'LL LEAVE IT ON FOR A LITTLE WHILE AND THEN RUB IT OFF!

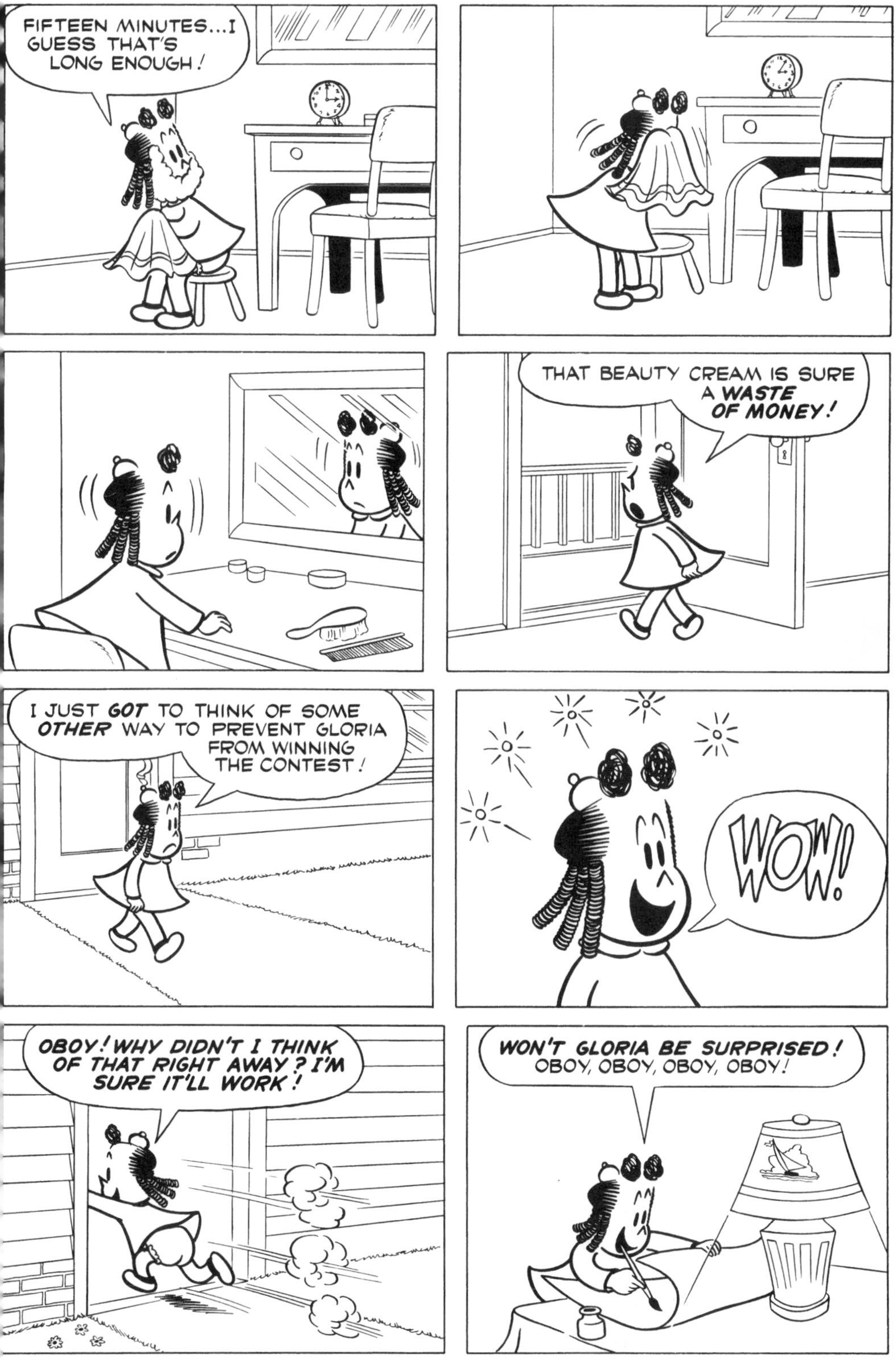
FIFTEEN MINUTES...I GUESS THAT'S LONG ENOUGH!
THAT BEAUTY CREAM IS SURE A WASTE OF MONEY!
I JUST GOT TO THINK OF SOME OTHER WAY TO PREVENT GLORIA FROM WINNING THE CONTEST!
WOW!
OBOY! WHY DIDN'T I THINK OF THAT RIGHT AWAY? I'M SURE IT'LL WORK!
WON'T GLORIA BE SURPRISED! OBOY, OBOY, OBOY, OBOY!

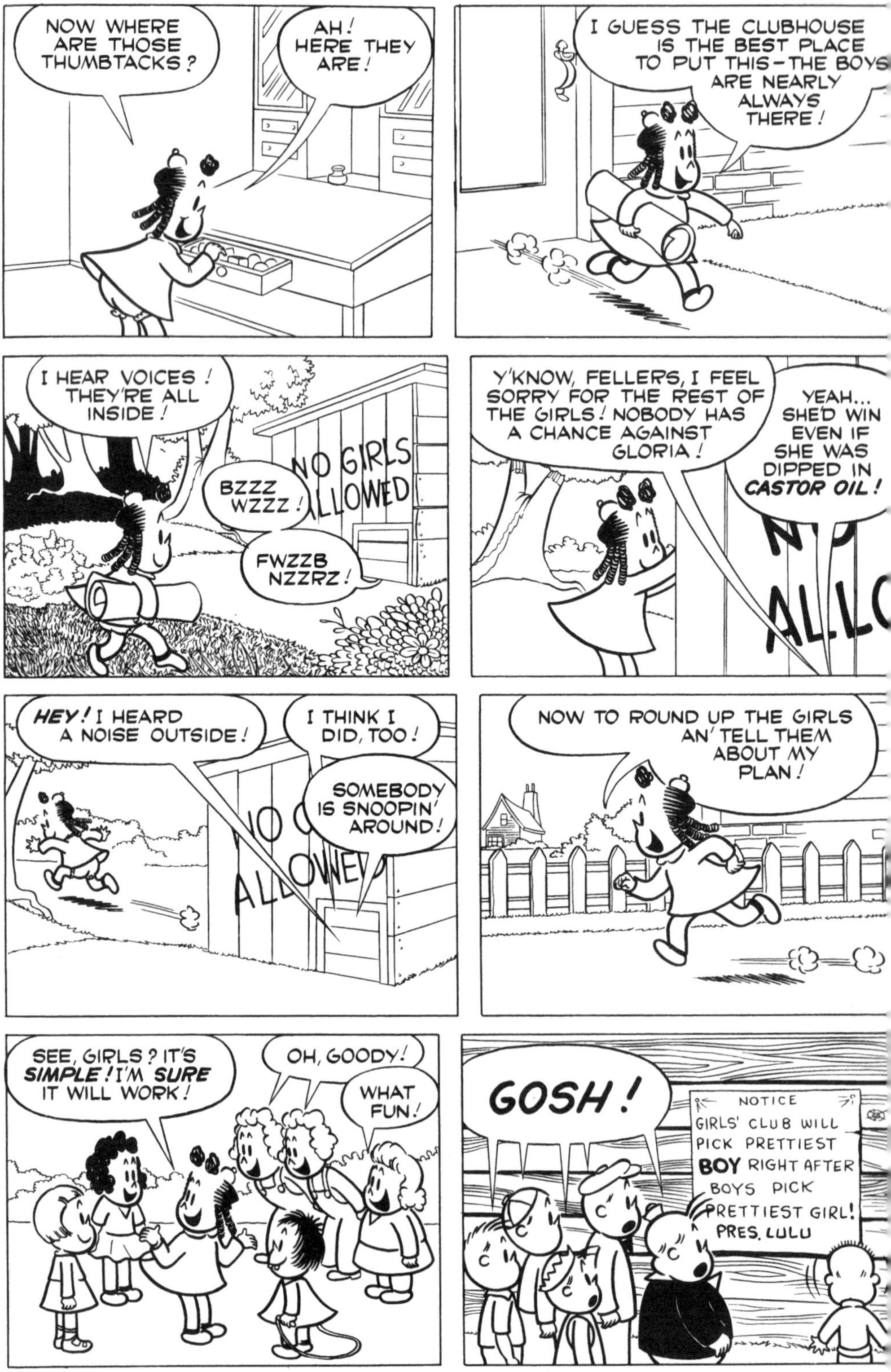
NOW WHERE ARE THOSE THUMBTACKS?
AH! HERE THEY ARE!
I GUESS THE CLUBHOUSE IS THE BEST PLACE TO PUT THIS—THE BOYS ARE NEARLY ALWAYS THERE!
I HEAR VOICES! THEY'RE ALL INSIDE!
NO GIRLS ALLOWED
BZZZ WZZZ!
FWZZB NZZRZ!
Y'KNOW, FELLERS, I FEEL SORRY FOR THE REST OF THE GIRLS! NOBODY HAS A CHANCE AGAINST GLORIA!
YEAH... SHE'D WIN EVEN IF SHE WAS DIPPED IN CASTOR OIL!
HEY! I HEARD A NOISE OUTSIDE!
I THINK I DID, TOO!
SOMEBODY IS SNOOPIN' AROUND!
NOW TO ROUND UP THE GIRLS AN' TELL THEM ABOUT MY PLAN!
SEE, GIRLS? IT'S SIMPLE! I'M SURE IT WILL WORK!
OH, GOODY!
WHAT FUN!
GOSH!
NOTICE
GIRLS' CLUB WILL PICK PRETTIEST BOY RIGHT AFTER BOYS PICK PRETTIEST GIRL!
PRES. LULU

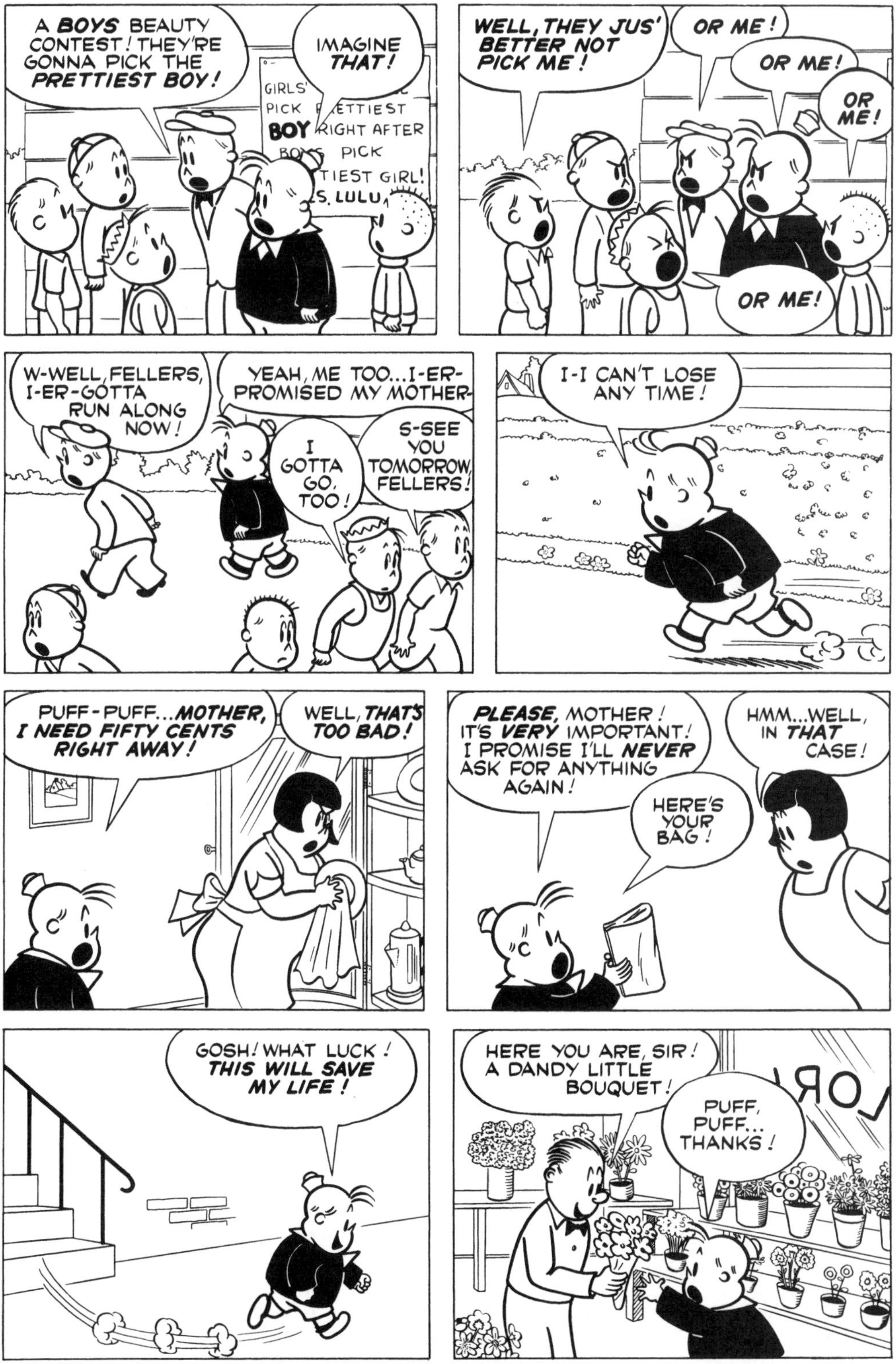
A BOYS BEAUTY CONTEST! THEY'RE GONNA PICK THE PRETTIEST BOY!
IMAGINE THAT!
GIRLS' ... PICK PRETTIEST BOY RIGHT AFTER BOYS PICK ...TIEST GIRL! ...S. LULU
WELL, THEY JUS' BETTER NOT PICK ME!
OR ME!
OR ME!
OR ME!
OR ME!
W-WELL, FELLERS, I-ER-GOTTA RUN ALONG NOW!
YEAH, ME TOO...I-ER-PROMISED MY MOTHER-
I GOTTA GO, TOO!
S-SEE YOU TOMORROW, FELLERS!
I-I CAN'T LOSE ANY TIME!
PUFF-PUFF...MOTHER, I NEED FIFTY CENTS RIGHT AWAY!
WELL, THAT'S TOO BAD!
PLEASE, MOTHER! IT'S VERY IMPORTANT! I PROMISE I'LL NEVER ASK FOR ANYTHING AGAIN!
HMM...WELL, IN THAT CASE!
HERE'S YOUR BAG!
GOSH! WHAT LUCK! THIS WILL SAVE MY LIFE!
HERE YOU ARE, SIR! A DANDY LITTLE BOUQUET!
PUFF, PUFF... THANKS!

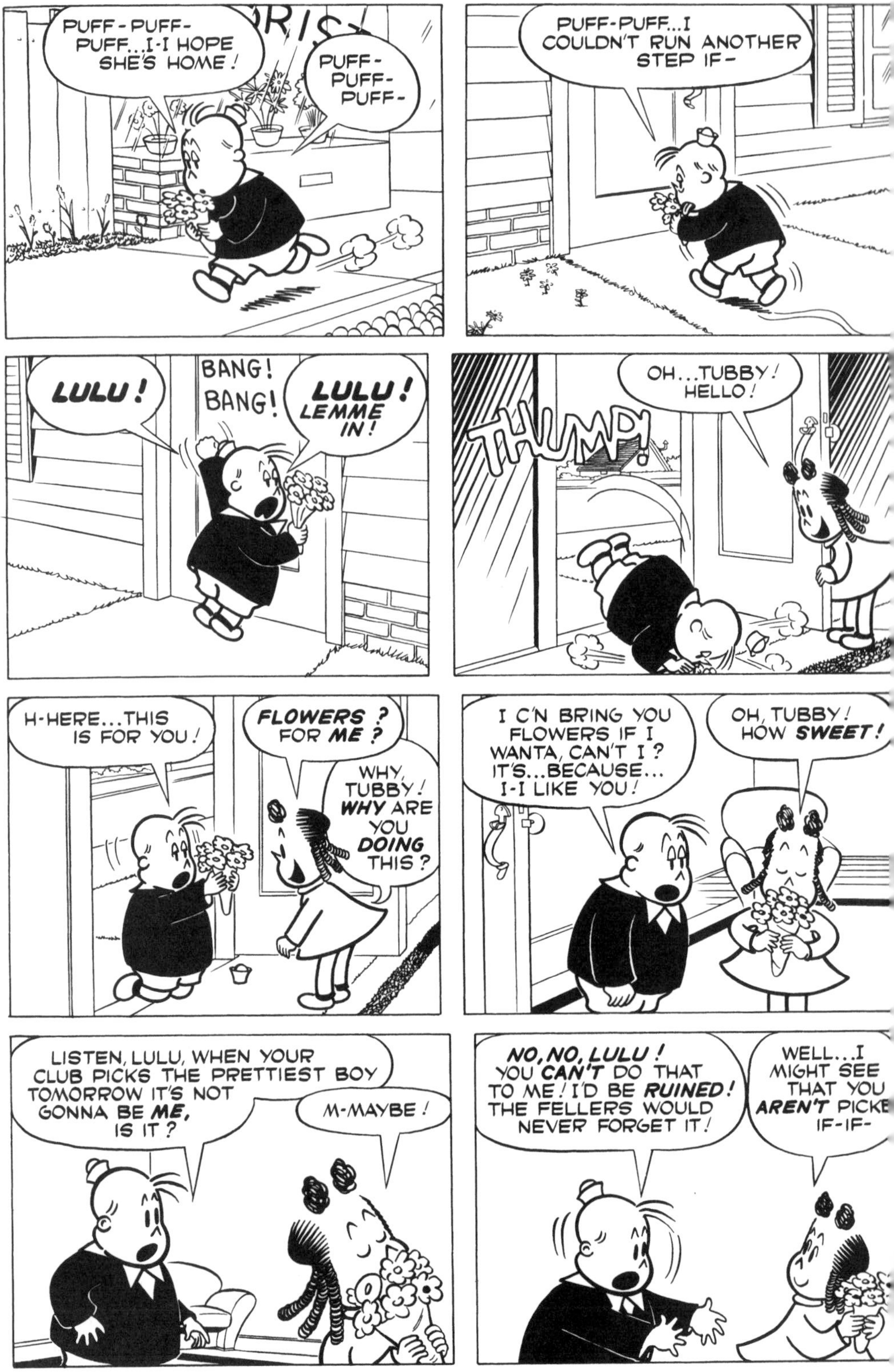

PUFF-PUFF-PUFF...I-I HOPE SHE'S HOME!
PUFF-PUFF-PUFF-
PUFF-PUFF...I COULDN'T RUN ANOTHER STEP IF-
LULU!
BANG! BANG!
LULU! LEMME IN!
THUMP!
OH...TUBBY! HELLO!
H-HERE...THIS IS FOR YOU!
FLOWERS? FOR ME?
WHY, TUBBY! WHY ARE YOU DOING THIS?
I C'N BRING YOU FLOWERS IF I WANTA, CAN'T I? IT'S...BECAUSE... I-I LIKE YOU!
OH, TUBBY! HOW SWEET!
LISTEN, LULU, WHEN YOUR CLUB PICKS THE PRETTIEST BOY TOMORROW IT'S NOT GONNA BE ME, IS IT?
M-MAYBE!
NO, NO, LULU! YOU CAN'T DO THAT TO ME! I'D BE RUINED! THE FELLERS WOULD NEVER FORGET IT!
WELL...I MIGHT SEE THAT YOU AREN'T PICKE IF-IF-

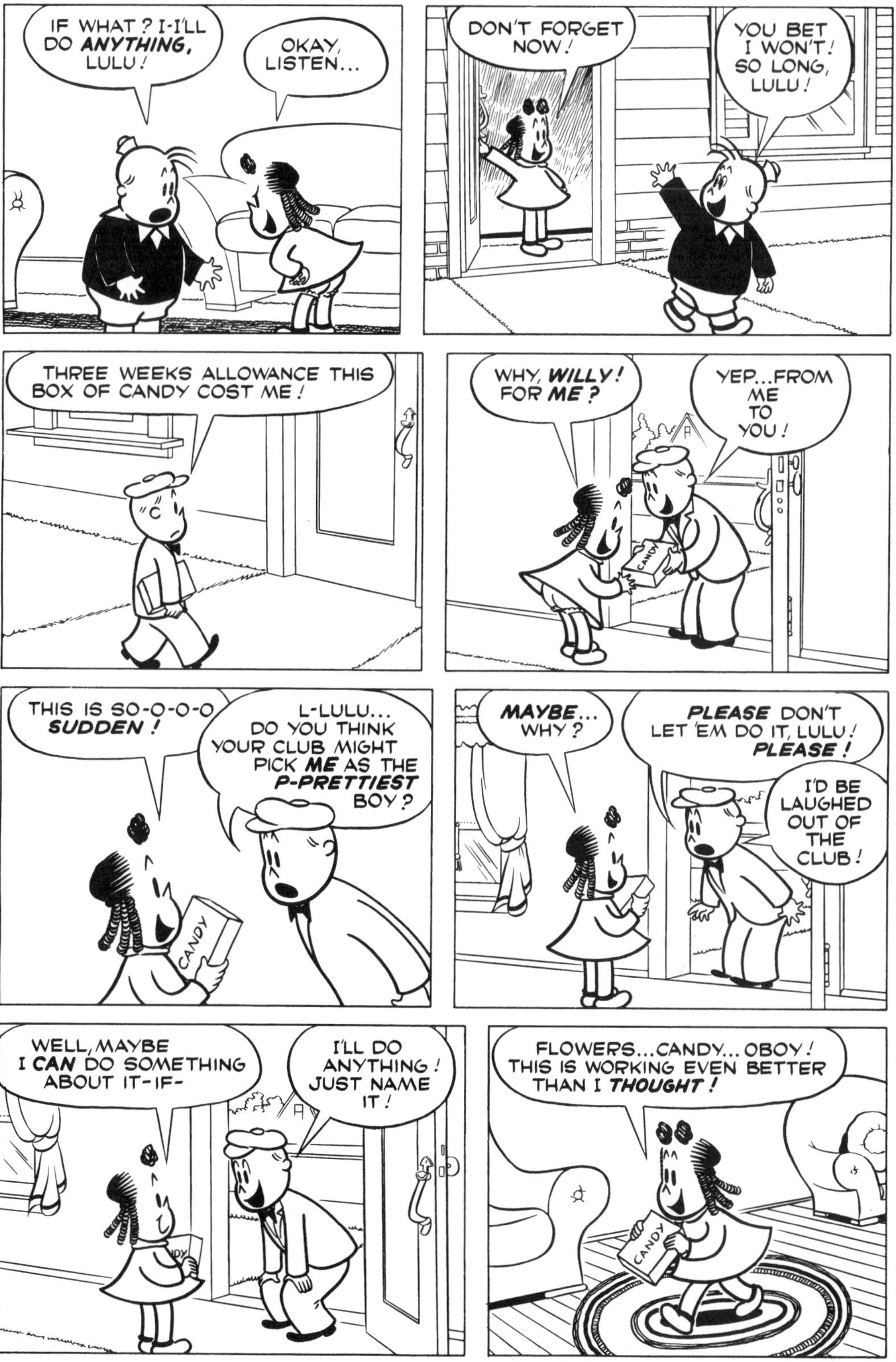
IF WHAT? I-I'LL DO **ANYTHING,** LULU!
OKAY, LISTEN...
DON'T FORGET NOW!
YOU BET I WON'T! SO LONG, LULU!
THREE WEEKS ALLOWANCE THIS BOX OF CANDY COST ME!
WHY, **WILLY!** FOR **ME?**
YEP...FROM ME TO YOU!
CANDY
THIS IS SO-O-O-O **SUDDEN!**
L-LULU... DO YOU THINK YOUR CLUB MIGHT PICK **ME** AS THE ***P-PRETTIEST*** BOY?
CANDY
MAYBE... WHY?
PLEASE DON'T LET 'EM DO IT, LULU! ***PLEASE!***
I'D BE LAUGHED OUT OF THE CLUB!
WELL, MAYBE I **CAN** DO SOMETHING ABOUT IT-IF-
I'LL DO ANYTHING! JUST NAME IT!
FLOWERS...CANDY...OBOY! THIS IS WORKING EVEN BETTER THAN I ***THOUGHT!***
CANDY

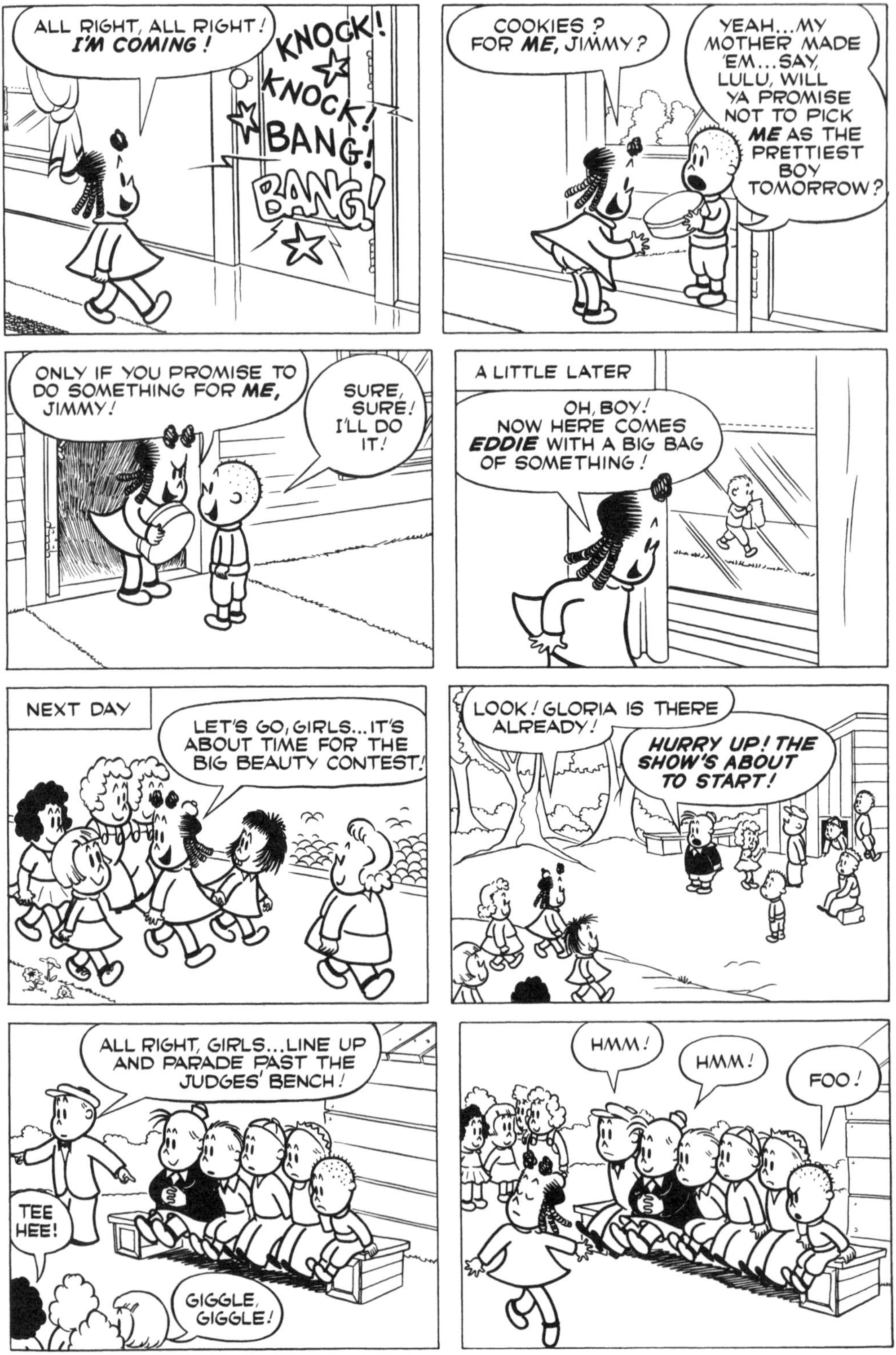
ALL RIGHT, ALL RIGHT! I'M COMING!
KNOCK! KNOCK! BANG! BANG!
COOKIES? FOR ME, JIMMY?
YEAH...MY MOTHER MADE 'EM...SAY, LULU, WILL YA PROMISE NOT TO PICK ME AS THE PRETTIEST BOY TOMORROW?
ONLY IF YOU PROMISE TO DO SOMETHING FOR ME, JIMMY!
SURE, SURE! I'LL DO IT!
A LITTLE LATER
OH, BOY! NOW HERE COMES EDDIE WITH A BIG BAG OF SOMETHING!
NEXT DAY
LET'S GO, GIRLS...IT'S ABOUT TIME FOR THE BIG BEAUTY CONTEST!
LOOK! GLORIA IS THERE ALREADY!
HURRY UP! THE SHOW'S ABOUT TO START!
ALL RIGHT, GIRLS...LINE UP AND PARADE PAST THE JUDGES' BENCH!
TEE HEE!
GIGGLE, GIGGLE!
HMM!
HMM!
FOO!

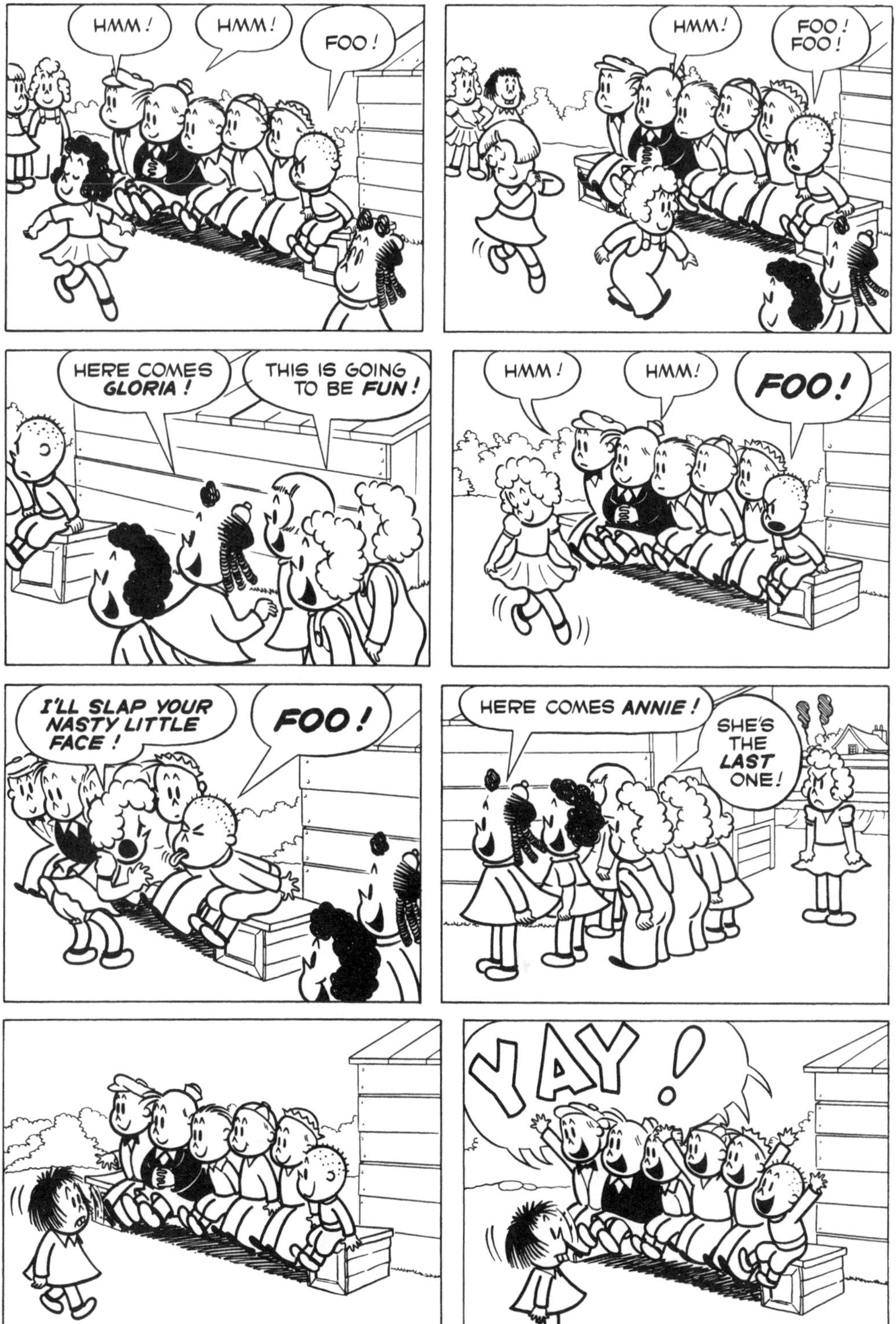
HMM!
HMM!
FOO!
HMM!
FOO! FOO!
HERE COMES GLORIA!
THIS IS GOING TO BE FUN!
HMM!
HMM!
FOO!
I'LL SLAP YOUR NASTY LITTLE FACE!
FOO!
HERE COMES ANNIE!
SHE'S THE LAST ONE!
YAY!

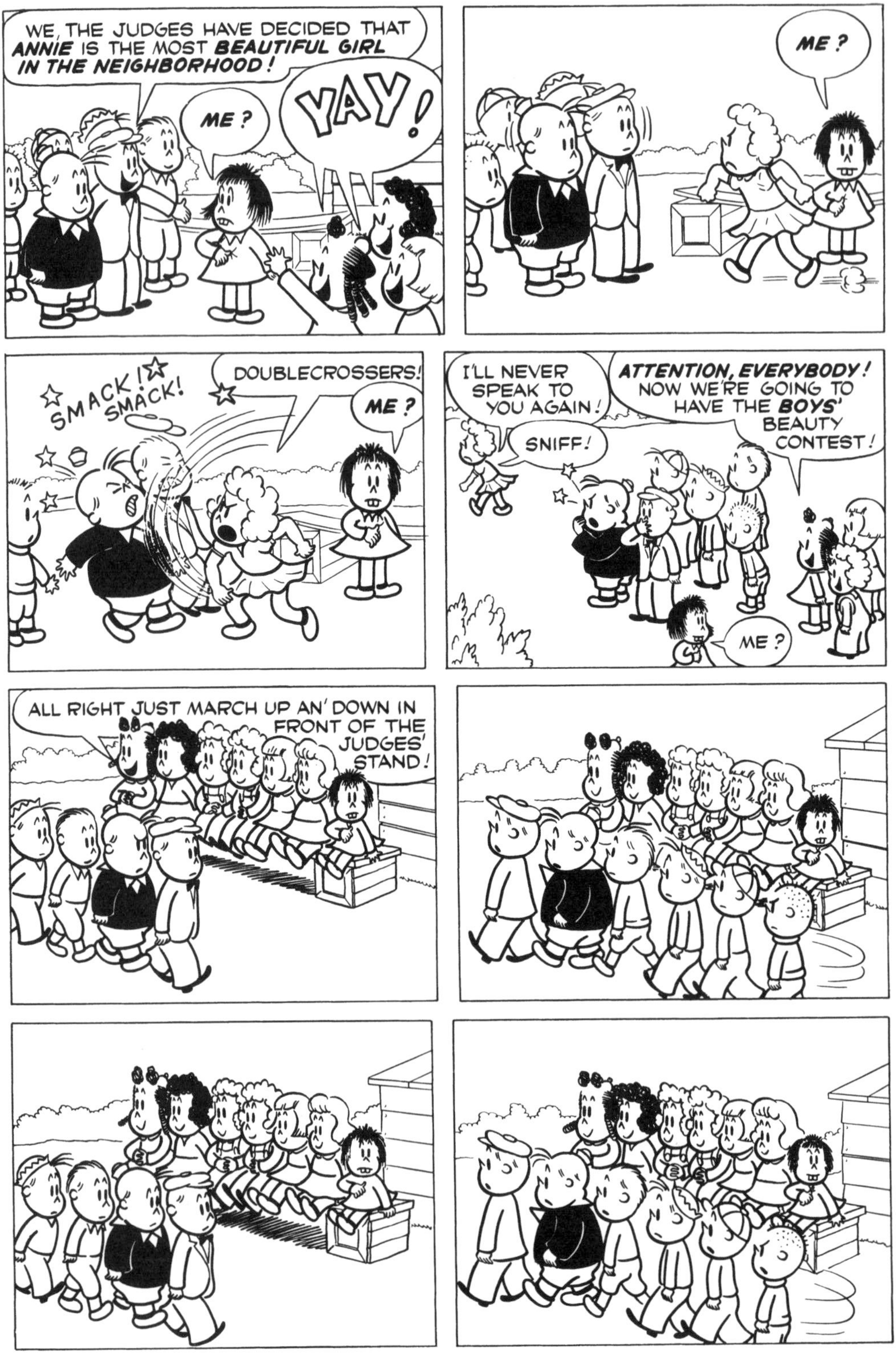

WE, THE JUDGES HAVE DECIDED THAT ANNIE IS THE MOST BEAUTIFUL GIRL IN THE NEIGHBORHOOD!
ME?
YAY!
ME?
SMACK! SMACK!
DOUBLECROSSERS!
ME?
I'LL NEVER SPEAK TO YOU AGAIN!
SNIFF!
ATTENTION, EVERYBODY! NOW WE'RE GOING TO HAVE THE BOYS' BEAUTY CONTEST!
ME?
ALL RIGHT JUST MARCH UP AN' DOWN IN FRONT OF THE JUDGES' STAND!

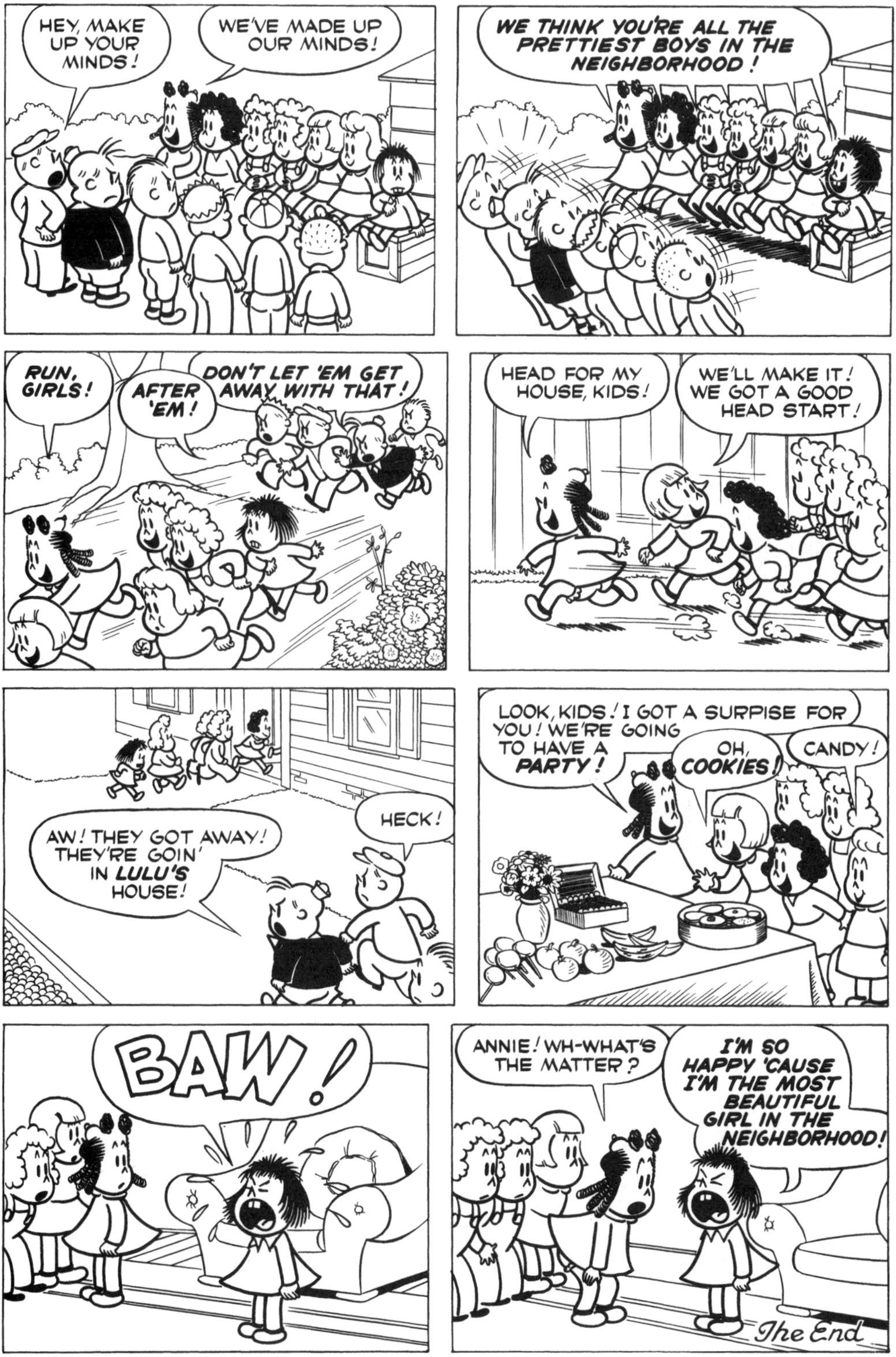
HEY, MAKE UP YOUR MINDS!
WE'VE MADE UP OUR MINDS!
WE THINK YOU'RE ALL THE PRETTIEST BOYS IN THE NEIGHBORHOOD!
RUN, GIRLS!
AFTER 'EM!
DON'T LET 'EM GET AWAY WITH THAT!
HEAD FOR MY HOUSE, KIDS!
WE'LL MAKE IT! WE GOT A GOOD HEAD START!
AW! THEY GOT AWAY! THEY'RE GOIN' IN LULU'S HOUSE!
HECK!
LOOK, KIDS! I GOT A SURPISE FOR YOU! WE'RE GOING TO HAVE A PARTY!
OH, COOKIES!
CANDY!
BAW!
ANNIE! WH-WHAT'S THE MATTER?
I'M SO HAPPY 'CAUSE I'M THE MOST BEAUTIFUL GIRL IN THE NEIGHBORHOOD!
The End

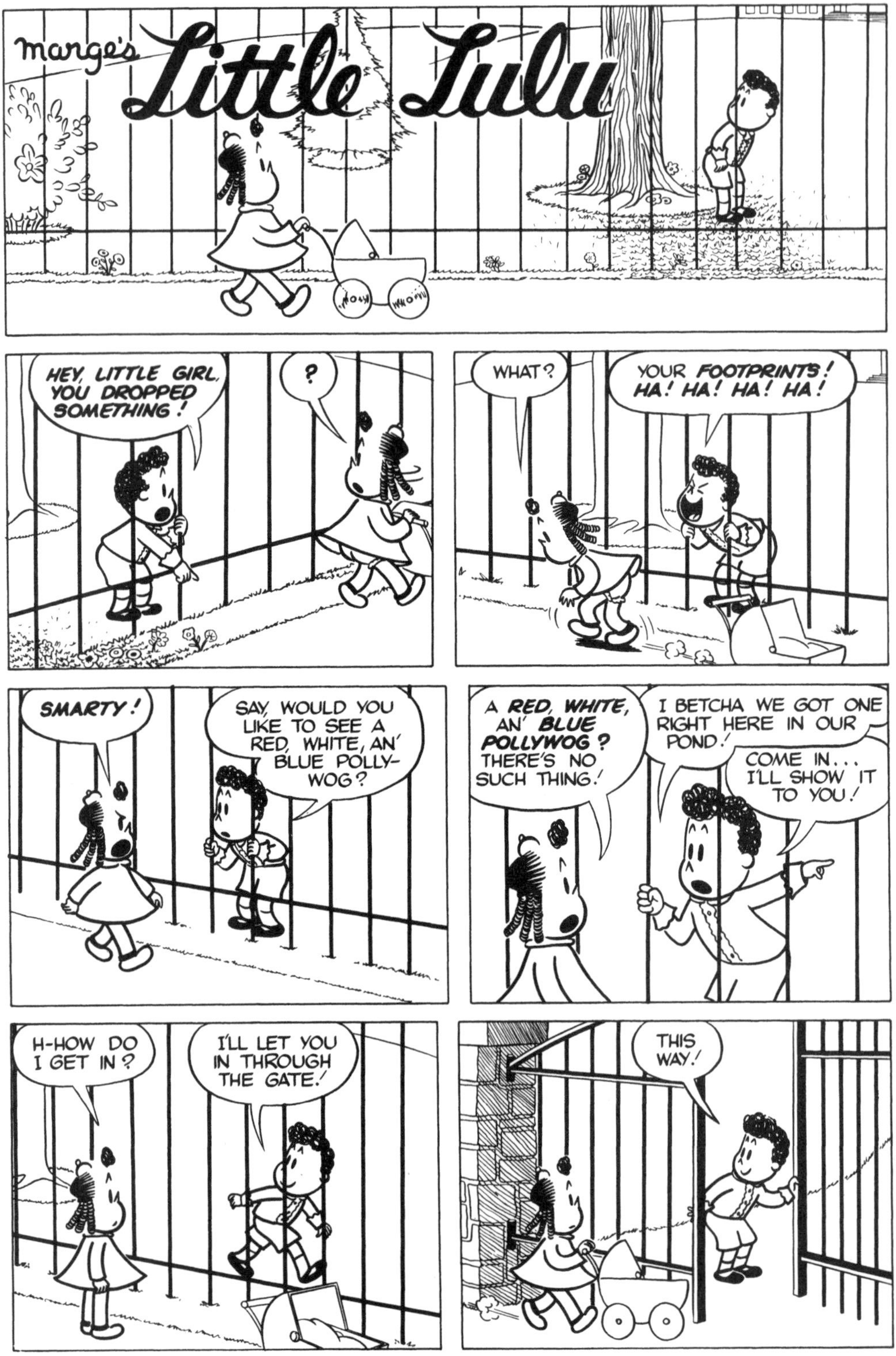
Marge's Little Lulu
HEY, LITTLE GIRL, YOU DROPPED SOMETHING!
?
WHAT?
YOUR FOOTPRINTS! HA! HA! HA! HA!
SMARTY!
SAY, WOULD YOU LIKE TO SEE A RED, WHITE, AN' BLUE POLLY-WOG?
A RED, WHITE, AN' BLUE POLLYWOG? THERE'S NO SUCH THING!
I BETCHA WE GOT ONE RIGHT HERE IN OUR POND!
COME IN... I'LL SHOW IT TO YOU!
H-HOW DO I GET IN?
I'LL LET YOU IN THROUGH THE GATE!
THIS WAY!

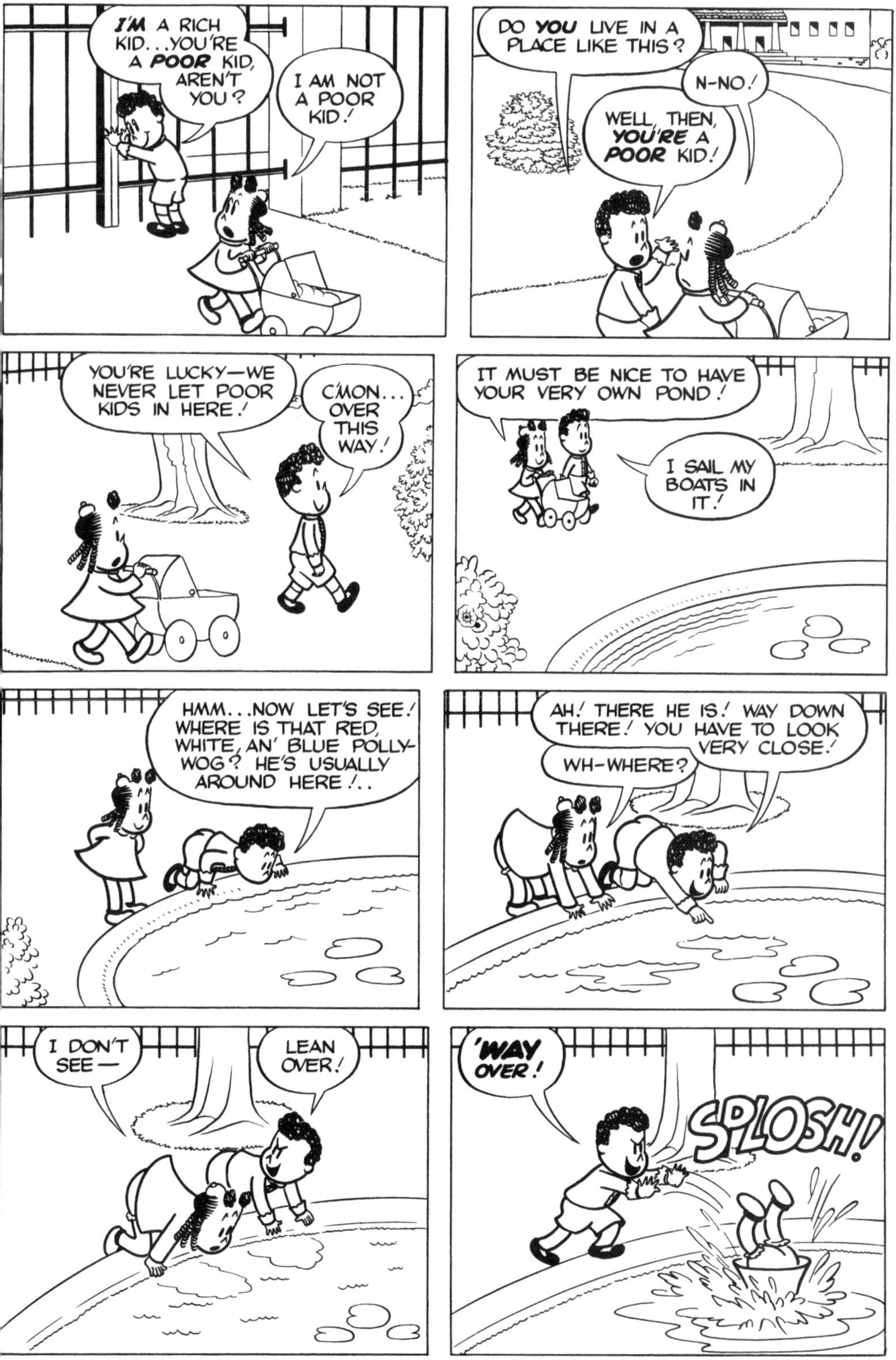
I'M A RICH KID...YOU'RE A POOR KID, AREN'T YOU?
I AM NOT A POOR KID!
DO YOU LIVE IN A PLACE LIKE THIS?
N-NO!
WELL, THEN, YOU'RE A POOR KID!
YOU'RE LUCKY—WE NEVER LET POOR KIDS IN HERE!
C'MON... OVER THIS WAY!
IT MUST BE NICE TO HAVE YOUR VERY OWN POND!
I SAIL MY BOATS IN IT!
HMM...NOW LET'S SEE! WHERE IS THAT RED, WHITE, AN' BLUE POLLY-WOG? HE'S USUALLY AROUND HERE!..
AH! THERE HE IS! WAY DOWN THERE! YOU HAVE TO LOOK VERY CLOSE!
WH-WHERE?
I DON'T SEE—
LEAN OVER!
'WAY OVER!
SPLOSH!

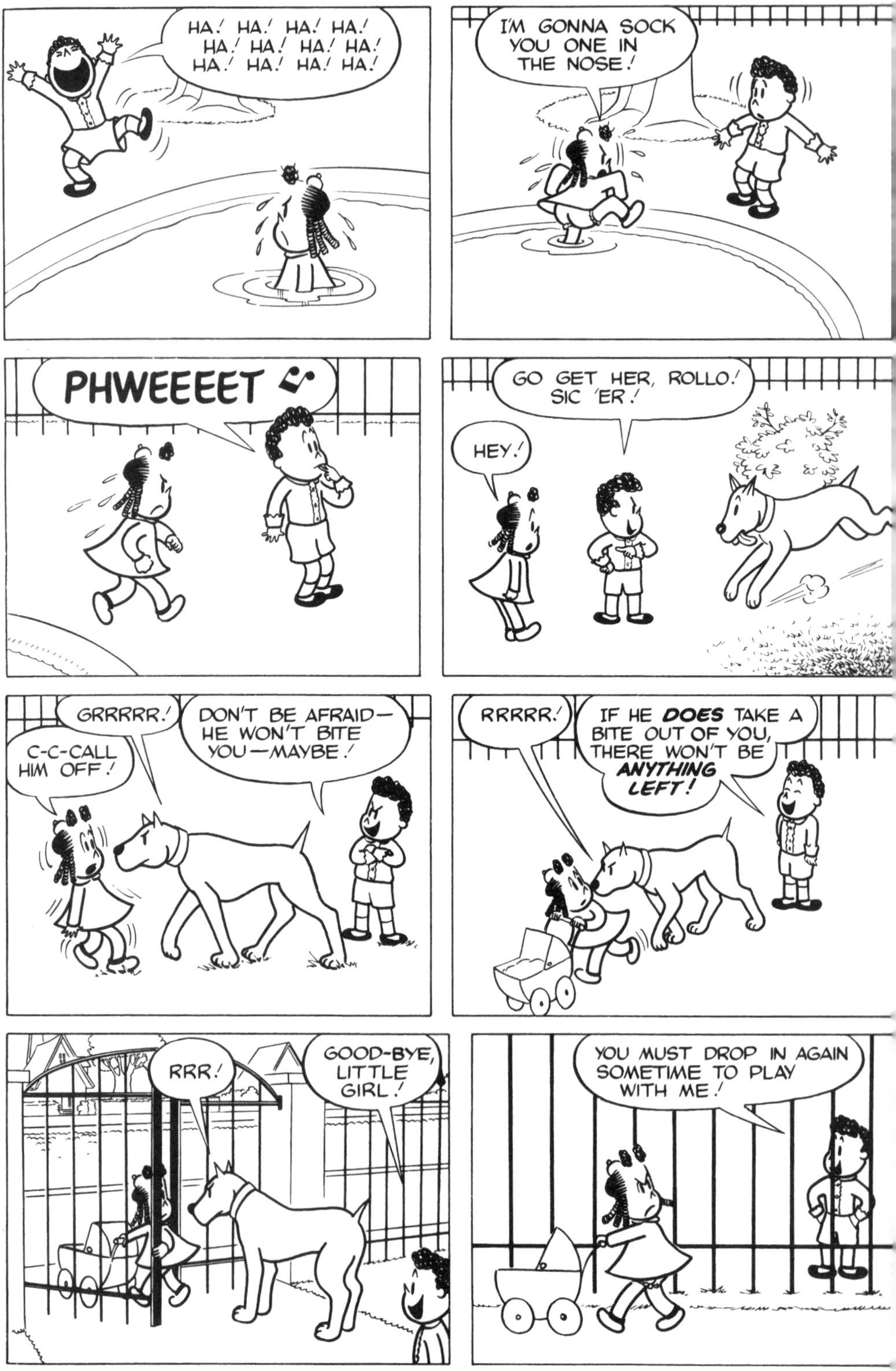
HA! HA! HA! HA! HA! HA! HA! HA! HA! HA! HA! HA!
I'M GONNA SOCK YOU ONE IN THE NOSE!
PHWEEEET
GO GET HER, ROLLO! SIC 'ER!
HEY!
GRRRRR!
DON'T BE AFRAID— HE WON'T BITE YOU—MAYBE!
C-C-CALL HIM OFF!
RRRRR!
IF HE **DOES** TAKE A BITE OUT OF YOU, THERE WON'T BE **ANYTHING LEFT!**
RRR!
GOOD-BYE, LITTLE GIRL!
YOU MUST DROP IN AGAIN SOMETIME TO PLAY WITH ME!

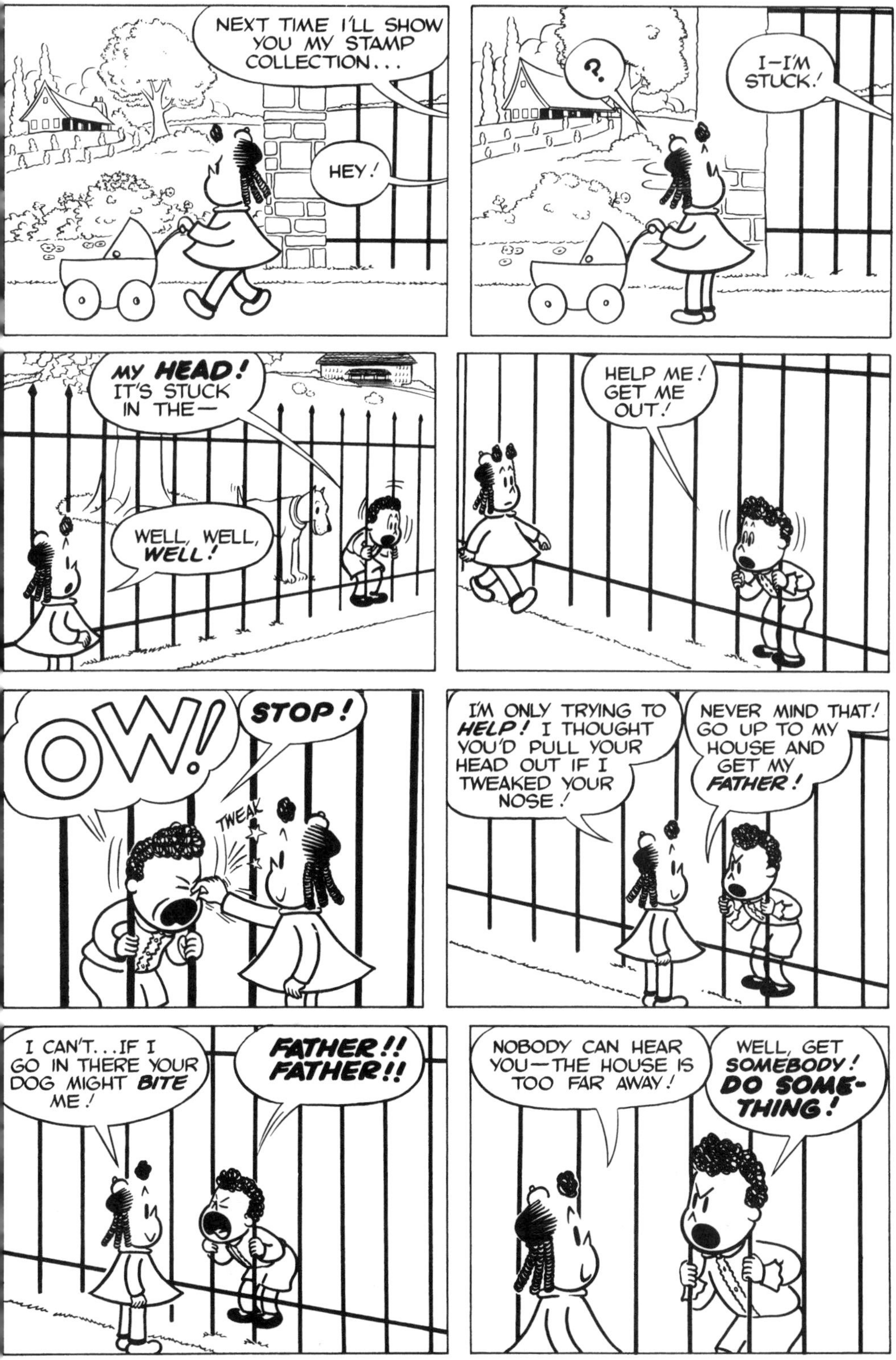

NEXT TIME I'LL SHOW YOU MY STAMP COLLECTION...
HEY!
?
I-I'M STUCK!
MY HEAD! IT'S STUCK IN THE—
WELL, WELL, WELL!
HELP ME! GET ME OUT!
OW!
STOP!
TWEAK
I'M ONLY TRYING TO HELP! I THOUGHT YOU'D PULL YOUR HEAD OUT IF I TWEAKED YOUR NOSE!
NEVER MIND THAT! GO UP TO MY HOUSE AND GET MY FATHER!
I CAN'T...IF I GO IN THERE YOUR DOG MIGHT BITE ME!
FATHER!! FATHER!!
NOBODY CAN HEAR YOU—THE HOUSE IS TOO FAR AWAY!
WELL, GET SOMEBODY! DO SOME-THING!

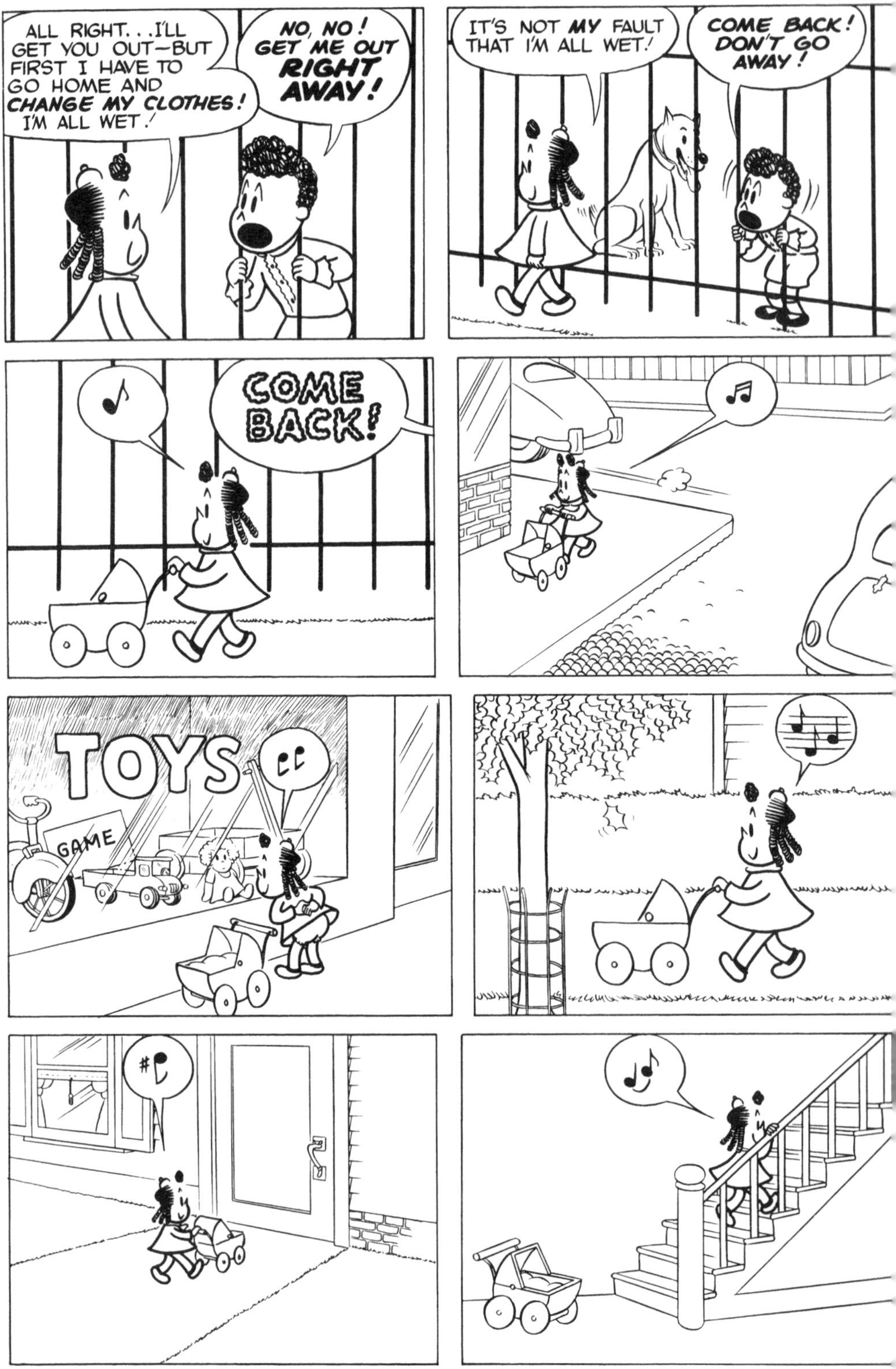
ALL RIGHT. . .I'LL GET YOU OUT—BUT FIRST I HAVE TO GO HOME AND CHANGE MY CLOTHES! I'M ALL WET!
NO, NO! GET ME OUT RIGHT AWAY!
IT'S NOT MY FAULT THAT I'M ALL WET!
COME BACK! DON'T GO AWAY!
COME BACK!
TOYS
GAME

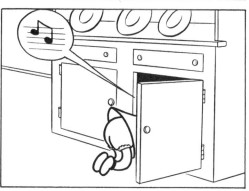

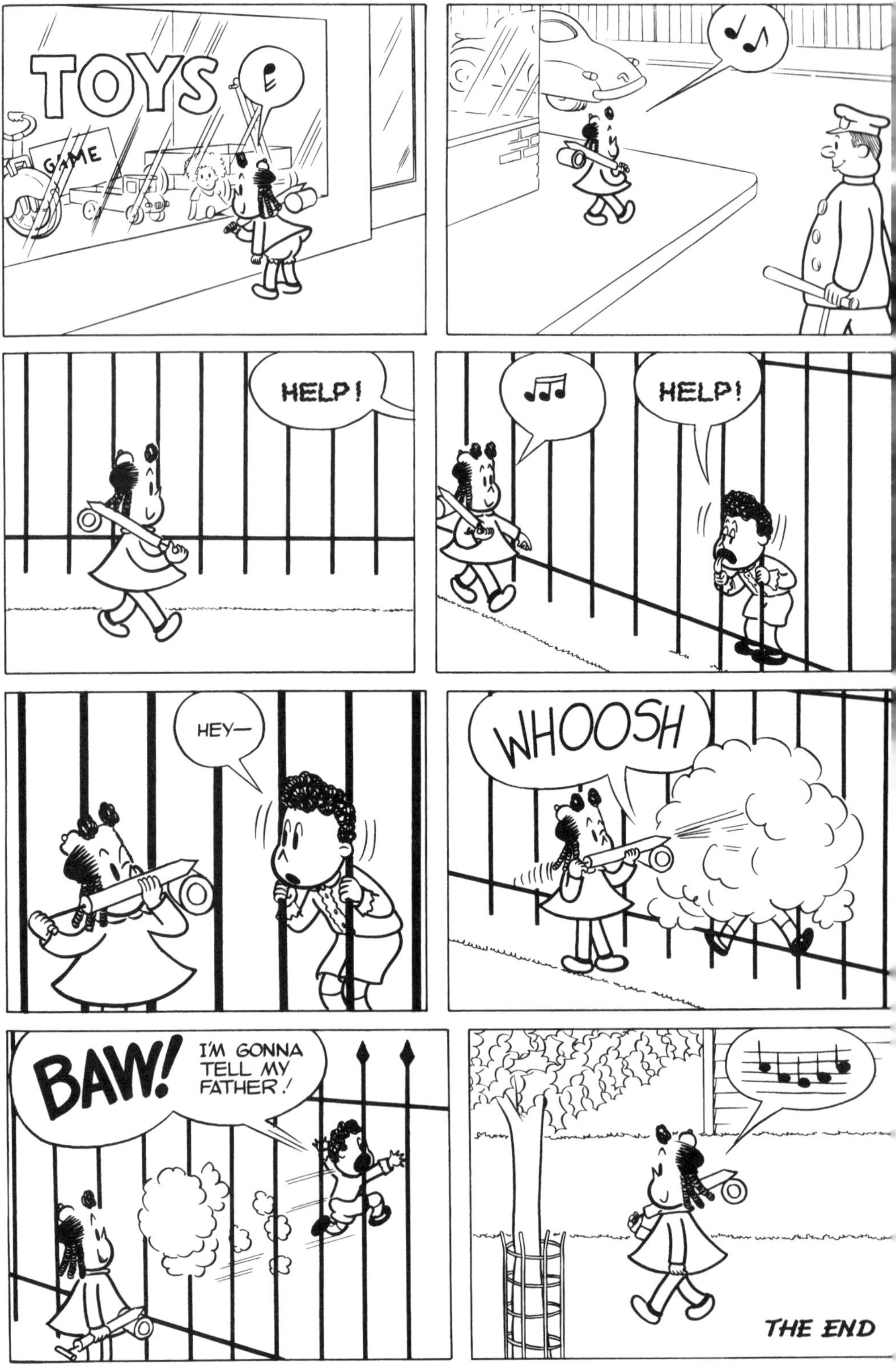
TOYS
GAME
HELP!
HELP!
HEY—
WHOOSH
BAW!
I'M GONNA TELL MY FATHER!
THE END

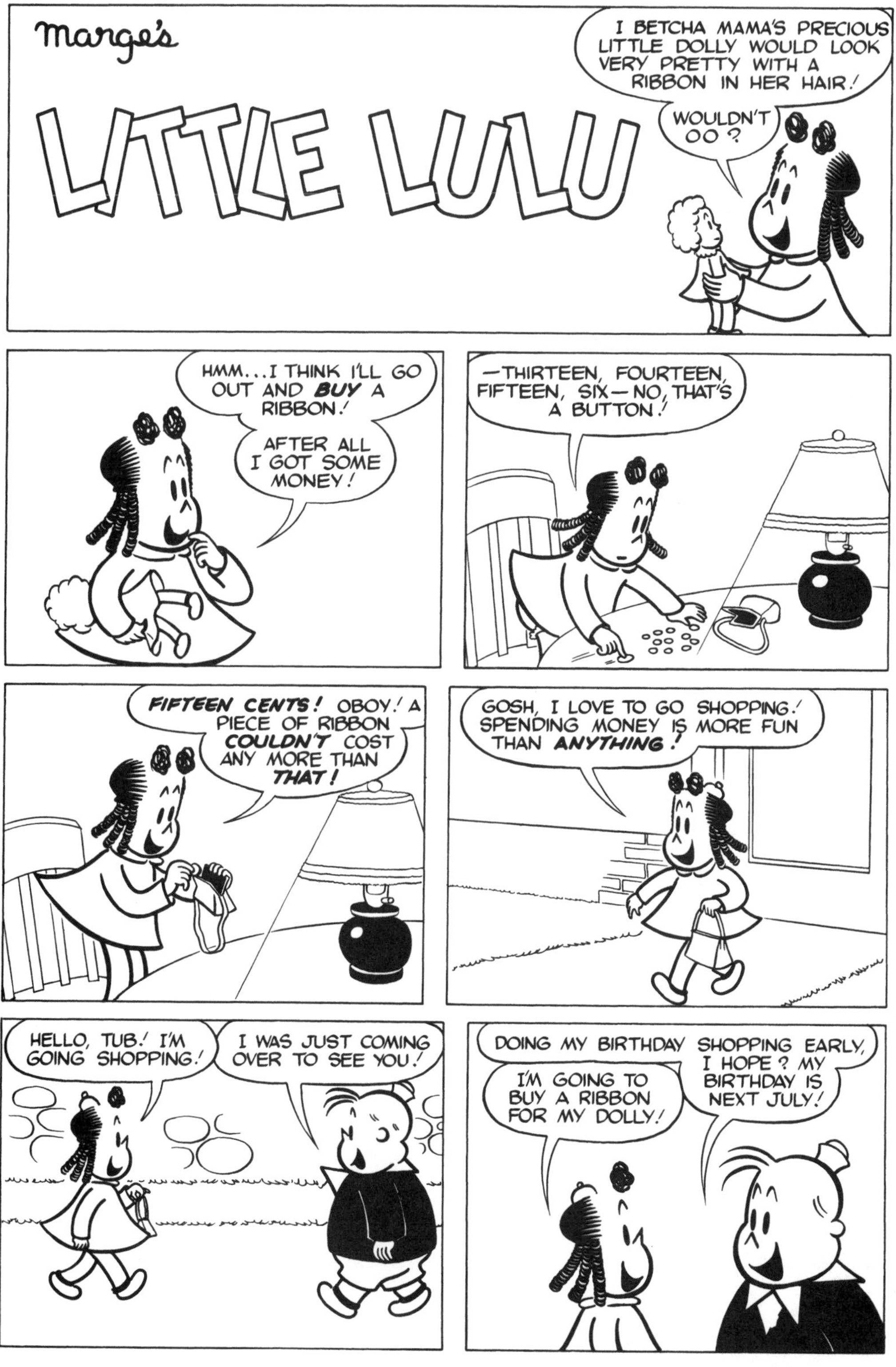
marge's
LITTLE LULU
I BETCHA MAMA'S PRECIOUS LITTLE DOLLY WOULD LOOK VERY PRETTY WITH A RIBBON IN HER HAIR!
WOULDN'T OO?
HMM...I THINK I'LL GO OUT AND BUY A RIBBON!
AFTER ALL I GOT SOME MONEY!
—THIRTEEN, FOURTEEN, FIFTEEN, SIX—NO, THAT'S A BUTTON!
FIFTEEN CENTS! OBOY! A PIECE OF RIBBON COULDN'T COST ANY MORE THAN THAT!
GOSH, I LOVE TO GO SHOPPING! SPENDING MONEY IS MORE FUN THAN ANYTHING!
HELLO, TUB! I'M GOING SHOPPING!
I WAS JUST COMING OVER TO SEE YOU!
DOING MY BIRTHDAY SHOPPING EARLY, I HOPE? MY BIRTHDAY IS NEXT JULY!
I'M GOING TO BUY A RIBBON FOR MY DOLLY!

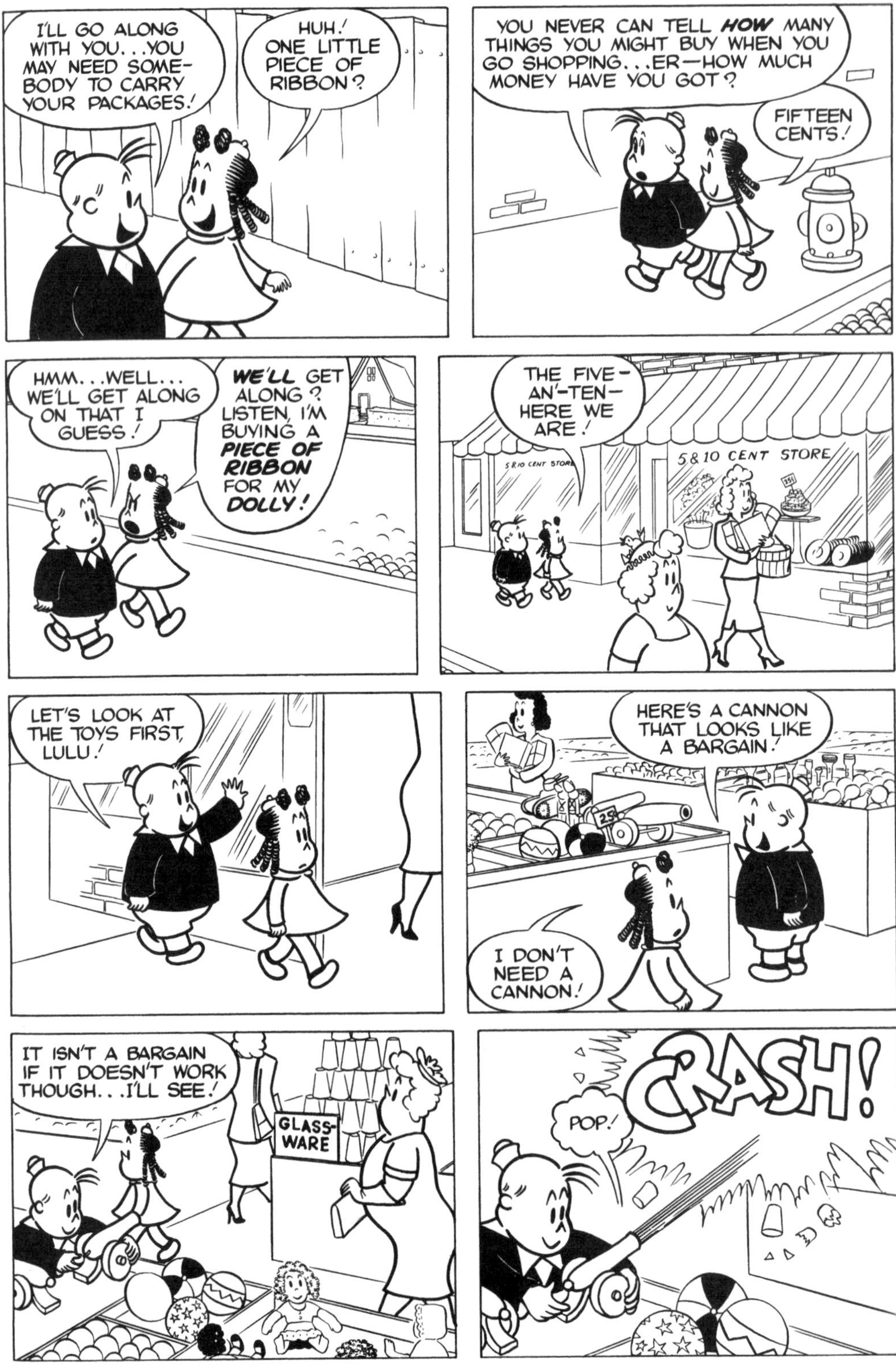
I'LL GO ALONG WITH YOU...YOU MAY NEED SOMEBODY TO CARRY YOUR PACKAGES!
HUH! ONE LITTLE PIECE OF RIBBON?
YOU NEVER CAN TELL HOW MANY THINGS YOU MIGHT BUY WHEN YOU GO SHOPPING...ER—HOW MUCH MONEY HAVE YOU GOT?
FIFTEEN CENTS!
HMM...WELL... WE'LL GET ALONG ON THAT I GUESS!
WE'LL GET ALONG? LISTEN, I'M BUYING A PIECE OF RIBBON FOR MY DOLLY!
THE FIVE-AN'-TEN-HERE WE ARE!
5&10 CENT STORE
5&10 CENT STORE
LET'S LOOK AT THE TOYS FIRST, LULU!
HERE'S A CANNON THAT LOOKS LIKE A BARGAIN!
25¢
I DON'T NEED A CANNON!
IT ISN'T A BARGAIN IF IT DOESN'T WORK THOUGH...I'LL SEE!
GLASS-WARE
POP!
CRASH!

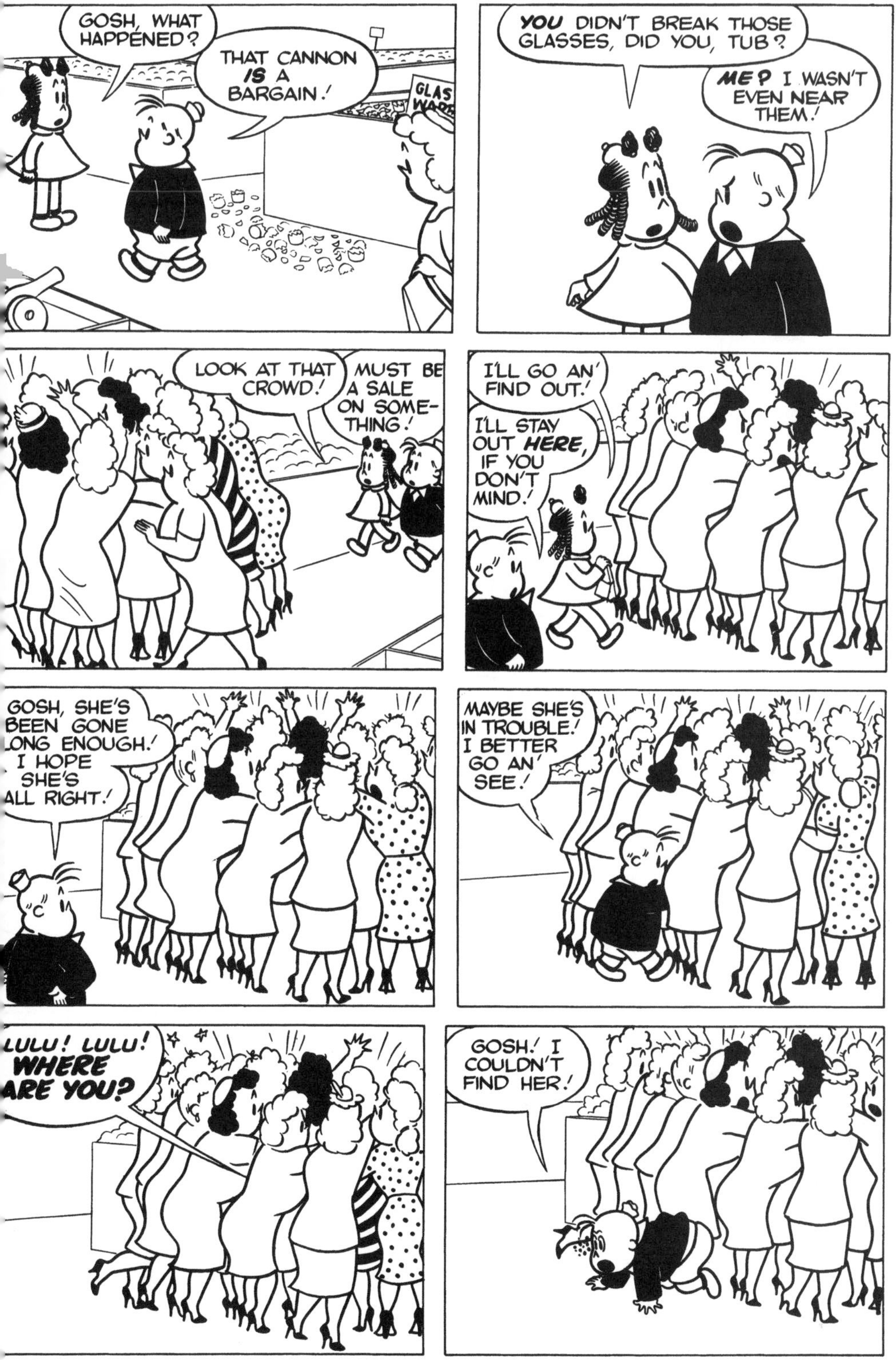
GOSH, WHAT HAPPENED?
THAT CANNON IS A BARGAIN!
GLAS WARE
YOU DIDN'T BREAK THOSE GLASSES, DID YOU, TUB?
ME? I WASN'T EVEN NEAR THEM!
LOOK AT THAT CROWD!
MUST BE A SALE ON SOME-THING!
I'LL GO AN' FIND OUT!
I'LL STAY OUT HERE, IF YOU DON'T MIND!
GOSH, SHE'S BEEN GONE LONG ENOUGH! I HOPE SHE'S ALL RIGHT!
MAYBE SHE'S IN TROUBLE! I BETTER GO AN' SEE!
LULU! LULU! WHERE ARE YOU?
GOSH! I COULDN'T FIND HER!

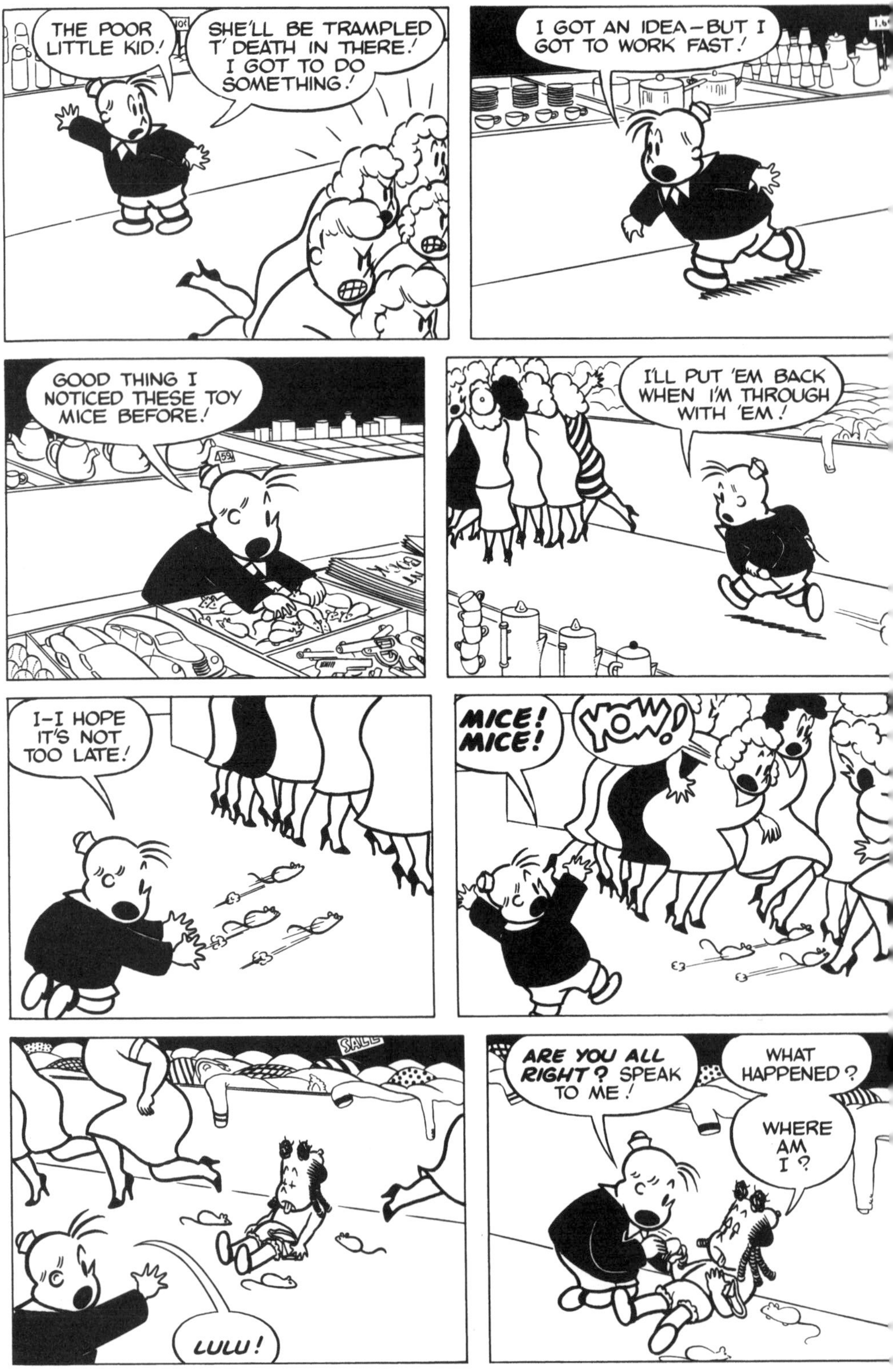
THE POOR LITTLE KID!
SHE'LL BE TRAMPLED T' DEATH IN THERE! I GOT TO DO SOMETHING!
I GOT AN IDEA—BUT I GOT TO WORK FAST!
GOOD THING I NOTICED THESE TOY MICE BEFORE!
I'LL PUT 'EM BACK WHEN I'M THROUGH WITH 'EM!
I-I HOPE IT'S NOT TOO LATE!
MICE! MICE!
YOW!
SALE
LULU!
ARE YOU ALL RIGHT? SPEAK TO ME!
WHAT HAPPENED?
WHERE AM I?

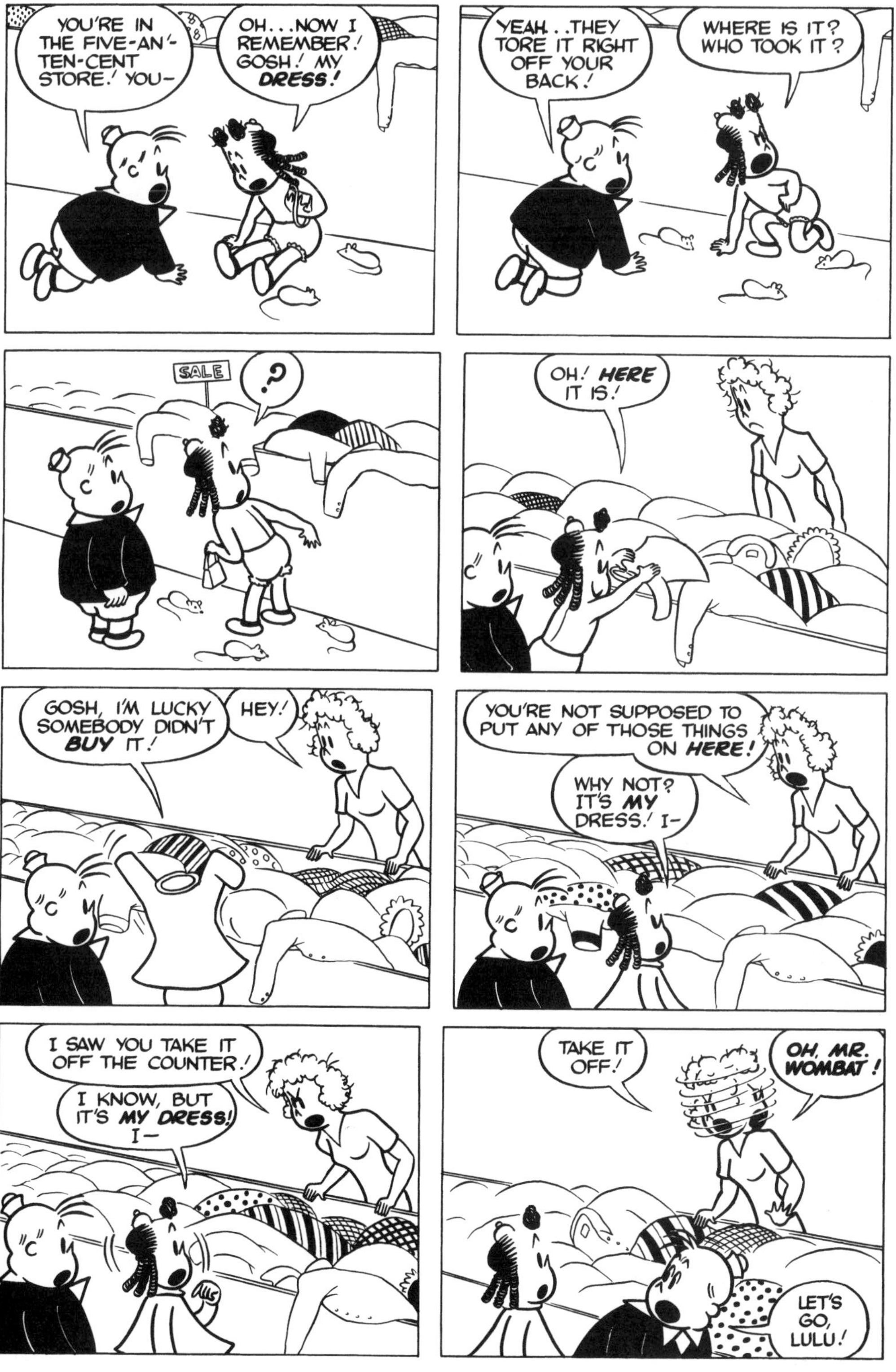
YOU'RE IN THE FIVE-AN'-TEN-CENT STORE! YOU–
OH...NOW I REMEMBER! GOSH! MY DRESS!
YEAH..THEY TORE IT RIGHT OFF YOUR BACK!
WHERE IS IT? WHO TOOK IT?
SALE
?
OH! HERE IT IS!
GOSH, I'M LUCKY SOMEBODY DIDN'T BUY IT!
HEY!
YOU'RE NOT SUPPOSED TO PUT ANY OF THOSE THINGS ON HERE!
WHY NOT? IT'S MY DRESS! I–
I SAW YOU TAKE IT OFF THE COUNTER!
I KNOW, BUT IT'S MY DRESS! I–
TAKE IT OFF!
OH, MR. WOMBAT!
LET'S GO, LULU!

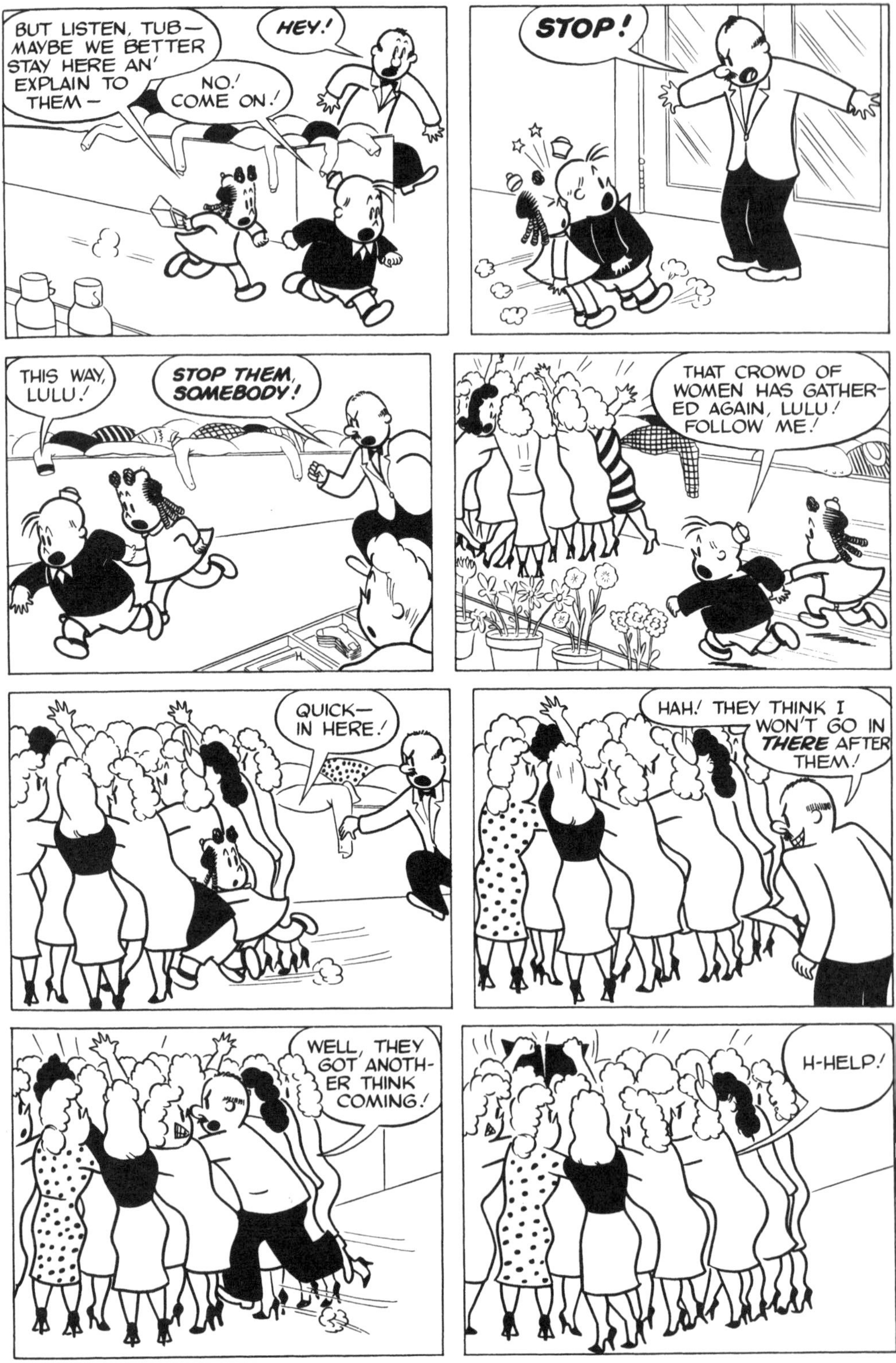
BUT LISTEN, TUB— MAYBE WE BETTER STAY HERE AN' EXPLAIN TO THEM—
HEY!
NO! COME ON!
STOP!
THIS WAY, LULU!
STOP THEM, SOMEBODY!
THAT CROWD OF WOMEN HAS GATHERED AGAIN, LULU! FOLLOW ME!
QUICK— IN HERE!
HAH! THEY THINK I WON'T GO IN THERE AFTER THEM!
WELL, THEY GOT ANOTHER THINK COMING!
H-HELP!

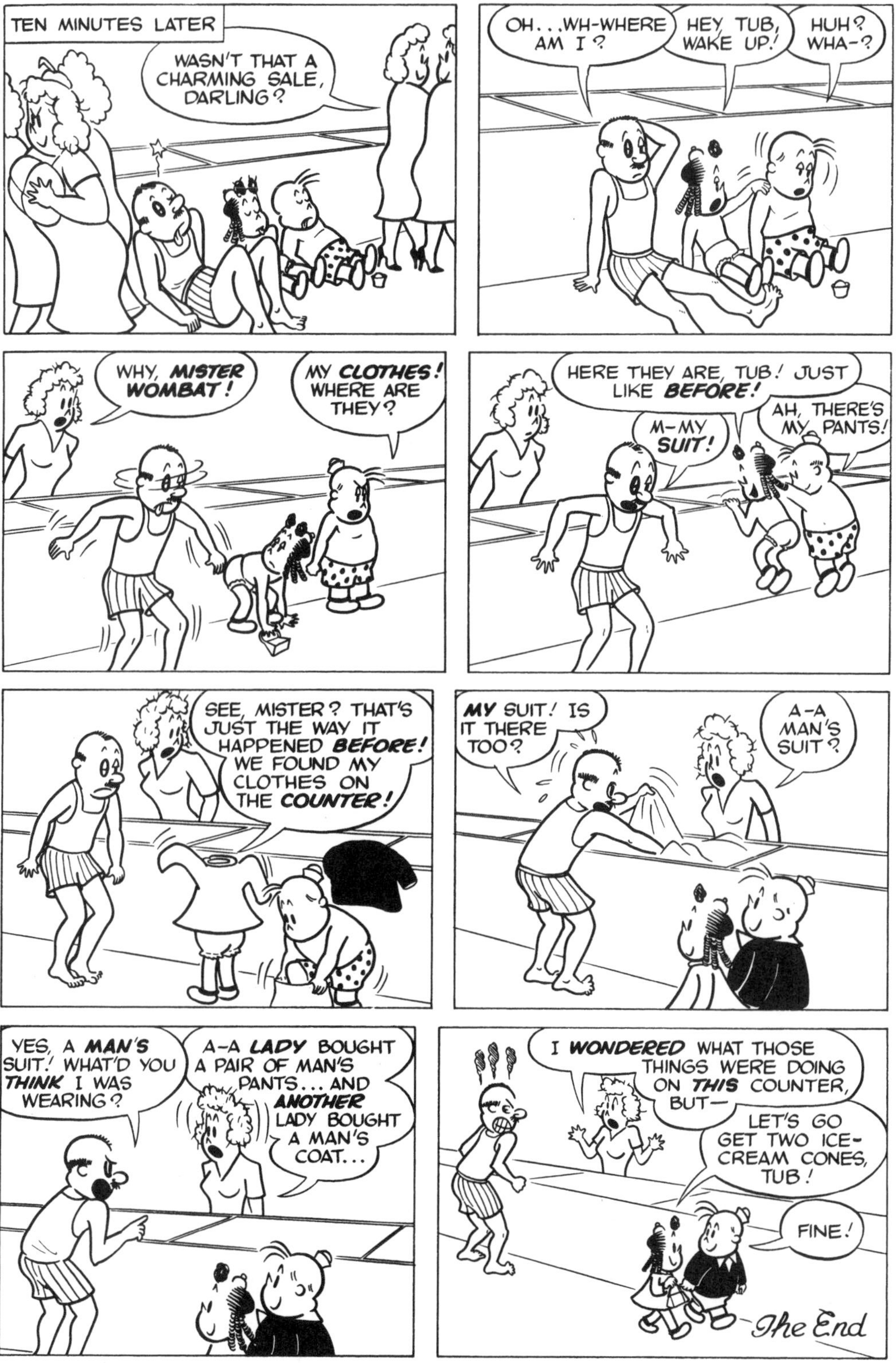
TEN MINUTES LATER
WASN'T THAT A CHARMING SALE, DARLING?
OH...WH-WHERE AM I?
HEY TUB, WAKE UP!
HUH? WHA-?
WHY, MISTER WOMBAT!
MY CLOTHES! WHERE ARE THEY?
HERE THEY ARE, TUB! JUST LIKE BEFORE!
M-MY SUIT!
AH, THERE'S MY PANTS!
SEE, MISTER? THAT'S JUST THE WAY IT HAPPENED BEFORE! WE FOUND MY CLOTHES ON THE COUNTER!
MY SUIT! IS IT THERE TOO?
A-A MAN'S SUIT?
YES, A MAN'S SUIT! WHAT'D YOU THINK I WAS WEARING?
A-A LADY BOUGHT A PAIR OF MAN'S PANTS... AND ANOTHER LADY BOUGHT A MAN'S COAT...
I WONDERED WHAT THOSE THINGS WERE DOING ON THIS COUNTER, BUT—
LET'S GO GET TWO ICE-CREAM CONES, TUB!
FINE!
The End

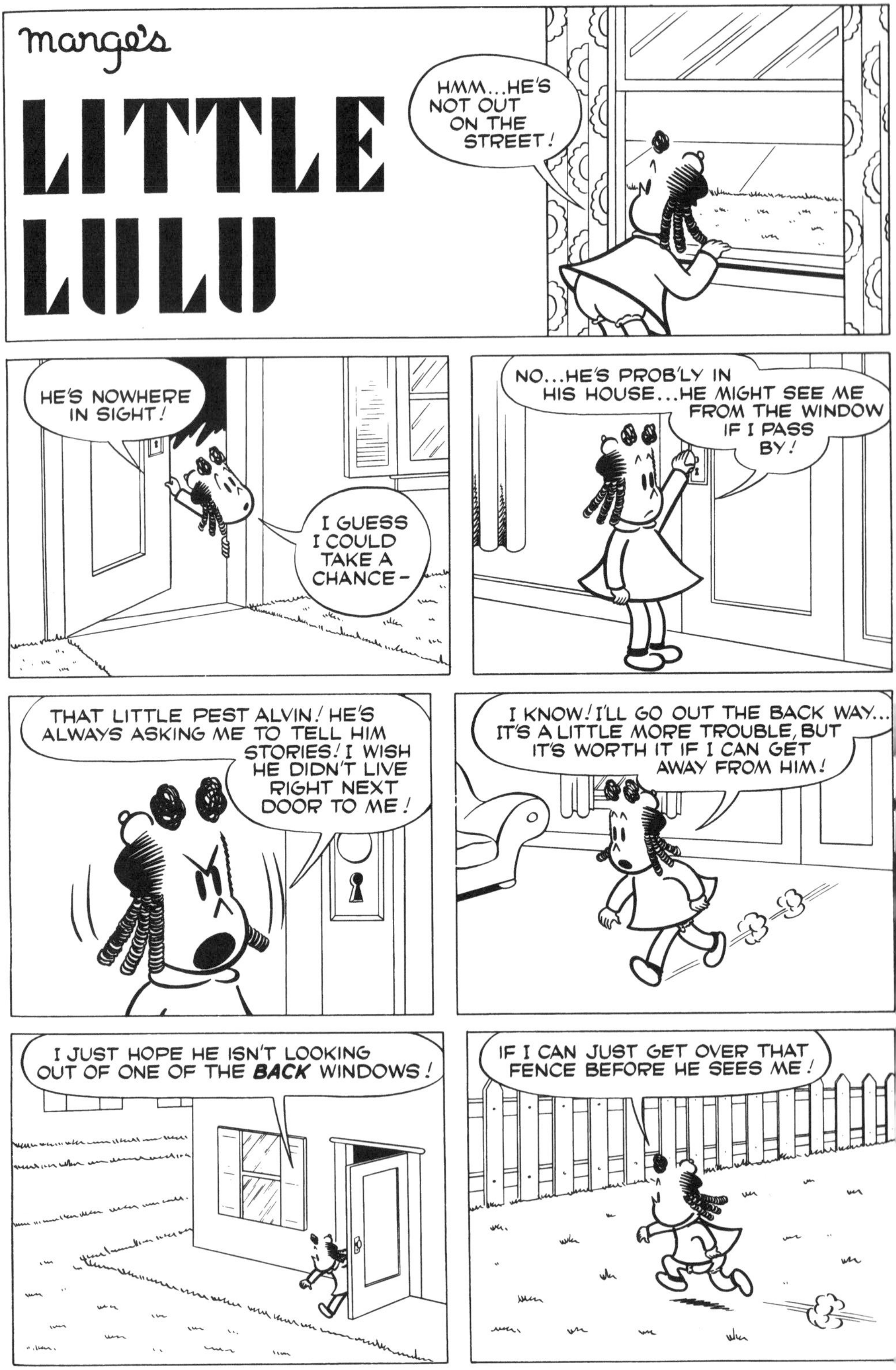
marge's
LITTLE LULU
HMM...HE'S NOT OUT ON THE STREET!
HE'S NOWHERE IN SIGHT!
I GUESS I COULD TAKE A CHANCE–
NO...HE'S PROB'LY IN HIS HOUSE...HE MIGHT SEE ME FROM THE WINDOW IF I PASS BY!
THAT LITTLE PEST ALVIN! HE'S ALWAYS ASKING ME TO TELL HIM STORIES! I WISH HE DIDN'T LIVE RIGHT NEXT DOOR TO ME!
I KNOW! I'LL GO OUT THE BACK WAY... IT'S A LITTLE MORE TROUBLE, BUT IT'S WORTH IT IF I CAN GET AWAY FROM HIM!
I JUST HOPE HE ISN'T LOOKING OUT OF ONE OF THE BACK WINDOWS!
IF I CAN JUST GET OVER THAT FENCE BEFORE HE SEES ME!

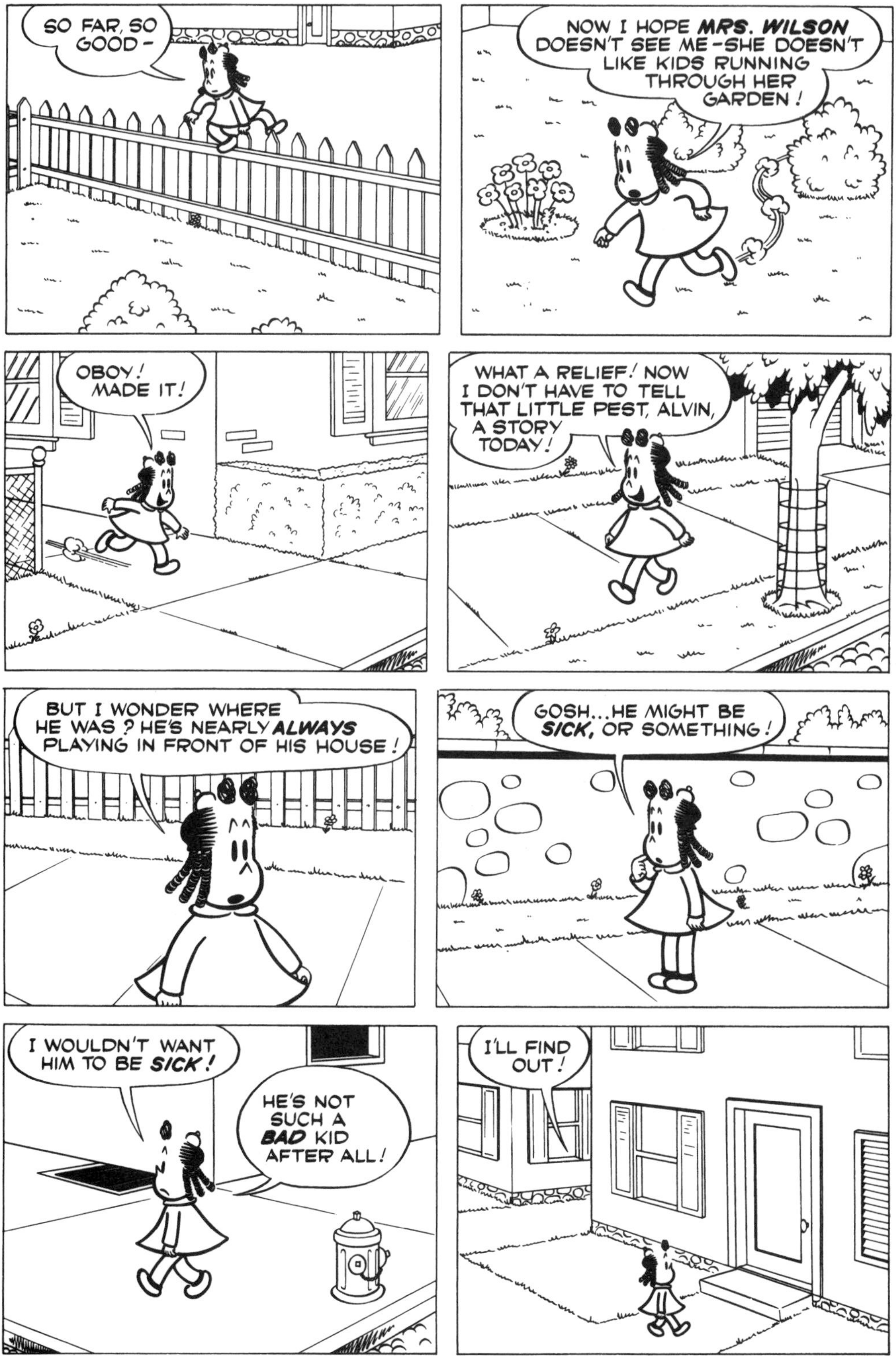
SO FAR, SO GOOD -
NOW I HOPE MRS. WILSON DOESN'T SEE ME - SHE DOESN'T LIKE KIDS RUNNING THROUGH HER GARDEN!
OBOY! MADE IT!
WHAT A RELIEF! NOW I DON'T HAVE TO TELL THAT LITTLE PEST, ALVIN, A STORY TODAY!
BUT I WONDER WHERE HE WAS? HE'S NEARLY ALWAYS PLAYING IN FRONT OF HIS HOUSE!
GOSH...HE MIGHT BE SICK, OR SOMETHING!
I WOULDN'T WANT HIM TO BE SICK!
HE'S NOT SUCH A BAD KID AFTER ALL!
I'LL FIND OUT!

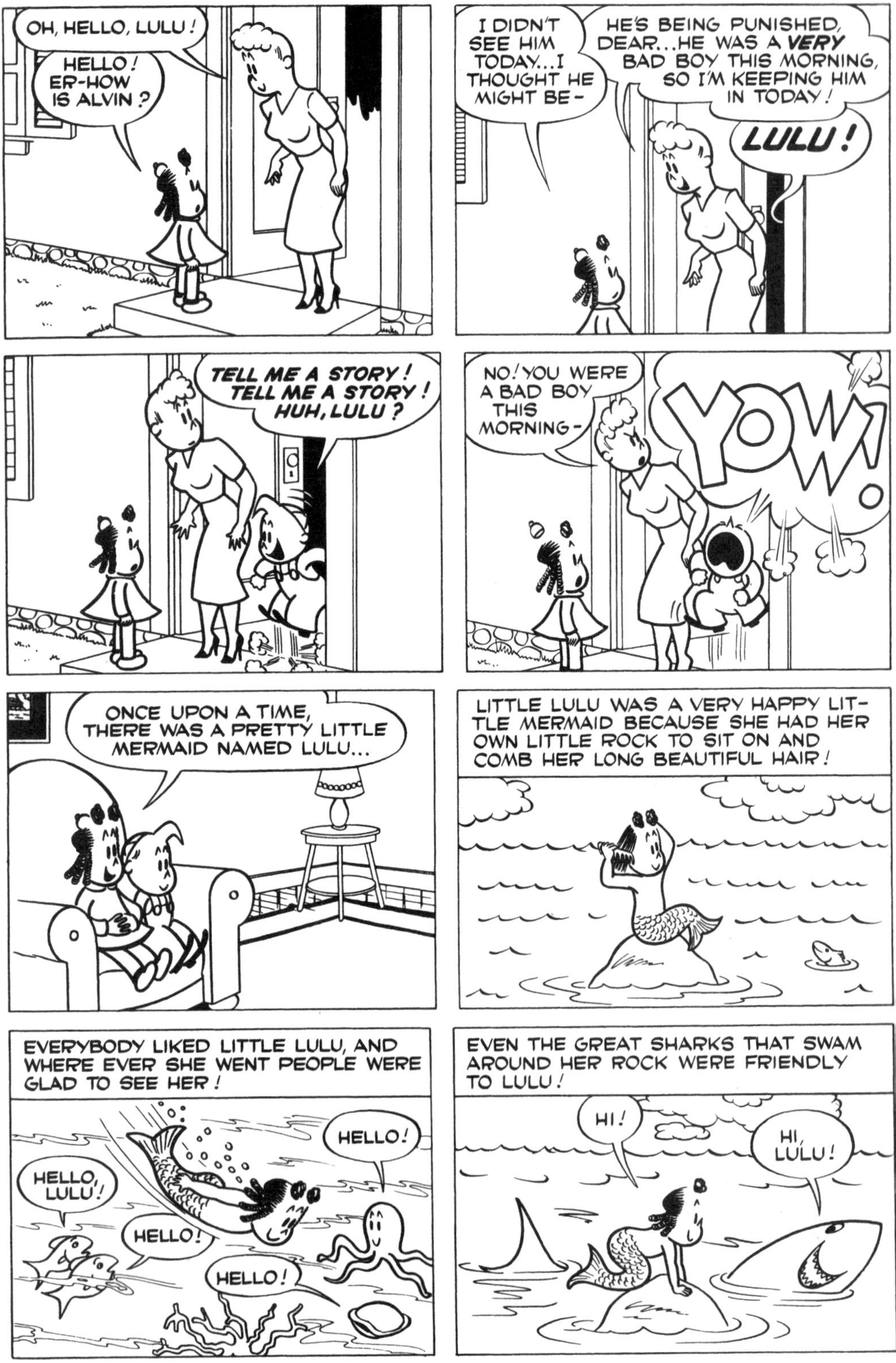
OH, HELLO, LULU!
HELLO! ER-HOW IS ALVIN?
I DIDN'T SEE HIM TODAY...I THOUGHT HE MIGHT BE-
HE'S BEING PUNISHED, DEAR...HE WAS A VERY BAD BOY THIS MORNING, SO I'M KEEPING HIM IN TODAY!
LULU!
TELL ME A STORY! TELL ME A STORY! HUH, LULU?
NO! YOU WERE A BAD BOY THIS MORNING-
YOW!
ONCE UPON A TIME, THERE WAS A PRETTY LITTLE MERMAID NAMED LULU...
LITTLE LULU WAS A VERY HAPPY LITTLE MERMAID BECAUSE SHE HAD HER OWN LITTLE ROCK TO SIT ON AND COMB HER LONG BEAUTIFUL HAIR!
EVERYBODY LIKED LITTLE LULU, AND WHERE EVER SHE WENT PEOPLE WERE GLAD TO SEE HER!
HELLO!
HELLO, LULU!
HELLO!
HELLO!
EVEN THE GREAT SHARKS THAT SWAM AROUND HER ROCK WERE FRIENDLY TO LULU!
HI!
HI, LULU!

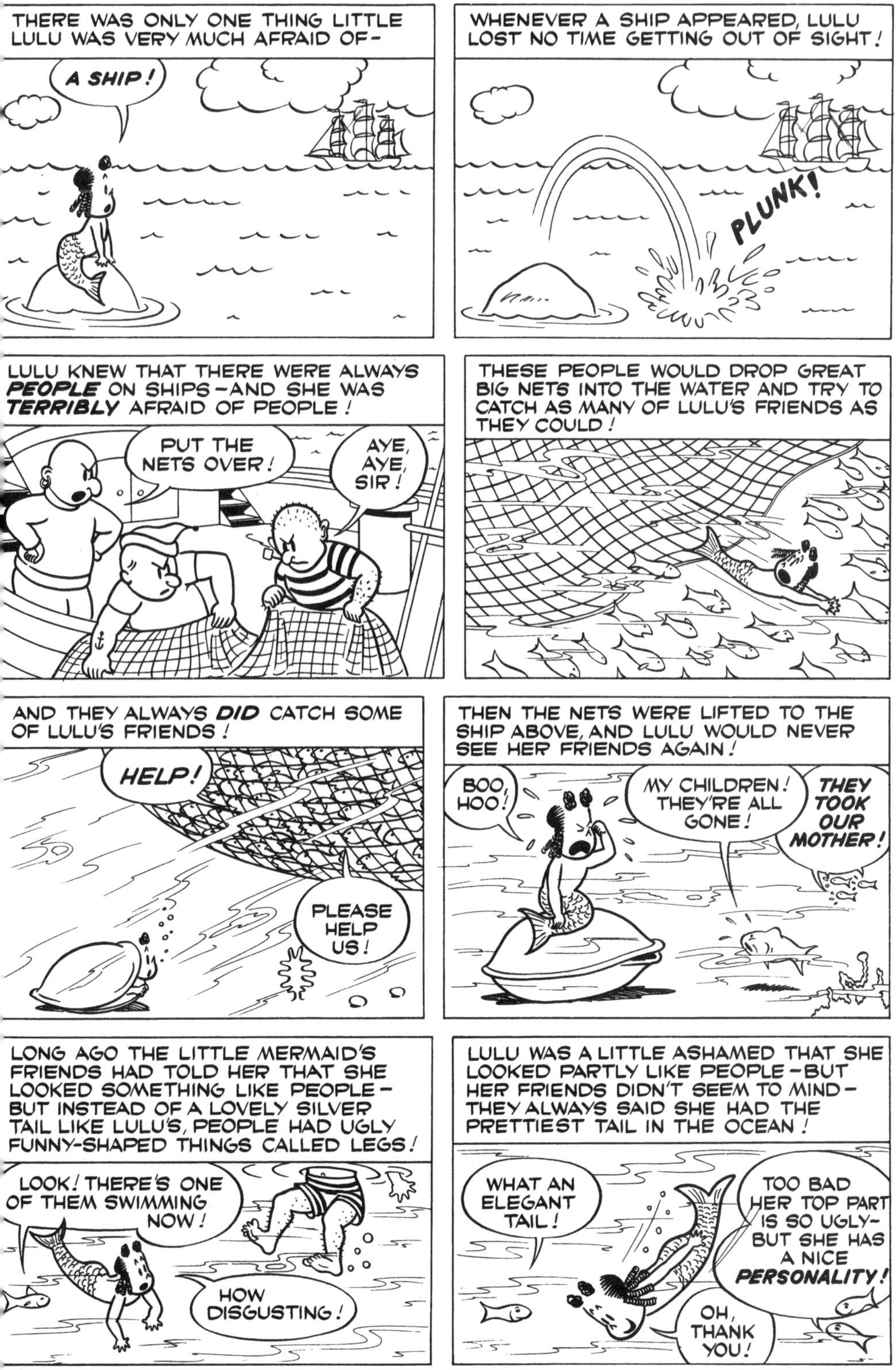
THERE WAS ONLY ONE THING LITTLE LULU WAS VERY MUCH AFRAID OF–
A SHIP!
WHENEVER A SHIP APPEARED, LULU LOST NO TIME GETTING OUT OF SIGHT!
PLUNK!
LULU KNEW THAT THERE WERE ALWAYS PEOPLE ON SHIPS–AND SHE WAS TERRIBLY AFRAID OF PEOPLE!
PUT THE NETS OVER!
AYE, AYE, SIR!
THESE PEOPLE WOULD DROP GREAT BIG NETS INTO THE WATER AND TRY TO CATCH AS MANY OF LULU'S FRIENDS AS THEY COULD!
AND THEY ALWAYS DID CATCH SOME OF LULU'S FRIENDS!
HELP!
PLEASE HELP US!
THEN THE NETS WERE LIFTED TO THE SHIP ABOVE, AND LULU WOULD NEVER SEE HER FRIENDS AGAIN!
BOO, HOO!
MY CHILDREN! THEY'RE ALL GONE!
THEY TOOK OUR MOTHER!
LONG AGO THE LITTLE MERMAID'S FRIENDS HAD TOLD HER THAT SHE LOOKED SOMETHING LIKE PEOPLE– BUT INSTEAD OF A LOVELY SILVER TAIL LIKE LULU'S, PEOPLE HAD UGLY FUNNY-SHAPED THINGS CALLED LEGS!
LOOK! THERE'S ONE OF THEM SWIMMING NOW!
HOW DISGUSTING!
LULU WAS A LITTLE ASHAMED THAT SHE LOOKED PARTLY LIKE PEOPLE–BUT HER FRIENDS DIDN'T SEEM TO MIND– THEY ALWAYS SAID SHE HAD THE PRETTIEST TAIL IN THE OCEAN!
WHAT AN ELEGANT TAIL!
TOO BAD HER TOP PART IS SO UGLY– BUT SHE HAS A NICE PERSONALITY!
OH, THANK YOU!

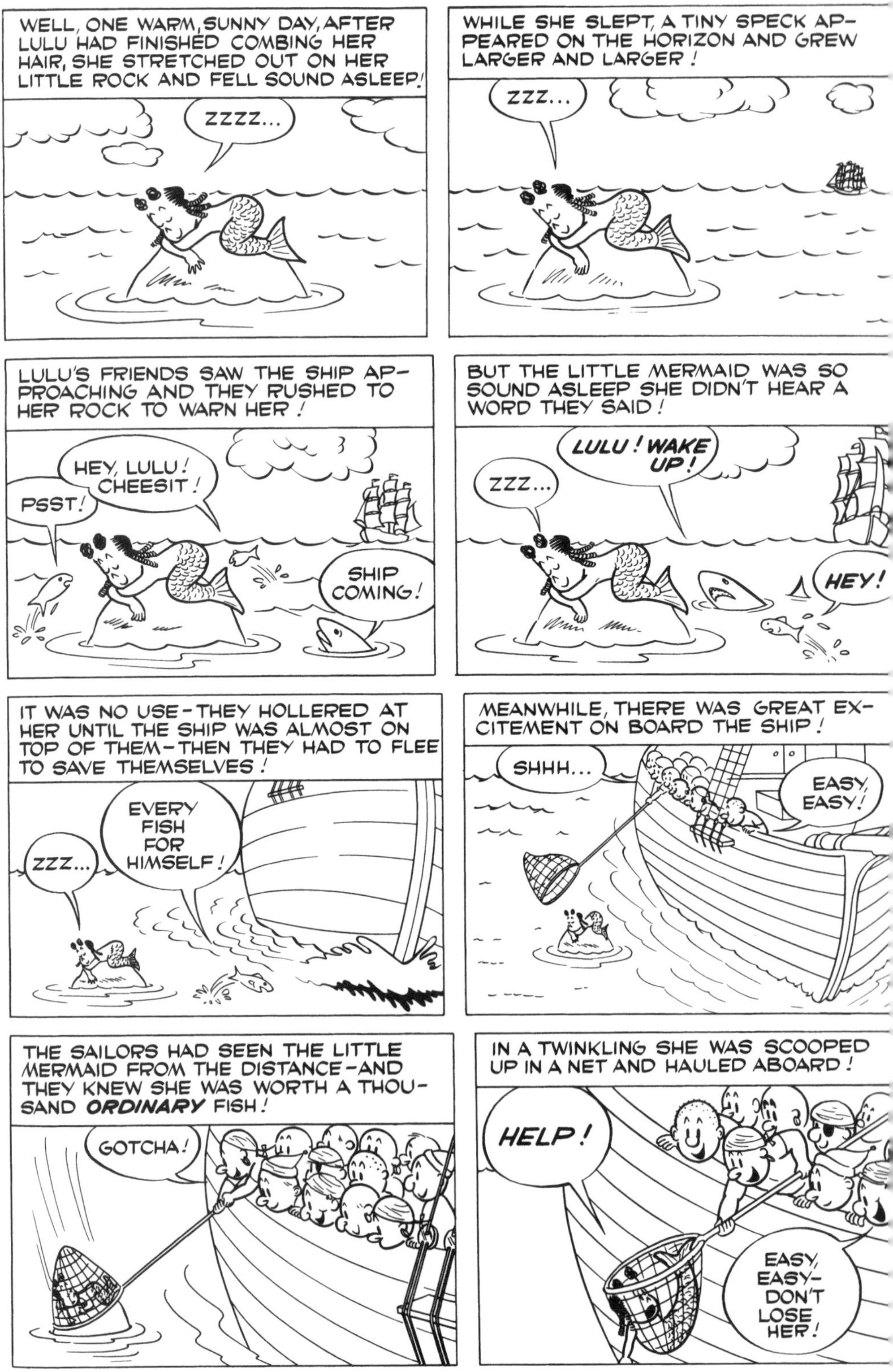
WELL, ONE WARM, SUNNY DAY, AFTER LULU HAD FINISHED COMBING HER HAIR, SHE STRETCHED OUT ON HER LITTLE ROCK AND FELL SOUND ASLEEP!
ZZZZ...
WHILE SHE SLEPT, A TINY SPECK APPEARED ON THE HORIZON AND GREW LARGER AND LARGER!
ZZZ...
LULU'S FRIENDS SAW THE SHIP APPROACHING AND THEY RUSHED TO HER ROCK TO WARN HER!
HEY, LULU! CHEESIT!
PSST!
SHIP COMING!
BUT THE LITTLE MERMAID WAS SO SOUND ASLEEP SHE DIDN'T HEAR A WORD THEY SAID!
ZZZ...
LULU! WAKE UP!
HEY!
IT WAS NO USE–THEY HOLLERED AT HER UNTIL THE SHIP WAS ALMOST ON TOP OF THEM–THEN THEY HAD TO FLEE TO SAVE THEMSELVES!
ZZZ...
EVERY FISH FOR HIMSELF!
MEANWHILE, THERE WAS GREAT EXCITEMENT ON BOARD THE SHIP!
SHHH...
EASY, EASY!
THE SAILORS HAD SEEN THE LITTLE MERMAID FROM THE DISTANCE–AND THEY KNEW SHE WAS WORTH A THOUSAND ORDINARY FISH!
GOTCHA!
IN A TWINKLING SHE WAS SCOOPED UP IN A NET AND HAULED ABOARD!
HELP!
EASY, EASY– DON'T LOSE HER!

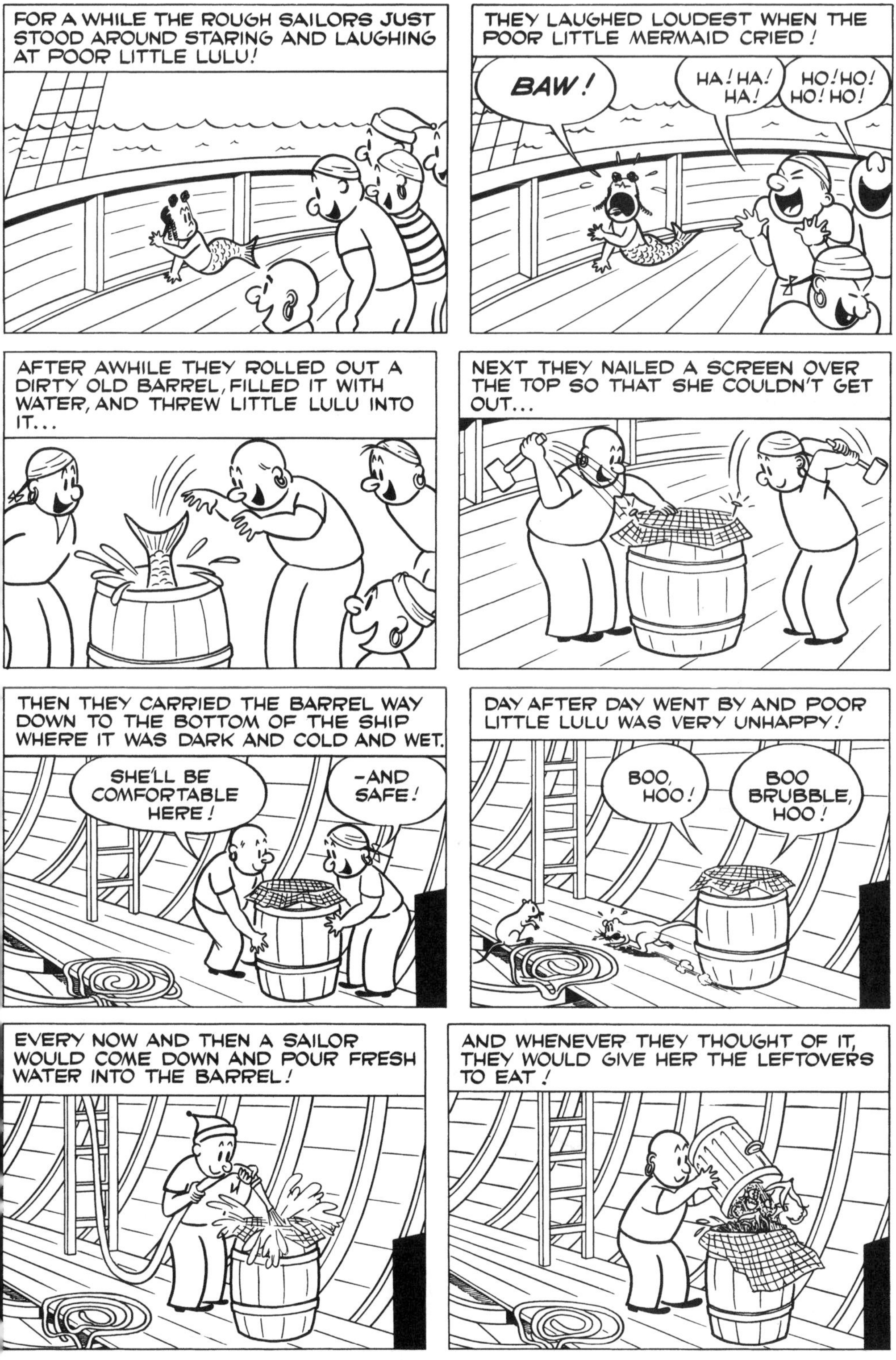
FOR A WHILE THE ROUGH SAILORS JUST STOOD AROUND STARING AND LAUGHING AT POOR LITTLE LULU!
THEY LAUGHED LOUDEST WHEN THE POOR LITTLE MERMAID CRIED!
BAW!
HA! HA! HA!
HO! HO! HO! HO!
AFTER AWHILE THEY ROLLED OUT A DIRTY OLD BARREL, FILLED IT WITH WATER, AND THREW LITTLE LULU INTO IT...
NEXT THEY NAILED A SCREEN OVER THE TOP SO THAT SHE COULDN'T GET OUT...
THEN THEY CARRIED THE BARREL WAY DOWN TO THE BOTTOM OF THE SHIP WHERE IT WAS DARK AND COLD AND WET.
SHE'LL BE COMFORTABLE HERE!
-AND SAFE!
DAY AFTER DAY WENT BY AND POOR LITTLE LULU WAS VERY UNHAPPY!
BOO, HOO!
BOO BRUBBLE, HOO!
EVERY NOW AND THEN A SAILOR WOULD COME DOWN AND POUR FRESH WATER INTO THE BARREL!
AND WHENEVER THEY THOUGHT OF IT, THEY WOULD GIVE HER THE LEFTOVERS TO EAT!

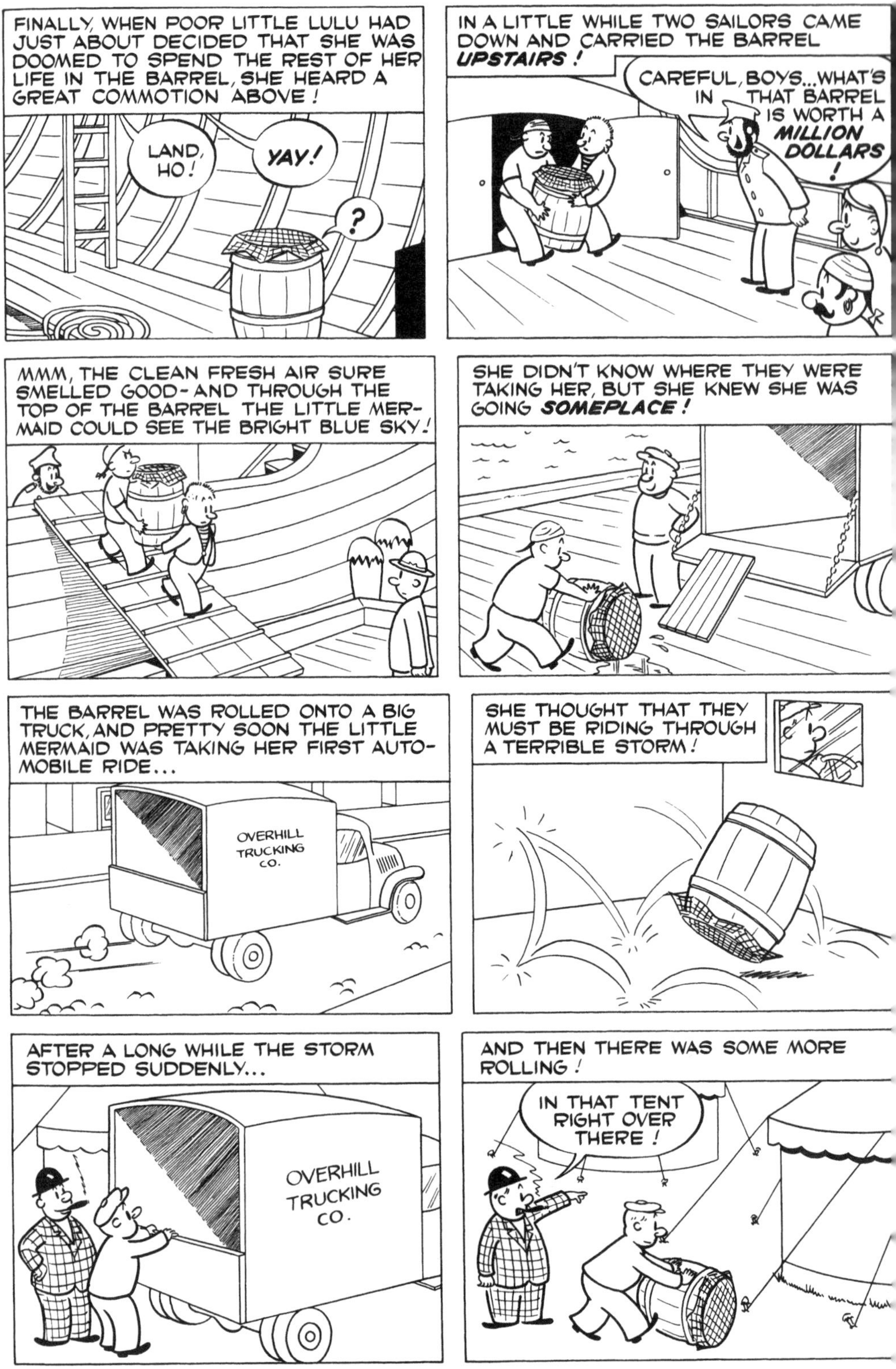
FINALLY, WHEN POOR LITTLE LULU HAD JUST ABOUT DECIDED THAT SHE WAS DOOMED TO SPEND THE REST OF HER LIFE IN THE BARREL, SHE HEARD A GREAT COMMOTION ABOVE!
LAND, HO!
YAY!
?
IN A LITTLE WHILE TWO SAILORS CAME DOWN AND CARRIED THE BARREL UPSTAIRS!
CAREFUL, BOYS...WHAT'S IN THAT BARREL IS WORTH A MILLION DOLLARS!
MMM, THE CLEAN FRESH AIR SURE SMELLED GOOD-AND THROUGH THE TOP OF THE BARREL THE LITTLE MERMAID COULD SEE THE BRIGHT BLUE SKY!
SHE DIDN'T KNOW WHERE THEY WERE TAKING HER, BUT SHE KNEW SHE WAS GOING SOMEPLACE!
THE BARREL WAS ROLLED ONTO A BIG TRUCK, AND PRETTY SOON THE LITTLE MERMAID WAS TAKING HER FIRST AUTOMOBILE RIDE...
OVERHILL TRUCKING CO.
SHE THOUGHT THAT THEY MUST BE RIDING THROUGH A TERRIBLE STORM!
AFTER A LONG WHILE THE STORM STOPPED SUDDENLY...
OVERHILL TRUCKING CO.
AND THEN THERE WAS SOME MORE ROLLING!
IN THAT TENT RIGHT OVER THERE!

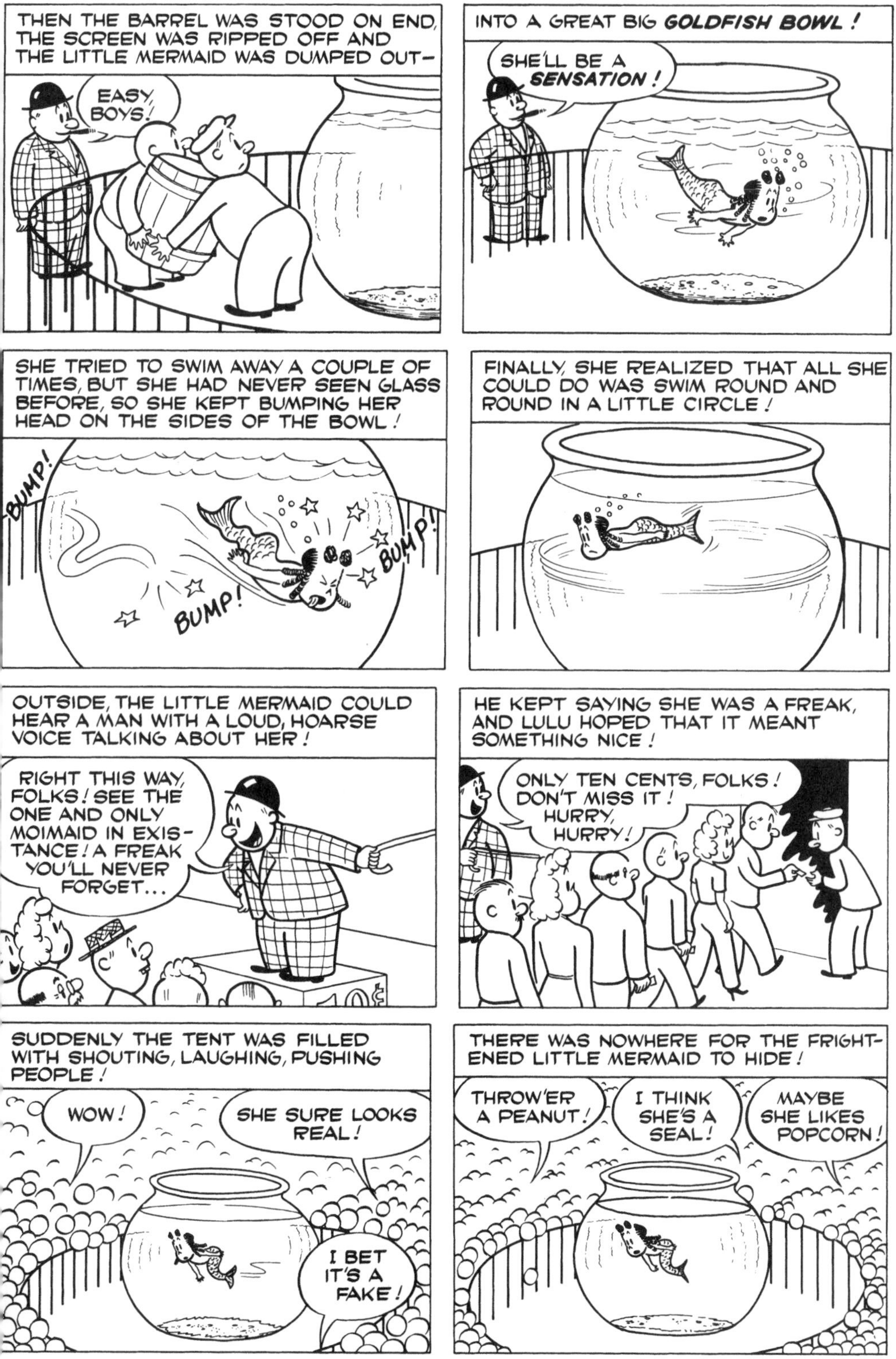
THEN THE BARREL WAS STOOD ON END, THE SCREEN WAS RIPPED OFF AND THE LITTLE MERMAID WAS DUMPED OUT–
EASY, BOYS!
INTO A GREAT BIG **GOLDFISH BOWL!**
SHE'LL BE A **SENSATION!**
SHE TRIED TO SWIM AWAY A COUPLE OF TIMES, BUT SHE HAD NEVER SEEN GLASS BEFORE, SO SHE KEPT BUMPING HER HEAD ON THE SIDES OF THE BOWL!
BUMP!
BUMP!
BUMP!
FINALLY, SHE REALIZED THAT ALL SHE COULD DO WAS SWIM ROUND AND ROUND IN A LITTLE CIRCLE!
OUTSIDE, THE LITTLE MERMAID COULD HEAR A MAN WITH A LOUD, HOARSE VOICE TALKING ABOUT HER!
RIGHT THIS WAY, FOLKS! SEE THE ONE AND ONLY MOIMAID IN EXISTANCE! A FREAK YOU'LL NEVER FORGET...
HE KEPT SAYING SHE WAS A FREAK, AND LULU HOPED THAT IT MEANT SOMETHING NICE!
ONLY TEN CENTS, FOLKS! DON'T MISS IT! HURRY, HURRY!
SUDDENLY THE TENT WAS FILLED WITH SHOUTING, LAUGHING, PUSHING PEOPLE!
WOW!
SHE SURE LOOKS REAL!
I BET IT'S A FAKE!
THERE WAS NOWHERE FOR THE FRIGHTENED LITTLE MERMAID TO HIDE!
THROW'ER A PEANUT!
I THINK SHE'S A SEAL!
MAYBE SHE LIKES POPCORN!

POOR LITTLE LULU TRIED TO HIDE BY BURYING HER HEAD IN THE PEBBLES AT THE BOTTOM OF THE GOLDFISH BOWL!

FINALLY, A LONG TIME AFTER, LULU PULLED HER HEAD OUT OF THE PEBBLES AND LOOKED AROUND...

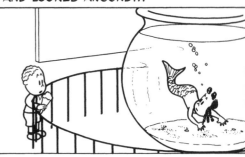

THERE WAS ONLY ONE LITTLE BOY LEFT IN THE TENT—BUT HE WASN'T LAUGHING—HE LOOKED SAD!

THE LITTLE MERMAID SMILED WHEN HE HELD OUT A HALF-EATEN ICE-CREAM CONE TO HER!

DAY AFTER DAY THE LITTLE BOY CAME BACK, AND HE ALWAYS STOOD IN THE SAME PLACE—NOT LAUGHING LIKE EVERYBODY ELSE—JUST SMILING SADLY!

ONE DAY WHEN NEARLY EVERYBODY HAD LEFT, THE LITTLE BOY LINGERED BEHIND AS USUAL—BUT HE SEEMED TO BE VERY NERVOUS, AND KEPT LOOKING OVER HIS SHOULDER!

FINALLY, WHEN THE LAST PERSON LEFT, HE SUDDENLY REACHED INTO HIS POCKET AND PULLED OUT SOMETHING THAT LOOKED VERY MUCH LIKE A BIG ROCK!

THEN TO THE GREAT SURPRISE OF THE LITTLE MERMAID, HE THREW IT STRAIGHT AT HER—OR SO SHE THOUGHT!

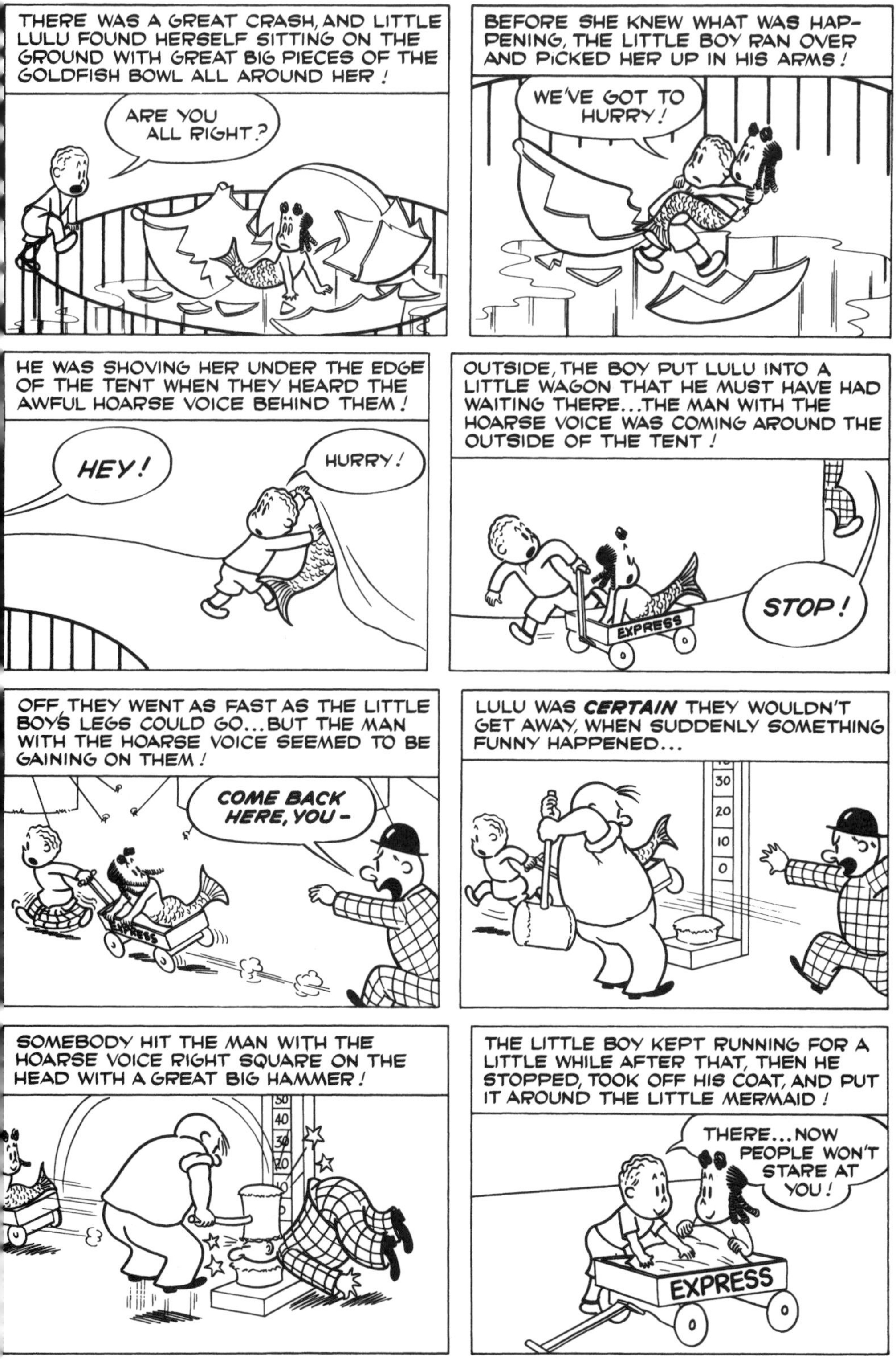
THERE WAS A GREAT CRASH, AND LITTLE LULU FOUND HERSELF SITTING ON THE GROUND WITH GREAT BIG PIECES OF THE GOLDFISH BOWL ALL AROUND HER!
ARE YOU ALL RIGHT?
BEFORE SHE KNEW WHAT WAS HAPPENING, THE LITTLE BOY RAN OVER AND PICKED HER UP IN HIS ARMS!
WE'VE GOT TO HURRY!
HE WAS SHOVING HER UNDER THE EDGE OF THE TENT WHEN THEY HEARD THE AWFUL HOARSE VOICE BEHIND THEM!
HEY!
HURRY!
OUTSIDE, THE BOY PUT LULU INTO A LITTLE WAGON THAT HE MUST HAVE HAD WAITING THERE...THE MAN WITH THE HOARSE VOICE WAS COMING AROUND THE OUTSIDE OF THE TENT!
EXPRESS
STOP!
OFF THEY WENT AS FAST AS THE LITTLE BOY'S LEGS COULD GO...BUT THE MAN WITH THE HOARSE VOICE SEEMED TO BE GAINING ON THEM!
COME BACK HERE, YOU -
EXPRESS
LULU WAS *CERTAIN* THEY WOULDN'T GET AWAY, WHEN SUDDENLY SOMETHING FUNNY HAPPENED...
30
20
10
0
SOMEBODY HIT THE MAN WITH THE HOARSE VOICE RIGHT SQUARE ON THE HEAD WITH A GREAT BIG HAMMER!
50
40
30
20
THE LITTLE BOY KEPT RUNNING FOR A LITTLE WHILE AFTER THAT, THEN HE STOPPED, TOOK OFF HIS COAT, AND PUT IT AROUND THE LITTLE MERMAID!
THERE...NOW PEOPLE WON'T STARE AT YOU!
EXPRESS

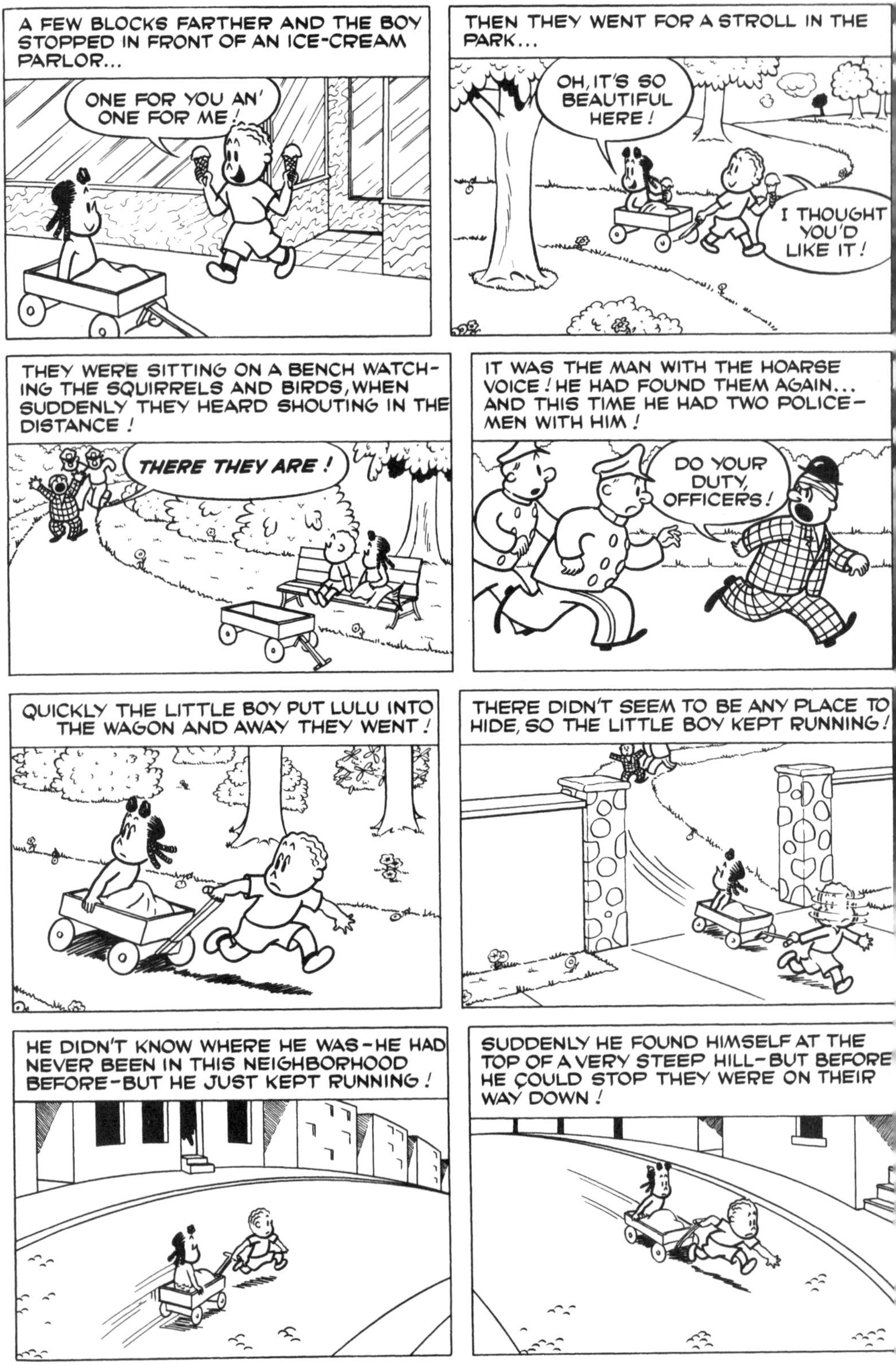
A FEW BLOCKS FARTHER AND THE BOY STOPPED IN FRONT OF AN ICE-CREAM PARLOR...
ONE FOR YOU AN' ONE FOR ME!
THEN THEY WENT FOR A STROLL IN THE PARK...
OH, IT'S SO BEAUTIFUL HERE!
I THOUGHT YOU'D LIKE IT!
THEY WERE SITTING ON A BENCH WATCHING THE SQUIRRELS AND BIRDS, WHEN SUDDENLY THEY HEARD SHOUTING IN THE DISTANCE!
THERE THEY ARE!
IT WAS THE MAN WITH THE HOARSE VOICE! HE HAD FOUND THEM AGAIN... AND THIS TIME HE HAD TWO POLICEMEN WITH HIM!
DO YOUR DUTY, OFFICERS!
QUICKLY THE LITTLE BOY PUT LULU INTO THE WAGON AND AWAY THEY WENT!
THERE DIDN'T SEEM TO BE ANY PLACE TO HIDE, SO THE LITTLE BOY KEPT RUNNING!
HE DIDN'T KNOW WHERE HE WAS-HE HAD NEVER BEEN IN THIS NEIGHBORHOOD BEFORE-BUT HE JUST KEPT RUNNING!
SUDDENLY HE FOUND HIMSELF AT THE TOP OF A VERY STEEP HILL-BUT BEFORE HE COULD STOP THEY WERE ON THEIR WAY DOWN!

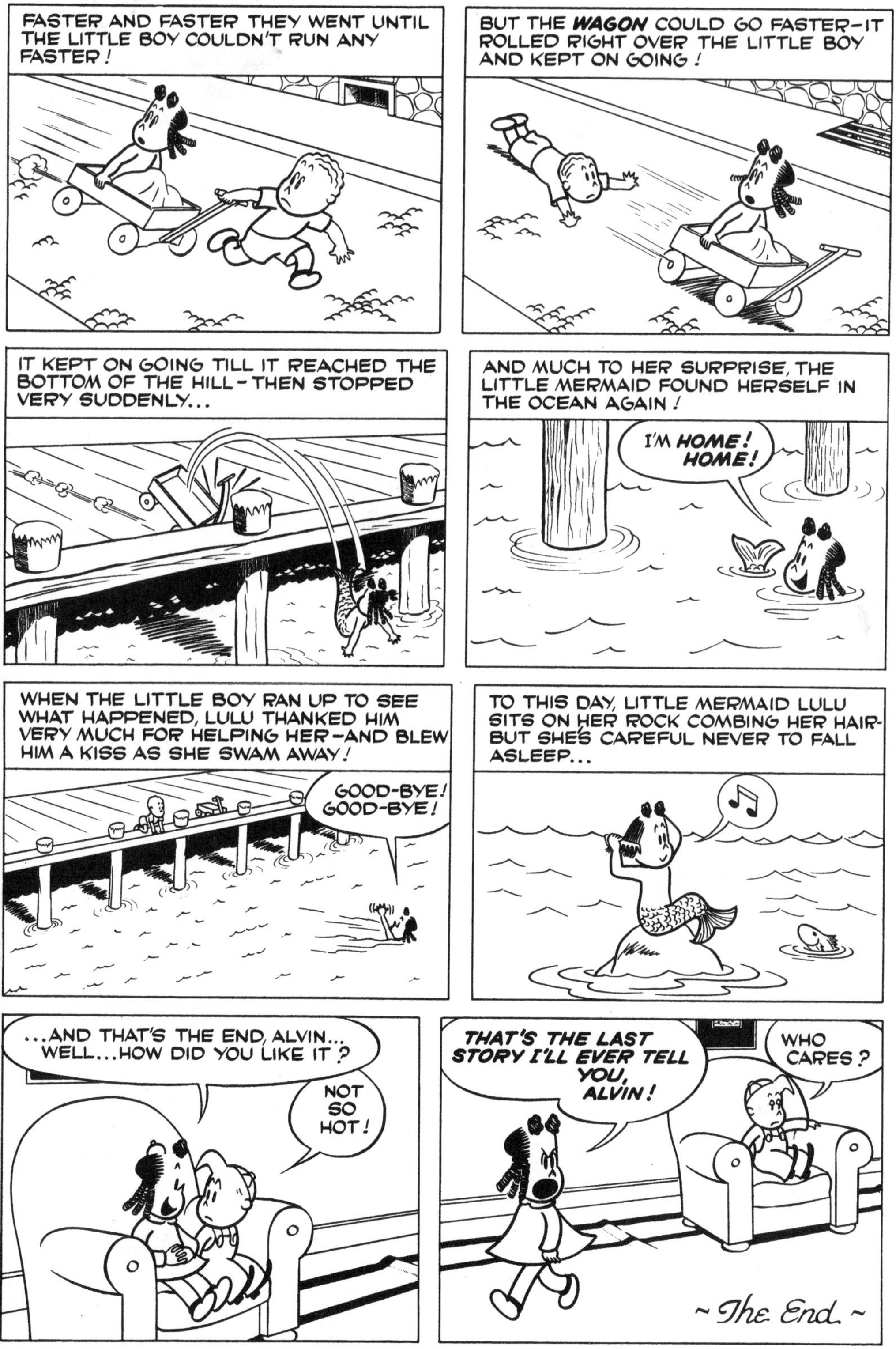
FASTER AND FASTER THEY WENT UNTIL THE LITTLE BOY COULDN'T RUN ANY FASTER!
BUT THE *WAGON* COULD GO FASTER—IT ROLLED RIGHT OVER THE LITTLE BOY AND KEPT ON GOING!
IT KEPT ON GOING TILL IT REACHED THE BOTTOM OF THE HILL—THEN STOPPED VERY SUDDENLY...
AND MUCH TO HER SURPRISE, THE LITTLE MERMAID FOUND HERSELF IN THE OCEAN AGAIN!
I'M *HOME! HOME!*
WHEN THE LITTLE BOY RAN UP TO SEE WHAT HAPPENED, LULU THANKED HIM VERY MUCH FOR HELPING HER—AND BLEW HIM A KISS AS SHE SWAM AWAY!
GOOD-BYE! GOOD-BYE!
TO THIS DAY, LITTLE MERMAID LULU SITS ON HER ROCK COMBING HER HAIR—BUT SHE'S CAREFUL NEVER TO FALL ASLEEP...
...AND THAT'S THE END, ALVIN... WELL...HOW DID YOU LIKE IT?
NOT SO HOT!
THAT'S THE LAST STORY I'LL EVER TELL YOU, ALVIN!
WHO CARES?
~ The End. ~

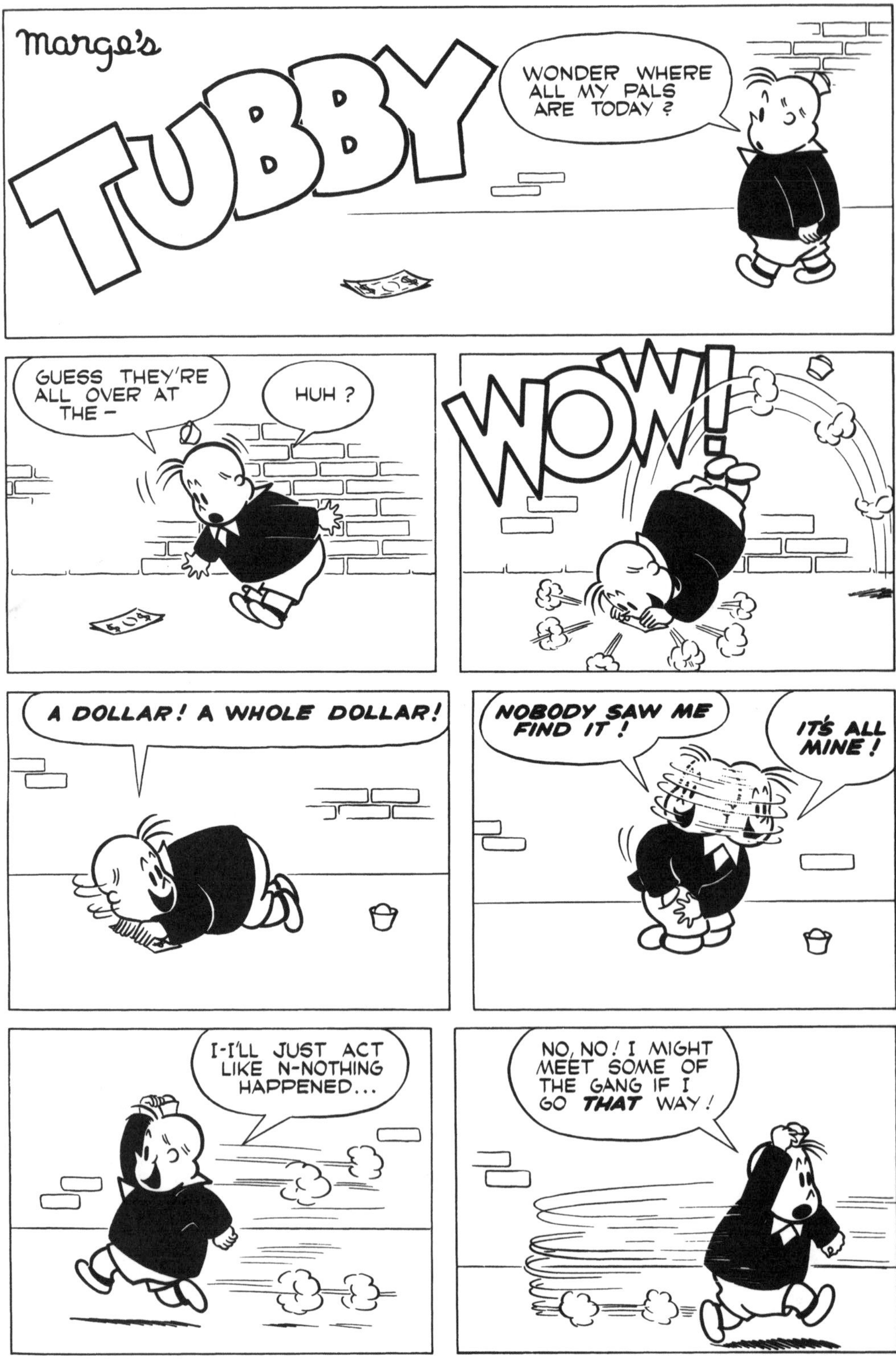

marge's
TUBBY
WONDER WHERE ALL MY PALS ARE TODAY ?
GUESS THEY'RE ALL OVER AT THE –
HUH ?
WOW!
A DOLLAR! A WHOLE DOLLAR!
NOBODY SAW ME FIND IT !
IT'S ALL MINE !
I-I'LL JUST ACT LIKE N-NOTHING HAPPENED...
NO, NO! I MIGHT MEET SOME OF THE GANG IF I GO THAT WAY !

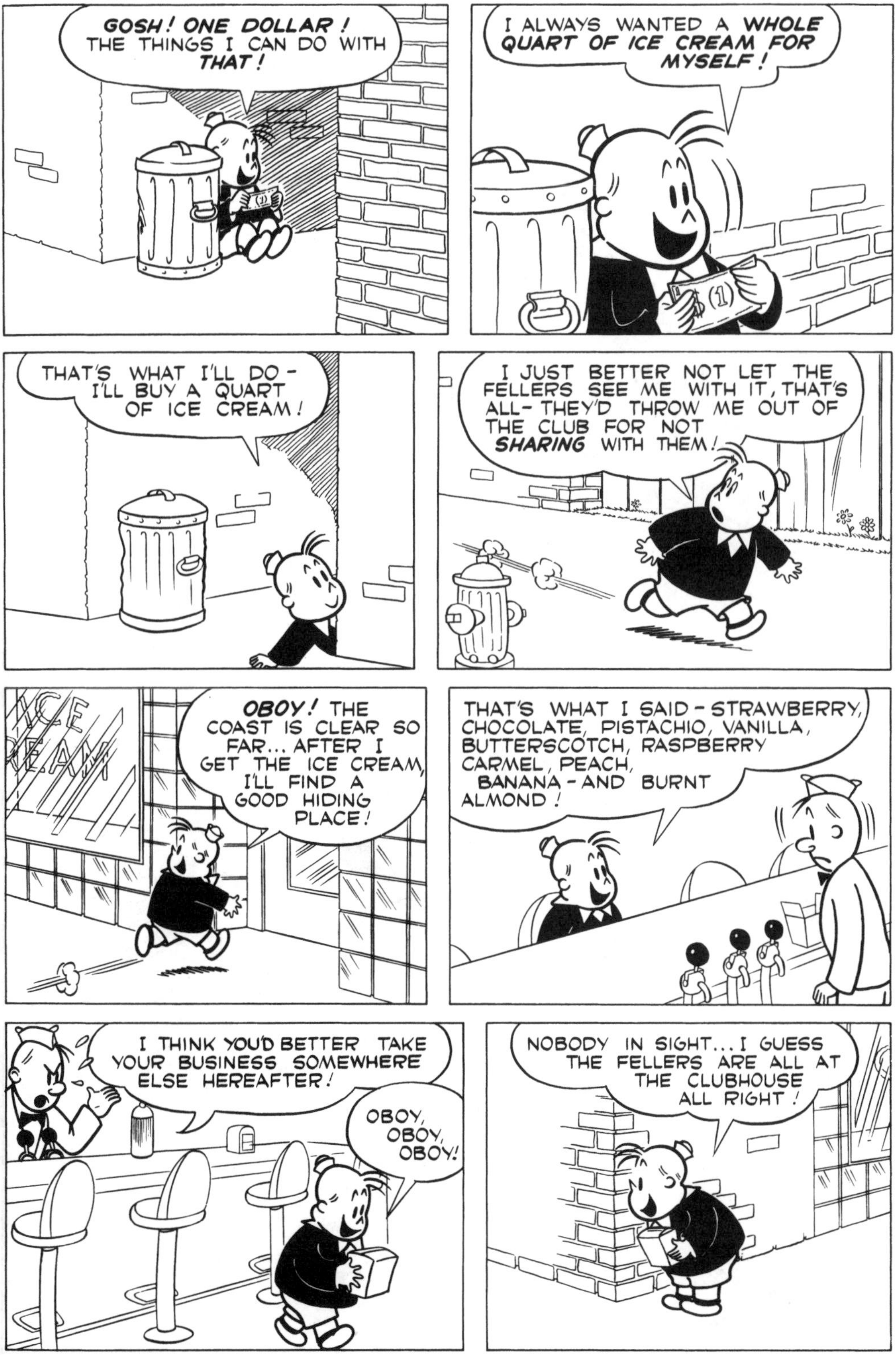
GOSH! ONE DOLLAR! THE THINGS I CAN DO WITH THAT!
I ALWAYS WANTED A WHOLE QUART OF ICE CREAM FOR MYSELF!
THAT'S WHAT I'LL DO - I'LL BUY A QUART OF ICE CREAM!
I JUST BETTER NOT LET THE FELLERS SEE ME WITH IT, THAT'S ALL- THEY'D THROW ME OUT OF THE CLUB FOR NOT SHARING WITH THEM!
OBOY! THE COAST IS CLEAR SO FAR... AFTER I GET THE ICE CREAM, I'LL FIND A GOOD HIDING PLACE!
THAT'S WHAT I SAID - STRAWBERRY, CHOCOLATE, PISTACHIO, VANILLA, BUTTERSCOTCH, RASPBERRY CARMEL, PEACH, BANANA - AND BURNT ALMOND!
I THINK YOU'D BETTER TAKE YOUR BUSINESS SOMEWHERE ELSE HEREAFTER!
OBOY, OBOY, OBOY!
NOBODY IN SIGHT... I GUESS THE FELLERS ARE ALL AT THE CLUBHOUSE ALL RIGHT!

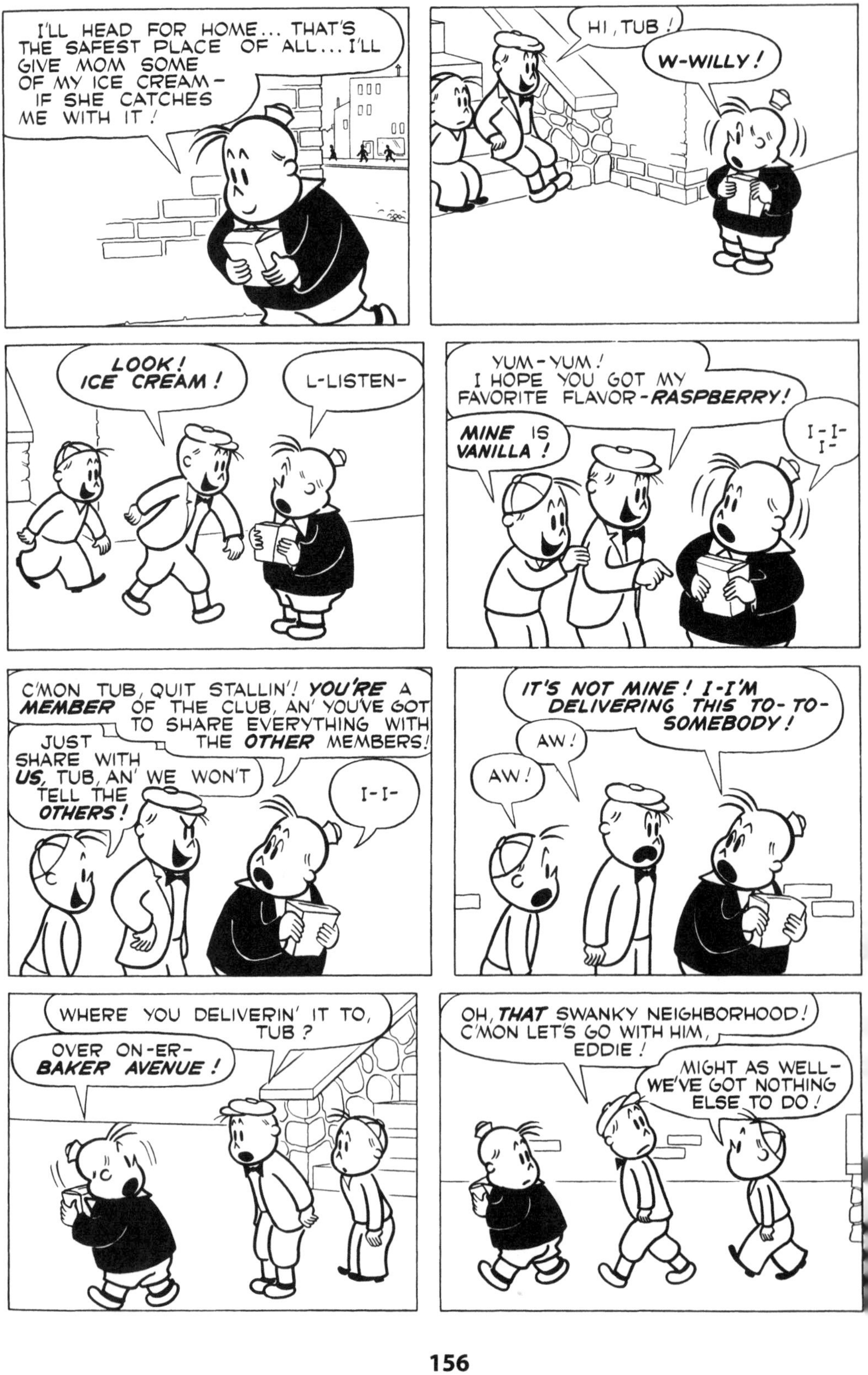
I'LL HEAD FOR HOME... THAT'S THE SAFEST PLACE OF ALL... I'LL GIVE MOM SOME OF MY ICE CREAM – IF SHE CATCHES ME WITH IT!
HI, TUB!
W-WILLY!
LOOK! ICE CREAM!
L-LISTEN-
YUM-YUM! I HOPE YOU GOT MY FAVORITE FLAVOR-RASPBERRY!
MINE IS VANILLA!
I-I-I-
C'MON TUB, QUIT STALLIN'! YOU'RE A MEMBER OF THE CLUB, AN' YOU'VE GOT TO SHARE EVERYTHING WITH THE OTHER MEMBERS!
JUST SHARE WITH US, TUB, AN' WE WON'T TELL THE OTHERS!
I-I-
IT'S NOT MINE! I-I'M DELIVERING THIS TO-TO-SOMEBODY!
AW!
AW!
WHERE YOU DELIVERIN' IT TO, TUB?
OVER ON-ER-BAKER AVENUE!
OH, THAT SWANKY NEIGHBORHOOD! C'MON LET'S GO WITH HIM, EDDIE!
MIGHT AS WELL-WE'VE GOT NOTHING ELSE TO DO!

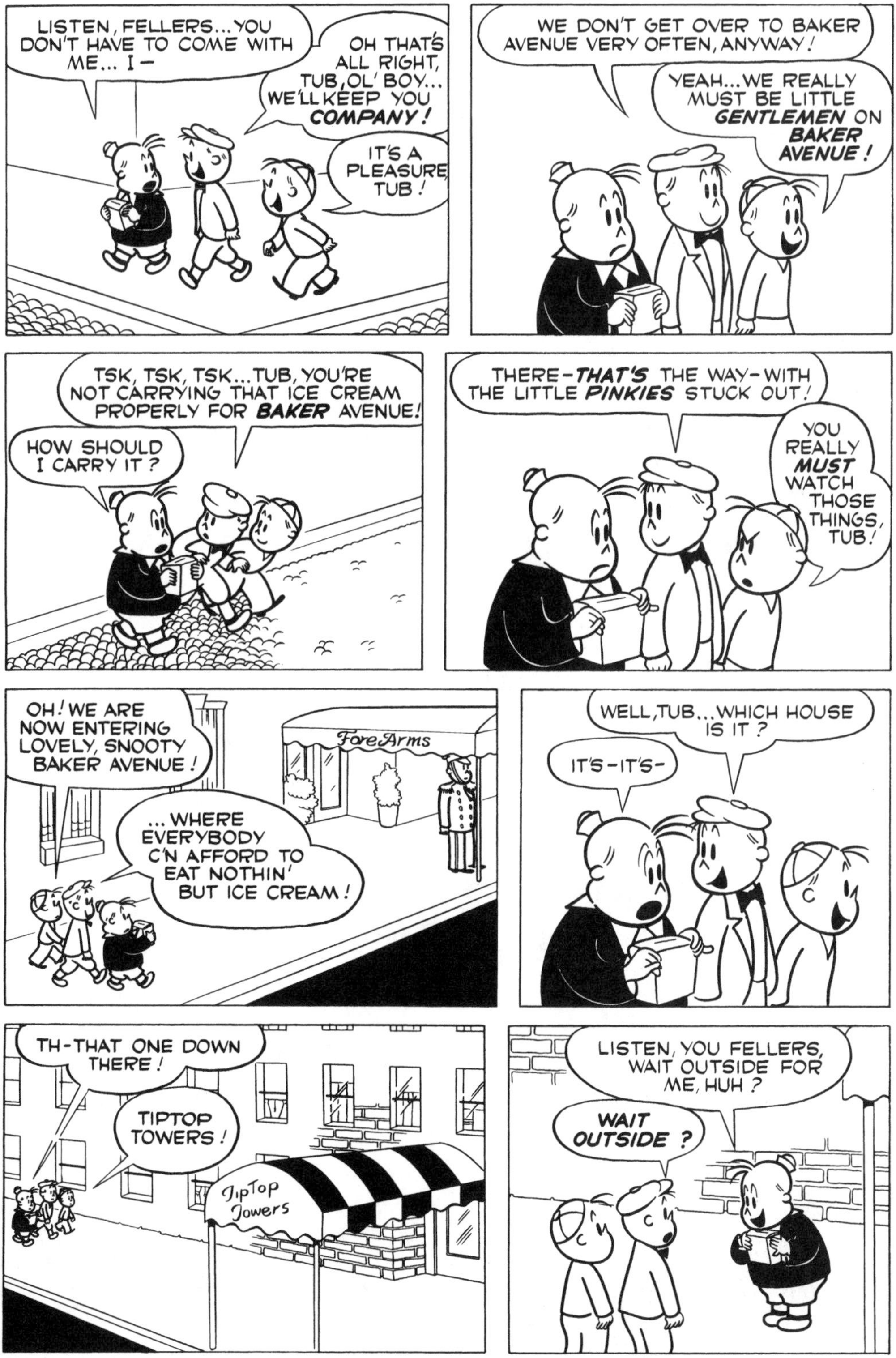
LISTEN, FELLERS...YOU DON'T HAVE TO COME WITH ME... I—
OH THAT'S ALL RIGHT, TUB, OL' BOY... WE'LL KEEP YOU COMPANY!
IT'S A PLEASURE, TUB!
WE DON'T GET OVER TO BAKER AVENUE VERY OFTEN, ANYWAY!
YEAH...WE REALLY MUST BE LITTLE GENTLEMEN ON BAKER AVENUE!
TSK, TSK, TSK...TUB, YOU'RE NOT CARRYING THAT ICE CREAM PROPERLY FOR BAKER AVENUE!
HOW SHOULD I CARRY IT?
THERE—THAT'S THE WAY—WITH THE LITTLE PINKIES STUCK OUT!
YOU REALLY MUST WATCH THOSE THINGS, TUB!
OH! WE ARE NOW ENTERING LOVELY, SNOOTY BAKER AVENUE!
Fore Arms
...WHERE EVERYBODY C'N AFFORD TO EAT NOTHIN' BUT ICE CREAM!
WELL, TUB...WHICH HOUSE IS IT?
IT'S—IT'S—
TH-THAT ONE DOWN THERE!
TIPTOP TOWERS!
TipTop Towers
LISTEN, YOU FELLERS, WAIT OUTSIDE FOR ME, HUH?
WAIT OUTSIDE?

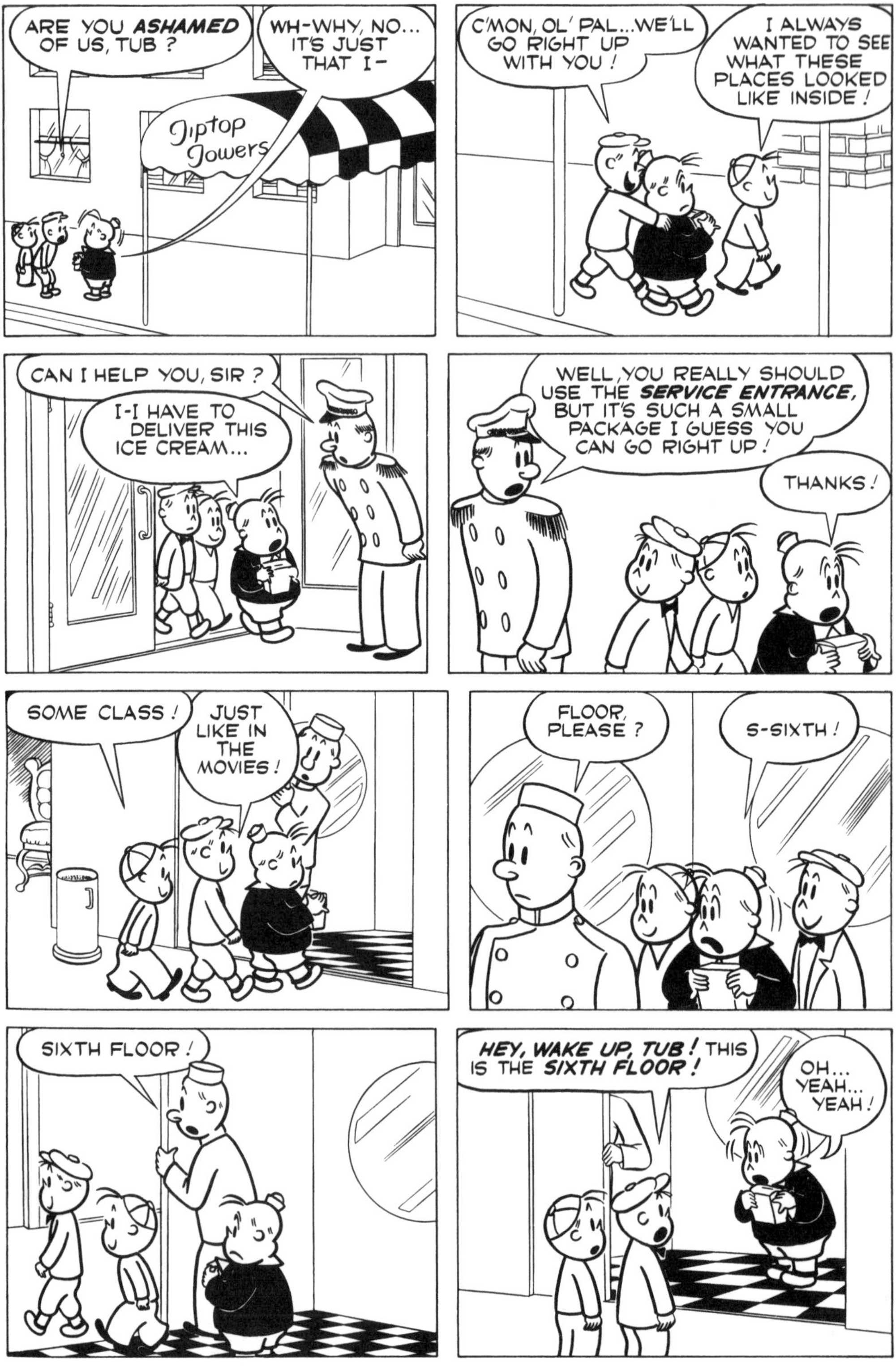
ARE YOU ASHAMED OF US, TUB ?
WH-WHY, NO... IT'S JUST THAT I-
Tiptop Towers
C'MON, OL' PAL...WE'LL GO RIGHT UP WITH YOU !
I ALWAYS WANTED TO SEE WHAT THESE PLACES LOOKED LIKE INSIDE !
CAN I HELP YOU, SIR ?
I-I HAVE TO DELIVER THIS ICE CREAM...
WELL, YOU REALLY SHOULD USE THE SERVICE ENTRANCE, BUT IT'S SUCH A SMALL PACKAGE I GUESS YOU CAN GO RIGHT UP !
THANKS !
SOME CLASS !
JUST LIKE IN THE MOVIES !
FLOOR, PLEASE ?
S-SIXTH !
SIXTH FLOOR !
HEY, WAKE UP, TUB ! THIS IS THE SIXTH FLOOR !
OH... YEAH... YEAH !

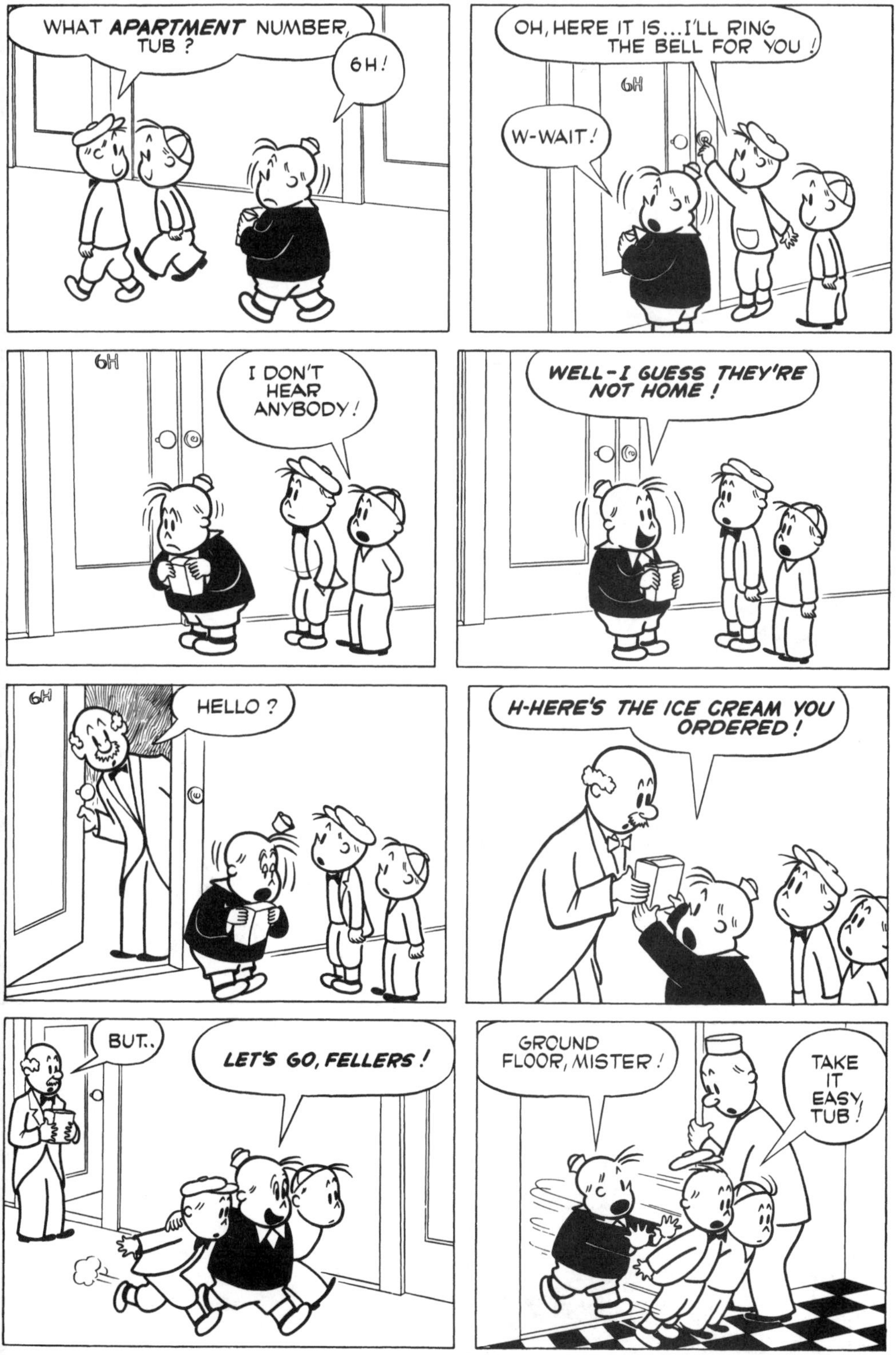
WHAT APARTMENT NUMBER, TUB ?
6H!
OH, HERE IT IS...I'LL RING THE BELL FOR YOU !
6H
W-WAIT!
6H
I DON'T HEAR ANYBODY!
WELL-I GUESS THEY'RE NOT HOME !
6H
HELLO ?
H-HERE'S THE ICE CREAM YOU ORDERED!
BUT..
LET'S GO, FELLERS !
GROUND FLOOR, MISTER!
TAKE IT EASY TUB!

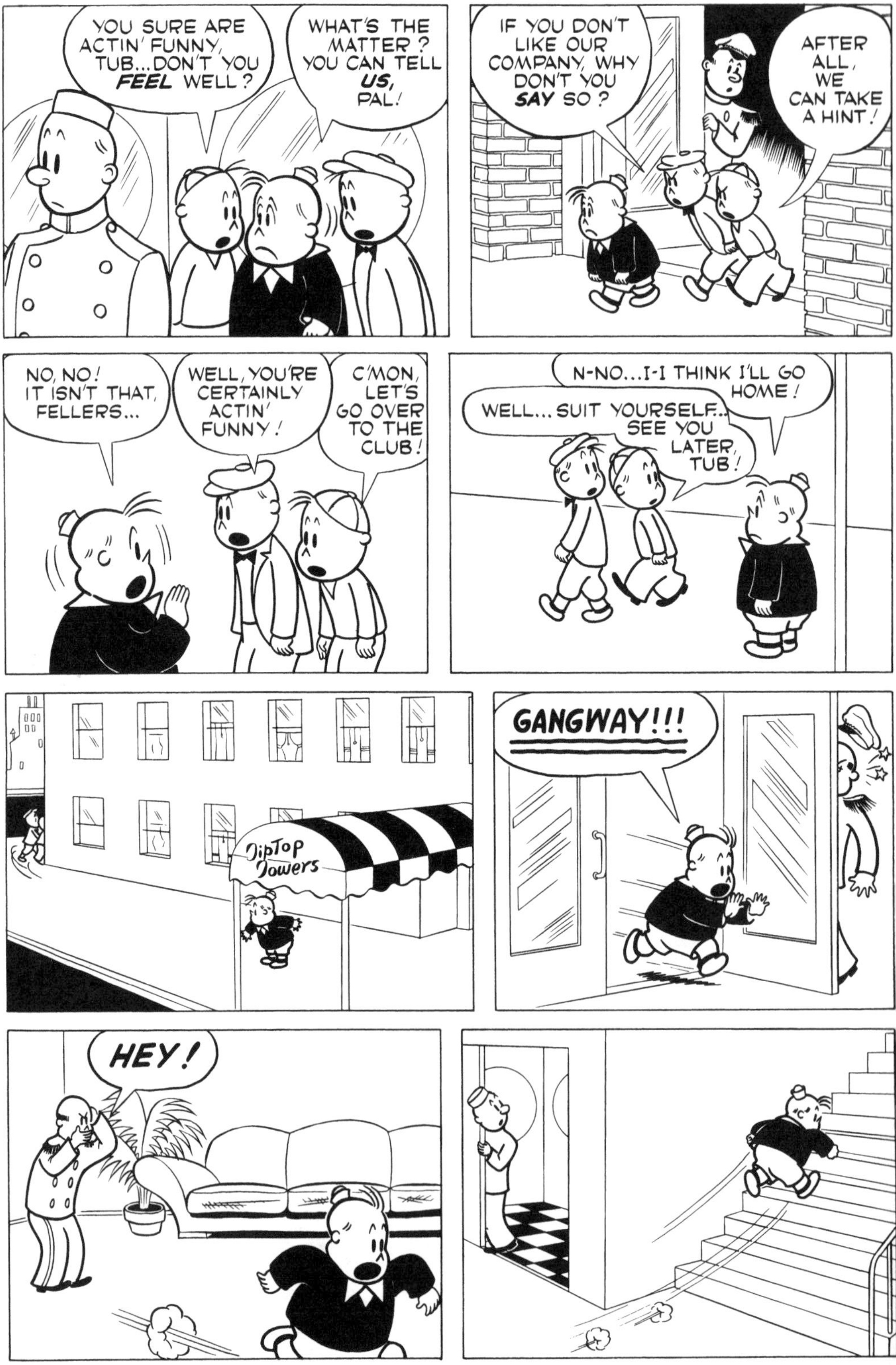

YOU SURE ARE ACTIN' FUNNY, TUB...DON'T YOU FEEL WELL?
WHAT'S THE MATTER? YOU CAN TELL US, PAL!
IF YOU DON'T LIKE OUR COMPANY, WHY DON'T YOU SAY SO?
AFTER ALL, WE CAN TAKE A HINT!
NO, NO! IT ISN'T THAT, FELLERS...
WELL, YOU'RE CERTAINLY ACTIN' FUNNY!
C'MON, LET'S GO OVER TO THE CLUB!
N-NO...I-I THINK I'LL GO HOME!
WELL... SUIT YOURSELF... SEE YOU LATER, TUB!
TipTop Towers
GANGWAY!!!
HEY!

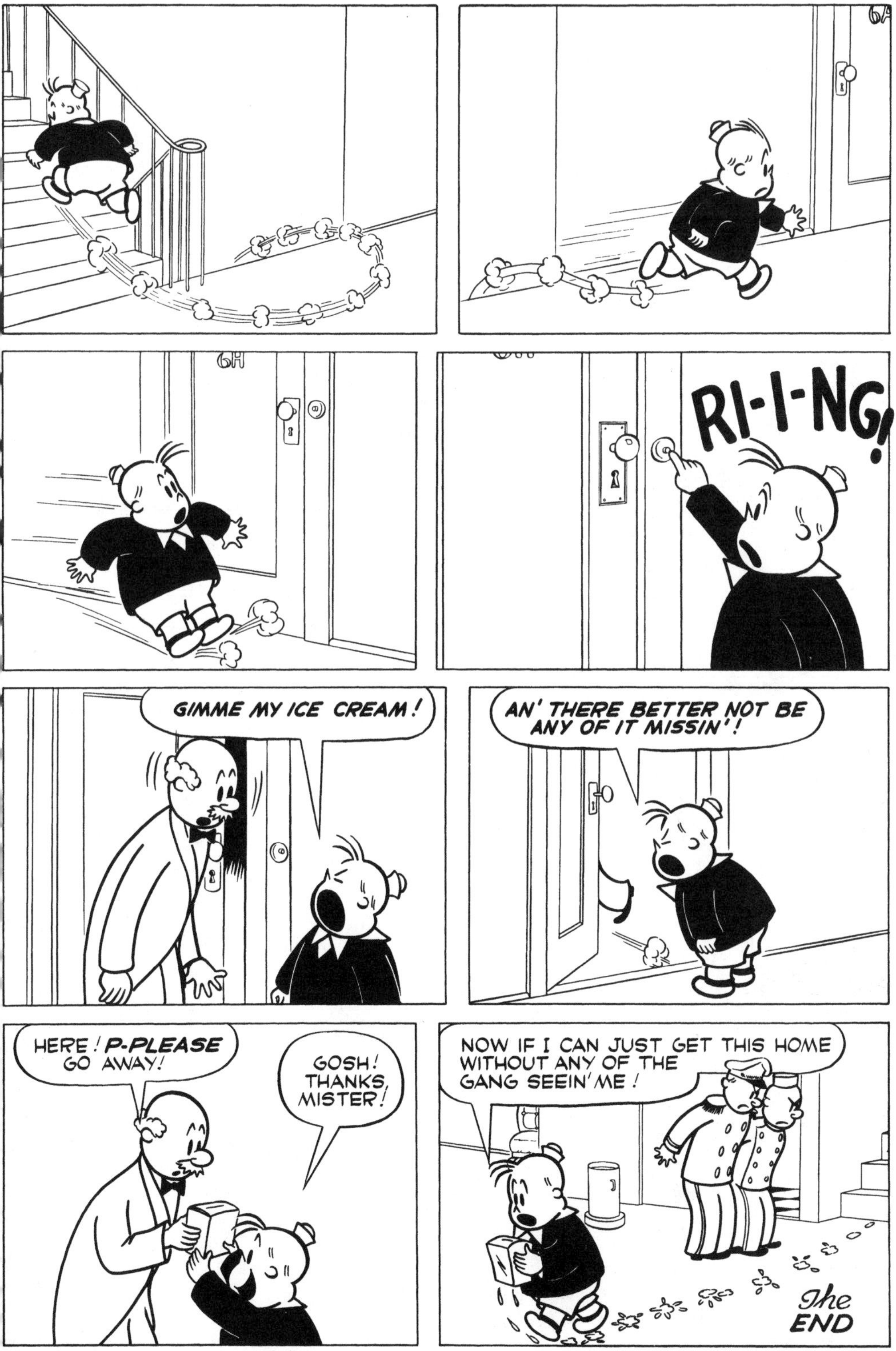
6A
6H
RI-I-NG!
GIMME MY ICE CREAM!
AN' THERE BETTER NOT BE ANY OF IT MISSIN'!
HERE! P-PLEASE GO AWAY!
GOSH! THANKS, MISTER!
NOW IF I CAN JUST GET THIS HOME WITHOUT ANY OF THE GANG SEEIN' ME!
The END

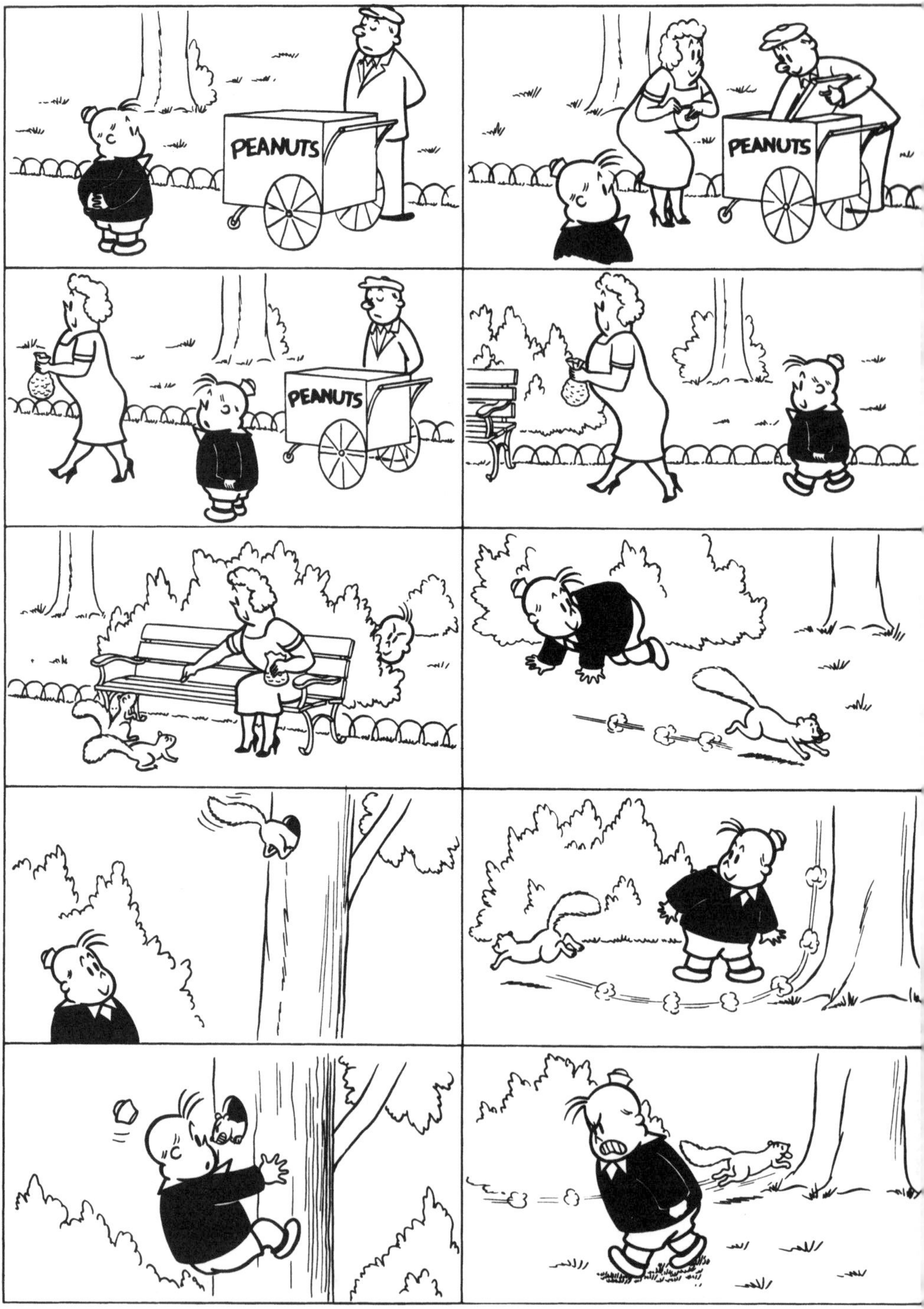
PEANUTS
PEANUTS
PEANUTS

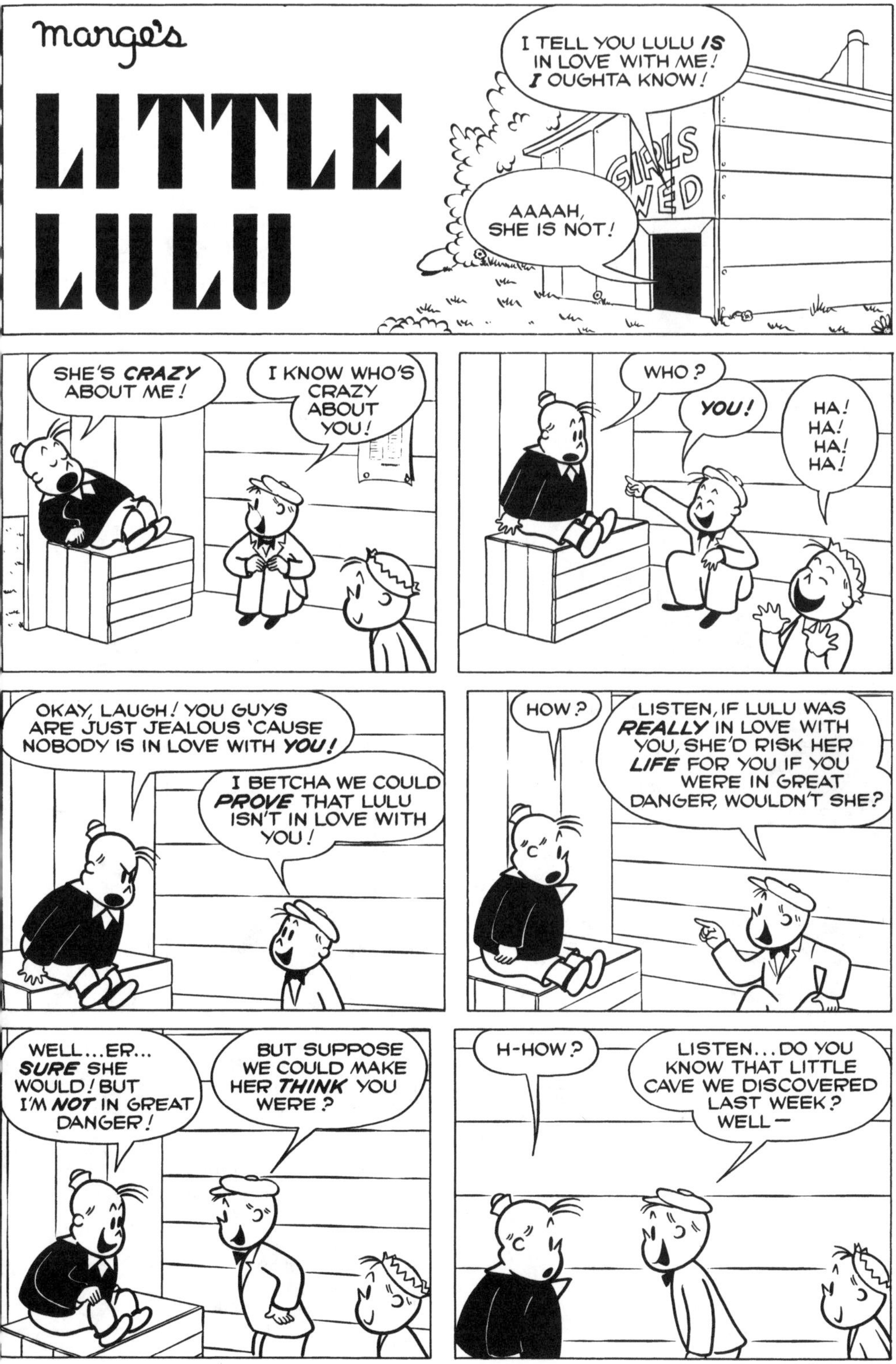
marge's
LITTLE LULU
I TELL YOU LULU IS IN LOVE WITH ME! I OUGHTA KNOW!
GIRLS WED
AAAAH, SHE IS NOT!
SHE'S CRAZY ABOUT ME!
I KNOW WHO'S CRAZY ABOUT YOU!
WHO?
YOU!
HA! HA! HA! HA!
OKAY, LAUGH! YOU GUYS ARE JUST JEALOUS 'CAUSE NOBODY IS IN LOVE WITH YOU!
I BETCHA WE COULD PROVE THAT LULU ISN'T IN LOVE WITH YOU!
HOW?
LISTEN, IF LULU WAS REALLY IN LOVE WITH YOU, SHE'D RISK HER LIFE FOR YOU IF YOU WERE IN GREAT DANGER, WOULDN'T SHE?
WELL...ER... SURE SHE WOULD! BUT I'M NOT IN GREAT DANGER!
BUT SUPPOSE WE COULD MAKE HER THINK YOU WERE?
H-HOW?
LISTEN...DO YOU KNOW THAT LITTLE CAVE WE DISCOVERED LAST WEEK? WELL—

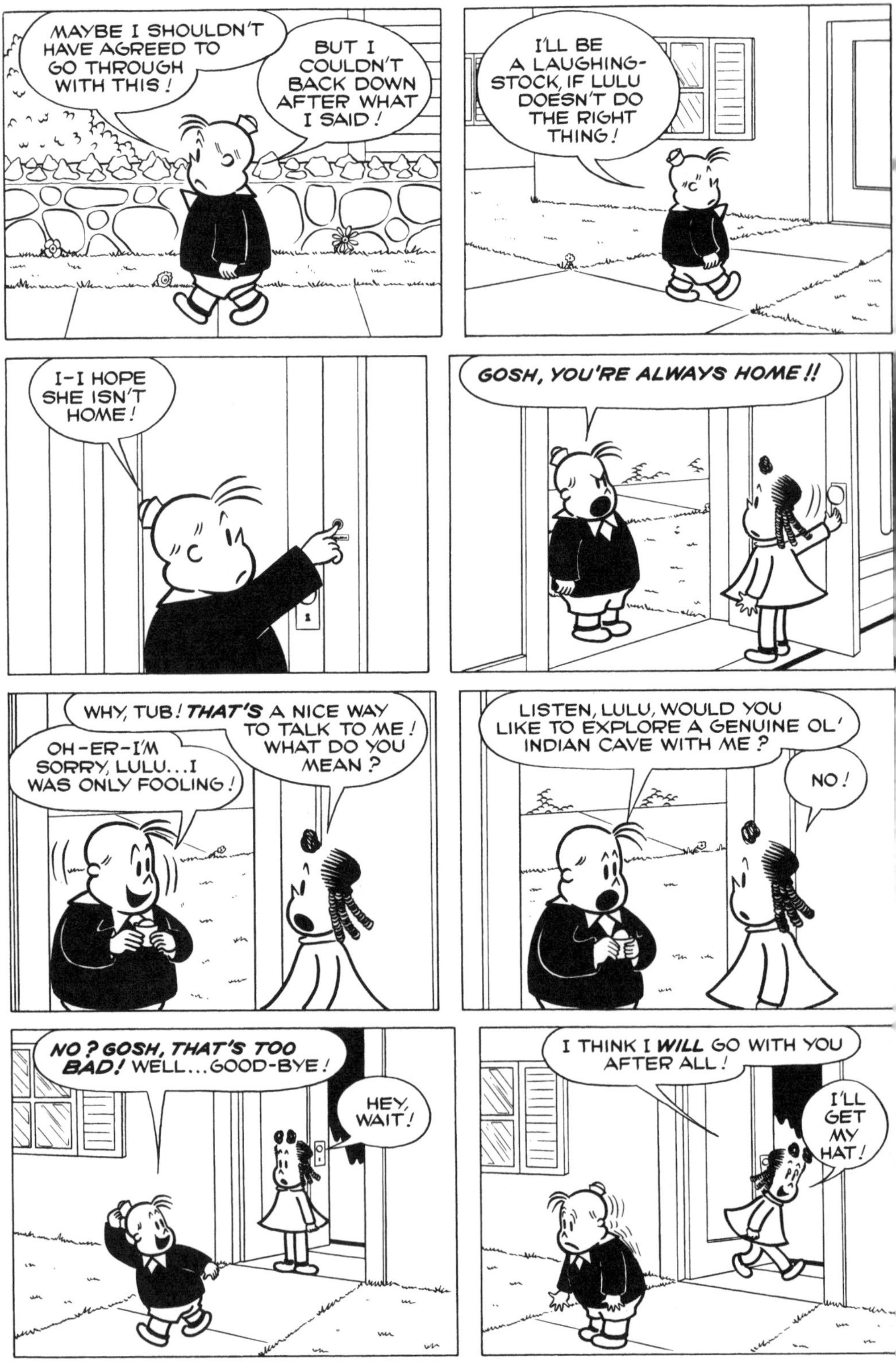
MAYBE I SHOULDN'T HAVE AGREED TO GO THROUGH WITH THIS!
BUT I COULDN'T BACK DOWN AFTER WHAT I SAID!
I'LL BE A LAUGHING-STOCK, IF LULU DOESN'T DO THE RIGHT THING!
I-I HOPE SHE ISN'T HOME!
GOSH, YOU'RE ALWAYS HOME!!
WHY, TUB! THAT'S A NICE WAY TO TALK TO ME! WHAT DO YOU MEAN?
OH-ER-I'M SORRY, LULU...I WAS ONLY FOOLING!
LISTEN, LULU, WOULD YOU LIKE TO EXPLORE A GENUINE OL' INDIAN CAVE WITH ME?
NO!
NO? GOSH, THAT'S TOO BAD! WELL...GOOD-BYE!
HEY, WAIT!
I THINK I WILL GO WITH YOU AFTER ALL!
I'LL GET MY HAT!

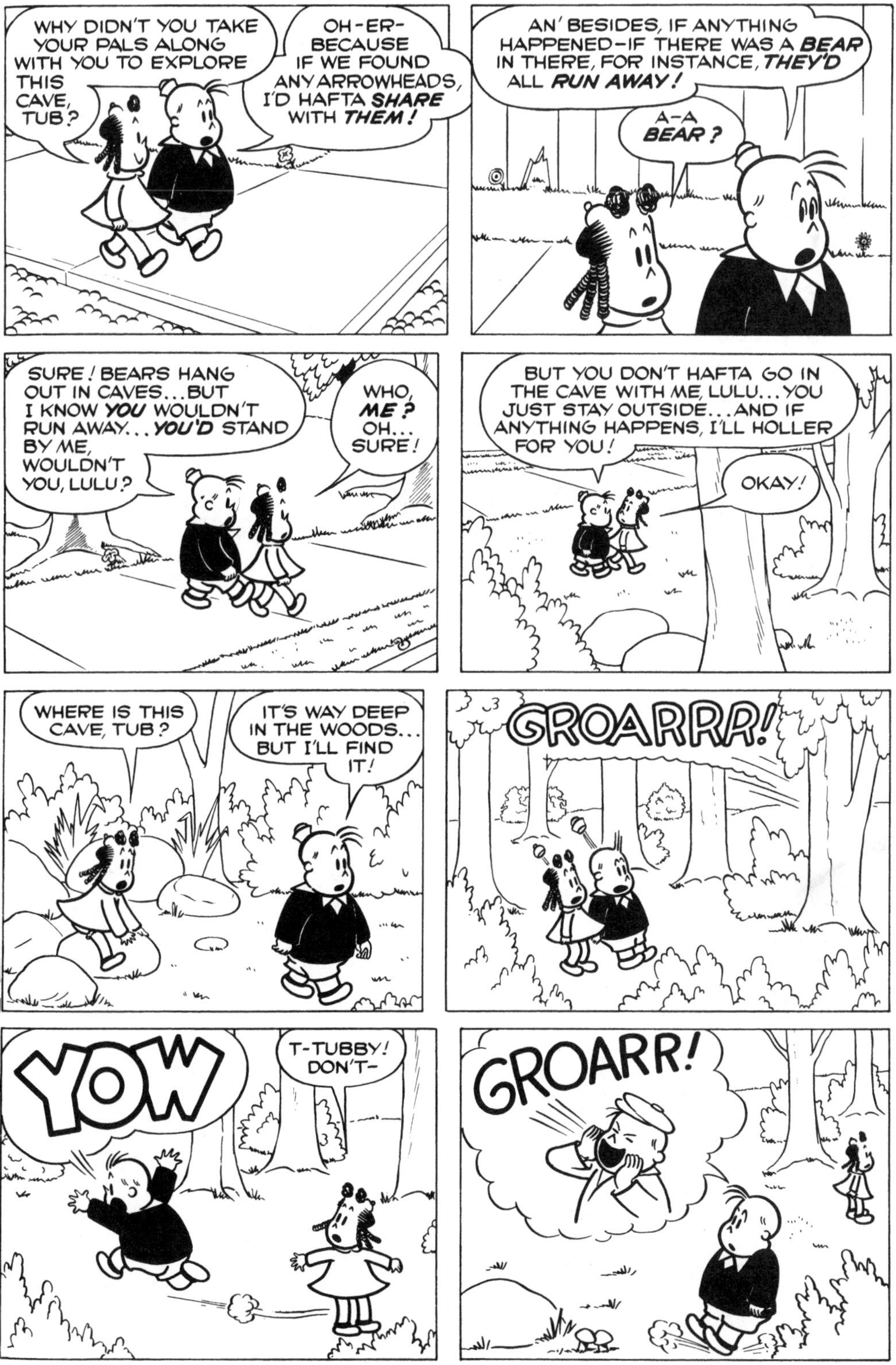
WHY DIDN'T YOU TAKE YOUR PALS ALONG WITH YOU TO EXPLORE THIS CAVE, TUB?
OH-ER- BECAUSE IF WE FOUND ANY ARROWHEADS, I'D HAFTA SHARE WITH THEM!
AN' BESIDES, IF ANYTHING HAPPENED-IF THERE WAS A BEAR IN THERE, FOR INSTANCE, THEY'D ALL RUN AWAY!
A-A BEAR?
SURE! BEARS HANG OUT IN CAVES...BUT I KNOW YOU WOULDN'T RUN AWAY...YOU'D STAND BY ME, WOULDN'T YOU, LULU?
WHO, ME? OH... SURE!
BUT YOU DON'T HAFTA GO IN THE CAVE WITH ME, LULU...YOU JUST STAY OUTSIDE...AND IF ANYTHING HAPPENS, I'LL HOLLER FOR YOU!
OKAY!
WHERE IS THIS CAVE, TUB?
IT'S WAY DEEP IN THE WOODS... BUT I'LL FIND IT!
GROARRR!
YOW
T-TUBBY! DON'T-
GROARR!

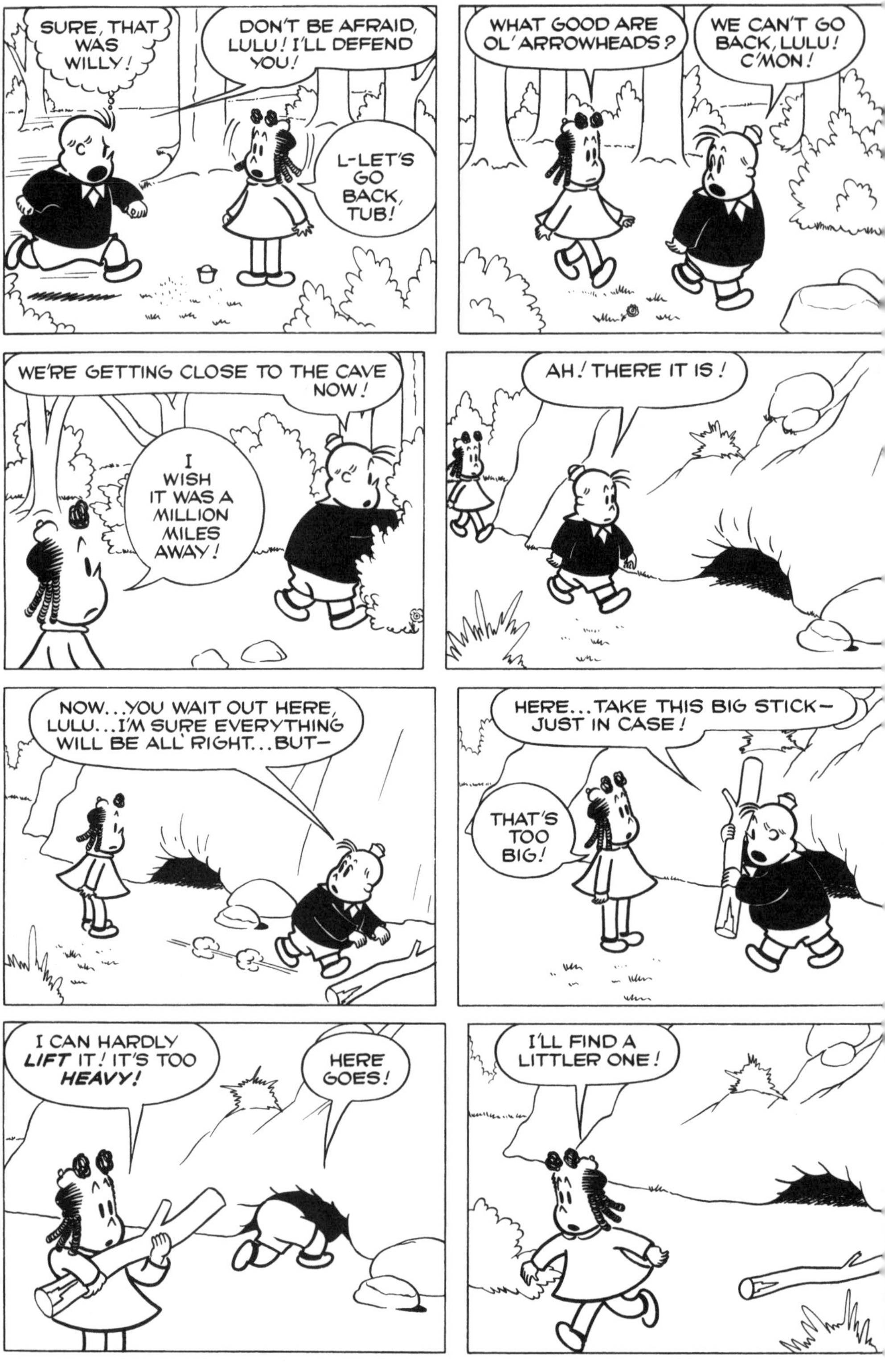
SURE, THAT WAS WILLY!
DON'T BE AFRAID, LULU! I'LL DEFEND YOU!
L-LET'S GO BACK, TUB!
WHAT GOOD ARE OL' ARROWHEADS?
WE CAN'T GO BACK, LULU! C'MON!
WE'RE GETTING CLOSE TO THE CAVE NOW!
I WISH IT WAS A MILLION MILES AWAY!
AH! THERE IT IS!
NOW...YOU WAIT OUT HERE, LULU...I'M SURE EVERYTHING WILL BE ALL RIGHT...BUT—
HERE...TAKE THIS BIG STICK—JUST IN CASE!
THAT'S TOO BIG!
I CAN HARDLY LIFT IT! IT'S TOO HEAVY!
HERE GOES!
I'LL FIND A LITTLER ONE!

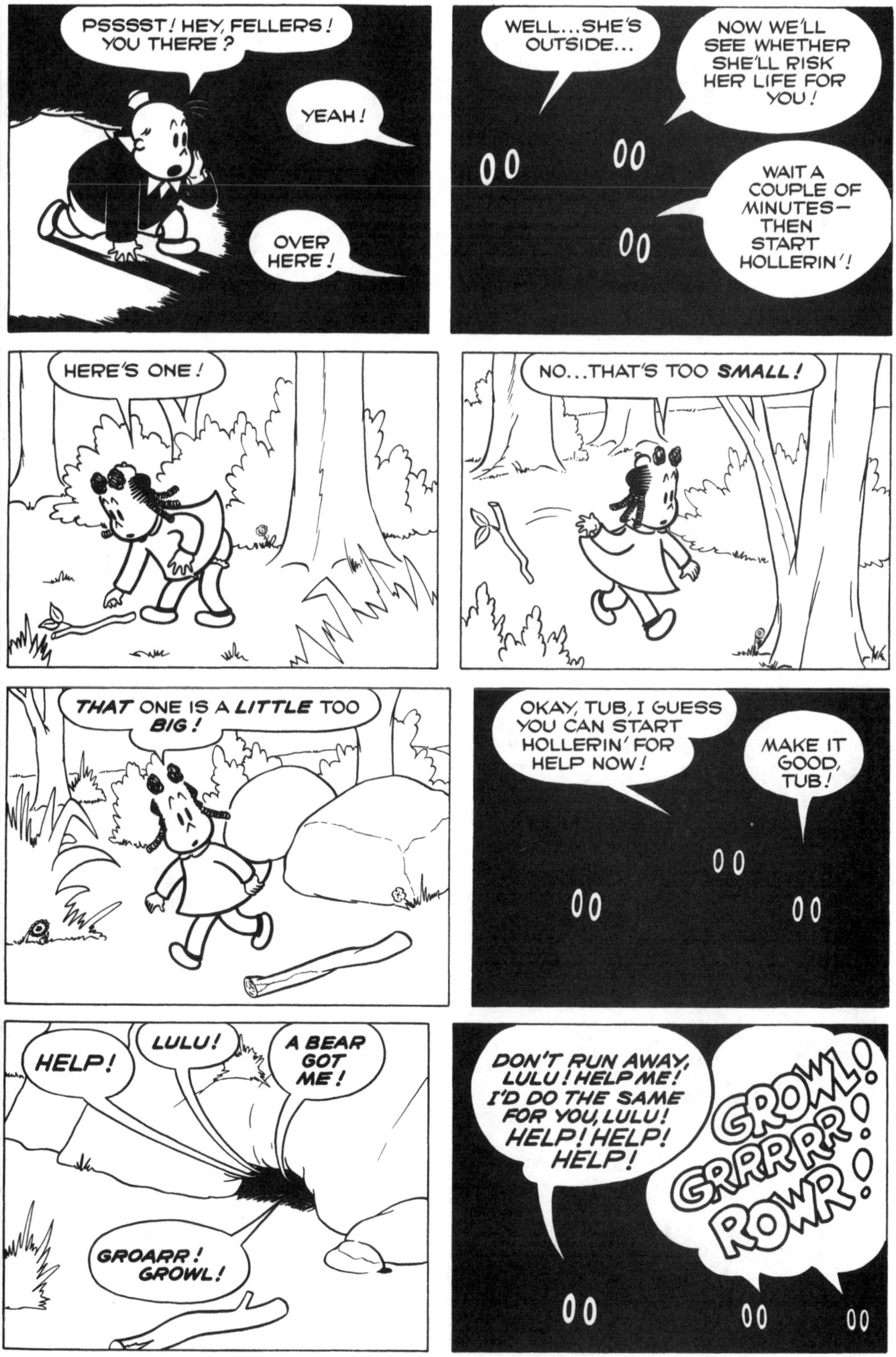
PSSSST! HEY, FELLERS! YOU THERE?
YEAH!
OVER HERE!
WELL...SHE'S OUTSIDE...
NOW WE'LL SEE WHETHER SHE'LL RISK HER LIFE FOR YOU!
WAIT A COUPLE OF MINUTES— THEN START HOLLERIN'!
HERE'S ONE!
NO...THAT'S TOO SMALL!
THAT ONE IS A LITTLE TOO BIG!
OKAY, TUB, I GUESS YOU CAN START HOLLERIN' FOR HELP NOW!
MAKE IT GOOD, TUB!
HELP!
LULU!
A BEAR GOT ME!
GROARR! GROWL!
DON'T RUN AWAY, LULU! HELP ME! I'D DO THE SAME FOR YOU, LULU! HELP! HELP! HELP!
GROWL! GRRRRR! ROWR!

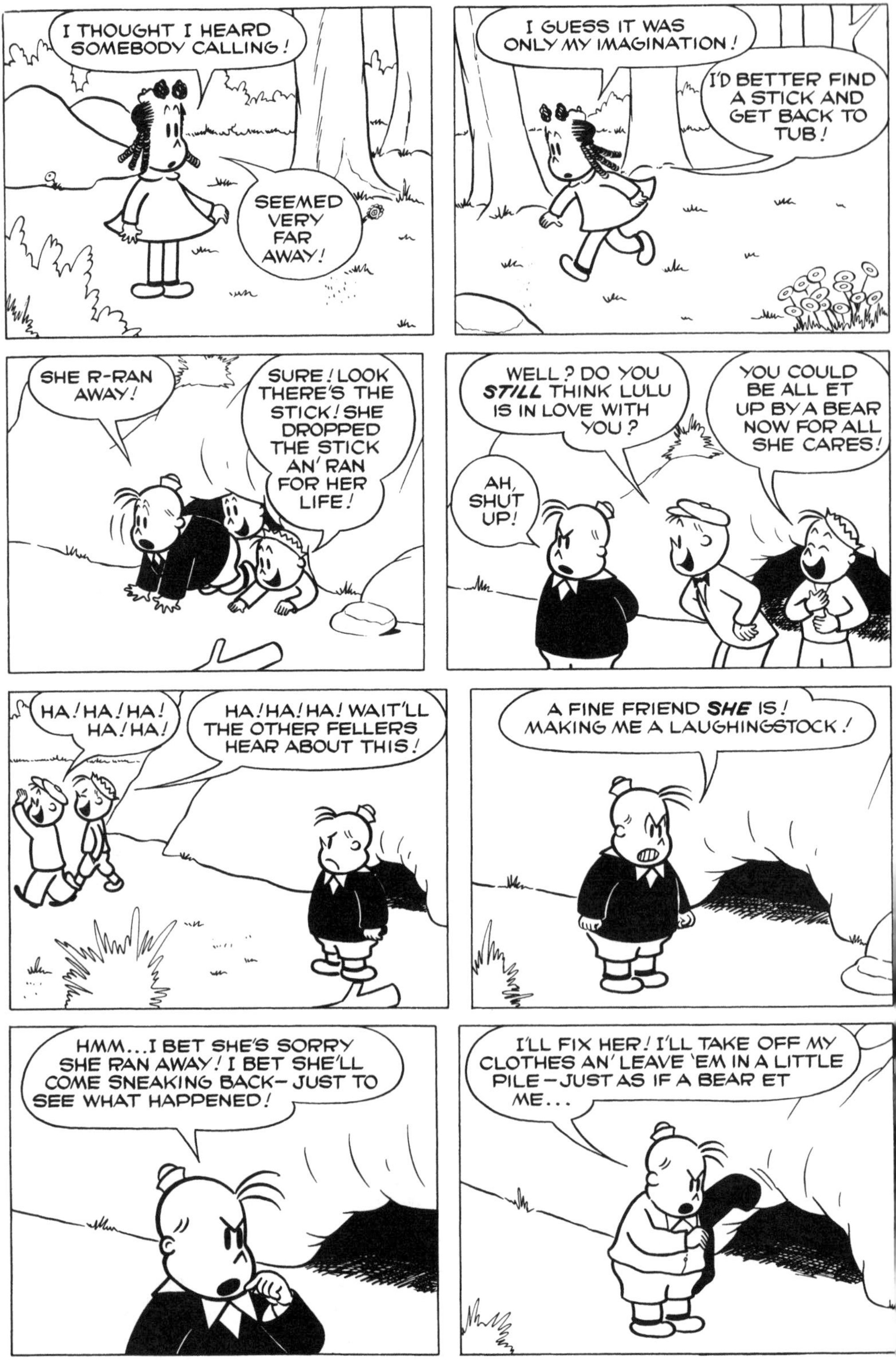
I THOUGHT I HEARD SOMEBODY CALLING!
SEEMED VERY FAR AWAY!
I GUESS IT WAS ONLY MY IMAGINATION!
I'D BETTER FIND A STICK AND GET BACK TO TUB!
SHE R-RAN AWAY!
SURE! LOOK THERE'S THE STICK! SHE DROPPED THE STICK AN' RAN FOR HER LIFE!
WELL? DO YOU STILL THINK LULU IS IN LOVE WITH YOU?
YOU COULD BE ALL ET UP BY A BEAR NOW FOR ALL SHE CARES!
AH, SHUT UP!
HA! HA! HA! HA! HA!
HA! HA! HA! WAIT'LL THE OTHER FELLERS HEAR ABOUT THIS!
A FINE FRIEND SHE IS! MAKING ME A LAUGHINGSTOCK!
HMM... I BET SHE'S SORRY SHE RAN AWAY! I BET SHE'LL COME SNEAKING BACK– JUST TO SEE WHAT HAPPENED!
I'LL FIX HER! I'LL TAKE OFF MY CLOTHES AN' LEAVE 'EM IN A LITTLE PILE–JUST AS IF A BEAR ET ME...

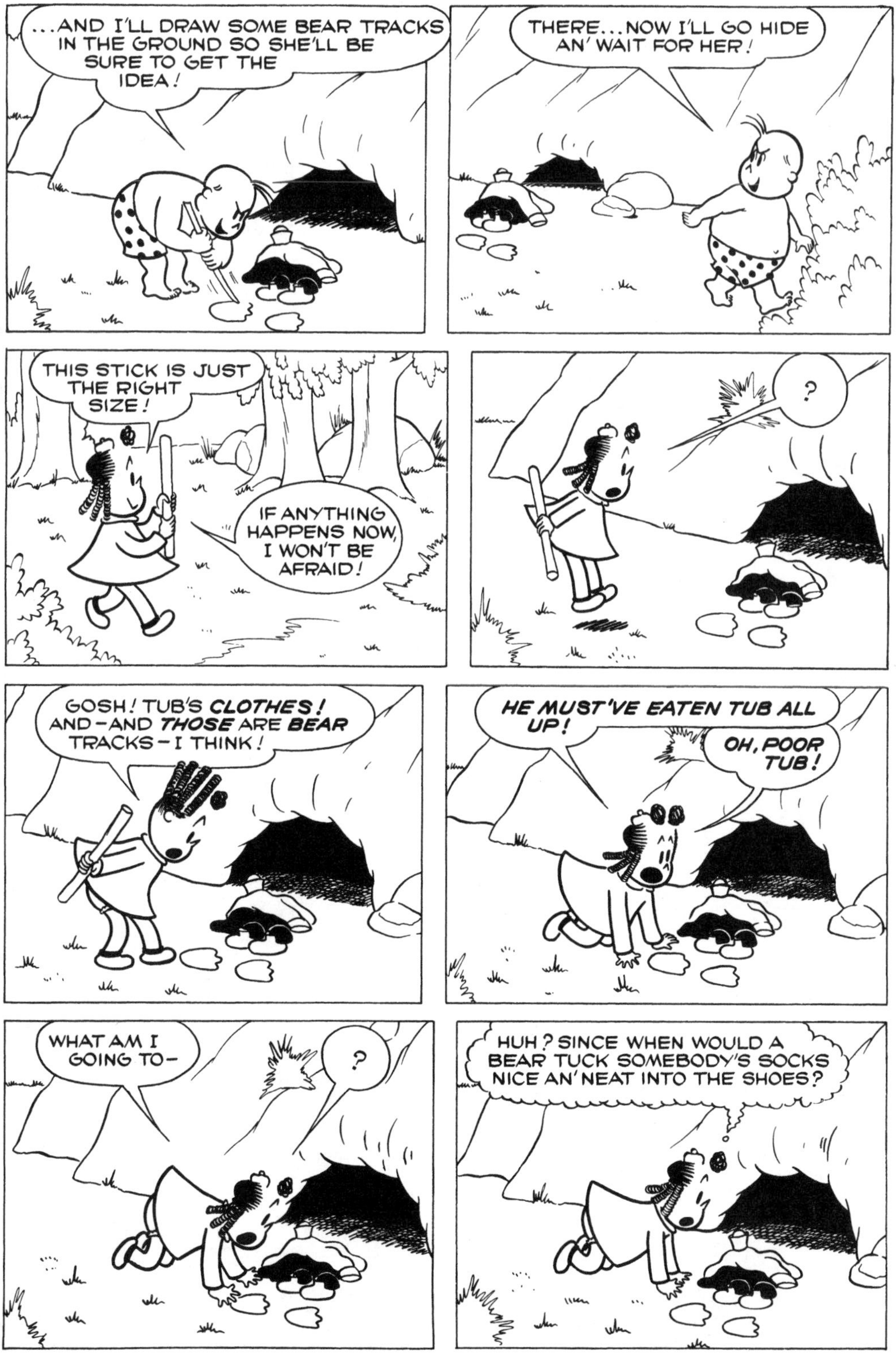
...AND I'LL DRAW SOME BEAR TRACKS IN THE GROUND SO SHE'LL BE SURE TO GET THE IDEA!
THERE...NOW I'LL GO HIDE AN' WAIT FOR HER!
THIS STICK IS JUST THE RIGHT SIZE!
IF ANYTHING HAPPENS NOW, I WON'T BE AFRAID!
?
GOSH! TUB'S CLOTHES! AND—AND THOSE ARE BEAR TRACKS—I THINK!
HE MUST'VE EATEN TUB ALL UP!
OH, POOR TUB!
WHAT AM I GOING TO—
?
HUH? SINCE WHEN WOULD A BEAR TUCK SOMEBODY'S SOCKS NICE AN' NEAT INTO THE SHOES?

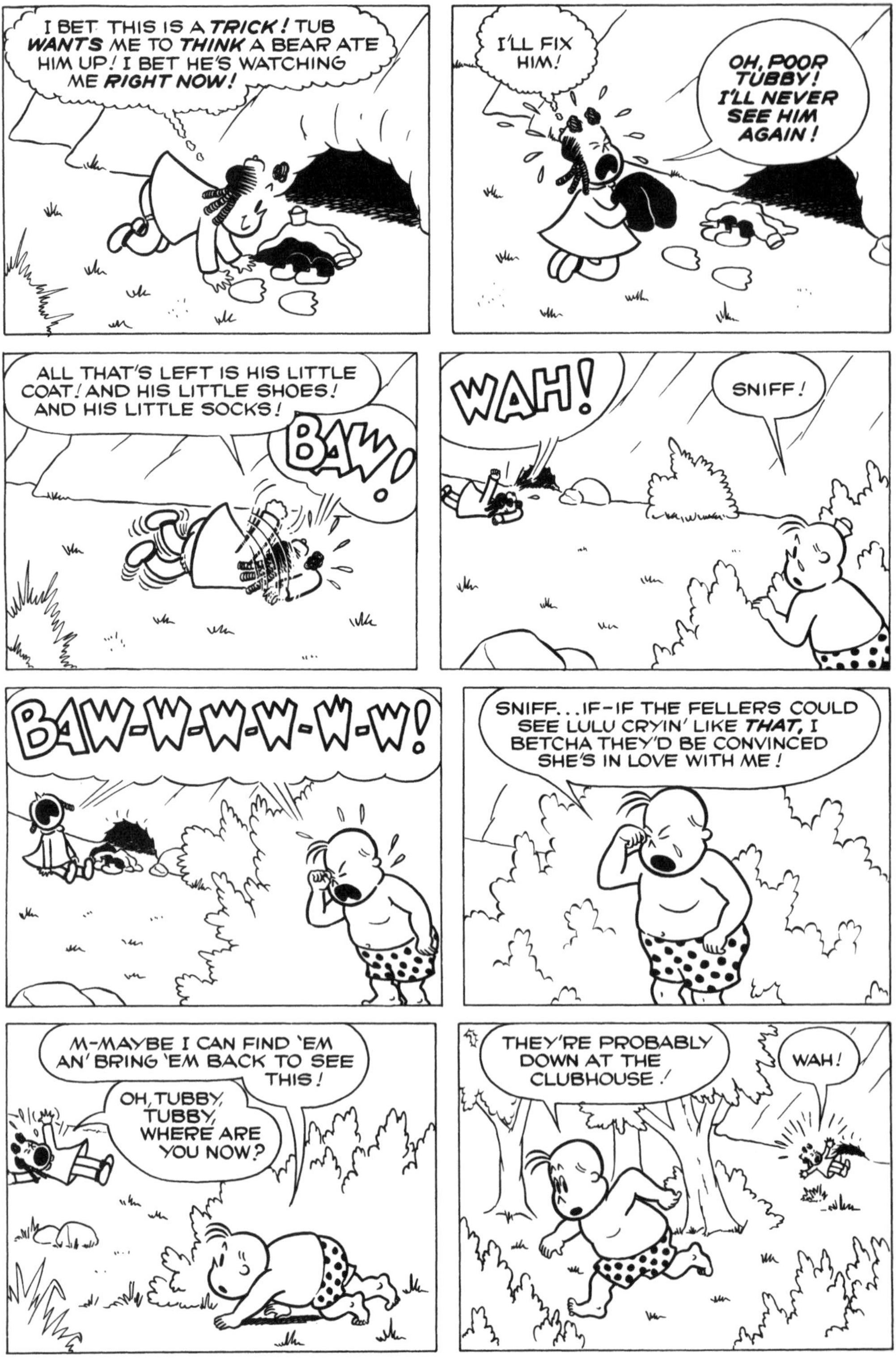
I BET THIS IS A TRICK! TUB WANTS ME TO THINK A BEAR ATE HIM UP! I BET HE'S WATCHING ME RIGHT NOW!
I'LL FIX HIM!
OH, POOR TUBBY! I'LL NEVER SEE HIM AGAIN!
ALL THAT'S LEFT IS HIS LITTLE COAT! AND HIS LITTLE SHOES! AND HIS LITTLE SOCKS!
BAW!
WAH!
SNIFF!
BAW-W-W-W-W-W!
SNIFF...IF-IF THE FELLERS COULD SEE LULU CRYIN' LIKE THAT, I BETCHA THEY'D BE CONVINCED SHE'S IN LOVE WITH ME!
M-MAYBE I CAN FIND 'EM AN' BRING 'EM BACK TO SEE THIS!
OH, TUBBY, TUBBY, WHERE ARE YOU NOW?
THEY'RE PROBABLY DOWN AT THE CLUBHOUSE!
WAH!

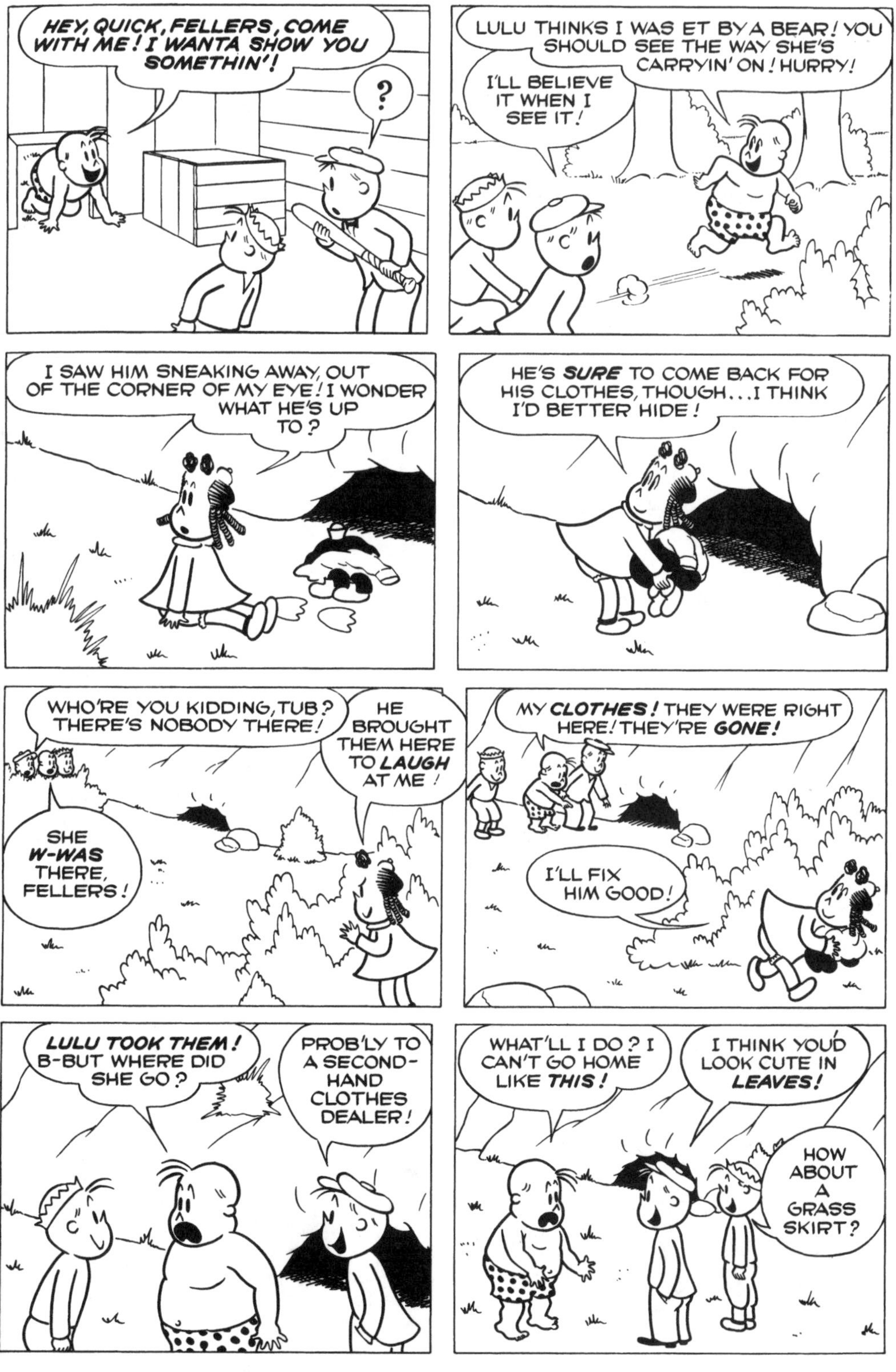
HEY, QUICK, FELLERS, COME WITH ME! I WANTA SHOW YOU SOMETHIN'!
?
LULU THINKS I WAS ET BY A BEAR! YOU SHOULD SEE THE WAY SHE'S CARRYIN' ON! HURRY!
I'LL BELIEVE IT WHEN I SEE IT!
I SAW HIM SNEAKING AWAY, OUT OF THE CORNER OF MY EYE! I WONDER WHAT HE'S UP TO?
HE'S SURE TO COME BACK FOR HIS CLOTHES, THOUGH...I THINK I'D BETTER HIDE!
WHO'RE YOU KIDDING, TUB? THERE'S NOBODY THERE!
SHE W-WAS THERE, FELLERS!
HE BROUGHT THEM HERE TO LAUGH AT ME!
MY CLOTHES! THEY WERE RIGHT HERE! THEY'RE GONE!
I'LL FIX HIM GOOD!
LULU TOOK THEM! B-BUT WHERE DID SHE GO?
PROB'LY TO A SECOND-HAND CLOTHES DEALER!
WHAT'LL I DO? I CAN'T GO HOME LIKE THIS!
I THINK YOU'D LOOK CUTE IN LEAVES!
HOW ABOUT A GRASS SKIRT?

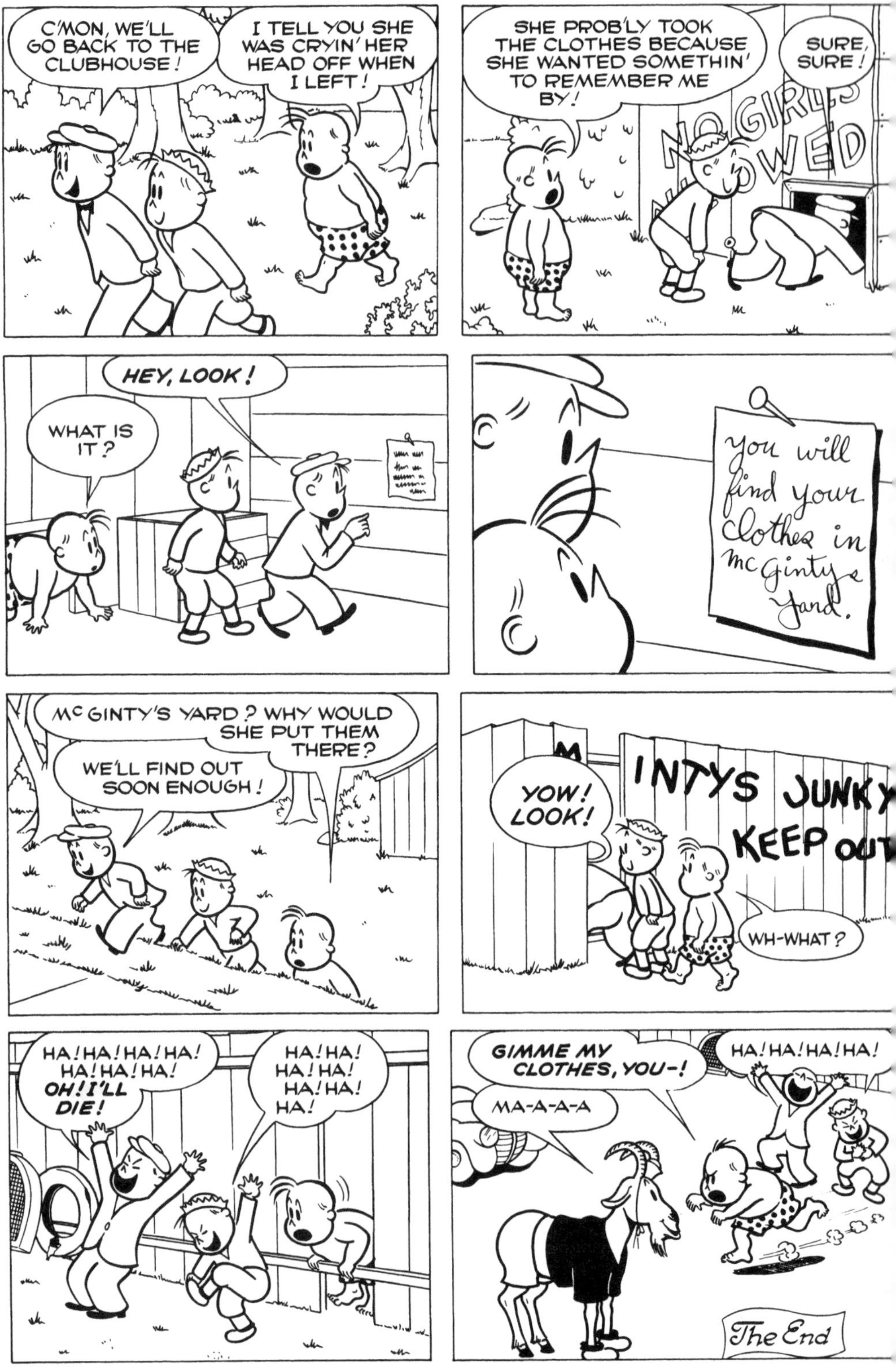
C'MON, WE'LL GO BACK TO THE CLUBHOUSE!
I TELL YOU SHE WAS CRYIN' HER HEAD OFF WHEN I LEFT!
SHE PROB'LY TOOK THE CLOTHES BECAUSE SHE WANTED SOMETHIN' TO REMEMBER ME BY!
SURE, SURE!
NO GIRLS
HEY, LOOK!
WHAT IS IT?
you will find your clothes in McGinty's yard.
McGINTY'S YARD? WHY WOULD SHE PUT THEM THERE?
WE'LL FIND OUT SOON ENOUGH!
YOW! LOOK!
INTYS JUNKY
KEEP OUT
WH-WHAT?
HA! HA! HA! HA! HA! HA! HA! OH! I'LL DIE!
HA! HA! HA! HA! HA! HA! HA!
GIMME MY CLOTHES, YOU-!
HA! HA! HA! HA!
MA-A-A-A
The End

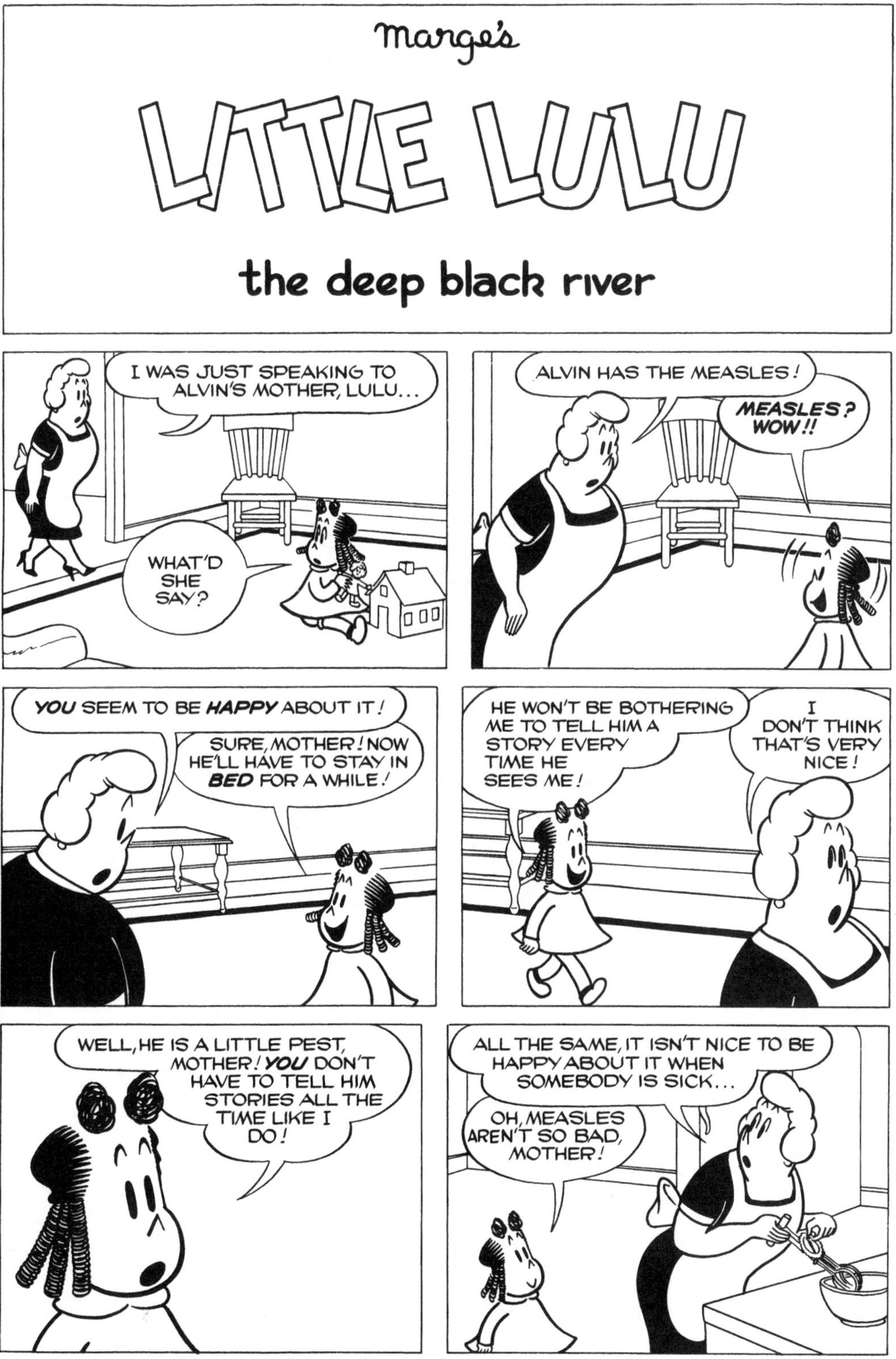
marge's
LITTLE LULU
the deep black river
I WAS JUST SPEAKING TO ALVIN'S MOTHER, LULU...
WHAT'D SHE SAY?
ALVIN HAS THE MEASLES!
MEASLES? WOW!!
YOU SEEM TO BE HAPPY ABOUT IT!
SURE, MOTHER! NOW HE'LL HAVE TO STAY IN BED FOR A WHILE!
HE WON'T BE BOTHERING ME TO TELL HIM A STORY EVERY TIME HE SEES ME!
I DON'T THINK THAT'S VERY NICE!
WELL, HE IS A LITTLE PEST, MOTHER! YOU DON'T HAVE TO TELL HIM STORIES ALL THE TIME LIKE I DO!
ALL THE SAME, IT ISN'T NICE TO BE HAPPY ABOUT IT WHEN SOMEBODY IS SICK...
OH, MEASLES AREN'T SO BAD, MOTHER!

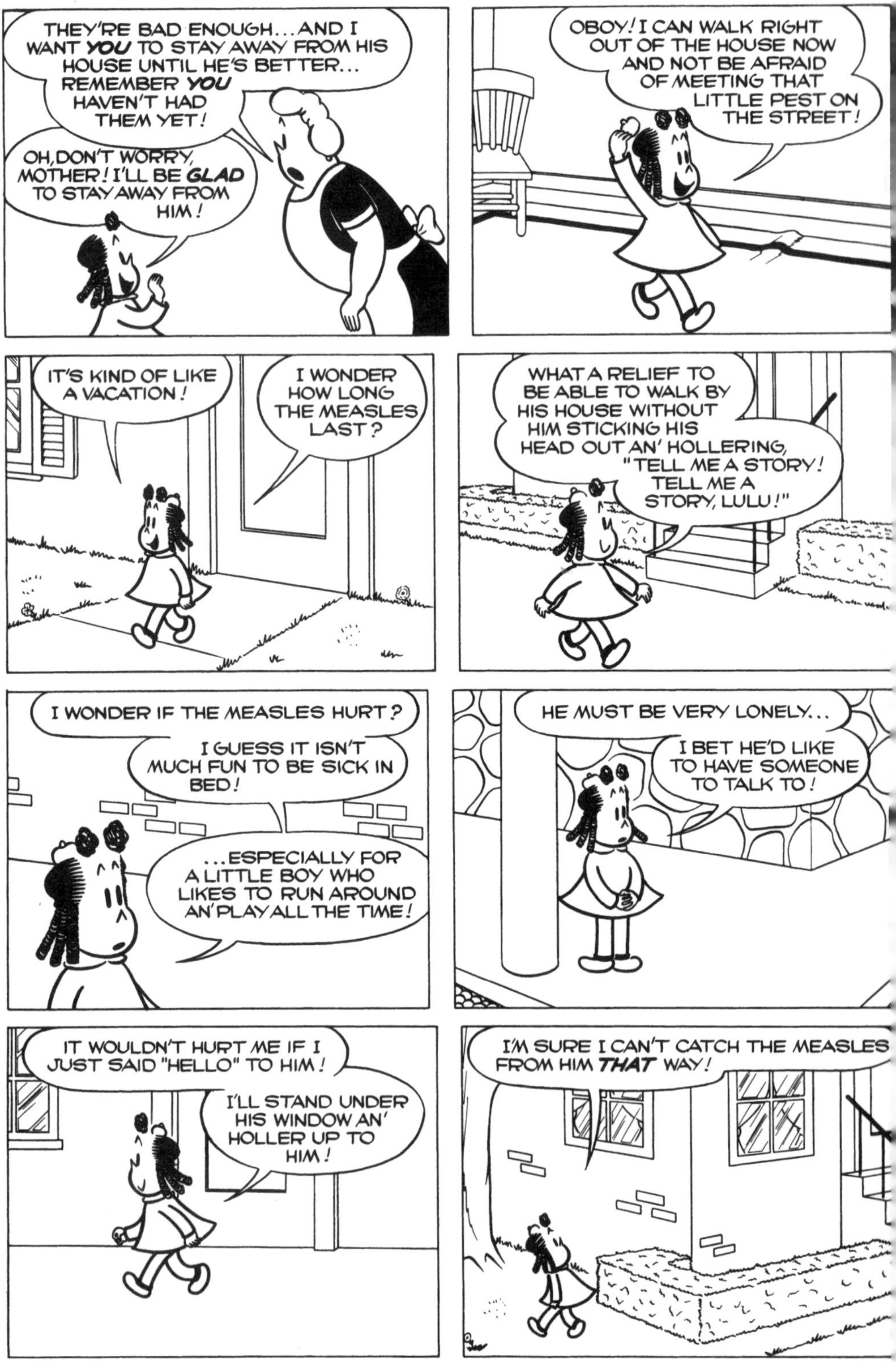
THEY'RE BAD ENOUGH... AND I WANT YOU TO STAY AWAY FROM HIS HOUSE UNTIL HE'S BETTER... REMEMBER YOU HAVEN'T HAD THEM YET!
OH, DON'T WORRY, MOTHER! I'LL BE GLAD TO STAY AWAY FROM HIM!
OBOY! I CAN WALK RIGHT OUT OF THE HOUSE NOW AND NOT BE AFRAID OF MEETING THAT LITTLE PEST ON THE STREET!
IT'S KIND OF LIKE A VACATION!
I WONDER HOW LONG THE MEASLES LAST?
WHAT A RELIEF TO BE ABLE TO WALK BY HIS HOUSE WITHOUT HIM STICKING HIS HEAD OUT AN' HOLLERING, "TELL ME A STORY! TELL ME A STORY, LULU!"
I WONDER IF THE MEASLES HURT?
I GUESS IT ISN'T MUCH FUN TO BE SICK IN BED!
...ESPECIALLY FOR A LITTLE BOY WHO LIKES TO RUN AROUND AN' PLAY ALL THE TIME!
HE MUST BE VERY LONELY...
I BET HE'D LIKE TO HAVE SOMEONE TO TALK TO!
IT WOULDN'T HURT ME IF I JUST SAID "HELLO" TO HIM!
I'LL STAND UNDER HIS WINDOW AN' HOLLER UP TO HIM!
I'M SURE I CAN'T CATCH THE MEASLES FROM HIM THAT WAY!

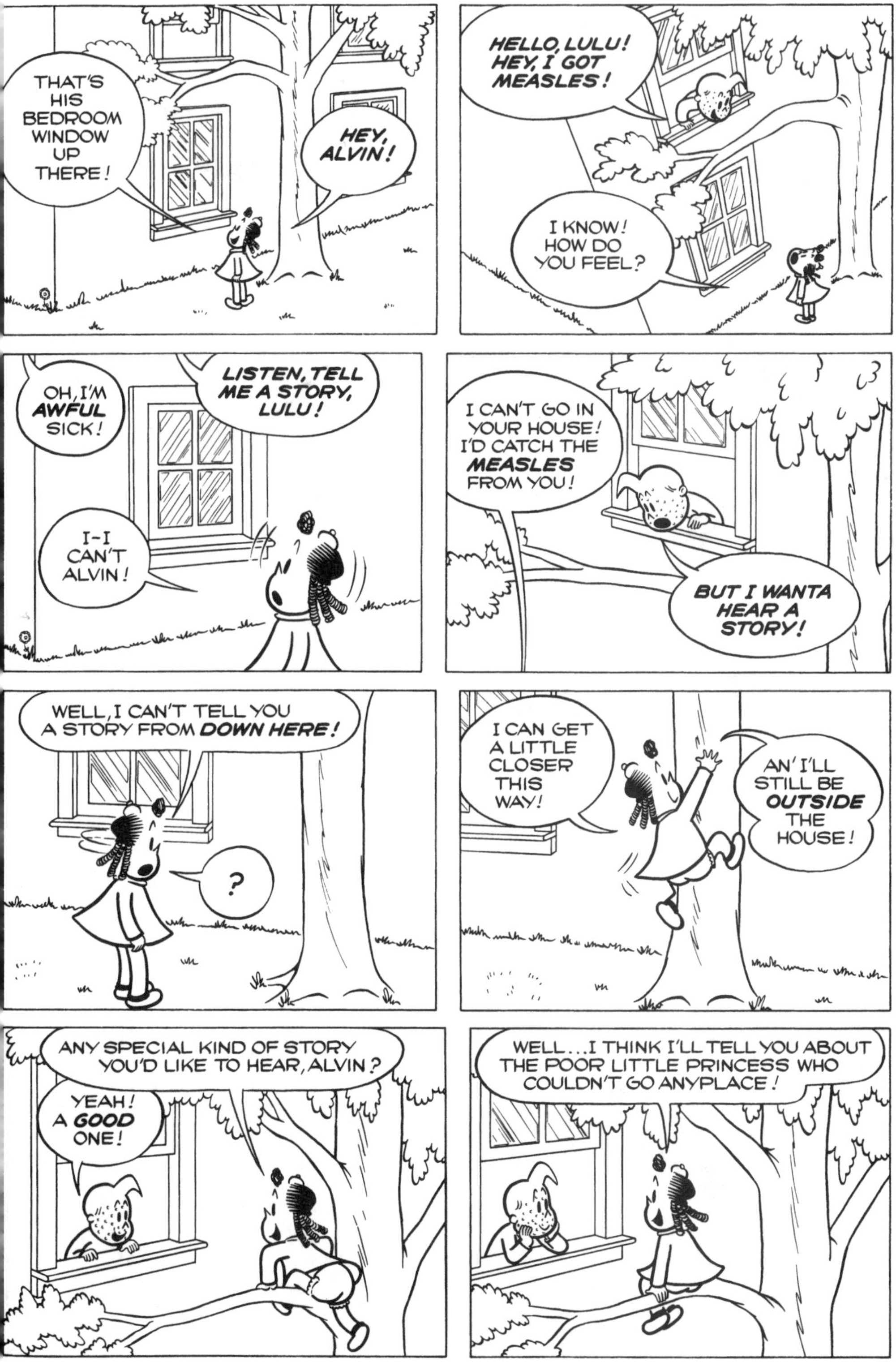
THAT'S HIS BEDROOM WINDOW UP THERE!
HEY, ALVIN!
HELLO, LULU! HEY, I GOT MEASLES!
I KNOW! HOW DO YOU FEEL?
OH, I'M AWFUL SICK!
LISTEN, TELL ME A STORY, LULU!
I-I CAN'T ALVIN!
I CAN'T GO IN YOUR HOUSE! I'D CATCH THE MEASLES FROM YOU!
BUT I WANTA HEAR A STORY!
WELL, I CAN'T TELL YOU A STORY FROM DOWN HERE!
?
I CAN GET A LITTLE CLOSER THIS WAY!
AN' I'LL STILL BE OUTSIDE THE HOUSE!
ANY SPECIAL KIND OF STORY YOU'D LIKE TO HEAR, ALVIN?
YEAH! A GOOD ONE!
WELL...I THINK I'LL TELL YOU ABOUT THE POOR LITTLE PRINCESS WHO COULDN'T GO ANYPLACE!

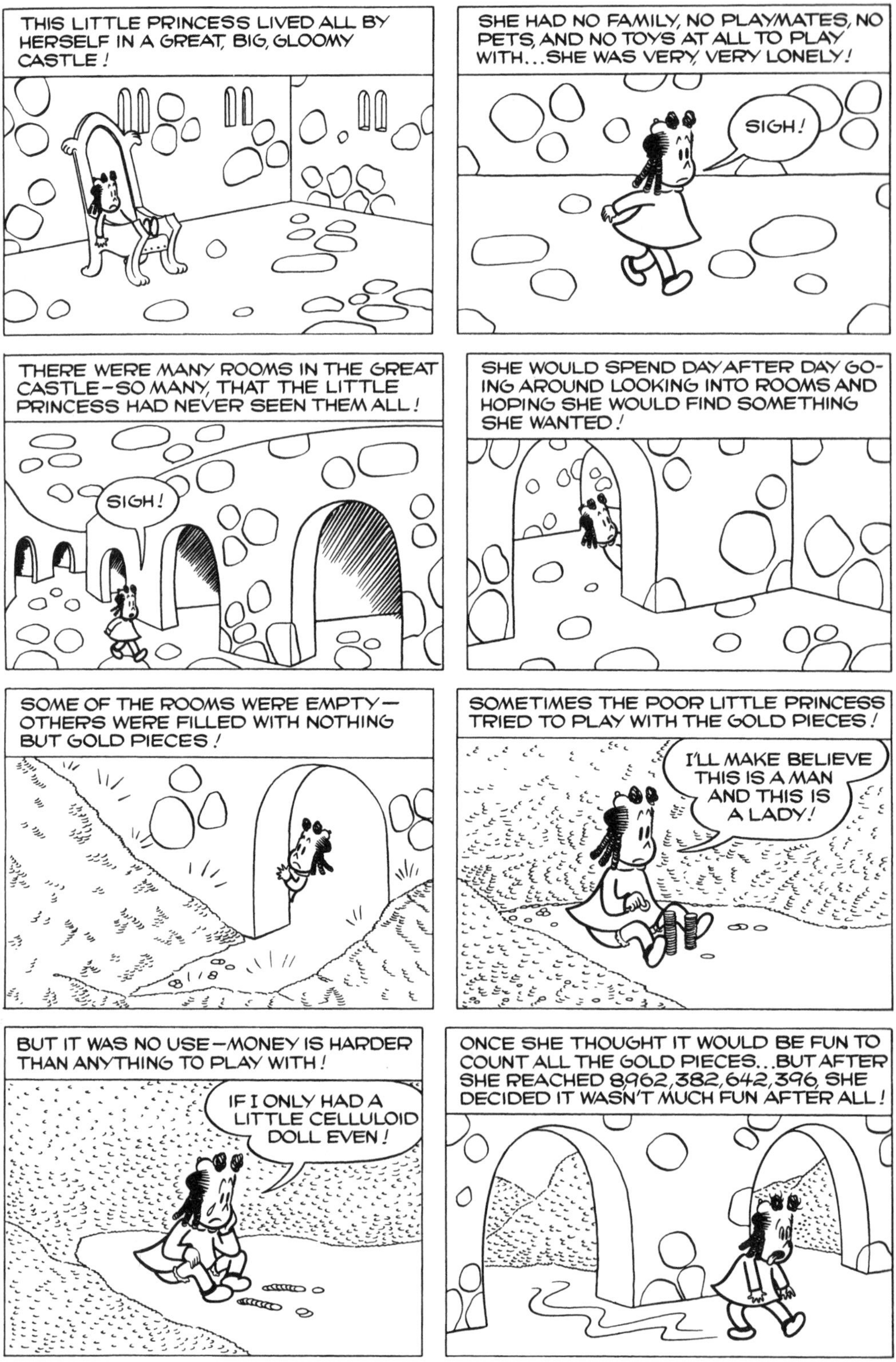
THIS LITTLE PRINCESS LIVED ALL BY HERSELF IN A GREAT, BIG, GLOOMY CASTLE!
SHE HAD NO FAMILY, NO PLAYMATES, NO PETS, AND NO TOYS AT ALL TO PLAY WITH...SHE WAS VERY, VERY LONELY!
SIGH!
THERE WERE MANY ROOMS IN THE GREAT CASTLE—SO MANY, THAT THE LITTLE PRINCESS HAD NEVER SEEN THEM ALL!
SIGH!
SHE WOULD SPEND DAY AFTER DAY GO-ING AROUND LOOKING INTO ROOMS AND HOPING SHE WOULD FIND SOMETHING SHE WANTED!
SOME OF THE ROOMS WERE EMPTY—OTHERS WERE FILLED WITH NOTHING BUT GOLD PIECES!
SOMETIMES THE POOR LITTLE PRINCESS TRIED TO PLAY WITH THE GOLD PIECES!
I'LL MAKE BELIEVE THIS IS A MAN AND THIS IS A LADY!
BUT IT WAS NO USE—MONEY IS HARDER THAN ANYTHING TO PLAY WITH!
IF I ONLY HAD A LITTLE CELLULOID DOLL EVEN!
ONCE SHE THOUGHT IT WOULD BE FUN TO COUNT ALL THE GOLD PIECES...BUT AFTER SHE REACHED 8,962,382,642,396, SHE DECIDED IT WASN'T MUCH FUN AFTER ALL!

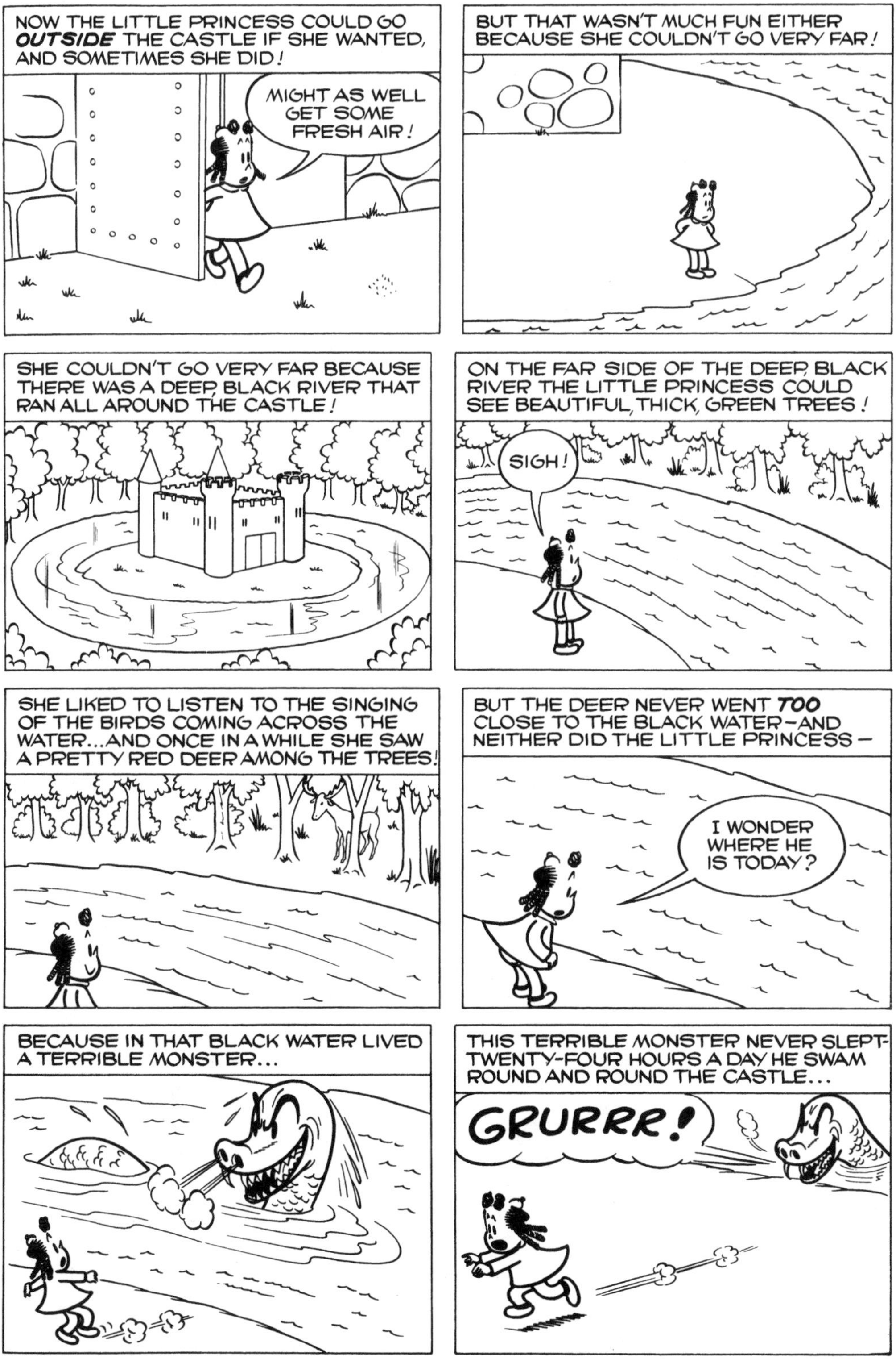
NOW THE LITTLE PRINCESS COULD GO *OUTSIDE* THE CASTLE IF SHE WANTED, AND SOMETIMES SHE DID!
MIGHT AS WELL GET SOME FRESH AIR!
BUT THAT WASN'T MUCH FUN EITHER BECAUSE SHE COULDN'T GO VERY FAR!
SHE COULDN'T GO VERY FAR BECAUSE THERE WAS A DEEP, BLACK RIVER THAT RAN ALL AROUND THE CASTLE!
ON THE FAR SIDE OF THE DEEP, BLACK RIVER THE LITTLE PRINCESS COULD SEE BEAUTIFUL, THICK, GREEN TREES!
SIGH!
SHE LIKED TO LISTEN TO THE SINGING OF THE BIRDS COMING ACROSS THE WATER...AND ONCE IN A WHILE SHE SAW A PRETTY RED DEER AMONG THE TREES!
BUT THE DEER NEVER WENT *TOO* CLOSE TO THE BLACK WATER—AND NEITHER DID THE LITTLE PRINCESS—
I WONDER WHERE HE IS TODAY?
BECAUSE IN THAT BLACK WATER LIVED A TERRIBLE MONSTER...
THIS TERRIBLE MONSTER NEVER SLEPT—TWENTY-FOUR HOURS A DAY HE SWAM ROUND AND ROUND THE CASTLE...
GRURRR!

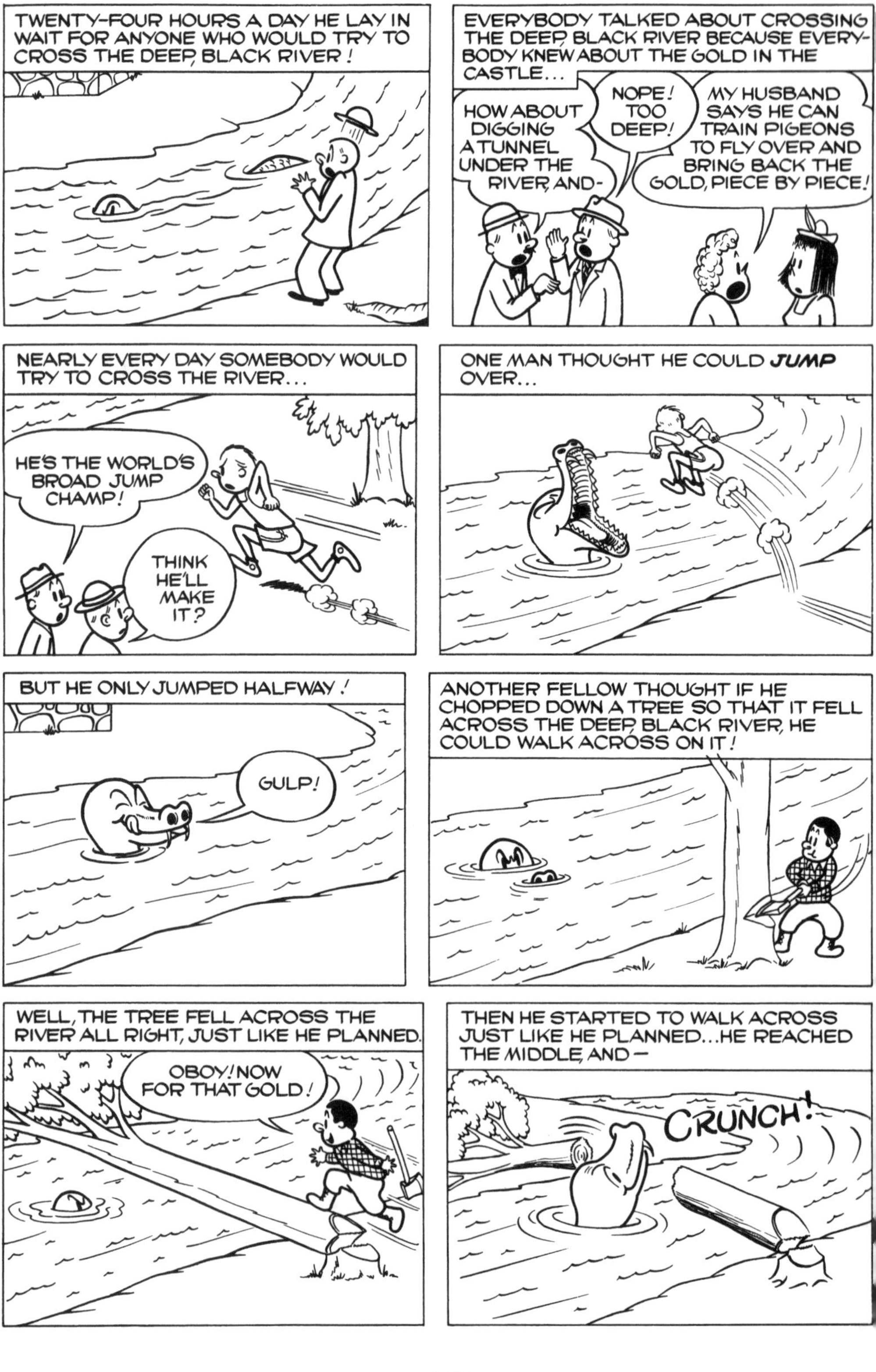
TWENTY-FOUR HOURS A DAY HE LAY IN WAIT FOR ANYONE WHO WOULD TRY TO CROSS THE DEEP, BLACK RIVER!
EVERYBODY TALKED ABOUT CROSSING THE DEEP, BLACK RIVER BECAUSE EVERYBODY KNEW ABOUT THE GOLD IN THE CASTLE...
HOW ABOUT DIGGING A TUNNEL UNDER THE RIVER, AND-
NOPE! TOO DEEP!
MY HUSBAND SAYS HE CAN TRAIN PIGEONS TO FLY OVER AND BRING BACK THE GOLD, PIECE BY PIECE!
NEARLY EVERY DAY SOMEBODY WOULD TRY TO CROSS THE RIVER...
HE'S THE WORLD'S BROAD JUMP CHAMP!
THINK HE'LL MAKE IT?
ONE MAN THOUGHT HE COULD JUMP OVER...
BUT HE ONLY JUMPED HALFWAY!
GULP!
ANOTHER FELLOW THOUGHT IF HE CHOPPED DOWN A TREE SO THAT IT FELL ACROSS THE DEEP, BLACK RIVER, HE COULD WALK ACROSS ON IT!
WELL, THE TREE FELL ACROSS THE RIVER ALL RIGHT, JUST LIKE HE PLANNED.
OBOY! NOW FOR THAT GOLD!
THEN HE STARTED TO WALK ACROSS JUST LIKE HE PLANNED...HE REACHED THE MIDDLE, AND—
CRUNCH!

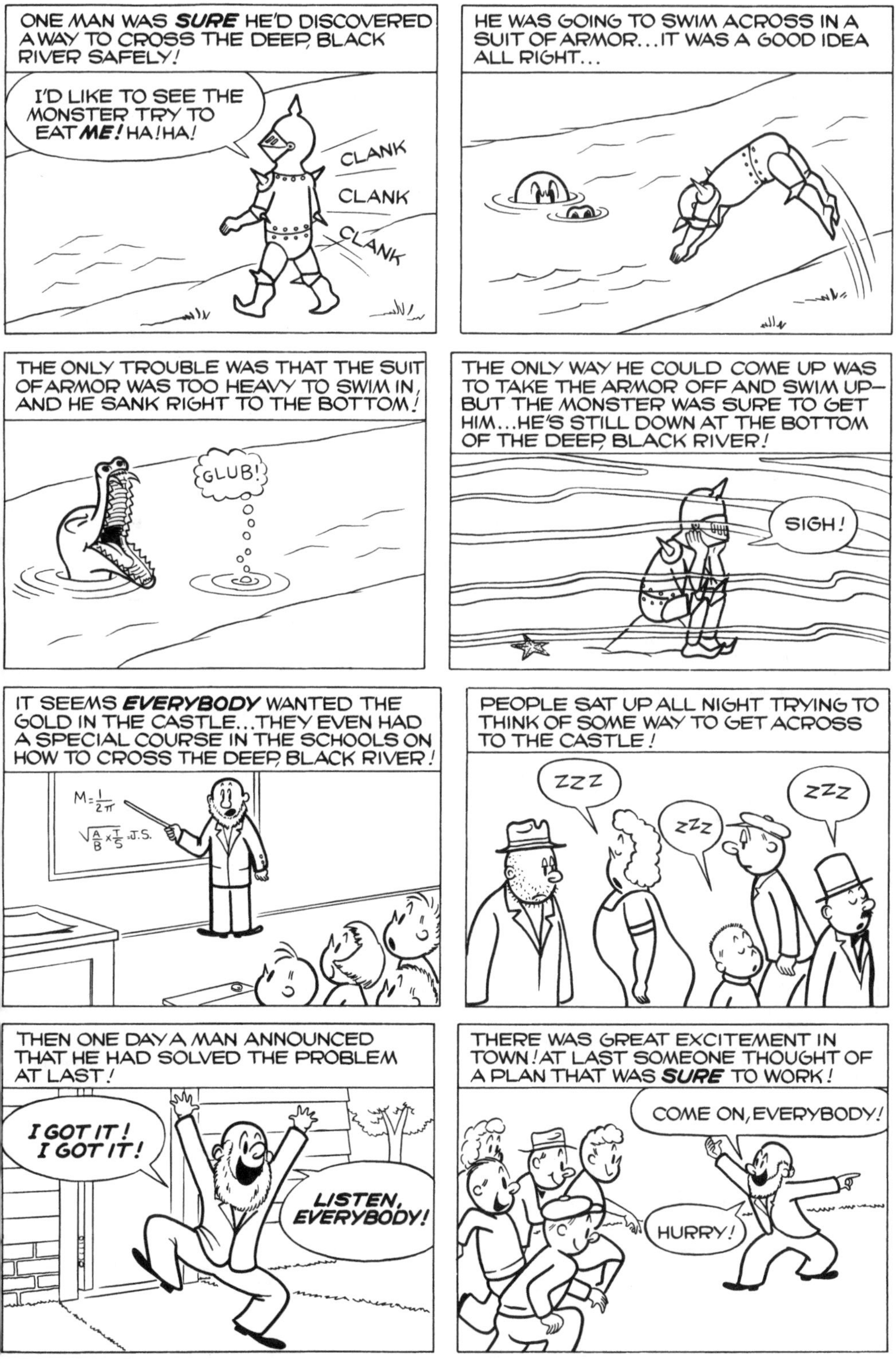
ONE MAN WAS SURE HE'D DISCOVERED A WAY TO CROSS THE DEEP, BLACK RIVER SAFELY!
I'D LIKE TO SEE THE MONSTER TRY TO EAT ME! HA! HA!
CLANK
CLANK
CLANK
HE WAS GOING TO SWIM ACROSS IN A SUIT OF ARMOR... IT WAS A GOOD IDEA ALL RIGHT...
THE ONLY TROUBLE WAS THAT THE SUIT OF ARMOR WAS TOO HEAVY TO SWIM IN, AND HE SANK RIGHT TO THE BOTTOM!
GLUB!
THE ONLY WAY HE COULD COME UP WAS TO TAKE THE ARMOR OFF AND SWIM UP—BUT THE MONSTER WAS SURE TO GET HIM... HE'S STILL DOWN AT THE BOTTOM OF THE DEEP, BLACK RIVER!
SIGH!
IT SEEMS EVERYBODY WANTED THE GOLD IN THE CASTLE... THEY EVEN HAD A SPECIAL COURSE IN THE SCHOOLS ON HOW TO CROSS THE DEEP, BLACK RIVER!
M = 1/2π
√(A/B × T/S) = J.S.
PEOPLE SAT UP ALL NIGHT TRYING TO THINK OF SOME WAY TO GET ACROSS TO THE CASTLE!
ZZZ
ZZZ
ZZZ
THEN ONE DAY A MAN ANNOUNCED THAT HE HAD SOLVED THE PROBLEM AT LAST!
I GOT IT! I GOT IT!
LISTEN, EVERYBODY!
THERE WAS GREAT EXCITEMENT IN TOWN! AT LAST SOMEONE THOUGHT OF A PLAN THAT WAS SURE TO WORK!
COME ON, EVERYBODY!
HURRY!

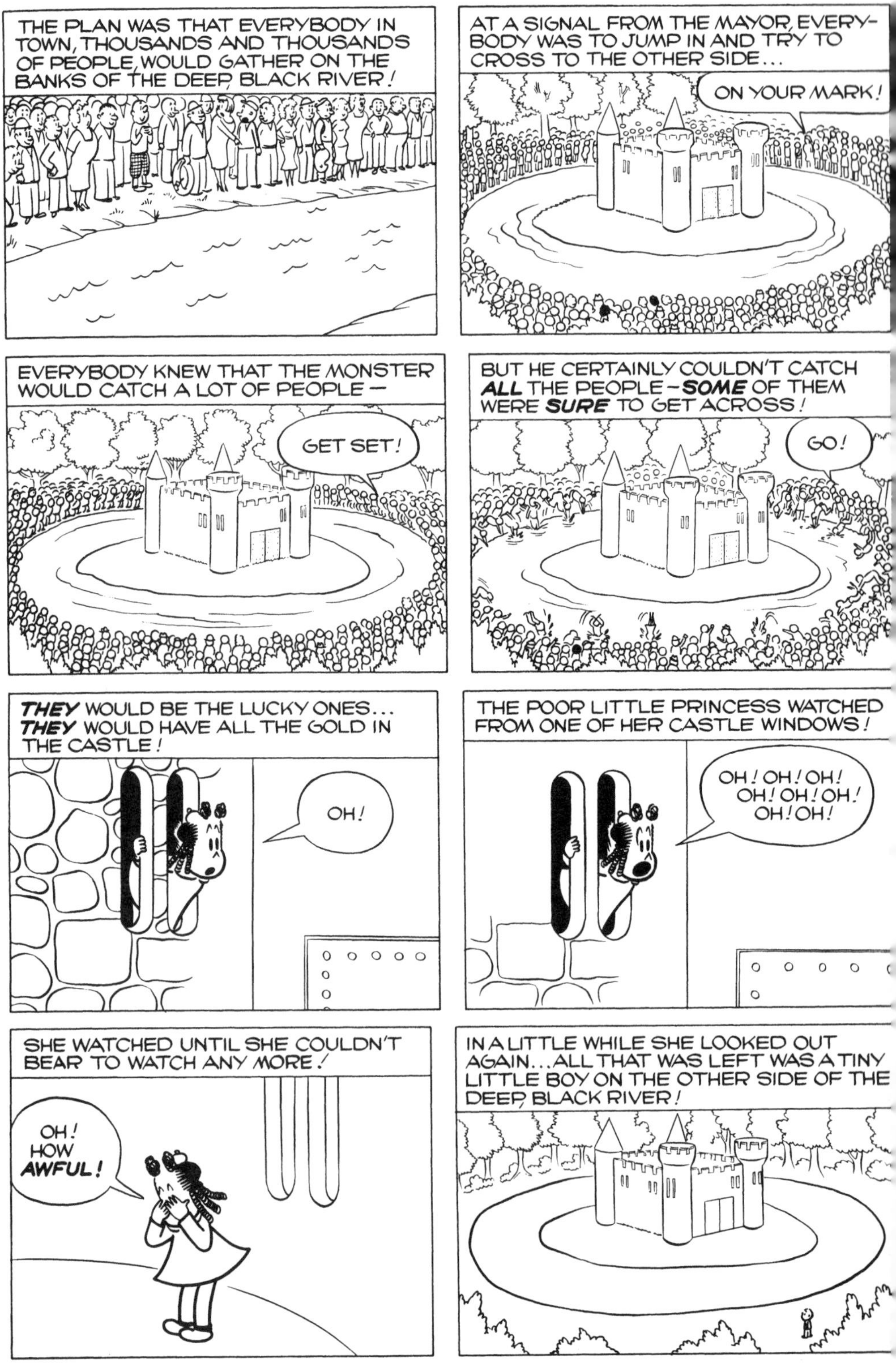

THE PLAN WAS THAT EVERYBODY IN TOWN, THOUSANDS AND THOUSANDS OF PEOPLE, WOULD GATHER ON THE BANKS OF THE DEEP, BLACK RIVER!
AT A SIGNAL FROM THE MAYOR, EVERYBODY WAS TO JUMP IN AND TRY TO CROSS TO THE OTHER SIDE...
ON YOUR MARK!
EVERYBODY KNEW THAT THE MONSTER WOULD CATCH A LOT OF PEOPLE —
GET SET!
BUT HE CERTAINLY COULDN'T CATCH **ALL** THE PEOPLE — **SOME** OF THEM WERE **SURE** TO GET ACROSS!
GO!
THEY WOULD BE THE LUCKY ONES... **THEY** WOULD HAVE ALL THE GOLD IN THE CASTLE!
OH!
THE POOR LITTLE PRINCESS WATCHED FROM ONE OF HER CASTLE WINDOWS!
OH! OH! OH! OH! OH! OH! OH! OH!
SHE WATCHED UNTIL SHE COULDN'T BEAR TO WATCH ANY MORE!
OH! HOW **AWFUL!**
IN A LITTLE WHILE SHE LOOKED OUT AGAIN... ALL THAT WAS LEFT WAS A TINY LITTLE BOY ON THE OTHER SIDE OF THE DEEP, BLACK RIVER!

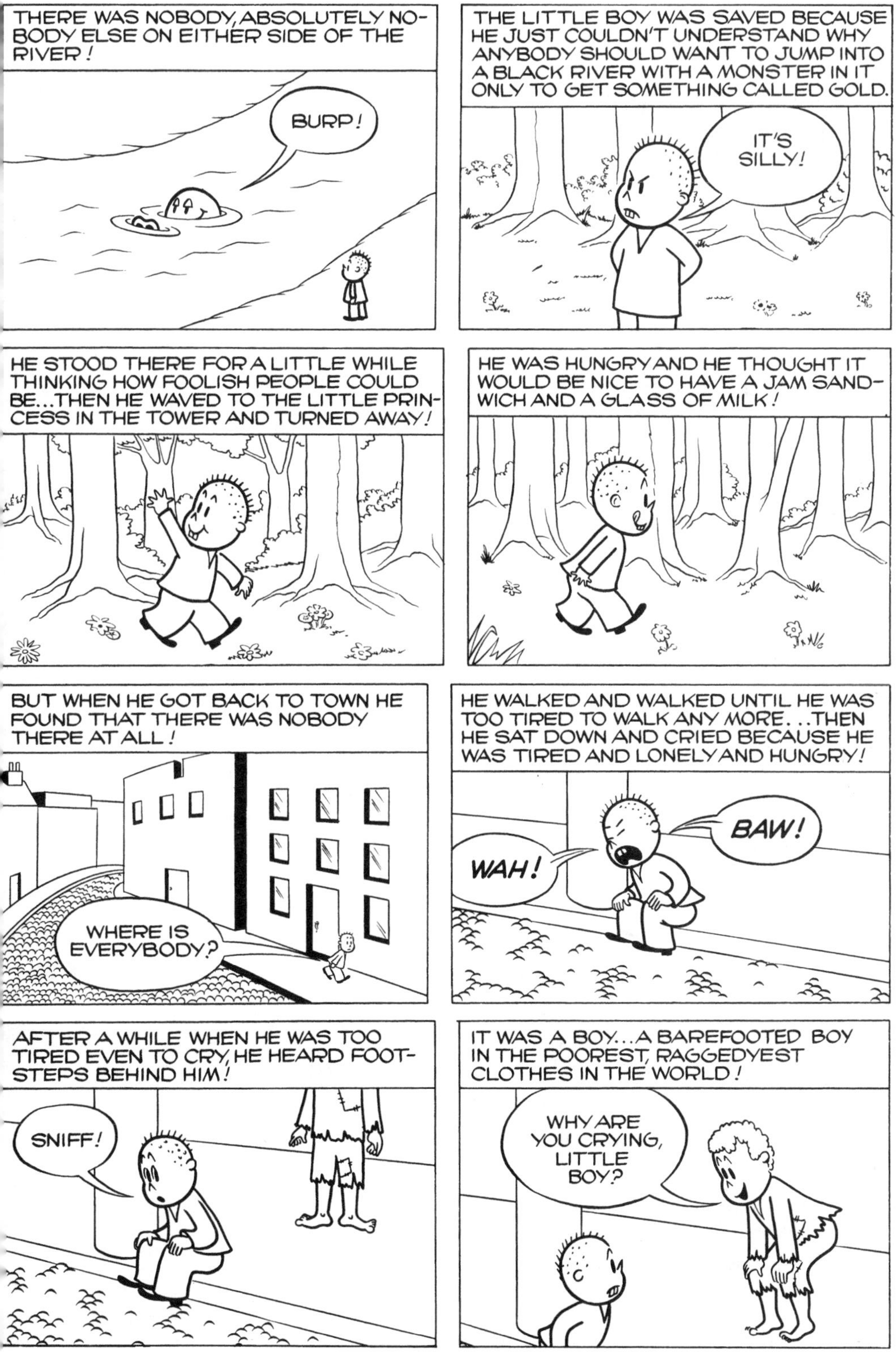
THERE WAS NOBODY, ABSOLUTELY NOBODY ELSE ON EITHER SIDE OF THE RIVER!
BURP!
THE LITTLE BOY WAS SAVED BECAUSE HE JUST COULDN'T UNDERSTAND WHY ANYBODY SHOULD WANT TO JUMP INTO A BLACK RIVER WITH A MONSTER IN IT ONLY TO GET SOMETHING CALLED GOLD.
IT'S SILLY!
HE STOOD THERE FOR A LITTLE WHILE THINKING HOW FOOLISH PEOPLE COULD BE...THEN HE WAVED TO THE LITTLE PRINCESS IN THE TOWER AND TURNED AWAY!
HE WAS HUNGRY AND HE THOUGHT IT WOULD BE NICE TO HAVE A JAM SANDWICH AND A GLASS OF MILK!
BUT WHEN HE GOT BACK TO TOWN HE FOUND THAT THERE WAS NOBODY THERE AT ALL!
WHERE IS EVERYBODY?
HE WALKED AND WALKED UNTIL HE WAS TOO TIRED TO WALK ANY MORE. . .THEN HE SAT DOWN AND CRIED BECAUSE HE WAS TIRED AND LONELY AND HUNGRY!
WAH!
BAW!
AFTER A WHILE WHEN HE WAS TOO TIRED EVEN TO CRY, HE HEARD FOOTSTEPS BEHIND HIM!
SNIFF!
IT WAS A BOY...A BAREFOOTED BOY IN THE POOREST, RAGGEDYEST CLOTHES IN THE WORLD!
WHY ARE YOU CRYING, LITTLE BOY?

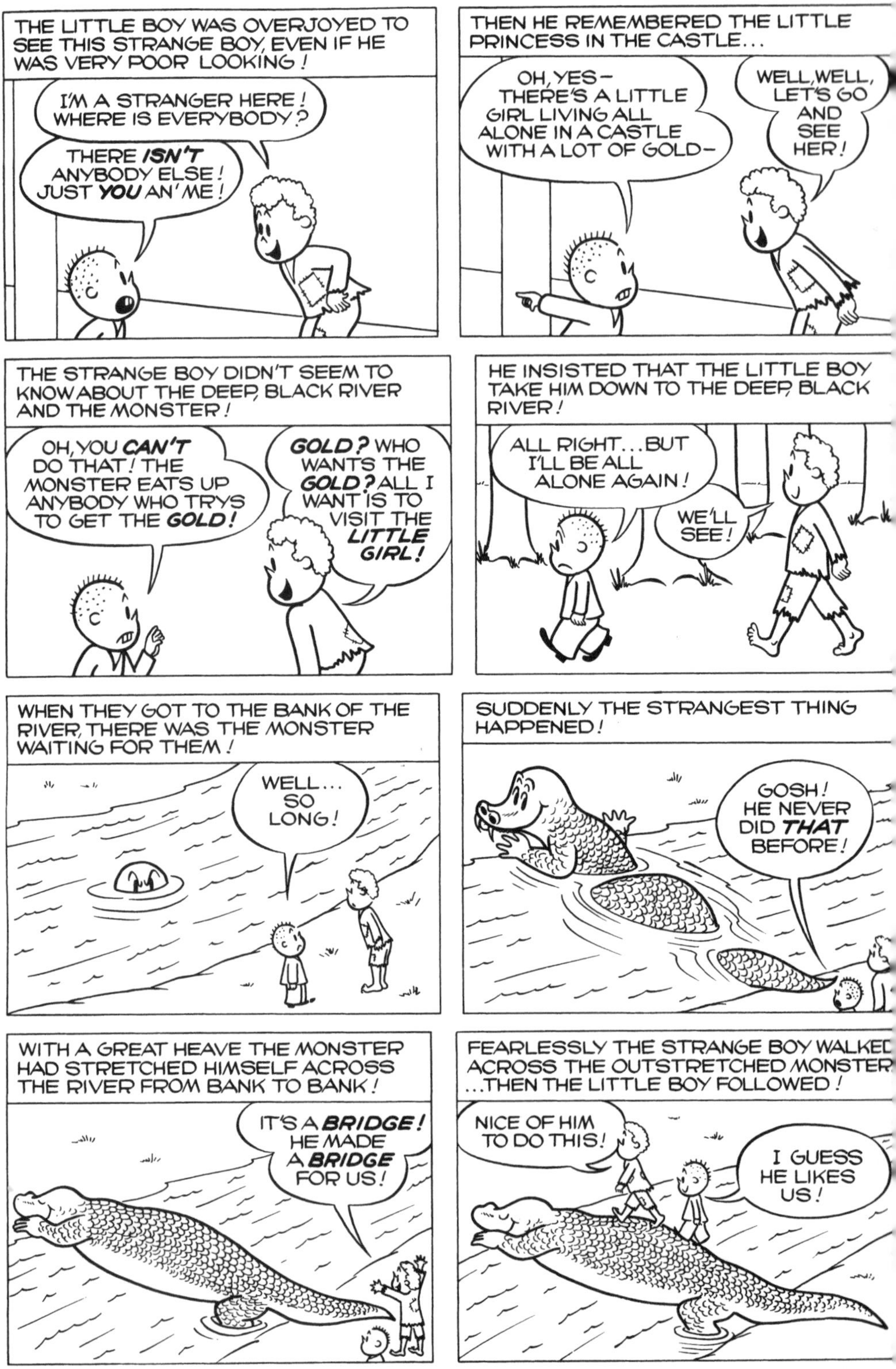

THE LITTLE BOY WAS OVERJOYED TO SEE THIS STRANGE BOY, EVEN IF HE WAS VERY POOR LOOKING!
I'M A STRANGER HERE! WHERE IS EVERYBODY?
THERE ISN'T ANYBODY ELSE! JUST YOU AN' ME!
THEN HE REMEMBERED THE LITTLE PRINCESS IN THE CASTLE...
OH, YES– THERE'S A LITTLE GIRL LIVING ALL ALONE IN A CASTLE WITH A LOT OF GOLD–
WELL, WELL, LET'S GO AND SEE HER!
THE STRANGE BOY DIDN'T SEEM TO KNOW ABOUT THE DEEP, BLACK RIVER AND THE MONSTER!
OH, YOU CAN'T DO THAT! THE MONSTER EATS UP ANYBODY WHO TRYS TO GET THE GOLD!
GOLD? WHO WANTS THE GOLD? ALL I WANT IS TO VISIT THE LITTLE GIRL!
HE INSISTED THAT THE LITTLE BOY TAKE HIM DOWN TO THE DEEP, BLACK RIVER!
ALL RIGHT... BUT I'LL BE ALL ALONE AGAIN!
WE'LL SEE!
WHEN THEY GOT TO THE BANK OF THE RIVER, THERE WAS THE MONSTER WAITING FOR THEM!
WELL... SO LONG!
SUDDENLY THE STRANGEST THING HAPPENED!
GOSH! HE NEVER DID THAT BEFORE!
WITH A GREAT HEAVE THE MONSTER HAD STRETCHED HIMSELF ACROSS THE RIVER FROM BANK TO BANK!
IT'S A BRIDGE! HE MADE A BRIDGE FOR US!
FEARLESSLY THE STRANGE BOY WALKED ACROSS THE OUTSTRETCHED MONSTER ...THEN THE LITTLE BOY FOLLOWED!
NICE OF HIM TO DO THIS!
I GUESS HE LIKES US!

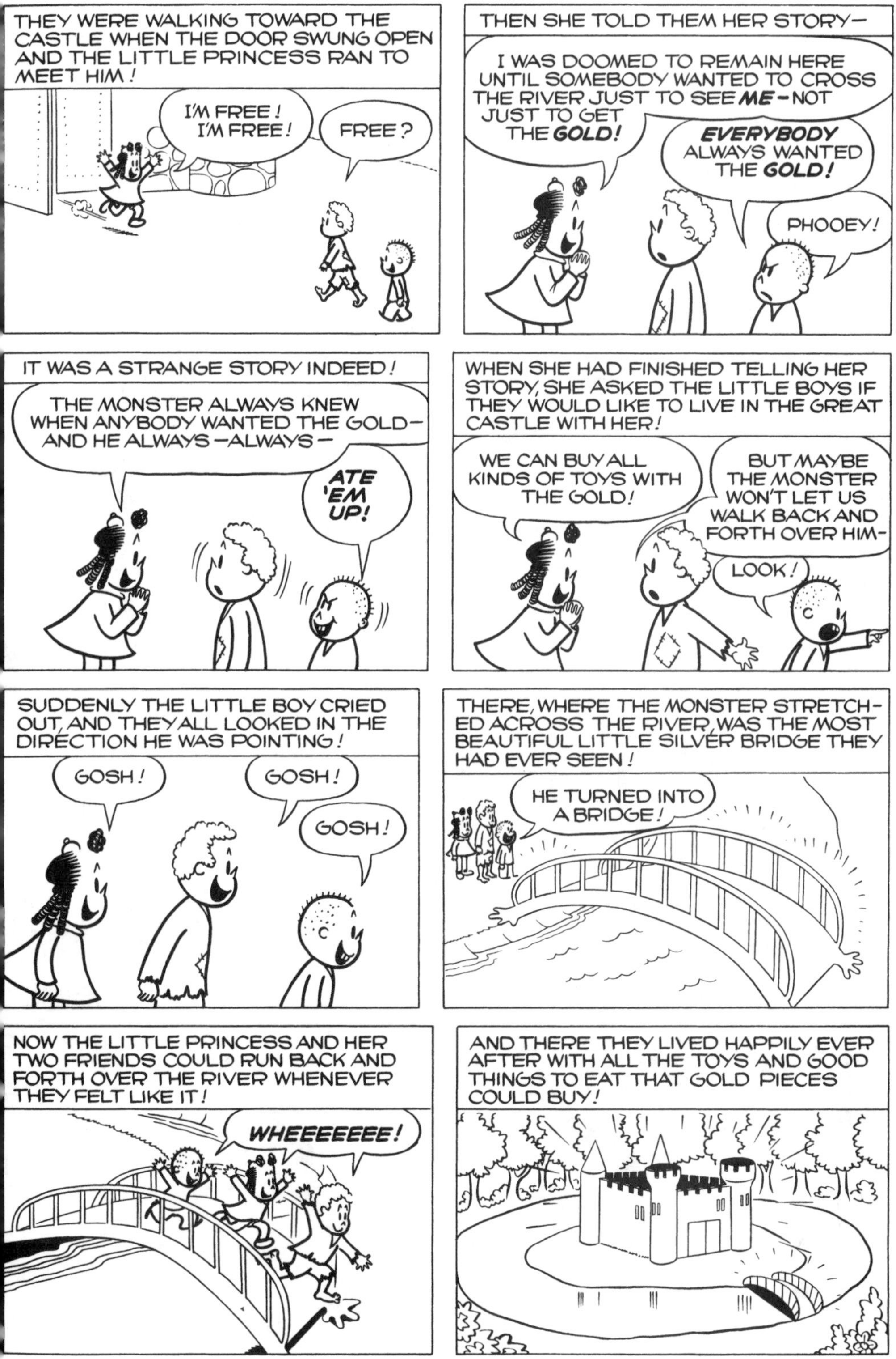
THEY WERE WALKING TOWARD THE CASTLE WHEN THE DOOR SWUNG OPEN AND THE LITTLE PRINCESS RAN TO MEET HIM!
I'M FREE! I'M FREE!
FREE?
THEN SHE TOLD THEM HER STORY—
I WAS DOOMED TO REMAIN HERE UNTIL SOMEBODY WANTED TO CROSS THE RIVER JUST TO SEE **ME**—NOT JUST TO GET THE **GOLD!**
EVERYBODY ALWAYS WANTED THE **GOLD!**
PHOOEY!
IT WAS A STRANGE STORY INDEED!
THE MONSTER ALWAYS KNEW WHEN ANYBODY WANTED THE GOLD— AND HE ALWAYS —ALWAYS—
ATE 'EM UP!
WHEN SHE HAD FINISHED TELLING HER STORY, SHE ASKED THE LITTLE BOYS IF THEY WOULD LIKE TO LIVE IN THE GREAT CASTLE WITH HER!
WE CAN BUY ALL KINDS OF TOYS WITH THE GOLD!
BUT MAYBE THE MONSTER WON'T LET US WALK BACK AND FORTH OVER HIM-
LOOK!
SUDDENLY THE LITTLE BOY CRIED OUT, AND THEY ALL LOOKED IN THE DIRECTION HE WAS POINTING!
GOSH!
GOSH!
GOSH!
THERE, WHERE THE MONSTER STRETCHED ACROSS THE RIVER, WAS THE MOST BEAUTIFUL LITTLE SILVER BRIDGE THEY HAD EVER SEEN!
HE TURNED INTO A BRIDGE!
NOW THE LITTLE PRINCESS AND HER TWO FRIENDS COULD RUN BACK AND FORTH OVER THE RIVER WHENEVER THEY FELT LIKE IT!
WHEEEEEEE!
AND THERE THEY LIVED HAPPILY EVER AFTER WITH ALL THE TOYS AND GOOD THINGS TO EAT THAT GOLD PIECES COULD BUY!

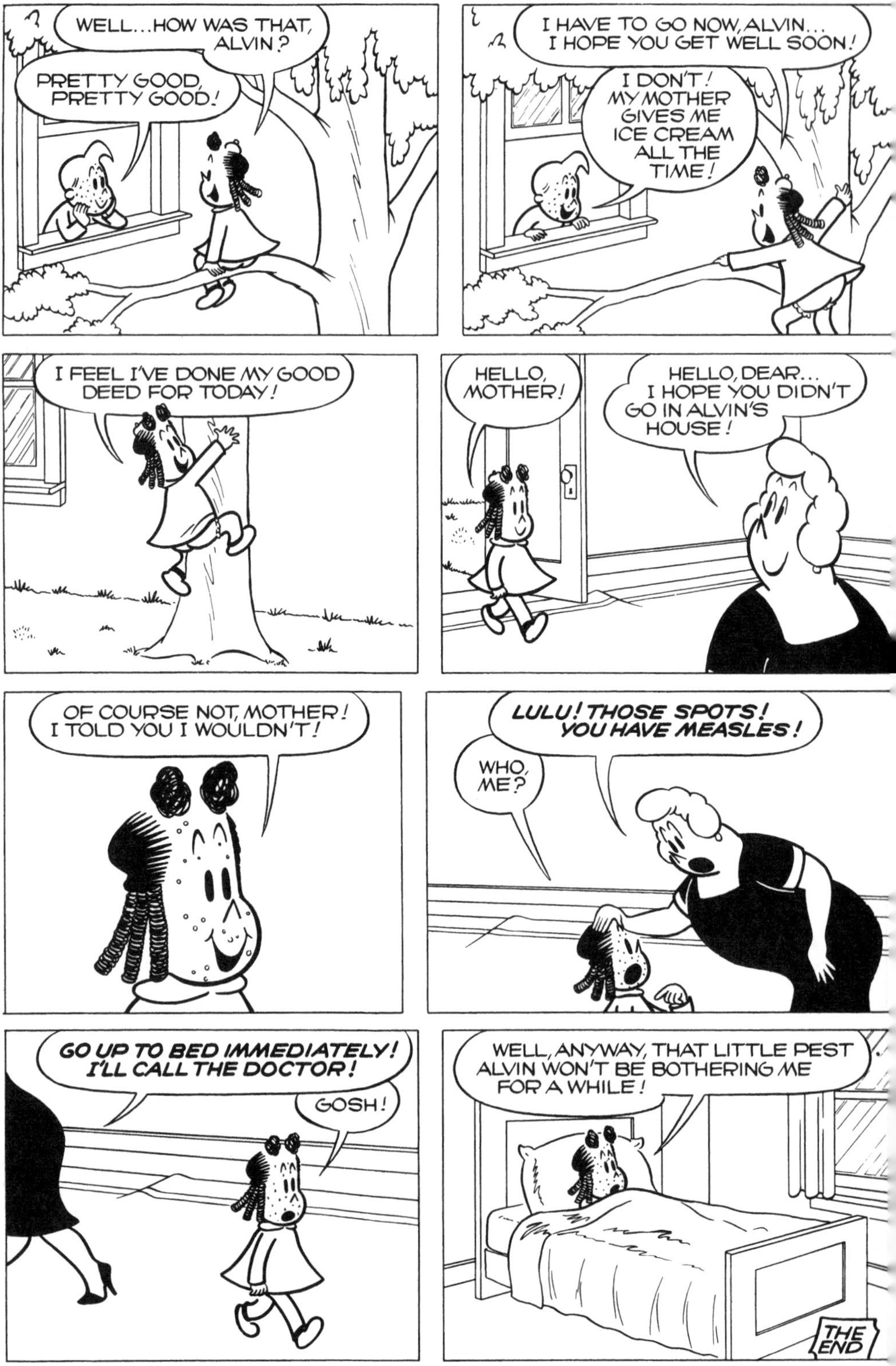
WELL...HOW WAS THAT, ALVIN?
PRETTY GOOD, PRETTY GOOD!
I HAVE TO GO NOW, ALVIN... I HOPE YOU GET WELL SOON!
I DON'T! MY MOTHER GIVES ME ICE CREAM ALL THE TIME!
I FEEL I'VE DONE MY GOOD DEED FOR TODAY!
HELLO, MOTHER!
HELLO, DEAR... I HOPE YOU DIDN'T GO IN ALVIN'S HOUSE!
OF COURSE NOT, MOTHER! I TOLD YOU I WOULDN'T!
LULU! THOSE SPOTS! YOU HAVE MEASLES!
WHO, ME?
GO UP TO BED IMMEDIATELY! I'LL CALL THE DOCTOR!
GOSH!
WELL, ANYWAY, THAT LITTLE PEST ALVIN WON'T BE BOTHERING ME FOR A WHILE!
THE END

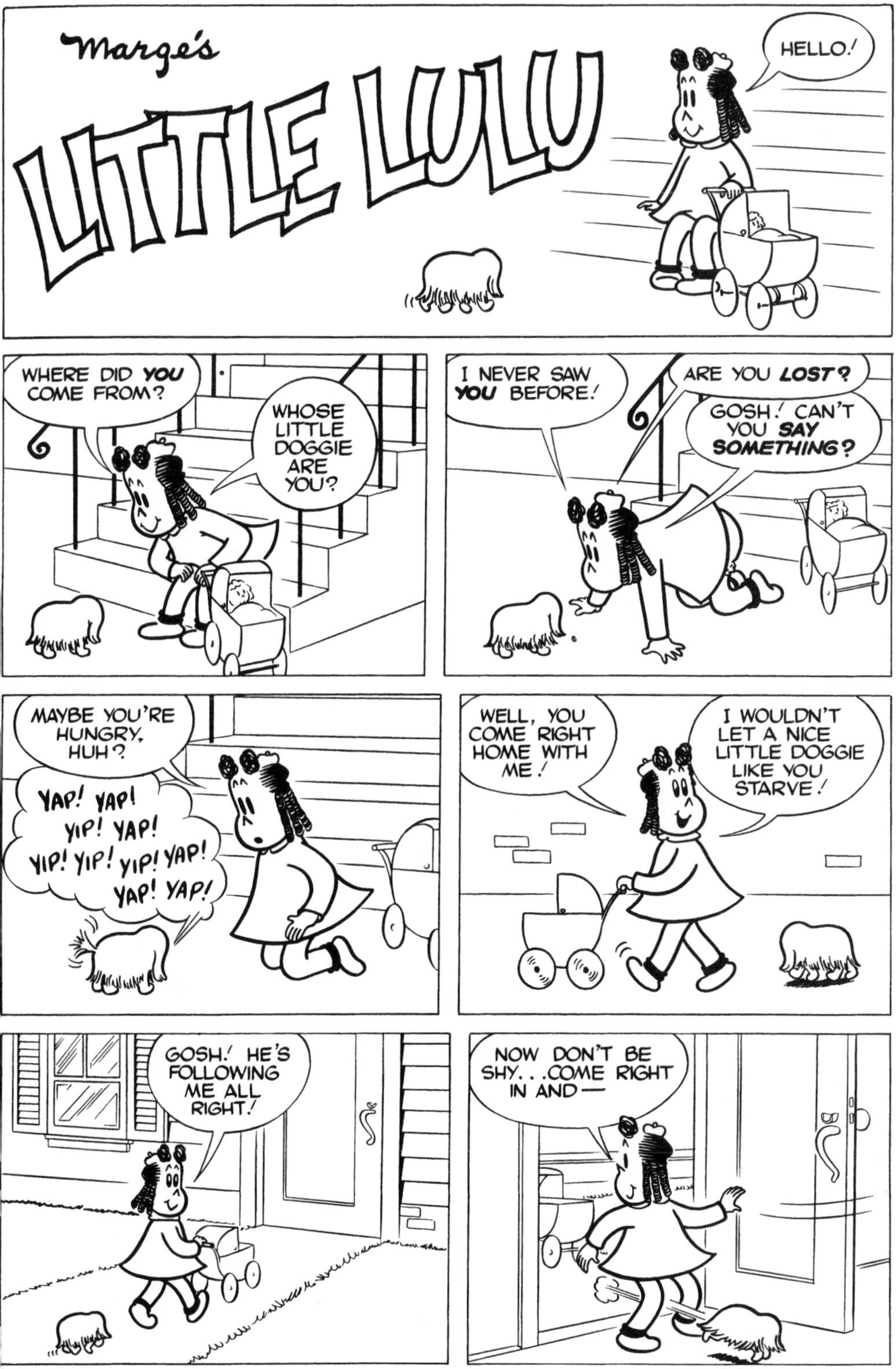
Marge's
LITTLE LULU
HELLO!
WHERE DID YOU COME FROM?
WHOSE LITTLE DOGGIE ARE YOU?
I NEVER SAW YOU BEFORE!
ARE YOU LOST?
GOSH! CAN'T YOU SAY SOMETHING?
MAYBE YOU'RE HUNGRY, HUH?
YAP! YAP! YIP! YAP! YIP! YIP! YIP! YAP! YAP! YAP!
WELL, YOU COME RIGHT HOME WITH ME!
I WOULDN'T LET A NICE LITTLE DOGGIE LIKE YOU STARVE!
GOSH! HE'S FOLLOWING ME ALL RIGHT!
NOW DON'T BE SHY...COME RIGHT IN AND—

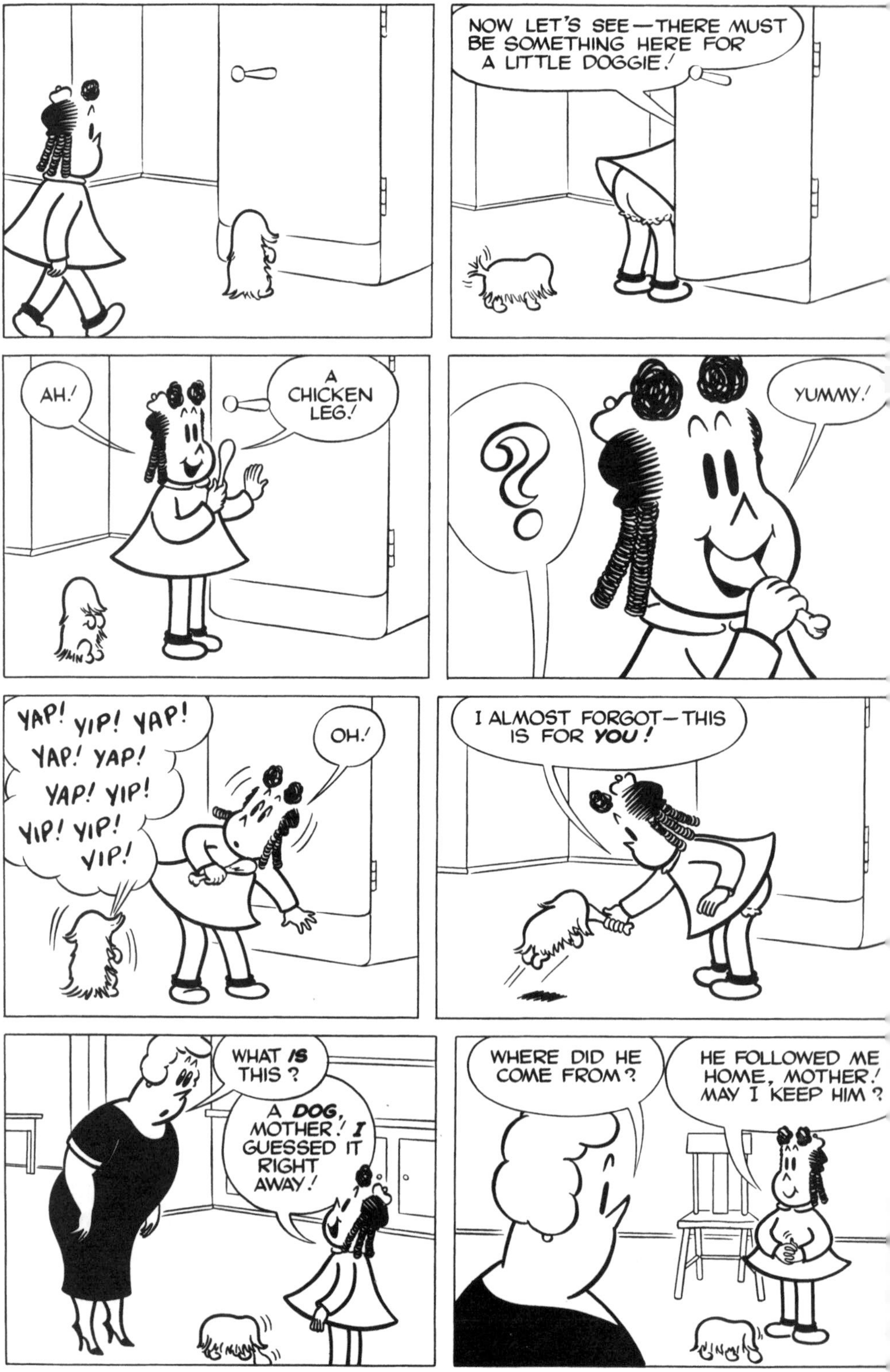
NOW LET'S SEE—THERE MUST BE SOMETHING HERE FOR A LITTLE DOGGIE!
AH!
A CHICKEN LEG!
?
YUMMY!
YAP! YIP! YAP! YAP! YAP! YAP! YIP! YIP! YIP! YIP!
OH!
I ALMOST FORGOT—THIS IS FOR YOU!
WHAT IS THIS?
A DOG, MOTHER! I GUESSED IT RIGHT AWAY!
WHERE DID HE COME FROM?
HE FOLLOWED ME HOME, MOTHER! MAY I KEEP HIM?

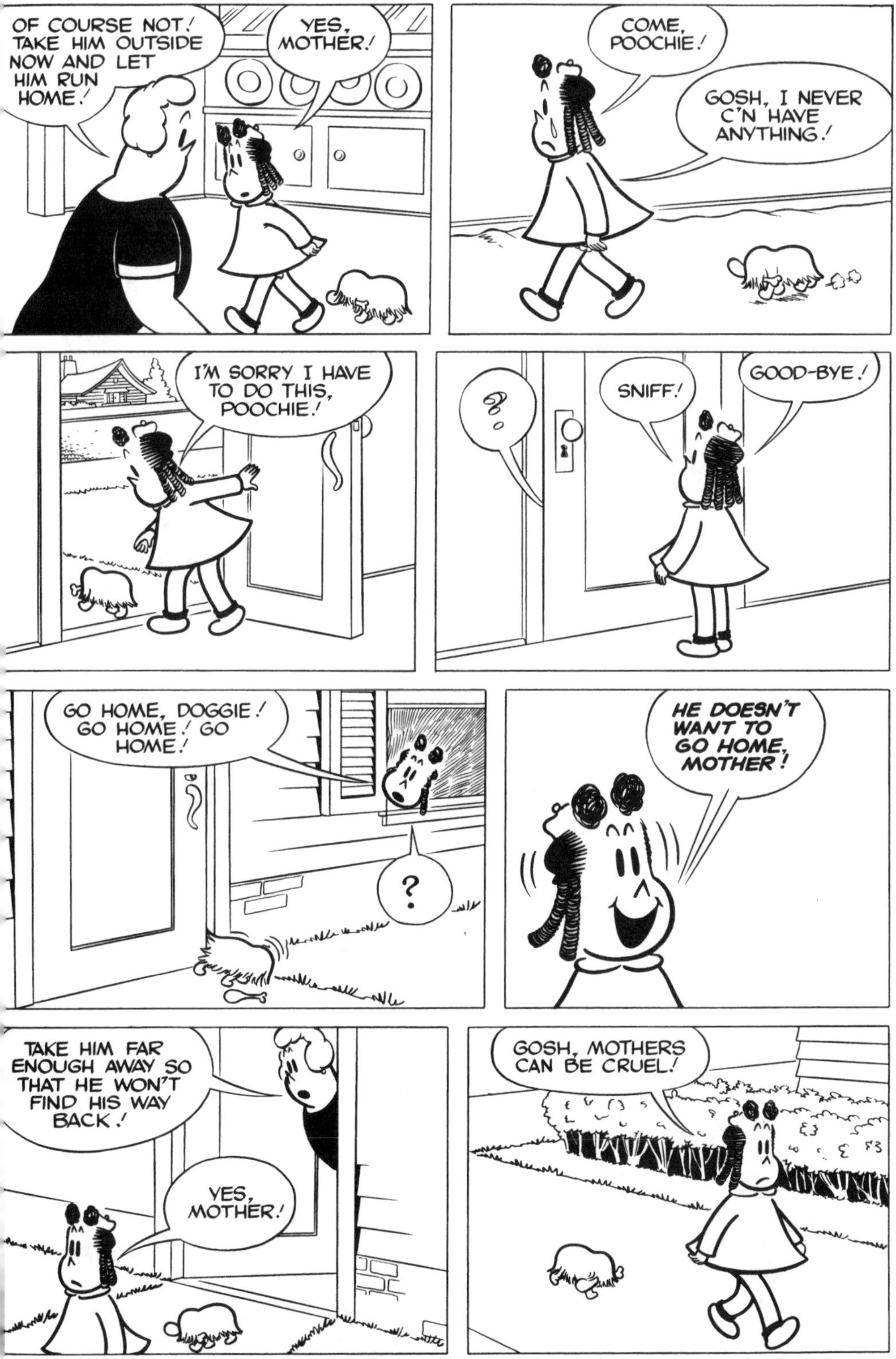
OF COURSE NOT! TAKE HIM OUTSIDE NOW AND LET HIM RUN HOME!
YES, MOTHER!
COME, POOCHIE!
GOSH, I NEVER C'N HAVE ANYTHING!
I'M SORRY I HAVE TO DO THIS, POOCHIE!
?
SNIFF!
GOOD-BYE!
GO HOME, DOGGIE! GO HOME! GO HOME!
?
HE DOESN'T WANT TO GO HOME, MOTHER!
TAKE HIM FAR ENOUGH AWAY SO THAT HE WON'T FIND HIS WAY BACK!
YES, MOTHER!
GOSH, MOTHERS CAN BE CRUEL!

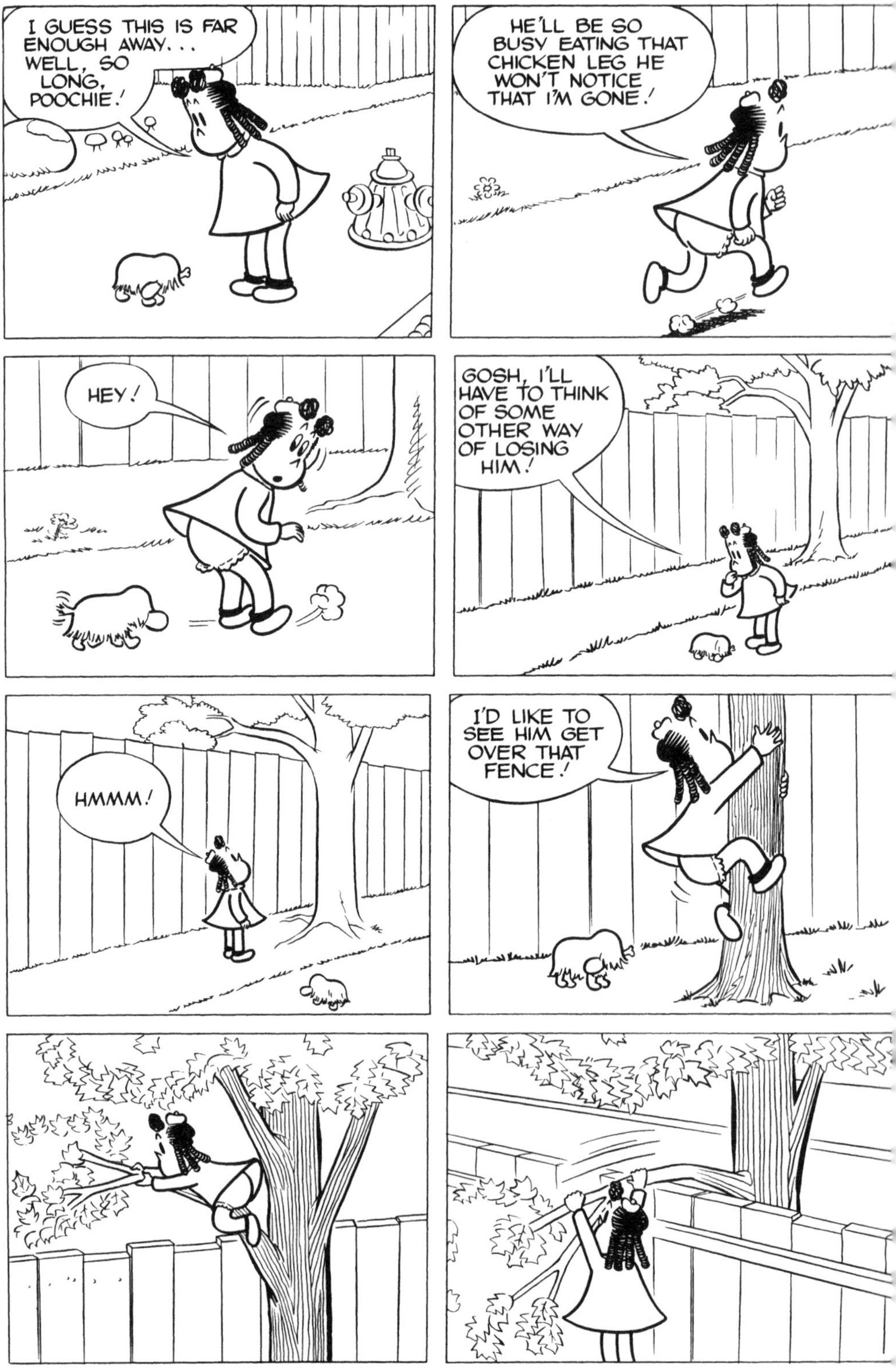
I GUESS THIS IS FAR ENOUGH AWAY... WELL, SO LONG, POOCHIE!
HE'LL BE SO BUSY EATING THAT CHICKEN LEG HE WON'T NOTICE THAT I'M GONE!
HEY!
GOSH, I'LL HAVE TO THINK OF SOME OTHER WAY OF LOSING HIM!
HMMM!
I'D LIKE TO SEE HIM GET OVER THAT FENCE!

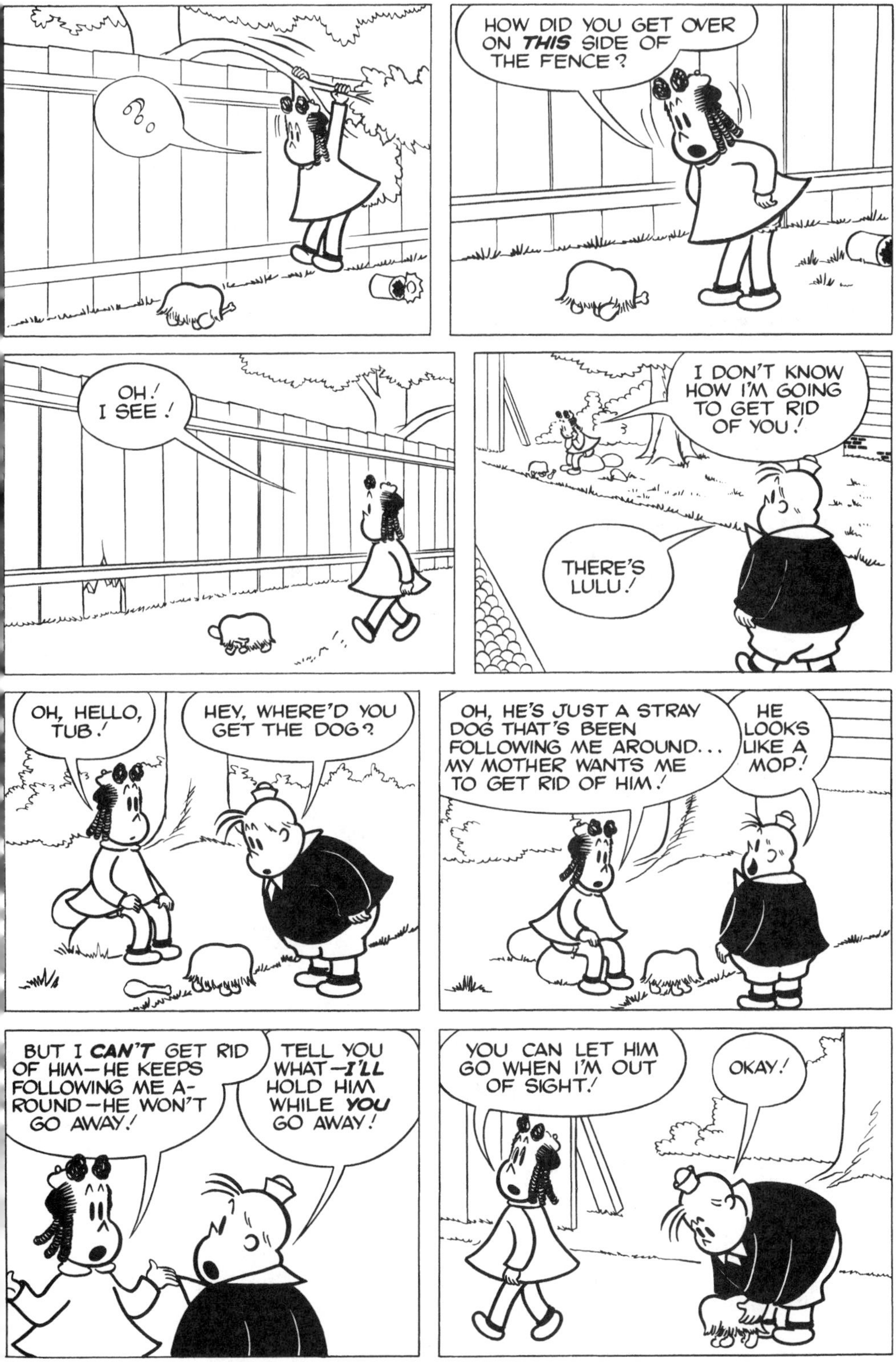
HOW DID YOU GET OVER ON *THIS* SIDE OF THE FENCE?
OH! I SEE!
I DON'T KNOW HOW I'M GOING TO GET RID OF YOU!
THERE'S LULU!
OH, HELLO, TUB!
HEY, WHERE'D YOU GET THE DOG?
OH, HE'S JUST A STRAY DOG THAT'S BEEN FOLLOWING ME AROUND... MY MOTHER WANTS ME TO GET RID OF HIM!
HE LOOKS LIKE A MOP!
BUT I *CAN'T* GET RID OF HIM—HE KEEPS FOLLOWING ME A-ROUND—HE WON'T GO AWAY!
TELL YOU WHAT—*I'LL* HOLD HIM WHILE *YOU* GO AWAY!
YOU CAN LET HIM GO WHEN I'M OUT OF SIGHT!
OKAY!

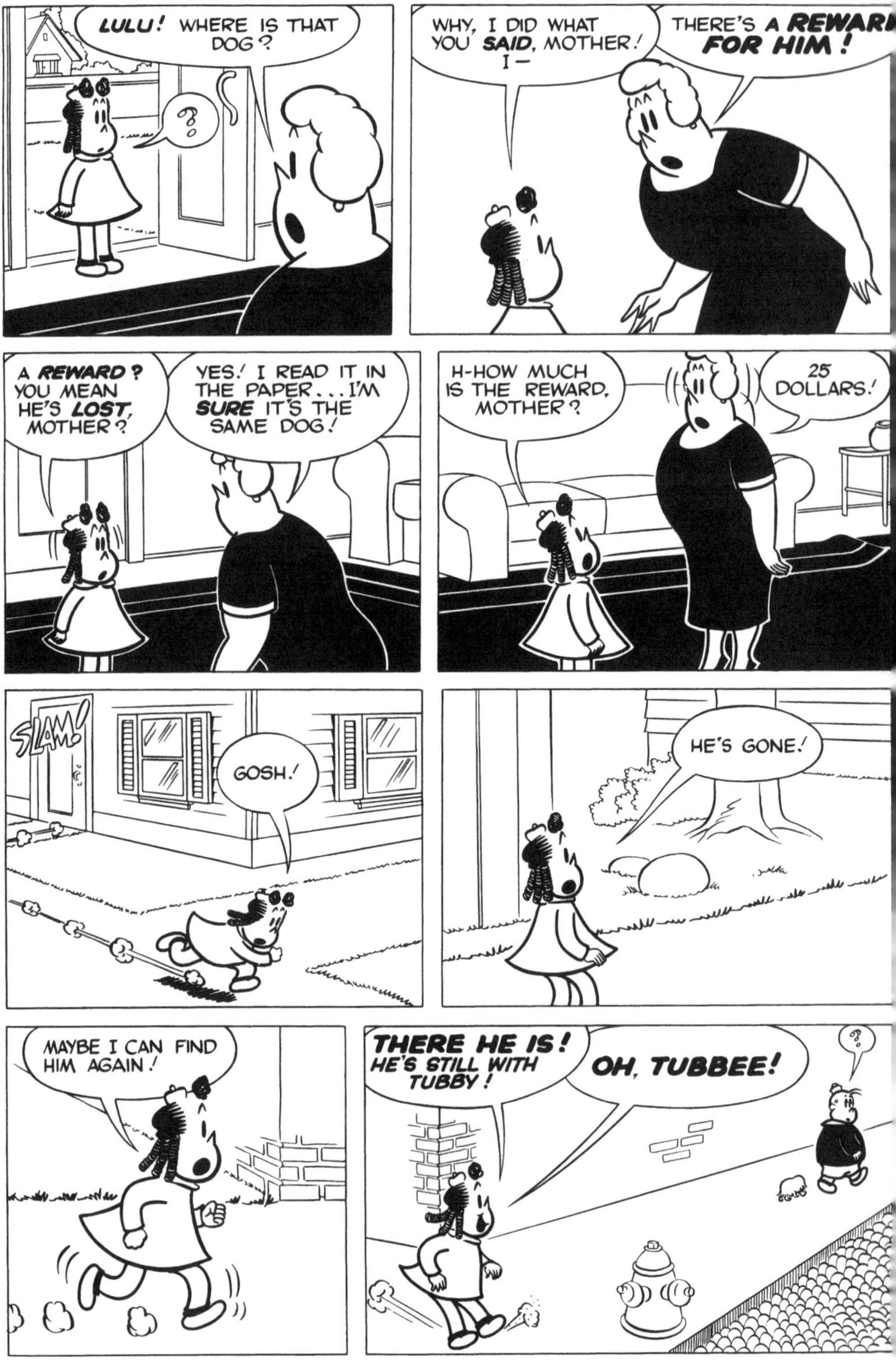
LULU! WHERE IS THAT DOG?
?
WHY, I DID WHAT YOU SAID, MOTHER! I—
THERE'S A REWARD FOR HIM!
A REWARD? YOU MEAN HE'S LOST, MOTHER?
YES! I READ IT IN THE PAPER... I'M SURE IT'S THE SAME DOG!
H-HOW MUCH IS THE REWARD, MOTHER?
25 DOLLARS!
SLAM!
GOSH!
HE'S GONE!
MAYBE I CAN FIND HIM AGAIN!
THERE HE IS! HE'S STILL WITH TUBBY!
OH, TUBBEE!
?

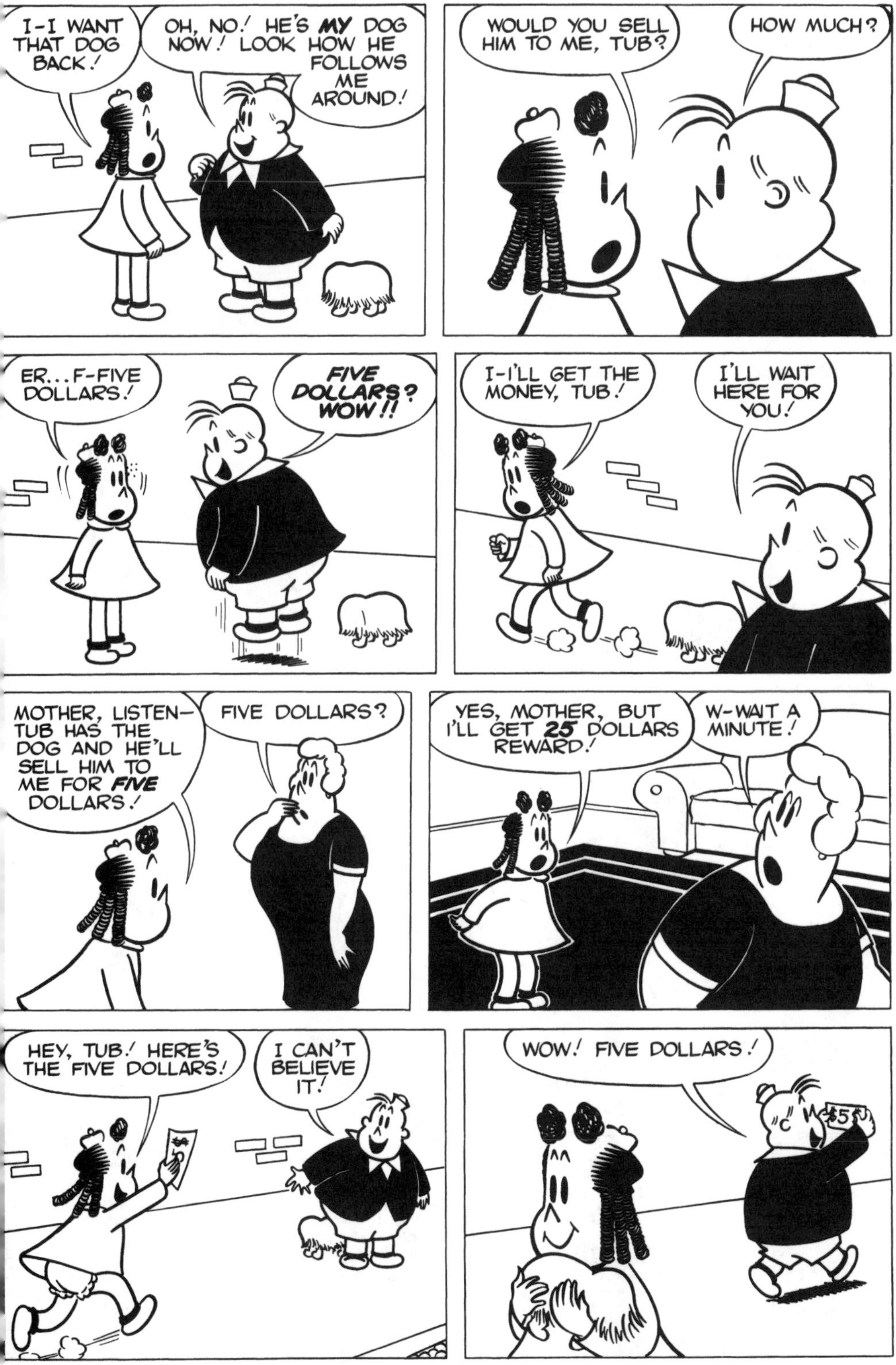
I-I WANT THAT DOG BACK.!
OH, NO.! HE'S MY DOG NOW.! LOOK HOW HE FOLLOWS ME AROUND.!
WOULD YOU SELL HIM TO ME, TUB?
HOW MUCH?
ER...F-FIVE DOLLARS.!
FIVE DOLLARS? WOW!!
I-I'LL GET THE MONEY, TUB.!
I'LL WAIT HERE FOR YOU.!
MOTHER, LISTEN—TUB HAS THE DOG AND HE'LL SELL HIM TO ME FOR FIVE DOLLARS.!
FIVE DOLLARS?
YES, MOTHER, BUT I'LL GET 25 DOLLARS REWARD.!
W-WAIT A MINUTE.!
HEY, TUB.! HERE'S THE FIVE DOLLARS.!
I CAN'T BELIEVE IT.!
WOW.! FIVE DOLLARS.!

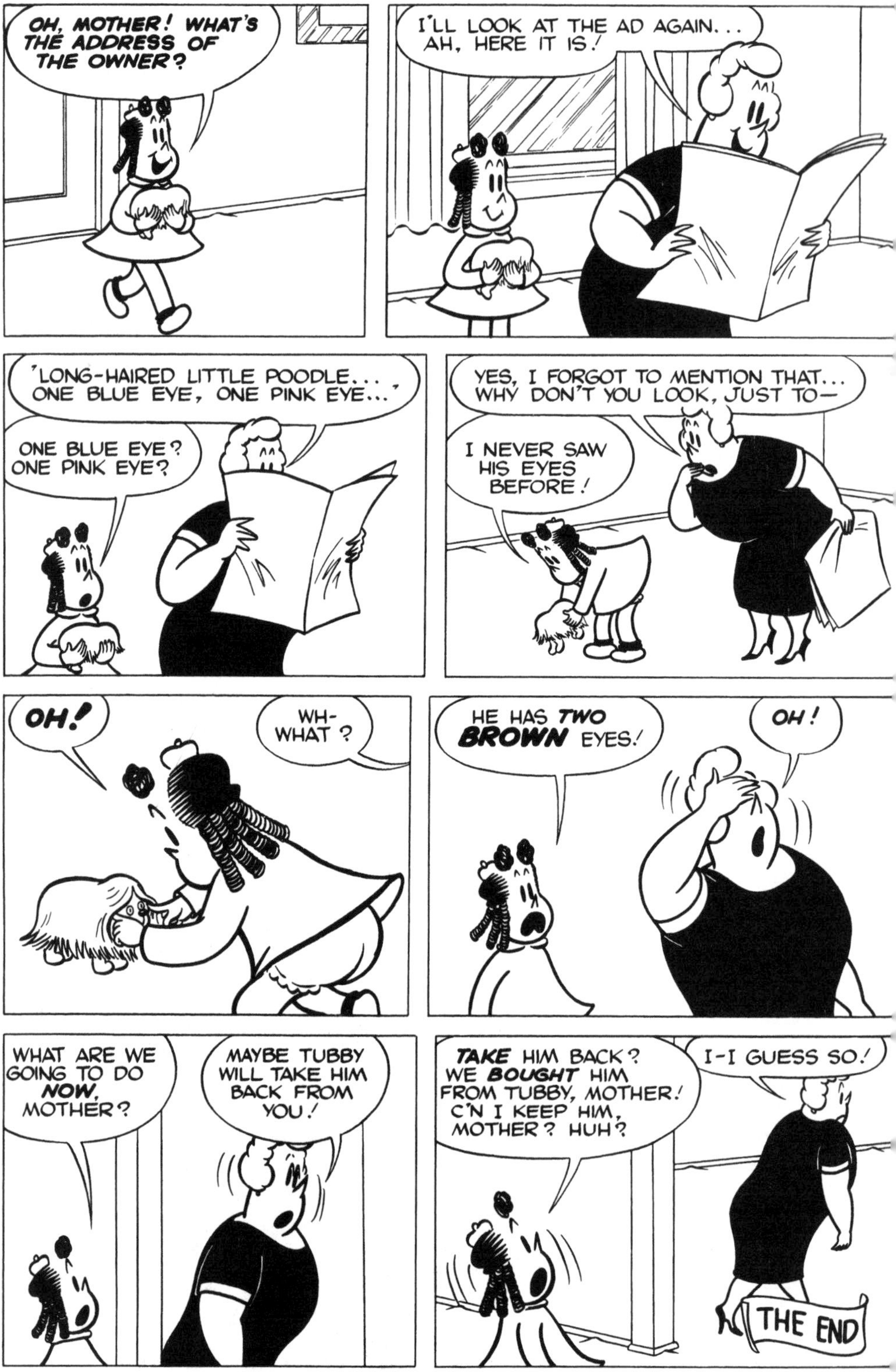
OH, MOTHER! WHAT'S THE ADDRESS OF THE OWNER?
I'LL LOOK AT THE AD AGAIN... AH, HERE IT IS!
'LONG-HAIRED LITTLE POODLE... ONE BLUE EYE, ONE PINK EYE...'
ONE BLUE EYE? ONE PINK EYE?
YES, I FORGOT TO MENTION THAT... WHY DON'T YOU LOOK, JUST TO—
I NEVER SAW HIS EYES BEFORE!
OH!
WH- WHAT?
HE HAS TWO BROWN EYES!
OH!
WHAT ARE WE GOING TO DO NOW, MOTHER?
MAYBE TUBBY WILL TAKE HIM BACK FROM YOU!
TAKE HIM BACK? WE BOUGHT HIM FROM TUBBY, MOTHER! C'N I KEEP HIM, MOTHER? HUH?
I-I GUESS SO!
THE END

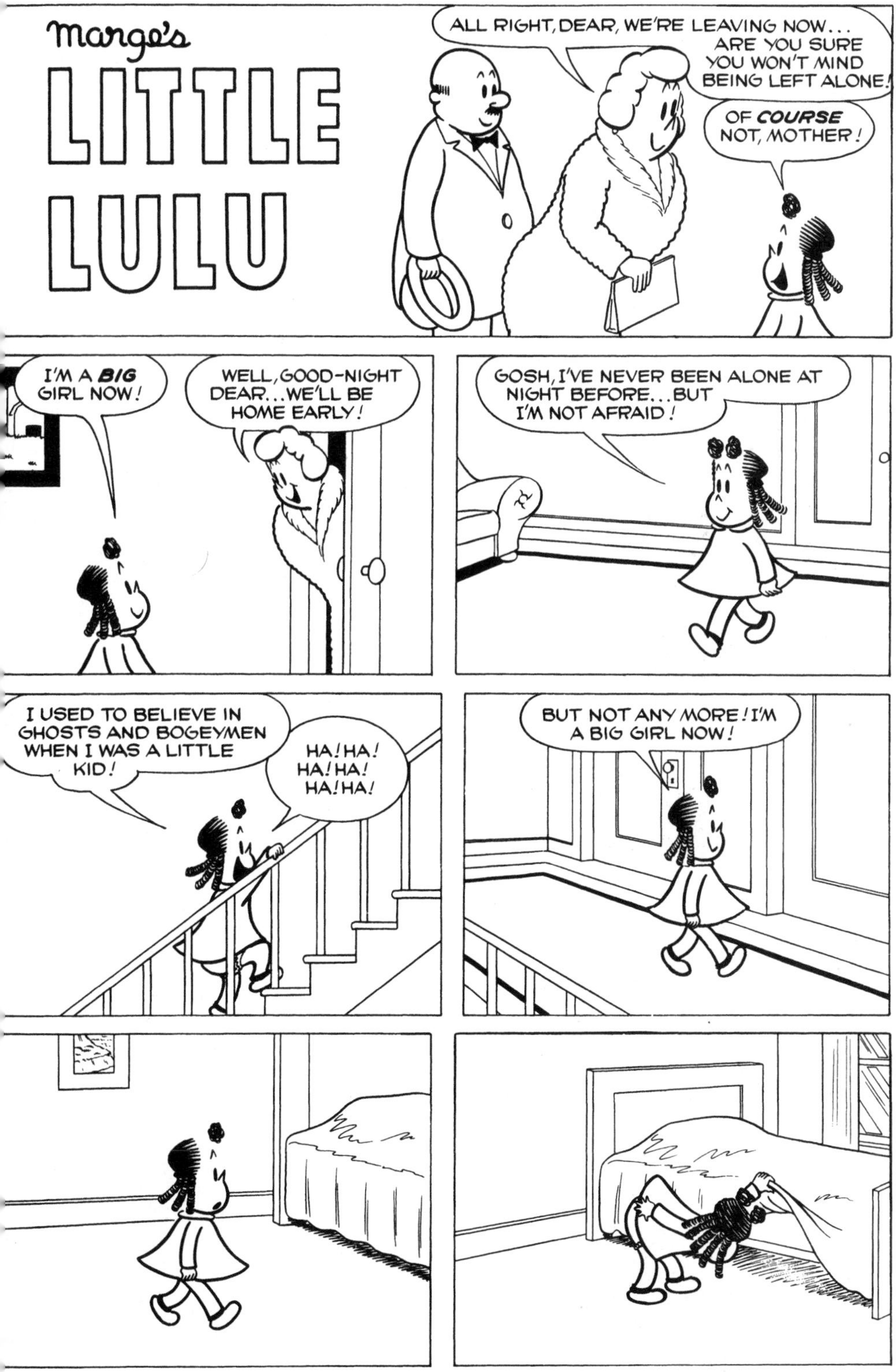
marge's
LITTLE LULU
ALL RIGHT, DEAR, WE'RE LEAVING NOW... ARE YOU SURE YOU WON'T MIND BEING LEFT ALONE?
OF COURSE NOT, MOTHER!
I'M A BIG GIRL NOW!
WELL, GOOD-NIGHT DEAR... WE'LL BE HOME EARLY!
GOSH, I'VE NEVER BEEN ALONE AT NIGHT BEFORE... BUT I'M NOT AFRAID!
I USED TO BELIEVE IN GHOSTS AND BOGEYMEN WHEN I WAS A LITTLE KID!
HA! HA! HA! HA! HA! HA!
BUT NOT ANY MORE! I'M A BIG GIRL NOW!

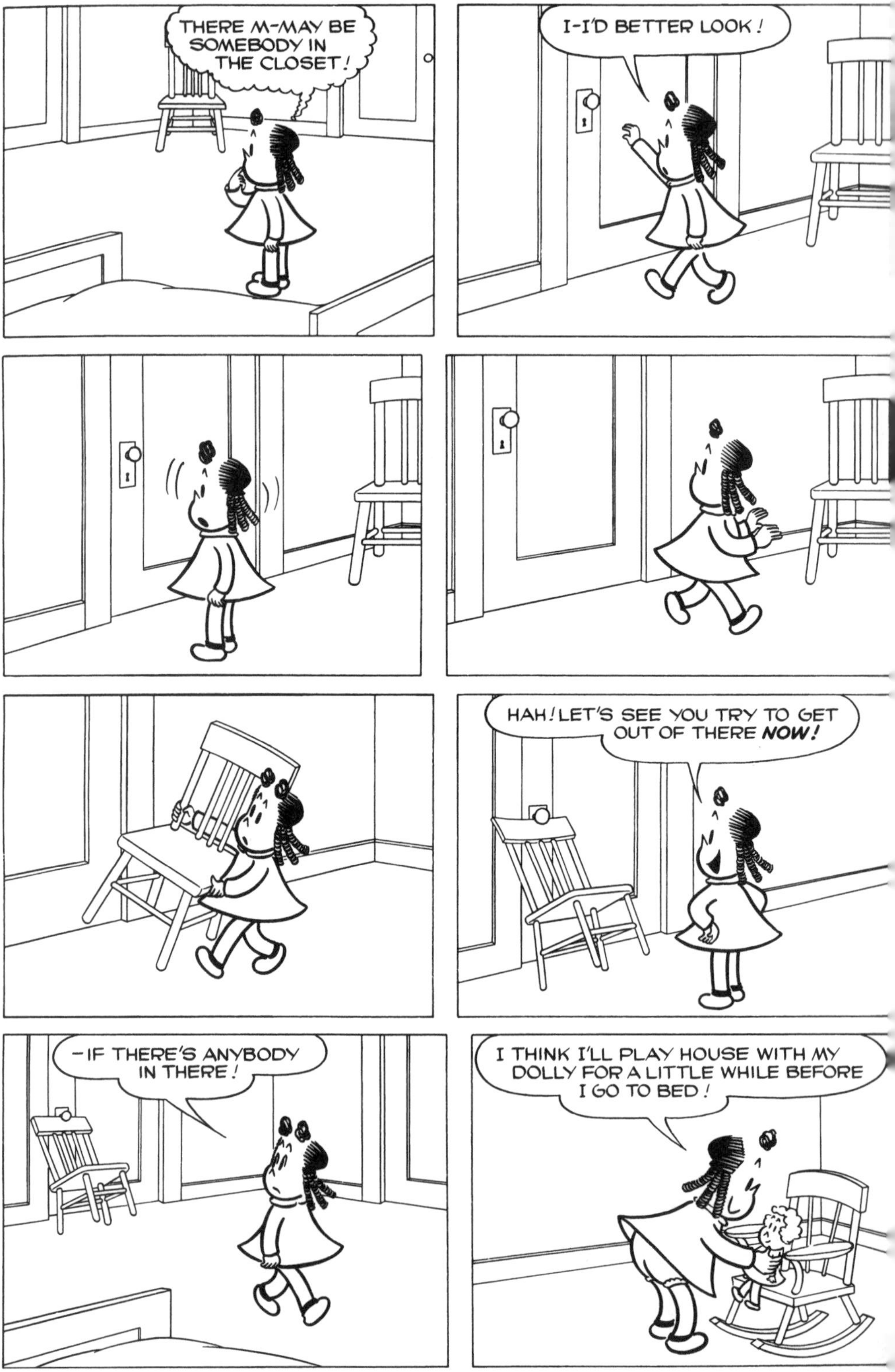
THERE M-MAY BE SOMEBODY IN THE CLOSET!
I-I'D BETTER LOOK!
HAH! LET'S SEE YOU TRY TO GET OUT OF THERE NOW!
-IF THERE'S ANYBODY IN THERE!
I THINK I'LL PLAY HOUSE WITH MY DOLLY FOR A LITTLE WHILE BEFORE I GO TO BED!

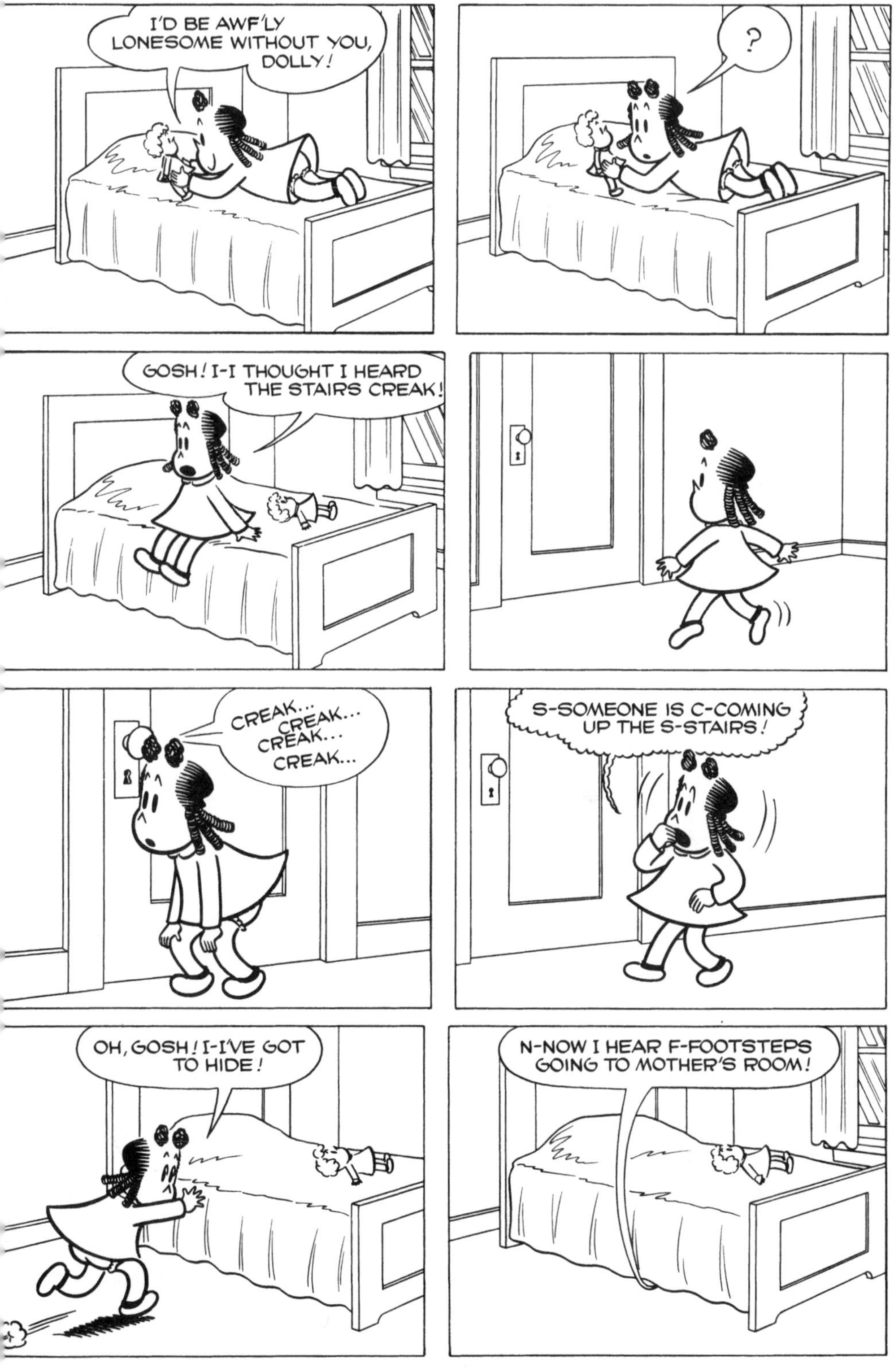
I'D BE AWF'LY LONESOME WITHOUT YOU, DOLLY!
?
GOSH! I-I THOUGHT I HEARD THE STAIRS CREAK!
CREAK... CREAK... CREAK... CREAK...
S-SOMEONE IS C-COMING UP THE S-STAIRS!
OH, GOSH! I-I'VE GOT TO HIDE!
N-NOW I HEAR F-FOOTSTEPS GOING TO MOTHER'S ROOM!

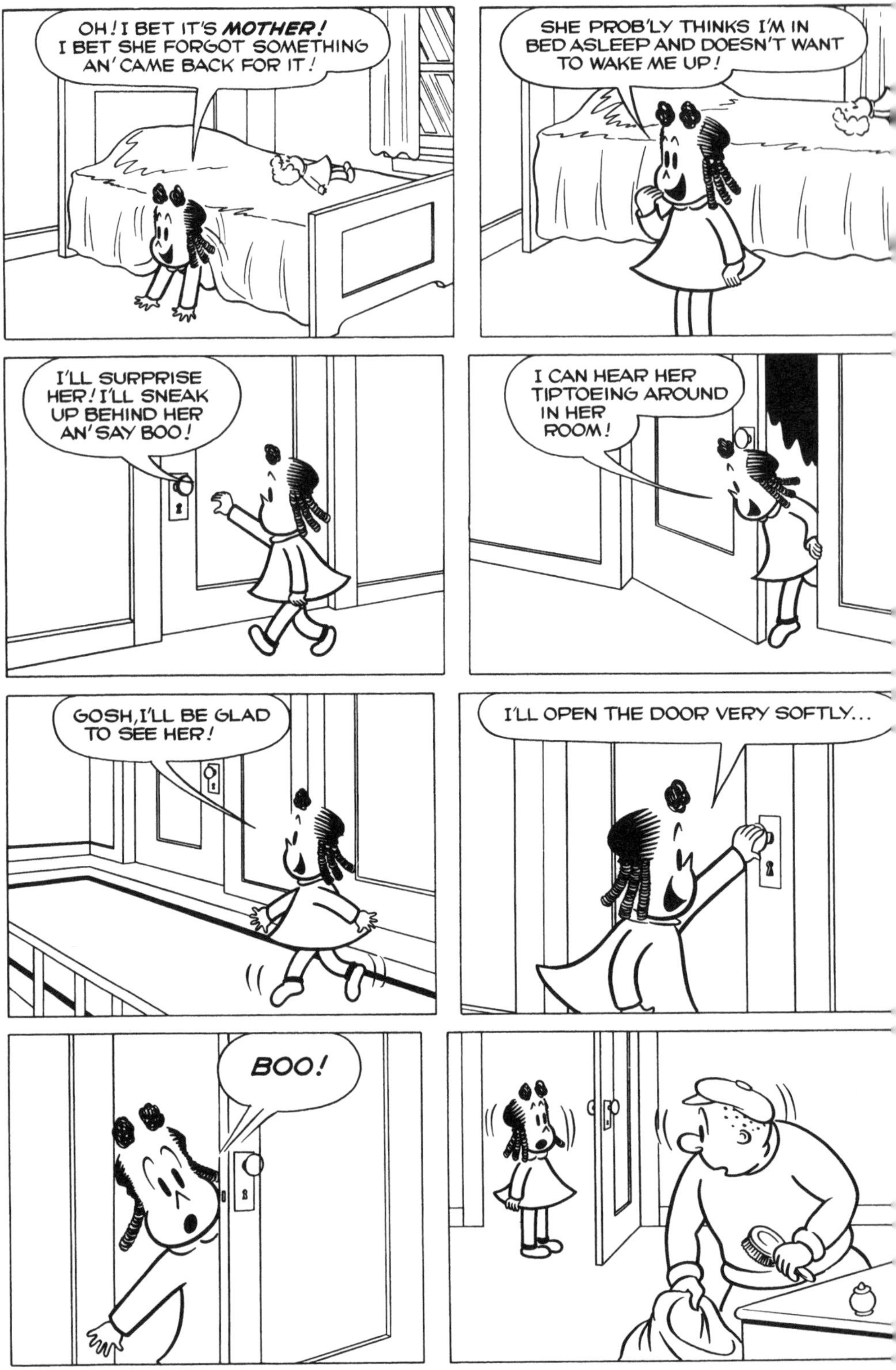
OH! I BET IT'S *MOTHER!* I BET SHE FORGOT SOMETHING AN' CAME BACK FOR IT!
SHE PROB'LY THINKS I'M IN BED ASLEEP AND DOESN'T WANT TO WAKE ME UP!
I'LL SURPRISE HER! I'LL SNEAK UP BEHIND HER AN' SAY BOO!
I CAN HEAR HER TIPTOEING AROUND IN HER ROOM!
GOSH, I'LL BE GLAD TO SEE HER!
I'LL OPEN THE DOOR VERY SOFTLY...
BOO!

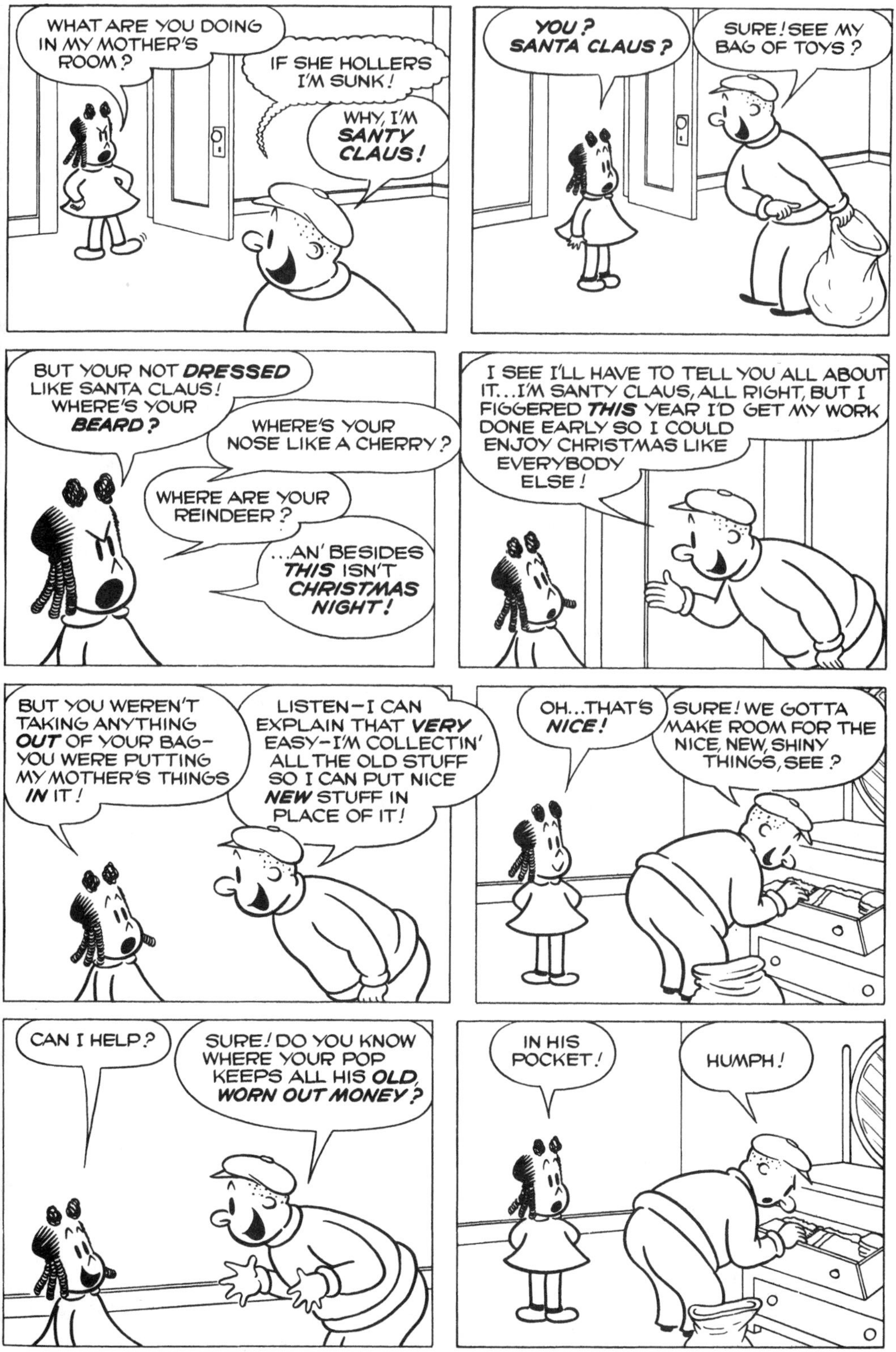
WHAT ARE YOU DOING IN MY MOTHER'S ROOM?
IF SHE HOLLERS I'M SUNK!
WHY, I'M SANTY CLAUS!
YOU? SANTA CLAUS?
SURE! SEE MY BAG OF TOYS?
BUT YOUR NOT DRESSED LIKE SANTA CLAUS! WHERE'S YOUR BEARD?
WHERE'S YOUR NOSE LIKE A CHERRY?
WHERE ARE YOUR REINDEER?
...AN' BESIDES THIS ISN'T CHRISTMAS NIGHT!
I SEE I'LL HAVE TO TELL YOU ALL ABOUT IT...I'M SANTY CLAUS, ALL RIGHT, BUT I FIGGERED THIS YEAR I'D GET MY WORK DONE EARLY SO I COULD ENJOY CHRISTMAS LIKE EVERYBODY ELSE!
BUT YOU WEREN'T TAKING ANYTHING OUT OF YOUR BAG- YOU WERE PUTTING MY MOTHER'S THINGS IN IT!
LISTEN-I CAN EXPLAIN THAT VERY EASY-I'M COLLECTIN' ALL THE OLD STUFF SO I CAN PUT NICE NEW STUFF IN PLACE OF IT!
OH...THAT'S NICE!
SURE! WE GOTTA MAKE ROOM FOR THE NICE, NEW, SHINY THINGS, SEE?
CAN I HELP?
SURE! DO YOU KNOW WHERE YOUR POP KEEPS ALL HIS OLD, WORN OUT MONEY?
IN HIS POCKET!
HUMPH!

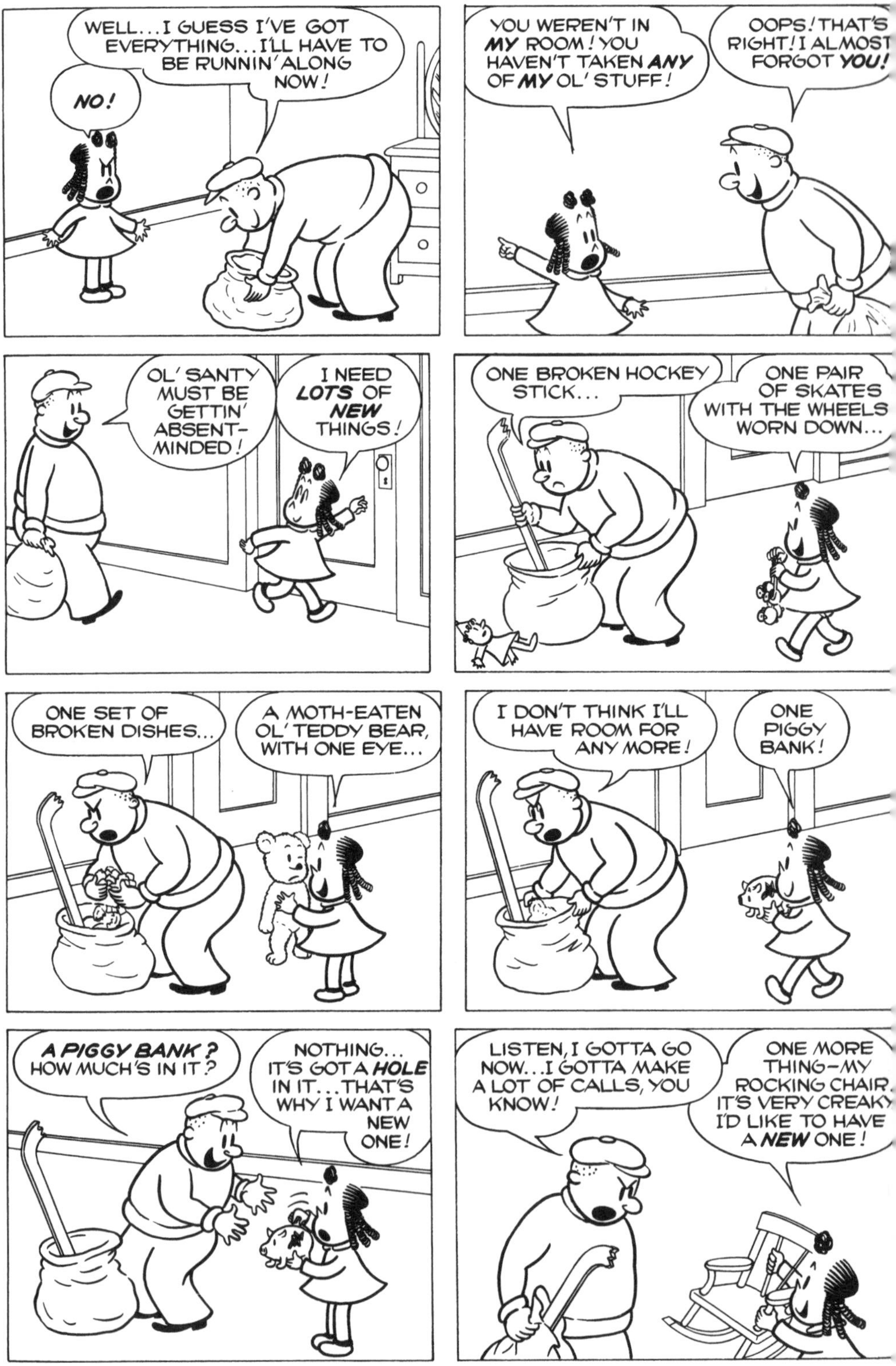

WELL...I GUESS I'VE GOT EVERYTHING...I'LL HAVE TO BE RUNNIN' ALONG NOW!
NO!
YOU WEREN'T IN **MY** ROOM! YOU HAVEN'T TAKEN **ANY** OF **MY** OL' STUFF!
OOPS! THAT'S RIGHT! I ALMOST FORGOT **YOU!**
OL' SANTY MUST BE GETTIN' ABSENT-MINDED!
I NEED **LOTS** OF **NEW** THINGS!
ONE BROKEN HOCKEY STICK...
ONE PAIR OF SKATES WITH THE WHEELS WORN DOWN...
ONE SET OF BROKEN DISHES...
A MOTH-EATEN OL' TEDDY BEAR, WITH ONE EYE...
I DON'T THINK I'LL HAVE ROOM FOR ANY MORE!
ONE PIGGY BANK!
A PIGGY BANK? HOW MUCH'S IN IT?
NOTHING... IT'S GOT A **HOLE** IN IT...THAT'S WHY I WANT A NEW ONE!
LISTEN, I GOTTA GO NOW...I GOTTA MAKE A LOT OF CALLS, YOU KNOW!
ONE MORE THING—MY ROCKING CHAIR. IT'S VERY CREAKY. I'D LIKE TO HAVE A **NEW** ONE!

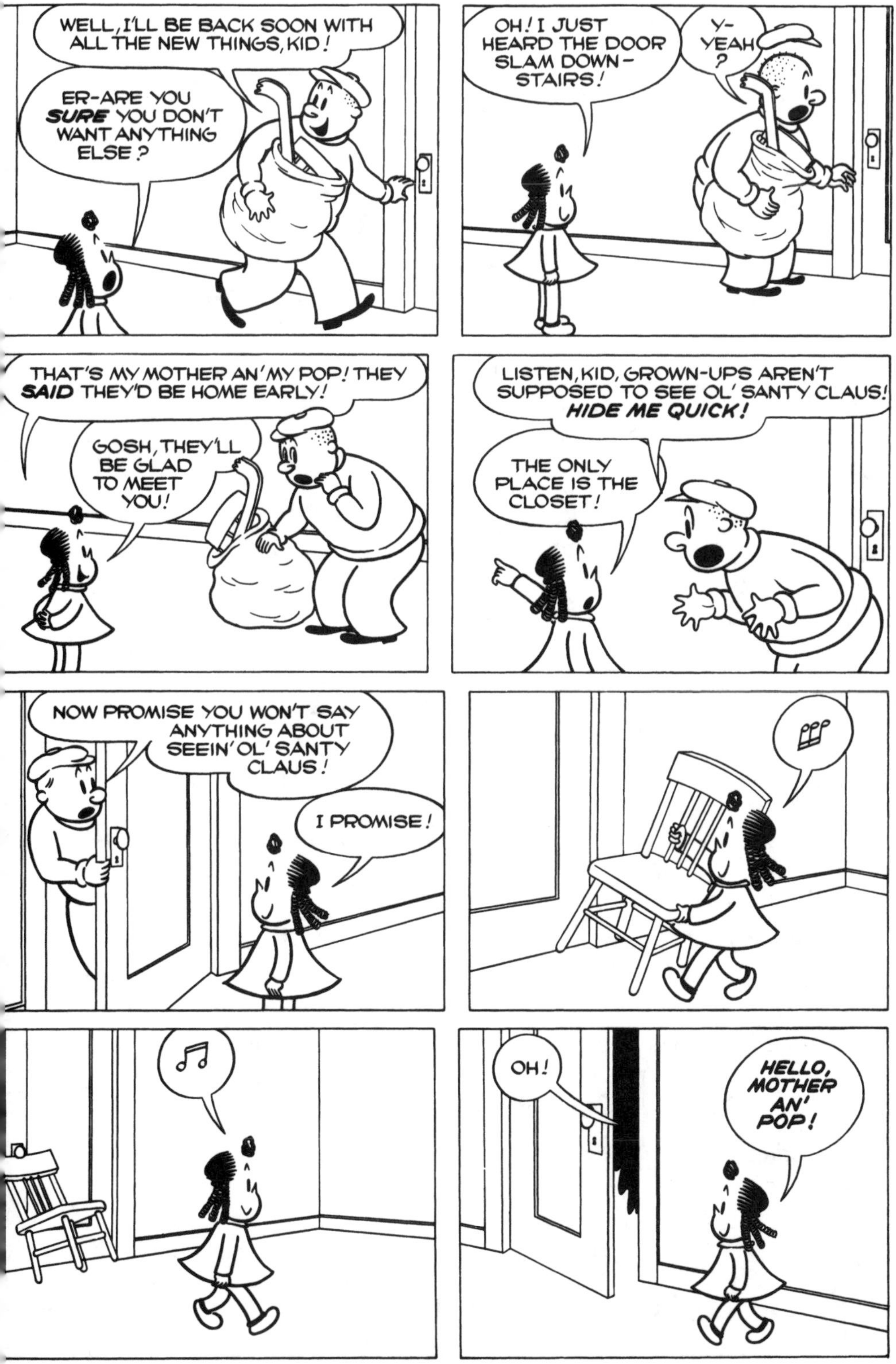
WELL, I'LL BE BACK SOON WITH ALL THE NEW THINGS, KID!
ER-ARE YOU **SURE** YOU DON'T WANT ANYTHING ELSE?
OH! I JUST HEARD THE DOOR SLAM DOWN-STAIRS!
Y-YEAH?
THAT'S MY MOTHER AN' MY POP! THEY **SAID** THEY'D BE HOME EARLY!
GOSH, THEY'LL BE GLAD TO MEET YOU!
LISTEN, KID, GROWN-UPS AREN'T SUPPOSED TO SEE OL' SANTY CLAUS! **HIDE ME QUICK!**
THE ONLY PLACE IS THE CLOSET!
NOW PROMISE YOU WON'T SAY ANYTHING ABOUT SEEIN' OL' SANTY CLAUS!
I PROMISE!
OH!
HELLO, MOTHER AN' POP!

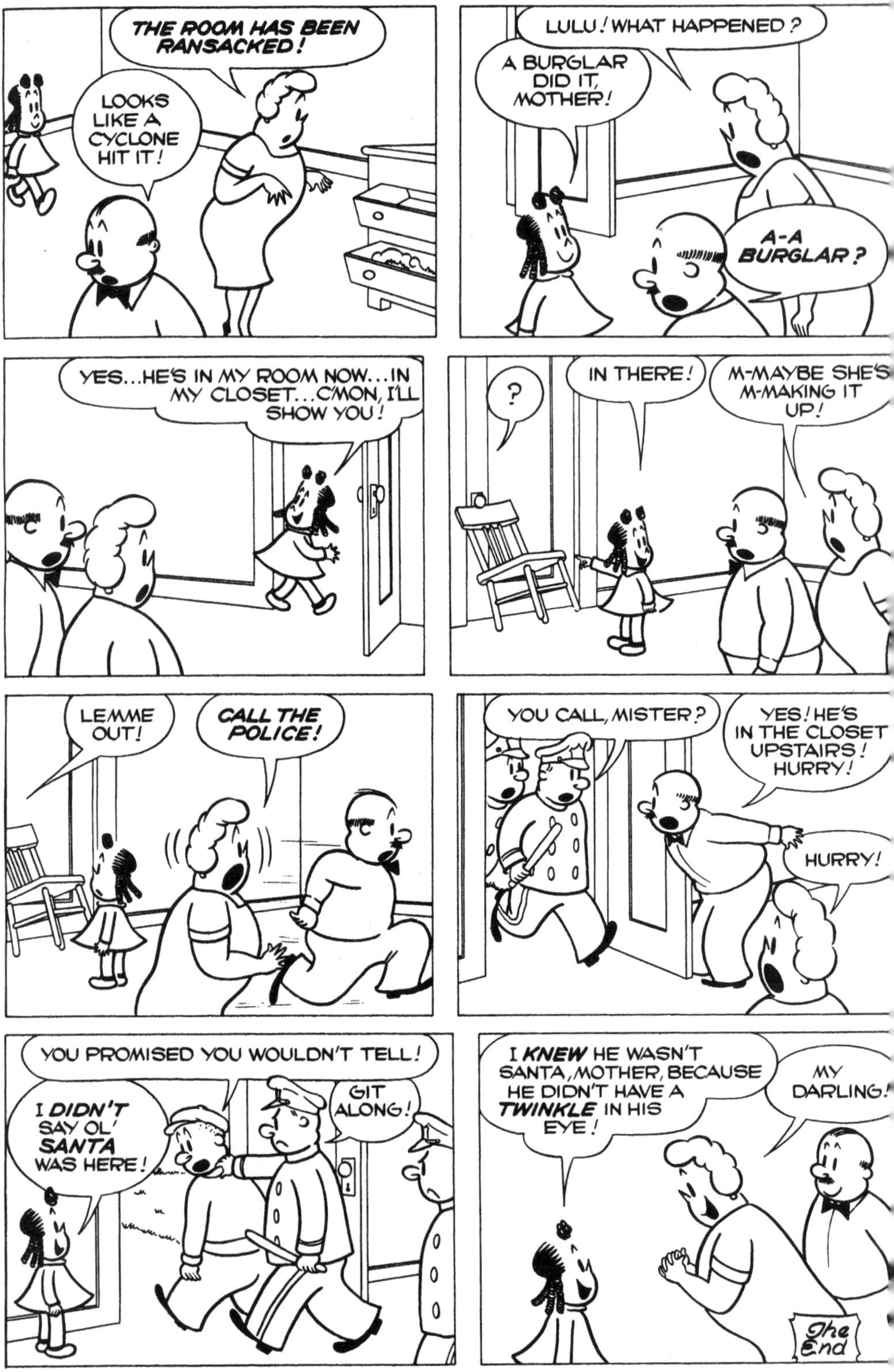
THE ROOM HAS BEEN RANSACKED!
LOOKS LIKE A CYCLONE HIT IT!
LULU! WHAT HAPPENED?
A BURGLAR DID IT, MOTHER!
A-A BURGLAR?
YES...HE'S IN MY ROOM NOW...IN MY CLOSET...C'MON, I'LL SHOW YOU!
?
IN THERE!
M-MAYBE SHE'S M-MAKING IT UP!
LEMME OUT!
CALL THE POLICE!
YOU CALL, MISTER?
YES! HE'S IN THE CLOSET UPSTAIRS! HURRY!
HURRY!
YOU PROMISED YOU WOULDN'T TELL!
I DIDN'T SAY OL' SANTA WAS HERE!
GIT ALONG!
I KNEW HE WASN'T SANTA, MOTHER, BECAUSE HE DIDN'T HAVE A TWINKLE IN HIS EYE!
MY DARLING!
The End

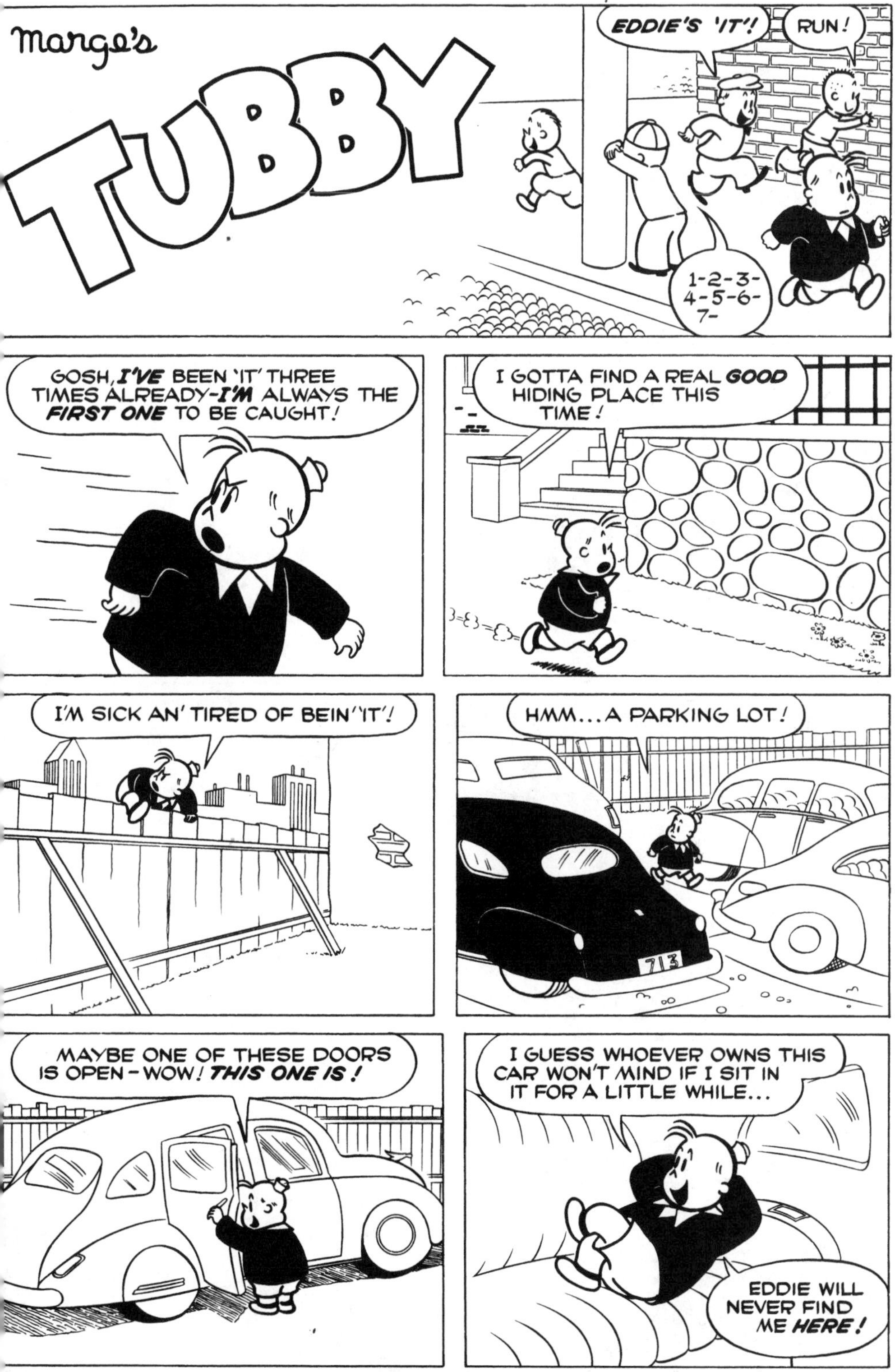
Marge's
TUBBY
EDDIE'S 'IT'!
RUN!
1-2-3-4-5-6-7-
GOSH, I'VE BEEN 'IT' THREE TIMES ALREADY-I'M ALWAYS THE FIRST ONE TO BE CAUGHT!
I GOTTA FIND A REAL GOOD HIDING PLACE THIS TIME!
I'M SICK AN' TIRED OF BEIN' 'IT'!
HMM...A PARKING LOT!
713
MAYBE ONE OF THESE DOORS IS OPEN-WOW! THIS ONE IS!
I GUESS WHOEVER OWNS THIS CAR WON'T MIND IF I SIT IN IT FOR A LITTLE WHILE...
EDDIE WILL NEVER FIND ME HERE!

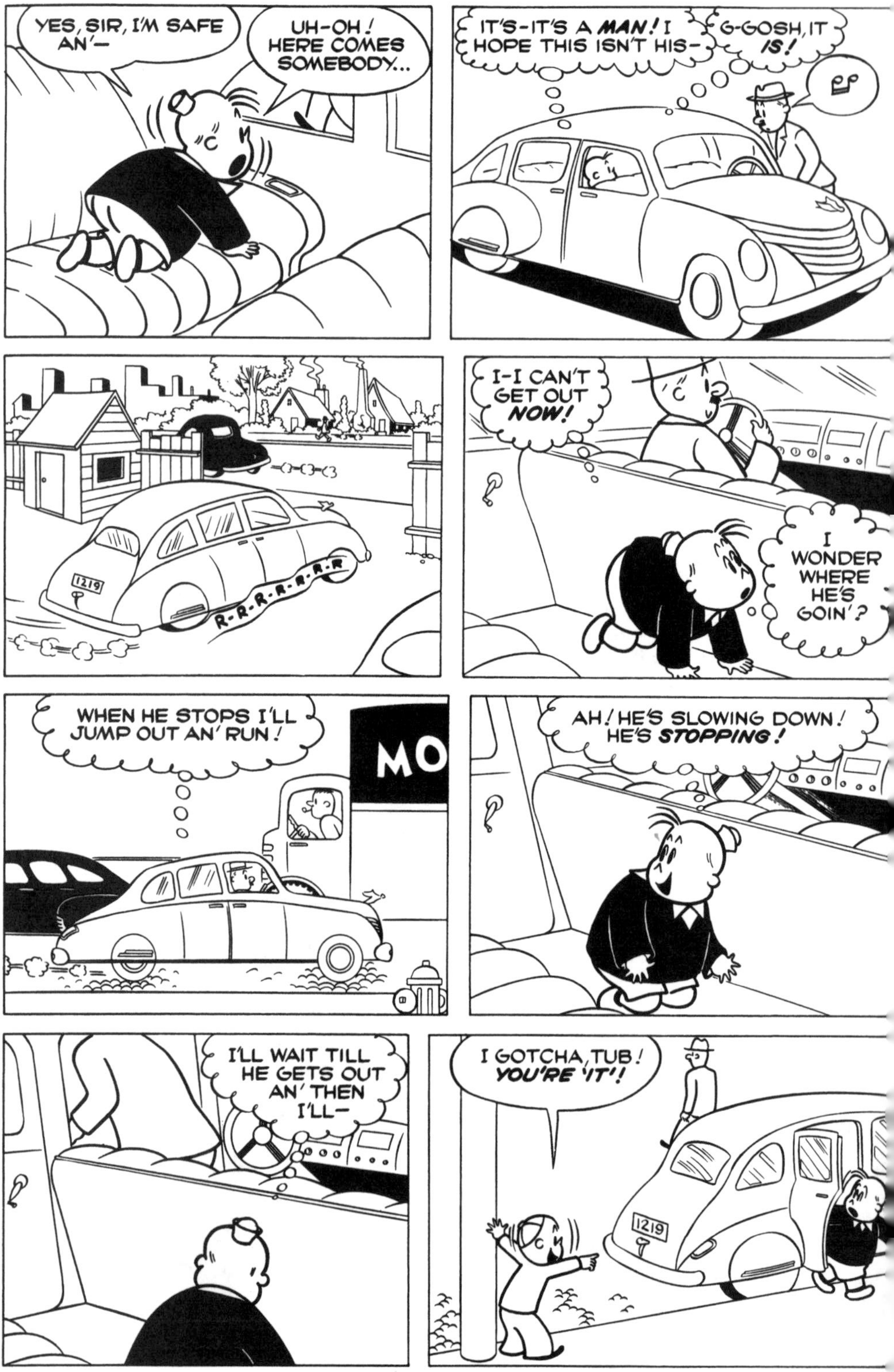
YES, SIR, I'M SAFE AN'—
UH-OH! HERE COMES SOMEBODY...
IT'S-IT'S A MAN! I HOPE THIS ISN'T HIS-
G-GOSH, IT IS!
R-R-R-R-R-R-R-R
1219
I-I CAN'T GET OUT NOW!
I WONDER WHERE HE'S GOIN'?
WHEN HE STOPS I'LL JUMP OUT AN' RUN!
MO
AH! HE'S SLOWING DOWN! HE'S STOPPING!
I'LL WAIT TILL HE GETS OUT AN' THEN I'LL—
I GOTCHA, TUB! YOU'RE 'IT'!
1219

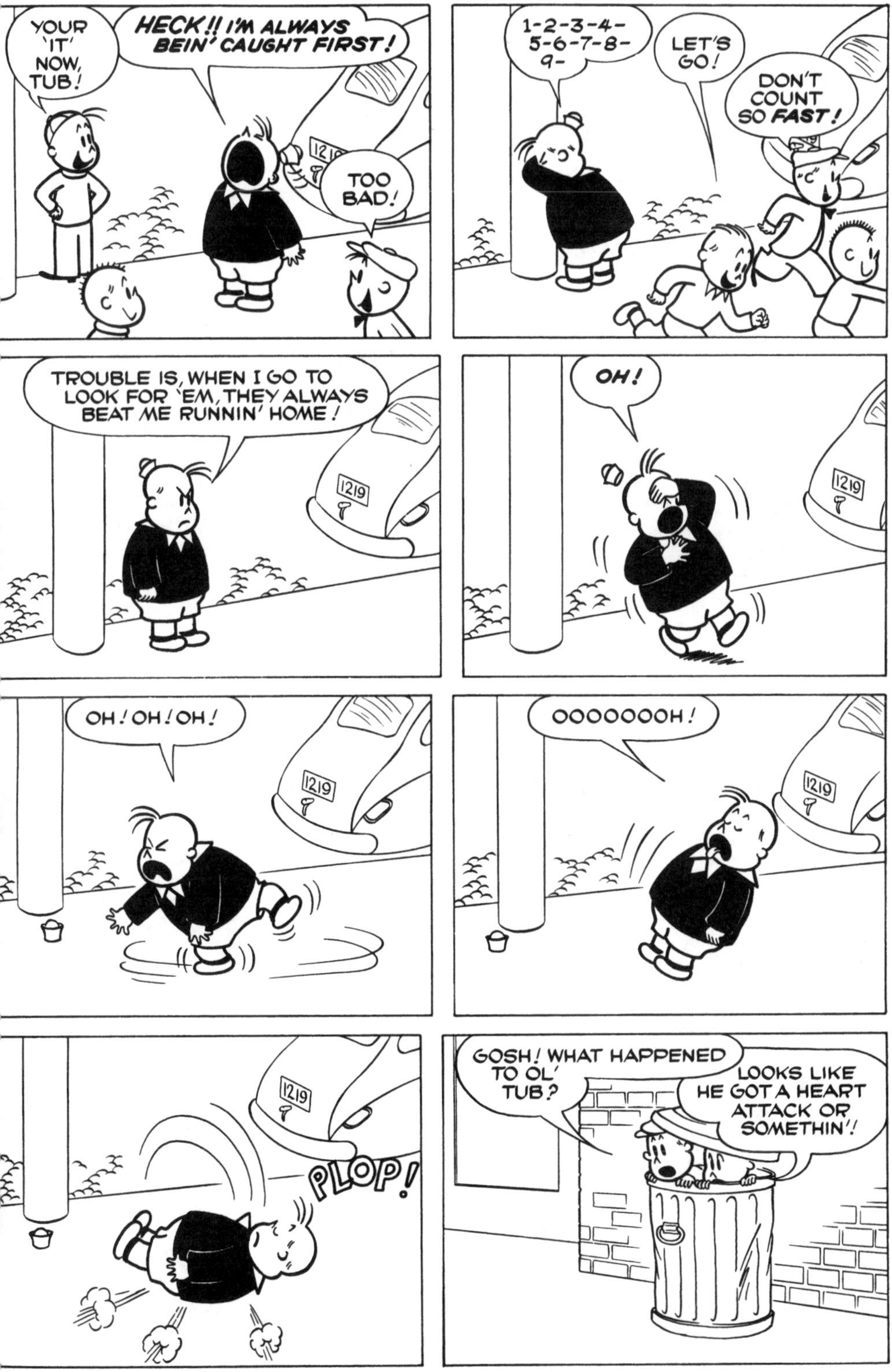
YOUR 'IT' NOW, TUB!
HECK!! I'M ALWAYS BEIN' CAUGHT FIRST!
TOO BAD!
1-2-3-4- 5-6-7-8- 9-
LET'S GO!
DON'T COUNT SO FAST!
TROUBLE IS, WHEN I GO TO LOOK FOR 'EM, THEY ALWAYS BEAT ME RUNNIN' HOME!
OH!
OH! OH! OH!
OOOOOOOH!
PLOP!
GOSH! WHAT HAPPENED TO OL' TUB?
LOOKS LIKE HE GOT A HEART ATTACK OR SOMETHIN'!

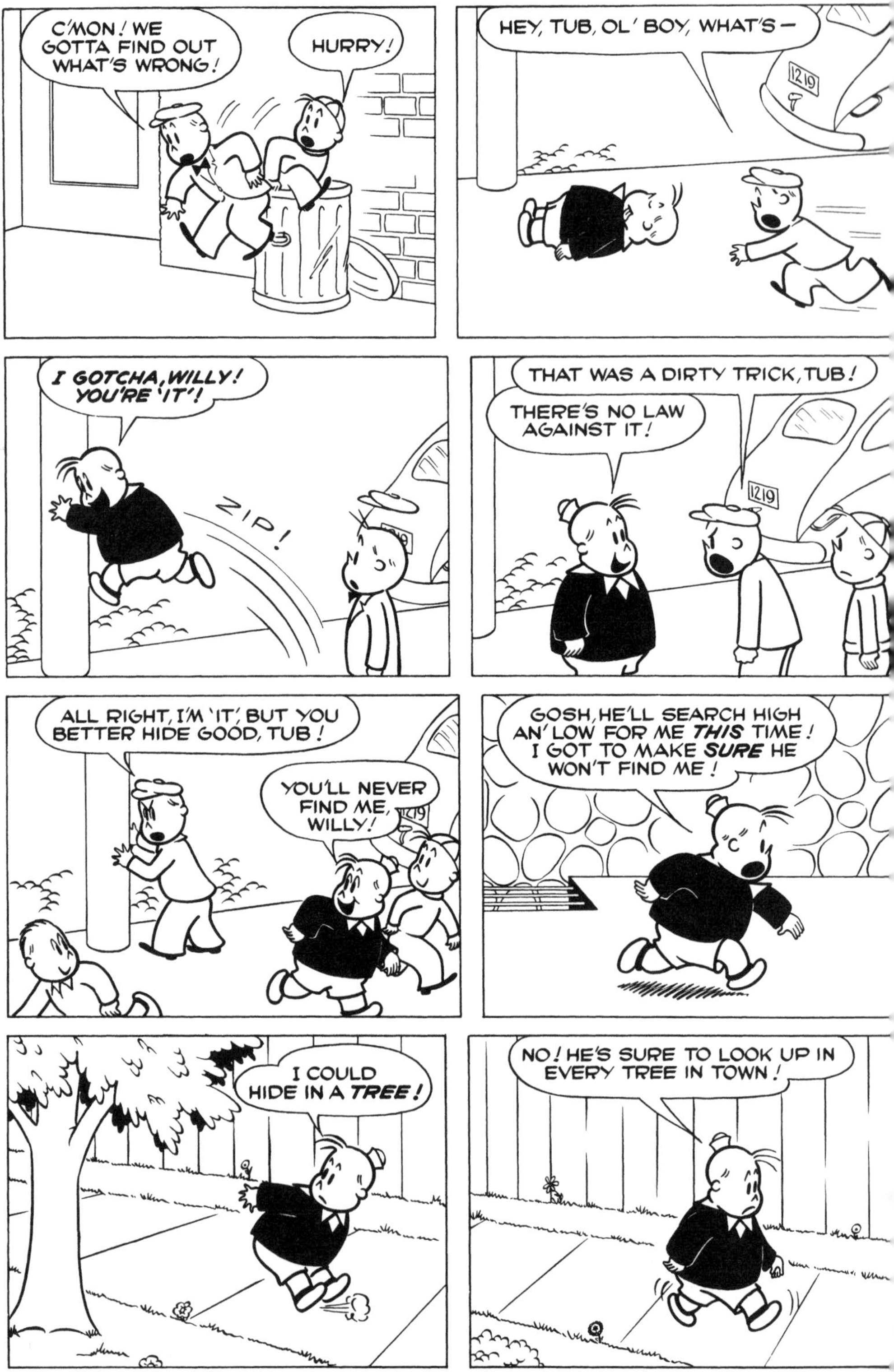
C'MON! WE GOTTA FIND OUT WHAT'S WRONG!
HURRY!
HEY, TUB, OL' BOY, WHAT'S —
1219
I GOTCHA, WILLY! YOU'RE 'IT'!
ZIP!
THAT WAS A DIRTY TRICK, TUB!
THERE'S NO LAW AGAINST IT!
1219
ALL RIGHT, I'M 'IT', BUT YOU BETTER HIDE GOOD, TUB!
YOU'LL NEVER FIND ME, WILLY!
GOSH, HE'LL SEARCH HIGH AN' LOW FOR ME *THIS* TIME! I GOT TO MAKE *SURE* HE WON'T FIND ME!
I COULD HIDE IN A *TREE*!
NO! HE'S SURE TO LOOK UP IN EVERY TREE IN TOWN!

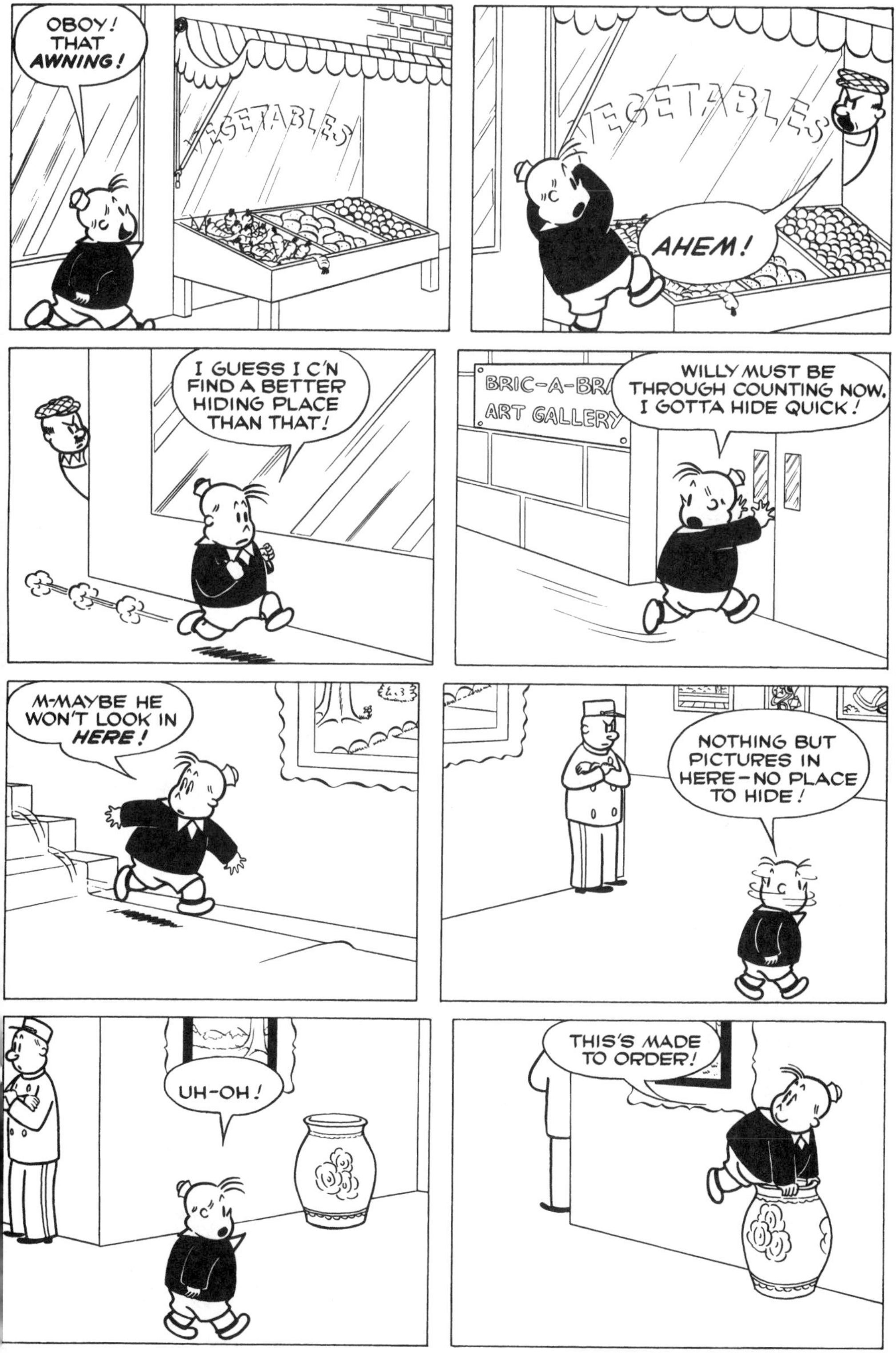
OBOY! THAT AWNING!
VEGETABLES
VEGETABLES
AHEM!
I GUESS I C'N FIND A BETTER HIDING PLACE THAN THAT!
BRIC-A-BRA
ART GALLERY
WILLY MUST BE THROUGH COUNTING NOW. I GOTTA HIDE QUICK!
M-MAYBE HE WON'T LOOK IN HERE!
NOTHING BUT PICTURES IN HERE—NO PLACE TO HIDE!
UH-OH!
THIS'S MADE TO ORDER!

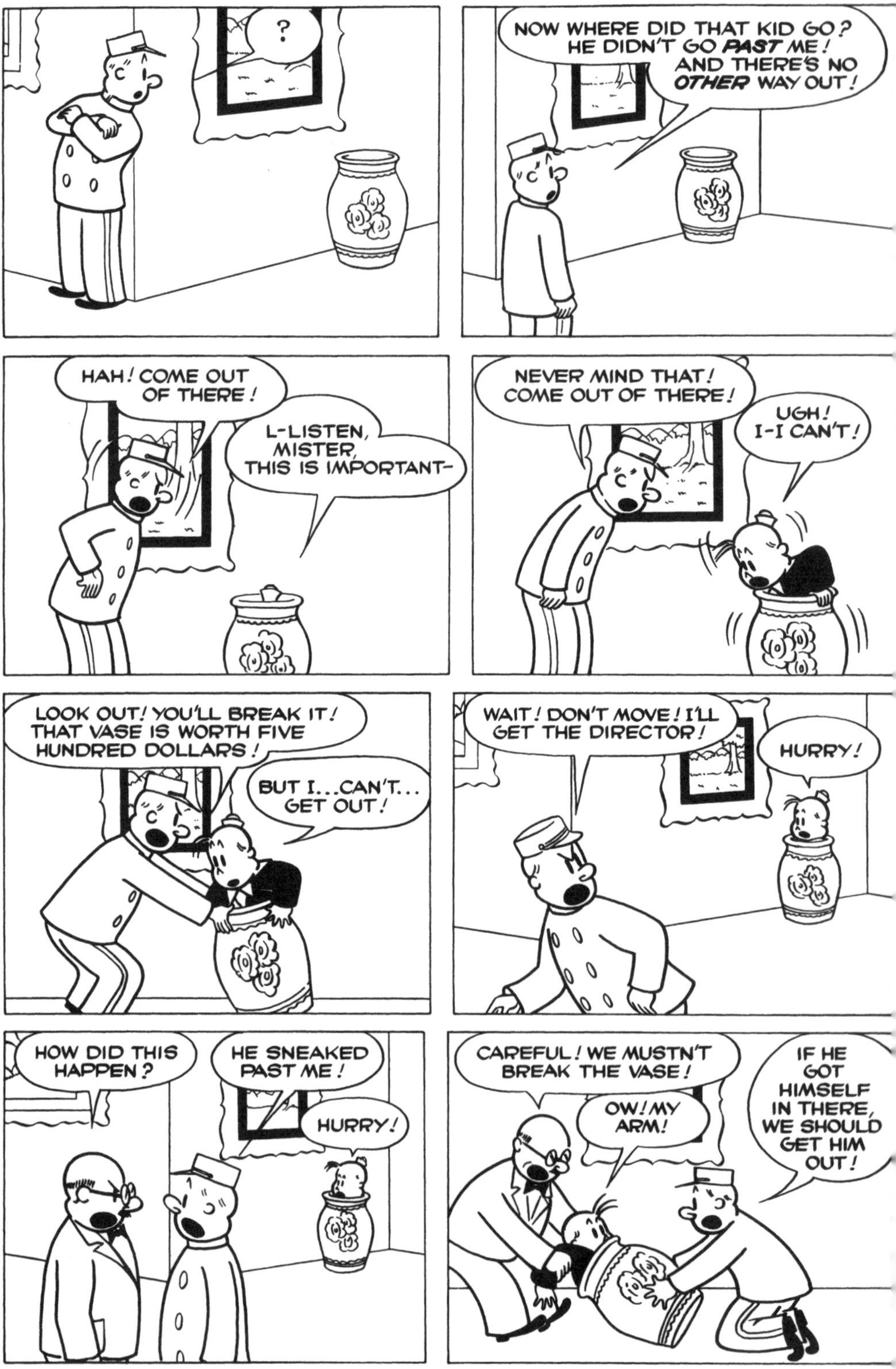
?
NOW WHERE DID THAT KID GO? HE DIDN'T GO PAST ME! AND THERE'S NO OTHER WAY OUT!
HAH! COME OUT OF THERE!
L-LISTEN, MISTER, THIS IS IMPORTANT-
NEVER MIND THAT! COME OUT OF THERE!
UGH! I-I CAN'T!
LOOK OUT! YOU'LL BREAK IT! THAT VASE IS WORTH FIVE HUNDRED DOLLARS!
BUT I...CAN'T... GET OUT!
WAIT! DON'T MOVE! I'LL GET THE DIRECTOR!
HURRY!
HOW DID THIS HAPPEN?
HE SNEAKED PAST ME!
HURRY!
CAREFUL! WE MUSTN'T BREAK THE VASE!
OW! MY ARM!
IF HE GOT HIMSELF IN THERE, WE SHOULD GET HIM OUT!

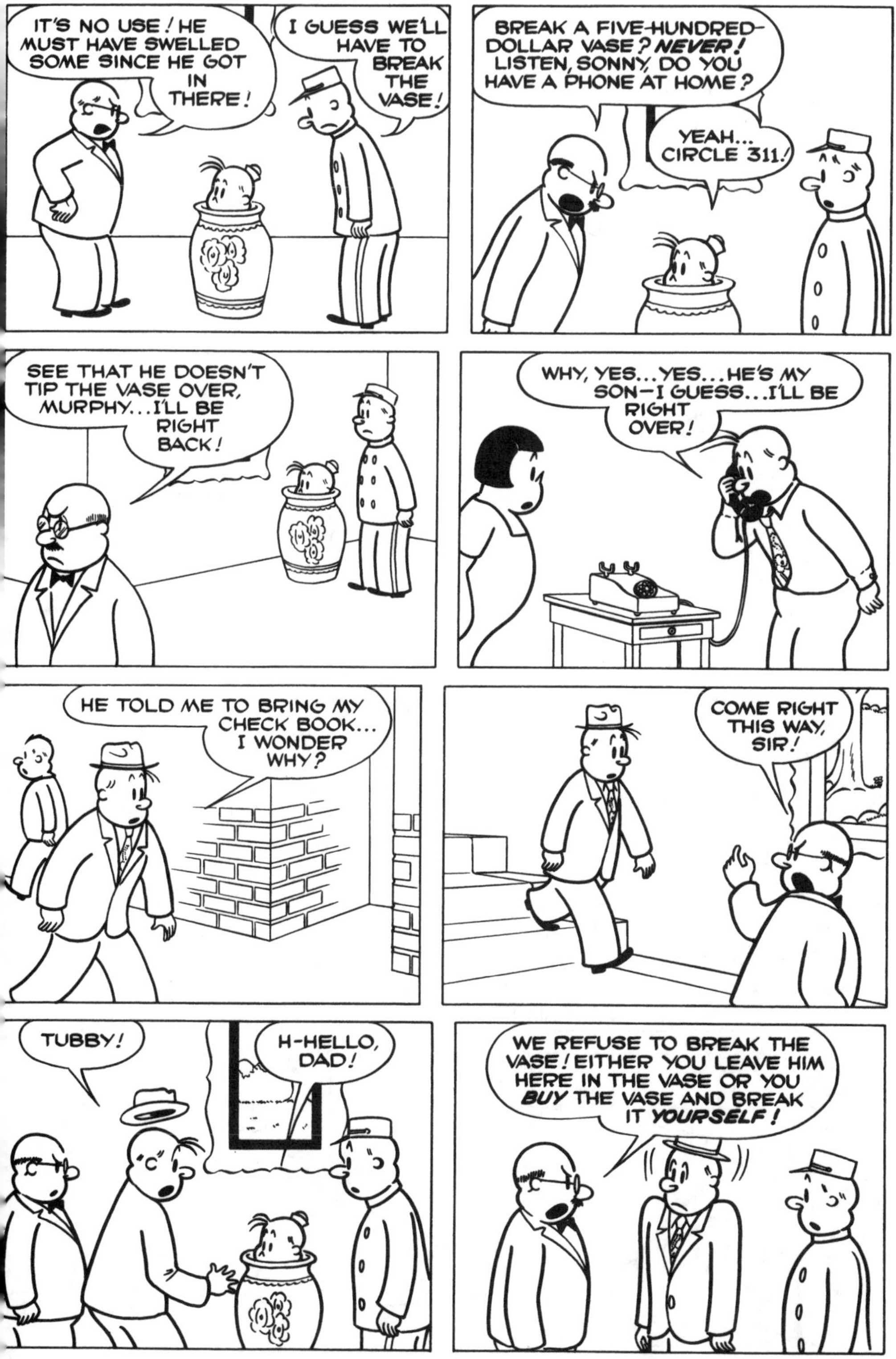

IT'S NO USE! HE MUST HAVE SWELLED SOME SINCE HE GOT IN THERE!
I GUESS WE'LL HAVE TO BREAK THE VASE!
BREAK A FIVE-HUNDRED-DOLLAR VASE? NEVER! LISTEN, SONNY, DO YOU HAVE A PHONE AT HOME?
YEAH... CIRCLE 311!
SEE THAT HE DOESN'T TIP THE VASE OVER, MURPHY...I'LL BE RIGHT BACK!
WHY, YES...YES...HE'S MY SON—I GUESS...I'LL BE RIGHT OVER!
HE TOLD ME TO BRING MY CHECK BOOK... I WONDER WHY?
COME RIGHT THIS WAY, SIR!
TUBBY!
H-HELLO, DAD!
WE REFUSE TO BREAK THE VASE! EITHER YOU LEAVE HIM HERE IN THE VASE OR YOU BUY THE VASE AND BREAK IT YOURSELF!

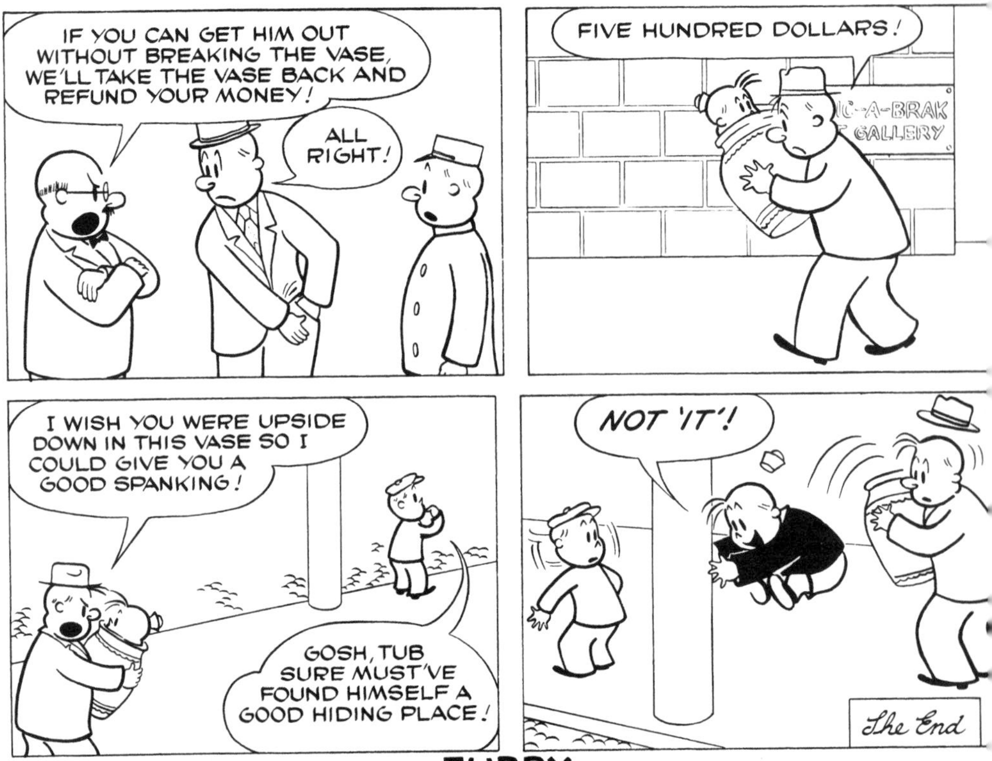
IF YOU CAN GET HIM OUT WITHOUT BREAKING THE VASE, WE'LL TAKE THE VASE BACK AND REFUND YOUR MONEY!
ALL RIGHT!
FIVE HUNDRED DOLLARS!
I WISH YOU WERE UPSIDE DOWN IN THIS VASE SO I COULD GIVE YOU A GOOD SPANKING!
GOSH, TUB SURE MUST'VE FOUND HIMSELF A GOOD HIDING PLACE!
NOT 'IT'!
The End

TUBBY

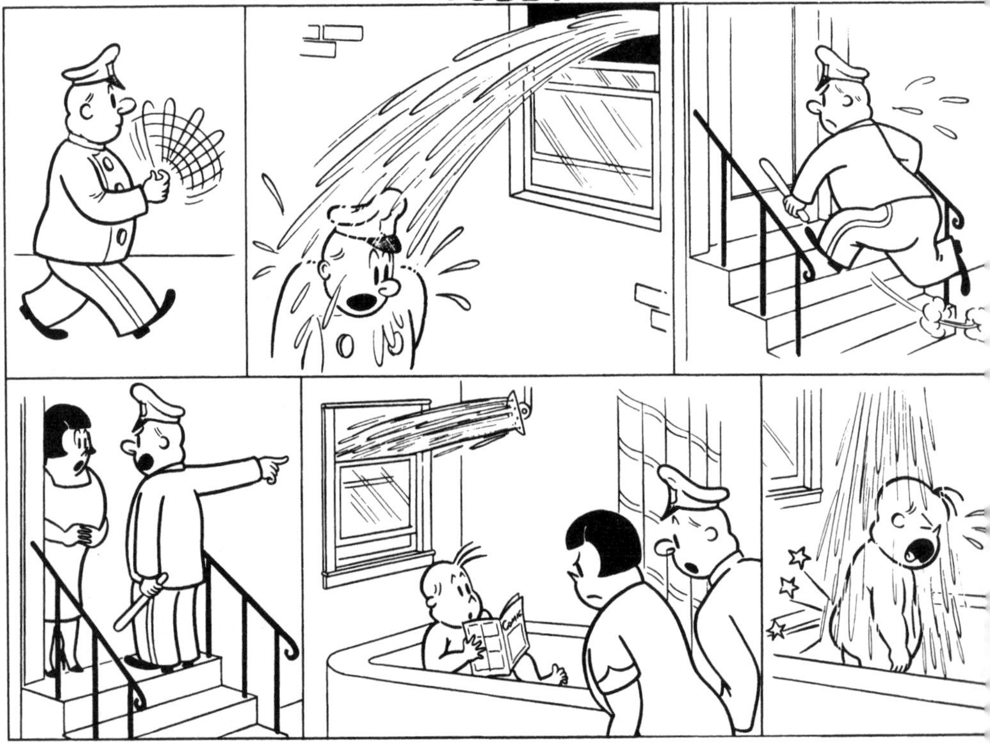

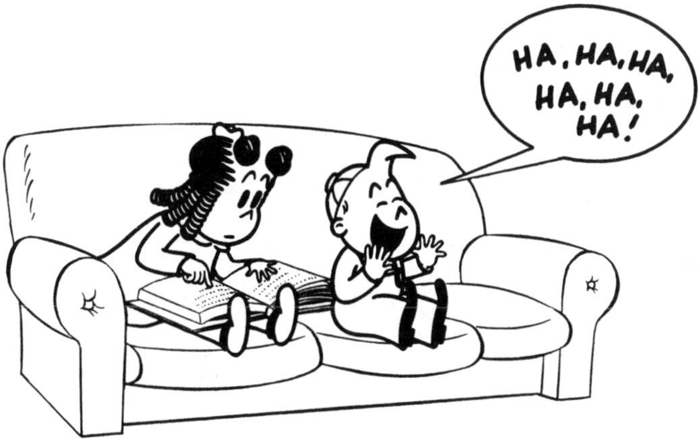
HA, HA, HA, HA, HA, HA!

Little Lulu®

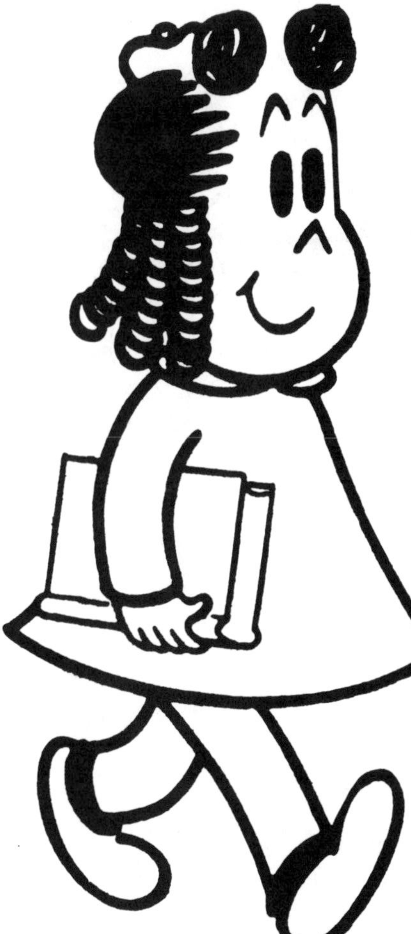

Little Lulu Volume 1:
My Dinner with Lulu
ISBN: 1-59307-318-6

Little Lulu Volume 2:
Sunday Afternoon
ISBN: 1-59307-345-3

Little Lulu Volume 3:
Lulu in the Doghouse
ISBN: 1-59307-346-1

Little Lulu Volume 4:
Lulu Goes Shopping
ISBN: 1-59307-270-8

Little Lulu Volume 5:
Lulu Takes a Trip
ISBN: 1-59307-317-8

Little Lulu Volume 6:
Letters to Santa
ISBN: 1-59307-386-0

Little Lulu Volume 7:
Lulu's Umbrella Service
ISBN: 1-59307-399-2

Little Lulu Volume 8:
Late for School
ISBN: 1-59307-453-0

Little Lulu Volume 9:
Lucky Lulu
ISBN: 1-59307-471-9

COMING IN JUNE!
Little Lulu Volume 10:
All Dressed Up
ISBN: 1-59307-534-0

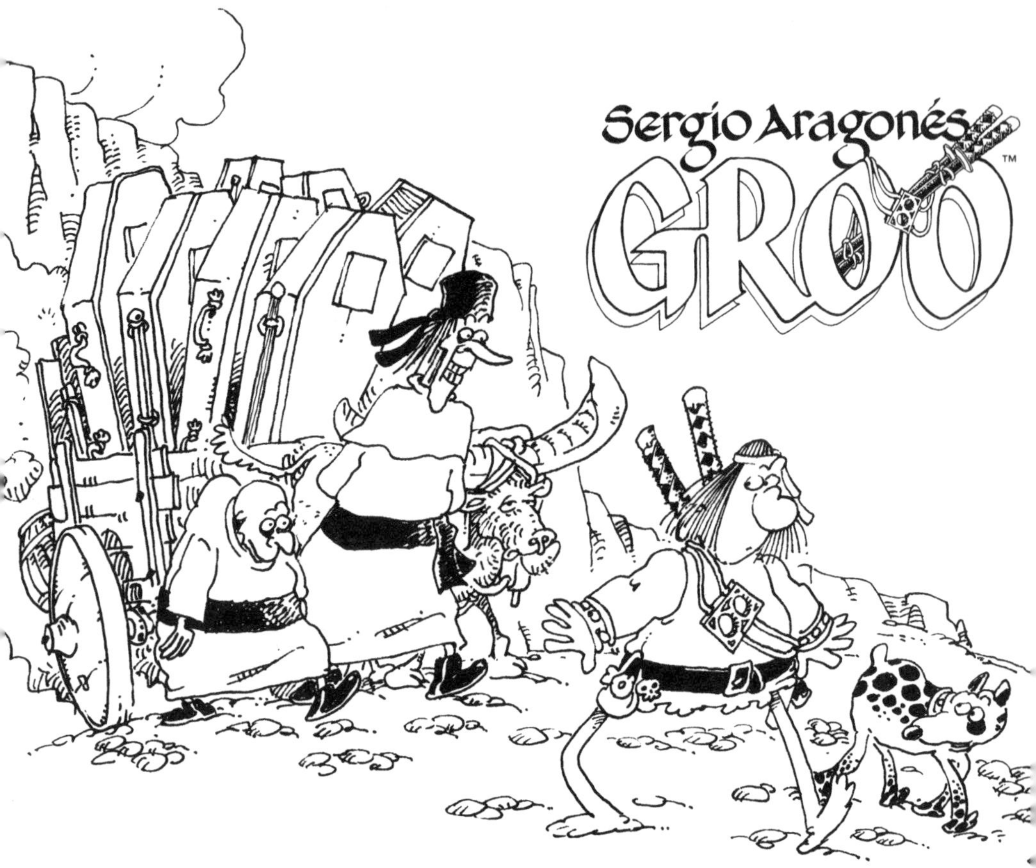
Sergio Aragonés
GROO™

The Groo Houndbook
ISBN: 1-56971-385-5 / $9.95

The Groo Inferno
ISBN: 1-56971-430-4 / $9.95

The Groo Jamboree
ISBN: 1-56971-462-2 / $9.95

The Groo Kingdom
ISBN: 1-56971-478-9 / $9.95

The Groo Library
ISBN: 1-56971-571-8 / $12.95

The Groo Maiden
ISBN: 1-56971-756-7 / $12.95

The Groo Nursery
ISBN: 156971-794-X / $11.95

The Groo Odyssey
ISBN: 1-56971-858-X / $12.95

The Most Intelligent Man in the World
ISBN: 1-56971-294-8 / $9.95

Groo and Rufferto
ISBN: 1-56971-447-9 / $9.95

Mightier than the Sword
ISBN: 1-56971-612-9 / $13.95

Death and Taxes
ISBN: 1-56971-797-4 / $12.95

AVAILABLE AT YOUR LOCAL COMICS SHOP OR BOOKSTORE!

To find a comics shop in your area, call 1-888-266-4226.
For more information or to order direct visit Darkhorse.com or
call 1-800-862-0052 Mon.-Sat. 9 A.M. to 5 P.M. Pacific Time

*Prices and availability subject to change without notice

Magnus, Robot Fighter Volume One
ISBN: 1-59307-269-4 / $49.95

Magnus, Robot Fighter Volume Two
ISBN: 1-59307-290-2 / $49.95

Magnus, Robot Fighter Volume Three
ISBN: 1-59307-339-9 / $49.95